INNOVATIONS IN CLIENT-CENTERED THERAPY

WILEY SERIES ON PERSONALITY PROCESSES

IRVING B. WEINER, *Editor*
Case Western Reserve University

INTERACTION IN FAMILIES
by Elliot G. Mishler and Nancy E. Waxler

SOCIAL STATUS AND PSYCHOLOGICAL DISORDER
by Bruce P. Dohrenwend and Barbara Dohrenwend

PSYCHOLOGICAL DISTURBANCE IN ADOLESCENCE
by Irving B. Weiner

ASSESSMENT OF BRAIN DAMAGE
by Elbert W. Russell, Charles Neuringer, and Gerald Goldstein

BLACK AND WHITE IDENTITY FORMATION
by Stuart Hauser

THE HUMANIZATION PROCESSES
by Robert L. Hamblin, David Buckholdt, Daniel Ferritor, Martin Kozloff, and Lois Blackwell

ADOLESCENT SUICIDE
by Jerry Jacobs

TOWARD THE INTEGRATION OF PSYCHOTHERAPY
by John M. Reisman

MINIMAL BRAIN DYSFUNCTION IN CHILDREN
by Paul Wender

LSD: PERSONALITY AND EXPERIENCE
by Harriet Linton Barr, Robert J. Langs, Robert R. Holt, Leo Goldberger, and George S. Klein

TREATMENT OF THE BORDERLINE ADOLESCENT
by James F. Masterson

PSYCHOPATHOLOGY
edited by Muriel Hammer, Kurt Salzinger, and Samuel Sutton

ABNORMAL CHILDREN AND YOUTH
by Anthony Davids

PRINCIPLES OF PSYCHOTHERAPY WITH CHILDREN
by John M. Reisman

AVERSIVE MATERNAL CONTROL
by Alfred B. Heilbrun, Jr.

INDIVIDUAL DIFFERENCES IN CHILDREN
edited by Jack C. Westman

STRUCTURE AND FUNCTIONS OF FANTASY
by E. Klinger

EGO FUNCTIONS IN SCHIZOPHRENICS, NEUROTICS, AND NORMALS
by L. Bellak, M. Hurvich, and H. K. Gediman

INNOVATIONS IN CLIENT-CENTERED THERAPY
edited by David A. Wexler and Laura North Rice

TROUBLED CHILDREN
by Leonore Love and Jaques Kaswan

INNOVATIVE TREATMENT METHODS IN PSYCHOPATHOLOGY
edited by Karen S. Calhoun, Henry E. Adams and Kevin M. Mitchell

THE CHANGING SCHOOL SCENE
by Leah Gold Fein

INNOVATIONS IN CLIENT-CENTERED THERAPY

Edited by

DAVID A. WEXLER
University of California,
San Francisco

LAURA NORTH RICE
York University

A WILEY-INTERSCIENCE PUBLICATION

JOHN WILEY & SONS   New York • Chichester • Brisbane • Toronto

Library of Congress Cataloging in Publication Data:

Wexler, David A. 1946-
Innovations in client-centered therapy.

(Wiley series on personality processes)
"A Wiley-Interscience publication."
1. Client-centered psychotherapy. I. Rice, Laura
North, 1920- joint author. II. Title.
[DNLM: 1. Nondirective therapy. WM420 W545i]

RC481.W49 1974 616.8'914 74-10538
ISBN 0-471-93715-0

Printed in the United States of America

10 9 8 7 6 5 4 3

Series Preface

This series of books is addressed to behavioral scientists interested in the nature of human personality. Its scope should prove pertinent to personality theorists and researchers as well as to clinicians concerned with applying an understanding of personality processes to the amelioration of emotional difficulties in living. To this end, the series provides a scholarly integration of theoretical formulations, empirical data, and practical recommendations.

Six major aspects of studying and learning about human personality can be designated: personality theory, personality structure and dynamics, personality development, personality assessment, personality change, and personality adjustment. In exploring these aspects of personality, the books in the series discuss a number of distinct but related subject areas: the nature and implications of various theories of personality; personality characteristics that account for consistencies and variations in human behavior; the emergence of personality processes in children and adolescents; the use of interviewing and testing procedures to evaluate individual differences in personality; efforts to modify personality styles through psychotherapy, counseling, behavior therapy, and other methods of influence; and patterns of abnormal personality functioning that impair individual competence.

Irving B. Weiner

Case Western Reserve University
Cleveland, Ohio

Preface

The chapters that make up the present volume were written especially for the book, and each one is an exploration of the ideas that are currently of most interest to each writer. The chapters vary in length, but each author was offered enough space to explore his ideas in any way that made sense to him. The book makes no attempt to give broad coverage to everything going on in the field, but gives intensive coverage to a few innovative ideas. Our goal is to make available to students, both undergraduate and graduate, as well as to professionals in clinical and counseling psychology and other applied areas, some of the new client-centered developments of the 1970s.

Those of us involved in teaching, training, and consultation have found that these developing ideas are exciting to the people with whom we work. The ideas seem to reach out to this generation of students, who are struggling to find some priorities for their own intellectual and professional commitments. There is a need for a new volume on client-centered therapy, one that focuses intensively on some of the ideas at the growing edges of the field. The research generated in the field is readily available in the journals, but with a long time lag from its original conception, and in the dry and condensed form necessitated by the journal format. The greatest gap in the literature seems to be in the discussion of ideas that are live and developing right now, ideas that one can bring to bear on one's own emerging thinking rather than reading about them as finished products 5 years later.

The contributors to this book were faculty members and/or graduate students at the University of Chicago Counseling and Psychotherapy Research Center, where Rogers spent the years 1945–1957, and where much of client-centered theory and practice took shape. They have since gone in a variety of directions, geographically, theoretically, and in their chosen areas of professional focus. Yet all of them have strong roots in client-centered theory and practice and have been deeply influenced by Carl Rogers and his thinking. Fortunately there has not grown up around Rogers the kind of orthodoxy that would require his formulations to be the last word on any issue. Rogers certainly would not welcome this kind of blind devotion, and would in fact view it as a failure in actualization. Each of us has had and is having his own experiences as a therapist and teacher, as well as in a variety of other roles, and must therefore arrive at his own formulations. Nevertheless Rogers' thinking has been a central influence on our development.

A second important influence was the strong commitment to research that characterized the staff of the Counseling Center. Perhaps a more fundamental way of putting this would be to call it a commitment to the demystification of psychotherapy. The conviction was that observing, describing, and understanding the events of psychotherapy would improve training and enrich both practice and the development of new theory. It was felt that not only would this *not* dehumanize the all-important therapy relationship, but it would allow the participants a fuller use of their potentials. It was this attitude that led to the electrical recording of therapy interviews in the 1940s, at a time when therapists from other orientations tended to regard this as a shocking infringement on their own mystique. It was this attitude that led to the pioneering research volume of Rogers and Dymond in 1954. The combination, usually within the same person, of a strongly humanistic approach with a strong commitment to empirical research aroused a certain amount of cognitive dissonance in our colleagues in psychology at Chicago, but it made sense to most of us then and still does.

A third potent influence has been the variety of disciplines, in addition to psychology, that were represented at the Chicago Counseling Center. Graduate students from the Religion and Personality Program at the Divinity School came for training in psychotherapy and counseling, and in the process opened up for the rest of us some of the important ideas current among theologians. There were students and faculty from the Committee on Human Development, with their emphasis on understanding the biological and social aspects of development. Others came from Education, Sociology, Anthropology, Philosophy, and Social Thought. This variety of backgrounds led to an openness in exploration, an absence of the kind of rigidity often found in groups whose backgrounds are too similar. Each of us had to take a close look at our own presuppositions; things that were taken for granted by one group were opened up for questioning by another. It is this diversity of backgrounds and viewpoints, together with some fundamental agreements on the nature of man, the nature of growth-promoting relationships and a commitment to seeking a detailed understanding of such facilitative relationships, that seems to us to give this book its special flavor.

San Francisco, California   DAVID A. WEXLER

Toronto, Canada   LAURA NORTH RICE

Contents

PART I INTRODUCTION   1

1. REMARKS ON THE FUTURE OF
   CLIENT-CENTERED THERAPY   7

   Carl R. Rogers

PART II THEORY   15

2. PERSONAL GROWTH AND CLIENT-CENTERED
   THERAPY: AN INFORMATION-PROCESSING VIEW   21

   Wayne Anderson

3. A COGNITIVE THEORY OF EXPERIENCING,
   SELF-ACTUALIZATION, AND THERAPEUTIC
   PROCESS   49

   David A. Wexler

4. THEORY AND PRACTICE OF CLIENT-CENTERED
   THERAPY: A COGNITIVE VIEW   117

   Fred M. Zimring

5. CONCEPTUALIZING AND MEASURING
   OPENNESS TO EXPERIENCE IN THE
   CONTEXT OF PSYCHOTHERAPY   139

   Pamela Howell Pearson

6. THE ICONIC MODE IN PSYCHOTHERAPY   171

   John M. Butler

PART III   PRACTICE   **205**

7. CLIENT-CENTERED AND EXPERIENTIAL PSYCHOTHERAPY   **211**

Eugene T. Gendlin

8. THREE DIMENSIONS OF PSYCHOTHERAPY: I–WE–THOU   **247**

Joseph R. Noel and Timothy K. De Chenne

9. CLIENT-CENTERED THERAPY AND GESTALT THERAPY: IN SEARCH OF A MERGER   **259**

Carolyn T. Cochrane and A. Joanne Holloway

10. THE EVOCATIVE FUNCTION OF THE THERAPIST   **289**

Laura North Rice

PART IV   BEYOND INDIVIDUAL PSYCHOTHERAPY   **313**

11. CARL ROGERS' PSYCHOLOGY AND THE THEORY OF MASS SOCIETY   **319**

Peter Homans

12. ON CREATIVENESS AND A PSYCHOLOGY OF WELL-BEING   **339**

Ned L. Gaylin

13. IT TAKES ONE TO KNOW ONE: EXISTENTIAL–ROGERIAN CONCEPTS IN ENCOUNTER GROUPS   **367**

Jim Bebout

14. PHASES IN THE DEVELOPMENT OF STRUCTURE IN THERAPY AND ENCOUNTER GROUPS   **421**

Ariadne Plumis Beck

15. CLIENT-CENTERED AND SYMBOLIC
PERSPECTIVES ON SOCIAL CHANGE:
A SCHEMATIC MODEL   465

William R. Rogers

CONTRIBUTORS   497

AUTHOR INDEX   501

SUBJECT INDEX   507

INNOVATIONS IN CLIENT-CENTERED THERAPY

Part I

INTRODUCTION

Since its "birth," so vividly described by Carl Rogers in the next chapter, client-centered therapy has had a tremendous impact on psychotherapy and counseling. This has been true not only among those trained in psychology, but in education, pastoral counseling, and, to a lesser extent, in psychiatry and social work. Originally called *nondirective,* later rechristened *client-centered,* and now often spoken of as *Rogerian,* it has changed and developed throughout the years as Carl Rogers and his colleagues and students have deepened their experience in working with troubled people and have extended their work to a widening group of different populations. Those of us who have been closely involved with this orientation tend to focus on the ways it has changed and developed. Yet, looking back from the present vantage point, one can see that there has been a surprisingly coherent and consistent body of ideas concerning the elements of a facilitative relationship, a relationship that will enable a person to change himself and the course of his life in growth-promoting directions.

Perhaps this body of ideas about the conduct of psychotherapy and counseling can best be seen in contrast with the orientations that were most influential at the time these ideas were developing. The most influential

1

orientation in psychotherapy at that time was psychoanalysis, not yet much modified by developments in ego psychology and object relations theory. Here we see some drastic contrasts with classical psychoanalysis, not just in theoretical formulations, but even more clearly in the things that took place in the therapy hour. One of the cornerstones of the Rogerian view has been the basic knowableness and trustworthiness of one's own inner awareness. If the right conditions are present, an individual can accurately symbolize these inner data, and can use them to reorganize and make choices. This assumption was in sharp contrast to the focus on unconscious motives and their derivatives, assumed by psychoanalysis to be unknowable except in highly disguised forms, requiring interpretation from outside in order to unmask them. Thus, passive free association, with the therapist intervening at intervals to point out hidden meanings, was replaced by having the client concentrate on trying to express what was going on in himself, what it was like to be him, with the therapist staying in the client's internal frame of reference, listening empathically, and giving back to the client what he understood him to be expressing. The client was encouraged to check this "reflection" with his own experience, thus creating an intensive inner dialog, in the sense that the person began to *listen to himself.*

The traditional psychoanalytic relationship with the therapist was designed to be ambiguous and thus to encourage transference of feelings and ways of relating that rightfully belonged to early childhood figures. This was replaced in client-centered therapy by a relationship in which the therapist showed that he cared about the client and that this caring involved no conditions of worthwhileness. The assumption was that the client probably would bring to the relationship expectations based on earlier experiences, but that if the therapist continued to be consistently caring, accepting the client just as he was, the client would discover these maneuvers to be irrelevant and unnecessary. Furthermore he would discover that such a relationship, free from games and countergames, could be a deeply satisfying one. Thus the interpretation of the transference was replaced by the establishment of a climate of acceptance, in which the client's communications were taken at face value.

A further assumption of this new approach was that whatever was important to the client would emerge in his present life experiences, including his interactions with the therapist. Thus the psychoanalytic push toward tracing back to early childhood family constellations was replaced by a willingness to deal with whatever was currently concerning the client. Although childhood events were sometimes recalled by the client, the emphasis was very much on present concerns.

A further emphasis was the focus on openness rather than on defense. The idea of defense still had a place in the theory, but in practice the classical psychoanalytic focus on the interpretation of defenses was replaced by an attempt on the part of the therapist to create a climate of safety, in which defenses might be found to be unnecessary. Thus nonjudgmental acceptance and the attempt to see the client's world as he saw it replaced the frontal attack on the client's defenses. It was assumed that if the interpersonal anxiety level of the client was lowered, he would then be more able to tolerate the intrapersonal anxiety of self-exploration.

The most fundamental point of difference, the one that made all these other things possible, was of course the assumption of a basic motivation toward growth and differentiation. This was a sharp contrast with the homeostatic or deficiency motivation of Freudian theory. Without such an assumption, Rogers found that he simply could not account for the fact that clients usually did not need to be pushed and steered toward change, but would move into intense self-exploration and find it satisfying even when it involved pain and anxiety. Once clients had accurate external and internal data, they consistently made choices leading to growth.

When the client-centered approach is compared with the eclectic and predominantly directive counseling approaches of that era, the most essential difference is that the Rogerian approach assumed that most people with problems had presumably been deluged with instruction and good advice from people around them, but were unable to act on it. It was assumed that if the person could achieve a clearer perception of who he really was and what was important to him, he could then make adaptive and satisfying choices. Thus the giving of information and advice was replaced by an effort to facilitate self-discovery.

Now, returning to the 1970s, it is clear that much of all this has been absorbed into many different orientations to therapy and counseling. Revolutionary though it seemed at the time, client-centered therapy is often spoken of now as one of the older therapies. Most people in the field have been exposed to Rogerian ideas in some form, and most are aware of the large volume of research that has been generated. Thus for some students exposed to client-centered thinking only through the usual course in theories of counseling and psychotherapy, the ideas seem to lack excitement. But perhaps it is not just that the ideas have been assimilated into the general therapy literature. The problem seems to be in part that these ideas have something of a flavor of benevolent passivity that is not very heady fare for this activist-minded generation. One of the major contributions of client-centered therapy was the emphasis on the capacity and responsibility of each individual for coming to grips with his own problems, an emphasis that contrasted strongly with the older paternalism in the helping professions. Students of today's generation take this for granted; their focus is now on how to be more effective in doing something about it. They are registering for psychology courses in droves, yet they often fail completely to find what they want there. Their question now is whether psychology in general and client-centered therapy in particular have anything to say about the questions that concern them: about the problem of achieving intimacy without distortion of the self; about ways of developing one's own creative potential, not just in order to turn out products, but for one's own satisfaction; about finding more constructive ways of living and working together in groups; about changing a society that often seems to have little to offer but technological luxuries.

Yet, there *are* exciting new directions developing in client-centered therapy, directions that do speak to some of those issues. On the theoretical side, the tie-in with information-processing theory, with its laboratory investigations of cognitive functioning, gives therapy theory a firmer base in experimental psychology. However, this base does not, like some learning theories, threaten to turn man into a machine, but suggests ways in which he can become more fully human. Developments on the practice side explore ways in which the therapist, working from certain baseline conditions, can incorporate specific ways to facilitate growth. The applications of client-centered principles to such areas as group functioning and community organization are increasingly becoming a focus of attention.

The book is divided into four parts. In the remainder of Part I, Carl Rogers traces some of the background of client-centered therapy and makes some predictions about its future. The chapters in Part II focus primarily on developments in theory, although most of them also suggest some implications of the theory for the conduct of therapy. Part III is mainly concerned with practice in the one-to-one situation. Although these developments are often rooted in new theoretical perspectives, the chapters have as their focus innovations in the practice of psychotherapy. Part IV goes beyond individual therapy into a larger context, into groups, the community, and issues that concern society as a whole. The introduction to each part is designed to integrate material in the separate chapters by outlining some of the trends that we see emerging from them. The remainder of this Introduction, together with Rogers' paper on the past and future of client-centered therapy, should serve as an introduction to the volume as a whole.

Although the chapters in this book are reassuringly different from each other and sometimes in fact represent opposing views on certain issues, some common themes do come out strongly. Although most of these will be discussed in the introductions to the various sections, it seems appropriate here to point to a few of them and to note to what extent they are foreshadowed in Carl Rogers' predictions, given in Chapter 1, concerning the future of client-centered therapy.

One theme that is common to practically every chapter is an insistence on attending to and seeking to understand the internal processes and structures that characterize man. These internal processes are not only viewed as legitimate objects of study, but as the direction most likely to lead to discovery and crucial research. This is completely in accord with Carl Rogers' prediction, which he sees as running counter to the behavioral emphasis that has formed the mainstream of American psychology. However, these chapters seem to reflect a greater optimism that this viewpoint need not lead to a choice between a humanistic and a scientific psychology. As several of the authors point out, the climate of psychology seems to be changing in directions that make such a split less necessary.

A second strong common element is the view of man as proactive, as basically motivated to seek out and organize new experiences that are likely to lead to growth and differentiation. As Rogers points out, this was considered an essential element in his 1940 statement, and is no less essential as a cornerstone of today's thinking. Although formulated quite differently in some of the chapters, this is still probably the basic assumption on which all other assumptions rest.

A third common element is the one with which Rogers closes his statement. Client-centered therapy has implications that go way beyond the one-to-one relationship—implications for groups of many different kinds, for community intervention, for prevention of emotional problems, even for the development of creativeness in individuals and societies. In his basic theory statement in 1959, Rogers presented a diagram showing that the understanding of the therapeutic relationship should have implications for family life, education, group leadership, and group conflict (Rogers, 1959). Nevertheless, the work of exploring the implications for these different areas in ways that take account of the complexities of each area is barely underway. Several of the chapters in Part IV have attempted such beginnings in new areas.

A fourth element that is present in several of the chapters on theory, and strongly present in the chapters on practice, is one that is not mentioned by Rogers. This is the assertive aspect of the therapist's functioning, the active decision process concerning the most appropriate way to function at any given moment. The basic attitudes of the therapist are still recognized as being decisive to the quality of the encounter, but there is more emphasis on particular kinds of therapist participation. The way in which this active choice process on the part of the therapist is made consistent with the deep human relationship that continues to be central in client-centered therapy is discussed at length in the introduction to the section on practice, Part III.

One further trend has been saved until last because it pervades all four sections of the book, and because it is basic to where client-centered therapy has been and where it is going. All the authors share with Rogers a hopeful view of man as able to transcend the limitations imposed by his environment, his past learnings, even his own structures, and create change in himself and his environment. (This is perhaps one reason why client-centered therapy still has an appeal for the current generation of students, and it is an element that they have found missing from most of psychology.) But these writings reflect not just an underlying optimism, but an explicit attempt to try to understand the mechanisms that make such transcendence possible. And they are asking about such mechanisms not just in individuals, but in groups, communities, and societies. How and under what circumstances can individuals, groups, and communities stop and resist the drift resulting from their own histories or from currently impinging circumstances? How is it possible for them to turn around on their own experience and discover and implement directions that will be more satisfying?

REFERENCES

Rogers, C. R. A theory of therapy, personality, and interpersonal relationships, as developed in the client-centered framework. In S. Koch (Ed.), *Psycology: A study of a science*. Vol. 3. *Formulations of the person and the social context*. New York: McGraw-Hill, 1959.

CHAPTER 1

Remarks on the Future of Client-Centered Therapy

Carl R. Rogers

It would seem quite absurd to suppose that one could name a day on which client-centered therapy was born. Yet I feel it is possible to name that day, and it was December 11, 1940. Let me explain what I mean.

Before that date, in my book on *The Clinical Treatment of the Problem Child,* for example, I felt that I was summarizing and pointing out the basic orderliness in the work that all sensible clinicians were doing. The only originality involved was that of trying to discover the order that existed in clinical practice.

During the period 1930–1940, I was developing a way of working with individuals, which was influenced by my Freudian training at the Institute for Child Guidance; by my own continuing experience with children and adults; by the Rankian thinking to which I had been exposed through individuals who had absorbed that approach at the Philadelphia School of Social Work; and by discussions in our own staff. But though I was aware that I was developing my own way of working with individuals, it again seemed to me that I was simply following a main current of therapeutic effort and that what I was doing was not different from the work of most counselors. When I went to Ohio State University in January 1940, I found that graduate students regarded my ideas as new, but I felt that this occurred because they had had little contact with practicing clinicians. I continued to regard myself as holding views common to most younger therapists and counselors.

This belief, however, changed on the date that I mentioned. I had been invited to come to the University of Minnesota to talk to their chapter of

[1] This chapter is a revised and updated version of unpublished remarks delivered at a symposium on "The Future of Client-Centered Therapy," at a meeting of the American Psychological Association, September 1964.

Psi Chi. I prepared a paper entitled "Newer Concepts in Psychotherapy." The title was again intended to indicate that I was trying to point up the emerging trends, acting as a summarizer or reviewer of those trends. I described older approaches that were being dropped—the giving of advice, the intellectual interpretation of personality dynamics, and so forth. I tried to spell out the elements in a newer psychotherapy, drawing on the recordings of interviews that some of us had been so laboriously making during the year 1940 at Ohio State.

I was totally unprepared for the furor the talk aroused. I was criticized, I was praised, I was attacked, I was looked on with puzzlement. By the end of my stay in Minneapolis it really struck me that perhaps I was saying something new that came from *me*; that I was not just summarizing the viewpoint of therapists in general. It was shortly after that I decided I would work toward a book presenting my point of view—a point of view drawn in large measure from others, nourished by others, but still a point of view that was my *own*. The Minnesota talk was revised to become Chapter II of the book and was entitled, "Old and New Viewpoints in Counseling and Psychotherapy." Thus it can be seen that the Minnesota paper marked a real turning point for me in which I began to believe that I might personally, out of my own experience, have some original contribution to make to the field of psychotherapy.

The four elements of this newer approach described in that Minnesota talk were these: (a) "It relies much more heavily on the individual drive toward growth, health, and adjustment." Therapy "is a matter of freeing (the client) for normal growth and development." (b) This therapy "places greater stress upon . . . the feeling aspects of the situation than upon the intellectual aspects." (c) "This newer therapy places greater stress upon the immediate situation than upon the individual's past." (d) "This approach lays stress upon the therapeutic relationship itself as a growth experience."

By and large I feel no apology for these four elements as I dimly understood them then. They have stood up well during the ensuing years. I will not try to speak of the childhood and adolescence of this orientation. There were so many positive experiences with an exciting group at the University of Chicago Counseling Center. There were so many attacks from all quarters on this ridiculous approach. The most common reaction was "It would be impossible to conduct psychotherapy in this way, and besides we're doing just this already." I look back with amusement on the social workers and psychiatrists who furtively entered our doors, because they had been told by their superiors that it was strictly "verboten" to set foot within the Counseling Center.

Now, over a quarter of a century later, all that is forgotten. This whole approach has been greatly enriched by many, many individuals, practitioners and research workers; its hypotheses have been explored in many research investigations; it has reached into different parts of this country, into many foreign countries, and into several different professions. Now it has seemed to some that it is time to take a look forward and to try to predict the future. I feel a bit embarrased by this task, but I also feel pleased. Client-centered therapy has become a sturdy 34-year-old, developed through the experience of many people in psychology, psychiatry, education, and social work. I am happy to think about the directions this 34-year-old is taking as he faces toward the future.

It has become a commonplace that one of the best ways to predict the future of a professional person is to study his past and present. These constitute the best prediction of what he is likely to do in the future. Consequently in my remarks I want to comment on some concepts, some values, that have been discernible in the past and the present of client-centered therapy and that consequently would seem to point toward the future.

1. A willingness to change, an openness to experience and to research data has been one of the most distinctive features of client-centered therapy. The incorporation of this element of changingness has set it apart, almost more than anything else I know, from other orientations to therapy.

The confidence of the client-centered therapist is in the *process* by which truth is discovered, achieved, and approximated. It is not a confidence in truth already known or formulated. Hence we have, I hope, been relatively free of dogmatism.

If we look toward the future, it seems quite clear that this process, the process in which we have our basic confidence, needs to be expressed in a new philosophy of science. Such a new formulation would find a place for intuitive and experiential insights—a rethinking of the creative side of science—as well as a rethinking of the objective, experimental, empirical, and confirmatory side. It is my hope and belief that individuals who ally themselves with the client-centered orientation will contribute to this development of a new philosophy of psychological and behavioral science. It seems to be quite desperately needed at the present time.

2. Client-centered therapy has seen the unique, subjective, inner person as the honored and valued core of human life. In taking this perspective the client-centered orientation has taken a stance that is in deep opposition to the major trend of American psychology—a trend that I see as viewing human life through a mechanistic, atomistic, deterministic scientism. I have been distressed at the narrow, and to me self-defeating, attitudes and behavior of American psychology. I am heartened by the fact that the group that has been stimulated by client-centered thinking has joined with

the other humanistic elements in American psychology in promoting a broader and, I believe, in the long run, a truer view of the human being and of the science that seeks to understand him.

I would not want to give the impression that client-centered therapy is in irreconcilable opposition to the hardheaded logical positivism of most of American psychology. Quite the contrary. It is simply a matter of primary values. The client-centered point of view puts a primary value on the subjective human being and believes that a thoroughly objective and empirical science can be utilized as one of the means and tools by which the human being can discover new ways to self-development and new *means* of achieving subjectively chosen goals. It thus places a secondary value on scientific method as a *tool*, rather than making scientific method a primary end in itself.

3. Another·emphasis in client-centered therapy that has been clear from the beginning has been the stress on the enormous potential of the individual. In this connection I would like to mention some strange experiments conducted at the Western Behavioral Sciences Institute while I was a member. It has been found that if you take a group member who has shown no signs of exercising leadership abilities and simply tell him, "We would like you to become the leader. We would like you to engage in the kind of behaviors that will cause you to become the leader of this group," he will follow these instructions. The amazing thing is that once he feels he has been given permission to be a leader he discovers within himself a wide repertoire of leadership behaviors on which he can call. Once he realizes he has been given permission to be a leader he calls upon the resources within himself to become a leader. I think in many respects this is quite analogous to what is accomplished in therapy. Therapy gives the client permission to be more of himself, and consequently he *becomes* more of his potential.

Inasmuch as our culture is so desperately in need of greater creativity, more responsible leadership, more effective competence in all its citizens, I feel that this concept of individual potential, and the learnings we have achieved as to how it may be released, will be an important part of the future of the client-centered orientation.

4. A fourth element to which I wish to call your attention is one that was not strongly present at the inception of client-centered therapy but has come to be a very prominent feature. This is the recognition that a deep human relationship is one of man's most crying needs today. Perhaps in some sense it has always been a deep need but our present-day culture, for many reasons that I cannot go into here, experiences this need more obviously, more intensely, than has even been true before. The individual

human being has a profound need to be fully known and fully accepted. Client-centered therapy, along with a number of other factors in modern life, has helped both to recognize and to meet this kind of need.

This recognition of the significance of the deep human relationship is one reason why client-centered ideas have interpenetrated with the group dynamics movement. The vast spread of T-groups, workshops in human relationships, basic encounter groups, and sensitivity training groups, bears testimony to the place that this hunger has in our modern society.

This stress on the development-inducing and growth-promoting character of the basic human encounter is one reason why the modern state hospital sees one of its most important functions as the training of aides and ward personnel in the genuine relationship skills they are able to release.

This recognition of the significance of what Buber terms the I–thou relationship is the reason why, in client-centered therapy, there has come to be a greater use of the self of the therapist, of the therapist's feelings, a greater stress on genuineness, but all of this without imposing the views, values, or interpretations of the therapist on the client.

This acceptance of the need of every individual for free, spontaneous, mutual, deep communicative relationships is one of the major reasons why I believe that client-centered therapy has an enormous potential in the field of prevention. More than most therapeutic theories and practice, it is oriented toward wellness, toward the development of more fully function-ing persons, toward enhancement of interpersonal relations. If such I–thou relationships can be achieved more frequently in the family, in schools, in work relationships, in basic encounter groups organized specifically for the purpose, I believe this will constitute a profound mental health resource that will prevent many, if not most, of the psychological disturbances that plague our culture.

5. Another concept that has developed in client-centered therapy over the years is that life exists in the moment—the belief that life is *lived now*. This differs from the concept that life at the moment is simply the automatic behavior of the organism as determined by its childhood experience or its prior operant conditioning. It is different from the view that life exists only in some to-be-achieved future. It has been a part of my own therapeutic experience that living fully in this moment is the only way of building con-structively on one's past without being owned by it, that living fully in the moment is the only effective way of living for all time.

Here it is quite clear that we link up with the whole existentialist approach to life, but I trust we will not accept slavishly the views of any one of the existentialist thinkers. I was moved by an article by Arthur Combs in which he points out that hardheaded American psychologists are turning to European existentialism, ignoring the fact that there has been more progress in a humanistic existential point of view among their own psychologists in this country than in the foreign group. He says that we turn toward European existentialism while "our studies on self-actualization are spelling out its nature and pointing the way to its achievement." This is in line with Rollo May's remark that when people have asked him, "Yes, but what do the European existential psychotherapists *do*?" his response has been, "Well, examine the work of Carl Rogers and his associates and you will get a pretty good idea of what existential psychotherapy is."

As we try—as therapists, as clients, as group members—to discover what it means to live fully in the moment, I predict that we will draw from that experience to formulate our own version of an existential point of view toward life.

6. There is one other emphasis of the client-centered point of view that I believe has rather profound implications for the future. From the beginning it has been believed that the training of the therapist is not cognitive only, but basically experiential. It is strange that this simple view has had such widening ramifications.

I can remember my great surprise when Dr. Hedda Bolgar said to me many years ago, "It is true, isn't it, that you were the first person to bring the training of psychotherapists into a university?" My first reaction was one of complete incredulity. She gradually convinced me that it was probably true that the first practicums in counseling and psychotherapy conducted at Ohio State may well have constituted the opening wedge into university life of an experiential training in human relationships.

If this is factually true, I would have to confess that at the time I certainly had no realization that this simple step would throw down a significant challenge to the whole educational system. Over the years, however, I have come to recognize that the moment you admit that you are trying to facilitate learning by the whole man—not dealing with his mind only, nor just with his ideas, but dealing with the *experiencing* of feelings, attitudes, and gut-level reactions, you have challenged the whole educational system, which loudly says that education has only to do with ideas, facts, and concepts. The experiential training of therapists, where it is expected that they will sense in themselves changing attitudes, feelings, and emotions, and that this sensing is a part of their learning—this unwittingly constitutes a challenge to the basic concept that education has only to do with man from the neck up. In deep opposition to this concept we are saying, in our training of therapists, that to function effectively man needs to be *all* there. He needs to be *present*, with his unverbalizable reaction, the feelings of which he is but dimly aware, the attitudes and values he holds, as well as the ideas he has learned and formulated, and the concepts and theories he has read in a book. This whole notion of significant learning, a learning that involves the whole man, is a threat to the members of our educational institutions and will, I think, come to be even more of a threat in the future. Who would have supposed that when a few poorly formed thoughts about counseling and psychotherapy were expressed in 1940, and when a practicum was formed in which individuals could experience themselves in the therapeutic relationship, that these unimportant events would have any implications for the whole educational system from kindergarten to the Ph.D.? I for one would have thought the notion ridiculous. Yet, I have come increasingly to believe that a portion of the impact of the client-centered orientation on education lies in its implicit belief that the best of learning is facilitated when the whole man learns, in a way that involves his feelings and his viscera as well as his intellect. There is every reason to believe that this impact will continue into the future.

These, then, are some of the emphases and the values in client-centered therapy that will, in my judgment, be evident in its future development.

It amused me as I was formulating these remarks that very little of what I have found myself wanting to say has to do directly with the long-term one-to-one relationship of psychotherapy. The things that seem to be seeking expression in me make me aware that it is my belief that client-centered therapy will have a significant outreaching impact on areas of life that include, but are much broader than, the one-to-one relationship of psychotherapy.

Part II

THEORY

Psychological theory is considered by many to be a network of abstractions, born from the minds of armchair thinkers rather than observers, having little contact with reality, but cast out on the world as a set of constructions to be imposed upon it. This is *not* the case with client-centered theory. Rogers' original theoretical statements grew from his experiences in therapy and from attempts to describe the richness of what he found there. Throughout the 34-year history of client-centered therapy, theory has been born from clinical practice and from attempts to understand that practice. Central to the client-centered tradition has always been a deep concern for the demystification of therapy—a concern for observing, isolating, describing, and researching the crucial components of the therapy process. Theory has come from listening and from the attempt to understand what is heard. It is this feature of client-centered theory that has always made it close to reality, close to the concrete events of therapy. But throughout its history, client-centered theory has not remained static. As new insights were gained from listening and reflecting on what was heard, the theory changed and evolved, always guided by the search for greater and greater differentiation and specificity in describing the central ingredients of therapy in all their richness of detail.

This search for a more differentiated level of description is just as characteristic of the chapters in the present volume. Their theorizing has also come from the practice of therapy and from the attempt to describe its richness. Each author has taken some crucial concepts or facets of client-centered therapy and sought to shed new light and understanding on them through greater specificity of theory. In this sense, these chapters are very Rogerian. Yet, these chapters, both individually and as a group, are also innovative in that they represent a marked departure from traditional Rogerian theory in the conceptual frameworks offered. In order to see where client-centered theorizing stands today, it would be well to consider the areas of common ground they share as a group, both in terms of how they follow from traditional Rogerian theorizing and how they depart from it.

The basic theme that is common to all chapters in this section is an emphasis on conceiving of therapy as a process, both in terms of the internal events occurring within the client and with respect to the inter-action of client and therapist. In all the chapters here we find a chief focus to be greater specification of the experiential processes occurring within the client and the ways in which the client–therapist interaction affects those processes. This concern with process rather than specific thematic contents or static personality structures is not new to client-centered theory. Although Rogerian theorizing during the 1950s (Rogers, 1951, 1959) had had something of a structural flavor to it, with its emphasis on the structure of the self-concept and its ensuring effects on the symbolization of experience, beginning in the late 1950s (Rogers, 1958) and on into the 1960s (Gendlin, 1962, 1964) the focus shifted to specifying the events of therapy and change in the client in terms of processes and their change. The focal concern in this shift was not on the self-concept, but on the experiential or feeling process occurring within the individual. Although all the theoretical chapters here share a common emphasis on process and thus are to some extent an outgrowth of this shift, what is new is the substance of the theorizing and the dramatically different form it takes from the client-centered theorizing of the last decade.

Perhaps the most striking thing that the reader will encounter in several of the chapters in this section is the heavy use of the concepts and language of cognitive and information-processing psychology. In Chapter 2, by Anderson, and Chapter 3, by Wexler, we find the client-centered notions of growth and actualization recast in an information-processing framework. In Chapter 3, the concept of experiencing is also reinterpreted from an information-processing standpoint. An information-processing perspective is also used by Anderson, Wexler, and Zimring (Chapter 4) to gain a better understanding of how the client-centered therapist's style of participtaion is effective in facilitating a more optimal mode of experiencing in the client. Chapter 5, by Pearson, does not formally employ the concepts and terminology of information processing, but her detailed specification of the process of openness to experience has a strong cognitive flavor.

This use of an information-processing approach to understand the events of therapy is new not only to client-centered theory, but to theory in the psychotherapy field as a whole. To some it may seem that client-centered theory and information-processing psychology make strange bedfellows. After all, information processing is fundamentally a laboratory psychology with a heavy emphasis on experimentation, whereas client-centered therapy is an applied psychology with theory typically being couched in phenomenological language and being constructed from naturalistic observation rather than experimentation. Yet, the two are not as divergent as it may seem on the surface. Like client-centered therapy, information-processing psychology is concerned with understanding the nature of internal events, and more particularly, processes occurring within the individual as he handles and organizes experience. What information processing fundamentally provides for the therapy theorist is a language, a language of events and processes that is free from many of the problematic assumptions of traditional personality theorizing, and unlike the phenomenological language of past client-centered theorizing, a language that is clearly rooted in empirical findings. Moreover, it is a language that is molecular, that gives a rich and detailed view of the complex internal events occurring within the individual. Given the client-centered theorists' concern with internal events and the manner in which the person processes his experience, and given their search for greater specificity in the description of the events of therapy, it is quite natural that they would adopt an information-processing perspective in their attempts to conceptualize the therapy process. It should also be pointed out that not only does the use of an information-processing framework offer the client-centered theorist a useful lens through which to view the events of therapy, but it also has the effect of bringing client-centered theory closer to the mainstream of psychology than it has been in the past. The trend to use an information-processing framework in therapy theory is one that we are very likely to see more of in the future.

Another common thread in many of the chapters here is the view of man as an active seeker of stimulation and novelty, an organism that seeks the assimilation of new experience and is permanently changed by the process. A number of authors (Anderson, Wexler, and Pearson) share a common theme in viewing a healthy mode of experiencing in terms of the increased use and assimilation, of the potential richness in information. Some (Anderson, Wexler, and Butler) specifically conceptualize the dynamics of client change in therapy, not in terms of change in personality *structure,* but rather the development of a processing *style* that makes enhanced use of the complexity and richness in information. Client-centered theory has always emphasized an optimistic and proactive view of man, but this view is given a firmer basis in being rooted in the context of the constructive nature of human information processing (Anderson) and the biological need for novelty and new experience (Wexler and Butler).

A theme that is also evident in the chapters in this section, and one that departs from traditional client-centered theorizing, is an increased interest in specifying just how the therapist's participation affects the client. This development parallels the renewed interest in therapist technique that is found in the practice section of this volume. In Rogerian theorizing there has typically been something of a gap with respect to the relationship between therapist technique and client change. There was specification of the orientation of the therapist (Rogers, 1957) and the types of changes that would probably occur in the client given effective implementation of that orientation (Rogers, 1958), but there was little theorizing on the hyphen in the therapist–client interaction. How the things that the therapist did were instrumenal in helping the client remained something of a mystery. This seems to be changing. The chapters by Anderson, Wexler, Zimring, and Butler all have as one of their principal aims the specification of how it is that client-centered technique is helpful to the client. In the chapters by Anderson, Wexler, and Zimring this is cast in an information-processing framework. Anderson describes how the therapist serves to help the client reallocate his attention so that he can make greater use of the richness that exists in information. Wexler elaborates how the client-centered therapist's style of responding serves surrogate information-processing functions for the client. On a moment-to-moment basis, the therapist is seen to serve attentional, organizing, or evocative functions for the client, compensating for where the client's style of processing might be deficient. Zimring elaborates how the therapist's interventions can assist the client at different points in the information-processing sequence so as to facilitate further processing in the client. Butler gives us new insight into the nature of empathy with his notion of the process of reconification of the client's feelings and how it affects the quality of the process occurring in the client. In all these chapters there seems to be a trend, more explicit in some than in others, to focus on empathic responding as the crucial therapist ingredient in client-centered therapy, and to deemphasize the importance of unconditional positive regard and congruence. In seeking a greater specificity in understanding the role of the therapist, there also seems to be a movement away from viewing the therapist as simply a reflector of feelings to viewing what he does in more complex and differentiated terms.

Just as there is a movement away from seeing the therapist's role in terms of the reflection of feelings, so too do the chapters here suggest a movement away from seeing client process in terms of the experiencing of feelings. In client-centered theory in the 1960s, the essence of client change was seen in terms of the experiencing of feelings. Feelings were taken as givens, both within the client and in theory. Feelings were assumed to exist within the client and effective therapeutic process entailed the client's symbolizing their richness. In theory there was little attempt to attack the problematic question of specifying the nature of feelings. Several chapters here suggest that this too is changing. Using Wittgenstein's philosophical framework as a basis, Zimring attacks the notion that feelings exist as entities within the client apart from their expression. Both Wexler and Butler also argue against the viewing of feelings as distinct entities. Wexler contends that feelings do not exist within the client prior to cognitive activity, but affect is produced within the client by the way he processes and organizes information. Butler views feelings, not as entities, but as aspects of ongoing neurophysiological processes upon which form is rendered and depicted by a process of iconification in the client.

A last common thread that should be mentioned is one that is only implicit, yet one that is vitally important in its possible implications for psychological theorizing on the nature of personality. Traditionally, personality theorizing has been a trait approach, with its emphasis on relatively enduring structural features of the person that show continuity in time. The view of personality that is implicit here is quite different. The behaviors of the person that are seen by an observer to reflect his personality are not seen to be the result of an organized network of structural features in the person, but rather are seen to reflect the characteristic style in which the person typically processes and organizes information. Personality is not a structure, but rather reflects the workings of processes in the handling of information. This view of personality suggests that the concepts and findings of information-processing psychology may potentially be a more fruitful vehicle for understanding the phenomena of personality than are concepts of traditional personality theory. Thus, we begin to see here the reinterpretation of traditional personality phenomena such as the self-concept (Zimring) and defense (Wexler), not in terms of personality structures, but rather in terms of the workings of a system of processes operating on and organizing information.

Thus, although the chapters here are an outgrowth of the traditional client-centered emphases on process and on achieving greater specificity in theorizing, they depart in numerous ways from traditional client-centered theorizing on the therapy process. None, however, is to be regarded as a finished system. At best they are only beginnings. Just as listening and reflecting on therapy has led the authors here to innovations and departures from traditional theorizing, so too will further listening and reflection lead to revision and change of frameworks offered here.

REFERENCES

Gendlin, E. T. *Experiencing and the creation of meaning.* New York: Free Press, 1962.

Gendlin, E. T. A theory of personality change. In P. Worchel & D. Byrne (Eds.), *Personality change.* New York: Wiley, 1964.

Rogers, C. R. *Client-centered therapy.* Boston: Houghton Mifflin, 1951.

Rogers, C. R. The necessary and sufficient conditions of therapeutic personality change. *Journal of Consulting Psychology,* 1957, **21**, 95–103.

Rogers, C. R. A process conception of psychotherapy. *American Psychologist,* 1958, **13**, 142–149.

Rogers, C. R. A theory of therapy, personality, and interpersonal relations as developed in the client-centered framework. In S. Koch (Ed.), *Psychology: A study of a science.* Vol. 3. New York: McGraw-Hill, 1959.

CHAPTER 2

Personal Growth and Client-Centered Therapy: An Information-Processing View

Wayne Anderson

> *So we create the necessity which then constrains us, constains ever more tightly day after day, so vindicating . . . our wisdom in having perceived from the outset we were not free. Finally we are bound hand and foot and may exclaim triumphantly how right we were.*
>
> **A. WHEELIS (1969, p. 61)**

> *The problem of rationality, of what man* will allow himself to *know and do, is the major problem of human existence.*
>
> **E. BECKER (1964, p. 221)**

A certain passivity inheres in experience. The world, without our seeming to have done anything to produce it, impinges upon us, and we are prey to emotions and thoughts whose origins defy any volition on our part. True, such is not the whole of it. For we do speak of intentions and desires, and plans, and in seeking to implement these we do gain awareness, even if dimly, of our role in "fashioning" our experience in order to give it form and substance. Yet to a great extent our functioning as artisans or craftsmen of our own experience, including its mapping into behavior, eludes us, so blinded are we by the "giveness" or the "reality" of that with which we deal.

Why is this so? To my mind it stems largely from two sources. For one thing, we have been unwilling to acknowledge the major role played by the person's own activities in perceiving, imagining, remembering, thinking, and behaving. For a second, we have ignored for too long the more extensive processes of which experience and behavior are but end products and so have failed to treat the "recipes" or "rules" by which these end products are formed. In short, we have been misled, over and over again, by the long-held doctrine of the person as a passive recipient of stimulus energies; as a simple "copier," "duplicator," and "warehouser" of external sensory events.

There are signs this is changing. There is a new tide arising in experimental psychology, a tide which undercuts such misleading assumptions and which can be used to free persons from their deadening influences. A few remarkable experimentalists and thinkers, such as Jean Piaget, Jerome Bruner, George Miller, Ulric Neisser, Joachim Wohlwill, Wendall Garner, Rudolph Arnheim, and J. J. and Elinor Gibson, have provided the major impetus for the tide. But its outreach can also be discerned in scores of studies—studies that view the perception, thought, and behavior of the child and the adult in terms of the extraction, transformation, storage, and use of stimulus information.

One major purpose of this chapter is to acquaint clinicians, educators, and others interested in the client-centered approach with some of the concepts and ideas of this new experimental trend and to show how closely related these are to the client-centered concern with human process and growth. The process scale of psychotherapy, about which Rogers (1961) has written so vividly, contains, for example, several implicit and explicit references to various information-processing operations. A second major purpose of the chapter is to extract from the new trend some thoughts about the individual's capacity and potential for personal growth when such growth is seen in the conceptual framework of information processing. A predominant concern here is the manner in which this capacity and potential can come under unduly restrictive constraints. Such constraints, conceived as rules or schemas by which perceptual activities are guided and directed and by which experience and behavior are produced, can be seen as contributing in large measure to the person's alienation from his own powers of self-growth. The final section of the chapter deals with the implications of the new experimental trend for the practice of psychotherapy.

INFORMATION PROCESSING AND PERSONAL GROWTH

Personal growth can generally be defined as the continued development and fuller use of one's potential and capacity. This definition is nearly synonymous with a view of experience and behavior that has been the central focus of a good deal of research in experimental psychology during the last two decades or so. The view growing out of research in the areas of perception, imagery, memory, thought, and skilled behavior, among others, is that of the person as an active, selective processor of information. Although this research is far from a unified body of knowledge, consisting as it does of varied models, diverse concepts, and differing interpretations of experimental data, some of its central tenets seem common enough to allow the following conclusions bearing on personal growth:

First, persons not only adapt, but grow psychologically, through the continuous extraction and use of information from stimulation. Second, such information extraction and use can be broadly conceived as information processing. Third, this information processing is unceasing from birth to death and draws upon both (a) the unending availability of information in external and internal stimulation and (b) previously extracted and used, or stored, information. Fourth, this information processing is always selective, and thus to a degree always optional, due to the person's limited information-processing capacities. Fifth, this information processing occurs in stages, takes time, and requires allocations of attentive capacity. Sixth, this information processing builds upon itself, resulting in a store of abstracted rules and schemas that come to guide and direct much of perception, imagery, memory, thought, and behavior. Seventh, these rules and schemas often prove inimical to personal growth, in part due to the very ease and economy with which they come to function and in part due to misleading conceptualizations of their function as primarily the duplication and reproduction of experience and behavior.

These conclusions can be seen to bear a close conceptual kinship to client-centered concerns with psychotherapeutic process and personal growth, particularly as described by Rogers (1961). They also carry certain theoretical and practical implications for the facilitation of personal growth in psychotherapy. These are matters elaborated upon in the next two sections of this chapter. In this section, however, the conclusions sketched above will be dealt with in more detail, drawing upon some of the models and ideas put forth in the study of human information processing.

As early as the 1950s, psychologists were beginning to take a look at the concept of stimulation in terms of information. Traditionally, stimulation had been seen in terms of physical, mechanical, and chemical energies. However, with the advent of cybernetics and communication theory, researchers in different areas found themselves dealing more and more with informational aspects of stimulation. This view did not deny the components of energy in stimulation. Rather it moved to a different level of analysis—that of the information carried by, or contained in, stimulation.

Accompanying this emphasis on the informational aspects of stimulation came a more subtle kind of conceptual shift. It was that the individual's own activities, whether voluntary or involuntary, contributed in great part to the obtaining of information from stimulation. It must be granted, of course, that stimulation can impinge upon us without our moving a muscle or batting an eye. We are, after all, born into a world that abounds with stimulus energies. Such energies activate our receptor systems, and we talk of the "sensations" arising from this activation.

But are these sensations truly information? Bartlett (1932) and Piaget (1950) are two experimental psychologists among others who have argued eloquently against the view of the person as a passive recipient of stimulation and sensations. A third voice recently raised against such a view is that of the perceptual psychologist J. J. Gibson (1966), who has argued for a distinction between *imposed* and *obtained* stimulation. The first, he notes, is ". . . forced on a passive organism [the second] . . . comes with activity [p. 44]." And it is only the second type that yields information—information, to quote Gibson (1966) once more, that ". . . is produced [inside or outside the individual] by his own action and in the course of action [p. 32]."

Thus, whether seen as "effective" or simply as "available," information is not to be identified with imposed physical, chemical, or mechanical stimulation. Rather it is what is discriminated, extracted, transformed, stored, or otherwise used by the individual from an everchanging internal and external flux of varied stimulus energies. In brief, in the information-processing view, it is the *individual* who "puts to work," or "makes use" of, the available or potential information in stimulation by his own actions and activities.

Information in this view is theoretically inexhaustible. Its potential is always within and without, waiting to be explored, mined, used, put to work. It is not raw sensory material, a chaotic flux awaiting the mind's organizing processes. It is potential information carrying structure from which features, invariant properties and relations, and higher-order patterns can be further structured, implemented, or used by the individual. In this sense, psychologists have erred in speaking of "unstructured situations." There are no unstructured situations. There are only situations with greater or lesser information potential.

For all of this abundance of potential information, one thing about it is certain. It cannot be fully exploited by the individual—either simultaneously or successively. The workings of the nervous system simply will not allow it. Some 15 years ago Miller (1956) suggested as much, documenting it with the then fairly new conceptual tool of information measurement and specifying in its terms the concept of limited channel capacity.

This concept stressed the rather severe limitations the spans of absolute judgment and immediate memory impose on the amount of information the person can receive, process, remember, and code into behavior. Although not a new idea in psychology, this formulation received impetus from the precise mathematical specification of "bits" of information in the amount of input mapped or coded by the individual into output. Such an emphasis highlighted the person's capacity to deal with but limited portions of stimulation at any one time, and a large amount of experimental work (e.g., Broadbent, 1958, 1971; Neisser, 1967; Norman, 1969) has explored this limitation and its implications. As a result of this work, a far more complex picture has arisen than that of the person as a simple "through-put" mechanism with a limited capacity for transmitting bits of information.

Some of the major elements in this more complex picture will be elaborated shortly, but first we should briefly touch upon the idea that the person's sensory organ and receptors are not passive, dormant instruments awaiting activation by stimulation. Rather their presence in the human being means an active, selective orientation through movements of the head, eyes, limbs, body, and so on, to limited portions of stimulation. This view owes its recent emphasis to J. J. Gibson (1966), who conceives of looking, hearing, tasting, smelling, and touching as *overt attentive acts* that are selective of the information contained in stimulation.

Such information to Gibson (1966) consists of the distinctive features, invariant properties, and high-order patterns that characterize objects and events. Moreover, he makes it clear that where, when, and how we look, hear, touch, taste, and smell are important factors in extracting this information. Perception thus is seen as active, selective, and exploratory, and Gibson (1966) suggests it is always open to new possibilities. As he puts it,

> The environment provides an inexhaustible reservoir of information. Some men spend most of their lives looking, others listening, and a few connoisseurs spend their time in smelling, tasting, or touching. They never come to an end. The eyes and ears are not fixed-capacity instruments, like cameras and microphones, with which the brain can see and hear. Looking and listening continue to improve with experience [p. 269].

Perception so conceived emphasizes both its selective limitations and capabilities. Stimulation carries more information than the person's receptors can ever deal with, so only portions of this information are selected and used. Yet there can be a progressive development in this selection and use—as well as the further search for, and discovery of, new features, properties, and patterns in information.

But perception does not exist in a vacuum. It is aided, abetted, and, on occasion, transcended by more "interior" processes. It cannot perhaps really be said to function apart from these. It is to these interior processes that we now turn as further elements in the picture of the person as an active, selective processor of stimulus information.

Much evidence makes it clear that perception and other information-processing activities occur temporally and in stages—at least four of which can be specified experimentally. In the first stage, which is most closely linked to the receptor systems, buffer stores appear capable of holding relatively undifferentiated, crudely articulated information for periods of up to a second. Some writers (e.g., Broadbent, 1969, 1971; Posner, 1969) refer to this stage as the preperceptual memory store and to the information in this stage as unencoded. Information held here is lost forever if it is not transferred into a second stage, often referred to as coding or categorization. But even if such coding or categorization takes place, it too is selective, as only portions of the buffer store can be so developed because of the rapid decay of the unencoded material.

Coding or categorization in the second stage requires allocations of attentive capacity. Posner (1969) offers a detailed analysis of this stage and suggests that in humans it often takes the form of naming or verbal codes. But he also notes there is evidence unencoded information can enter with or without naming or verbal activity into other abstract codes, such as motor programs, visual imagery, and schemas. The application of these codes, however, also requires the use of attentive capacity.

Information that has gone through the second stage still may be lost unless it enters a third stage of processing. This stage often is referred to as *short-term memory*, and information held in it must be rehearsed or "recycled" to prevent its loss. This stage also requires the use of attentive capacity. Broadbent (1971) has likened the third stage to the recent acquisitions shelf in a library and sees it as the final stage before transfer into a fourth stage or long-term memory—the "permanent library."

One striking thing about this description of the fate of stimulus information is that it possesses different characteristics in different stages. A second striking thing is that to be effectively extracted and used, the information contained in stimulation must be at least minimally, and in most cases, more extensively attended to by the person. One thus can imagine buffer stores in the first stage as continually teeming with crude, shortlived, multichanneled information, only portions of which attention can select for somewhat more lasting, or more permanent, storage and more detailed coding and processing. This very selection means, however, the rejection, filtering out, or the undetailed passive monitoring, of the multiciplicty of information continuously existing in the first stage.

One appealing model for dealing with these aspects of the fate of stimulus information is offered by Neisser (1967), who sees information processing proceeding both sequentially and in parallel. Parallel processing, which Neisser (1967) refers to as *preattentive,* does not demand large allocations of attention. It segments and isolates crude features, properties, and relations, and these can be used to guide perceiving, thinking, remembering, and behaving in a crude, holistic way. I need not, for example, note the make and design of every car on the expressway in order to drive to work. But for perception, imagery, memory, thought, or behavior to become more detailed, complex, and articulated requires that attentive capacity be focused successively upon selected aspects of input. This is sequential or serial, in contrast to parallel, processing.

Neisser's (1967) model, as well as the other experimentally based observations described above, emphasizes that the stimulus flux around and within us abounds with vast amounts of potential information—only a fraction of which is abstracted and used at any one time. They also emphasize that information selection *and* rejection are facts of life and that the finer and more detailed the extraction and use of information at any moment, the less is attentive capacity available for the processing of other potential information. It follows that much of what we experience and do is optional. Stimulus information is replete with choice, and a critical question is how we deal with such a supply of riches.

One answer to this question is the person's uses of attentive capacity. The allotment of attentive capacity has already been alluded to in the earlier discussion of Gibson's (1966) conceptualization of overt attentive acts and other conceptualizations of more covert interior attentive acts. Because of the overwhelming potential of information in stimulation, it is clear that what a person perceives, imagines, remembers, thinks, and does hinges to a great degree on how he allocates his limited, but precious, resources of attentive capacity.

Much research in human information processing is concerned directly or indirectly with the uses and limitations of attention, measured by rate of information transfer or degree of interference between simultaneous tasks. As a result of this work, Neisser (1967) sees selective attention as ". . . an allotment of analyzing mechanisms to a limited region of the field [p. 88]," and Norman (1969) describes it as ". . . our ability to extract the one message of concern out of many that might simultaneously be present [p. 177]." He elaborates:

This selective ability is also a limitation, for we are unable to do more than a very limited number of complex activities at the same time. We choose the message to which we attend by selectively restricting our attention to those physical cues and meaningful contents that we think will be relevant. We can lose the message if either the physical or the meaningful cues change or are interfered with by other, distracting messages [pp. 177–178].

The renewed experimental attack upon attention promises many rewards—not only in how it may serve adaptation, but also in how it may serve personal growth. The Gibsons (1966, 1969) have theorized, for example, that education is largely training in the allocation of attentive capacity. A number of years ago Schachtel (1959) also suggested that attentive acts, as manifested in the exploration of, and renewed approaches to, objects and events, were critical to enriched perception, thought, and memory. But unlike the Gibsons (1966, 1969), Schachtel (1959) did not limit such exploratory activity to overt acts. He defined focal attention as the person's capacity ". . . to *center* his attention on an object fully, so that he can perceive or understand it from *many* sides as clearly as possible [p. 251; italics added]."

These ideas are now receiving experimental study, and just how powerful a factor the education or training of attentive capacity may be is hinted at by Moray (1970), who wrote:

. . . it is common for experimenters in the field of attention to find after some time that they can achieve performance levels in competitive and selective tasks which far exceed the performance levels attained by their subjects [p. 194].

The importance of attentive capacity in moment-by-moment functioning raises at least two larger questions. One is, what happens to what is attended to and attended to well? A second is, what captures, guides, directs, and terminates attentive activities. The partial answers proposed to these questions will also speak to the issue raised earlier regarding the person's dealing with the overabundance of information in stimulation. In brief, much of perception, imagery, memory, thought, and behavior, and the attentive acts associated with these, are guided by abstractions from former experiences and behaviors. This is not to say percepts, images, memories, thoughts, and behaviors "reappear." They do not, although they may seem to do so due to the application of rules and schemas. It is as if we forget, as Laing (1969) has put it, that,

Our experience is a product, formed according to a recipe, a set of rules for what distinctions to make, when, where, on what. Rules are themselves distinctions in action. Operations between distinctions already constructed are carried out continually according to further rules [p. 23].

Such rules, or *schemas,* as Piaget (1950) refers to them, can be inferred early in childhood and throughout the individual's life from stable, recurring organizations of behavior. To Kagan (1970), for instance, "The child's encounters with events result, inevitably, in some mental representation of the experience, called a schema [p. 299]." According to Kagan:

A schema is defined as an abstraction of a sensory event that preserves the spatial or temporal pattern of the distinctive elements of the event . . . [A schema] . . . is to be regarded as a functional property of the mind that permits the organism to recognize and retrieve information . . . It is neither a detailed copy of the event nor synonymous with the language label for the event [p. 299].

Even beginning in childhood, then, rules and schemas—whether manifested in sensorimotor, imaginal, conceptual and/or symbolic forms—come to be powerful guides governing what the individual sees, hears, remembers, imagines, thinks, and does. In one sense, of course, rules and schemas can be viewed as adaptive. Indeed, it can be said they are essential for survival. For one thing, they provide "tests," "matches," or "templates," for recognizing previously experienced or behaved sequences of events. For another, they provide means for the modeling or representation of events distantly remote in space and time. One tells or acts out, for example, an episode from childhood. Rules and schemas also are highly economical. They conserve information-processing capacity and time by allowing us to generalize to many more instances than have ever been encountered before. As Talland (1968) wrote,

Children do not learn all over the motions of running down stairs with each rise and depth of the tread; they learn a skill that is adjustable to the varied demands of different sized stairs, including the use of their bottoms if the gradient is too steep for their legs . . . [It is a] process by which stairs of diverse shapes, sizes, and surfaces are brought under a common rule of locomotion [p. 32].

So, too, may various other sequential acts, such as those involved in perceiving, remembering, thinking, and imagining, come to be guided by common rules and schemas adjustable to varied demands or instances. It is just this generalization function of rules and schemas that makes them at once a blessing and a curse. On the one hand, they are economical, adaptive, and helpful to acts of discrimination, recognition, memory, thought, and behavior. In perception, for example, they often supplement gaps in current input, making exhaustive searches of available evidence unnecessary or redundant. One glimpse of smoke, and we assume a fire. On the other hand, rules and schemas can be blinding and maladaptive, just because of their generalization and gap-closing functions. Gaps may be real or imagined, and when rules or schemas are brought into play to help fill them, the options inherent in information may be drastically limited and important available evidence ignored or overlooked.

Ideally rules and schemas should undergo constant elaboration and diversification. To Piaget and Inhelder (1969), for example, there is continual reciprocal interplay between the person's information-processing activities and the information to which such activities are addressed. These authors wrote,

> ... the point of view of assimilation presupposes a reciprocity $S \rightleftarrows R$; that is to say, the input, the stimulus, is filtered through a structure that consists of the actions-schemes (or at a higher level, the operations of thought), which in turn are modified and enriched when the subject's behavioral repertoire is accommodated to the demands of reality. The filtering or modification of the input is called *assimilation;* the modification of internal schemes to fit reality is called *accommodation* [p. 6].

In a similar vein, Neisser (1967) argues learning may consist largely of storing information about processes (rules and schemas) rather than about contents (products of processes). As he put it, "Mental activities can be learned; perhaps they are the only things that are ever learned. [p. 296]."

The point is that too often our stored abstractions of former experiences in the form of rules and schemas lead us to view our current percepts, images, memories, thoughts, and behaviors not as freshly synthesized products created anew at each moment, but as mere replicas or duplicates of the past. A dead hand thus may come to rest on much of what we see, hear, imagine, remember, think, and do, thanks to what Neisser (1967) refers to as the *Reappearance Hypothesis.* According to that notion, prevalent in psychology for decades, the individual learns and stores percepts, images, memories, and acts, which then are simply reactivated upon need or demand as exact replicas or duplicates of those earlier events. Neisser (1967) has written of this notion as follows:

> This assumption is so ingrained in our thinking that we rarely notice how poorly it fits experience. If Reappearance were really the govern-

ing principle of mental life, repetition of earlier acts or thoughts should be the natural thing, and variation the exception. In fact, the opposite is true. Precise repetition of any movement, any spoken sentence, or any sequence of thought is extremely difficult to achieve [p. 282].

An important consequence of this misleading conceptualization is that we tend to overlook the novelty that characterizes many, if not all, of our percepts, images, memories, thoughts, and much of our behavior. What's more, in overlooking such novelty, we blind ourselves to what is unique and special in our experience and behavior and so fail to make use of its unending potential, of the options in it available to us. We become liable, in Gibson's (1966) terms, to "an overselection of information," or brutally "schematic" and literal in what we experience and do. As Gibson (1966) has described such a process in perception:

> After things are discriminated and their properties abstracted, their number is reduced to a few categories of interest and the subcategories or cross-categories neglected. At this stage only the information required to identify an object need be picked up and all the other information in the array, whatever makes it unique and special, can be neglected. Hence the percept of the object becomes a mere caricature or schema of what it would be if the perceiver took the time to scan the . . . structure of the object . . . The object may in fact be unique or special, that is, an exceptional one that is not in one of the observer's categories of interest. An overselection of information has occurred [p. 309].[1]

So a picture is emerging from the new experimental trend of the remarkable potential that human beings possess for continuous psychological development and growth. The new, the novel, the special, the unique exist everywhere, in each percept, each image, each thought, each memory, each act. The person, for all of his limited capacity, also possesses a remarkable ability to put into brief storage systems a large amount of information—and he possesses as well the ability to determine selectively the future development of information held in these brief storage systems.

A number of degrees of freedom thus exist for the person throughout the temporal course of experience and behavior to integrate, shape, and articulate the perceptual, imaginal, memorial, and behavioral products of his activities. These integrating, shaping, and articulating operations may take the form of overt adjustments and exploratory movements of the body, head, limbs, fingers, eyes, tongue, and so on, by which distinctive

---

[1] Reprinted by permission of Houghton Mifflin Company.

features, invariant properties, and higher-order patterns are extracted and used as information from stimulation. Or the operations may take the form of more covert and internal processes, such as naming, rehearsing, matching, classifying, seriating, or otherwise dealing with current or past input by means of stored sensorimotor, imaginal, or conceptual rules or schemas that may or may not be accompanied by observable overt activities. The ground of it all is in the individual's own information-processing activities and to what he chooses, either overtly or covertly, to direct those activities.

Personal growth in this view rests on the foundation of the great order of creativity and variation inherent in experience and behavior. Working with the information contained in stimulation, each person continuously synthesizes and fashions anew his own individualistic "works of art," whether these be percepts, images, memories, thoughts, and/or acts. The rules or schemes by which these "works of art" are produced may give many of them a striking resemblance to previous works, but they are new nonetheless. Yet the very ease and economy with which these rules or schemas come to function, and old, misleading views about how humans deal with stimulation, often obscure this basic creative capacity, stifling its optimal effect.

Generally, then, it is the recognition and use of this creative capacity, whatever the endeavor, that characterizes personal growth—which consists, for one thing, of the person's more active awareness of his own role in the shaping and fashioning of his experience and behavior. It also consists of the individual's expanded view of the inexhaustible informational riches contained in stimulation and of the options and possibilities open to him in making use of this stimulation. There is no end to this potential, and in personal growth the individual capitalizes upon it by actively searching for and extracting and using fresh features and patterns of information to ever enhance and enrich his experience and behavior.

INFORMATION PROCESSING AND THE PROCESS SCALE OF PSYCHOTHERAPY

So far this chapter has treated of some general notions concerning information and how individuals deal with it by active, selective attentive processes and the application of rules or schemas. Of particular concern has been the person's limited capacity, which can lead to an overselection of information and to a misapplication and/or general improverishment of rules and schemas. Also of concern have been misleading conceptualizations of the person as a passive recipient of stimulation and of the function of rules and schemas as primarily reproductive, rather than productive, of experience and behavior. Underlying all these concerns has been their influence on personal growth.

The facilitation of such growth is a major thrust in client-centered psychotherapy, and in the late 1950s and early 1960s researchers in the client-centered framework began to develop a variety of rating scales designed to assess the process of personal growth as it seemed to occur in psychotherapy. A description of this process has been offered by Rogers (1961). He conceives of it as movement along a continuum of personal functioning, several characteristics of which appear to bear a close conceptual kinship to the view of the person as an active, selective processor of information.

This section points to some aspects of this kinship. One is Rogers' (1961) emphasis in the process scale on the differentiation and recognition of feelings and personal meanings. Differentiation and recognition are concepts also stressed by the Gibsons (1966, 1969) in their work on perception, and it is argued that differentiation and recognition, whether of internal or external information, are perceptual and cognitive acts that involve certain information-processing activities and allocations of attentive capacity on the part of the individual. A second topic is a consideration of some of the characteristics of the process scale viewed in terms of different levels of use, or allocations of, the person's information-processing capacities. A final topic concerns the "peak" functioning of the individual as manifested in the process scale and how such functioning is congruent with certain ideas and principles derived from the experimental study of human information processing.

Writing of personal growth in psychotherapy, Rogers (1961) distinguished seven stages of such growth. Keeping in mind that these stages are seen as existing along a continuum, some sense of the overall view can be gained from considering simply its ends or extremes. In describing one of these extremes, Rogers (1961) noted:

> The client has now incorporated the quality of motion, of flow, of changingess, into every aspect of his psychological life, and this becomes its outstanding characteristic. He lives in his feelings knowingly and with basic trust in them and acceptance of them. The ways in which he construes experience are continually changing as his personal constructs are modified by each new living event. His experiencing is process in nature, feeling the new in each situation and interpreting it anew, interpreting in terms of the past only to the extent that the new is now identical with the past . . . He values exactness in differentiation of his feelings and of the personal meanings of his experience . . .

He lives fully in himself as a constantly changing flow of process [pp. 154–155].[2]

By contrast, consider Rogers' (1961) description of the extreme opposite end of his scale's continuum:

> The individual has little or no recognition of the ebb and flow of the feeling life within him. The ways in which he construes experience have been set by his past, and are rigidly unaffected by the actualities of the present . . . Differentiation of personal meanings in experience is crude or global, experience being seen largely in black and white terms . . . The individual at this stage is represented by such terms as stasis, fixity, the opposite of flow or change [p. 133].

Some of the characteristics of personal functioning upon which Rogers (1961) has based these descriptions and their relationship to information processing will be dealt with in more detail later in this section. Of particular interest at this point is Rogers' emphasis on the person's differentiation and recognition of feelings and personal meanings.

In this emphasis on differentiation and recognition, Rogers (1961) sounds a note similar to the Gibsons (1966, 1969). They also are interested in differentiation but in a different context—that of an information-processing view of perceptual development. They also are concerned with recognition as a perceptual act. True, almost all of the Gibsons' (1966, 1969) work is directed toward the person's processing of external information, whereas Rogers is more concerned with differentiation and recognition as they apply to internal events or feelings and personal meanings. But from the perspective of this chapter a person's information-processing capacities can be allocated in diverse ways, including the further development and use of information available in internal, as well as external, stimulation.

Thus it is possible to think of the processing of internal information as proceeding along much the same lines as those proposed by the Gibsons (1966, 1969) for the processing of external stimulation. In this view, dreams, fantasies, fleeting thoughts and images, the feelings that accompany many of our activities—all can be seen as potential or partially developed information available to be further differentiated, searched, explored, and used. Its structure may be more difficult to specify, its properties less immediately adaptive than the information extracted and used from external information, but its processing by the person is essentially the same as with external information. In other words, it involves the active, selective extraction of differential features, invariant properties, and higher-order patterns and the simultaneous filtering out of other variables, all or much of which is accomplished by attentive acts and the application of rules and schemas.

An example of how such processing can occur with external information is offered by E. Gibson (1969). She writes:

> I had never seen a Russian olive tree and did not know there was one in the yard. But when some Boy Scouts rang the doorbell of my temporary residence and asked me to see the Russian olive tree, it was quite easy to differentiate it from other trees, because it passed the tests of an olive tree: its characteristic shape, gray-green foliage and so on. The differences from other oilve trees were detectable, but so were the features of an olive tree . . . Thus the imaginal representation transfers to new discriminations and permits perceptual learning by providing the opportunity both for matching and for detection of differences [p. 154].[3]

Just as an imaginal representation helps E. Gibson match and detect differences in olive trees, so too may such internal representations help us discriminate, detect, articulate, and deal with feelings. A person has a lifetime of feelings. But how he regards any current feelings will be affected by how he has learned and/or has been taught to deal with them. In dealing with internal information, the person may not have devoted enough attentive capacity to it to make even crude discriminations—or, at the opposite extreme, he may have developed elaborate and articulate schemas and rules for processing internal events, including sophisticated recognitions and differentiations of these events.

All of this, I take it, is what Rogers (1961) means by "valuing exactness in differentiation" of one's feelings or by the individual's having "little or no recognition of the ebb and flow of the feeling life within him." Differentiation and recognition, in information-processing terms, turn out to be complex phenomena. Each thing, object, event, or sequence of events, turns out to be experienced and behaved within a context of a lifetime of things, objects, events, or configurations of these. Every information-processing act—whether an adjustment of the eyes, head, body, tongue, or a gating of visual, auditory, olfactory, gustatory, or tactile modes, or dealing with the external to the exclusion of the internal or vice versa, or some combination of all of these—spells one more step along a line of information-processing development. The use of certain capacities, or the allocation of attention to certain modes or channels, precludes the use and development of others. The recognition and differentiation of one's feelings are no exception to this. As a matter of personal growth, Rogers (1961) believes that the recognition and differentiation of feelings are important and that their exclusion as information-processing acts suggests impoverishment of the person, a failure to achieve the status of the fully functioning human being.

Thus, from an information-processing view, Rogers can be seen as stressing the importance in psychotherapy of the allocation of selective attention to certain kinds of information—in particular, feelings and personal meanings. So too, in some of the characteristics we will examine, and which are seen by Rogers (1961) as descriptive of the different stages in his process scale, the implication is always of attentive capacity at work, but at work in ways that can be seen as representing some freedom of choice. These options open up as one approaches the final stages of information processing, but one must recognize that the exercising of these options puts constraints on whatever else might have been attended to or dealt with. The characteristics Rogers (1961) describes also imply that rules and schemas may either impoverish or enrich experience and behavior.

To take again the extreme ends of the continuum as illustrative, some characteristics of the stage of psychological fixity and remoteness of experiencing are seen in these terms by Rogers (1961):

Feelings and personal meanings are neither recognized nor owned.
Personal constructs . . . are extremely rigid.
There is an unwillingness to communicate self. Communication is only about externals.
Close and communicative relationships are construed as dangerous.
No problems are recognized or perceived at this stage.
There is no desire to change.
There is much blockage of internal communication [p. 132].

As one moves to, say, a midpoint on the scale, there are a number of changes signaling personal growth. Some of these are described by Rogers (1961) as:

The client describes more intense feelings of the not-now-present variety.
Feelings are described as objects in the present.
There is a tendency toward experiencing feelings in the immediate present, and there is distrust and fear of this possibility.

There is little open acceptance of feelings, though some acceptance is exhibited.

Experiencing is less bound by the structure of the past, is less remote, and may occasionally occur with little postponement.

There is a loosening of the way experience is construed.

There are some discoveries of personal constructs; there is a definite recognition of these as constructs; and there is a beginning questioning of their validity.

There is an increased differentiation of feelings, constructs, personal meanings, with some tendency toward seeking exactness of symbolization.

There is a realization of concern about contradictions and incongruencies between experience and self [pp. 137–138].[4]

Viewed in information-processing terms, one can see that some of the changes in the characteristics described by Rogers (1961) in the scale suggest shifts in the allocative use of attentive capacity. There also can be seen in the changes a richer, more varied application and use of rules and schemas—one that takes more into account the inexhaustibility of information and the continuous workings of the brain and nervous system.

A great deal more attentive capacity appears devoted, for example, to internal events, making possible the recognition and beginning acceptance and ownership of feelings. Along with this, as might be expected from the ideas we have reviewed, comes an increased diffrentiation of feelings and personal meanings and their more articulated verbal coding. In moving toward more immediacy of experience, the person's attentive processes appear more closely attuned to the preattentive processes and all their abundance of multichanneled information. The new, the novel, the unique, the special begin to be processed. Experience opens up, magnifies, and internal communication is enhanced.

The loosening of the way experience is construed and the fact that "experiencing . . . is less remote, and may occasionally occur with little postponement" not only point to greater accessibility to preattentive information, but also suggest an enrichment and elaboration of the person's rules and schemas. There also is a greater awareness on the individual's part of his own role in the selection, coding, retrieval, and use of information. So he makes "some discoveries of personal constructs," and there is a "beginning questioning of their validity," paving the way for less overselection of information and a reworking and refurbishing of rules and schemas by fresh input.

There is also a beginning exploration of the self-schema as a high-level abstraction against the many instances of which it is made up and the discovery of contradictions and incongruities. Here attentive capacity is directed to one of the most, if not the most, crucial schemas a person stores, resulting in the integration of new and novel aspects of self arising from information previously neglected, ignored, or filtered out. A new self-schema thus begins to emerge, based less on the structure of the past than on a fresh ground of current experiencing.

These same shifts in information processing are even more dramatically evident in Rogers' (1961) description of the seventh, or "peak," stage in the personal growth continuum. In his key phrases, the stage is characterized by the following:

New feelings are experienced with immediacy and richness of detail . . . The experiencing of such feelings is used as a clear referent.

There is a growing and continuing sense of acceptant ownership of these changing feelings, a basic trust in his own process.

Experiencing has lost almost completely its structure-bound aspects and becomes process experiencing—that is, the situation is experienced and interpreted in its newness, not as the past.

The self becomes increasingly simply the subjective and reflexive awareness of experiencing. The self is much less frequently a perceived object, and much more frequently something confidently felt in process.

Personal constructs are tentatively reformulated, to be validated against further experience, but even then, to be held loosely.

Internal communication is clear, with feelings and symbols well matched and fresh terms for new feelings [pp. 151–154].[5]

Here we see described a person who functions much as the information-processing view implies a person is uniquely equipped to function. Rogers (1961) places special emphasis upon the experiencing of feelings in "immediacy and richness of detail"—an emphasis that suggests a special allocation of attentive capacity to internal events or information. But it is also an emphasis that suggests that the person is more in touch with the multiple possibilities of his experience and more open to its options and potential. Stress is also placed upon the person's experience and interpretation of situations in terms of newness and uniqueness rather than on resemblance to the past.

To me there is a striking similarity in some of the observations derived by Rogers (1961) from the study of personal growth in psychotherapy and some of the ideas and findings of those interested in the broad application of the principles of information processing to human experience and behavior. Neisser (1967), Piaget (1950), and the Gibsons (1966, 1969), as well as others referred to in this chapter, all stress the potential of the person for continuous psychological development and growth. They conceive of perception, imagery, memory, thought, and behavior not only as active and selective, but as very much here-and-now processes that carry constant potential for the enhancement and enrichment of experience.

At the very heart of this potential is but a handful of resources. For the tools of personal growth turn out to be the uses of attention and a store of extracted rules and schemas. Yet they are resources powerful enough to enhance and enrich or to devastate and impoverish personal experience and behavior.

IMPLICATIONS FOR PSYCHOTHERAPY

Much of the foregoing suggests that the refocusing or retraining of attentive capacity is an important factor contributing to personal growth in psychotherapy. This retraining or refocusing brings into play neglected aspects of current external or stored information and puts the person into closer contact with the myriad possibilities of experience and behavior. It also leads to the elaboration and articulation of rules and schemas, making them adequate and effective in dealing with the richness and variety of information contained in stimulation.

Such a view provides a major theme for this section. A second theme is that the aim of psychotherapy is not so much to get the person perceiving, imagining, remembering, thinking, or behaving differently as it is to bring him to a realization of the options inherent in these activities. One other point to bear in mind is that although in what follows it may seem as if the sole concern is with the one-to-one, or the more traditional, form of psychotherapy, this is not the case, and references will be made to work with couples, families, and groups under the general designation of "interpersonal networks." The issues to be touched upon here are of import in helping relationships of all kinds.

These issues include (a) the role of therapist selectivity, particularly in the client-centered approach, in articulating emotional, as well as other, dimensions of information to which attentive capacity may be devoted;

(b) some information-processing principles that may make such articulation more or less effective; (c) the view that the client-centered approach to therapy not only communicates empathic understanding by the therapist's adoption, in so far as possible, of the person's or network's rules and schemas, but that it also "vivifies" and "amplifies" these rules and schemas, leading to their progressive development and change; (d) an altered outlook on the emphasis in client-centered of perceptual change as the key to behavioral and personality change; and (e) the suggestion in line with this that structured exercises, such as those used by Gestalt therapists and in group work, may be valuable adjuncts to more traditional client-centered methods.

In the previous section it was noted that one characteristic of personal growth in psychotherapy was the increased differentiation, recognition, and ownership of feelings. A shift also occurred, if psychotherapy was successful, from dealing with feelings associated with past events to feelings experienced in the present. There was nothing said, however, about the therapist's role in producing these changes. They were simply seen as indicators of personal growth in psychotherapy, and the suggestion was made that they implied the allocation of the person's attentive capacity to heretofore neglected or rejected information.

These changes probably occur, at least in part, as a result of the therapist's consistent selective response to affective components in client or network messages. The effect, in a sense, is that of drawing the client's or the network's attentional resources again and again to the interpenetration of feelings with all that is perceived, imagined, remembered, thought, and done. The so-called *reflection-of-feelings* response has long been regarded as a basic technique in client-centered therapy. The term is somewhat misleading inasmuch as the client-centered therapist does not necessarily ignore components of client or network messages that are not related to feelings. Rather, the effort is to capture an integrated message—one that seeks to articulate as fully as possible what it is the client or network is expressing as well as feeling. Nonetheless, focal attention is limited, and its allocation to extract and use certain dimensions of information, including feelings, more effectively, excludes the extraction and use of other dimensions, and the therapist's role in this regard can be construed as the retraining or reeducation of attentive capacity.

It is too simple, of course, to speak of attending to feelings as the sole source of gain in psychotherapy. If such feelings habitually or typically have been ignored or rejected, their inclusion as a major object of attention implies the likelihood of a greater differentiation and recognition of such feelings and their integration into other aspects of personal or network functioning. Certainly, too, it can be maintained that cultural attitudes toward feelings as a source of information lead to their relative neglect in this society and that their fuller integration into experience and behavior by attentive retraining stands to enrich personal and network functioning.

At the same time however, it is not only feelings, but also all kinds of neglected, ignored, or rejected information, that can spell trouble for the individual or for the interpersonal network, and any focus by the therapist on these aspects of information can be seen as an effort to open the client's or network's attentive resources to a richer, more varied informational field. More than 20 years ago Fromm-Reichman (1950) advocated encouraging individuals to pay attention to and to verbalize marginal thoughts and images in psychotherapy. She also suggested individuals be trained to observe and describe physical sensations and symptoms as they arose in the therapeutic hour. Instructions to the individual in psychotherapy to report day and night dreams, as well as other fantasy material, also can be seen as efforts by the therapists to direct attentive capacity to ignored or neglected aspects of information.

One effect of this retraining or refocusing of attention is to make more accessible to use by the person or network information generated by the preattentive processes. As stressed earlier in this chapter, this information can be viewed as the teeming ground or field out of which can be articulated more finely detailed percepts, images, memories, thoughts, and behaviors. Neisser (1967) has gone so far as to suggest that preattentive information is analogous in many respects to Freud's primary process. Preattentive information, in contrast to information developed by the serial or successive focusing of selective attention, is profuse, rich, chaotic, and abundant. As such, it offers inexhaustible new resources for personal and network growth, resources that may be overlaid by too much cultural or personal emphasis on sequential or serial processing. As the Russells (1959) have suggested,

> The maintenance of a personality depends on free access by the attention to any kind of current or recorded input. It has been obvious since Freud (and in some ways before him) that none of us has a completely integrated personality in this sense. It was a master stroke of Freud to emphasize accessibility. Both common sense . . . and a great deal of experimental evidence . . . agree in stressing the advantage of delegating the control of skilled performance to mechanisms which are not continually attended to, and the fact that this delegation continually occurs . . . But all such delegations should be reversible, and

it should be possible to scan and readjust them whenever necessary. As long as this is so, they are not unconscious in Freud's sense [pp. 544–545].[6]

The so-called unconscious thus may not exist in repressed memories or stored information, but only in misapplications of attentive capacity or stored and abstracted rules for retrieving such information. By accentuating neglected, ignored, or rejected sources of information, the therapist can be viewed as working in psychotherapy to induce changes in the person's or network's uses of attentive capacity toward a fuller exploration and integration of information available in usable or retrievable forms.

None of this is to imply that a therapist can willy-nilly direct attention to whatever suits his whim or fancy. He can, of course, in hopes of striking some untapped resource in the person that will facilitate personal growth. But without some kind of rooting in the person's or network's preattentive processes or stored rules and schemas, information to which the therapist seeks to direct attentive capacity is not likely to result in meaningful development and use. Any topic presumably may be introduced in psychotherapy by the therapist and will represent a source of potential information. Yet to what degree such information can effectively be worked with by the client or network depends on its prior grounding in stored rules and schemas and/or the features, properties, and patterns currently available in preattentive material. Although this stance could be seen to reflect a client-centered bias, it also reflects findings from information-processing studies suggesting that information not stored or in current buffer "holds" does not exist as such and cannot be further processed.

Graphic examples of this have occurred in my own experience in therapy when I have sought to call the client's or network's attention to certain nonverbal components of behavior accompanying speech. If the behavior is not spoken to within a relatively brief duration of time, it may be impossible for the client or network to recover or reconstruct the component so that it can be meaningfully fitted into the ongoing sequence of therapeutic events. Similarly, my attempts to recover, or to bring the client's or network's attentive capacity to bear on events that have occurred in past therapy hours, often have met with bafflement and misunderstanding or, at best, polite compliance.

So in the present view the therapist must try to bring focal attentive capacity to bear on what he perceives, imagines, or thinks, is currently available information for the client or network. The information perhaps is being excessively filtered, neglected, ignored, and/or rejected, but it is available, if only in preattentive forms. A therapist's construction of events, perceptions, images, thoughts, memories, feelings, and the like is certainly a source of potential information, no matter how far removed it may be from the individual's or network's store of rules and schemas for making a similar construction or from information readily available in short-term buffers. But by selectively dealing with information in this fashion, the therapist runs the risk of simply bypassing the client's or network's capacity for personal growth by ignoring the principles inherent in experimental studies of information processing.

As I have understood and practiced it, the client-centered approach tends to "go with" the person's or network's allocation of information-processing capacities, particularly in the early stages of the therapeutic endeavor. It is "where the client is," what he chooses to "deal with," and so on, to which the client-centered therapists also devotes his information-processing capacities. It is as if, in the language of this chapter, the therapist becomes a "co-artist" or fellow artisan aiding the individual or network in shaping, forming, molding, and developing perceptual, imaginal, memorial, and behavioral products. Also, in using a here-and-now approach, the client-centered therapists opts not only for shared product or picture-making but, in my view, emphasizes and models process as well. He seeks, in short, to capture by paraphrasing, by reflecting, by trying to reconstruct the client's or network's meanings, the very rules and schemas by which the person fashions and creates his experience and behavior. Hayek (1962) has referred to this process as "rule perception." He likens it to the ability of individuals to use language in accordance with rules of which they may be totally unaware. Its effects, therefore, do not lie necessarily in the therapist's explicit grasp of the client's or network's rules or schemas, but rather in the patterning of the therapist's responses— a patterning that displays the intelligibility to the therapist of the client's or network's experience and behavior.

The concrete result of this process is the communication of empathic understanding by the therapist to the person or interpersonal network. It is, of course, a central tenet of client-centered theory that such under-standing must be communicated for personal or network growth to occur. However, this entrance into the client's or network's fashioning of experi-ence and behavior serves at least one other important function. It is that of vivifying or amplifying how the client or network applies rules and schemas to produce certain percepts, images, memories, thoughts, and behaviors.

In this process the therapist devotes his information-processing capa-cities to articulating the person's or network's experience and behavior as concretely, specifically, and vividly as he can. In so doing he puts into bold relief not only the content produced by the client or network, but, at the same time, some of the selective, extractive, and abstractive operations that go into the production of the content. Such an articulation, if the therapist is picking up the experience and behavior fairly accurately, allows the client or network to discern and begin to deal in their own terms with excessive filtering, repetitious patterning, and stereotyped or inadequate abstracting in their extraction and use of information. For what is occurring is a training or an education in the *how,* as well as the *what,* of experience and behavior. It is an emphasis upon process as much as upon content and, as such, is in keeping with the idea quoted from Neisser (1967) earlier in this chapter that content may be little more than the ever-renewed product of learned activities. In his words, once again, "Mental activities can be learned; perhaps they are the only things that are ever learned [p. 296]."

Such a perspective puts into doubt an overly simplified central tenet of early client-centered therapy, prior to its greater elaboration into process notions. It was that therapy sought only to bring about a change in the troubled individual's perception of himself. Under the influence of the Gestalt tradition, behavior was seen as following upon perception, and as one's image of oneself changed, then behavior changed, and much research (e.g., Rogers & Dymond, 1954) sought to substantiate this relationship.

Client-centered therapy has had a hard time shaking this notion that perception is somehow prior to, and vitally affects, all behavior. In the view here, the converse is equally true, and that in part is what this chapter is about. For, as we have tried to demonstrate, perception itself is but a product, a product shaped to a great degree by the person's own information-processing activities.

So where the person looks, the frequency of his eye movements, how he uses his various receptor systems via postural adjustments, to what he overtly or covertly chooses to attend, and the internal sets of operations by which information is rejected, rehearsed, stored, or otherwise dealt with —all of these become critical in determining what is perceived and what is retained or worked with out of what is perceived. Although the importance of perception and its impact on behavior should not be understated, it is equally important to realize that perception, thought, and behavior are all of a piece, and trying to posit one as prior to the other is misleading.

As client-centered therapy evolved from a concern with content to a concern with process, there was probably an implicit recognition of the individual's manufacturing of perception. Thus, studies making use of Rogers' process scale and other important work by Butler, Rice, and Wagstaff

(1962) on client and therapist expressivity, began to understore the client's own behavior and acts in creating percepts, images, memories, thoughts, and verbal abstractions of these. It is in this widening of the client-centered approach that we see one of its major convergences with the information-processing view.

As a consequence of my own interest and exposure to this view, I now feel less uneasy than I formerly did about asking clients to engage in new behaviors—either in the therapy hour or outside of it. Such prescribed behaviors may take the form of role-playing, nonverbal exercises, changes in daily routines and so on. In prescribing these activities I believe that the person's altered behaviors may give rise to new percepts, images, memories, thoughts, and feelings.

Role-playing, for example, means that the person tries to pattern his actions, speech, mannerisms, and the like so that that they depict these same characteristics as manifested by another person. To be able to do this with any degree of success the person must apply or induce rules or schemas different from his own. He thus may come to see not only the options inherent in the sequencing and articulation of various behaviors, but also that the induction and application of rules and schemas other than his own give rise to new percepts, images, memories, and thoughts. Changes in daily or habitual routines may serve a similar purpose, even to the extent of the person experiencing considerable difficulty in using new or different rules and schemas to guide his behavior, so that a greater appreciation is gained of the role they play in his life. Nonverbal exercises often bring into greater awareness the kinds of sensorimotor codes by which we orient and adjust ourselves to the social and physical environment and a keener recognition of how verbal codes guide and direct selective attention.

To me, in these prescribed or directed activities lies one of the appeals of Gestalt therapy, for it often explicitly requires definite, guided reallocations of attention or information-processing activities on the part of the client. What am I doing moment by moment? and, How am I doing it? are questions often asked of the client by the Gestalt therapist. He also often calls attention to overt actions of the client—foot-tapping, huddling in the chair, clutching of the throat with the hand, or whatever—and asks him to amplify these to see what experience such amplification generates. Such an amplification demands use of selective attention, which may result in more articulated rules and schemas and easier accessibility to activities that are usually preattentive.

The Gestalt therapist also asks clients to act out various aspects of themselves—or the personages, objects, landscapes, and other things that clients create in their dreams. These techniques are reported often to lead the client to a new experience of himself—or to the discovery of many overlooked (nonattended to?) aspects of this experience. In effect, Gestalt therapy recognizes the important role of behavior in generating fresh experience or information. It also, in line with the assumptions of this chapter, places primary stress on the person's creating or fashioning his own experience and behavior.

A similar argument can be adduced for the whole spectrum of structured exercises that have arisen from developments in the last decade of group work. Variously known as *T, encounter, sensory awareness,* or *sensitivity training* groups, these groups often make use of noncharacteristic ways of behaving in order to make the individual aware of how he manufactures, creates, or fashions his own experience through his own actions. A further characteristic of such groups is that the focus is often upon the allocation of information-processing capacities, including attention, to stimulus patterns arising from sources not ordinarily attended to. Thus a pencil, a painting, a landscape, a piece of music, or a certain set of feelings, may be assessed in great detail, its various configurations noted, its qualities allowed to emerge without verbal labeling, and so on. Or the attentive capacity of the person may be focused upon a certain portion of his body —with instructions to process or deal with information only from that area and perhaps to provide feedback to the area verbally or by imagery.

These methods entail the directed use of selective attention, with consequent enrichment of rules and schemas and a greater recognition of personal choice in the allocation of attentive capacity. As such, they lead to a greater awareness on the individual's part of his own role in the production of his experience and behavior. The objective is not so much to get the client perceiving, imagining, remembering, thinking, or behaving differently as it is to bring him to a realization of the options inherent in all these activities. It is toward this end that much of client-centered therapy can be seen to be directed, and explicit recognition of some of the information-processing mechanisms involved may make us not only more aware as therapists of what we are doing, but more effective as well.

For the truth is, we create by being. We are not passive recipients of experience. Nor are we simple behavior respondents. Information-processing studies teach us that we produce throughout our lives—less systematically at first, more systematically later—a constant stream of perceptual, imaginal, memorial, and behavioral objects. The bulk of these are fleeting, ephemeral, and quickly lost. But they are just as quickly replaced by newly fashioned experiential and behavioral products. As artists in this process, we perhaps all need to possess the skills, as Gibson (1966) has suggested, of a good caricaturist. For, in the view presented in this chapter, *all* perception, imagery, memory, thought, and/or behavior are caricatures. It cannot be otherwise. The only question is: Do we produce, or help others to produce, good or bad caricatures?

REFERENCES

Bartlett, F. C. *Remembering.* Cambridge, England: University Press, 1932.

Becker, E. *The revolution in psychiatry.* New York: Free Press, 1964.

Broadbent, D. E. *Perception and communication.* London: Pergamon, 1958.

Broadbent, D. E. Communication models for memory. In G. A. Talland & N. C. Waugh (Eds.), *The pathology of memory.* New York: Academic Press, 1969.

Broadbent, D. E. *Decision and stress.* New York: Academic Press, 1971.

Butler, J. M., Rice, L. N., & Wagstaff, A. K. On the naturalistic definition of variables: An analogue of clinical analysis. In H. H. Strupp & L. Luborsky (Eds.), *Research in psychotherapy.* Vol. 2. Washington, D.C.: American Psychological Association, 1962.

Fromm-Reichmann, F. *Principles of intensive psychotherapy.* Chicago: University of Chicago Press, 1950.

Gibson, E. J. *Principles of perceptual learning and development.* New York: Appleton-Century-Crofts, 1969.

Gibson, J. J. *The senses considered as perceptual systems.* New York: Houghton Mifflin, 1966.

Hayek, F. A. Rules, perception, and intelligibility. In *Proceedings of the British Academy.* London: Oxford University Press, 1962.

Kagan, J. The determinants of attention in the infant. *American Scientist,* 1970, **58,** 298–306.

Laing, R. D. *The politics of the family.* Toronto: CBC Publications, 1969.

Miller, G. A. The magical number seven, plus or minus two: Some limits on our capacity for processing information. *Psychological Review,* 1956, **63,** 81–96.

Moray, N. *Attention: Selective processes in vision and hearing.* New York: Academic Press, 1970.

Neisser, U. *Cognitive psychology.* New York: Appleton-Century-Crofts, 1967.

Norman, D. A. *Memory and attention.* New York: Wiley, 1969.

Piaget, J. *The psychology of intelligence.* New York: Harcourt, Brace, 1950.

Piaget, J., & Inhelder, B. *The psychology of the child.* New York: Basic Books, 1969.

Posner, M. I. Representational systems for storing information in memory. In G. A. Talland & N. C. Waugh (Eds.), *The pathology of memory.* New York: Academic Press, 1969.

Rogers, C. R. A process conception of psychotherapy. In *On becoming a person.* Boston: Houghton Mifflin, 1961.

Rogers, C. R., & Dymond, R. F. (Eds.) *Psychotherapy and personality change.* Chicago: University of Chicago Press, 1954.

Russell, C., & Russell, W. M. S. Raw materials for a definition of mind. In J. Scher (Ed.), *Theories of the mind.* New York: Free Press, 1959.

Schachtel, E. C. *Metamorphosis.* New York: Basic Books, 1959.

Talland, G. A. *Disorders of memory and learning.* Baltimore: Penguin, 1968.

Wheelis, A. How people change. *Commentary,* May 1969, 56–57.

CHAPTER 3

A Cognitive Theory of Experiencing, Self-Actualization, and Therapeutic Process[1]

David A. Wexler

The concepts of self-actualization and experiencing have, to a large extent, been the cornerstones upon which client-centered theory and practice have been built. The tendency toward self-actualization is seen as providing the basic motivational force by which a client in therapy moves toward enhanced functioning and greater psychological health. This movement is defined largely in terms of changes in the quality of the client's experiencing, and the role of the therapist is typically seen as one of facilitating the client's experiencing. Carl Rogers' theorizing on self-actualization and experiencing enjoys considerable popularity in humanistic psychology today. The concepts have, however, stimulated relatively little systematic investigation in scientific psychology; their molarity and ambiguities in the way in which they are defined have made them difficult to operationalize and investigate empirically. It is unfortunate that this is the case, for self-actualization and experiencing refer to phenomena that are crucial to an understanding of human functioning and represent an important area for scientific inquiry. The aim of this chapter is to set forth a new theoretical framework for understanding self-actualization and the process of experiencing with the hope that it will provide not only a clearer conceptual basis from which both these concepts might be investigated in future empirical work, but also a framework that will help us to understand better how a client changes in therapy and how the therapist helps to facilitate this change.

[1] Work on this chapter was facilitated by a Biomedical Sciences Support Grant to the author while he was at Rutgers University. The author would also like to thank Juliana van Tellingen and Lawrence Ward for their useful comments and suggestions on the material in this chapter.

The first section of this chapter will critically examine how self-actualization and experiencing have been traditionally viewed, with an eye to pointing out basic difficulties in the manner in which they have been conceptualized. In light of the difficulties raised, the next section will develop a new theoretical framework for understanding the concepts. Experiencing in therapy will be seen to reflect the manner in which information is processed on a moment-to-moment basis, and self-actualization will be seen as reflecting the person's characteristic style of processing information. Using this framework as a basis, the final section of this chapter will consider how the client-centered therapist's style of participation functions to facilitate the client's experiencing on a moment-to-moment basis.

SELF-ACTUALIZATION AND EXPERIENCING:
THE TRADITIONAL VIEW

Rogers has seen self-actualization as a basic organismic tendency to move toward the progressively greater realization of inherent potentials (Rogers, 1963).[2] Rogers sees this striving toward the fulfillment of inherent potentials as rooted in the biological nature of the organism and says it constitutes the one basic motivational force in life that moves the organism toward self-enhancement and growth (Rogers, 1963). Thus, Rogers gives us a statement both about the nature of the force (realization of inherent potentials) and about its source (rooted in the biological nature of the organism). Yet, as to its source, Rogers does not provide any clear conceptual or empirical basis for anchoring self-actualization in the basic biological nature of the organism; he simply postulates that it is so rooted.

Not only is there a lack of clarity with respect to the biological foundation of self-actualization, but there is also some ambiguity with respect to viewing its nature as the realization of inherent potentials. Although the realization of potentials is seen as the essence of self-actualization, Rogers does not specify what the substantive nature of these potentials might be, or even how their nature might be determined (since presumably they vary from person to person). Instead, when attempting to characterize self-actualized persons, he has emphasized the characteristics of openness to experience, organismic trusting, and existentiality (Rogers, 1961). These characteristics do not refer to inherent substantive potentials, but

[2] In different contexts Rogers has used the term "self-actualization" to refer both to the general organismic tendency to realize inherent potentials and to a more specific tendency to maintain the slf-concept. Here the term will be used to refer to the more general tendency to realize inherent potentialities.

to qualities of the person's experiencing. Although these characteristics have intuitive appeal in depicting an ideal mode of experiencing, the definitions of these notions are also problematic and lack precision, and they add little conceptual clarity to the construct of self-actualization.

According to Rogers (1961), if the person were fully open to his experience, "every stimulus—whether originating within the organism or in the environment—would be freely relayed through the nervous system without being distorted by any defense mechanism [pp. 187–188]." Such a state, however, would really not be optimal, for it would mean in effect that the person would find himself overwhelmed by the multitude of stimuli that impinges on him at any given moment in time. One of the basic characteristics of the organism is its ability to select relevant stimuli for processing while ignoring other, irrelevant, stimuli. Such behavior is not only necessary for adaptive behavioral functioning, but also essential for sheer physical survival. Yet, from the way Rogers defines openness to experience it would seem that such selection would be precluded.

If the person who is supposedly open to experience does indeed select only some stimuli for symbolization, how would his selection differ from selection in the service of defense (denial or distortion)? Rogers does not answer this question specifically, but if he did, his answer would probably lie in his notion of organismic trusting. Organismic trusting means that the person's locus of evaluation for the symbolization of experience and for the guidance of behavior is his own immediate bodily reaction (organismic valuing process), rather than conditions of worth introjected from others in the process of socialization (Rogers, 1959). Although there is intuitive appeal to the notion of behavior guided by one's own reactions, the distinction between the organismic valuing process and conditions of worth is problematic. Whether an immediate bodily reaction one has and uses to guide behavior is "really" one's own or is a result of the influence of others through socialization is basically unknowable. Consequently, there is really no clear basis for distinguishing in practice conditions of worth from the organismic valuing process, and, hence, distinguishing defensive selection in the symbolization of experience from selection that would supposedly be nondefensive.

By existentiality Rogers means that the person lives each experience freshly in the moment and discovers the structure of experience in the process of living it (Rogers, 1961). Although this quality of processing in which experience is handled in a fresh, fluid way also has intuitive appeal, it is somewhat amorphous. Thus it is difficult to pinpoint precisely what the concept refers to. The net effect is that there is no clear basis for observing or assessing this quality.

Not only are the notions of openness to experience, organismic trusting, and existentiality somewhat problematic in themselves, but the relationship of these qualities of experiencing to the realization of inherent potentials is also obscure. In reality, Rogers has basically said very little about the realization of inherent potentials with respect to self-actualization. Not only in his view of the self-actualized person (Rogers, 1961), but also in his writings on both personality (Rogers, 1959) and the process of change in therapy (Rogers, 1958), he has emphasized the way in which the person experiences and not the fulfillment of potentials. Furthermore, Gendlin (1964) does not see growth in terms of the realization of inherent potentials, but rather builds a theoretical model of personality change around his view of the dynamics of the experiencing process.

Although it is seen to be the essence of self-actualization, the notion of the realization of potentials has, in effect, really received little elaboration with respect to self-actualization. Not only is the defining of self-actualization in terms of the fulfillment of potentials not really integrated with the overriding emphasis on experiencing that is found in client-centered theory, but it is not altogether clear that this definition is particularly informative to begin with. How much understanding is gained by saying that people become what they potentially can be? What else could a person become, other than what he can be? While people do seem to move toward an enhanced state of personal functioning, simply invoking a motive to realize one's potentials as an explanation for this change does not tell us much about the nature of the phenomenon. Rogers does give us a promising lead into understanding this movement with this insightful observations that this enhanced state of functioning fundamentally involves changes in the way the person experiences. It would seem then that a conception of self-actualization that is both clearer and more in keeping with these observations and with the traditional client-centered emphasis on experiencing might be possible if it were not defined in terms of the realization of potentials but were instead explicitly based on a well-defined theoretical model for the experiencing process.

A paper by Gendlin and Zimring (1955) laid the groundwork for such a model, and the concept of experiencing has undergone more theoretical elaboration in subsequent work by Gendlin (1962, 1964) and also by Rogers (1961). As is the case with self-actualization, there are some problems with client-centered theorizing on the dynamics of the experiencing process.

Before considering the view of experiencing offered by Gendlin, Rogers' ideas on the process will be examined. His most current view of the experiencing process is elaborated in the context of specifying the process of change in therapy (Rogers, 1961). Experiencing is seen largely in terms of the awareness of feelings, and productive changes in the client's experiencing are basically seen to involve an increased tendency for the client to experience the immediacy and richness of his subjective feelings. Conceiving of movement in therapy as a series of stages, Rogers sees lower-process stages as involving an incongruence between experience and what is recognized in awareness. There is a rigidity and remoteness in the experiencing of feelings in that they are neither owned nor recognized. Upper stages of the process continuum, on the other hand, are characterized by a congruence between awareness and experience; there is a changing flow of feelings that the clinet accurately symbolizes in awareness. In short, the client is seen as fluidly in process; he *is* the reflexive awareness of the subjective feelings he is experiencing in the moment. Although this view of the upper stages of the process continuum is consistent with the characteristics of openness to experience, organismic trusting, and existentiality that Rogers has attributed to the self-actualized person, and thus carries some of the difficulties pointed to earlier, as a view of experiencing there are some additional problems with Rogers' position that should be discussed here.

One general difficulty leading to a number of specific problems is the way in which the notion of feelings is used. In Rogers' view of experiencing, and in client-centered thinking in general, a great premium is placed on the experiencing of feelings; the fuller awareness and symbolization of one's feelings is seen to be the crucial ingredient, not only of successful client participation in therapy, but of a healthy way to live as well. There is in fact a strong tendency in client-centered thinking to use and invoke the experiencing or nonexperiencing of feelings as an all-encompassing explanation for distinguishing what is good and bad. Although there is intuitive appeal to such a position, taking recourse in the view that experiencing reflects the degree to which the person is "in touch" with and aware of his feelings only provides a grossly molar view of experiencing that serves to preclude gaining a more explicit understanding of a client's participation in the therapy process. Moreover, this view rests on some problematic assumptions about the nature of feelings.

Rogers seems to assume that feelings have a "thing-like" quality that sets them apart and makes them a special class of experience, independent of and distinct from other types of experience. Feelings are neither things in themselves nor are they distinct from other types of experience. Feelings should not be confused with emotions, for inasmuch as it is quite common in the therapy process for affect to be present, it is rare that clients speak in terms of specific emotions per se (e.g., joy, sadness, anger). Rather, they say things like "I feel uninvolved," "I feel like I haven't been living the way I should," or "There's a real feeling that I have something to live for." Sometimes affect will be evoked when such things are said and sometimes it will not. When affect is present with such statements, however, it is difficult to identify a particular emotion being expressed. Feeling "uninvolved," for example, is not a specific emotion, but is an abstraction of the common meaning of substantive information the client may be attending to (e.g., lying in bed instead of going out of the house, or being a wallflower at parties). To simply say in such a case that the client is experiencing his feelings fails to recognize the fact that affect is being generated by the client in the context of creating a cognitive organization for a particular subset of information in his life. Feelings then are not things, devoid of substantive information, but are *generated* in the process of organizing such informaion. However, in the therapy hour clients are always generating organizations for substantive information, but not always evoking affect in the process. What is it about the *nature of the information* to be organized that determines whether or not affect will be generated? The result of invoking feelings as distinct entities in themselves rather than seeing affect as generated in the context of organizing substantive information not only renders one unable to answer this question, but keeps one from asking it in the first place. It is also important here to ask why, given a particular sample of information, some cognitive organizations of this information generate affect, whereas other organizations of the same information do not. To say simply that in one instance the client is in touch with or experiencing his feelings, and in the other instance he is not, is at best uninformative and at worst tautological. Moreover, this view precludes looking at what it might be about the *way* in which information is processed and organized that in one instance evokes affect and in another instance does not.

There is a further difficulty with Rogers' position that makes conceptualizing optimal experiencing in terms of the experiencing of feelings problematic. To hold this view, Rogers must assume that a richness of feelings exists outside of awareness, prior to symbolization. In so doing, he posits a duality between awareness on the one hand, and emotional experience outside of awareness on the other. Lower stages on his process continuum involve an incongruity between awareness and feelings (feelings are not owned or recognized), whereas higher stages involve an increased congruence between the two (the richness of feelings is fully experienced in awareness). Although it is clear that Rogers' view specifically posits the existence of feelings that are not experienced in awareness, he does not provide a basis upon which such a duality can be postulated. It seems that he would have to assume that outside of awareness there is some sort of reservoir, perhaps not unlike the Freudian unconscious, where a richness of feelings resides and exists. In productive therapy process, the client seemingly would draw upon this reservoir and experience the richness of his feelings in awareness.

Just as it is questionable to assume that feelings exist as entities in themselves independent of and distinct from other types of experience, it is also questionable to assume that they exist outside of awareness. It is clear that individual clients differ both over time and from other clients in the richness of their affective experience in therapy; however, this does not necessarily mean that the inner affective experience of the client low in the process continuum is basically rich, only he is not in touch with or aware of that richness. The inner affective experience of such a client may very well be simply barren and impoverished; the way he processes information in the therapy hour may create little in the way of richness of affect. It is one thing to say that a client is *unaware* of the richness of his feelings, and it is another thing to say that the client's affective experience *might be made* richer. The latter statement assumes only what is readily observable—that the richness of affective experience can vary; the former statement posits something there is no basis for assuming—that a richness of affective experience already exists somewhere outside of awareness.

It would seem that the notion of feelings may be invoked a bit too glibly in client-centered thinking. The presence of affect may be associated with productive client process, but simply saying that optimal experiencing involves the experiencing and symbolization of feelings should not make us content that we have "understood" the phenomenon. Such a level of explanation not only necessitates making some problematic assumptions about feelings, but it also keeps us from looking beyond it and inquiring into important questions with respect to the occurrence of affect in therapy.

There is another serious difficulty with Rogers' view of experiencing that transcends the way in which the notion of feelings is used. The process of experiencing is essentially viewed by Rogers as a passive one —the person is *open* to his experience; he lets in and receives all incoming stimuli and symbolizes the changing flow of his experience in awareness. In discussing the notion of openness to experience, we commented on the difficulties in viewing the full symbolization of all stimuli as an optimal state of affairs. It is important to note here that the Rogerian man is basically seen as a recipient of experience and not as an active agent who is the creator of his own experience. Viewing experiencing as a passive process leaves us with a paradox, for client-centered theory with its distinctly humanistic stance is usually thought of as emphasizing the proactive nature of man.

Viewing man as a recipient of experience quite naturally follows from the positing of a duality between experience and awareness. If one posits, as does Rogers, that experience exists outside of awareness, then in conceptualizing the process of experiencing it is quite natural to see man as something of a gatekeeper who may or may not let that experience into awareness. The greatest problem with viewing man as a recipient of experience is that this view is basically inconsistent with the main thrust of work in cognition and information processing, which has pointed to and stressed the active and constructive nature of attentional, perceptual, and memory processes (e.g., Bartlett, 1932; Neisser, 1967; Norman, 1969). Whether a person is engaged in a task of recognizing a letter of the alphabet or remembering a complex event in his life, work in these areas suggests that what is experienced is not a passive and literal representation of information being "received," but is an active construction generated from the information being attended to and processed. Experience is not something that already exists to which we may be open or not open, but is *created* by the *activity* of processing information. If a theory of experiencing is to be indeed viable it should be consistent with what is known about cognitive processes, and therefore should be built on a view of man as an active agent and molder of his experience and not on a view of man as a passive recipient who is "open" to experience.

Gendlin (1962, 1964), elaborating the process of experiencing more fully, basically sees it as an interaction between symbolization and implicit feelings. Implicit feelings function as the "direct referent" for symbolization, and they represent the "felt meaning" of experience (Gendlin, 1964). Gendlin (1964) further says that this " 'implicit' or 'felt' datum of experiencing is a sensing of body life [pp. 113–114]." As such, implicit feelings are seen as preconceptual, and because they are implicit they are also incomplete, awaiting explicit symbols. For Gendlin, experiencing is the process of attending to and focusing on the implicitly felt meaning of experience and attempting to articulate it with explicit symbols. If this is done, then there is an "unfolding" of the implicit feeling, consisting of the emergence of new facets of experience related to the direct referent. These new facets constitute a change in the meaning in what is implicitly felt, and thus a new direct referent is produced to be further attended to, focused on, and symbolized.

Although Gendlin's view of experiencing does not avoid all the problems discussed with respect to Rogers' view, it does avoid some of them. Unlike Rogers, Gendlin does not seem to postulate a basic duality between symbolization in awareness and experience outside of awareness. Gendlin (1964) states that both explicit symbols and the implicit felt meanings to which they refer are in awareness (p. 112). Moreover, whereas Rogers' view of experiencing is essentially passive, Gendlin's view has something of an active thrust to it in that experiencing is brought about by the attempt to focus on and symbolize implicit feelings.

It should be noted that Gendlin, perhaps more so than any other writer, has placed at the core of his theorizing one of the most striking characteristics of client behavior in client-centered therapy and perhaps all dyadic therapies—the client's continued attempt to organize as clearly as possible in symbols facets of information in his life that are of concern to him. In seeing experiencing as the back-and-forth movement between symbolization and implicit feelings, Gendlin views the process as a continuous interaction occurring intrapsychically between two poles: explicit symbols and the implicit feelings to which they refer. Although an interactive model is a fruitful one for attempting to explicate a process, the utility of such a model ultimately rests on the clarity with which the two poles are conceptualized. Given the striking characteristic of client behavior mentioned above, it is quite natural to see symbolization as one of the poles. Whereas it is reasonably clear what symbolization refers to, it is not so clear what "implicit feelings" really are, and it is here that the problem lies.

Gendlin asserts that implicit feelings are neither entities nor are they necessarily particular emotions (Gendlin, Beebe, Cassens, Klein, & Oberlander, 1968). However, because they are conceived of as being "a sensing of body life" and also have meaning implicit in them, it is not at all clear that they do not have a thing-like status attributed to them. It is also doubtful that something that is preconceptual has meaning in it prior to symbolization. Although it is a long-standing philosophical argument whether things have meaning in them or whether meaning is a construction of the perceiver, the main thrust of the research in cognitive psychology mentioned earlier, which stresses the constructive nature of all information processing, strongly suggests that things do not have meaning *in* them: people bestow meaning *on* them. It is probably more correct to say that meaning can be generated to organize information coming from internal sources than it is to say that such information already has meaning implicit in it. However, simply to call such information "feelings," as if to make it something of ultimate value in and of itself, does not tell us much about the nature of such information and how it differs from other information that would not be called feelings. It seems that with the notion of implicit feelings, Gendlin is resorting to classic mind–body dualism in order to invoke some sort of primal, but amorphous, element in mental life, perhaps clear with respect to its function (to be explicated with symbols), but unclear with respect to its nature. Like Rogers, Gendlin takes recourse in and invokes the notion of feelings at the expense of clearly explicating both their nature and what it is about the processing of information that in some instances evokes affect and in other instances does not. Although Gendlin may be offering us a promising lead in viewing experiencing as an interactive process in which symbolization is one of the poles, a clearer picture is needed of what the referent for that process might be. After recasting the concept of experiencing in the framework of information processing, we will return to Gendlin's notion of implicit feelings, in an attempt to clarify what it might refer to.

Our discussion would suggest that although the concepts of self-actualization and experiencing are central in client-centered thinking, theorizing on these concepts is not without its problems. In recasting these concepts it will be important to do so in light of the problems and difficulties raised by this discussion, with an eye toward their clarification.

With all the emphasis in client-centered thinking on how a person processes experience, it is quite surprising that client-centered theorists have largely ignored work in the areas of cognition and information processing, as the processing of experience is the central focus of work in these fields. It is unclear whether ignoring these areas is simply due to a lack of knowledge about them, or due to the possibility that client-centered theorists find the impersonal and objective nature of cognitive concepts incompatible with their own emphasis on the personal and subjective nature of the meanings people place on experience. Whatever the reason, ignoring these areas is quite regrettable because drawing on the concepts and findings of cognition and information processing could very well help to rectify some of the problems discussed here and to provide a firmer conceptual basis for understanding the phenomena traditionally placed under the notions of experiencing and self-actualization. Our recasting of these concepts will be based on a consideration of the basic principles that govern human information processing. Although our view will be recast in the framework of human information processing, it will not be incompatible with the client-centered emphasis on the personal and subjective way in which meaning is construed. Indeed, the view of experiencing that will emerge will combine an information-processing perspective with one that emphasizes the personal meanings people place on experience.

A COGNITIVE THEORY OF EXPERIENCING
AND SELF–ACTUALIZATION

Because we have maintained that a view of self-actualization should ideally be rooted explicitly in the workings of the process of experiencing, we will first concentrate on recasting the concept of experiencing with the aim of rectifying what our previous discussion pointed to as wanting in the traditional view of the process. Rather than simply invoking the experiencing or nonexperiencing of feelings as the core of the process, we will elaborate the dynamics of experiencing and an optimal style of client experiencing in terms of the manner in which information is processed in the therapy hour. This view will be based on a consideration of the constraints and capabilities of human information processing and the tendencies that underlie the workings of these constraints and capabilities in the therapy hour. Rather than seeing self-actualization as a basic motivational force to fulfill one's potentials, self-actualization will be seen to reflect the characteristic tendency to engage in an optimal mode of experiencing.

The Dynamics of Experiencing

Before turning to the process of experiencing in therapy, it is probably best to begin at the beginning and clarify what is meant by experience. Rather than thinking of experience as something that has existence prior to the functioning of cognitive processes and something to which the person is ideally open, it is more appropriate to view experience as created by the person who experiences. This is not a philosophical position that denies the existence of a world outside one's window or an inner world of memories or bodily sensations. Rather, it is a statement derived from work in psychology that suggests that our experience of these worlds is mediated by and is the result of complex processes of transforming information derived from them. Although once upon a time it was fashionable in psychology to think of the person as a passive system that receives stimuli, as was mentioned earlier, it is more appropriate, given what we now know, to think of the person as actively selecting, operating on, organizing, and transforming information in his environment. This change has been largely the result of work in the areas of attention, perception, and cognition that has stressed the active and constructive nature of these processes (see Neisser, 1967 for a comprehensive treatment of work in these areas), and work in the area of human information processing that shares a basic commonality in pointing to the active nature of organizing and transforming processes (e.g., Miller, Galanter, & Pribram, 1960; Norman, 1969). Experience is not something already existing to be open to, but is *what is created by the functioning of cognitive processes.*

To develop a view of the process of experiencing it is useful to make a basic distinction between the operation of cognitive processes and what they operate on. Cognitive processes act on and transform *information.* Information is the raw data or input for the process of experiencing and it may come from stimulus sources external to the person or from stimulus sources internal to him. Raw input from external sources refers to the vast multitude of information existing at any given moment in time that can potentially be processed through the different sensory modalities (e.g., visual, auditory, tactile). Raw information coming from internal sources may be of two basic types: (a) sensory input from internal sources (e.g., muscle movement, arousal, etc.), and (b) stored information from long-term memory. Whatever the source, this information itself does not constitute experience; experience is a construction generated *from* this information, produced within the constraints and capabilities of the system operating on the information. In order to provide a basis for understanding the process of experiencing in therapy, it is first necessary to describe briefly the principal capabilities and constraints of this system.

CONSTRAINTS AND CAPABILITIES OF INFORMATION PROCESSING[3]

Whether the person is processing information from external sources, from internal sensory sources, from long-term memory, or from all three simultaneously, the universe of information available to be processed at any one instant in time is of staggering magnitude. The major constraint of the system is that at any instant it can only operate on and process an extremely limited amount of information, usually thought to be five to nine units of information (Miller, 1956). The net effect is that some information must be selectively attended to, while a large amount of information is inevitably lost for further processing. Inasmuch as a loss in the richness of information is inevitable, it is also essential, for without it life would be chaotic in terms of the overwhelming influx of information.

Whatever the source of information, it first travels in a raw, uncondensed, and unprocessed form through a series of buffers, in between which some initial analysis or "preprocessing" of the material takes place. This preprocessing of information consists primarily of putting it into units (e.g., configurations of features, phonemes, letters) for analysis of its meaning later on in the processing sequence. These units are then held

[3] The description here of information processing will be highly general and will only be given in enough detail to provide the necessary components for understanding the model of client experiencing that will be elaborated. Detailed and comprehensive reviews of work in information processing can be found in Hunt (1971), Lindsay and Norman (1972), Neisser (1967), and Norman (1969). Because the ultimate concern here is therapy, and hence higher mental processes, our discussion will focus on the handling of information in short-term memory and will not consider the preliminary series of sensory and intermediate buffers in between which overlearned, preliminary feature analysis of sensory information takes place. Consideration of information processing at these stages can be found in Hunt (1971) and Neisser (1967).

temporarily for further processing in short-term memory. Short-term memory is something like the waiting room of the information-processing system. It is here that information is held to be worked on for processing of its meaning in the chief operating room of the system, which might be called the central processing unit. As a holding area, short-term memory is extremely limited in the amount of information it can hold. Moreover, if the information held there does not enter fairly quickly into the central processing unit to be operated on, it is interfered with by other information coming into short-term memory and will become less accessible for processing. One way that information can be retained in short-term memory for subsequent processing is through rehearsal. Although this capability of the system will not be particularly relevant when we consider client-experiencing in therapy, it will be of importance when we consider how the therapist facilitates the client's experiencing. The net effect of the limitations of this stage is that only some of the information contained in short-term memory is attended to and processed further, and other information is necessarily lost. While the information available for processing at any moment in time is infinitely rich, what man harvests from that richness is relatively little.

Although the constraints on how much information can be processed in the central processing unit necessitate that some information will never enter it because of loss from short-term memory, the capabilities of the processing system also permit a considerable richness of information to be retained and transferred to long-term memory. The principal means by which processing limitations are transcended and a richness of information is retained within the limitations in processing capacity is through the activity of "chunking" (Miller, 1956) or organizing the information in the central processing unit. Organizing information may involve grouping a number of units of information into a smaller number of units (as in grouping the digits of a telephone number into two or three units), or it may involve elaborating on and transforming the information into a structure (as a word, phrase, or image). It is the activity of operating on and organizing information into structures in the central processing unit that enables a considerable richness of information to be preserved and transferred to permanent storage in long-term memory. It is also this activity of attending to and organizing information that enables us to make "sense" out of our world, and it is this activity we call *experiencing*.

The organization of information generated in the central processing unit and transferred to storage in long-term memory is not a literal representation of the information in short-term memory, but an organization constructed and transformed from this information. Information is constructed and transformed into organizations through the use of *rules*.

Rules refer to procedures used in selecting, distinguishing, sorting, and grouping elements in the structure of information (Reitman, 1965). The concept of rules has found similar expression in psychological theory under the terms "plans" (Miller, Galanter, & Pribram, 1960) and "schemata" (Piaget, 1963). As information is held in short-term memory, rules that are appropriate for the handling of that information enter from long-term memory into the central processing unit to operate on and organize that information. Long-term memory, then, not only contains stored information to be fed back into the system via short-term memory, but also contains the repository of procedures for handling information. In its latter role, long-term memory is analogous to the program library of a computer (Hunt, 1971), containing systems for operating on and managing data being processed in the system. In its other role it is also the repository of data (stored information) for processing.

The range of rules available in the system is of crucial importance in determining the fate of information held in short-term memory. If the system contains no rules for handling some of the information held in short-term memory, that information cannot then be operated on and organized in the central processing unit and transferred to long-term store. This information then will go no further in the system and be lost in short-term memory as it is interfered with by other information. There is also another, less-than-optimal fate that can befall information held in short-term memory. Although a richness of information may exist in short-term store, rules available that enter the central processing unit for the handling of that information may only be capable of organizing some of the features of the information, and incapable of dealing with others. Consequently, only some of the relevant features of that information will be attended to, processed, and organized, while other features will be lost.

Though it may not be very apparent, most personality theorists (Rogers not excluded) have a concept that is functionally equivalent to that of rules. In personality theorizing this concept is generally represented in terms of an internalized organization, against which the suitability of information being processed is judged for its acceptability or its unacceptability. Acceptability is usually defined as consistency with the internal organization, and if the information is inconsistent with the standard it is seen as threatening and is either denied or distorted accordingly, so as to make it consistent. In Rogers' (1959) personality theory, the functionally equivalent concept is the self-concept; in Freud's (1927) it is the superego; and in Kelly's (1955) it is the personal construct system. In the view here, the phenomena traditionally termed *defense* are seen to be the case either where there are no rules present for organizing the information and it is lost in short-term memory and not processed further in the system (denial), or, the rules available can only organize some of the features of the information contained in short-term store and not others; hence the organization does not adequately reflect all that can be seen to be contained in the information (distortion).

There are two basic reasons why such an information-processing perspective might be a more fruitful vehicle for conceptualizing the phenomena referred to as defensive than that offered by traditional personality theory. First, unlike rules, each of the functionally equivalent concepts in personality theory is relatively constricted in the domain of content it refers to. In the case of Rogers' (1959) theory the domain is organized statements about the self; in Freud's (1927) theory it is introjected prohibitions vis à vis sexuality; in Kelly's (1955) system it is constructs for perceiving and construing people. Just given how different the above domains are, it is questionable that any one (or even perhaps all three together) can sufficiently account for the system through which the extremely diverse information in life is organized. Rules serve the same heuristic function in theory without imposing such content restrictions on the nature of the information being processed.

The second reason why the functioning of rules may be a preferable vehicle for understanding defense is that it makes unnecessary a very problematic assumption contained in personality theorizing on defense. In invoking a structure that contains the standards against which the acceptability of information is judged, personality theorists then have to invoke, explicitly or implicitly, another structure whose function is to judge the information as acceptable or unacceptable, and if the latter, deny or distort it accordingly. So as to be effective, this process is traditionally seen to take place outside of awareness. This structure is explicitly named in Freud's theory and is the unconscious portion of the ego. In Rogers' position and in Kelly's the structure is not named, but is usually referred to as "the person." In Rogers' theory the person "subceives" that information is inconsistent with the self-concept and then denies the information or distorts it to be consistent. The phenomenon is similar in Kelly's position with respect to information that would disconfirm the individual's personal construct system. All theories then explicitly or implicitly invoke an unconscious homunculus or "man within the man." This "little man" functions to perceive the meaning of the information without the person's actually being aware of this meaning. This inner entity then denies or distorts the information to make it consistent with the internalized standard.

Psychologists and philosophers alike have long been troubled by the postulating of such remarkable functions and purpose to an unconscious inner entity. The working of rules in the processing of information, however, makes the invoking of a "little man" unnecessary. Information is not "subceived" to be inconsistent with an internalized standard and then "denied" or "distorted." Rather, either information for which there are no organizing rules can simply not be processed further in short-term memory and is lost (denial), or rules process those features that can be handled and those that cannot be handled are lost (distortion). There is no need to invoke a little man with remarkable powers of subception, subterfuge, and purpose. Information simply cannot be handled and organized, or it can be handled and organized only partially. Indeed, what the observing theorist attributes purpose or intent to under the terms "denial" and "distortion," internally to the person may simply be the case of either the absence of rules or the presence of inadequate rules to organize the information.

Although the range of rules a person has for organizing information is of crucial importance in determining whether information can be processed adequately or whether it will be lost or processed inadequately, one's repertoire of rules need not remain fixed. When one is faced with organizing the set of features in some new formation, although no single rule when applied may be sufficient for handling the information, it may be that several rules, applied simultaneously in some new combination may prove adequate for its organization. This occurrence, analogous to what Piaget (1963) has termed "accommodation" or the "differentiation of schemata," can generate a new rule that represents the unique combination of the existent rules that have been applied. This new rule can then be stored in long-term memory, along with the person's existing repertoire of rules, for future use in the organizing of information. Thus, expanding one's repertoire of organizing rules (hence one's ability to handle diverse information) is basically dependent on a fluid use of existent rules where they are flexibly used with one another in new combinations.

We have said that the organization of information is the principal way processing limitations are transcended. Generating an organization for information not only preserves a richness of the information being processed by subsuming it in an organization, but the activity of doing this transfers the information from short-term store to permanent storage in long-term memory, thus preserving the information for future use. Perhaps the principal way that the influx of information at any given moment in time is organized and transformed is through the creation of *meaning structures*. A meaning structure is a symbolic, organized synthesis, in thought or speech, of information from external and/or internal sources. Such an organization refers not only to the generation of linguistic structures to organize information, but also to the creation of images to synthesize relevant attributes and features of the information being attended to. Whether a person says "This is a chair," or "I feel helpless," or he is describing a vivid scene he has imagined, we may think of him as creating meaning structures to order the particular information he is attending to at the time.

Although the creation of meaning structures enables us to organize a considerable influx of information and give order and shape to our world, such structures are necessarily created within the constraints and limitations of the information-processing system. Thus, the diversity of meaning structures one can create to give order to one's world ultimately rests on the diversity and flexibility of the processing rules one has in long-term memory. Moreover, creating a structure to organize information means that only some information is being attended to, and in the process, other information will inevitably be lost in short-term memory. Thus, although the extraordinary ability to find meaning in information enables man to organize and preserve a considerable diversity of information in his world, a price is paid for this activity in terms of the loss of an enormous richness of information that exists at any moment in time.

TENDENCIES UNDERLYING INFORMATION PROCESSING
IN THE THERAPY HOUR

To create meaning structures to organize information is to engage in a process that is ubiquitous in adult human functioning. Whether we are looking at a sunset, attempting to understand why we did something, trying to discover what is wrong with a broken motor, or telling someone how we "feel," we are engaged in a process of generating meaning and structuring some portion of our current *psychological field*. The psychological field, or *life space* as it is sometimes called, refers here to the person's subjective representation of his psychological environment. Following Lewin's (1935, 1938) suggestion, this environment includes the person's organization of both his external and internal worlds. It includes not only his representation of the present, but also his past and future as they are represented by him in the present. The activity of creating meaning structures to organize information and structure a portion of the psychological field is what a client is principally doing in the therapy hour. Whether the client is talking about his exhilaration, his failures, his aspirations, how his mother made him the way he is, or what happened to him on the way to the therapist's office, the client is engaged in a process of organizing information and structuring some portion of his life space. The process of creating meaning structures to organize information in the therapy hour does not differ in its working from the processing of information in more mundane situations in life, and hence takes place within the constraints and capabilities of the information-processing system just described. However, what does tend to make the therapy hour different from information processing in other situations in life is that the information being processed is often highly significant to the client and occupies a major portion of his psychological field.

We may in fact regard much of what a client does in therapy as a concerted attempt to achieve change and reorganization in the portions of his field that are of major concern to him. Whether the client is attempting to change his attitudes toward his spouse, alleviate his anxieties in interpersonal situations, or find more meaning in a seemingly barren and pointless existence, the client in therapy is fundamentally attempting to elaborate and reorder information so as to achieve a basic change and reorganization in the structure of a significant portion of his field. We may think of two very basic but somewhat opposing tendencies that underlie this attempt: a need for *organization and order* in processing information and structuring the field, and a need for *new experience and change* in the field. Man's penchant for organization has been stressed by the theorists of cognitive consistency (e.g., Festinger, 1957; Kelly, 1955) and also by the Gestalt theorists (e.g., Koffka, 1935) under the concept of *closure*. As we have elaborated, organization is also a major characteristic of the information-processing system and the principal means by which a multiplicity of information can be handled.

Although organization is of the utmost necessity in enabling the person to construe his world in a stable way, it can also become overly constricting and prevent the person from seeing what is novel and unique. Moreover, the organizations one generates for construing the world tend to grow old and sterile. Just as the seeking of organization is a pervasive tendency in human functioning, so too is the seeking of new experience and change. Whereas psychoanalytic and drive reduction theories were built upon the notion of a nervous system that sought quiescence and tension reduction, work in many areas of psychology (e.g., Duffy, 1962; Fiske & Maddi, 1961; Hebb, 1955; Leuba, 1955; Schultz, 1965) has pointed to the contrary in establishing both the existence of a basic hunger of the nervous system for stimulation and the importance of new experience and change for adaptive behavioral functioning and psychological well-being. However, unlike a rat, which may explore a maze for change in stimulation, man need not be dependent on the external environment for change, but can create it for himself via his own processing of information. *Through his ability to create meaning, man has the potential to be his own source for creating reorganization and change in experience by distinguishing and synthesizing new facets of meaning in the diverse and complex information in his life.* An optimal style of client experiencing is heavily dependent on the use of this potential and *consists of the activity of elaborating and organizing information so as to create reorganization and change in his field.*

Although the elaboration and reorganization of information so as to create change constitutes the ideal, rarely do clients seem to be able to do this for themselves. That is why they come to therapy. Indeed, clients' problems may not be what they think their problems to be, but rather *the way in which they think about their problems.* Clients' problems may fundamentally be deficiencies in the way they process information; their processing style is such that they are not able to process and organize information so as to create change and reorganization with respect to their concerns.

Our task then in elaborating the dynamics of experiencing in therapy and the components of an optimal style of experiencing is to explain how, within the constraints and capabilities of the information-processing system, a client can process and organize information so as to create change and reorganization in his field.

It should be said at the outset that this is not a brief, one-shot affair that takes place in but a moment of time. Rather it is characterized by groping, searching, repetition, continued refining of what is meant, the bringing in of additional information, and the exclusion of other information. Basically it is a process of elaborating new information and reorganizing it by finding new meaning in it. The elaboration of information is essential, because the creation of a meaning structure to organize information can only produce a significant reorganization and change in the field, if the material it refers to and is attempting to organize has been made relevant so as to occupy a significant portion of the field. For example, in psychoanalysis a meaning structure geared to explicating causation will not produce constructive insight and change unless the material it refers to has been made relevant so as to occupy a significant portion of the life space. Thus, a statement by the patient that points out the similarity between what he demands from his wife and the needs that were never satisfied by his mother will only produce reorganization and change if he has spent much time elaborating the nature of his relationship with his wife and also what his childhood was like with respect to his mother.[4] A similar situation exists in client-centered therapy, the difference being, however, that the structures the client creates tend to be

---

[4] Much of the work of psychoanalysis, especially in its early stages, probably consists of making a certain class of information (i.e., developmental) relevant so it will occupy a significant portion of the field. In general, for any given client or patient there is nothing absolute or predetermined about what particular information needs to be elaborated and made present in the field. It is only a question of the information being elaborated and taking on a significant portion of the field so it can then be reorganized. Although childhood experiences retrieved from long-term memory are certainly one type of information to make present and central in the field, it is questionable whether it is indeed necessary to engage in the time-consuming task of *making* this historical information relevant and significant in the field just so it can later be reorganized with the analyst's interpretations. There is undoubtedly information more current in the field with respect to the person's concerns that can serve as the substrate for elaboration and reorganization.

oriented toward description rather than causation. Clients will frequently come into therapy hour and say something like "I feel hopeless," creating little reorganization and change in their field. However, if made after considerable elaboration of information (e.g., recent attempts and failures at establishing relationships, remembered frustrations in attaining important goals) such a statement can accurately encapsulate the common meaning of the information and give organization and structure to the field. The activity of elaborating information and reorganizing its meaning is perhaps the most pervasive feature of dyadic psychotherapy, and this activity is part and parcel of the client's attempt to achieve reorganization and change in his field.

The key to understanding the dynamics of how a client in therapy elaborates information and organizes it so as to achieve reorganization and change is in explicating the joint working of two processes: *the differentiation of meaning and its integration.* Both processes take place within the constraints and capabilities of information processing and represent an ideal balancing of the needs for organization and new experience. These two crucial processes, however, occur on a moment-to-moment basis, so in order to understand them fully it will be necessary to look at what a client does in a more microscopic fashion than is typical in client-centered theory. We will examine below an isolated moment in therapy in order to explain the nature of these two processes, but it should be kept in mind that differentiation and integration do not occur only in one single isolated moment in therapy, but characterize what the client is doing continuously. In the process of our examination, in addition to pointing to what constitutes the ideal mode of processing, we will point to how clients typically deviate from the ideal.

Before turning our attention to the processes of differentiation and integration of meaning, it is essential to specify one further aspect of the creation of meaning structures as they are generated by the client in therapy. In addition to organizing the information held in short-term memory and structuring some portion of the field, the client's activity of creating a meaning structure also typically *evokes output* for further processing. This output consists of information generated in internal sources. Thus, it may consist of crude information evoked momentarily in highly condensed forms in memory locations in long-term memory (such as other facets of information in the experience being attended to, memories of past experiences, images, and associations) and/or kinesthetic stimuli (such as arousal, or a parched throat). Whatever the particular information evoked, it is fed back into short-term memory, where it is held, in its crude, unrefined form, for subsequent organization in the central processing unit. It is this range of evoked information that provides the client with a substrate for further processing, and it is from the information evoked by his meaning structures that the client can bring new information into his field by attending to it and organizing its meaning in his subsequent processing. The fate of information evoked internally, however, is uncertain. Many clients typically are oriented to allocating their attention and processing capacities to information derived from external sources rather than to information evoked internally. To use the terminology of Witkin (Witkin, Dyk, Faterson, Goodenough, & Karp, 1962) they are field dependent rather than field independent. Such clients will typically not fully attend to the information that may be evoked internally and held in short-term memory, and hence will not use it effectively as a substrate for further processing. Moreover, the full allocation of the client's attention and processing capacities to the information evoked internally does not guarantee in and of itself an optimal use of the information as a substrate for further processing. Frequently, the range of crude information evoked internally is far richer than what can be processed within the limitations in processing capacity. The client then must selectively attend to some of the information for further processing and organization in a subsequent structure, and other information will inevitably be lost in short-term memory. Usually, what the client selectively attends to will be what his repertoire of rules allows him to process and organize most readily. With such selection, however, comes the possibility that the information not attended to and lost might have provided the potential informational substrate for subsequent change and reorganization in the field.

DIFFERENTIATION AND INTEGRATION OF MEANING

The *differentiation of meaning* refers to the activity of elaborating a more particular facet of meaning in the information being processed. More specifically, it involves creating a meaning structure that organizes the meaning of some facet(s) of information evoked in raw form by a previous meaning structure. The structure created can be seen as subordinate to the first insofar as it functions to unpack and distinguish a more particular aspect of the meaning of the previous structure. Let us consider an example to illustrate how meaning is differentiated on the basis of information evoked by a previous meaning structure. Let us take a client who in describing his state of depression says, "I feel very much alone." This may evoke in highly condensed and crude form a whole range of information, which, for illustrative purposes, might include the following: fleeting thoughts of a lack of someone who cares for him, a desire for a meaningful relationship, fragmentary memories such as the image of himself lying on his bed staring at the ceiling on a Saturday night, seeing the cold faces on the streetcar staring indifferently ahead, or walking alone on a rainy night looking up at the brightly lighted windows in an apartment building. This information, however, is evoked only momentarily and is held temporarily in its crude, unprocessed form in short-term memory for subsequent processing and organization of its meaning. As information impinging on the client, it is some facet of this information that will provide the referent for a subsequent meaning structure.

Given the limitations of processing capacity, the range of information illustrated above, however, is likely to be far, far richer than what the client can meaningfully process at one time. Hence, the client will selectively attend to some facet(s) evoked while ignoring others. If the client lacks familiarity with the rather poignant memories evoked as a possible aspect of loneliness (i.e., has no rules for organizing such information in the context of his present experience) these facets evoked are likely to be ignored, and other facets that the client can process more readily in the present context are likely to be attended to and to constitute the substrate for subsequent organization. If the client has familiarity with the notion that nobody caring for him is a component of loneliness for him (i.e., possesses a rule for organizing such information in the context of his present experience) this facet is likely to be attended to and further processed and transformed from its raw form into a subsequent meaning structure. After saying "I feel very much alone" the client then goes on to say, "Like nobody really cares what happens to me." This second statement represents a subordinate structure to the first, in that it distinguishes a more particular aspect of what being "very much alone" means to the client.

In attending to and distinguishing this facet, however, the other information momentarily evoked and held in raw form in short-term memory has been ignored. This information will then be subject to interference, both from the activity of operating on and organizing the information attended to and from new facets of information, evoked by the new organization created, which are fed back into short-term store. Consequently, the information evoked but not attended to originally will become crowded out and become increasingly more difficult to retrieve. Thus, in allocating his attention and processing capacity to one facet of the information, the memories that were evoked become lost as a substrate for further elaboration.

On the basis of new information evoked by the subordinate structure "nobody cares what happens to me," the personal meaning of loneliness can be further differentiated. The client then goes on to say "Kind of brings to mind this picture of one of those old people you see who just kind of exist in their one-room apartments. Nobody in the world even caring they exist." Here his statement about nobody caring for him has evoked on the basis of similarity a rather poignant remembered image, which he does attend to and process. The first part of this third statement referring to the elderly people in their one-room apartments represents a subordinate structure to the second statement in that it differentiates and elaborates in more detail what nobody caring for him is like to him. The last part of this statement about the elderly people (nobody in the world even caring they exist) differentiates further the meaning of the memory in implicitly elaborating its relation to his current field.

By the activity of differentiating the meaning of what loneliness is like to him, the experience has become more meaningful to him in that he has brought, from memory, new information into his current field. Whereas the original experience of seeing the elderly people may have had an impact on him that was never explicitly organized with respect to the meaning it had for him, it is now reprocessed and organized with respect to his current field. By bringing in this memory and articulating its similarity to his current experience, his experience of loneliness takes on new meaning. By the activity of differentiating further the more particular meaning of loneliness, there is movement and change in his field, in that the experience comes to occupy a greater portion of the field. From an observer's standpoint the client may look more "involved" or "more into his feelings." What the client has done concretely, however, is to distinguish new facets of meaning on the basis of evoked information.

The differentiation of meaning, such as what is illustrated above, may be seen to have four effects. First, the client creates change in experience by this activity. Second, by distinguishing new facets of meaning in the experience, it becomes more meaningful and occupies a greater portion of the field. Third, in producing a number of new facets of meaning in the experience, the client may then organize these facets with a new superordinate structure that captures their common meaning. Fourth, the new facets of meaning that have been differentiated may provide an informational substrate from which the new superordinate structure can reorganize the portion of the field that has been differentiated.

After clients have differentiated a number of more distinct facets of meaning in an experience, they will typically say something more general that refers to the whole or to some portion of the constellation of facets that have been elaborated. This reflects the two principles elaborated earlier. Whereas in differentiating meaning the client has created new experience and change in some portion of his field, there is also a need to give order to this change by generating a structure that captures its meaning. The *integration of meaning* refers to the activity of synthesizing the meaning of the different facets that have been distinguished. More specifically it involves creating a superordinate structure that captures a common meaning in these differentiated facets. An integrating structure is based on the range of information held in short-term store that has been evoked by the structures that have been differentiated. As was the case with the differentiation of meaning, depending on the rules available for organizing information, some evoked facets will be attended to and utilized, whereas others will be ignored. The superordinate structures created will be a common meaning of those facets evoked by the subordinate structures that are attended to and utilized. An integrating meaning structure should not be thought of as a mere summation of the subordinate structures. Rather, it is an actively synthesized construction generated from information evoked by those structures. This synthesis not only organizes the differentiated structures with respect to one another, but in so doing they take on new meaning, because they are now embodied in and subsumed by a new structure. If there has been a change in the structure of the field due to the elaboration of new facets of meaning, then, ideally, this synthesis, in capturing the common meaning of these new facets, will represent a reorganization of that portion of the field.

Let us return to the client we have been discussing to illustrate how a portion of the field, changed through the differentiation of meaning, can be reorganized through the integration of meaning. After having differentiated loneliness in terms of a lack of somebody caring for him and the associated memory of the elderly people, the client goes on to say "I am very scared that for my whole life I will always be alone." In abstracting a new meaning from loneliness and nobody caring for him, in light of the memory that was evoked and processed, this statement represents a superordinate structure that generates a common meaning in and gives a new organization to the preceding statements. We might infer that the memory of the elderly people evoked in him a consideration of his own future in relation to his construal of his present situation (nobody caring for him). His subsequent statement explicitly organizes the meaning this relationship has for him in terms of a temporal continuity between his construal of his present situation and his future. In so doing there has been a movement and reorganization in a portion of his field in that his sense of being alone has been reorganized with respect to remembered material and changed to a fear of spending the rest of his life lonely. This new integrating structure will also likely evoke a new range of information that will provide the substrate for further differentiation.

The process of experiencing then is ideally self-perpetuating; it involves an ongoing and continuous activity of differentiating and integrating meaning to achieve a change and reorganization of the field. Although this is the ideal, clients are in therapy because their characteristic style of processing is such that they do not adequately differentiate and integrate meaning for themselves in such a way that change and reorganization are produced by their processing. We may point to some difficulties that typically arise in the manner in which clients differentiate and integrate meaning.

One source of difficulty is that some clients may attend to and elaborate information with reference to a very small portion of their field. These are clients who tend to see their problems as highly circumscribed (e.g., a problem in relating to one's boss, a problem in overeating). They may differentiate and integrate meaning with respect to their problem, but they are highly restrictive in the information they include as relevant to it and they fail to explore its meaning in a larger context. Because they only differentiate and integrate meaning with respect to a highly limited domain of their field, there is little significant reorganization and change created through their processing.

Most clients do differentiate and integrate meaning with respect to things that occupy a significant portion of their life space. There frequently are deficiencies, however, in the manner in which meaning is differentiated. A major difficulty with the processing style of many clients is that meaning is inadequately differentiated. As a result, the client's processing activity fails both to create change in experience and to provide the necessary elaboration of information whereby a subsequent meaning structure can serve to reorganize the field. Provided a richness of information has indeed been evoked internally and fed back into short-term memory, inadequate differentiation may stem from a constricted allotment of attention to the information or the application of a restricted set of rules for organizing it. As a result, either the information will be largely ignored and lost, or only those facets of information that can most readily be processed will be attended to and organized, while a richer informational substrate for subsequent differentiation will be lost.

To illustrate the situation of inadequate differentiation, let us suppose that after the client had said "I feel very much alone—like nobody cares for me," he said "It's a real bad feeling." This statement would be an integration of meaning, as it represents a superordinate structure abstracting a common meaning in the two previous statements. Assuming that the memory of the elderly people was in fact evoked and held in short-term memory, the client's processing rules may not have been able to organize the memory, and hence attention was alloted to other facets of information that could more readily be organized. A price, however, is paid for this selection. Calling his experience "bad" does not represent a change and reorganization of the portion of the field being attended to, as had occurred when his experience of loneliness was changed and reorganized after further differentiation to a fear of always being lonely. In calling his experience of loneliness bad, the client has achieved a premature closure in unpacking the meaning of his experience, and has cut off further differentiation of its meaning. As was the case when the memory was attended to, this further differentiation might have brought new information into the field, enabling there to be meaningful movement and reorganization.

Inadequate differentiation may appear in a number of forms. It is found in clients who repeat and rehash the same material over and over again in an attempt to achieve a reorganization of the material. Because they differentiate the meaning of the material inadequately, their attempts at reorganization are thwarted, and they must go back and try again to find crucial facets of meaning that will permit reorganization and change. Inadequate differentiation is also manifested in the client whose processing style is diffuse. This is the client who disconnectedly jumps from topic to topic. Here no one theme is continuously focused on, attended to, and differentiated; rather, tangential information is attended to and processed instead. Quantity of different material being processed is substituted for quality in the processing. Consequently, there is no meaningful differentiation of any one portion of the field and hence little success at reorganization.

Inadequate differentiation may also arise because the structures the client generates evoke little internally in the way of an informational substrate for further organization. For continuous differentiation and integration to take place, the structures created must function not only to organize information but also to evoke a rich substrate of new information for further processing. Frequently, the structures clients create evoke little and hence there is an impoverished substrate for further processing. The statement "It's a really bad feeling" serves to illustrate this point. "Bad" is not very evocative in that it is so general as to have little in the way of concrete associations and connotations. Moreover, feeling "really bad" is something of a cliché, inasmuch as it tends to be said so habitually that it is almost meaningless. It is analogous to what happens in semantic satiation experiments, where, in repeating a word over and over, its range of connotations becomes lost and the word becomes meaningless. As a result, such a phrase is likely to evoke little internally in the way of potential information for subsequent differentiation.

Reflecting the utilization of a narrow range of rules to organize information, clients frequently generate such habitual structures to articulate the meaning of information they are attempting to organize. In so doing, they fail to evoke in themselves a rich substrate from which further differentiation can occur. The implication here is that an optimal mode of experiencing involves forgoing the habitual and using a multiplicity of rules to construe information in new, expressive ways. Hence, when clients are engaged in an optimal mode of experiencing, they will tend to ascribe meaning to their experience in highly vivid forms such as metaphor and imagery. Because such forms are rich in terms of the information they evoke, they are an extremely potent vehicle for providing an enriched substrate of new information for further processing.

We have seen how an unproductive mode of experiencing may arise from a failure to adequately differentiate meaning. In this case new information, which might provide the substrate for a meaningful reorganization of the field, is not elaborated and brought into the field. So too may an unproductive mode of experiencing arise from a failure or inability to integrate meaning. Ideally, in differentiating meaning the client brings a multiplicity of new information into his field, creating movement and change in it. If this multiplicity of information is not organized with an integrating structure that captures its meaning, disorder in the field may result. When this occurs, the client's experiencing seems chaotic and he will appear anxious. He is in a sense overwhelmed by information he cannot adequately organize. This information need not necessarily be the result of information differentiated by his own processing in the course of the therapy hour. It may also come from recent or not-so-recent events in his life that are still present in his field, but which he has been unable to organize effectively. The client may use the therapy hour to elaborate this information in an attempt to generate order in it.

In terms of the two opposing principles that guide the processing of information, a failure or inability to integrate meaning can be understood as an overabundance of experience and change at the expense of organization. It is the situation that generates anxiety. Anxiety, however, should not be looked at as a distinct affect outside of the context in which it arises. Rather, anxiety *is* the subjective experience arising from an inability to organize significant information in the field. If in such a situation the client says something to the effect that he "feels anxious," this should be regarded as an integrating structure that ascribes a meaning to the state of disordered information that occupies his field and any arousal that may accompany it. As an integrating meaning structure, however, it will usually not serve to reorganize the field, but rather will often serve as a starting point for differentiating the components of the anxiety (i.e., the information that the client is unable to organize).

It is a frequent occurrence that in elaborating to another why one is anxious, there is a reduction in the anxiety. By way of explanation we tend to say one has ventilated his anxiety or gained insight into it. Such terms, however, do not really serve to explain adequately how anxiety can be reduced through such elaboration. In elaborating possible causes for the anxiety, one is generating structures that serve to give order to disordered information. There is a reduction in anxiety when one "understands" its cause, not because the understanding one has is "true," but because the cause elaborated is plausible and functionally serves to provide order in an otherwise disordered field.[5]

In addition to producing anxiety, a failure to integrate meaning will affect the future accessibility of the information that has not been integrated. It is a well-known finding from memory studies (see Mandler, 1967) that the organization of information facilitates its future accessibility in long-term memory. By integrating meaning the client gives increased organization and structure to information by subsuming the differentiated facets in a superordinate structure. Consequently, the accessibility of this information in long-term memory for activation in future processing is enhanced. A failure to integrate meaning is in effect then a failure to supply this added organization, and as a result, the facets of meaning that have been differentiated will be less accessible for future processing by the client. Indeed, for some clients much of the work of therapy may consist of the client's retrieving from long-term memory information that was never adequately organized in the first place, and elaborating it so that it can then be meaningfully reorganized.

What is likely to cause an inability or failure to integrate the meaning of a multiplicity of information contained in the differentiated structures? One factor operative here may be that the amount of information contained in those structures is more than the client is characteristically able to handle. There are individual differences in the range of rules people possess for handling information, hence there are differences in the amount of information that can effectively be attended to and organized. In terms of its sheer quantity, the information may simply be too much for the client to integrate. An inability or failure to integrate meaning may also be a result of the quality of the information contained in the differentiated structures. If this information contains much diversity, the client may not possess a sufficient breadth of rules for organizing it. In terms of the present view, clients who are anxious and seek help to reduce their anxiety are indeed likely to be those who lack a sufficient range of organizing rules, and are therefore characteristically unable to handle and

[5] A similar situation probably exists with respect to the psychoanalyst's interpretations. It is not that the causal relationships the analyst offers his patient as an explanation for his present behavior are "true." Rather, to the patient who has spent much time and energy elaborating historical information so as to make it significant and central in his field (see previous footnote), the interpretations offered are plausible and serve to give order to his field.

organize the multiplicity and diversity of information in their lives.

We have discussed how a client's mode of experiencing may not create new experience and change in that he may inadequately differentiate meaning and not provide a substrate from which reorganization can take place, or he may fail or be unable to integrate meaning adequately to achieve this reorganization. It should be pointed out that clients who are unable to integrate meaning in a multiplicity and diversity of information are, in fact, likely to be those who inadequately differentiate meaning. The same insufficient range of rules for handling information that results in an inability to organize a multiplicity and diversity of information (integration of meaning), will also lead one to be unable to attend to and distinguish new facets of information evoked internally that might be held in raw form in short-term memory. We may speak of such clients as rigid or defensive and say their experiencing is constricted or, to use Gendlin's (1964) term, "structure-bound." Given that people must organize information, there is probably no such thing as non-structure-bound experiencing; it is only a question of whether the structures that people create distinguish and organize new facets of meaning in experience. Those clients who possess a narrow range of processing rules will only attend to readily organizable information and will tend to construe it in habitual ways. Hence, they will create little reorganization and change through their processing. It is not that such clients tend to "deny experience in awareness." Rather, their processing style is only able to handle a constricted amount and range of information. A richness of experience is not denied; it simply tends not to be created. If it is indeed evoked, the information that could provide the substrate for creating new experience and change in the field is not attended to, processed, and organized, and it is hence lost. We will later elaborate how the therapist helps to facilitate the differentiation and integration of meaning so that the client will engage in a more optimal mode of processing. Now, having examined the dynamics of experiencing in terms of how the moment-to-moment use of the operations of differentiation and integration can function to achieve reorganization and change, it is time to speak more generally about the characteristics of an optimal mode of experiencing and about its effect on the client.

Productive Experiencing: The Optimal Mode

An optimal mode of client experiencing should not simply be seen to involve a state of being "open" to a richness of experience that exists somewhere outside of awareness. Rather, an optimal mode of experiencing is the *activity* of differentiating and integrating meaning so as to *create* a richness of experience. Experiencing is productive and optimal when the client's cognitive processes are functioning to their fullest capabilities (within the constraints of the information-processing system) to create change and reorganization in experience through vigorous differentiation and integration of meaning.

From our model of the dynamics of experiencing we can describe some of the general characteristics of an optimal mode of experiencing. When engaging in a productive mode of experiencing, the client's processing will appear to be fluid and unfolding. When the client is taking an active stance toward the differentiation and integration of meaning, new facets of meaning will be continually distinguished and elaborated, and thus the structure of the client's field will be changing and evolving rather than static. The client's attention will not be focused on what can be most readily processed and organized, but will be focused instead on the unique facets of information evoked internally. Because this will entail attending to and processing features of information that are not yet well organized in the present context of experience, the client will have to forgo closure and tolerate uncertainty as to the outcome of his processing. When a richness of facets of meaning have been differentiated in the field, they will be synthesized by the client so as to capture the fullness of the total meaning. In order to capture the unique features of information evoked and to generate a rich substrate for further processing, the structures created to organize information will tend to be vivid and novel, rather than habitual and ordinary. In continuously elaborating and organizing the meaning of the emerging facets of information evoked, the client's statements will not be disjointed and fragmented, but will tend to unfold into a thematic unity.

Several consequences of engaging in an optimal mode of experiencing may be specified. One of the most important, perhaps, is that the client creates reorganization and change in his experiencing of things in his field that are of concern to him. This change is the immediate effect, but there are also likely to be more enduring effects on the mode in which he will process information in the future. Because it satisfies his basic need for new experience and change, engaging in an optimal mode of experiencing will be intrinsically reinforcing for the client. The client is then likely to engage in this mode more frequently. By engaging in an optimal mode of experiencing, basically *the client learns that he can be his own source for creating new experience and change via his own cognitive functioning.*

Engaging in an optimal mode of experiencing is also likely to increase the client's processing capacity for organizing information. By using organizing rules in flexible combination with one another to generate novel and vivid organizing structures, the client will also be adding to his existent repertoire of ways for organizing and construing information. Thus, the client's capacity for processing a richness and complexity of information in the future will be enhanced. It is commonly thought that productive experiencing will produce "expanded" awareness. The present view does not contradict this, but rather provides a framework for understanding what expanded awareness involves. Awareness is not some internal entity looking at what is being attended to and processed. Rather, awareness *is* the activity of attending to, processing, and organizing information. Awareness is likely to be expanded by engaging in an optimal mode of processing because the person has increased his capacity to process a greater richness and complexity of information and thus tends to create, handle, and organize more information in his system at any given moment in time.

In addition to enhancing the client's capacity for handling information, experiencing in an optimal mode will also directly result in making more information available for future processing. Vigorous differentiation and integration in effect imposes heightened structure on information. Thus, the information will be more organized in long-term store, hence more easily activated to serve as a substrate during future processing.

Although viewing a productive mode of experiencing in terms of vigorous differentiation and integration of meaning is relatively new, there is some empirical work bearing on its validity. A recent study (Wexler, 1974) assessed the relationship of the moment-to-moment use of the operations of differentiation and integration of meaning to subjects' voice quality as they described their experiencing of emotions. Voice quality was assessed using a classification system developed by Rice and associates (Butler, Rice, & Wagstaff, 1962; Rice & Wagstaff, 1967) that has been found to be a sensitive index of productive and unproductive processing styles (Rice & Gaylin, 1973) and a good predictor of success and failure in therapy (Rice & Wagstaff, 1967). The relationship found between the degree of differentiation and integration of meaning and the presence of the voice quality indicative of a productive mode of processing (focused voice quality) was highly significant ($r = .84$), suggesting that a productive style of processing does indeed involve vigorous differentiation and integration of meaning. Consistent with the present view of experiencing, this study also found that associated with vigorous differentiation and integration of meaning were the tendencies to organize information in highly vivid structures and to organize a diversity of information in the structures created. Research is presently in progress to assess directly the relationship between the activity of differentiating and integrating meaning and what is traditionally conceptualized and assessed (Klein, Mathieu, Kiesler, & Gendlin, 1970) as a depth of experiencing.

It is important to note that the present viewpoint and the more traditional client-centered viewpoint would not differ in *what* is identified as optimal experiencing. Rather, they differ as to the *way* in which the phenomenon is conceptualized. It should be made explicit how the present viewpoint differs from the traditional view of experiencing, and in so doing point out how it rectifies some of the difficulties discussed earlier with respect to traditional theorizing on the process.

Instead of seeing experiencing as a passive process in which the client is conceptualized as ideally being "open to experience," the present view emphasizes the active and constructive nature of the process. Experiencing optimally is not a matter of the richness of experience that is let in and received, but rather a matter of the richness that is produced through one's processing activity.

The present viewpoint also differs rather sharply with Rogers' notion of openness to experience. It was pointed out earlier that a complete openness to stimulation would be overwhelming and chaotic. The ability to select some information for processing and organization and exclude other information is a highly adaptive feature of the organism that should not be done away with lightly. Indeed, although selection may become overly constricting, it is also what enables man to avoid the habitual and construe new meaning in his experience. From the present framework, optimal experiencing is seen to involve not complete openness, but a selective process of attending to, processing, and organizing attributes of information that permit new facets of meaning in experience to be distinguished and synthesized.

The present view of experiencing also differs from the traditional client-centered view in another very important respect: little has been said here about the experiencing of feelings. Our failure to speak of feelings has not been an oversight; it has been quite intentional. It stems from our previous discussion, which both pointed to problems and ambiguities in the use of the notion of feelings in client-centered thinking and suggested that the experiencing of feelings is, in fact, used as something of a catch-all in client-centered theory, and serves to give a grossly molar view of the process of experiencing. It also precludes looking at two important questions: (a) what is it about some information that will produce affect when the information is processed and organized, and (b) given that the processing and organizing of some particular sample of information sometimes will produce affect and sometimes will not, what is it about the *way* in which information is processed and organized that in one instance creates affect and in the other does not. Having elaborated a view of the dynamics of experiencing and its underlying tendencies, we should now reconsider the matter of feelings, and in so doing, suggest some tentative answers to these two questions.

Gendlin (1964) has contended that personality change nearly always "involves some sort of intensive affective or feeling process occurring in the individual [p. 105]." We would not disagree. Affect will undoubtedly be present when a client is productively processing information so as to create change and reorganization, and through his processing efforts the client will certainly "feel" different. Because affect is present when experiencing is optimal does not mean, however, that the essence of an optimal mode of experiencing should be seen as the symbolization and experiencing of feelings. Such a view not only necessitates seeing feelings as a distinct class of bodily events or mental entities that exist in and of themselves outside of awareness awaiting symbolization, but it also fails to recognize the fact that affect occurs in therapy when the client is dealing with substantive information. Rather than seeing change as *resulting* from an "intensive affective or feeling process," the present view sees affect as *produced* by the activity of processing substantive information. Affect in therapy is a by-product of the client's activity of distinguishing and synthesizing facets of meaning that create reorganization and change in the field.[6]

The present view leads us to consider the question of why it is that affect will be present with the processing of some information, but not all. One factor of obvious importance here is the significance or centrality in the field of the information with which the client is working. It is, for example, far more likely that affect will be present when the client's processing is focused on his basic aspirations in living than when it is focused on the furnishing in the therapist's office or on remembering what he ate for lunch. Although significance of information may be a necessary condition for the occurrence of affect, it is not a sufficient condition. Focusing one's processing on one's basic aspirations or goals in living certainly will not always produce affect; the client, for example, who simply retrieves from memory and enumerates his aspirations as he has construed them in the past is not likely to experience affect in the process. The elaboration of significant information that is already well organized does not produce affect. Let us examine the conditions under which we do indeed see a client experience affect.

One condition under which we observe affect is when the information that is elaborated has the effect of producing *disorganization* in the client's

---

[6] We use the term "affect" rather than "feelings" because the former term implies less a thing-like status and more a general state of the person than does the latter term.

field. It is quite common, for example, to observe affect when a client elaborates information that is inconsistent or incompatible with other information present in his field. The client who describes in the therapy hour how recent events in his life make the attainment of his basic aspirations impossible (i.e., the events elaborated are incompatible with the holding of these aspirations) is quite likely to experience affect in the process. It is also readily observable outside the therapy situation that when a person is overwhelmed by events in his life that he cannot organize, he experiences affect. How are we to understand these observations? Are we to understand them as consisting of an awareness and symbolization of feelings? Or, is it not more plausible to say that the affect occurs as the *result* of the presence of disorganized information in the field? As therapists we know that it is relatively easy for us to elicit affect in our clients. It is easy to predict, for example, that if we confront a client with information that is inconsistent with the information he is elaborating, some sort of affective reaction will likely be produced in the client. How are we able to predict that this will be the case? It would be difficult to say that it is because we know there to be an existing feeling somewhere in the client and doing such confronting causes him to get "in touch" with it. Rather, it is because we know that the information we will confront him with will be inconsistent with what he is saying, and we know, either explicitly or implicitly, that if disorganization is created in a person's field, affect will be produced.

The second condition under which we see a client experience affect is when the information being processed has the effect of producing *change* and *restructuring* in the client's field. It is frequently observed that affect will be experienced when a client comes to new realizations or looks at things in new ways. Thus, if the client who has had his basic aspirations in living thwarted is subsequently able to go on to distinguish new facets of meaning that give new purpose to his life, he is also likely to experience affect, but this time of a more positive nature. Is this the result of becoming aware of some new feeling existing within him? It seems much more appropriate to say that the affect has been produced by the restructuring of his field. It is commonly observed in psychoanalysis that a statement, either by the patient or the analyst, that produces insight will often be accompanied by affect. How can this observation be explained? Such statements can hardly be seen as attempts to depict some feeling and bring it more fully into awareness. Basically, statements geared to producing insight are attempts to give a new organization to the material the patient has been discussing (i.e., information that is present in his field). Affect can occur as a result of such statements because they basically serve to produce a restructuring of the patient's field.

The foregoing discussion indicates that the occurrence of affect in therapy is not a matter of symbolizing distinct, internal entities but is the result of elaborating substantive information that produces either disorganization or restructuring of the field. However, after doing such processing clients often will make statements that seem geared to labeling or depicting some affective state. Do these statements represent the symbolization of some distinct class of entities called "feelings?" To answer this question let us examine a few such statements. Consider again the client who has produced disorganization in his field by elaborating how recent events in his life make fulfilling his basic aspirations impossible. Let us suppose that after elaborating these events the client then says something like "I feel hopeless" or "I feel like my life is empty." These statements should not simply be viewed as the symbolization of some distinct internal entity existing prior to and outside the context of the information being processed. Rather, such statements, in part, represent integrating structures that capture a common meaning in and give organizations that are appropriate to the particular information existing at that moment (i.e., having basic aspirations thwarted). Let us suppose that after having produced a restructuring of his field by elaborating new facets of meaning that give new purpose to his life, he then goes on to say something that seems to point to a different affective state such as "I feel hopeful" or "I feel like the clouds have silver linings." These statments do not represent the symbolization of some new internal entity of which he is now aware. Rather, they represent, in part, organizations that capture the meaning of the particular substantive information that has changed the structure of the field (i.e., the realization of new purpose in living).

We have used the words "in part" in speaking of statements geared to depicting affective states because generating structures that capture the common meaning of the particular substantive information producing disorganization or change is not all that is involved in the occurrence of affect in therapy. To be sure, affect is not all cognition; it also involves bodily processes. However, it would be a mistake to view affect largely in terms of bodily processes for we shall see in a moment that we are not in a position to simply see the occurrence of affect in therapy as "a sensing of body life" and the symbolization of its "implicit meaning" (Gendlin, 1964); cognition does indeed play the major role in the process.

Although the presence of visceral changes may seem to distinguish affective experience from nonaffective experience, we should not assume that the almost infinite universe of states preceded by the words "I feel," or even the basic emotions (e.g., anger, sadness, euphoria), can be distinguished from one another and identified solely on the basis of different bodily states. Through the years it has been argued back and forth whether different emotions involve distinctly different physiological patterns (cf. Arnold, 1960; Cannon, 1929; James, 1884), but research by Schacter (Schacter & Singer, 1962; Schacter & Wheeler, 1962) has shown quite conclusively that different emotions do *not* involve different visceral reactions. Using drugs to induce relatively homogeneous visceral patterns in subjects and then putting them in different experimental conditions, Schacter showed that the same visceral pattern would produce drastically different emotions. The particular emotion experienced would not be a function of a particular visceral pattern, but would rather be a result of the person's cognitions about his situation.

The Schacter research showed that the role of bodily processes in the occurrence of affect is at best a very general one: all emotional experience seems to have a basic commonality in involving a gross change in bodily arousal. However, a change in bodily arousal neither determines that one specific affective state, rather than another, will be experienced, nor does it even ensure that affect will be experienced at all. A change in arousal will be a condition for the occurrence of affect only when the person lacks an appropriate explanation or interpretation (i.e., organizing structure) for the arousal. Thus, for example, the client who breathlessly sits down in the therapist's office after having bounded up the stairs will be experiencing a change in bodily arousal but is unlikely to be experiencing affect, the reason being that he has an appropriate explanation for organizing his change in arousal. The Schacter research indicated that when a person lacks an appropriate cognition or interpretation for a change in bodily arousal, the arousal at best only functions as a general, nonspecific signal for the presence of affect; it does not determine *what* particular affective state the person will experience. The particular affect that is experienced is not a function of the bodily state but is a function of the person's cognitive interpretation of his current situation (i.e., the particular information in his current field). The person attributes a particular affective meaning to his change in arousal on the basis of the particular substantive information that is present in his field, and he "selects" his affective state on the basis of the affective labels that he has learned are appropriate for describing such information. Statements clients make, then, to describe seemingly different affective states are not attempts to depict different bodily states; rather, they are attempts to give organization to a general change in bodily arousal in terms of the particular content of the information present in the field. Thus, the attributing of an affective label to describe a change in arousal can be viewed as an attempt to provide an interpretation and structure for that arousal where one was lacking.

The Schacter research indicates that we must reject Gendlin's (1964) view that the occurrence of affect involves a symbolization of the "implicit meaning" in "body life." Schacter's research strongly suggests that the multitude of different affective states described by clients does not simply represent the processing of distinct patterns of information from internal sensory sources. There appears to be no meaning intrinsic in bodily states that distinguishes one affect from another. Rather, people bestow a particular meaning on a general change in bodily arousal on the basis of the particular information present in their field.

Having suggested that the occurrence of affect in therapy involves (a) the processing of information that produces either disorganization or restructuring in the field and (b) a general change in bodily arousal in the client, it should be pointed out that the two typically occur together in therapy. Whereas it is possible for a change in arousal to occur without disorganization or restructuring in the field (as with the client who has just run up the stairs), disorganization or restructuring in a significant portion of the field is not likely to occur without an accompanying change in arousal. Thus the client who elaborates how recent events in his life are incompatible with and make impossible the fulfillment of his basic aspirations in living is likely to experience a change in arousal as a result of the presence of this incompatible information in his field.[7] Similarly, the realization of new purpose in living that restructures the client's field is also likely to produce a change in arousal. However, as the Schacter research would indicate, whether the resulting affective state is construed as a "hopeless feeling" or a "hopeful feeling" is not a function of a differing bodily state. Rather, it is a function of attributing a different affective meaning to a general change in bodily arousal on the basis of the particular content of the information being processed at the moment.

The second question raised concerning the occurrence of affect in therapy was as follows: given that the processing of a particular sample of information will sometimes evoke affect in a client and sometimes not, what is it about the *way* the client processes information that in one instance evokes affect and the other instance does not? Our previous discussion has already suggested an answer to this question. The particular

[7] The elaboration of significant recent events that are difficult to organize is only one of the ways in which the client can produce disorganization in his field in the therapy hour. Disorganization can also occur as a result of the retrieval and elaboration of early events in one's life. It is frequently observed in psychoanalysis that the elaboration of early traumatic events that have been "repressed" in the "unconscious" will be accompanied by affect (often termed catharsis). It is probably not that this material has been actively repressed, but rather that it was never adequately organized in the first place and hence not easily retrievable from long-term store. Affect accompanies the retrieval of such information from long-term store, not because there is repressed affect tied to the material, but because it produces a state of disorganization in the field when retrieved.

class or type of information that we are concerned with is information that has significance or centrality in the client's field. By this we mean basically information that is relevant to the major concerns of the client. However, as was indicated earlier, clients frequently process information relevant to their central concerns but do not always produce affect through their processing. A client's failure to produce affect does not simply stem from a failure to "own or recognize his feelings." Rather, it stems from a failure in the client's processing activity. When a client is speaking about things that are significant to him, but he is not experiencing affect in the process, it is because he neither elaborates facets of information that produce any change in the structure of his field nor produces any change in arousal through his processing activity. Whereas events in the outside world often *elicit* a change in bodily arousal, and hence, an affective reaction, in client-centered therapy we are principally dealing with *self-produced* arousal, that is, arousal the client generates in himself. When a client's mode of experiencing is optimal, he contributes to his arousal in two ways: (a) his heightened processing activity is itself a source of arousal, and (b) the facets of meaning he differentiates and integrates produce a change in the structure of his field, and hence a change in arousal. When clients speak about their experience in terms that are highly global and nondescriptive, it is not that they are out of touch with their feelings. Rather, they are failing to create affect through their processing; their processing activity produces neither a change in arousal nor the elaboration of information that would change the structure of their field.

Before we leave the area of affect, we might briefly reconsider Gendlin's (1964) notion of "implicit feelings" which he sees to be the referent for symbolization in the process of experiencing. We have already indicated that we cannot view this referent simply in terms of the meaning implicit in "body life." From our information-processing perspective, we would suggest that the referent for symbolization in therapy is crude information, whether activated in memory locations in long-term store or in internal sensory sources, that is held in its relatively unprocessed form in short-term store. When the client "feels" that his words have not accurately captured his internal experience, it is not that he has failed to explicate the implicit meaning of a feeling. Rather, he has failed to generate a structure that adequately organizes the information held in short-term store. What the client "feels" is the presence of information impinging on him that has not been adequately organized. We would also suggest that when Gendlin (1969) has people "focus" on their implicit feelings he is basically instructing them to redirect their attentional and processing capacities away from information derived from external sources, and instead, reallocate these internally to the processing of information central in their field.

Unproductive Modes of Experiencing

Having elaborated a view of both the dynamics of the experiencing process in therapy and its optimal mode, we are in a position to gain more insight into how clients typically deviate from the ideal. In describing the dynamics of experiencing, we have already indicated some of the ways in which clients are deficient in the manner in which they differentiate and integrate meaning and thus fail to create reorganization and change through their processing. These deficiencies, however, can appear in different forms. We will now briefly describe three different unproductive modes of processing commonly found in clients.[8] From the standpoint of our view of the optimal mode of experiencing, we will also indicate the major processing deficiencies characteristic of each mode.

DEPRESSED MODE OF PROCESSING

Such clients seem anergic and listless, and their affective experience is bland and impoverished. Fundamentally, their approach to processing is passive; they do little in the way of elaborating distinct facets of meaning in their experience. The structures characteristically generated to organize information are extremely general and vague, and therefore evoke little richness of information to serve as a substrate for further differentiation. Because their processing style is extremely limited in the amount of information created to enter into reorganization, their processing generates little movement or change in experience and their field remains static and unchanging. The fact that such people frequently speak of meaninglessness in their lives may well be due to the fact that they do little in the way of actively differentiating and integrating new facets of meaning to produce change and reorganization in experience.

[8] Two of the unproductive processing modes described here and also the optimal mode described earlier parallel the different client-voice-quality patterns assessed in therapy research by Rice and associates (Butler et al., 1962; Rice & Wagstaff, 1967; Rice & Gaylin, 1973). Rice's voice-quality classification system may represent a useful means for assessing these modes on the basis of vocal style. The depressed, rigid, and optimal modes of processing parallel Rice's *limited, externalizing,* and *focused* voice qualities respectively. The findings cited earlier (Wexler, 1974) indeed showed a strong relationship between vigorous differentiation and integration of meaning and focused voice quality, suggesting that with respect to the optimal mode the parallel is very close.

RIGID MODE OF PROCESSING

This mode characterizes those who are usually thought of as having a vigilant style of defense. It is similar to the depressed mode in only one basic respect—little reorganization and change typically result from the processing activity. Unlike the depressed mode, this style of processing information is active and energetic. However, the activity and the energy are directed not toward the elaboration and organization of new information, but toward fitting information in the field into preexistent structures. In generating meaning structures to organize information in their lives, such clients characteristically are constricted in the range of organizing rules utilized. As a result, only the information that the client can most readily organize is attended to and processed; a richness of information that might provide the substrate for change is lost because of an inability to organize it. These clients then typically do very little in the way of differentiating and integrating new facets of meaning. Because these clients are able to organize only a constricted range of information they are familiar with, the structures generated to organize it tend to be those used habitually in the past. Inasmuch as the structures are habitually used, such clients typically evoke little new information, if any, through their processing. Generally, then, this mode of processing is characterized by a tightness in elaborating and organizing information. The price paid for this organization is lack of change. Because this processing style produces little reorganization and change, it also produces little in the way of affect. It is not that these clients are not in touch with their feelings, or that they defend against their feelings, as is commonly thought, but rather that their mode of processing simply does not generate affect.[9]

DISORDERED MODE OF PROCESSING

This mode differs from the other two in that there are characteristically many facets of meaning elaborated and present in the field. The inability lies in synthesizing and integrating. People with this mode are characterized by a disorganized field, and hence anxiety. The information in their field is greater in amount and/or complexity than what they are optimally able to process. The verbalizations of such clients will frequently be disconnected, with the client disjointedly going from one facet of experience

[9] Using Rice's *externalizing* voice quality as an index of this processing style, pretherapy Rorschach scores do indeed suggest that such clients have a dearth of inner affect (Rice & Gaylin, 1973). Other research (Wexler, 1974) also lends support to the view that those with this processing style do little in the way of differentiating and integrating meaning when talking about their emotions, and also tend to organize a constricted range of information in the structures created.

to another in an attempt to elaborate parts that might permit synthesis and reorganization. However, in jumping from one facet to another, typically they are never able to attend to the mass of facets as a whole and are therefore unable to synthesize a common meaning in the array and give organization to their field. Frequently, a client with this processing style will leave the therapist with a disordered mass of information to respond to—but a mass that the therapist must respond to if he is to synthesize the meaning of what the client is attempting to organize.[10]

We will later consider how the therapist can differentially respond to the client according to his particular processing deficiencies. Before doing so, however, we should first reconsider the concept of self-actualization in light of the cognitive view we have been developing.

Self-Actualization

Earlier, in considering the way in which self-actualization has been conceptualized by Rogers, we saw how the overall emphasis in characterizing self-actualized persons was on the manner in which the person experienced, rather than on the realization of inherent potentialities. Moreover, we saw that the qualities of experiencing Rogers theorized to be characteristic of self-actualized persons, though perhaps intuitively appealing, were somewhat problematic. Now, having elaborated a model of experiencing, with respect to both its dynamics and its optimal mode, we are in a position to reconsider the concept of self-actualization, with the hope that our model will not only provide a firmer basis for rooting self-actualization in the experiencing process, but also enable us to be clearer in the way we conceptualize the characteristics of the self-actualized person.

In considering self-actualization, it is useful to make a basic distinction between self-actualization as a tendency, and self-actualization as a set of characteristics. A *tendency* refers to a directional force, whereas *characteristics* refer to structural features implied by the expression of a direc-

---

[10] Clients with this processing style do tend to be less difficult to work with than clients with either of the other two unproductive processing styles, as they do elaborate information to serve as a substrate for reorganization. The task of the therapist is mainly facilitating the organization of the differentiated material. It is a commonly observed fact, and one that is well documented in therapy outcome research (see Luborsky, Chandler, Auerbach, Cohen, & Bachrach, 1971), that clients who are anxious tend to have a good prognosis for therapy. It is not simply that they are in a state of discomfort and therefore "motivated" for therapy as is commonly thought. Rather, they are the clients who indeed provide and present a differentiated field for reorganization.

tional force (Maddi, 1972). In considering self-actualizaton as a tendency, rather than seeing it as the unfolding of substantive potentials, the present framework views it as a greater utilization of a potential process. Self-actualization is seen as the development and utilization of the capacity to process and organize information in such a way that the person is able to be his own source for the creation of new experience and change through his cognitive functioning. *Self-actualization then is seen as the characteristic propensity to engage in an optimal mode of experiencing.* Although man generally possesses the capacity to use his own cognitive processes for generating new experience and change, few individuals utilize it effectively. People's characteristic mode of processing and organizing information in their lives is such that they typically do not create new experience and change for themselves through their own cognitive functioning. What leads one person and not another characteristically to utilize this capacity effectively is likely to be intimately connected to the course of cognitive and perceptual development. A consideration of these developmental factors, however, is far beyond the scope of this chapter, and it will be sufficient for present purposes to view self-actualization as an increased tendency to utilize one's capacity to engage in an optimal mode of experiencing.

In seeing self-actualization as rooted in the basic organismic need for new experience, the present view picks up on the reinterpretation of self-actualization advanced by Butler and Rice (1963) in providing a conceptual basis for anchoring self-actualization in the biological nature of the organism. Butler and Rice saw self-actualization as originating in the basic stimulus hunger of the organism, and they conceptualized self-actualization in terms of the person's functioning to be his own source for new experience. To Butler and Rice's position we would add that adient motivation and the satisfaction of stimulus hunger must be tempered and balanced with organization in experience. Our view of the dynamics of experiencing has also provided a framework for understanding how cognitive processes can indeed function to create new experience and change through the differentiation and integration of meaning.

In elaborating the characteristics of the self-actualized person we are leaving the therapy hour behind and speaking of how the person appears in his experiencing "in the world." Our emphasis will be on those cognitive characteristics that are likely to be found in the person who typically engages in an optimal mode of experiencing. We will first briefly sketch a general picture of the self-actualized person, and then consider in a bit more detail some of the important characteristics of his cognitive functioning.

The chief characteristic of the self-actualized person is that he will continually be construing new facets of meaning in his experience. By distinguishing and synthesizing a richness of new facets of meaning in experience, the world of the self-actualized person will be one that is continually changing and unfolding into richer and more varied patterns. This is the case for his construal of both his external world and his internal world. In processing and organizing information from his external environment, the self-actualized person will distinguish new facets in what he takes in through his senses. Thus, as Butler and Rice (1963) have contended, the self-actualized person will be continually renewing his interest in his environment by re-creating it. It is not that he is completely open to all external stimulation; rather he creates new experience from his environment by allocating his attention and processing capacities to distinguishing and synthesizing new facets of meaning in it. Although the self-actualized person, then, will tend to process and organize a richness of information from his external world, he is not dependent on the external environment for providing a source for new experience. He is also autonomous in being able to create new experience and change for himself via his own cognitive functioning. Thus, in tending to differentiate and integrate a richness of facets of meaning from information evoked internally, the self-actualized person can create new experience and change independently of his environment. The affect of the self-actualized person is likely to be rich and varied; not because he symbolizes feelings, but because he creates them in the process of distinguishing and synthesizing new facets of meaning in his experience.

In viewing self-actualization as the tendency to engage in an optimal mode of experiencing, we can enumerate more specific characteristics of the cognitive functioning of the self-actualized person. These characteristics follow from our consideration of what constitutes the optimal mode of experiencing, and although they are largely not empirically supported at present, they can be put forth as propositions that can be readily investigated in future empirical work.

RULE UTILIZATION AND RULE GENERATION

Because the self-actualized person must be able to construe new facets of meaning in information, we would expect that he would have available and characteristically utilize a wide range of rules in processing and organizing information. This would enable him to distinguish unique aspects of meaning in information and to construe them in a manner that is multidimensional rather than unidimensional. Although the utilization of a wide range of rules will enable him to differentiate a diversity of facets of meaning in information, it will also enable him to organize and synthesize commonalities in this diversity. In utilizing rules in unique combinations to generate novel organizations for information, we would also expect the self-actualized person to be simultaneously adding to his existent repertoire of rules that can be used in future processing.

AMOUNT AND COMPLEXITY OF INFORMATION

Although self-actualized persons must necessarily process information within the constraints of the information-processing system, they will also make optimal use of its capabilities. Some information, whether from internal or external sources, will inevitably be lost to the self-actualized person; however, because a wide range of rules is utilized in handling information, the organizations created will tend to deal more adequately with the potential richness of information than organizations created by the person who is not self-actualized. We would expect, then, self-actualized persons to be capable of processing and organizing both a greater amount of information and a greater complexity in the structure of that information than those who are relatively un-self-actualized.

MEMORY

As elaborated earlier, both short-term memory and long-term memory represent crucial components in the information-processing system; short-term memory being the holding area for information waiting organization, long-term memory being the repository of stored information that can be activated and evoked to enter into ongoing processing. We would expect self-actualization to involve enhanced functioning in both these memory systems. If the self-actualized person characteristically organizes a relative richness of information, this might in part be due to an increased capability of short-term memory to hold information for processing. If the self-actualized person tends to meaningfully process and organize a relative richness of information, this would also mean that a relative richness of information is transferred to permanent storage in long-term memory. Although permanent storage does not necessarily mean that the information can be readily activated, as we elaborated earlier, vigorous differentiation and integration have the effect of imposing increased organization on information, and thus it will tend to be accessible for activation in the future. Thus, as the self-actualized person organizes information in his life, we would expect that a richness of information will be evoked in long-term store, thereby providing an enriched informational substrate for his processing.

ATTENTION

If the self-actualized person has a heightened capacity to handle and organize information with respect to both amount and complexity, then self-actualization might also entail a heightened capacity to attend simultaneously to a variety of information that is evoked in him. Although attention must necessarily be selective, we would not expect the self-actualized person to allocate his attention to what can be most readily organized. Rather, we would expect him to allot his attention to unique features of information evoked in him. This might entail an *internal scan* (Sternberg, 1970) of the variety of information activated, and an allotment of attention to the novel and unique features of the information.

PERCEPTION

If self-actualized persons can handle and transform a greater amount and complexity of information than relatively un-self-actualized persons, then at the perceptual level they may characteristically take in more information from external sources inasmuch as they are better able to handle it. In this regard, research by Zimrink, Nauman, and Balcombe (1970) found that the greater the elaboration a person's conceptual activity showed with respect to emotional experience, the more information he was able to attend to in a selective attention task.

Although there is not at present empirical support for most of the above assertions concerning the characteristics of the self-actualized person, there is some preliminary empirical work lending plausibility to the view that self-actualization does indeed involve the characteristic tendency to engage in an optimal mode of experiencing. Wexler (1974) found that the degree to which people differentiate and integrate meaning in describing their experiencing of emotions showed a significant positive relationship to their score on an inventory assessing self-actualization. Whether the characteristics of cognitive functioning proposed here are indeed associated with self-actualization represents an exciting and important area for investigation in future research.

THERAPEUTIC PROCESS

Views on what it is that changes in successful psychotherapy are perhaps almost as diverse as the numerous approaches to therapeutic practice that exist. To be sure, man interacts with an exceedingly complex environment, and given that complexity we can often identify changes accompanying successful psychotherapy in any number of areas—behavior, attitudes, relationships with others, self-esteem, and so on. However, if we look at what is basic and central to man—that he is a processor and organizer of information—we are also likely to see other basic changes stemming from successful psychotherapy.[11] The essence of successful therapy is seen here to involve a *change in the characteristic style in which information is processed*. The aim of therapy is to make people more self-actualized. By this we do not mean that the client realizes in himself some sort of innate substantive potential to be one sort of person instead of another sort of person. Rather, we mean that the client fundamentally learns that he can be his own source for creating reorganization and change in experience through his cognitive functioning. Basically, we would view therapy as a learning situation; the aim of the client-centered therapist is to help the client engage in an optimal mode of experiencing. Although the immediate consequence of engaging in such a mode in therapy will be that the client will experience reorganization and change with respect to his concerns, the more important consequence is that he will learn a mode of processing he can engage in outside of the therapy hour. Therapy will be successful when a client learns he can be truly self-sufficient in creating reorganization and change for himself through his own cognitive functioning.

The client-centered therapist is not a teacher of an optimal mode of experiencing. However, when he is functioning optimally he serves, on a moment-to-moment basis, as a very potent facilitator in helping the client engage in a more productive mode of experiencing. Our task then in understanding the role of the client-centered therapist will be to elaborate how his style of participation functions to help the client engage in a more optimal mode of experiencing. We will regard the therapist basically as serving information-processing functions; his manner of responding is geared to helping the client transcend deficiencies in the style in which he characteristically elaborates and organizes information so

---

11 The viewpoint expressed here is in agreement with that expressed in another context by Simon (1969). Man need not be seen as complex; it is only his interaction with a highly complex and varied environment that makes him appear complex. The processing system that acts on information received from that environment, although perhaps elegantly geared to adaptive and flexible functioning in the varied environment, may itself be relatively simple. Although we find from our research, in the laboratory or with therapy outcome tools, or whatever, that man does indeed seem to be complex, we should remember that we have in a sense elicited that complexity with our measurement procedures. What we are basically assessing is the variability that the processing system can show in responding to our measures or our experimental situations; we are not assessing the complexity of the processing system itself.

that he can engage in a more productive mode of experiencing in the therapy hour.

The Role of the Therapist: The Therapist as a Surrogate Information-Processor

Traditional client-centered views on how the therapist helps to facilitate change have tended to be couched in terms that are molar and general. In the most general form, the therapist is seen to provide a special relationship for the client, with help being seen as a by-product of the client's experiencing of this relationship (Rogers, 1962). The curative effect of the relationship is seen to stem from the therapist's providing an "understanding" atmosphere that permits growth and change. Though there may be some general truth in such a view, it does not give us much insight into the specific properties of understanding and what its direct effects are.

Rogers (1957) has postulated three therapist conditions (empathy, unconditional positive regard, and congruence) to be essential for successful therapeutic change. Over the years these three therapist conditions have come to be thought of as the identifying characteristics of client-centered practice, and some (e.g., Truax & Carkhuff, 1967) have even argued that they represent the essential ingredients in all modes of therapeutic practice. Though held in great reverence by many, the postulating of empathy, unconditional positive regard, and congruence as the dictums of client-centered practice presents problems, both for the novice attempting to learn client-centered technique and for the theoretician attempting to understand how client-centered practice helps the client on a moment-to-moment basis. These problems basically stem from the fact that the three therapist conditions are conceptualized as *attitudes,* not as specific *behaviors.* Attitudes refer to states or ways to be; they do not readily translate into specifiable overt behaviors. Thus, the novice attempting to learn client-centered practice is told what he is to *experience,* but there is little concrete specification of what he is to *do.* The theoretician also finds no clear specification for how these therapist attitudes help the client on a moment-to-moment basis. The relationship between therapist conditions and client process is stated perhaps somewhat simplistically as an "if–then" situation: if the therapist experiences and communicates these attitudes and a vulnerable client perceives them, then therapeutic change will take place in the client (Rogers, 1957).

It is doubtful whether the communication of attitudes alone is a particularly potent therapeutic tool to be relied upon. Therapists do indeed do specific things on a moment-to-moment basis that have observable effects. The client-centered therapist is no exception. In elaborating how the client-centered therapist functions on a moment-to-moment basis in helping the client engage in an optimal mode of experiencing, our focus will be on understanding the properties and functions of empathic responding. Our emphasis on empathy stems from the fact that of the three therapist conditions elaborated by Rogers, empathy is the only one that is directly translated into overt behavior, and it is the one that functions as a potent facilitator of client experiencing. After discussing the properties and functions of empathic responding, we will show how the notions of unconditional positive regard and congruence not only fail to be manifested in overt behavior but also are already implied in and subsumed by the task of responding empathically. Our discussion of empathy will not question the importance it can have therapeutically. Indeed, Rogers' discovery of the therapeutic value of empathic responding probably represents one of the most significant contributions to the practice of therapy, if not to the whole area of human relations. The aim of our discussion is to use the cognitive model developed here to gain more theoretical insight into how empathic responding does indeed function as such a potent therapeutic tool.

EMPATHIC RESPONDING

We use the term "empathic responding" rather than "empathy" to stress the fact that it is not merely an attitude but a consistent style of overt behaviors given as responses to a client. Rogers (1957) sees empathy as involving the therapist's perceiving and understanding the experience of the client "as if" it were his own, and communicating that understanding to the client. Although empathy is seen as a basic therapist attitude, it is perhaps more appropriate to view it as the activity of generating a particular type of response. What are the properties, then, of an empathic response?

One way that an empathic response has been frequently characterized is as a *reflection of feelings* (Shlien, 1961). Such a view is quite consistent with seeing optimal experiencing in terms of the experiencing of feelings; a therapist's response ideally reflects the feelings that the client is "really" feeling so as to enhance the client's experiencing of those feelings. We have commented at length how the viewing of client process in terms of the experiencing of feelings both rests on an ill-defined and ambiguous concept of feelings and precludes gaining a better understandinng of the process of experiencing. The same is also true for seeing empathic responding in terms of the reflection of feeling. Such a view necessitates both attributing a special thing-like quality to feelings and assuming that a richness of feelings exists outside of awareness in some sort of reservoir. Moreover, seeing the role of the therapist as simply a reflector of feelings also precludes gaining a more explicit understanding of the properties of an empathic response and the important processing functions it serves.

An empathic response is an attempt to organize and articulate the *meaning* of the information the client is processing. When it is optimal, *an empathic response is a structure or group of structures that more fully captures, and better organizes, the meaning of the information in the field that the client is processing than had the structure(s) the client had generated himself.* An empathic response is basically an organization of information generated by the therapist and held out to the client. It is an organiation that attempts to encapsulate, fully and accurately, the meaning of all or some of the information in process in the client. The information that the therapist works with and attempts to organize may be that existing in the client just prior to the structures the client generated or that which is subsequently evoked in the client by the creating of those structures. In functioning as an alternate organizer of the meaning of the particular information in the field the client is processing, the therapist serves on a moment-to-moment basis as a *surrogate information-processor.* The term "surrogate" is important here. The therapist works with the information the client is attempting to process, but also, to the extent that the client's processing is less than optimal, the therapist's organizations held out to the client can function to compensate for where the client's processing is deficient. It is in its being a more accurate organization of meaning that an empathic response can have its effects in serving to facilitate a more optimal mode of experiencing. In capturing more fully the meaning of the particular information the client is processing, an accurate empathic response can serve to differentiate or integrate the meaning of the client's experience more effectively than the structures the client generated himself.

In its effect empathic responding does far more than give the client the message "I am with you" (Truax & Carkhuff, 1967, p. 46) or communicate to the client that he is understood. Indeed, on a moment-to-moment basis the organization of information contained in an empathic response can serve three vitally important processing functions for the client: (a) an attentional function, (b) an organizing function, and (c) an evocative function. In serving these three processing functions, the therapist takes over processing functions from the client and compensates for where the client's processing might be deficient in preventing him from effectively differentiating and integrating meaning so as to achieve reorganization and change in experience.

To understand how empathic responding can serve an important attentional function for the client, it is important to recall that in the ongoing processing of information in the therapy hour, information evoked at a given instant in time and held in short-term memory is often far more than what can be meaningfully attended to and organized by the client at the time. The consequence is a selective allotment of attention by the client. Two problems may arise from such selection. First, information that can most readily be organized with the client's existent rules may be attended to for further processing at the expense of richer information not so readily organized. Second, evoked information may momentarily be attended to and organized by the client in a meaning structure but subsequently dropped as a substrate for further elaboration due to the presence of other information impinging on him. In diverting attention to the organization of other information, the client may leave an important facet of meaning in experience insufficiently elaborated. Common to both cases is the fact that potentially rich information is crowded out by other information to which the client attends instead, and a rich substrate for subsequent processing may be lost.

Although the client's attention may be diverted, the therapist's need not be. The information evoked in the client that impinges on him and makes demands on his attention and processing capacities is typically greater than the information the client evokes in the therapist. Thus, the attentional demands on the therapist are less and he can shift his attention more readily among the different facets of information evoked in him than can the client. We do not mean to imply that attending to the different facets of information being communicated by the client is an easy task for the therapist. On the contrary, it is a very demanding one. We only mean to say that as a listener there is less impinging on him and he can more loosely attend to the different facets of information communicated by the client and hence formulate his response on a less constricted basis. By focusing his response on the information the client's attention has been diverted from, the therapist can serve an important processing function in refocusing the client's attention and hence, his subsequent processing, on what would otherwise be lost. In information-processing terms, the therapist is basically serving a rehearsal function. Whereas without the therapist's response, the information would become lost in short-term memory by being crowded out by other information, the therapist's response maintains the information in a high-priority position in short-term store so that it will be reattended to and further processed.

It should be clear that in serving this attentional function the therapist is directing the subesquent processing of the client by holding out to him facets of information to be attended to and further processed. Popular opinion to the contrary, it is a myth to think of the client-centered therapist as nondirective. He is only nondirective in the sense of working with and responding to information that is already in process in the client. However, in working with that information he is quite directive, though his direction takes a subtle and noncoercive form. By selecting some facets of information and ignoring others in organizing his responses, the therapist is continually directing and redirecting the subsequent processing of the client. We call the direction given by the therapist noncoercive because, while it is demanding of the client's attention, the therapist will typically not persist on the point if the client does not pick up on the direction offered.

Seeing the therapist's response as serving to refocus the attention and subsequent processing of the client raises the question of what the therapist should use as his guide for making his selection in what to respond to and what to ignore. The traditional client-centered answer would be that the therapist should respond to feelings. We have previously suggested that affect occurs only because the processing of information has certain effects on the client. We further suggested that affect was most likely to be produced when information occupying a significant portion of the client's field is processed and when the processing has the effect of producing either disorganization or change in the structure of the field. Consistent with this position, the therapist should listen carefully for and select those facets of information that seem to refer to central aspects of the client's functioning and that either seem to have an unfinished flavor for the client or seem to present processing difficulties for him.

Although the content of what the client says will be the principal means by which a therapist will pick and choose facets of information to respond to and focus the client's attention, the therapist should not be bound solely by the words the client says. Frequently, clients will not verbalize facets of information evoked in themselves that are problematic, and which they cannot readily organize. This is often the case with clients who have what was described previously as a rigid processing style. With such clients often a quaver of the voice, a quiver of the mouth, or a postural shift can serve as a far more reliable signal to the therapist that the client is moving into significant territory than the particular words he says. The therapist may not know the particular content of what was evoked, but he knows "something" was evoked, and his response can be geared toward getting an elaboration of the content. Thus, the therapist might well ignore what the client has said and instead say something like "I sense there's something about that which disturbs you," thereby redirecting the client's attention to elaborating the problematic information evoked but not verablized.

The most obvious processing function that empathic responding continually serves in helping the client to engage in a more optimal mode of experiencing is an organizing function. We have noted earlier that one of the most striking characteristics of a client's behavior is his continued attempt to organize and articulate as clearly as possible the meaning of information in the field he is attempting to give order and form to. However, due to deficiencies in their existent repertoire of rules, clients typically do not generate an organization that either distinguishes and accurately captures the meaning of some new facet of information evoked, or synthesizes and encapsulates the meaning of a number of differentiated facets. As a result of this inability to generate an adequate organization that gives order to the information they are attempting to process at the moment, further processing is either hindered or stopped. The client lacks an organized substrate from which he can go on to further differentiate and integrate meaning. In such a situation, some clients will keep trying to search for the exact words to generate that organized substrate, whereas other clients will give up and go on to something else.

Although the client's processing deficiencies may hinder or prevent him from generating an adequate organization from which he can go on, the therapist can provide this organization in the response he holds out to the client. Whereas the client's existent repertoire of rules may make him unable to generate such an organization, the therapist is not bound by the organizing rules of the client. On a moment-to-moment basis, the therapist in his response can serve a vitally important processing function in providing an organization which more accurately captures the meaning of the information the client is attempting to organize than had the organization the client had generated. The effect of a good empathic response on the client is always further differentiation and integration of new facets of meaning; an accurate empathic response serves to provide an organized substrate from which the client can go on and distinguish and synthesize new facets of meaning that emerge from the organization.

To function effectively as an alternate organizer of information will require that the therapist's language be concise. Responses that are long or diffuse will have minimal impact on the client. Instead of providing the client with a clear, accurate organization, such responses will themselves make heavy demands on the client's processing. They will produce an overload of information in short-term store and the client will have to devote all his energies to attending to, retrieving, and decoding all the different aspects of the complex response the therapist has given him in order to discover an organization. Most clients can not or will not expend such energy. Typically the client will then either attend to only one small facet of the therapist's response, and hence become diverted from the central theme he is pursuing, or he may ignore the therapist's response altogether. In either case, the therapist will have failed in providing an effective organization from which further processing can proceed.

An optimal mode of client experiencing not only necessitates that the client both attend to new facets of information evoked by his processing and accurately organizes their meaning, but it also requires that the structures he generates evoke a rich substrate of information for further processing. Very frequently the structures clients generate evoke little. As we noted earlier, clients often utilize general and inexpressive structures to organize the meaning of the information they are attending to and processing. The quality of their processing suffers, because they do not evoke for themselves a substrate that can serve as the basis for further differentiation and integration of new facets of meaning.

Just as the structures the client generates can serve not only to organize input but also to evoke output, so too can the structures the therapist holds out to the client. Whereas the client's structures may evoke little in the way of new information for further processing, the therapist's structures can serve an important surrogate function in evoking new facets of information for the client to attend to. Thus, the therapist functions to provide the evoked substrate for further processing that the client had not provided for himself. If the client is talking about some experience in the past, the therapist's response can serve to evoke other important facets of the experience that may be in long-term store but not activated by the client's processing. If the client is elaborating some present facet of his experience, the therapist's response can function to evoke new aspects or implications that the experience might potentially have for the client, but which his own processing had not evoked.

The evocative function of empathic responding places a premium on the vividness of the therapist's language as well as its conciseness. A response lacking conciseness is likely to produce too much information in short-term store. A concise response, however, is not necessarily evocative. There are many possible organizations that the therapist can generate to give order and meaning to the information the client is processing at a given moment in time. As Butler and Rice (1963) note, all these possible organizations will not be equally evocative. Therapist's responses that use general and inexpressive language may be reasonably accurate but they will be minimally evocative. In responding to the client, the therapist must choose his words carefully; the words he picks should be sharp and poignant, and be rich in terms of the connotations they evoke. Earlier, we noted that metaphor and imagery are particularly potent means for evoking an enriched substrate for subsequent processing; however, they are not the only means. Responses that use active verbs and vivid adjectives, or those that juxtapose language can also be effective.

To many therapists of other orientations, and even to some therapists who consider themselves client-centered, empathy is seen as something relatively easy to achieve. Viewing empathy as an attitude to be communicated to the client, these therapists tend to see empathy as a rather passive task involving merely paraphrasing, summarizing, or reflecting what the client has said, so as to show him he is understood and encourage him to go deeper. Effective empathic responding is neither easy to achieve nor is it a passive task. The task of generating responses that can serve attentional, organizing, and evocative functions for the client demands a full and active use of the therapist's processing capacities at every moment. To serve an attentional function effectively, at any given moment the therapist must listen and attend carefully to all the different facets of information that might be potentially evoked in the client. He must do an extensive scan of this information and select those facets that seem most meaningful and significant to the client. Given that he has selected what aspects to respond to, if he is also to serve an organizing function, he must then transform this information into concise words that capture the precise meaning the information has for the client. Contrary to popular stereotypes, the effective client-centered therapist is not a wooden responder who merely paraphrases or repeats in summary fashion what the client has just said. He selects those facets evoked that are most meaningful and live for the client, and then actively synthesizes and transforms these into structures that more accurately capture their meaning. If the response is also to serve an evocative function, the therapist must carefully choose the words that will have maximum impact in evoking an enriched substrate for further processing in the client. The task may be difficult and demanding, but it is also rewarding. In being effectively empathic, the therapist can compensate for deficiencies in the client's style of processing that prevent him from engaging in a more optimal mode of experiencing.

When the therapist is functioning most effectively as a surrogate information-processor, there is a sense in which the responses he holds out to the client are a slight bit ahead of the client's processing in pointing him toward a more optimal mode of experiencing. The structures the therapist holds out to the client do not merely summarize or paraphrase, but actually take off from the client's previous response and go a step further in integrating or differentiating the meaning of the information the client is processing. A competent client-centered therapist does not respond merely to the literal meaning of the words the client has just said. He also responds to the meaning of the information that was likely evoked in the client by what he just said. Thus, when optimally empathic, therapists' responses tend to take the form of what the client might say next were he attending to what his processing evokes and productively distinguishing and synthesizing new facets of meaning so as to achieve reorganization and change in his field.

For heuristic purposes we may distinguish two basic forms that an empathic response may take on a moment-to-moment basis: (a) an integrating form or (b) a differentiating form. A therapist's response that is *integrating* serves to synthesize and organize for the client a common meaning evoked by the different structures the client has just created. A *differentiating* response focuses on a particular facet evoked by one or a few of the client's structures and further distinguishes for the client a more particular aspect of its meaning. At times the distinction between the two forms may be somewhat blurred, for in differentiating a more particular facet of meaning, the therapist may have to focus on and synthesize the common meaning evoked by a subset of the client's structures. It is useful, however, to distinguish these two forms, for depending on the nature of the client's processing of the moment, one form will be more appropriate than the other in facilitating further processing in the client.

Frequently, a client in his verbalizations will differentiate a number of distinct facets of meaning in his experience that can be seen to evoke a common meaning not articulated by the client. However, for reasons discussed earlier, he may not synthesize the common meaning evoked by them and generate a superordinate structure that organizes the differentiated facets. Although he has differentiated meaning and created change in his field, an organization of the meaning of what has been differentiated is lacking. As a result, the client will lack a clear organization from which he can then go on to differentiate new facets of meaning. In such a situation, the therapist's response should take an integrating form. In capturing the common meaning evoked by the differentiated facets, the therapist's response can provide the organization that the client has not provided for himself, and in so doing, provide the basis from which the client can go on and differentiate new facets of meaning that emerge from the organization. With clients who have a disordered mode of processing, the therapist's responses will frequently take an integrating form, inasmuch as these clients will tend to elaborate a number of different facets of meaning in experience but be unable to attend to them and synthesize their common meaning.

A very common occurrence in therapy is that a client will insufficiently differentiate the meaning of a particular facet of experience. As we discussed earlier, most clients do not take an active stance toward distinguishing new facets of meaning in experience. Instead, they tend toward premature closure in their processing, leaving significant facets of meaning that might be generated from what is evoked unelaborated. As a result, they fail both to create change in the structure of their field and to provide the necessary informational substrate whereby a meaningful reorganization of the field can occur. In such a situation the therapist's response should take a differentiating form. The aim of the therapist should be to focus on a significant facet of information evoked but not adequately elaborated by the client, and hold out to the client an organization that more uniquely distinguishes its meaning. Here the therapist's response compensates for inadequate differentiation by the client in further unpacking the meaning of the client's experience. Because inadequate differentiation is generally the rule rather than the exception, this is perhaps the most pervasive form that a therapist's response should take on a moment-to-moment basis. In serving to differentiate new facets of meaning from what is evoked in the client but not adequately elaborated, the therapist plays on a moment-to-moment basis a vitally important role in helping the client both to create change in the structure of his field and to provide the necessary informational substrate for meaningful reorganization.

Let us first examine an excerpt from therapy that will illustrate how a therapist's response can serve to integrate a common meaning evoked by a number of differentiated facets, thereby facilitating further differentiation. Our example will also illustrate the attentional, organizing, and evocative functions an empathic response can serve. For illustrative purposes the therapist's response given here serves all three functions simultaneously, but it should be noted that at any given moment in time, depending on the nature of the client's processing, the therapist can emphasize one of these processing functions in his response rather than the others. The client, a woman who is considering leaving her husband, is discussing her relationship with him. To facilitate reference for later discussion we will indicate what could be considered the structures generated by the client and therapist with lower-case letters.

Client	I feel like I don't have to feel so guilty that I didn't love him (a). I feel like I've cared about him (b). But I think maybe it's good (c)—maybe some people you can care about only so much (d) and other people you can care about more (e). And I know that I can care about somebody much more (f) than I care about him (g). Or else maybe I'm kidding myself (h). I don't know (i).
Therapist	But that's the way you feel (x). Like—somehow he—you can't care for him with all the caring you've got in you (y).
Client	That's it! (j) And that's what I want to do (k). You know—[care] as much as I can (l). And I want to have somebody care about me, as much as they can (m) . . . .

Before examining how the therapist's response serves to integrate meaning for the client, let us consider what the client is saying in her first statement. We may see structures b–g as basically serving to differentiate the meaning of why the client thinks she should not feel guilty for not loving her husband (a). These structures can be seen to evoke consistently an implicit contrast and discrepancy between her actual feelings for her husband and some possible state she thinks is both more optimal and desirous. We see this first in her implicit distinction between caring (b) and love (a). The contrast is more directly made, though in a more generalized form, when she talks of people to whom only limited caring is possible (d) as compared to people for whom it is possible to have a heightened experience of caring (e). She then goes on to make this general contrast more specifically related to herself when she asserts a possibility that there might be somebody for whom she can care about more (f) than she cares for her husband (g). However, rather than attending to and directly organizing the meaning of this implicit contrast and discrepancy, which has been continually evoked by this series of structures, in the absence of such an organization she begins to doubt the validity of what she is expressing (h and i) and stops further processing of the information.

The first part of the therapist's response (x) basically serves to affirm the subjective validity of what the client has expressed and to redirect her attention to what she had been processing previously. The second part of the therapist's response (y) refocuses her attention directly on what was previously evoked, and it is this part that serves to integrate the common meaning evoked by the facets she had differentiated. The statement "You can't care for him with all the caring you have in you" organizes in a simple but precise and elegant way the basic contrast and discrepancy evoked by the client's structures. Whereas the client had failed to organize the common meaning evoked by what she had differentiated, the therapist's response serves to organize, effectively and explicitly, the contrast between what the client actually feels toward her husband and what she would like to feel toward somebody. However, the therapist's response does more than integrate meaning and serve an organizing function. It also evokes in the client an enriched substrate for further processing. In using a form of the word "care" in the context of both poles of the contrast, the therapist's structure creates a link between the two poles that directly juxtaposes the actual state with a possible state. The effect is to evoke in the client and focus her subsequent processing on an intensified sense of the discrepancy between the two. In this juxtaposition the therapist's response also clearly reevokes in the client an intensified sense of an untapped reservoir of caring that was implicit in and likely evoked in the client by what she had said previously (e and f). The effect of evoking this informational substrate is that the client is able to go on and more clearly elaborate what she yearns for (k, l, and m). Whereas the client at the end of her first statement had stopped further processing, in accurately capturing and emphasizing the basic discrepancy implicit in her differentiated structures, the therapist provided an organization that optimally fitted the information in the field she was attempting to give order to. In so doing, he provided an organization and evoked a substrate from which the client could continue processing and further differentiate new facets of meaning that emerged from the organization.

Let us now examine another excerpt from therapy to illustrate how a therapist's response can serve to differentiate further the meaning of a particular facet of information evoked in the client but not adequately elaborated. Again, we will point to the attentional, organizing, and evocative functions of the therapist's response. The client is a student who, in the context of talking about the state of depression he has been experiencing, is describing his passive attitude with respect to school. We will again identify the structures of the client and therapist with lower-case letters to facilitate later discussion.

Client   I'm not sure what I'm really doing in this place [school] (a). I see myself getting up in the morning (b), eating breakfast (c), going to this class and to that one (d), just sitting in there (e), not even listening (f)—day after day (g). There doesn't seem to be too much point in it (h). It's really bad (i). And I'm really starting to get worried (j). I have this work just piling up (k). There are so many things I have to read for school (l) and a mess of papers I have to write (m). (pause) I just wish I could get it done (n), but I never seem to be able to get myself started (o).

Therapist   I sense that when you look at your life you can really see yourself just going through motions (x). From empty motion to empty motion (y), day in and day out (z).

Client   (pause) It's all just motions (p)—meaningless motions (q). I'm removed from it (r)—uninvolved (s). With school (t), my attempts at relationships with girls (u). Like I'm sort of bystander (v)—just sitting there watching my life go by (w).

Before examining how the therapist's response further differentiates the meaning of a particular facet of meaning evoked and serves processing functions for the client, we will examine what the client has said in his first response. In elaborating the doubt he expresses about being in school (a), the client generates a series of structures (b–g) that are situationally descriptive of his mode of participating in school. These structures evoke a particular sense of repetitiveness and emptiness in his style of involvement in school, which is alluded to (h), but not explicitly elaborated.

Because this aspect of repetitiveness and emptiness could potentially have great significance, not just in reference to his participation in school but also in relation to his whole style of involvement in life in general, it would probably be productive, in terms of subsequent processing, were it explicitly distinguished and explicated. However, instead of attending to and differentiating the meaning of this particular facet of information evoked, the client then goes on to evaluate the general quality of his involvement in school with the nondescriptive structure "bad" (i). Rather than unpacking the meaning of this general structure in terms of what in particular was "bad" about the information evoked, the client's attention and subsequent processing turn instead toward other things that are "bad," and he goes on to describe the mounting pressures at school and his inability to meet those pressures (j–o).

Although the therapist could have responded to the situationally specific worries that the client had turned to in the latter part of his statement (j–o), he chose to ignore these worries. Instead, he chose to refocus the client's attention on the aspect of repetitiveness and emptiness that was likely evoked in the client by the earlier part of his statement but inadequately attended to and insufficiently differentiated due to interference by other information (situational school worries). Inasmuch as the evoked facet the therapist selected to respond to was likely to refer to a number of areas of experience in the client's life space other than school, and thus to represent a more general style of involvement in life, the therapist's choice was probably a wise one. The therapist's structures distinguish with far greater specificity than had the client's just what seems "bad" to the client about the style of involvement described in structures b–g. The words of the therapist (x–z) explicitly organize for the client the repetitiveness and emptiness that had been evoked but not fully elaborated. The therapist, however, has also done something quite subtle. He has indeed perceived the more general significance of what the client is saying and frames his response, not in the context of the client looking at his involvement in school, but rather in looking at his involvement in life (x). In so doing, the therapist is subtly directing the client's attention to scanning other areas of experience for possible relevance in the present context. The therapist's response serves to differentiate the meaning of a particular facet of the client's experience, but it also simultaneously serves to evoke an enriched substrate for further processing. With his effective repetition of words (y and z), the therapist reevokes the repetitiveness and emptiness of the client's style of involvement and places it in a high-priority position for subsequent processing by the client.

The effects of the therapist's response on the client's subsequent processing are quite dramatic. We might infer from his pause that the client is indeed processing what the therapist's response has evoked in him, for he then goes on to differentiate with more richness of detail other aspects of his basic style of involvement (q–s). Then, probably due to the lead of the therapist, he expands its relevance to a greater portion of his field (t and u). Having done this differentiation, what was originally left as something that was merely "bad" now results in a rather poignant reorganization of information and realization of a very basic and pervasive orientation to living (v and w).

It should be clear from our discussion that effective empathic responding should be neither a matter of merely paraphrasing or summarizing what the client has said nor simply a matter of reflecting feelings. Rather, if it is to serve processing functions for the client, it is a matter of carefully attending to and selecting from the different facets of information contained in what the client has said and what might have been evoked, and then transforming this information into effective linguistic organizations that serve to further differentiate or integrate meaning for the client and evoke in him an enriched substrate for further processing.

Our discussion raises an important practical question, but one that also has theoretical implications: to what extent must the therapist be optimally empathic in actively differentiating and integrating new facets of meaning for the client in order to help him engage in a productive mode of therapeutic process? Just as there are differences in the extent to which clients "work" at differentiating and integrating new facets of meaning, so too are there differences in the degree to which therapists must work at helping their clients to engage in a more optimal mode of experiencing. It is a common observation of experienced client-centered therapists that it is far more difficult with some clients to respond effectively so as to help them engage in a richer mode of experiencing than it is with other clients. It is also a common observation that with a given client the degree to which the therapist will have to work at his responses will vary. When the client's experience lacks richness, the therapist will have to be maximally accurate and effective in his responses if the client is to engage in a more productive mode of therapeutic process. However, when the client's experiencing is rich and at a "peak," the therapist will often have to do little. In fact, the therapist can even be inaccurate in his responses and miss what the client is saying and the quality of the client's processing will typically not suffer. In such a situation, the client will keep on his track and continue in his rich mode of experiencing.

Our view of the therapist as a surrogate information-processor helps us both to understand these observations and to answer the question of how active and optimal in his responses the therapist must be. The relationship between the quality of client process and quality of empathic responding can be stated as an *inverse function*: if therapeutic process is to take place, the degree to which the therapist must be active and optimally empathic will be inversely related to the quality of the client's processing. In the terms of the present viewpoint, at a given moment in time the less productively the client is differentiating and integrating meaning, the more active and optimal the therapist will have to be both in serving attentional, organizing, and evocative functions for the client and in differentiating and integrating new facets of meaning for him.

In delineating the properties and functions of the client-centered therapist's style of participation, our focus has been on showing how the therapist, through empathic responding, serves as a surrogate information-processor for the client and in so doing serves important processing functions for him. On a moment-to-moment basis an empathic response compensates for processing deficiencies in the client that prevent him from engaging in an optimal mode of experiencing. It is this that makes the client-centered therapist's style of participation therapeutic, and it is this that makes the consistent use of empathic responding such an extremely potent tool in helping the client engage in and learn an optimal mode of experiencing.

In our discussion we have said little about unconditional positive regard and congruence, the other therapist conditions seen by Rogers as essential for therapeutic change. We have emphasized empathic responding rather than these two conditions because what the therapist does overtly in terms of his behavior is to hold out structures to the client, structures that attempt to capture the specific meaning of the information in process in the client. As we shall see, the therapist does not overtly express unconditional positive regard and congruence to the client. Ascribing such importance to these two conditions emphasizes the role of the therapist as one of experiencing and communicating attitudes to the client and fails to deal adequately with what the therapist *does* and what are the functions served by what he does. In discussing the role of the client-centered therapist in terms of the properties and processing functions of empathic responding, we have attempted to shed some light on how what he does is instrumental in facilitating change. In light of our discussion, we should now briefly reconsider the conditions of unconditional positive regard and congruence. We will suggest that not only do each of these two conditions fail to find overt expression in the behavior of the therapist, but if we do indeed wish to think of them as something experienced internally in the therapist, they are in fact already implied in and subsumed by the task of responding empathically.

UNCONDITIONAL POSITIVE REGARD

By unconditional positive regard Rogers (1957) means that the therapist does not differentially approve or disapprove of any particular class of behaviors or experiences of the client; all the behaviors and experiences are equally prized and accepted by the therapist as worthwhile. Unconditional positive regard does not refer to something that the therapist overtly expresses to the client; the therapist does not tell the client of his unconditional positive acceptance of him. Rather, the term refers to the *absence* of any differential evaluation by the therapist. The therapist simply accepts whatever the client may be saying or experiencing and neither approves nor disapproves of it. As such, this nonevaluative stance is already implicit in the task of responding empathically. If the therapist is functioning optimally as a surrogate information-processor, what he is doing is attempting to organize as accurately as possible the meaning of the information in process in the client, whatever the nature of its content. Judgment, evaluation, approval, or disapproval are simply not involved in the task.

Not only is it questionable to view unconditional positive regard as something that is overtly expressed to the client, but it is also doubtful that it is something the therapist even experiences internally on a moment-to-moment basis. Given the complexity and difficulty of the task of responding empathically, it is quite unlikely that the therapist sits there on a moment-to-moment basis experiencing the unconditional positive regard or warmth he has for the client. Just as the attentional and processing capacities of the client have limits, so too do those of the therapist. To function on a moment-to-moment basis in an optimally empathic manner necessitates that all the therapist's attentional and processing capacities be allocated to understanding the meaning of the information in process in the client, and to organizing a response that accurately captures this meaning. If instead the therapist were to attend to and process some sense of unconditional positive regard he experiences for the client, he could not fully attend to what the client is experiencing, and the effectiveness of his responses would greatly suffer.

It is also questionable to contend, as Rogers (1957) has, that the client must perceive the unconditional positive regard of the therapist if therapy is to be successful. We should not confuse what an observer might perceive in listening to a taped recording of therapy or what a client might reconstruct about the therapist in answering a questionnaire (see Barrett-Lennard, 1962) with what the client actually processes and perceives on a moment-to-moment basis in the therapy hour. In hearing a therapist's response it is highly doubtful that the client stops to process and perceive whether the therapist is accepting or not. What he does process and perceive immediately is an organization that may or may not fit the information in process in him. If the therapist's response "hits," the client will go on to elaborate new facets of meaning that emerge. If not, he probably will correct, refine, or ignore what the therapist says.

CONGRUENCE

By congruence Rogers (1957) means that the therapist is "genuine" or "whole" in his relationship with the client, there being no discrepancy between what he overtly expresses and what he internally experiences. Congruence, then, basically refers to the presence or absence of a discrepancy in the therapist and not to something that he overtly expresses to the client. In fact, in his paper on the necessary and sufficient conditions of therapeutic personality change, Rogers (1957) is quite clear that it is a state of the therapist, and unlike empathy and unconditional positive regard it is not to be viewed as something that needs to be communicated to and perceived by the client. As a state of the therapist it too is already implied in and subsumed by the task of responding empathically. As was noted earlier, empathic responding involves the full allocation of the therapist's attentional and processing capacities. If the therapist is fully engaged in the task of attending to the client and responding empathically, then ideally the only information in process in him would be that which might be in process in the client; there would be nothing else. If he is successful in organizing the meaning of this information in his response to the client, he will not only be empathic, but insofar as his expression fits the information in process in him he will also be what Rogers calls congruent.

We would reinterpret the notion of congruence as basically pointing to the importance of the therapist's devoting all his attentional and processing capacities to the task of understanding the client and responding empathically. As Butler (1958) has noted, congruence really only becomes an issue when the therapist is failing in his task of attending to and understanding the client, and instead experiencing something else such as boredom or annoyance with the client. Such a situation represents a failure on the part of the therapist to allocate all his attentional and processing capacities to the client. Given the fact that the amount of information that can be processed at any moment in time is severely limited, anything else occupying the attention and processing of the therapist will surely function as a source of interference and severely detract from his ability to understand the client.

In the past few years there has been an increasing trend among many client-centered therapists (see Rogers & Truax, 1967) to view congruence not as something that naturally follows from being optimally empathic and only arising as an issue when the therapist is functioning in a less than optimal manner, but rather as something that is primary and an end in itself. It is unclear whether this development is a reaction to the stereotype of the client-centered therapist as a passive responder, a result of the impact of experiences with encounter groups, or due to the possibility that genuineness or "realness" in a relationship may represent some sort of "condition of worth" for many client-centered therapists. Whatever the cause for this shift, it has had a rather disturbing and unfortunate consequence on the way some therapists practice client-centered therapy. Congruence has come to be seen as the equivalent of therapist self-expression, and therapists have come to think of their task as reacting to the client rather than understanding him. As a result, under the banner of being honest, egalitarian, and genuine in engaging in a "real" human encounter, a number of therapists from a client-centered orientation have used the concept of congruence as some sort of license for relying heavily on the expression of their reactions to their clients as a therapeutic tool.

In introducing and relying on the expression of their reactions, these therapists have not only abdicated the very potent processing functions they can play through the active use of empathic responding, but they have also significantly departed from the basic client-centered orientation in introducing material that is external to the frame of reference of the client. What is unique about the client-centered therapist is that he does not introduce information that from an external frame of reference might be seen as significant; instead, he works in the client's frame of reference with the information that the client thinks is significant. In fact, it is usually only when the therapist who relies on self-expression thinks the client is *not* doing anything significant that he chooses to express something like boredom or annoyance. Though done under the guise of "honesty" and congruence, it is probably more honest to say that it is done as an attempt to make the client experience something that is deeper or more significant than whatever it is that he is talking about. If a client is not engaged in a productive mode of experiencing and is producing little movement or change in his field, there is probably no surer way to produce rapid change in his field than for someone in the position of a therapist to tell him that he is bored or annoyed with the client. What the therapist has basically done is use self-expression as a substitute for empathic understanding in attempting to change the quality of the client's experiencing.

When a client is not engaged in a productive mode of experiencing and seems defensive, it is a difficult task to listen carefully for significant facets of information evoked to respond to. It is far easier to conjure up and create significant experience for the client than it is to engage in this difficult task and work with the information in process in the client. Generally, it is much easier to tell people our reactions to them than it is to understand them. If one is predisposed to think of the task in therapy as reacting to the client, then one is indeed likely to have reactions to the client. If, however, we think of the task as attending, understanding, and effectively communicating that understanding to our client, then not only are we far less likely to have reactions to the client, but we are also likely to be much more effective in responding empathically to him.

In attempting to understand how the client-centered therapist is an instrumental agent in facilitating change, we have stressed the role of the therapist as a surrogate processor of information. In serving important processing functions for the client, empathic responding, when used with sensitivity and accuracy, is an extremely potent tool in enabling the client to transcend his processing deficiencies and engage in a more optimal mode of processing. To some it may seem that our view of the therapist as a surrogate processor who organizes the meaning of the information in process in the client is one that makes the therapist seem like some sort of response machine, devoid of human qualities. Such is not the intent. Neither has our intent been to poeticize and romanticize what the therapist does. Our intent has only been to conceptualize what it is the therapist overtly does and what are its effects. The task of responding empathically is not a passive task that is mechanical and wooden. To the contrary, it is an extremely active task that draws heavily on all the sensitivities and capabilities of the therapist. It is a task that makes heavy demands on all his attentional, organizing, transforming, and linguistic capacities. These are not "nice" words that are highly evocative and easy to resonate to. Yet, they are indeed the qualities that make people human.

REFERENCES

Arnold, M. B. *Emotion and personality.* Vol. 1. New York: Columbia University Press, 1960.

Barrett-Lennard, G. T. Dimensions of therapist response as causal factors in therapeutic change. *Psychological Monographs,* 1962, **76** (43, Whole No. 562).

Bartlett, F. C. *Remembering: A study in experimental and social psychology.* Cambridge: Cambridge University Press, 1932.

Butler, J. M. Client-centered counseling and psychotherapy. In D. Brower & L. Abt (Eds.), *Progress in clinical psychology.* Vol. 3. New York: Grune & Stratton, 1958.

Butler, J. M., & Rice, L. N. Adience, self-actualization and drive theory. In

J. M. Wepman & R. W. Heine (Eds.), *Concepts of personality*. Chicago: Aldine, 1963.

Butler, J. M., Rice, L. N., & Wagstaff, A. K. On the naturalistic definition of variables: An analogue of clinical analysis. In H. Strupp & L. Luborsky (Eds.), *Research in psychotherapy*. Vol. 2. Washington, D.C.: American Psychological Association, 1962.

Cannon, W. B. *Bodily changes in pain, hunger, fear and rage.* (2nd ed.) New York: Appleton-Century-Crofts, 1929.

Duffy, E. *Activation and behavior*. New York: Wiley, 1962.

Festinger, L. *A theory of cognitive dissonance*. Palo Alto, Calif: Stanford University Press, 1957.

Fiske, D. W., & Maddi, S. R. (Eds.) *Functions of varied experience*. Homewood, Ill.: Dorsey, 1961.

Freud, S. *The ego and the id.* London: Institute for Psychoanalysis, and Hogarth Press, 1927.

Gendlin, E. T. *Experiencing and the creation of meaning*. New York: The Free Press of Glencoe, 1962.

Gendlin, E. T. A theory of personality change. In P. Worchel & D. Byrne (Eds.), *Personality change*. New York: Wiley, 1964.

Gendlin, E. T. Focusing. *Psychotherapy: Theory, Research, and Practice*, 1969, **6**, 4–15.

Gendlin, E. T., Beebe, J., Cassens, J., Klein, M., & Oberlander, M. Focusing ability in psychotherapy, personality, and creativity. In J. M. Shlien (Ed.), *Research in Psychotherapy*. Vol. 3. Washington, D.C.: American Psychological Association, 1968.

Gendlin, E. T., & Zimring, F. The qualities or dimensions of experiencing and their change. *Counseling Center Discussion Papers*, **1**(3). Chicago: University of Chicago Library, 1955.

Hebb, D. O. Drives and the C.N.S. (conceptual nervous system). *Psychological Review*, 1955, **62**, 243–254.

Hunt, E. What kind of computer is man? *Cognitive Psychology*, 1971, **2**, 57–98.

James, W. What is an emotion? *Mind*, 1884, **9**, 188–205.

Kelly, G. A. *The psychology of personal constructs*. Vol. 1 New York: Norton, 1955.

Klein, M. H., Mathieu, P. L., Kiesler, D. J., & Gendlin, E. T. *The Experiencing Scale: A research and training manual*. Madison: University of Wisconsin, Bureau of Audio-visual Instruction, 1970.

Koffka, K. *Principles of gestalt psychology*. New York: Harcourt, Brace & World, 1935.

Leuba, C. Toward some integration of learning theories: The concept of optimal stimulation. *Psychological Reports*, 1955, **1**, 27–33.

Lewin, K. *A dynamic theory of personality: Selected papers.* New York: McGraw-Hill, 1935.

Lewin, K. The conceptual representation and the measurement of psychological forces. In D. Adams & H. Lundholm (Eds.), *Contributions to psychological theory.* Vol. 1, No. 4. Durham, N.C.: Duke University Press, 1938.

Lindsay, P. H., & Norman, D. A. *Human information processing: An introduction to psychology.* New York: Academic Press, 1972.

Luborsky, L., Chandler, M., Auerbach, A. H., Cohen, J., & Bachrach, H. M. Factors influencing the outcome of psychotherapy: A review of quantitative research. *Psychological Bulletin,* 1971, **75,** 145–185.

Maddi, S. R. *Personality theories: A comparative analysis.* (Rev. ed.) Homewood, Ill.: Dorsey, 1972.

Mandler, G. Organization and memory. In K. W. Spence & J. T. Spence (Eds.), *Psychology of learning and motivation.* Vol. 1. New York: Academic Press, 1967.

Miller, G. A. The magical number seven, plus or minus two: Some limits on our capacity for processing information. *Psychological Review,* 1956, **63,** 81–97.

Miller, G. A., Galanter, E., & Pribram, K. H. *Plans and the structure of behavior.* New York: Holt, Rinehart & Winston, 1960.

Neisser, U. *Cognitive psychology.* New York: Appleton-Century-Crofts, 1967.

Norman, D. A. *Memory and attention: An introduction to human information processing.* New York: Wiley, 1969.

Piaget, J. *The origins of intelligence in children.* New York: Norton, 1963.

Reitman, W. R. *Cognition and thought.* New York: Wiley, 1965.

Rice, L. N., & Gaylin, N. L. Personality processes reflected in client vocal style and Rorschach performance. *Journal of Consulting and Clinical Psychology,* 1973, **40,** 133–138.

Rice, L. N., & Wagstaff, A. K. Client voice quality and expressive style as indexes of productive psychotherapy. *Journal of Consulting Psychology,* 1967, **31,** 557–563.

Rogers, C. R. The necessary and sufficient conditions of therapeutic personality change. *Journal of Consulting Psychology,* 1957, **21,** 95–103.

Rogers, C. R. A process conception of psychotherapy. *American Psychologist,* 1958, **13,** 142–149.

Rogers, C. R. A theory of therapy, personality, and interpersonal relations as developed in the client-centered framework. In S. Koch (Ed.), *Psychology: A study of a science.* Vol. 3. New York: McGraw-Hill, 1959.

Rogers, C. R. *On becoming a person.* Boston: Houghton Mifflin, 1961.

Rogers, C. R. The interpersonal relationship: The core of guidance. *Harvard Educational Review,* 1962, **32,** 416–429.

Rogers, C. R. Actualizing tendency in relation to "motives" and to consciousness. In M. Jones (Ed.), *Nebraska symposium on motivation*. Lincoln: University of Nebraska Press, 1963.

Rogers, C. R., & Truax, C. B. The therapeutic conditions antecedent to change: A theoretical view. In C. R. Rogers (Ed.), *The therapeutic relationship and its impact: A study of psychotherapy with schizophrenics*. Madison: University of Wisconsin Press, 1967.

Schacter, S., & Singer, J. Cognitive, social, and physiological determinants of emotional state. *Psychological Review*, 1962, **69**, 379–399.

Schacter, S., & Wheeler, L. Epinephrine, chlorpromazine and amusement. *Journal of Abnormal and Social Psychology*, 1962, **65**, 121–128.

Schultz, D. *Sensory restriction: Effects on behavior*. New York: Academic Press, 1965.

Shlien, J. M. A client-centered approach to schizophrenia: First approximation. In A. Burton (Ed.), *Psychotherapy of the psychoses*. New York: Basic Books, 1961.

Simon, H. A. *The science of the artificial*. Cambridge: M.I.T. Press,1969.

Sternberg, S. Memory scanning: Mental processes revealed by reaction-time experiments. In J. S. Antrobus (Ed.), *Cognition and affect*. Boston: Little, Brown, 1970.

Truax, C. B., & Carkhuff, R. R. *Toward effective counseling and psychotherapy: Training and practice*. Chicago: Aldine, 1967.

Wexler, D. A. Self-actualization and cognitive processes. *Journal of Consulting and Clinical Psychology*, 1974, **42**, 47–53.

Witkin, H. A., Dyk, R. B., Faterson, H. F., Goodenough, D. R., & Karp, S. A. *Psychological differentiation*. New York: Wiley, 1962.

Zimring, F., Nauman, C., & Balcombe, J. Listening with the second ear: Selective attention and emotion. Paper presented at the meeting of the American Psychological Association, Miami, September 1970.

CHAPTER 4

Theory and Practice of Client-Centered Therapy: A Cognitive View

Fred M. Zimring

Client-centered therapy started 34 years ago with a description of practice. This was followed by various theoretical statements, which tried without great success to explain the effects of the practice. One reason for their lack of success is that although the practice of this therapy was based on some new and startling assumptions about the nature of man, the assumptions underlying the theoretical statements were those current in the zeitgeist, or intellectual climate, at that time. Hence the explanations neither informed the practice nor aided the training for or research about it. Because of changes in the zeitgeist since the original formulations and because of resulting advances in cognitive psychology, it has now become possible to offer a more closely matching description and explanation of the practice, perhaps permitting gains in both research and training.

One such change in the zeitgeist is that the individual is no longer seen as inescapably separate from other people and from the environment. Instead, people are now seen as shaped by others. Similarly, there has been a change from the perception of the person as interactive, first affecting the environment and then being affected by it (like a Ping-Pong game), to one of the person as transactive, as part of the environment, as in the present view of ecology.

Another, somewhat similar, change has been in the view of the lack of communication between people. Earlier, the individual was thought to be basically unknowable and private, with "privileged access" to his own thoughts and experience; now, however, it is felt that the barrier to communication is a lack of caring, an unwillingness to receive communication.

Allied to these changes have been some shifts in assumptions about knowledge and truth. Both psychoanalysis and client-centered therapy grew in an atmosphere that assumed that a single, static, correct truth exists and that knowing this truth will solve your problems or "set you free." Today there is much less trust in the effect of knowledge of an unchanging truth and more emphasis upon the effect of interacting with the everchanging world. Thus, there has been a change in emphasis in the concept of the main goal of psychotherapy. The psychologically healthy person, previously seen as one who knows the truth about himself, is now seen as one who is experiencing, engaged and involved—in process rather than simply processing knowledge. These present emphases in the zeitgeist come much closer to matching the practice of client-centered therapy than did those emphases that guided the original explanations 30-odd years ago.

These changes in the intellectual climate have included changes in modern experimental psychology, where a similar shift in assumption has taken place, so that the emphasis upon structural constructs such as "habit family hierarchies" has changed to include interest in mechanisms and processes. Because these interests are consistent with the implicit assumptions underlying the practice of client-centered therapy, the terms they have produced allow for a new description of this therapy and an explanation of why its methods produce the results they do.

In order to arrive at this explanation, the correspondence between the assumptions underlying the practice and those underlying the theory of client-centered therapy will be assessed. Then a short discussion of Ludwig Wittgenstein's philosophy will help to clear away some obstacles and will provide the broad framework for the explanation. A survey of cognitive processes will furnish terms for the new description of the practice in the concluding section of the chapter.

CLIENT–CENTERED THERAPY: THE CORRESPONDENCE BETWEEN PRACTICE AND THEORY

In this section six aspects of the practice of client-centered therapy are discussed, with reference to how well they have been accounted for in previous theories or descriptions.

The Duality Between Awareness and the "Truth"

Most methods of psychotherapy attempt to move the client from a state of error or blindness to one of truth. The client is perceived as distorting, defending, living incorrectly. A gap is seen between where he is at present and where he should be, a goal toward which he should move. This perception generally rests on one or both of two assumptions. One is that there are mistakes in behavior, living patterns, or assumptions, such as the mistakes in living postulated by the Adlerians. This assumption of error or mistake is no different from that made in many problem-solving situations. The dynamic psychotherapies add another assumption: that the cause of the problem exists in the person, that the threatening experiences, feelings, and urges are presently in existence. Because the first of these assumptions (to solve a problem, first find the error) is general in our society, when an unconscious is assumed it is taken as self-evident that insight (emotional or intellectual awareness of this unconscious material) will lead to adjustment and freedom from neurosis.

The assumptions of client-centered practice (as opposed to various theoretical explanations of this practice) differ diametrically from the assumptions just discussed. No truth that will free the client is looked for, because there is no faith in a static truth, and because there is no assumption of an existent unconscious. There is no knowledge that the therapist thinks desirable for the client to possess, and there is no unconscious or unaware materials to which the client should be directed: the therapist is not aware of and does not direct the client toward any particular content. Thus, for example, in respect to the client's inability to talk about certain topics, there is no attempt to analyze in terms of hidden or unconscious feelings, experience, or wishes.

Because the therapist does not work with a duality betweeen awareness and truth, he is not aware of any incongruity between what the client says and what he would be saying if he were "healthier" (realized his true experience or feelings). Thus, the therapist does not use a map to direct the client toward any particular truth.

It is this attitude that is hardest to understand about the practice of client-centered therapy. We are so accustomed to solving problems by analysis, to correcting a difficulty by finding its cause, that it is hard to believe that client-centered therapists do not do this. Therapists trained in other methods sometimes assume that the client-centered therapist possesses but has learned to suppress or ignore hypotheses about the cause of the difficulty. This is not so.

The consistency of any therapy practice is tested when the therapy is failing. When the client does not seem to be changing in the direction the client-centered therapist considers good and is reporting increased anxiety and inability to handle the world, what does the therapist do? Does he attempt to find what is "really wrong," or what should be changed in the client's life, or how the client is distorting, and so on? No, in actual practice, the client-centered therapist only attempts to understand more fully what the client means, and he may have another therapist listen to the recordings of the therapy session to see if there is a failure of understanding. Thus, even when under this pressure, the therapist does not look at the content outside the client's frame of reference such as history, symptoms, or the like. No duality is seen between the content of the client's awareness (or experience) and a more healthy, "more valid" knowledge.

Even though this duality did not exist in the practice of client-centered therapy, it did exist in previous theories that attempted to explain and describe the practice. Thus, in the self-theory of Rogers (1951, Ch. 11), anxiety and rigidity were seen as the result of the discrepancy between the self as perceived (the self that you think you are) and the self as experienced (your actual experiences). If a woman saw herself (self as perceived) as a good mother (one who is not angry) and if her self as experienced included the experience of anger, then this experience could not be allowed into awareness (i.e., could not be symbolized). As discrepancy between the self as perceived and the self as experienced increased, so would anxiety and rigidity. If the mother engaged in more angry behavior, she would feel increasing threat and exhibit increasing rigidity because of the growing discrepancy between her self as perceived and self as experienced. This duality was carried through Rogerian theory until theories emphasizing experiencing and the process of psychotherapy became important.

Duality in the Therapist's Behavior

The possible incongruence between awareness and experience is only one of the dualities that have been important in client-centered theory. In discussions of the behavior of the therapist, the necessity for congruence between what he feels and says has sometimes been stressed. Rogers and Truax (1967) said that unless the therapist is integrated and genuine within the therapeutic encounter, neither understanding nor unconditional positive regard can exist. This means that the therapist is "openly being the feelings and attitudes which . . . are flowing in him . . . that the feelings that the therapist is experiencing are . . . available to his awareness, and also that he is able . . . to communicate them if appropriate [pp. 100–101]." Here there is concern with a duality between awareness and expression, as well as with the one between feelings and awareness. All of these dualisms follow, of course, from the assumption of a static construct, such as the self, with a continuing structure.

The Therapist's Focus

So far the discussion has been limited to what client-centered therapy does not do. If it does not assume a truth, if it does not try to solve a problem by analysis, how does it achieve its desired effect? Its general method is the therapist's focusing upon the client's world from within that framework. This means that the therapist neither gives information to the client about aspects of the client's world from the therapist's standpoint nor asks questions about the client's world, but instead tries to understand what the client means and how he sees his world at present. The therapist does not try to connect previous material talked about with present material.

The hypotheses that the therapist forms in the moment-to-moment interaction in therapy are not about the cause of the client's difficulty or what the client is experiencing at the moment at an unconscious level: instead, they are about the meaning to the client of the client's last statement. It is this habit of mind that is typical of the experienced client-centered therapist and distinguishes him from the novice: hypotheses about what is meant have replaced those about causes. Most theories of client-centered therapy, in their assertion that the client's framework is the focus, have matched this characteristic of practice.

The therapist focuses on the client's world and communicates his understanding, but he cannot focus on all aspects of it. He must select, condense, or summarize. Previous theories and descriptions have not specified in any detail what material he should choose. In recent Rogerian theory (Rogers, 1959; Gendlin, 1962) the emphasis upon the client and his experiencing has provided both a goal—an increase in experiencing— and additional description of the object of the therapist's focus—the felt experiencing of the client. This description is close to the practice of client-centered therapy.

The Therapist's Goals for the Client

Because the therapist is not interested in any particular content of the client's experiencing or in the client's arrival at a desired truth or state, he does not assume any particular goal for the client. He does not assume that it would be a good thing for the homosexual client to become heterosexual, nor for the failing student to pass, nor even (in all cases) for the client to become less anxious. The therapist does not assume the client's goal. If the client's presenting problem is an inability to study, the therapist does not assume that the therapy is successful when this is remedied.

The therapist's goals are general and have to do with the experiencing and the report of feelings of the client. The therapist hopes that by the end of therapy the client will be reporting richer experiencing, but he does not hope for an increase of any particular experiencing—for more anger or sexual feelings, for example.

This attitude is based on an implicit assumption that the client will live better if his present sensitivity in his ongoing experiencing is increased. More fundamentally, it is based on the assumption that there is no single truth or static cause of difficulty. Instead, there is an ongoing process that can be facilitated. It is only from this perspective that the basis of client-centered therapy can be understood. This is why hypotheses about causes and diagnosis are not formed: they are irrelevant because for client-centered therapy practice the only effective possibility is that the experiencing of the client be entered into and changed through the verbal interaction.

This aspect of client-centered therapy has been discussed adequately in client-centered theory. In discussions of openness to experience and the fully functioning person, it has been asserted that the goal of client-centered therapy is maximal, full experiencing, rather than a more specific objective on the part of the therapist.

Unconditional Positive Regard

Another aspect of client-centered practice is that the therapist's response to the client is mildly positive and constant, free of fluctuations in evaluation. Everything that the client says is taken at a constant level. This constancy means that the practice, at least as an ideal, avoids using the therapist's approval or disapproval as a force for change through reinforcement or extinction. This aspect of practice has been adequately specified by the theories and descriptions of client-centered therapy, written since the initial publications.

The Mechanism of Change

So far, we have seen that the general mechanism posited in previous theoretical explanations or descriptions was the therapist's focus on the client's world and the goal posited was an increase in the client's sensitivity to his experiencing. In previous explanations there has been little discussion of how the former produces the latter (i.e., discussion of the mechanism of change). An exception was Gendlin's (1964) experiencing theory, in which his major concern was the method (focusing) used by the client to bring change, especially in personality structures. He was not directly concerned with what the therapist does to aid in this process.

That there have been so few theories concerned with how the therapist's action produces the client's change may have been a deliberate avoidance based on the premise that attitudes are more important than technique, that technique by itself is manipulation. If emphasis upon technique leads to dealing mechanically with the client, then therapy should not be taught in this way. However, this is an empirical question—does training in technique lead to this undesirable result? If not, and if the operations by which the therapist should select material for responding in therapy can be specified, we will be able to train more rapidly and to measure the processes that bring change. Lack of measurement of the change agent within the therapy hour has been a large deficiency in psychotherapy research.

In summary, previous theories and descriptions of client-centered therapy have been most deficient in matching the practice in two respects. One has been the assumption of dualities that do not exist in practice— dualities between where the client is and where he should be and between the content of his awareness and what he might be aware of. This dualistic emphasis in client-centered theory grew from the zeitgeist, one that also spawned psychoanalytic theory, and was based on several assumptions. One was that psychological difficulties grow from an existent present cause, the way an infection grows from a germ. Another was that emotions, feelings, and thoughts exist as internal objects that can cause behavior and experience. We think that it is the anger within a person that causes him to slam a door, whether or not he is aware of the anger. We would not make the same assumption about the physical world; we would not assume that there is a concept of gravity within a drop of water that causes it to run downhill.

Newer theories in client-centered therapy moved away from this dualistic emphasis and focused on experiencing in the client. Instead of a self having experiences that are not in awareness, there is only experiencing, which can be barren or rich. However, these theories stopped short of considering the only material the therapist has to work with, the client's statements as part of his experiencing. This is an indication of the second deficiency of previous descriptions of client-centered therapy.

This second deficiency is that, with the exception of the explanation of Gendlin (1964), previous descriptions did not discuss the mechanism of change, that part of the interaction between therapist and client that modifies the client's experiencing processes. Changes in the zeitgeist have now made possible a description of the mechanism of change, because the practice of client-centered therapy, although incompatible with the earlier assumptions, does match some of the exciting aspects of the present intellectual climate. This climate has been strongly influenced by Ludwig Wittgenstein (1953, 1958), and there are grounds in his philosophy for resolving the dualities between feelings and behavior and between feelings and experience. In addition a basis is provided for viewing what the client says as an essential part of his frame of reference and his experiencing. Thus Wittgenstein's philosophy makes it possible to describe the client–therapist processes in new ways.

WITTGENSTEIN'S PHILOSOPHY

The relevant aspects of Wittgenstein's philosophy are those concerned with the status of feelings, ideas, and other internal "furniture." Wittgenstein expended much energy in showing that to assume that ideas or feelings have thing-like characteristics is an error. For him a feeling such as sympathy is not an entity standing behind the behavior of weeping; instead it *is* this behavior. The term "sympathy" is simply a concept that organizes or encompasses the various relevant aspects of our experience. This concept encompasses both our weeping and whatever images we have about ourselves in negative or painful circumstances.

Wittgenstein was not denying that feeling constructs incorporate both internal and external experience. Most important, however, he was denying that the internal necessarily causes or stands prior to the external behavior. Indeed, the internal representation does not have to exist for the behavior to take place. If deeply engrossed in talking you will not be conscious of a fully formed idea or concept. However, if you are interrupted and have to wait to speak, then a formed idea occurs. Thus an idea (in the sense of a formed concept or entity) is not necessary for you to make a complicated point, although it may be necessary for you to retain all aspects of it.

The cohesiveness of the inner and outer experience is not seen as emanating from a single entity such as sympathy; there is no identical core to each experience of sympathy, but rather only similarity. Thus each instance of sympathy (e.g., crying, talking about some things and not others) is similar, but does not share a substance. The analogy used by Wittgenstein is of brothers, who are members of the same family but who share no identical substance.

His philosophy, in its argument against any discrepancy between an inner entity and outer expression, is relevant because the client-centered therapist in practice does not assume a duality. He does not assume that what the client says is a manifestation of some entity lying behind the statement. The therapist is interested only in the present process of describing experience. Just as Wittgenstein argued that the expression is the essence, so the client-centered therapist treats expression as the only possible focus.

In addition to correcting errors in the theorizing about client-centered practice, the Wittgensteinian framework permits a more accurate description of the way the therapist changes the processing of the client. We can begin to see this by applying Wittgenstein's perspective to the construct of a frame of reference. According to previous Rogerian descriptions of practice, the therapist's job was to understand the client's frame of reference. There it was assumed that the client would bring to the therapy a fully formed frame of reference the therapist could understand. From Wittgenstein's perspective, however, a small but vital difference in the view of this interaction becomes apparent: the client's frame of reference is not envisioned simply as a series of views or statements about the world that exist within the client's head, any more than sympathy is a feeling or entity within the client. Instead, the client's frame of reference is what he talks about, plus what he is capable of saying but may not choose to say. Many of the statements that he makes depend upon what is said to him. As envisioned in the earlier client-centered writings, the client's frame of reference is like an object to be photographed, and the therapist is like a photographer. The object remains the same whether or not the photographer takes a picture of it. As viewed using the Wittgensteinian analysis, however, the client's talk in therapy is like a seed growing—a result of the processes encompassing both seed and environment. Thus in therapy the interaction produces statements by the client, and these statements are as integral a part of the frame of reference as the weeping is a part of sympathy. If the therapist did not interact with the client to produce these statements, they would not be produced and the frame of reference would be different to that extent. Thus the therapist does not simply "reflect" statements that exist independently of that interaction.

This discussion of one aspect of client-centered therapy illustrates how the application of the Wittgensteinian framework permits a description of the ways in which the client and therapist enter into a joint process. We will see later that this joint process results in a change in the experiencing of the client.

Like all valid philosophic clarification, the Wittgensteinian framework tells us *how* to talk about psychotherapy but does not tell us *what happens*. To describe what happens in the combined client–therapist process, a framework for the description of empirical events that satisfies the Wittgensteinian prescriptions must be employed. That there is such a framework is no coincidence: it was one influenced by the Wittgensteinian revolution.

THE COGNITIVE FRAMEWORK

Thirty-odd years ago the frameworks used by scientific psychology were useless to client-centered therapy because scientific psychology concentrated on the description and prediction of responses to particular stimuli. On the other hand, client-centered therapy was interested in the internal, the individual framework occurring between stimulus and response. An exciting change, which has occurred in psychology during the last 30 years, is that an interest in "inside" events has become respectable and an extensive framework has developed for the description and investigation of these events.

This change occurred as scientific psychology became more interested in mechanisms and organization. Previously, the view was that the human being was a collection of small basic units like associations or S–R bonds which, like bricks, could be combined into larger units. Now, due to the developments in the cognitive and linguistic areas, mechanisms, organizations, structures, and processes all exist in their own right and are seen as basic to the explanation of behavior. Just as we have seen that the practice of client-centered therapy cannot be correctly understood from a framework that emphasizes knowledge rather than knowing, so the cognitive framework in scientific psychology emphasizes the knowing rather than the known, the mechanism rather than the trace, the search rather than that which is searched for. Thus the emphasis is no longer on what is learned and filed inside the head to be read or recaptured. Awareness is not seen as influenced by the contents of awareness but instead is seen as a process of reconstruction. One's "awareness" of the letter *A* is a series of cognitive operations.

Information can be retained as a visual or an auditory image for a very short period of time (somewhat less than a second) without processing. If it is not processed it fades and is lost. The processing involves transferring some of the information from the visual or auditory image to the short-term store. It is transferred by being read from the image (as one might read from a printed page) or by being coded. Here *coding* means the use of a system for identifying, grouping or handling information, usually, as we shall see, by using some organization from the long-term store. Some experts such as Broadbent (1958) have felt that it is at this point between the image and the short-term store that the selectivity of attention takes place (i.e., irrelevant information is filtered out and lost and relevant information is selected for future processing). Other experts (e.g., Deutsch & Deutsch, 1963) think this happens later in the sequence.

The short-term store is a workshop containing the material being worked with at the moment. Material enters from the visual and auditory stores and the long-term store. Most importantly, the potential organization for material in the system enters from the long-term store. If, for example, there were 11 numerals, 2, 4, 6, 8 . . . 22, the organization of them as "even numerals starting with 2 and ending at 22" is given by our long-term store knowledge about sequences of numerals.

One of the interesting aspects of the short-term store is that it is limited. Although initially (Miller, 1956) this limitation was thought of in terms of items—that seven plus or minus two items is the maximum number of items that can occupy the short-term store workroom at one time—it is more accurate to describe this limitation in terms of the number of operations (assembling, grouping, etc.) that can occur at the same time. Thus, if you were told a strange telephone number and were immediately to start to do an arithmetic problem, you probably would not be able to retain the number. This limitation is an advantage because it forces the organization of material. In the previous example, the organization of the sequence of numbers gave fewer items to be retained in the short-term store. Generally speaking, the more organization imposed upon the material, the fewer the operations necessary to handle the information and the more material capable of being retained in the short-term store.

As mentioned, organization is imposed through the attachment of long-term store material to material in the short-term store. Another way of retaining material is through rehearsal (as you might rehearse a telephone number). This method is more vulnerable to interference and loss than is the use of long-term store organization for retention.

The organization or coding of short-term store material from the long-term store may be of several types. Substitutive coding takes place when a rule is used, substituting long-term store material for the information, as in the previous example, where the necessity for remembering all 11 numerals was eliminated by use of a rule for generating the sequence. In elaborative coding, long-term store information is added to the original information, as in the use of a rhyme to remember a name. Still another kind of coding uses temporal groupings of stimuli (e.g., the use of rhythm to remember a chain of digits).

In addition to the organization going from the long-term store to the short-term store, organization sometimes goes into the long-term store for future use. Thus the discovery of a new concept may mean an addition of organization to the long-term store, which can be used in the future to group material in the short-term store.

After the information has been processed and is ready for use, relevant hierarchies of skill for performance or behavior are activated. These may be automatic, like routine habits used in driving an automobile, and so occupy little processing space. If not automatic, as when one takes an unusual action while driving, these skills or processes may occupy all possible "mental space."

The discussion to this point has assumed that these stages in the processing of information occur in sequence. However, what determines or organizes these sequences is of importance. Even in the simplest of tasks the subject may use a variety of operations in different sequences. For example, if asked to remember nonsense syllables, the subject may associate them with similar words and put these associations into a sentence, and he may decide that he can remember more if he concentrates on the early and the late syllables, rather than those in the middle of the list.

Both the type of strategy used by the subject and the conditions under which one strategy rather than another will be chosen have been investigated in concept attainment research (Bruner, Goodnow, & Austin, 1956). In an important and influential book, *Plans and the Structure of Behavior,* Miller, Galanter, and Pribram (1960) saw the broad organization of sequences of behavior by plans and purposes as being a critical and ignored variable in psychology.

Several aspects of this very brief description should be emphasized. First, unless processed, information is retained for only a brief period. Second, only a small portion of information impinging on a person can be retained. Third, organization is of great effect in retaining information. Fourth, organization can be learned and is itself retained. Fifth, the organization of patterns of processes is done by purposes, habits, and plans.

A general characteristic of the information-processing framework is that it does not separate inner structure and outer behavior. Instead, a response is seen as part of a sequence of operations that have both inner and outer components. Thus images are treated with as much respect as verbal associations. This characteristic is one that grew directly from Wittgenstein's assertion that the expression is part of the process itself.

The cognitive framework is not dualistic in separating knowledge from knowing; both knowledge and knowing are viewed as different aspects of a single process of construing the world. In addition, this framework provides the elements of a process consistent with Rogers (1959) and Gendlin's (1962) emphasis on experiencing. Thus it is consonant with the current view of man—people as process. The difference between this and the old zeitgeist's emphasis on the possession of knowledge is clear.

A reformulation of client-centered therapy in information-processing terms holds promise of more accurate description of the finer-grained aspects of the process of therapy, especially of how the therapist affects the client in their interaction.

INFORMATION PROCESSING AND PSYCHOTHERAPY

In the examples used in the section on cognition, nonemotional information was used. Although in psychotherapy emotional information is the focus, the differences between emotional and other kinds of information is immaterial for our purposes. This is so because there is no difference insofar as processing is concerned, just as there is no essential difference between the radio receiver's operations in transmitting jazz or classical music.

What we have said about organization and cognition applies with ease to psychotherapy. Does an insight change the way we see and act in the world? An insight, in cognitive terms, is organization that is transferred to the long-term store and is then used to organize material as it comes into the short-term store. Is it ineffective to tell someone what his distortion or maladjustment is (even if what is said is true)? Viewed cognitively, a statement about experience is an organization that results from certain aspects of the image being attended to, maintenance of these aspects within the short-term store, and, finally, the coding and organizing of the aspects in the long-term store. This organized material in the long-term store will again serve as an organizer for future bits of information. An externally supplied statement (e.g., "your basic problem is not facing your anger") has not resulted from any of these processes within the person and so may not be stored in the long-term store as an organizer for future bits of information.

This application of information-processing concepts to psychotherapy is valuable for the formulation of an adequately detailed description of the client–therapist transaction, which is being postulated here as the core element of client-centered practice.

The Initial Stages of Information Processing and Therapeutic Interaction

The experiencing of the client starts with the processing of information from the initial image. Only what is read or taken from this initial image can be part of the further processing. Therefore, if what is taken from the image does not have to do with his own immediate experience, the client will not be able to discuss or to use his experience in further steps in the processing. That is, it will not enter awareness.

An example of a client taking other than his immediate experience from his sensory image is the following from Mr. Bebb (discussed in "An Analysis of a Failure Case," Rogers & Dymond, 1954).

Client   Lazy, and . . . had no ambition or no backbone. And . . . also in the school I went to . . . which was . . . well, it's a sort of an orphanage and sort of a . . . institution . . . which I was put into after my father and my mother was divorced. And there the . . . well, the kids always made fun of me because I was sort of a dull, inactive . . . in their activities, and . . . which I'm quite sure gave me sort of inferiority complex. And this happened throughout my stay in my country, I mean, even in the merchant marine, I mean they used to say, I wasn't made to be a seaman, or that . . . but . . . well, I like to travel and things like that, even though it was generally (words lost) during the war. Then in '46 I came to this country, and I didn't . . . I didn't know any English. And . . . I picked up the language pretty readily after I'd been here a little while, and spoke it fairly well; and people told me that I spoke English very nice, and thought I was a nice young man. And . . . intelligent and all that stuff. And it struck me as very funny because it was such a complete contrast to what had . . . been said about me in my country. Then after two years in this country I . . . well, I'd been in the merchant marine here, I thought I'd . . . I mean, I'd all the time liked to read, and things like that. Thought that I'd try to take the entrance exam at the university here, just for, I mean, I hadn't expected to be accepted. I knew the competition with native Americans, things like that, but then I was accepted and . . . here's where my hunch and my theory comes in. I fear that perhaps back home, because of lacking attention or . . . lack of manifestations of interest in my personality, or love, or similar emotions, I tried to cultivate all sorts of friendships just because I wanted the attention, I wanted the friendship. Whereas over here people, they . . . indicated that they didn't think I was quite as bad as I thought myself and maybe that has . . . in turn has made me more choosey. The people whom I associate with. This is only a possibility. And . . . I don't know just how to explain . . .

Therapist I'd like to see if I understand some of that. That is, in the institutional school, you were lazy and dull and so forth. And at home you were regarded as lazy and didn't hold a job and so forth. And in the merchant marine the same way. And under that kind of an attitude, you felt a good deal of need to make friends with anyone and everyone, I suppose.

In the latter part of this rather long comment, Mr. Bebb is talking about why "back home" he cultivated "all sorts of friendships" but here he is more "choosey." In this discussion of why his behavior in respect to other people changed, he is not looking at his experience.

An experienced counselor is aware of the necessity of reading the experiential information from the image and will wait for this material to be presented. It is this that frequently determines when the counselor responds. For example, in the case of Mrs. Oak:

Client   (Laughing) I just came from the hospital. Apparently things have been going all right. I suppose they know what they are doing. Peggy's doctor is going to be out of town for two months. And in the meantime Peggy is to see a certain psychiatric social worker . . . rather on the young side. And I feel it's too bad but yet I've got to assume that they know what they're doing. Peggy's attitude is pretty much that it's a waste of time. I mean sort of a, well quote, it's, "Why should I go over and shoot the breeze with this girl."

If the counselor had chosen to respond at this point, he would have been responding to Mrs. Oak's perception of her daughter's experience and not to Mrs. Oak's perception of her own experience. Thus the counselor waited until Mrs. Oak said in addition, "But it's just one of those things, it's kind'a disturbing to me, but . . ." and then the counselor said, "Kind of disappointing things to have occur." Here the counselor was referring to the client's immediate experience of the incident, thereby maximizing the chances that this information will enter into further processing.

Intermediate Stages of Information Processing and Therapeutic Interaction

If some experiential aspects are taken from the image but there are no organizing principles employed for this material in the short-term store, this material will be lost and not be available for further processing, as in the case of Vera:

Client   I'm getting to the feeling where I don't know . . . and the same thing is happening in school, like I ditch first period and I know I shouldn't do it but I do it and stay out of school you know and find excuses to stay home and do too many things, get hall passes and go places I know I'm not supposed to go like during lunchtime, get out of homemaking you know I do things like that that I know I shouldn't . . . and it's gotten to the point now where I don't dare do anything more before . . .

Therapist   You don't like the kind of person you see yourself becoming.

Client   I'm too lazy and too tired to do anything about it.

Therapist   Just kind of go along and do these things rather than making some effort . . . it feels like . . . what . . . you're just too tired and lazy is that the way it feels . . .

Client   I don't know . . . kinda bored . . . I just . . . (sneeze)

Therapist   Kleenex are . . .

Client   I have hayfever or something . . . I sneeze constantly . . . I'm wondering can it be psychological, sneezing or anything like that or can getting bumps . . . hives kinda like and then going down. Maybe I just convinced myself that I'm allergic to our kittens and maybe I am . . . everytime I get near them . . . everytime I lie on our couch I start sneezing . . . everytime I get near a kitten, I touch the kitten and rub my eyes my eyes break out . . .

Here the counselor did not pick up the "boring" construct as an organizer for the client's immediate experience. Because it was not used, it was lost; the client changed the topic and began talking about her sneezing, rather than considering the quality of her experience of school.

Growth and Transfer of Organization

In addition to the organizing of experience for further processing, another process can occur in which *new* organization is transferred to the long-term store for use in organizing experience in the future. Insight is organization that orders our experience at the moment in new ways and then is transferred to the long-term store for later use.

Client   Yes, he has it (pause). Of course, ah, if you were to scratch the surface, his anal eroticism is one thing that I've noticed very strongly, or his mother attachment. I suppose that all is an indication of the other things at work, for instance, I tell him that a child's love towards his mother is, ah, not on the spiritual plane that we like to think it is. Why, he has a fit when he hears that because it probably hits him in the fact that his love—in other words, we are touching something that is close to him. Me thinkest thou protesteth too much . . . that sort of idea, you know. But on the whole my relationship with Arnold is satisfactory. Sexually, ah, it could be better, I think.

Ah, it isn't as successful as it was with Joseph, the fellow that I had an affair with before. I know why, and there I'm in the same vicious circle again. Knowing why doesn't help the matters any, you see. I know that Joseph, he's feminine, not homosexual, but effeminate enough for me to be the, ah, take the lead you see, and to feel that I have the matter in control at all times. I know that, although maybe at the time I perhaps didn't realize it until after I started to analyze the reasons.

Therapist You think now you do realize that, ah, satisfaction has been greater for you where you were the predominant person.

Here the therapist holds up an image of the experience—the feeling of satisfaction when she was a dominant person. These experiential aspects become the stimulus for the next response and hence remain available for further processing at the moment. They may also be organized in a way that can be transferred to the long-term store for ordering of experience in the future. Thus, after the construct "being the predominant person leading to more satisfaction" has been used as an organizer, it may be stored and may organize similar experience in the future.

The therapist, by selecting and organizing (here by juxtaposing the comments about being dominant and feelings of satisfaction more closely), opened up the possibility for her of a higher level, more inclusive organization combining both aspects of the organization that she used. Many of her comments had experiential aspects, so that the therapist's task here was not simply to read off and emphasize those aspects, but rather, given those aspects, to provide an organization that was natural for her. For another client, the counselor's task might be to be sensitive to these experiential aspects and concentrate on listing, emphasizing, or underlining, rather than organizing them.

What the counselor does will depend upon the particular aspect of the information processing of emotional information in which the client is deficient. As we saw with Mr. Bebb, if the client does not read experiential data from the immediate image for processing, the counselor can help at that point. This is the familiar case of the client who does not talk about his feelings. Here the counselor does not discuss feelings (in the sense of constructs like angry or uncomfortable) but emphasizes the experiential aspects of the client's immediate experience. He draws attention to the quality of the experience, rather than to a symbolized feeling. Thus a therapist might repeat to a client how "hard" it was to get to the office on a particular day or that it was "bad" for someone to do what he did to the client—all adjectives that qualify or refer to the experience of the client, rather than to feeling constructs such as anger and depression.

If the client is at another processing stage, if he is capable of talking about these experiental qualities, then the task of the therapist is to see that these qualities are not crowded out from the short-term store workroom but instead are kept there long enough to be worked with. This is one of the more prevalent types of response in client-centered therapy—the response that summarizes the qualitative aspects of the client's experience and serves as a focus for the client's next remark. An example might be the therapist's emphasizing that several quite different experiences were all similarly boring. This deflects the client from the nonexperiential aspects of the interaction or experience he is describing, such as how someone else felt about it, or the circumstances under which it took place.

If, moving further down the information-processing chain, the client has transferred or captured experiential elements before they have faded and has managed to keep them in the short-term store so that they are not crowded out by irrelevant aspects, then these qualitative aspects are capable of being organied or related. It is at this level of information processing that the client's "feelings" are reflected. Here the therapist is not only emphasizing the qualitative aspects of the client's experience— the fact that he felt "tight" or that his experience felt "heavy"—but is also organizing these aspects. Thus the therapist draws attention to the regularity of the client's experience by selecting from what he says and repeating and hence emphasizing that he felt tight and his experience felt heavy whenever he had to talk to either a parent or a teacher. This process of selecting and reflecting back organization for further processing continues as the organization of the elements gets more complex and abstracted. Thus, in the client's subjective language, that "father thing" can refer (for both the client and the therapist) to a whole organization of experiential elements having to do with fear of failure in providing for others.

As we can see from these examples, client-centered counselors do not just reflect or select feelings. Instead they select and reflect experiential elements and, when appropriate, the organization of these experiential elements. They may reflect feelings, either as experiential elements or as symbols of particular organization. Thus the word "anger" may simply be the qualitative aspect of a particular experience. Conversely, it may serve as a known symbol for a particular organization for both the client and the therapist when they have talked about the feelings of anger and rage that occur in a very particular kind of situation.

The fact that the counselor can only work effectively at or slightly beyond the client's level of information processing of emotional material is one reason why particular responses are inappropriate. A counselor who reflects back organization of qualitative aspects of an experience before the client has isolated these aspects for himself will not further the information processing of the client. For example, if the client says, "My wife shouldn't have done that. I've told her a number of times that she shouldn't, and yet she never listens to me" and if the response is "It makes you angry when she doesn't do what you tell her to do," the counselor is organizing experiential elements (anger) or the client's experience which the client has not worked with as yet, and so the client cannot use the organization.

ORGANIZATION AND THE SELF–CONCEPT

The self-concept is a type of organization that has been important for client-centered theory. The self-concept was seen as controlling the awareness of immediate experience when that experience material was incongruent with the perceived self-concept and thus was threatening. The cognitive explanation offered here gives a different rationale, that material is not symbolized, not because of threat, but because it is unorganized and so lost in the confusing overload of information at the moment. This is similar to why you could not retain a passage heard in a language you do not understand. If you think of yourself as a calm (nonangry) person, then you might not describe your action as angry after you slam the door when someone says something abrupt to you. The older frameworks might say that it is too "threatening" for you to perceive yourself as being angry—that it would threaten a condition of worth. Alternatively, in the explanation given here, you may have no concept of anger for perceiving your action. Instead you may have concepts that would organize the same behavior under a concept of "tired," or you may lose the experience: it may be dropped completely. Here the perceived self is not a censor controlling the information coming into the system; instead it is a collection of organizing statements about the world that serve to retain and process information consistent with these statements.

What difference does it make if the explanation is that of a lack of organizing concepts, rather than the threat of the incongruent material? It is important because the latter explanation is inconsistent with the *practice* of client-centered therapy. In that interaction, threat is not a diagnostic entity: it does not tell the therapist that he is near sensitive material, nor is it a signal for him to avoid an area. In his behavior in therapy the client-centered therapist acts in line with the explanation given here—he does not work with avoidance, reassurance, interpretation, or other ways of handling or manipulating threat or anxiety.

Also, the cognitive explanation permits the shedding of some surplus baggage, in that to assume threat because of inconsistency with the perceived self-concept necessitates a second self-system with a subceiver or unconscious censor to eliminate the inconsistent or threatening experiences before they are perceived.

This discussion indicates that every stage of the client's functioning is just as real as any other and does not have to be defined in terms of the presence or absence of (or closeness to or distance from) underlying feelings. In addition, this description shows that it is possible to see the client's utterances about emotional material as being influenced by cognitive processes, rather than as resulting from a unique process. Thus it may be possible to view the person as a whole: without separate systems for processing emotional and nonemotional material.

Another result of this description is that it provides a basis for a classification of counselor responses and of the different stages at which the client may be. Perhaps some of our perplexities about the lack of progress of particular clients may be answerable in a new way: a client's inability to proceed in therapy may be influenced by where he is cognitively.

SUMMARY AND CONCLUSION

In this chapter the practice of client-centered therapy and previously offered theories and descriptions of it were explored. It became clear that an adequate theory of client-centered practice should explain the change of the client in terms that are consistent with the practice, that is, without the assumption of long-term structures such as the self, but with the moment-to-moment interaction of client and the therapist as its sole concern. Although this discussion has been couched in information-processing terms, it is not these terms that the most essential, but rather the following basic concepts:

1. The important components in the process discussed above are the experiential elements in the client's frame of reference.

2. These experiential elements can be organized to a greater or lesser degree.

3. The degree to which these elements are organized determines whether they will be utilized or lost.

4. The process of client-centered therapy has as its goal an increase in experiential organization and therefore in the ability to utilize experiential elements.

5. The therapist achieves this goal through an interaction involving joint processing of the client's experience. The therapist works both at the same level with and slightly ahead of the client's ability to organize, thus facilitating his processing.

6. What is retained by the successful client over a period of time is an increased ability to organize experiential data, that is, to have fuller, richer experiencing.

It becomes clearer why the assumptions of the older zeitgeist that "knowledge would set you free" were not a fertile soil for the growth of an adequate theory of client-centered practice: it is not what the client knows that is important but rather how he organizes his experience.

REFERENCES

Broadbent, D. E. *Perception and communication.* Oxford: Pergamon, 1958.

Bruner, J. S., Goodnow, J., & Austin, G. *A Study of thinking.* New York: Wiley, 1956.

Deutsch, J. A., & Deutsch, D. Attention: Some theoretical considerations. *Psychological Review*, 1963, **70**, 80–90.

Gendlin, E. T. *Experiencing and the creation of meaning.* New York: Free Press, 1962.

Gendlin, E. T. A theory of personality change. In P. Worchel & D. Byrne (Eds.), *Personality change.* New York: Wiley, 1964.

Miller, G. A. The magical number seven, plus or minus two: Some limits on our capacity for processing information. *Psychological Review*, 1956, **63**, 81–96.

Miller, G. A., Galanter, E., & Pribram, K. H. *Plans and the structure of behavior.* New York: Holt, Rinehart & Winston, 1960.

Rogers, C. R. *Client-centered therapy: Its current practice, implications, and theory.* Boston: Houghton Mifflin, 1951.

Rogers, C. R. A tentative scale for the measurement of progress in psychotherapy. In E. A. Rubinstein & M. B. Parloff (Eds.), *Research in psychotherapy.* Washington, D.C.: American Psychological Association, 1959.

Rogers, C. R., & Dymond, R. F. *Psychotherapy and personality change: Co-ordinated studies in the client-centered approach.* Chicago: University of Chicago Press, 1954.

Rogers, C. R., & Truax, C. B. The therapeutic conditions antecedent to change: A theoretical view. In C. R. Rogers (Ed.), *The therapeutic relationship and its impact: A study of psychotherapy with schizophrenics.* Madison: University of Wisconsin Press, 1967.

Wittgenstein, L. *Philosophical investigations.* New York: Macmillan, 1953.

Wittgenstein, L. *The blue and brown books.* (2nd ed.) New York: Harper, 1958.

CHAPTER 5

Conceptualizing and Measuring Openness to Experience in the Context of Psychotherapy

Pamela Howell Pearson

No concept is more central nor more important in Rogers' (1959) theories of personality and psychotherapy than is the concept of openness to experience. When persons are fully open to experience, they are optimally actualized within themselves and in the world. Such persons function fully, that is, live and experience in rich and complex ways that accord with the full realization of their inherent potential. They are neither limited by debilitating defenses nor misdefined by false identities that hamper the full and ongoing expression of their inner potential. They are persons in process, in flux, everchanging and growing. Complete openness to experience also describes the ideal outcome in client-centered therapy. During the psychotherapy process, the therapist strives to facilitate openness to experience and to remove defensive perceptions learned in social interaction.

A more complete and deeper understanding of the goals of the therapist and how to implement them remains limited as long as the concepts, or tools of understanding, exist as pie in the sky, vague concepts. Complete openness to experience remains the impossible dream, a tantalizing fantasy, an unfulfilled promise for human potential. Left as unspecified ideals, vague abstractions do little to further understanding, techniques of therapy, or the therapists' own growth as persons. As it has existed in client-centered writings, openness to experience has been a vague, broad, and not very useful construct.

The aim of this chapter is to present a new, extended, modified, and more specific conceptualization of openness to experience that ties the concept to measuring operations in the psychotherapy context. If reliable and valid operations can be derived, then, this conceptual–operational package can provide a stepping-stone for fruitful empirical work, which, in turn, can revamp and modify the present proposal. This rational analysis of the concept of openness to experience builds upon Rogers' (1951, 1959) prior theorizing, as well as upon previous conceptual and empirical work of my own (Pearson, 1968, 1969, 1972).

Openness to experience is here defined as a three-phase assimilation process serving both information and identity functions concurrently. In its normal operation, the assimilation process provides the person with accurate, up-to-date information about his or her private experiences. Concurrently, these same experiences are being assimilated into and becoming part of self-structure. Normally, persons are expected to change and grow as a result of the continuing assimilation of their ongoing experience, thereby changing in their identities in the typical course of living. When defense blocks the assimilation process, both information and identity functions are ill served. Defense restricts the scope and nature of information available to the person. The person no longer has absolute access to accurate, complete, and current information. At the same time, identity formation is arrested and blocked, and the process of assimilation is halted. Defense occurs because previous, introjected aspects of self are threatened by the person's present experience. In a defensive state, persons are cut off from their feelings and from psychological growth.

ROGERS' CONCEPT OF OPENNESS TO EXPERIENCE IN ITS THEORETICAL CONTEXT

As a first step in reformulation, it is important to define the concept as Rogers views it, and to note its interplay with other important concepts in his theory, namely defense, threat, conditions of worth, and self-structure. Defense and threat both interfere with the accurate registration of information; conditions of worth prevent the assimilation of new experience into the structure of self.

Complete openness to experience is an attribute of both the human infant, prior to socialization, and the fully functioning person who has no defenses. Rogers (1959) defines the concept as follows:

. . . . to be open to experience is the polar opposite of defensiveness. The term may be used in regard to some area of experience or in regard to the total experience of the organism. It signifies that every stimulus, whether originating within the organism or in the environment, is freely relayed through the nervous system without being distorted or channeled off by any defensive mechanism. . . . [p. 206].[1]

What does the concept cover? If we divide the concept into a stimulus portion and a response portion, we can more easily see the extent of psychological space included. The term "experience" denotes the stimulus portion, and includes the totality of psychological stimulation, sensations, feelings, and cognitions that originate from both external and internal sources. Excluded are those stimuli that are incapable of being registered psychologically, such as changes in blood sugar. For Rogers, the concept of experience emphasizes the here-and-now, the events in focal attention experienced by the person in the moment, but also includes the events in the ground of perception, and memories of past experience, as perceived at the moment. In responding to this wealth of input, the term "open" denotes the response portion, namely the capacity for symbolization. Total openness means that a person is capable of symbolizing each stimulus or event with total accuracy, not necessarily verbally. Practically speaking, the open person does *not* symbolize all of ongoing experience. If no part of experience is denied to, or distorted in, awareness, then the person stands in the center of his or her experience with complete freedom to pick and choose any portion as a focus. This psychological state of openness is possible only when no threat to current self-structure exists.

When threat does exist, the individual is no longer able to pick and choose at will. Instead, experience becomes selectively viewed through a lens that distorts or blots out that portion of experience incompatible with the existing conditions of worth in the self-structure. According to Rogers (1959), the self-structure is characterized by a condition of worth whenever "a self-experience or set of related self-experiences is either avoided or sought solely because the individual discriminates it as being less or more worthy of self-regard [p. 209]." These parts of self-structure were learned in situations in which the individual received conditional positive regard, when they were valued as persons only when they met the expectations of significant others. Gradually, the persons themselves incorporated the same attitudes toward their own experience and behavior, and "pseudoassimilated" (Perls, 1947) these same attitudes into the self-structure. When ongoing, direct experience challenges a self-perception based on a condition of worth, threat arises, and defense ensues to "protect" self-structure. Threat, in Rogers' view, is both a necessary and sufficient condition for the occurrence of defense, the distortion or denial of an experience to conscious awareness.

[1] All quotations in this chapter from Rogers (1959) reprinted by permission of McGraw-Hill.

Defense prevents the occurrence of four negative consequences for the individual. If defense did not occur, "the self-concept would no longer be a consistent gestalt, the conditions of worth would be violated, and the need for self-regard would be frustrated. A state of anxiety would exist [Rogers, 1959, p. 227]." The state of inconsistency of the self-concept is no doubt the least threatening of the four consequences, as inconsistency per se is not avoided. It is only when inconsistency goes arm in arm with the violation of conditions of worth, with the frustration of positive self-regard, and with the state of anxiety ensuing from a near encounter of experience and pseudoassimilated experience that it is also avoided.

If large portions of self-structure have been formed on the basis of the conditions of worth, then persons tend to become generally rigid and inaccurate in their perceptions. It is then psychologically necessary for these persons to distort perceptions relatively constantly, and thus, to lose the accuracy of perception characteristic of the optimal open state. Moreover, such defensive persons are characterized by intensionality, a term referring to the person's tendency to "see experience in absolute and unconditional terms, to overgeneralize, to be dominated by concept or belief, to fail to anchor his reactions in space and time, to confuse fact and evaluation, to rely upon abstractions rather than upon reality-testing [Rogers, 1959, p. 205]." Thus, persons range in the degree and frequency of defense from very little to a great deal. In principle, of course, the range is absolute.

How does it happen that persons become enmeshed in defensive operations when such operations clearly interfere with optimal functioning? According to Rogers, the infant at a very early age develops a need for positive regard whose satisfaction depends on the positive regard of significant others. If these significant others, usually parents, communicate conditional positive regard to the child, he or she is placed in a choice situation. In order to please the parents, and to receive positive regard, the child must behave or feel in a way that is incongruent with his or her authentic experience. Because the need for positive regard is so strong and compelling, the child typically chooses to receive the positive regard from others, at the expense of ultimately falsifying his or her own experience. Thus, rather inevitably, when such choice situations occur, children choose love over self, the positive regard of others over their own experience. Rogers (1959) speaks of the inevitable choice and the alienation it produces in the following way. The choice is "a natural—and tragic—development in infancy" and accounts for "the basic estrangement in man. He has not been true to himself, to his own natural organismic valuing of experience, but for the sake of preserving the positive regard of others has now come to falsify some of the values he experiences and to perceive them only in terms based on their value to others [p. 226]." Once values are formed on the basis of the values of others, they are introjected into and become part of the self-structure, representing attitudes about experience and behavior that are not congruent with what the person values. Borrowing Perls' (1947) term, they are incorporated into the self-structure by a pseudoassimilation process, described in detail later. More concretely, direct experience is falsified by the person because in the past he or she was told that this type of experience meant that he or she was a "bad" or unworthy person. A new encounter with a similar area of experience revives the conditioned positive regard for the person and sets into motion an "unworthy self" dynamic that has the potential for producing unpleasant anxiety, fear, and self-hatred.

Now that we have considered the concepts of openness to experience, defense, threat, and conditions of worth and their interactions, let us consider how and if one can measure the concept of openness to experience as it has been defined and described. We can conceive of openness to experience and defensiveness as representing two extreme poles on a continuum of access to experiential data. At one extreme, openness denotes the complete and unlimited access to such data. In contrast, defensiveness denotes completely limited access, a psychotic condition. For any one particular experience, we can measure openness to experience if we could assess the extent to which a person is capable of accurately symbolizing all aspects or parts of that experience. To the extent that a person is unable to symbolize all aspects of the experience (denial) or to symbolize those aspects in an accurate form (distortion), he or she would be considered defensive. Defined as an abstract capacity, ideal measurement would consist of noting all aspects of potentially conscious experience, comparing these potentially available experiences with actual organismic experience, and obtaining a difference score between the two. Such a methodological feat is possible only in our fantasies because, in practice, we cannot directly measure either potentially available experience or organismic experience.

Inasmuch as it does not seem to be possible to measure openness to experience in this abstract form, the construct must be defined and described more concretely as a functioning process in personality. Given that a person has the capacity to be fully open to experience, how does the capacity function in practice? How can we tell when someone is open to experience? How can we tell when someone is defending? Is the person who is totally open to experience deprived of mechanisms of stimulus structuring and selection? Is the person who is totally open adrift in a sea of stimulation?

In his earlier writings, Rogers (1951) clearly states that both stimulus selection and structuring are normal, appropriate organismic functions, and thus occur in the person who is fully open to experience. Openness to experience, as it functions in practice, does not result in experiential bombardment and a chronic state of overstimulation.

Stimulus selection is construed as an ongoing process that operates according to the criterion of relevance of experience to the self-structure. Rogers (1951) discusses the criterion for stimulus selection as follows: "As experiences occur in the life of the individual, they are either (a) symbolized, perceived, and organized into some relationship to the self; (b) ignored because there is no perceived relationship to the self-structure; or (c) denied symbolization or given a distorted symbolization because the experience is inconsistent with the structure of self [p. 503]." Thus, if a particular stimulus is ignored and not present in consciousness, that stimulus may be either irrelevant to self or it may be defensively excluded from awareness. The process governing the selection of relevant stimuli for the person who is fully open to experience is the organismic valuing process, a continually operating process that orients the individual toward the satisfaction of his or her needs and actualization. When functioning properly, the organismic valuing process guides the individual toward stimuli relevant for stimulus selection, valuing, and action for the total unified organism, because for the person fully open to experience, there is no disparity between the actualization of the organism and the actualization of self. When such disparity exists, as it does in most persons socialized in Western culture at least, the organismic valuing process functions improperly. Experiences can be perceived as organismically satisfying when in fact this is not true (Rogers, 1959). An implication to be drawn from such observations is that individuals can and do experience satisfaction in perceptions that are defensively determined. A preliminary analysis of the concept of organismic valuing is presented in an earlier paper (Pearson, 1969).

Not only is stimulation differentially valued and selected, according to Rogers, but awareness of stimulation is configural and structured, according to gestalt figure-ground relationships. Rogers (1959) quite clearly maintains that experience is structured when he states, "this representation (of stimulation in awareness) may have varying degrees of sharpness or vividness, from a dim awareness of something existing as ground, to a sharp awareness of something which is in focus as figure [p. 198]." The person in an open state does not perceive a confused, unorganized disarray of stimulation, but rather perceives "good" gestalts of changing stimulation as guided by the organismic valuing process. For the person in a defensive state, experience may be of several varieties. The person is more likely to experience anxiety, uneasiness, and tension as the experience approaches symbolization in awareness (Rogers, 1959). Conversely, anxiety is less likely to be experienced by the person when a distorted or denied experience is remote from symbolization. The concept of anxiety, as it is used here, refers to a phenomenological state of uneasiness or tension, not to a permanent, "trait" anxiety, nor to "bound" anxiety, as described in the psychoanalytic literature.

RESTRICTIONS ON THE DOMAIN OF OPENNESS TO EXPERIENCE

In the present analysis, the stimulus domain, or part, of the concept is restricted to self-relevant experience. Although this restriction may appear obvious, a few words need to be said about it. From the last section, it is clear that such a restriction is amply justified in Rogers' (1951) own writings, as he proposes that stimulation that is appraised as non-self-relevant is ignored by the person. At the same time, his later definition (Rogers, 1959, p. 206) of openness to experience explicitly includes all of experience. For the purpose of further specifying and measuring the construct, the restriction makes the task a bit easier because it makes the domain of the construct somewhat smaller. From this point on, we will be discussing a smaller target construct, openness to self-relevant experience. A similar, although not identical, restriction was utilized in previous analyses (Pearson, 1968, 1969, 1972).

SELECTION OF AN APPROPRIATE CONCEPTUAL MODEL FOR OPENNESS TO SELF–RELEVANT EXPERIENCE

A next step in the reformulation of openness to self-relevant experience was a choice about the most appropriate conceptual model. Such a choice is an important step in reconstruing, because the model chosen sets guidelines for further analytic work. In Rogers' writings about the concept of openness to experience, he implicitly and explicitly uses the four typical conceptual models used in construing nonmotivational personality constructs, namely state, trait, stylistic, and process models. Given an interest in maintaining consonance between the present reformulation and Rogers' theory, any of these models could have been selected.

The selection of a model rested on three separate, but interwoven conceptual and operational criteria. First, it seemed clearly important to choose a model that could end up with a comparison of persons both over time and over situations, thereby yielding more generality. Second, the target concept of openness to self-relevant experience is so broad in its conception that a crucial conceptual goal was the analysis of the target construct into smaller and more homogeneous parts. A model lending itself to analytic operations was thus highly desirable. Finally, directness as opposed to indirectness of measurement was a goal. Does the model correspond directly to the nature of the concept?

According to these three criteria, both the state and stylistic models were rejected. The state model was excluded because it emphasizes the moment-to-moment variation of open and defensive states. Although such a model is frequently utilized in Rogers' formulations, it does not readily lend itself to the criteria of generality over time, nor does it suggest how one might analyze the construct. Also rejected was the stylistic model, even though at one point in his writings, Rogers defines openness to experience as the way an internally congruent person meets new experience. Because this particular model of construing openness to experience was insufficiently elaborated by Rogers, it would be difficult to determine even the nature of the psychological constructs to be studied.

A typical global-trait model was also rejected, although it is clearly appropriate. Using this model, one could define a set of target constructs aimed at measuring the general consequences of defense over time, namely perceptual rigidity, reality testing, and intensionality (Rogers, 1959). But such target constructs suffer from conceptual indirectness, and from Rogers' writings, at least, there are no guidelines to direct the more specified analyses of these three concepts.

A combination of the analytic-trait and process models was chosen as the most suitable on a variety of grounds. First, the trait model, emphasizing the generality over time and situations, seemed clearly desirable. Second, the process model seemed definitely in order, because it emphasizes the private experiencing of the person, and is described by Fiske (1971) as "a hypothesized sequence of internal activities, initiated by a stimulus and sometimes concluding with an action or overt response [p. 297]." Using a process model offers the advantage of directness and suitability to the nature of the construct. Moreover, both the analytic-trait and process models readily lend themselves to further analytic operations. Moreover, a process conception is especially suitable for the psychotherapy context, because observations can be systematically collected over time and sessions. Thus, we can look at and compare the different parts of the construct over time and situations.

Now that an appropriate model has been selected for reconceptualizing the concept of openness to experience, we can begin the critical task of further explicating the construct. In the analysis to follow, openness to experience is recast as an active process of assimilating experience. This active process operates continually in two separate contexts, information and identity. Each of these important contexts will be separately described and discussed, and assimilation, as it occurs in each of the contexts, will be analyzed into conceptually distinct phases. In the last section of the chapter, a proposal for measuring assimilation in the context of information will be presented and tied to psychotherapy process.

THE CORE OF THE CONCEPT OF OPENNESS TO EXPERIENCE

How do I feel about that? Who am I?

These questions concerning self, and others like them, express the needs for private information and for identity that the process of openness to experience, when functioning appropriately, provides.

The essence, core, or basic substance of the concept of openness to experience is defined as the process of assimilating self-relevant experience. This perceptual–symbolic process operates continually, processes self-relevant information, and provides the person with answers to informational questions about self (How do I feel about that?) and with answers to identity questions (Who am I?). As mentioned earlier, the assimilation process serves two functions concurrently. The informational function provides data that keep the person in moment-to-moment contact with current, ongoing internal and external stimulation. It yields information for reality testing whether one tests the internal or external reality. Interconnected and interdependent with the informational function is the identity function. When operating normatively, as it does in the infant and in the fully functioning person, the data from self-relevant information is continually integrated into and changes the structure of self. Normatively, self is constantly maintaining, changing, growing, and becoming.

In the present analysis, the assimilation process is proposed to operate in an active, multidimensional manner within the confines of physiological restrictions and in the context of a matrix of ongoing experience. The discussion to follow will consider each of these characteristics as they apply to the process of assimilation when it is not disturbed by defensive interventions. Or, phrased in other terms, assimilation will be considered as it functions in the fully functioning person free of defenses. The effects of defense and the three phases of assimilation will be considered somewhat later.

Assimilation is, in all cases, proposed to be both an active and a reactive process, in contrast to an inactive and passive process. Assimilation is viewed as an energetic, busy, working, lively process that causes action and change, hence, is active. It is reactive in the sense that it is affected by forces outside as well as inside the person. Such forces produce noticeable changes in the perceptual and emotional field of the persons involved. Persons are not inert organisms. Similarly, assimilation process is not inactive nor is it passive. Contributing to the basic active nature of the assimilation process is the adoption by the person of an active sense of responsibility for his or her own experience. This stance is an attitude toward *all* experience irrespective of whether the experience was originally instigated by external or internal self-relevant events. The active stance seizes responsibility for itself. In such a stance, one claims one's own experience. In contrast is the passive, inert stance, in which individuals implicitly or explicitly relinquish responsibility for their own experience, and in effect, conceive of themselves as being at the mercy of other persons, or more abstractly, fate. Such a passive stance produces a definite stumbling block in therapy because it blocks assimilation, and indeed, can be considered one major avenue of defense. I have become accustomed to calling such a passive stance the "Poor Pitiful Pearl" stance because it is typically adopted by women, in part because of the passivity associated with the stereotypically feminine role. By exclaiming loudly how terrible things keep happening to her, and professing equally loudly that she has no control over any of it, the client dooms herself to stasis. For other clients, operating from an active stance, change is produced by an encounter, a transaction, an integration, an active coming together of the person and the experience. It should be noted that the active stance is independent of the person's actual ability to control the external or internal event. Whether a particular event has "happened" to the person or whether the person has taken some initiative in choosing or creating the particular event, assimilation requires an active stance to flow naturally.

Along with its active nature, the assimilation process also operates in a multidimensional fashion, the content and direction an idiosyncratic function of the particular person. It is clearly complex, involving gestalts of changing experience, and is not subject to rational, linear, undimensional analyses. In its progression, it is difficult, if not impossible, to predict the content of the next step in advance, except for the general outlines. Often, such steps in therapy "feel right" to a client viewing the process from inside out. When subjected to rational considerations, such steps may appear absurd when the vantage point is outside in. Even the persons themselves may be surprised when they experience the next step. Many dimensions of experience are involved, and multiple levels of depth of meanings may also be involved, depending upon the experience. For example, in processing the death of a loved one, the first dimension of processing may involve the grieving; a second may involve the experiencing of personal loss; a third could involve reliving the experiences shared with the person; a fourth could be the feelings of relief that the person has died; a fifth could consider the changes in life style after the person died, and so on. Gendlin (1962) provides us with a detailed account of such inner experiencing.

This active, multidimensional assimilation process is proposed to occur within the confines of physiological restrictions on stimulus input, which, of necessity, limit the amount of data that can be processed in time. The present proposal draws upon activation theory (Fiske & Maddi, 1961) in proposing that there are optimal levels of activation, or stimulus input, for individuals. If these optimal, or characteristic, levels are exceeded, persons experience negative affect as a result of overstimulation and respond by reducing their stimulus input. On the other hand, if stimulus input is too low, persons respond by increasing their stimulus input.

An important implication to be drawn from activation theory is that even in the case of ideal assimilation, undisturbed by defense, persons would at times cease processing when intolerable levels of high activation were experienced. Such natural ebbing and flowing would not be considered evidence for defense, but would be viewed as part of the natural assimilation process. In general, then, assimilation is proposed to occur within the boundaries of the physiological limitations on stimulus input, and would presumably, as does everything, show individual differences.

In the fully functioning person, who is totally open to experience, the continued operation of the assimilation process provides for both psychological maintenance and growth within the confines of these physiological limits. Although the concepts of maintenance and growth-processing overlap, it seems worthwhile to make the distinction. Maintenance-processing refers to the present, to the here-and-now, to keeping "experiential" account current at the moment. It refers to the need for processing of the information from the day's activities, events, feelings, thoughts, and reactions. When completed, such maintenance-processing in effect maintains the person at his or her present level of functioning. Given the complexity and the overload conditions of living, however, backlogs in processing may develop because of a temporary overload of events to be processed. As soon as there is experiential space, however, these events are processed to completion, because there is no interference from defensive processes. In ideal functioning, the choice of the situation most relevant for processing will be selected by the organismic valuing process. Other experiences would be held in check in an organismic "holding pattern" during that time. An analogy may be drawn between such an occurrence and the landing pattern at a busy airport. Each plane has its assigned place in the scheme of things and awaits its turn to land. But such a state of affairs is temporary.

The concept of *experiential space* deserves description and requires comment. It is defined as the amount of psychological room to process significant, self-relevant events. It assumes that all persons have both physiological as well as psychological limits on the amount of stimulation processed. The physiological requirement sets broad limits on stimulus input; no one can process too many events at once. Psychologically, input from significant events and defensive processes both take up experiential space. Thus, defense takes up valuable experiential space, and deprives the person of room to maintain and grow.

Growth-processing, in contrast to maintenance-processing, refers to processing in the direction of increasing self-actualization. Growth means dealing with issues that are on the "growing edge" of the person. Following Rogers (1951, p. 488), growth is evidenced by personality changes characterized by greater differentiation and complexity, including greater breadth and depth of inner experiencing. Growth is also characterized by experience and behavior that is in the direction of increased autonomy, toward socialization but not conformity, and toward increased novelty in experiencing. The person in the midst of growth-processing would be continually changing and growing, would be constantly in process, and typically unpredictable insofar as specific behaviors are concerned.

In the ideal case, assimilation occurs in the natural flow of a person's living, and is not an instantaneous process in most cases. Although serving both maintenance and growth functions, it is also subject to physiological limitations. Persons typically attempt to maintain activation at characteristic level and within the band suitable for them. Three properties of stimulation contribute to total impact: (a) intensity, (b) meaningfulness, and (c) variation (Fiske & Maddi, 1961). In general, the greater the intensity, meaningfulness, and/or variation, the longer the processing time for a particular self-relevant event. *Intensity* refers to the physical intensity; *meaningfulness* to the subjective importance of the event for the person; *variation* refers to the extent to which the event is unique, different from other events experienced by the person. All other things being equal, it should be faster to assimilate an event like an insult from a friend than it would be to assimilate the tragic death of a parent. Presumably, the insult would be a moderately meaningful, low-intensity and low-variety, event, whereas the death would be a highly meaningful, highly varied, and low-intensity event.

Thus far, the process of assimilation has been considered as a general process as it naturally occurs with no disruption from defensive processes.

Unfortunately, children of Western culture that we are, we have no recourse but to consider the pervasiveness of defense, its genesis, and its consequences. In the analysis to follow, the assimilation process will be considered in two separate, functional contexts. In the *information* context, assimilation is contrasted with nonassimilation, the arresting or disruption of the assimilation of experience by defensive processes. In the second context, that of *identity formation*, assimilation is proposed as the counterpole of *pseudoassimilation*, a process during which experience is introjected into the self-structure, creating the fabric of the "false" self. Such pseudoassimilated experience, when interwoven into the self-structure, provides both necessary and sufficient conditions for subsequent defensive functioning. It is because of introjected self-perceptions that defense occurs in human functioning.

The Context of Information: Assimilation Versus Nonassimilation

In its operation in the context of information, the assimilation process consists of a series of three cyclic phases. Given an event of importance to the person, assimilation begins anew. At the high end of the scale, openness to relevant experience means that a person has successfully completed each of the phases; defensiveness, on the other hand, indicates that a person has completed none or some of them. In any one phase, a person is either open or defensive.

A brief overview of the phases may well be helpful at this point. In the Attention–Recognition phase, openness involves attending to, focusing upon, and verbally recognizing important affective–cognitive cues in a self-relevant event. In this first phase, the person begins to move toward the more unified experiencing that is characteristic of the next two phases. In the Reaction phase, openness means sensing the personal import of the experience. Such sensing implies the conjoint occurrence of three separate phenomenological states: a state of affective–cognitive unity, an awareness of oneself as the locus of feeling, and an active, experiential sense of responsibility for one's own experience. In the final phase, Exploration–Closure, openness is characterized by the continuing inner exploration of facets of personal meaning until closure is reached. At the end of this phase, the person experiences a shift or change in inner experiencing and the sense of a finished experience. For each of the three phases, defensiveness is indicated by the absence of the open response. The maximally defensive response is exemplified by the person who neither attends, recognizes, reacts, explores, or finishes an important experience. A familiar clinical example is that provided by the defense mechanism of repression.

In ideal assimilation, each early phase must occur before its next succeeding phase. Thus, each early phase is posited to be a necessary, but not sufficient condition for the occurrence of its next succeeding phase. The successful completion of the Attention–Recognition phase is a necessary condition for entering into the Reaction phase, because a person has to attend to a situation before he or she can react. Attending, recognizing, and reacting are viewed as necessary conditions for exploring, delving into personal meanings. Thus, Attention–Recognition and Reaction, when successfully completed, provide the necessary conditions for moving into the Exploration phase. Finally, exploration of personal meanings provides the necessary conditions for achieving closure. At the closure point, a new matrix of experiential meanings in the self-structure forms. A new gestalt of self is born. Whatever the phase or subphase the person is experiencing, the open person has access to all information provided by the process. The defending person, on the other hand, is aware only of experience as it is distorted by the lens of defense, and has access only to that information. When defense occurs, assimilation is blocked or halted.

Although the successful completion of each early phase is necessary before entering into later phases, the successful completion is not a sufficient condition. Defensive process can intrude at any point in the assimilation process and block its continued operation. Defensive perception is manifested by avoidance—of significant affective and/or cognitive portions of experience, of experiencing self as the locus of affect, of taking responsibility for one's experience, of exploring one's inner experience.

A detailed consideration of the phases including more specific definitions of openness and defensiveness follows.

ATTENTION–RECOGNITION

Given that a self-relevant experience has occurred, the person in an open state responds in an adient manner, orienting toward, approaching, and attending to central, relevant affective cues in the event. Such a person actively selects and cognitively approaches the major affective cues in the experience. For the open person, these affective cues occupy the figure, not the ground, of the perceptual field. Although the open perceptual field will be flexible and constantly in flux, the open person can always cognitively recognize and verbally report relevant, central affective cues in the experience. In contrast, the defending person does not do so. Avoidance is the key feature of the defensive response. The defending person may avoid the event in totality, its potential or latent affect, or its emerging personal meaning. The extreme of avoidance is illustrated by the client who does "not want to talk about it." If the therapist brings up the subject, the client may actively avoid in several ways, by changing the subject, by denying that the event has any importance, or by "forgetting" it. In intermediate avoidance, the client may talk about the event in purely cognitive terms and thereby avoid the affective component. Recourse to cause-and-effect, rational explanations, and endless recounting of minor, as opposed to major, aspects of the experience are two stratagems used to avoid. Another common tactic is to minimize the importance of the event as in "oh, well, no big thing . . . on with life."

More specifically defined, the open response in phase one, Attention–Recognition, involves the cognitive, symbolic recognition of affective cues in a self-relevant experience. Such recognition is conscious and can be verbally reported. In phase one, openness does not require the experiencing of the affective import. The defensive response is defined as the absence of approach toward and/or symbolic recognition of central, relevant affective cues in the experience. Such defensive responding may be indicated by the active avoidance of the experience in totality or by active avoidance of the recognition of the affective component.

REACTION

Once a person has achieved openness in phase one, he or she moves into the second phase of assimilation quite naturally, provided that defense does not intervene. The Reaction phase could well be called the gateway to the assimilation process because during this phase three necessary inner states must be experienced concurrently by the open person. This phase is a difficult one, because all three states can and do present major barriers to the assimilation process. The presence of each of the states is necessary for continuing forward motion in the process of assimilation. As was mentioned earlier, the three states are (a) a state of affective–cognitive unity, (b) a state of awareness of oneself as the locus of feeling, and (c) a state of experiential responsibility for one's own experience. They are now described in detail.

The first inner state is aptly depicted by Rogers' concept of experiencing feelings. The concept "denotes an emotionally tinged experience, together with its personal meaning. Thus, it includes the emotion, but also the cognitive context of the meaning of the emotion in its experiential context. . . . it thus refers to the unity of emotion and cognition as they are experienced inseparably in the moment [Rogers, 1959, p. 198]." There are three separable features to the state: the affective, the context or external stimulus, and the cognitive component. An illustration is provided by the client who, in responding to a put down by a friend, says "Boy, it really hurt me when he said that." Such a statement exemplifies the three main features of the open response. The client's statement includes the affective reaction word "hurt"; it indicates an awareness of the context, "when he said that"; and it shows the importance of the cognitive component, indicated by the verbalization of the event in words.

The person in an open state is not just mouthing affect or reaction words nor talking about his or her experience from the remote perspective of an observing spectator. The open person speaks from an experiential vantage point; the person is into feelings, not talking about them. From the vantage point of the empathic therapist or from that of the sensitive observer, it is clear both from content and voice quality cues that the person speaking is experiencing his or her feelings. He or she is not intellectualizing about them. If the content of a client's verbalizations is "I feel very angry at him for that," the same therapist or observer senses no nagging doubt about the genuineness of the open response. Thus, the person experiencing a state of affective–cognitive unity accurately communicates the genuineness of his or her experiencing. But it should be pointed out that the mere use of affect words by themselves do not constitute sufficient grounds for categorizing a response as open. One must, in addition, utilize nonverbal, voice quality cues before making such a judgment. In the voice–quality classification system developed by Rice and Wagstaff (1967), an open response would be rated as focused or emotional and would not be rated as externalizing or limited.

Defense in the reaction phase does not typically manifest itself in the purely cognitive use of affect or reaction words. The avoidance of affect is rather blatant; it is avoided in totality. Typical of such direct affect avoidance are the defenses of intellectualizing, rationalizing, and ruminating. From the presence of such processes, one might quite reasonably infer the presence of a disturbing stimulus, even though the nature of the stimulus is hardly apparent. Because they illustrate cognitive-approach, affect-avoidance responses, these three defenses may be considered intermediate defensive maneuvers, as would cognitive-avoidance, affect-approach responses. The latter defense is aptly illustrated by the so-called hysterical outburst during which "uncontrolled" emotionality reaches its peak. The extreme form of defense in the Reaction phase is illustrated by a total unawareness and avoidance of personal impact or significance, both affective and cognitive.

The second requirement for the open response in phase two is that the person accurately perceive that the feeling or reaction is in self and belongs to self. If a feeling of anger is perceived, but is disowned by self, the person may well use projection to account for that feeling. Necessarily, then, self must be experienced as the locus of feeling when indeed this is the case.

The third and final requirement for the open response in the Reaction phase is that the person experience a sense of responsibility for his or her own feelings and reactions, as opposed to relinquishing responsibility, blaming others, or fate. The sense of responsibility centers in self. Some examples. The hysterical outburst implicitly gives up the responsibility for the expression of emotion, and in so doing, places the burden for control of self on the external world, usually other people. "You're making me angry." The crucial assumption behind this response is that the other person is responsible for and causes his or her anger. If one's response is not one's own, then one feels powerless to change it. Responsibility has to be assumed before change is possible.

To summarize this all too sketchy discussion, an open response during the Reaction phase has at least three major components. The first is the state of cognitive–affective unity about a self-relevant experience. Either cognitive and/or affective avoidance is defined as defensive. Second, an open response requires that the person accurately perceive an internal locus of feeling and personal meaning. If the locus of feeling is not experienced within self, the response is designated as defensive. One may in such a case project the feeling: "You're angry at me." Third, in the open response, the person accepts experiential responsibility for the nature of one's own feeling or reaction. If both the nature of the reaction, for example, anger, and the locus of feeling are accurately perceived (e.g., "I am angry"), it is still possible to defend by externalizing and blaming others: "I am angry; you made me angry; it is all your fault, so I'm going to freak out at you." To be classified as open, one must claim ownership for one's feelings and reactions. One must accept active responsibility. "I am angry at you; you didn't make me angry (because you can't make me do anything); I am angry because that is how I am reacting to you right now." Such ownership of one's own reactions creates a situation of maximum freedom for the individual. The person is free to respond in any way to the stimulus because he or she can perceive the locus of change as residing within oneself.

Defense, in contrast, is indicated by the absence of any of the three necessary components or any combination thereof. Defense may involve the avoidance of affect and/or cognition. It may be manifested by the avoidance of experiencing oneself as the internal locus of affect or feeling. It may also involve the denial of responsibility for one's feelings and/or expressive actions. The occurrence of any *one* type of avoidance is a sufficient condition for a response to be designated as defensive.

EXPLORATION–CLOSURE

Successfully completing the Attention–Recognition and Reaction phases, a person proceeds into the third and final phase of the assimilation process. As in the Reaction phase, the open person must engage in affective–cognitive approach, must perceive self as the locus of feeling, and must assume responsibility for his or her feelings. What differentiates openness in the Exploration–Closure phase from openness in the Reaction phase are two additional criteria. First, the open person must adopt a stance of inner exploration, must turn into inner experiencing. Second, the open person must actually engage in the process of inner exploring to the point of closure. In the exploration process, a person increasingly differentiates aspects or facets of a self-relevant experience, using an experiential "trial and error" and a "trial and success" approach. The person tries on different symbolizations of his or her experience, the criteria being what "feels right" to the person. Typically, during inner exploration, feelings become more differentiated, shift, and change according to inner meanings, which in Gendlin's (1962) theory, emerge and are created during the process. A person is totally absorbed in following the track of the inner experiencing. Closure, the endpoint of the phase, is achieved and experienced when, in Rogers' term, the feelings are experienced fully. At the closure point, the person senses the changed and finished experience. "I don't know why, but I just don't feel bad about that anymore." At this point, the experience would be considered fully assimilated into becoming part of the self-structure.

Defense in the Exploration phase is indicated by failure to adopt a stance of inner exploration, failure to engage in exploration and/or failure to achieve closure about the experience. If defense intervenes at the beginning of the phase, the process of inner exploration may simply not occur. But, defense can also occur at any other point during exploration. For example, the client may draw a blank while in the midst of searching for the meaning of an important event. It is almost as if the shutters of experiencing, once open, shut suddenly, shutting off a crucial part of the meaning of the experience. A sudden, marked shift in the depth of a client's experiencing can also occur, when he or she quickly moves out of a deep level of feeling to a more superficial level. Many times, clients return in a later session, resume the track, and finish the experience. If an experience is not finished, it remains a sore point for the person, and adds to the backlog of experiences that need to be processed to completion.

It is a common experience that clients enter therapy with a pressing need to assimilate a large number of unfinished experiences. These experiences have accumulated over time because their complete assimilation has been blocked by defensive intervention. One of the major tasks of psychotherapy is to facilitate the assimilation of unfinished experiences, to complete the deficiency-processing. This term refers to the organismic need to assimilate completely the accumulation of prior, self-relevant experience whose processing has been blocked by defensive intervention. At different points in his theory of psychotherapy, Rogers (1959) refers to the importance of processing this backlog of past, unfinished experience, which, of necessity, reorganizes the self-structure. Once such deficiency–processing has been completed, the client can return to the normative maintenance- and growth-processing.

The Identity Context: Assimilation Versus Pseudoassimilation

At the endpoint of the process of assimilation, new experience and self-structure reintegrate into a new gestalt. For the fully functioning person, this continuing assimilation provides for psychological growth and a continually changing self. Unfortunately, however, few persons enjoy selves formed entirely on the basis of assimilation of their direct, ongoing experience.

Instead, the alternate process of pseudoassimilation provides much of the fabric of self. Pseudoassimilation is defined as the process during which aspects of self are incorporated into self-structure, those aspects being inaccurate and false attributes of self. These inaccurate aspects of self have their genesis in the perceptions and values of significant others, not in the direct experience of the person. Pseudoassimilation, as opposed to assimilation, becomes the primary identity process in situations in which individuals feel that they will lose the positive regard of significant others if they follow their own track. In such cases, people feel that they have to choose between love and self, that they will lose the positive regard of significant others if they remain true to themselves, their experience, and their values. Typically, such choice situations are not symbolized clearly in awareness.

Consistent with Rogers (1951), identity is thus formed by the integration of information from two sources, direct, ongoing experience (assimiltaion) and the distorted symbolization of experience based on the values of others (pseudoassimilation). The resultant self-structure, itself a gestalt, is an interwoven tapestry of both assimilated and pseudoassimilated experience. Within the self-structure, both types of experience interconnect, intertwine. Consistent with Rogers' (1959) definition, self-structure is viewed as a potentially conscious, conceptual gestalt comprised of self-perceptions and the values attached to those perceptions.

These values are derived from two distinct sources: their usefulness in actualizing the organism, and their utility in obtaining *conditional* positive regard from significant others. In the first instance, valuing is organismic; in the second, valuing is based on the desires and values of others.

In order to obtain a preliminary understanding of how pseudoassimilation takes place, it is useful to divide the process into a series of three phases: Conflict, Choice, and Incorporation. Note that these phases occur only in those situations where obtaining positive regard is an issue for the person. It is only when the individual feels that positive regard can be obtained at the expense of his or her feeling, valuing, and behaving that the process of pseudoassimilation becomes a possible route for the formation of self.

From Rogers' (1951, 1959) writings, we can infer that the Conflict phase entails an approach–approach conflict between the tendency to actualize the organism, on one hand, and a quest for positive regard, on the other. The motive to obtain positive regard from significant others is, according to Rogers (1959), the stronger of the two, especially for the infant. When both motives cannot be satisfied in any one situation, the person experiences a state of conflict.

But the conception of a simple approach–approach conflict holds only for the newborn. In the developing child and in the adult, an avoidance component emerges as an added feature. Over time and situations, persons learn to avoid not receiving positive regard because of the severity of the negative consequences. Those consequencs, whether intended by the significant other or not, involve a state of holistic, negative self-disapproval. The absence of positive regard can be, and often is, construed to mean generalized disapproval of self. Powerful conditioning is underway when the entire worth of the person can be linked to specific disapproval for specific actions. Rogers (1959) states that the infant, unable to differentiate well, is especially prone to misconstrue specific disapproval as generalized disapproval. Further, he proposes that the infant learns to view self as do others, liking or disliking self as a total configuration. The incessant need to obtain positive regard can be understood more fully if we stop and consider that not obtaining such regard plunges the person into a state of holistic, negative self-appraisal. Such an unpleasant state, once experienced, will typically be arduously avoided, even when emerging selfhood is at stake. The conflicted individual is caught in a terrible bind and the stakes are high.

In phase two of pseudoassimilation, the individual chooses which of the two routes to take. It seems clear that the infant, without benefit of clear symbolization, falls easy prey to opting for conditional positive regard. Once a child can symbolize the nature of the choice, however, he or she has more power of choice and degrees of freedom. If the nature of the choice can be clearly perceived, one can choose not to receive conditional positive regard. In so choosing, one must bear the brunt of experiencing the holistic, negative self-disapproval attendant upon making that choice. The extent of disapproval is a function of the prior conditioning of self-worth over time and over situations. Persons then return to utilizing the assimilation process to work through these negative feelings about self.

During the course of psychotherapy, clients grapple with such choices. In order to undo the conditioned, negative sense of self-worth attendant upon choosing to hold onto their own realities, they must suffer, and move through the "bad me" dynamic. In this dynamic, a powerful conditioner of human experience and action, persons must explore and experience the fullness of their perceptions that they are bad, unworthy, guilty, and undeserving persons. In many cases, the fear and the negativity of such deep convictions are difficult to bring into consciousness, much less directly experience. The less that self-worth has been conditioned in a holistic negative way, the easier it is for the person to make a choice in his or her own favor.

If the choice in phase two involves opting for the conditional positive regard, a person moves into the Incorporation phase of the pseudoassimilation process. During this phase, the falsified experiences become part of self-structure. Rogers (1951) explains the consequences of pseudoassimilation as follows: "Behavior is regarded as enhancing the self when no such value is apprehended through sensory or visceral reactions; behavior is regarded as opposed to the maintenance and enhancement of the self when there is no negative sensory or visceral reaction. It is here, it seems that the individual begins on a pathway which he later describes as 'I don't really know myself' [p. 501]." Unlike assimilation, the incorporation of experience involves the lodging of overgeneralized aspects of experience into self-structure. These global attributes—"I am an intelligent person"—are owned and positively valued by the person, dictating his or her behavior in many specific situations. In contrast, experience that is assimilated is typically situation-specific, "I behaved intelligently when I took the chemistry test." These global self-perceptions must be maintained in order to keep the person's self-worth intact. As a result, persons work quite hard to "prove" that these incorporated characteristics are part of self and describe self accurately.

Client-centered psychotherapy endeavors to dissolve the "false self" based on pseudoassimilation by creating an optimal set of interpersonal conditions that work toward undoing the results of the pseudoassimilation process. In his theory of the necessary conditions for psychotherapy,

Rogers (1959, p. 213) proposes that the therapist be congruent in the relationship, experience unconditional positive regard toward the client, and have an empathic understanding of the client's internal frame of reference. In essence, the therapy condition re-creates the necessary conditions for psychological growth. Undoing, or reversing the process of pseudoassimilation, can be viewed as involving a series of three phases: Differentiation, Choice, Redefinition of Self.

If the client can perceive the necessary therapist conditions, he or she can also begin to question the expectation that the therapist, as have other persons, is offering conditional positive regard. Simply put, clients can begin to relax and trust that the therapist is "in their corner." This means that the therapist is for them as persons, for their growth. Neither will the therapist disapprove of them as persons, nor will he or she reinforce the holistic negative regard that the person experiences about self. A discordant situation arises, because the client no longer finds a significant other who reinforces the conditions of worth. Instead, the therapist views the person as worthy, important, and interesting, regardless of the specific content of feelings and behavior. Once a client no longer has to be concerned about obtaining positive regard, he or she can turn to the concerns about self. Here the empathic understanding of the therapist serves at least two important functions. First, it helps the person clarify, hence differentiate and discriminate, present and prior experience. Second, the understanding promotes exploration and reevaluation of experience. It facilitates sharing and the rediscovery of self. The therapist's understanding contributes to the client's reappraisal of experience. "I don't feel so weird anymore, now that I know that you understand that" is not an uncommon comment.

The combination of prizing, empathy, and the psychological climate these produce then functions as a generalized fear reducer, enabling the client to feel safe. Persons can then take advantage of the inherent motivation to symbolize their experience accurately (Rogers, 1959). Clients can begin the long overdue deficiency-processing using the assimilation process. In deficiency-processing, the crucial differentiations involve separating the direct experiencing of self from the overgeneralized, incorporated aspects of self. Viewing an earlier preception of self, a client may remark, "but that's not really me. I don't really *want* to be doing that. I just did it to please my father. It was his trip, not mine." Once pseudoassimilated experience is adequately differentiated, choice can reoccur. Persons can again choose to follow the dictates of others or the values of self. In any case, they will no longer blindly follow the values of others. In successful therapy, clients tend to follow their own valuing, although part of that valuing will take into account the needs, interests, and values of other persons. In the third, and final phase, Redefinition, self is altered along the lines of what the person wants, consonant with the organismic valuing process.

As clients continue to differentiate and to reassimilate aspects of self, they also begin to experience a generalized dissolution of the conditions of worth, and to begin to feel unconditional positive self-regard. Once such an attitude toward self can be consistently experienced, the person will have no pseudoassimilated experience, and no need for the utilization of defense. As a result, the normal assimilation process can be used for the person's continuing identity formation. The process of undoing pseudoassimilation, and replacing it with assimilation, is difficult and typically lengthy. Both the difficulty and length are in part functions of the extent to which persons have relied on pseudoassimilation as the basic process for identity formation. The interested reader is referred to Perls (1947) for another discussion of pseudoassimilation.

A PROPOSAL FOR MEASURING THE PROCESS OF ASSIMILATION AND ITS PHASES

The basic strategy used to measure assimilation addresses itself to tracking each of the three phases of the process and to rating two dimensions of the psychological event being processed by the person. By so doing, we could examine both the situation and the response concurrently as well as independently. The actual proposal consists of the presentation of a tentative classification system for rating two important contributors to the "difficulty" of a particular psychological event: (a) the meaningfulness, and (b) the frequency of occurrence. These two dimensions of stimulation, drawn from activation theory (Fiske & Maddi, 1961), contribute additively to the total impact of any psychological event. Their measurement, along with the measurement of the three phases of the assimilation process, can, in principle, allow us to consider both the situation and the response. This differentiated measurement strategy, based upon Fiske's (1971) directives, can hopefully yield a system of increased complexity and fruitfulness. In the rest of the chapter, this tentative system will be presented along with suggestions for its use.

Classification of Self-Relevant Events

Earlier in the chapter, ideal assimilation was proposed to vary as a function of the intensity, meaningfulness, and variation of any one particular event in a person's life. The greater the physical intensity, the meaningfulness, and/or the variation, the greater the total impact of the event. Impact is here considered to be equivalent to "difficulty," and contributions to impact add to difficulty level. Hence, the greater the impact of an event, the harder the event is to process, assuming an ideally functioning assimilation process.

Why measure difficulty at all? In principle, we would like to be able to order the situations or events so that we can estimate the basis for individual differences in response strengths. Such ordering guards against the possibility that one client has processed "easy" experience, whereas another has processed "hard" experience, their equal levels of processing being a stimulus, and not a response, function. If we have no estimate of the difficulty level of the experience, we are working with the uncomfortable assumption that clients generally process at the same level of difficulty, an assumption that does not fit my experience as a therapist.

Difficulty can be indexed in at least two ways. First, difficulty is reflected in the amount of processing time, given an ideally functioning assimilation process. In other words, aside from defensive intervention, the amount of assimilation time would be expected to covary positively with the total impact of an event. Inasmuch as both meaningfulness and variation contribute to impact, the greater the meaningfulness and/or variation, the greater the amount of time spent processing the event. This hypothesis, drawn from activation theory (Fiske & Maddi, 1961), is clearly empirically testable. Difficulty can also be reflected by the frequency and/or amount of defense elicited by a particular experience. Here again, total impact of an event is proposed to covary positively with total amount of defensive intervention. This prediction is based on the assumption that defense in the general population reflects the general social consensus regarding a particular experience. In other words, those experiences that are negatively valued by the culture at large would be those same experiences that are reflected in the individual as conditions of worth. The more society at large "defends" against a particular experience, the more likely it is that individuals will have learned conditions of worth about that experience. The individual in need of processing experience has to contend with two separate difficulties. On one hand, the more impactful the experience, the harder it is to process. On the other hand, the more impact, the greater the likelihood that he or she has learned conditions that obstruct the successful and rapid processing of that event.

The present rating scheme is illustrated in Table 5.1. Here, one client, prior to entering therapy, has indicated the experiences in her life that are troubling her. These experiences would be classified as those in need of

Table 5.1.   Rating by One Client of the Subjective Meaningfulness and Frequency of Occurrence of Self-Relevant Events

Meaningfulness of Self-Relevant Event	Frequency of Occurrence		
	Continuing	Intermittent	Infrequent
High	Conflict over sex with spouse	Conflict about closeness with significant others	Rape
	Constant feelings of guilt	Uncomfortable interactions with others	Parental death
Moderate	"Having to" go to store each week	Conflicts with boss at work	Witnessing auto accident
	Getting up every morning to take dog out	Negotiating a money hassle with spouse	Getting lost in scary neighborhood
Low	Fear of driving, not driving	Uncomfortable encounters with co-worker	Mild insult by friend
	"Having to" iron	Talking over TV	Yearly checkup at doctor

"deficiency" processing, experiences that need to be worked through in the process of psychotherapy. After listing each of those experiences, she was asked to rate the relative levels of meaning or subjective importance for her, and to indicate the relative frequency of occurrence of those events. A 3 point scale was used for both meaningfulness and frequency of occurrence in this one case. Any rating scheme should not only consider the number of points on the scale that can be used to make profitable distinctions, but should also attend to specific operational definitions of the points on each of the scales. Prior to utilizing these dimensions in rating experience, it would be profitable to try out several different rating scales to determine their differential fruitfulness and reliability. More discussion about these two dimensions is available in Fiske and Maddi (1961).

In addition to obtaining the client perspective, it is also important to obtain the comparative perspective of the therapist on the rating of the meaningfulness dimension. Data from both client and therapist vantage points would certainly contribute to unraveling the almost mysterious independence of the two separate vantage points. One theoretical point that must be taken into account concerning these two perspectives is that clients cannot be considered accurate raters of the meaningfulness of their own experience. Organismic valuing, or the process that provides the information regarding the value of experience, is disrupted by the presence of conditions of worth in the self-structure. Hence, events can be distorted in their levels of importance by such defensive disruption. Persons in paranoid states often view extremely minor events as exceedingly important, thereby departing significantly from the norm of consensual validation. Similarly, one of the major payoffs of repression is its diminution of the importance of meaningful experience. Again, the contrast between the client's subjective estimate and the norm is marked. However, we can study both vantage points, analyze the divergent groups in detail, and learn more about the differing perspectives of client and therapist. The present measurement strategy allows for this type of comparative perspective.

Classification of Open and Defensive Responses

The general scheme for classifying open and defensive responses in each of the three phases of the assimilation process is presented abstractly in

Table 5.2. Necessary and Sufficient Conditions for Rating Openness and Defense in Each of the Three Phases of the Process of Assimilation

Phase	Rating Cues	Necessary and Sufficient Conditions for Openness	Sufficient Conditions for Defense
Attention–Recognition	Content	Cognitive approach	Cognitive avoidance
Reaction	Content Voice quality	Conjoint affective–cognitive approach	Absence of affective and/or cognitive approach
		Acceptance of self as locus of affect	Denial of self as locus of affect
		Acceptance of experiential responsibility for one's feelings and expressions	Denial of experiential sense of responsibility for one's feelings and expressions
Exploration	Content	As in Reaction phase	As in Reaction phase
	Voice quality	Stance of inner exploration	Absence of stance of inner exploration
		Exploration of inner experience, inner meanings	Absence of inner exploration, inner meanings
Closure	Content Voice quality	Experiential sense of finished experience	Absence of experiential sense of finished experience

Table 5.2. From examination of the table, it is readily apparent that the rating system is complex. As a result, raters should be thoroughly trained to a criterion of adequate reliability before actually rating. In addition, familiarity with client-centered psychotherapy process and/or sensitivity to both voice quality and content cues should be preliminary requirements for these raters.

For any one psychotherapy session, both client and therapist will note the frequency, the nature, the meaningfulness, and the frequency of occurrence of all events discussed during that session. Inasmuch as all sessions will be tape recorded, it is also possible to have the objective raters note these events. For any event, its progress in being assimilated is to be rated in each of the three phases.

Following the outline presented in Table 5.2, rating in the Attention–Recognition phase requires a judgment concerning the client's cognitive approach to that event. If the client verbalizes statements indicative of cognitive approach, the response is scored as open. On the other hand, if the event is cognitively avoided, the response is scored as defensive. To be classified as open, the approach behavior must be directed toward a central or important aspect of that event, as opposed to a trivial detail. Enter the problem of estimating the importance or centrality of parts of the experience. Keeping a detailed record of such judgments will allow us to define centrality more carefully. Once an event has been deemed self-relevant, a client may obtain a defensive rating because he or she turns to more important events. Again, it would be wise to make detailed notes concerning that sequence.

In the other two phases of assimilation, the rating cues are more complicated, and it is critical to track and rate each of the necessary conditions separately. In the Reaction phase, it is necessary to rate three separate aspects of the client's phenomenological state, an open rating on all three dimensions constituting the sufficient conditions for an overall rating of open. Defense is given as the overall rating if one or more of the necessary conditions for openness is not met.

In the Reaction phase, conjoint affective–cognitive approach is the first necessary condition for openness. Both content and voice quality cues must be utilized to ensure an accurate rating. The content cues typically involve the use of reaction (e.g., hit, bother) and/or affect words (e.g., hurt, angry). Voice quality cues communicate the sense of the immediacy versus the remoteness of the experiencing. It might well be helpful to cross-reference to a previously devised classification system, and to point out some of the similarities. In the classification system devised by Rice and Wagstaff (1967), open responses would be considered as either focused or emotional in voice quality. On their expressive stance dimension, an open response would be classified as a subjective reaction, not a static feeling description.

In the Reaction phase, the second necessary condition for an open response is the client's acceptance of him/herself as the locus of affect, given that affect is being experienced. A person must impart a sense of self as the experiencer of his or her experience. In rating this condition, the rater is alerted to the use of disowning projection. In this instance, the client would be accurately aware of the content or nature of a particular feeling, but would be denying it as a self-experience. Instead, the same feeling would be seen in others, but not in self. Such denial and projection might have to be repeated over situations before raters would have sufficient confidence in their judgments.

An experiential sense of acceptance of the responsibility for one's experience is the third criterion for openness in the Reaction phase. Again, the rating cues are found in both content and voice quality. Acceptance is indicated by any content statement suggesting acceptance and substantiated by behavior. The adoption of an inward searching stance is an important rating cue. It is almost as if the client asks "What am *I* doing to contribute to this situation?" In addition, voice quality cues communicate an inner, as opposed to outer, stance. In the Rice and Wagstaff (1967) voice-quality system, they would be considered focused. Content can reflect defense by showing either an explicit or implicit denial of responsibility. Any reaction that in effect blames the world or other persons for one's feelings constitutes a sufficient condition for rating that response as defensive.

In both the Reaction and the Exploration–Closure phases, all three conditions must be present for an open response. The absence of any one is considered a sufficient condition for defense. If the client moves beyond defensive responding, and so changes from defensive to open, credit is given for the openness, provided that the client does not return to defensive maneuvers during the Reaction phase.

For the purposes of rating, the Exploration–Closure phase has been broken into two parts. During the Exploration portion, an open response is indicated by a stance of inner exploration, a focus on inner experience, and participation in an exploration process. Again, both voice quality and content serve as rating cues. Focused voice quality (Rice & Wagstaff, 1967) and the emergence of differentiated, unusual, individualized inner meanings highlight the cues that are necessarily present to designate the response as open. During the exploration process, the client lets go of rational schemes for ordering his or her experience, and proceeds as if directed by an affective process, focusing on and reporting a changing gestalt of unified affective–cognitive experience. Often it seems as if the client is searching for the "right" meaning, the meaning that fits the particular flow of experiencing. Defense in the Exploration phase is indicated by the omission of any of the five criteria for openness, specifically including the absence of a stance of inner exploration and/or by the absence of the actual exploration process.

Closure, or the endpoint of the assimilation process, is indicated by both content and voice quality cues. Any content suggestive of the subjective sense of an emotionally finished experience is an important rating cue. Clients will often remark, "I don't know why, but I just feel better now. It feels gone." Typically, clients cannot construct a cause-and-effect explanation for the change, no matter how hard they try. In contrast, defense is indicated by the absence of a sense of a finished experience. The absence of closure is often shown by the client's awareness that something keeps nagging him or her.

As presented, the proposal for measurement is clearly in a tentative, preliminary stage. Its implementation should consider the reality that the context of psychotherapy, while, on one hand, highly appropriate for observing and tracking the process of assimilation, is, on the other hand, a seminaturalistic setting. Because stimuli in such a setting cannot be preselected to be construct-relevant, we are limited to using a simple frequency model, counting the frequency of open and defensive responses. For any one subscore, depending on how one wants to combine the two dimensions of "difficulty," the frequency of occurring behavior is the index. This frequency must be judged relative to a standard period of observation to obtain a base. Because it has been used effectively in other studies, 20 sessions of individual psychotherapy, each roughly consisting of 50 minutes, is suggested. Continuous audio or video taping would provide data collection, and would allow the preliminary classifications to be rechecked if need be.

For a pilot measurement project, clients should be preselected so that they represent a wide spectrum of initial level of openness to experience. One possible preselection procedure would be interviewer ratings at the time of intake, using a 5-point scale to rate globally openness versus defensiveness. A second would be the utilization of the measure of the Reaction phase of openness to experience (Pearson, 1969) since the construct validity of the measure has already been investigated. We are not trying to control for initial level. Preselection is important to guarantee adequate variation in the pilot population. For construct-validation purposes, however, it would be well to obtain an independent measure of openness.

It is also crucial to measure, but more preferable to control, the therapist characteristics that have been shown to affect the client's level of openness to experience, namely unconditional positive regard, empathy, and congruence (Rogers, 1967). By taking these therapist characteristics into account, we can not only estimate their effects on the dependent variables, openness and defensiveness, but we can also coordinate therapist conditions and the entire measurement scheme presented here. Ultimately, of course, we would like to be able to obtain a differentiated view of client–therapist transaction. If therapist characteristics are viewed along with client, we can make a first step in that direction.

Because of its exploratory nature, the initial implementation of this measurement project should attempt to gather as much data as possible. The raters who listen to all the therapy sessions would be expected to follow the course of all self-relevant events, both within and over sessions. In fact, it might be well if raters were assigned to follow specific clients throughout. Notes would be taken to refine and clarify the criteria for openness and defensiveness. If we can gather as much information as possible, we can fill in this preliminary scaffold with more clearly articulated definition, which, in turn, will lead to more reliable ratings.

Usefulness of System

Once the basic, difficult work of obtaining reliable ratings of the phases of assimilation and the concurrent task of obtaining ratings on the meaningfulness and frequency of occurrence of self-relevant events have been accomplished, the next step is to attempt construct-validation studies using the system. One major focus of these studies would be to determine the fruitfulness of the measurement itself. We would address ourselves to answering questions concerning the phases themselves. Are intercorrelations among the phases equivalent to 1.0, or are the conceptual distinctions fruitful? Do the meaningfulness and the frequency of occurrence aspects of stimulation behave as we would expect? Do they in fact positively covary with the difficulty of processing experience? Is it harder to process highly meaningful and infrequent events, or is it equally difficult to process highly meaningful and continuing events? Once some of the answers based on theoretical predictions can be tested, then we can have more confidence in our measures. Another important area of construct validation involves operating within the framework of Rogers' (1959) theory, and testing predictions involving both openness to experience and psychotherapy. Do clients progress further in their assimilation of experience if therapists can offer high levels of the necessary conditions? Does increasing assimilation go hand-in-hand with increasing organismic valuing? Once a context of validation can be established, then one can turn to using this system in other ways.

One important use would be to consider the system as a moment-to-moment tool. We can look at the type of therapist intervention in combination with a certain point in the assimilation process. If the type of defense utilized by the client is mainly in the Reaction phase and consists of disowning his or her experience, what is the most effective therapist intervention? Is confrontation effective? Is unconditional positive regard by itself enough to move the block? How are these techniques differentially effective? And are they differentially effective for a particular type of experience? Is confrontation more effective with highly meaningful, infrequent events than it is with moderately meaningful, intermittent events? Such questions can be addressed to this measurement scheme, once the initial validation has been accomplished.

A final use of the scheme is the potential for measuring the individual both prior to and after psychotherapy. Because we have attended to the issues needing deficiency-processing, we can track the client's progress on each of the issues, thereby obtaining a clearer and more definitive picture of what has changed during the course of therapy. For any particular client, we can spot trouble, and locate issues that don't move in therapy. Overall, of course, we would expect clients in successful therapy to decrease their need for deficiency-processing and to learn to keep their accounts current in their daily living.

REFERENCES

Fiske, D. W. *Measuring the concepts of personality.* Chicago: Aldine, 1971.

Fiske, D. W., & Maddi, S. R. (Eds.) *Functions of varied experience.* Homewood, Ill.: Dorsey, 1961.

Gendlin, E. T. *Experiencing and the creation of meaning.* New York: Free Press of Glencoe, 1962.

Pearson, P. H. A conceptual and methodological study of three Rogerian constructs. Unpublished doctoral dissertation, The University of Chicago, 1968.

Pearson, P. H. Openness to experience as related to organismic valuing. *Journal of Personality,* 1969, **37**, 481–496.

Pearson, P. H. A rational analysis of Rogers' concept of openness to experience. *Journal of Personality,* 1972, **40**, 349–365.

Perls, F. S. *Ego, hunger and aggression.* London: Allen & Unwin, 1947.

Rice, L. N., & Wagstaff, A. K. Client voice quality and expressive style as indexes of productive psychotherapy. *Journal of Consulting Psychology,* 1967, **31**, 557–563.

Rogers, C. R. *Client-centered therapy.* Boston: Houghton Mifflin, 1951.

Rogers, C. R. A theory of therapy, personality and interpersonal relationships, as developed in the client-centered framework. In S. Koch (Ed.), *Psychology: A study of a science*. Vol. 3. *Formulations of the person and the social context*. New York: McGraw-Hill, 1959.

Rogers, C. R. (Ed.) *The therapeutic relationship and its impact*. Madison: University of Wisconsin Press, 1967.

CHAPTER 6

The Iconic Mode in Psychotherapy[1]

John M. Butler

> *Since feeling has form*
> *Who pays attention to the syntax of things*
> *Will never really know you . . .*
>
> (Paraphrase)

It is more than 20 years since the writer (Butler, 1952b, 1953) expressed the opinion that one feature of the psychotherapeutic situation is an increase in total self-expressiveness and that differentiated complexity is the most distinguishing feature of the self-actualizing person. These views were based not so much upon theoretical considerations as upon participation in thousands of hours of psychotherapy. During the intervening years my convictions about the importance of expressiveness and of the attainment of differentiated complexity in psychotherapy have been strengthened; also some insight into the way in which differentiated complexity was related to self-actualization, motivation, and learning was attained (Butler & Rice, 1963).

But less progress was made solving the problem of clinically observed increase in expressiveness. The problem here was twofold. First, I could not arrive at an adequate understanding of the nature of feelings although my colleagues and I were discussing feelings all along. Second, the impact upon me of psychotherapeutic hours was primarily esthetic in nature. Good and peak therapeutic hours seemed to me to possess a type of beauty, and, to be honest, I felt that employing the entrancing esthetic

[1] I wish to express my appreciation to Dr. Alvin Mahrer and to the editors for helpful suggestions about the content and organization of this chapter.

appeal of expressiveness as a basis for understanding psychotherapy and personal change in psychotherapy smacked of selfish gratification. After all, clients live in a world, have much coping to do, and, it seemed, had problems to solve in which self-knowledge, almost in the sense of self-description, was of high importance. What was the utility of esthetic self-expression in coping with these realities—however obviously and stubbornly true it seemed to be that clients in Rogerian therapy dealt mainly with self-engendered feelings tending toward what might be called intrinsic self-expressiveness? However, with the publication of Langer's remarkable work on feeling (Langer, 1967) things began to fall into place with respect to the relation of feelings, motivation, and learning as they operate in psychotherapy, and with the relation of feelings to self-expressiveness. The discussion of feelings appearing here is based upon that of Langer.

Although it may not be obvious that an adequate view of the nature of feelings must be obtained before one can understand expressiveness, I am not going to make a case for my conclusion. Rather I am going to attempt to develop the theme implied by my view.

THE NATURE OF FEELING

The first thing to say about feelings is that we do not have feelings; what we tend to call feelings are not items or entities. Feelings are organized processes that have form, although not necessarily complete form. Having form, they may be regarded as items of experience; that is, the form of a feeling is an item of experience. Those organized processes we call feelings are neurophysical processes, but not all such processes are feelings. Feelings constitute a subset of the set of neurophysiological processes. It must be emphasized, however, that feelings do not constitute a special kind of neurophysiological process. Rather, feelings are aspects of ongoing neurophysiological processes. From psychological studies we know that a weak stimulus can generate a neurophysiological process that is not sensed, is not a feeling. But increasing the strength of the stimulus changes the state of affairs to the point where a feeling appears. Feelings appear just as a glow appears when metal becomes sufficiently hot. That is, feelings as organized neurophysiological processes are appearances (not mere appearances) and represent aspects of neurophysiological functioning that appear as that critical point, the threshold, is passed. They are the result of heightened neural activity and are phases of neural states, just as water, ice, and steam are phases of H_2O. A feeling, however, is not coterminous with the process of which it is an aspect. That is, a process in which feeling appears may begin and end in a state that is not the state of feeling.[2]

One advantage the view of feeling, as delineated above, has is that one is not required to believe, implicitly or explicitly, that feelings are mysterious products of neural processes, for they are not products at all; one is required only to view them as part and parcel of neural processes, having to do with intensity rather than with presence or absence. The vexing question, considered by a myriad of writers, of how neural impulses break through to the province of the mental becomes irrelevant. What does become relevant is the question of the conditions under which neural impulses come to the point at which feelings appear; that is, the point at which the mental or psychical appears. It turns out that trains of physical events change conditions to the point where we are in the province of the nonphysical or mental.

From psychophysics it is known that those feelings aroused by stimulation do not arise except when the stimulus (impingement) has a certain strength or energy level. Below that energy level, nerve impulses may be entrained via the stimulus, but feelings do not appear; above that level, feelings appear as an aspect of the occurrences of neural activity. As the stimulus becomes stronger and stronger new feelings appear. It seems, therefore, that the degree of excitation of nerves and neuronal assemblies has to do with the appearance of feeling.

The living organism, biological evidence has clearly shown, is an inherently active system. In particular, the nervous system is itself spontaneously active, as shown, for example, in the single pacemaker cell regulating the heartbeat in crabs. If the nervous system can function at those levels of excitation where feelings appear, independent of stimulation external to itself or to the organism, then the organism is a supplier of experience to itself; that is, feelings appear that are self-engendered.

There is reason to believe that the human organism functions so that self-engendered feelings appear (Butler & Rice, 1963). It would seem that such feelings appear, to the subject organism, or come to appear, to be different in origin than feelings originating in impingement, encounter, stimulation. Given this view of feelings, the objective is that which appears to originate from outside in impingement and encounter; the subjective is that which appears to be self-engendered or engendered from within. That is, the objective and the subjective are themselves feelings, not mere definitions. Note, however, that all feelings, as aspects or phases of neural

---

[2] Paradoxically, feeling processes have structure in the sense that, as is now well-established, nerve impulses are patterned and have a spatiotemporal organization (Bullock, 1961). Hence, feeling processes are structures in the sense that they partake of the organized neurophysiological processes of which they are aspects.

processes, are "subjective" in the usual sense of being private. They are appearances only to the organism in which they occur. They are also "objective" in the sense that they are aspects of ongoing biological processes. As such they are physical events capable of being observed as such (but not as feelings) in practice or in principle.

To clinicians, at least, to objectify feelings usually implies a defensive process in which a person attains psychological distance from an emotionally arousing painful process or event. This is *not* the usage employed here. To objectify a feeling is used here to denote the process by which all varieties of feelings are brought into being and moved from the province of the subjective to that of the objective and perceptible. In so doing, feelings are in a very real sense brought out into the world so that the form of feelings becomes actually perceptible. In a given instance the process of objectification may serve the function of defense, but defensiveness does not inhere in the process of objectification of feeling in the usage of this discussion.

THE COMMUNICATION OF FEELING

Feeling processes are mental events. Sensings, perceivings, imaginings, fantasyings, thinkings, plannings are feelings or trains of feelings. In particular, emotional feelings constitute just one subclass of feelings. There are many varieties of feelings and, of the great variety and number of human feelings, some are suited to discursive (logically organized) language and some are not. Those that are mainly have to do with coping with the world, with the milieu, the society, the group, and relationships; they have, in short, to do with impingement and encounter.

Mathematics and logic are most suitable for discursive language or discourse. At the opposite pole from mathematics and logic is the unsuitability of discursive thought and language for communicating much of that class of feelings that we designate as emotional. True, we have names for some emotional feelings but they are broad class names such as joy, fear, grief, anxiety. It seems that, in fact, discursive language is not only unsuited to communicating emotional feelings, but it cannot do so; emotional feelings cannot be communicated but can only be implied or conveyed by language.

Thus, we have what seems to be a paradox. As I said at the beginning of this paper psychotherapy is concerned with expressive behavior or self-expression. But, in accenting expressive behavior and self-expression, something revealing of the nature of the feelings of the client is being accented. Yet, we are saying that the expressive and mainly the linguistic behavior of the client is unsuited to the understanding of emotional and vital feeling. How then can emotional feeling be understood by the therapist when the client is using language to express feeling?

Part of the answer is obvious. Convention allows understanding. Clients, at times, communicate rather standard feeling names such as joy, guilt, fear, or anger. Yet, if a client says "I am angry" and stops there, the communication is quite enigmatic. However, one can sometimes seem (and seemingly successfully so) to use discursive language to communicate feeling. Supposedly, for example, empathic understanding involves understanding of feeling. But if knowledge of empathy were in liquid form, it would scarcely fill a thimble. True, we can "understand" feeling but how do we arrive at the understanding?

The answer is radical. Feelings are not actually communicated or understood at all. They are rendered or depicted. Feelings, to be understood, must be *objectified* so that they exemplify the shape or form of feelings with the result that the feelings can be clearly *perceived*. It is the exemplification or objectification of feeling that is of paramount importance in the understanding of another's feelings. Objectifying feeling is most often done via language and dramatic gesture; that is, through the use of logically arbitrary and conventional symbolizations, even though the language may not be being used conventionally and arbitrarily. The extent to which language is successful in objectifying feeling is dependent upon figurative language, dramatic gesture, voice quality, and word usage (all of which are quite transitory unless tape or video recorded).

OBJECTIFICATION OF FEELING

Therapists, when exposed to a client's poetic, metaphorical, figurative language and the component of dramatic gesture, tend to describe their clients as alive and describe such clients as "good" or as good prognosis clients. Oddly enough they are liable to perceive the form of the feeling of their client more fully than the client himself. But they are, after all, much more in the position of the involved spectator watching a painter engaged in the process of painting. More accurately perhaps, they are watching the painter paint and they continue to contemplate the painting when the artist has finished it.

I mean to be quite literal here. Poets and painters both objectify feeling but in different modes. Painters, however, may be representing something else and be intending to represent something else when they objectify their own feeling, but poets are most often focusing on representing or depicting feelings themselves and nothing else.

In taking the stance of empathically understanding client feelings, the therapist, when confronted with well-objectified feelings, experiences them as impingement or encounter. In perceiving these feelings accurately he is, of course, doing what anyone perceiving objects does; he subjectifies them. The objectified feelings of the client are transformed to become subjectified feelings of the therapist. If an aim of the therapist is to reflect the feelings of the client, his task is then to reobjectify the client's feelings. If he can do this well the tables are turned. The client is now in somewhat the same position as the therapist was when the client rendered and objectified feelings to be perceived by the therapist. Disentangled from the causal process of rendering and objectifying his own feelings, the client perceives and recognizes these feelings as rendered and objectified by the therapist; and experiences recognizable semblances of his own feelings in terms of impingement, impact, and encounter. Need it be said that consistently encountering a recognizable semblance of one's own feeling *out there in the world* is rather rare in human experience? It is in this quite deep sense that the reflection of feeling, a singularly misleading phrase, results, as Rogers said early on, in clarification, in coming to know oneself.

When this complex interactional process occurs many times, the client experiences encounter with himself or rather with actual objectified images of self that have the character not only of encounter but of information. He comes to a kind of self-knowledge, symbolic but not necessarily logically organized, akin in nature to the knowledge one obtains when he encounters good paintings, poetry, music. Indeed, the self-knowledge is almost necessarily *not* conceptualized in the discursive mode; that is, logically organized.

With respect to the therapist response, there is a further comment to be made. As renderings of client feelings, themselves derived from client rendering of his own feelings, therapist responses carry their own distinctive hallmark. The therapist has subjectified the objectified images of the client's feelings; that is, he has appropriated them and they have become his own. In the process of reobjectifying, the form of the therapist's own feelings is exhibited, for the very process of rendering involves an act of creation. Therefore, the client is also encountering his therapist, but this encounter with the therapist is, again, self-encounter as well. The therapist's imprint on the reobjectified feeling has, literally, vital importance. As, in the life and vitality of a painting, a painter's feelings are projected into whatever may be being represented, it is the embodiment of feeling that gives what is being rendered its sense of life and vitality. The client simultaneously perceives the living vitality of himself and his therapist.

Thus, there may be a double objectification of feeling in psychotherapy. The therapist may be reobjectifying client feeling and objectifying his own feeling simultaneously. Then the client has a dual encounter with self and other. This duality of encounter may be of decisive importance in psychotherapy, for in this duality the participants become both the knower and the known.

The word "image" as used so far refers to personal events, the subjective processes that have not yet been expressed and are embodied and moved from the province of the subjective to that of the objective. Hereafter, the expression "objectified image" will be taken as being synonymous with the word "icon." An icon is an object that is an idol or representation of something else. It has many of the properties of that which it represents (adapted from English & English, 1958).

The usage of the word "icon" is not restricted to a usage common in information-processing psychology in which "icon" refers to a representation of information from a visual modality. As an object that represents something else, an icon fulfills the definition of symbol.

In an overall sense it seems fair to say that therapy in which the kind of understanding based on the perception of objectified images of the participants' feelings plays a predominant role, is therapy in the *iconic mode*. In this iconic mode the client, in his encounter with his therapist, encounters his own feelings, feelings iconically realized via his therapist. It is in this iconic encounter, where the client meets objectively realized images of his own feelings, that he can be freed from the process of producing images of his own feelings and perceive or meet himself and thus gain self-knowledge. This avenue of self-knowledge exists by way of subjectification of iconic self-realization, and not by way of literal, discursive, propositional, analytical conceptualization.

CHARACTERISTICS OF ICONS

As was stated above an icon is something that represents something else and is thus a symbol, an abstraction. But what kind of a symbol or abstraction is a rendered image, an icon?

First, an icon represents a feeling, an appearance; the feeling it represents is unperceptible. Second, an icon may also represent a something, an object or event in the province of the objective that occasioned the feeling. Thus an icon cannot be viewed simply in terms of the resemblance between two or more somethings; it must be viewed in terms of a created resemblance. Third, an icon is not just a copy; it is not identical with what it represents, suggests, or resembles. Fourth, an icon is unique but does not uniquely resemble a particular something. Thus, if an icon represents a cat to someone, an endless number of other icons may also represent a cat. Similarly, if an iconic response represents a self-engendered feeling, many other iconic responses may represent the same feeling. Fifth, an icon is not an imitation; a perfect imitation would be a copy. This difference between an icon and any actual object is essential.

From the above characteristics it can be seen that an icon is a symbol and that many different icons may represent the same object. Because icons are symbols and involve both suggestive representation from the point of view of the process of creating them, and presentation from the standpoint of their creators, it would seem that this kind of abstraction is quite different from logical abstraction. Iconic abstraction probably is the minimum example of symbolizing. Also, there is not one set of existent rules, nor is there likely to be, governing icon formation. Iconic abstraction may be the primal, intellectual process whereby feeling is rendered with perceptible form and each and every icon is unique. Thus, iconic abstraction is just the creation of perceptible form and, as such, involves creation of enriched perceptual experience rather than the stripping down and impoverishment of experience, as in generalization.

IMPLICATIONS FOR PSYCHOTHERAPY

If in psychotherapy we are interested in client feelings and especially if we are interested in the form of client feelings, then we should reiconify client feelings to the end that the client perceives, but not necessarily logically understands, the form of his ongoing vital feeling processes. This task obviously becomes easier when the client creatively iconifies his own feelings. But often it is difficult for clients to iconify or, at least, to iconify well. When this is the case the therapist has problems. First, the client who cannot iconify his feelings well is difficult to perceive accurately. Second, the therapist then has the problem of facilitating the iconification of client feeling, one outcome of which is that he may more clearly perceive the client. One way to deal with the problem of improving client iconification of feeling is to stimulate clients directly by better iconifying their feelings than they themselves do. This is discussed later in this chapter. Another way would be to train clients toward more creative self-expression, that is, to train them to better iconify the images of their own feelings. This could no doubt be done. One relatively immediate effect of the improvement in the iconification of feelings by the client would be an *increase* in the responsiveness of the therapist; that is, the therapist can better iconify his own feelings, for he too will be stimulated by the expressive embodiment of feelings. Thus, in a very real sense the therapist can increase his own responsiveness by directly influencing the client to better iconify his own feelings or by training the client to do so.

The central task of a client-centered therapist is threefold. First, to encourage and facilitate the expressive embodiment of feeling; second, to encourage and facilitate the expression of well-rendered representations of client feelings (objectifications); third, to himself create well-rendered images of client feelings. I believe that prizings (or unconditional positive regard), congruence, genuineness, and the like are ancillary, although important, to the conduct of therapy.

RELATION TO ADIENT MOTIVATION

In addition to the direct self-knowledge possible through client encounter with the reiconification of his own feelings by the therapist, there is a motivational aspect inherent in the process of creating iconic representations of one's own feelings. This motivational aspect has centrally to do with experiential processes, both those originating in impingement or encounter and those that are self-engendered.

The motivational aspects of experiential processes, especially self-engendered experiential processes, have been discussed at some length (Butler & Rice, 1963) under the heading of adience. On the basis of evidence originating in experimental work in neurophysiology, sensory deprivation, and exploratory behavior, the conclusion was reached that there is a biological requirement for experience shared by animals and men alike. That this need for experience is such that extreme sensory deprivation results in anomalous neural and behavioral development is now well established (see Riesen, 1966). On the motivational side, it has been shown that animals, when deprived of stimulation (transactional experience), will both work to get it and acquire new responses in the process. And no less an authority than Riesen (1966), on reviewing the work on visual deprivation, has stated that there is ". . . a basic motivational component in stimulus-seeking behavior. Exploratory behavior appears to be no less physiologically motivated than other drives. . . . Since diffused light is insufficient for maintaining neural structures and functions in some individual cells of the visual systems, the drive for stimulus complexity can serve to maintain optimum neural metabolism in such cells . . . a special category of nonphysiological drive is no longer required in theoretical formulations [p. 141]." And Riesen also points out that the use of sensory neurons results in the development to larger size, more complex structure, and increased physiological reactivity. What Riesen is emphasizing is that patterned experience originating in impingement and transaction (stimulation) is necessary for optimal growth and development of the neural sensory systems; and that primates will work and acquire new responses in order to obtain it. It now can be said, with some assurance, that there is a fundamental requirement to have complex, new experience. This requirement is deeply rooted in the biological nature of organisms; and this requirement, when not met, results in developmental anomalies in the neural, perceptual and behavioral domains. It can also be said that this requirement, although not requiring a formulation in terms of drive, is amenable to the drive paradigm in the sense that new and complex experience can be shown to act as a reinforcing agent, and that new responses and trains of behavior can be acquired when complex, patterned experience (stimulation) is used to reinforce responses.

Stimulation undoubtedly serves to heighten the activity of the nervous system, and therefore, results in the phase of neural functioning that has been labeled as feeling. Animals are by the very constitution of their nervous systems limited largely to stimulation, exteroceptive and/or interoceptive, for new experience, and thus, are dependent upon their environment for the fulfillment of the vital need for new experience. When deprived of stimulation, they rather quickly show the effects of deprivation. With human beings, however, it is quite different; they can often withstand long periods of stimulus deprivation when able to create their own experience.

Human beings are so constituted that an almost endless variety of feelings arise out of the intrinsic action of the nervous system. It is plausible, if not certain, that the constant, everchanging flow or appearance of symbolic feelings can, as Rice and I (Butler & Rice, 1963) have indicated, have many of the same biological consequences as a train of transactional experiences (or stimuli), and satisfy needs for new experience.

Thus, the very occurrence of these processes that are called cognitive processes is inherently reinforcing or rewarding. Hence, that special form of cognitive experiencing that has been called encounter with icons of one's own feelings results in both self-knowledge and reward or reinforcement.

Those cognitive processes that are designated by the name of differentiation and elaboration are especially significant. In differentiating and elaborating feelings, either those that originate directly from stimulation or those that are self-engendered, a rewarding, reinforcing process is going on as well. The process of differentiating and elaborating feeling not only enlarges the phenomenal field or life space, but also is a reinforcing and rewarding process that fulfills a biological need and provides a double justification of usefulness if such is required. It is just in this process of elaboration and differentiation that the individual acquires autonomy. The creation of new cognitive structures, especially those created by way of elaboration and differentiation of self-engendered feelings, mediates between stimulus and response. This mediation alters the impact of the individual upon his environment; consequently the impact from the environment, especially the environment of others, can to a great extent originate with the individual himself.

This aspect of the theory of adience has been perceptively extended by Wexler (1971) under the headings of the constructive processing of experience and constructive productivity. He has found that a type of voice quality, previously found to be positively related to the outcomes of psychotherapy, was also related positively to differentiated cognitive processing (Wexler, 1974).

On the other hand, a type of voice quality negatively related to the outcome of therapy was also negatively related to constructive information processing. Furthermore, in a group of nonclinic subjects, both the type of voice quality that had positively related to therapy outcome and constructive information processing were positively related as well to an index of self-actualization. Contrariwise, the type of voice quality negatively associated with the outcome of therapy was negatively related to the index of self-actualization, and for those subjects with this type of voice quality, constructive processing of experience was low.

Voice quality, as a paralinguistic feature of oral communication, is iconic in nature. Thus, in the frame of reference here employed, Wexler found that voice quality, in revealing the form of feeling, also indexed the extent of and the manner in which subjects exhibited types of cognitive processes theorized to be self-actualizing in their nature and in their consequences. It is gratifying, therefore, to note that Wexler found voice quality and constructive productivity not only highly related each to the other, but also to an index of self-actualization.

In reiconifying the images objectified by clients, the therapist presents the client with a symbolic transformation of the client's own feeling. In the process of subjectifying this new icon of his feelings, the client not only experiences clarification but he is also having a new experience of what is familiar. This newness in familiarity is, in part at least, rooted in the client's disentanglement from the client's own process of himself objectifying the form of his feelings; this experience, even when painful, is, as is so evident from recordings, rewarding in nature and evocative in effect. The evocative effect of iconic representation is a heightening of experience, an increase in the amount of subjective feeling in which the client carries forward to a more inclusive completion in the form (or gestalt or theme) embodied in his earlier responses. This feature is so characteristic of Rogerian therapy conducted in the iconic mode that the therapeutic interview as a whole may have a quite decided thematic structure.

It is a curious fact that, when I have played back recordings of what I regard as peak Rogerian hours, conducted in large part in the iconic mode, the hours have seemed quite natural. The remarkable and evident esthetic impact of the client's responses has seemed to those listening to possess a kind of inevitability, and to have little or nothing to do with the therapist. The thematic development (or carrying forward) has seemed quite inevitable. Yet, when I have stopped the recording after a therapist's response, and said to those listening "Predict what the client will say next," I have gotten few takers and even fewer accurate predictions. What seems natural, inevitable, and right in retrospect is often largely unimaginable in prospect; this unpredictability in inevitability is characteristic of much of the structure of the best in art, poetry, and music. How does such thematic development occur?

In the therapeutic situation client and therapist are interacting expressively, not merely talking to each other. Clients present therapists with an endless array of expressive gestures, inflections, paces, rhythms, cadences, tensions, strains, continuities, discontinuities, and figurative expressions, which, to the therapist, refer to the forms of feeling that the external form, the "communication," embodies. Most often in our sobersided Anglo-Saxon civilization, in which literal discourse is valued and the poetic and dramatic are devalued, people embody their feelings in gestures and voice quality. And a great deal can be embodied via these avenues. Consider the following client response occurring in the second hour of therapy. The client has been talking about her plans and impulses, extending over a period of eight months, to commit suicide: "There's a whole lot of what I remember the whole thing—It was like a sudden panic—It's afraid of something but I don't know what—Just afraid and I won't face up to it whatever it is. I just won't." During this response her voice quality conveyed a complex blend of fear, refusal, helplessness, impossibility, and determination. She cannot and will not reveal or admit the source of her fear, and this is readily perceivable by listeners not trying to understand in terms of a model of personality or therapy.

In this response the client's language was not very expressive, but her voice quality was such that it evoked a flood of images in the therapist. It was thus easy for him to respond figuratively and metaphorically in the interest of evoking responses more directly revealing of the form of these feelings.

BLOCKS TO RENDERING OF FEELINGS

It should not be supposed that the evocative effect of iconifying feelings, with consequent development of the form of one's feelings to a more vivid and well-defined form or gestalt is always or even often a smooth process. Many people have developed a generalized fear of thematically developing their feelings and of objectifying their feelings (self-disclosure). The very process of so doing has become a cue for anxiety. The remedy for the anxiety so engendered is to in some way interrupt the process of thematic development, to return to the familiar territory of the repeated and the well-worn. This can be accomplished by explaining away, by self-devaluation, by distancing and talking about (intellectualizing), by projecting against norms, criteria, ideals, and so on.

Although anxiety and interruptive processes work against development of the form of client feelings, adient motivation is working in favor of it, for the generation of new experience by way of one's own responses and also the therapist's is inherently reinforcing (or rewarding). The situation is reminiscent of that in approach–avoidance conflict in which rewards and punishments are contiguous in time and place. An illustrative excerpt follows from the same client quoted above. The client vividly renders her feelings all right, but from time to time she interrupts her own process of generating new experience by attributing it to mere imagination, to mental sickness, to perverted feelings, and the like. At the same time, however, she also reveals a certain satisfaction or pleasure in expressing herself. By the time the excerpt ends she says excitedly in a tone expressing discovery "Maybe I'm so bored I gotta invent things to have feelings about. . . . Maybe that's it I bet you." Also by the time the excerpt ends there is vivid development and depiction of some of her feelings. This is particularly true of the relation between boredom (diminished experience) and the generation of new experience through fantasy and hallucination.

Client (C)   Yeh, that's what I experience. Fear. It's just a panic. Like you would run out of this building if it were burning— only just the opposite, like you'd feel compelled to run into it.

Therapist (T)   Because you're so afraid, huh?

C   Well because you had to remove yourself—you had—must not be around, and it felt like after I couldn't, I didn't have phenobarbitol so I figured I could hit an artery you know, and I got a stiff hand which will get better. I was lucky you know, but things, I mean like that are upsetting to me.

T   I didn't quite get that about your hand.

C Well, I thought, I could, had studied the book, and I could get an artery, and I didn't. But it's frightening. It makes me feel kind of vicious [voice is becoming flat and monotonous] and it cost a lot of money, and it's aggravating now. I'm lucky because if I use my hand enough, I'll get back the full use of it, but I don't know—to be crippled. [Here the client has interrupted the development of her feelings just after expressing fright and upset.]

. . . .

C Yeh—You know something, I haven't mentioned. After that I'd walk around; then I'd touch the door, and I'd imagine that there was blood on the door, you know. I can imagine that's how it was like with William Heirens [a murderer] after he cut her up. I thought: gee it must be the same feeling.

T That's what you were like, like he'd been huh?

C Yeh—I hear he's always near someone else's person.

T Pretty horrifying huh?

C Maybe it's the word. It's like a hallucination or what do you call it— just imagination. I was thinking how they describe like how vampires die with a stake in their heart, and I used to feel like that—wasn't even thinking about a vampire; it came to me later—of how I must be feeling like a vampire—but later on I felt I had something sticking down through the middle of me—and it was just imagination. [in horror-stricken tone of voice]

T This imagination of you was kind of horrifying, huh?

C That's right.

T And you are afraid that underneath there's really something horrifying about you.

C Yeh—I feel kinda like, you know, like one of those horror movies, but different than the other kind of feelings like the Tennessee Williams. The other one is just like the insane doctor—cut him up in the cellar bit—like that.

T Kind of like you're cruel and bloodthirsty huh? [Tone of voice conveys client's expression of relish in the preceding response]

C I like that—What's wrong with having some kind of pervert—I'm kind of perverted—right? Yeh . . . [Client interrupts process by characterizing herself as perverted.]

. . . .

T It's good to feel strong in some way or another.

C Um Hum [with emphasis]. Like this morning I fixed up my garden, you know, and I had to get all the dirt out of the grass clumps. So I got tired and sat down to do it, you know. And all of a sudden I had this funny feeling, you know, just imagination. But it was like after the atomic bomb thing, and I felt like a kid you know, sitting on the dirt. Only the dirt seemed to me like bodies see. You know, arms, and legs on the earth all blown apart. [weeping] And like uh, life if I was a kid I wouldn't know it was anything gruesome you know. Just pick one up and use it for a toy or something, and I felt like that. It was imagination, but there was nothing to be left to wonder about. It was just like it was just happening, and I felt that way. [Tone of voice is removed and distant.]

T You were in it? Lonesome.

C Yes, and sad and lost. Where'd they all go? [wonderingly and pathetically]—I just—

T Where did they all go, there's only these parts, huh?

C Yeh—I didn't know there was anything bad about them you know. Just played with them. It was lonesome to pick 'em up. Never did that kind of thing happen to me. I didn't feel like it did. Why would I have been, you know, growing up in this country, but nothing like that was in this country—

T How could I have felt such things then?

C Just imagination that's all.

T I think so, but you're afraid it's not imagination; you're afraid that you've really been there, or lived some other life. You know something that you don't know.

C Yes I do. I always did, a lot. But that's some kind of mental sickness.

T I gather it's part of your fear.

C There's a whole bunch of that other stuff, and [in a rising voice] I think I'm making it all up. I wasn't there. [Here and in the last two responses the client is interrupting the development of her own feelings.]

T You're not making up the feelings though.

C No, it's real. All kinds of stuff like that.

T But where did they come from?

C [taking the therapist literally] The earth. It's afraid—bad things—oh bad things—[weeping] Oh I don't know what it's all about because I—It don't have anything to do with me. How?—I don't get it.

T I see, it's not you.

C Well, I mean not me like this life I lived.

T It's not got to do with *your* life at all.

C   Yeh—But I don't even remember anything like that. Except just one Russian story of this way.

T   Yes—The Red Laugh, huh? [in tone of recognition]

C   Yeh. I can't remember the story.

T   It really frightens you. There's something in you you just don't know about huh?

C   What?

T   Is that it?

C   Yes.

T   *It* takes hold of you.

C   Yeh. You know my family comes from Russia. All the family but I never talked about it. The Red Laugh?

T   That's the story you were talking about wasn't it?

C   Yeh—I read that quite awhile ago. I don't remember it now.

T   I think you remember it alright.

C   [with much emphasis and a certain hostility] No!

T   I don't mean that—I mean what happened in the garden.

C   Did that happen in the garden? I don't remember.

T   Something like that.

C   You mean I read a story, and it made such a vivid impression on me that all of a sudden I'm playing it out in my mind?

T   That could be.

C   Maybe I am so bored I gotta invent things to have feelings about.

C   Could that be? [excitedly]

T   That could be.

C   Cause—

T   You really suspect that huh?

C   Could that be? (excitedly)

T   Yeh that could be.

C   Maybe that's it. I bet you. [excitedly]

T   That's one way to live huh? Create some feelings.

In the preceding excerpt the client is iconifying her feelings quite well, better than the therapist is iconifying them. In the following excerpt from the same interview the first therapist response is a quite good iconification of client feeling. The client responds by carrying forward with the development of feeling, but almost immediately interrupts the process with an introjected value. It is quite likely that the heightening of feeling stimulated by the therapist response is also a cue for anxiety.

C I don't see why I should feel that way though. You know what I was
thinking yesterday? I was thinking and thinking and if I'm not happy
with my husband, why in the world did I go back to him? And if I
ever came back to him and I'm not happy, why can't I figure out to
leave him. And I am figured out to—you know how I feel about him.
When I feel better toward him all of a sudden (but I don't understand
that) I feel like I don't have to feel so guilty that I didn't love him. I
feel like I've cared about him. But maybe it's good—maybe some
people you can care about only so much and other people you can
care about more. And I know that I can care about somebody much
more than I care about him. Or else maybe I'm kidding myself. I
don't know.

T But that's the way you feel. Like—somehow he—[grunts with effort,
then with a cadenced rhythm and a highly inflected voice] you can't
care for him with all the caring you've got in you.

C [Excitedly] That's it! And that's what I want to do. You know—as
much as I can. And I want to have somebody care about me, as much
as they can.

T Give yourself and be given to.

C [with emphasis] That's right. That's exactly what I want. Really I
don't know if I can get it—then I'll probably get so I want to live,
[with a falling voice]—and yet that's not meeting up with things.

. . . .

C I mean that's being spoiled isn't it? If I can't have it just the way I
want it, it won't do.

T I suppose that's being spoiled but I'm not so sure that's what you're
saying [C: Well] That's kind of the way you sum it up isn't it? [C:
Well I gotta think. Like—] Maybe that means I'm spoiled, insisting,
not having everything.

C Yes, yeh—What if we'd been married 10 years (nine with the year
added) what if—I feel so obligated to him then that if I leave him
again, I'll feel so guilty about it that I won't let myself be happy; so I
better stay with him. That's feeling trapped, and I don't like it.

T Kind of feel trapped by the guilt you would have.

. . . .

C Thank you. I think what happened Saturday we went to the arena
and—my husband and me, and it worked out okay. Fairly okay. I expressed what I felt like and I started explaining things, and he was
saying things out of panic and I could realize it and not get carried
away and arguing about it—pointless things. And I could say to him:

Well all right, what's he really got? What's he really trying to say you know and get down to it and after it was all over we had to go downtown to go shopping and all of a sudden I sensed that I didn't have to figure it out in words what I sensed was that those certain feelings I used with him—There was a whole bunch of other feelings left out that were deeper, in back and these feelings were the ones I was thinking about Joe—that's his name. It's the same thing you know really the way a person is you want really to live with what's the deepest in you and I—[pause]

T   That he can't fill you—that he can't take up the thoughts in the back of your mind.

C   [excitedly] That's it. Oh—That's it exactly it—yeh—We talk a little bit, and he's lost and that's it. Does that mean that I'm brighter than he is or just that I think differently than he does?

These excerpts, scattered over much of the range of a therapeutic hour, show how the thematic development of feelings is interrupted by norms, criteria, and ideals, each of which implies self-devaluations: in this case of being unrealistic and inauthentic. This kind of interruption of feeling processes can be discussed from many points of view, but from the writer's point of view, these stereotyped self-interruptions, stated in a stereotyped, by-the-way manner, function most significantly to limit the range of experience. For this client, there are several effects. First, as she says herself, she is in conflict, caught between anxiety and ennui. Second, she lives to a large extent in a world of fantasy. Third, she experiences her fantasy world as more real (vivid, alive) than anything else. Fourth, she has begun to feel a loss of identity and to feel that she has lived some life and had some experience that she doesn't know about; this leads her to the conclusion that she is out of control and is crazy, a fearsome thought for her. The very prospect of fully developing her feelings about her husband, of fully experiencing herself, is a cue for anxiety and for a self-devaluing interruption of the development of her experiential processes. But her need to experience rises; she feels bored, and resorts, as she says, to "making dramatics" because she is so bored and frustrated. Thus to come to closure has become an aversive process and whole areas of experience have become out of bounds. She is afraid to develop her feelings fully, and self interruptions reduce her anxiety.

BOREDOM VERSUS ANXIETY: THE EXISTENTIAL DILEMMA

The self-limitations upon experience, upon freely developing one's feelings, lead to frustrating, painful ennui, with the alternative being anxiety and self-devaluation. Yet clients often choose anxiety in order, as they so often indicate, to have an alternative to the suffering and meaninglessness of diminished experience.

Thus, much of what both therapists and their clients construe as psychopathology constitutes an actual existential dilemma. The client's own learned fears of experiencing, especially of self-engendered creative experiencing and conduct based thereon, lead to frustrating, emotionally arousing interruptions of developing the form of his own feeling processes. The consequences are triple in nature: the client lacks experience; he suffers from the lack of positive reinforcement that comes from not fulfilling his need for experience; and he cannot or does not iconify his feelings or does not do so well. Thus, his deficits have to do with the amount of experience; the satisfaction of completing the form of his own feeling processes; and the reduction of actual encounter with icons of his own feelings. The total outcome is that the kind of self-knowledge available through iconification of his feelings is either unavailable or drastically reduced.

Completion of the incipient form of one's feeling processes is constitutive of the experiencing process. Indeed, it would seem that the experiencing process is the primitive version of what has been called the drive for meaningfulness, for only wholes are meaningful.

Human beings have the doubtful privilege of reversing a natural order by way of self-induced interruptions of their own feeling processes in order to avoid or reduce anxiety. Mandler and Watson (1966) have shown that the interruption of organized behavioral sequences leads to anxiety, but when the process of experiencing has itself become a cue for anxiety, it is by interrupting the process, by not experiencing the development of one's own feelings, that anxiety is avoided. This is accomplished at the price of frustration of motive and under the penalty of remaining relatively undifferentiated and unelaborated with consequent boredom and inanition. That is, the person lacks a basic satisfaction, and has a less than optimal basis for transcending himself in his own situations.

EXISTENTIAL PRESENCE: FACILITATING DIRECT
SELF-COMPREHENSION

Implicit in the foregoing discussion is the notion that in iconifying feeling a person is literally becoming existentially present in the world; that is, he is coming into the province of the objective for both self and others. And especially when a person is iconifying self-engendered feelings, he is actually bringing something new into the world; something truly original is coming into the province of the objective of self and others that is literally perceivable by self and others.

An aura of mystery sometimes seems to surround iconification of self-engendered feelings because such icons present what was not previously in the province of the objective both for self and others. They seem emergent or presentational rather than representational in character, especially to others. But to self, they tend to seem representational rather than presentational.

When self's iconifications of feeling are subjectified by another and then reiconified, self has more of an opportunity to self-comprehend because he has now had two opportunities to encounter himself as existentially present in the area of his own objective. The first opportunity came when self created the icon; the second, when the other reiconified the feeling. But the second opportunity occurs under different conditions than the first. The first occurs when the person is in the process of creating; the second, when self is perceiving the other creating a reiconification of self's icons. Thus, self is no longer engaged and focused upon presenting self. Rather he is encountering self when he is set to perceive what the other is engaged in. Thus it is that the reiconification of feeling is more likely to result in self-comprehension, the creation of further self-experiencing, and developing further the incipient form of his own feelings. As Gendlin (1968), would put it, the person is more likely to stay on his own experiential track. Thus it is also that a person does not further explore himself, what he does do is further express himself, presenting further iconifications of his own feelings with the result that his own tendency to divert himself, to interrupt the train of his own experiencing, is less likely to come into play. In following the experiential track of a client by reiconifying feeling, a therapist helps the client do something that the earlier illustrations show is difficult for many clients to do; namely, stay on their experiential tracks or further develop the forms of their own feelings for this is just what they are afraid to do. Developing the forms of their own feelings is just the process that has become anxiety evoking.

Of course when a client encounters a reiconification of his own feeling he is also encountering his therapist for his therapist has encountered him, has subjectified the iconification of the client's feelings, and has, through the process of reiconifying, created a recognizable semblance of client feelings that the client does indeed recognize as a semblance of his own feelings. That is why in the dual encounter of self and other in the reiconified feeling the client recognizes self and experiences being understood by his therapist. But he also perceives the feelings that have been evoked in the therapist by encounter with the icons of the client's own feelings. Thus the client comprehends his therapist as well as himself when the therapist has reiconified his feelings. It would seem therefore that the therapist is known in a very real sense as a person right from the start when he accurately reiconifies the client's feelings, and that the therapist is in the nature of the case self-disclosing when reiconifying the feelings of the client; just as a client is self-disclosing when being himself existentially present.

Usually neither the client nor the therapist comes to as full direct comprehension of the therapist as of the client in psychotherapy because the therapeutic enterprise is usually explicitly directed toward enhancing the self-comprehension of the client. Thus the therapist may become known or directly comprehended by the client in bits and pieces because the therapist is more engaged in reiconifying client feelings and furthering the development of the form of client feelings than either the client or the therapist is in developing further the form of therapist feelings. However, there seems to be no reason why developing the form of the feelings of both participants could not be accomplished were the participants to aim at mutual development of the form of feelings, each of the other.

When a client knows a therapist through the reiconification of his own feelings by the therapist, he is known in the here-and-now of the therapist; he is confronted by the therapist in terms of the present responsiveness of the therapist to him; this is, to say the least, unusual. For most of us are used to being known in terms of the reactiveness of others. That is, most of us are used to being reacted to in terms of the past of others, in terms of reminding others of this and that, of calling into being revivals of the experience of others that have little to do with us. And this roundabout fashion of getting to know the other is so usual that we feel we do not know the other when we do not know him via his past. Furthermore, direct knowledge of others via their existential presence through the iconic presentation of feelings is not usually construed as knowing. Only logical conceptualization in which a person is "figured out" with his past entering into the logical conceptualization is construed as constituting knowledge of the other.

Iconifications, however, are presentational or representational abstractions not following our rules for logically organized conceptualization. And in encounter with the unique iconic representations of feelings, with all of its vivid impact, perception becomes a form of direct knowledge and comprehension that requires no analysis, because, for icons, meaning and perception are one.

Being an abstractly organized symbol, an icon is preconceptual in the sense that it appears before the conceptualization of self and of experience. It seems likely that not only does iconification of feeling precede conceptualization but that it is the ground for conceptualization. More important, it is probably the ground for one's sense of identity; without iconification of feeling the sense of identity cannot become stable for it is by way of iconification of feeling that one becomes existentially present. It is only then that a person can encounter himself in the world and come to comprehend himself directly as he directly comprehends anyone or anything else in the province of his objective.

Below are some illustrative excerpts from the eighth interview of a client in which the therapist endeavored to be more expressive in each and every response than was the client in the preceding response; that is, he attempted to iconify client feeling better than the client himself did. In so doing, it was thought, the result would be that the client would to some extent have his needs for new experience satisfied by the therapist; would come to satisfy his own need for experience; and would become more self-expressive. In other words, the client would, it was hoped, better iconify his own feelings and further develop the form of his own feelings. He would arrive thus at a fuller and more direct comprehension of self through the dual encounter of himself with himself by way of self and therapist iconification of his own feelings. The eighth hour was the only hour in which the therapist endeavored to be more expressive than his client for it was desired to compare hours later than the eighth hour with the eighth and earlier therapy hours.

The client chosen for this "therapeutic experiment" was thought to be a poor prognosis client and to be quite disturbed. During therapy hours he sat without moving, his face expressionless, and stared straight ahead with the middle finger of each hand placed carefully on the crease in his trousers over the knee. His voice quality and style of expression were of a type found (Butler, Rice, & Wagstaff, 1962; Rice & Wagstaff, 1967) to characterize poor-prognosis clients in client-centered therapy. His expressive stance was one of objective analysis. He talked about his experiences, seeming to recount them and not generate experience for himself in the process. Indeed, experience seemed to happen to him rather than to be an activity he was engaged in.

In striving to be somewhat more expressive than his client, the therapist strove to inflect his voice somewhat more than did the client, and also to employ somewhat more in the way of dramatic or expressive gesture. It was considered that the use of a more figurative language represented a higher level of expressiveness than just an inflected voice because such language is usually already accompanied by increased inflection and increased use of dramatic or expressive gesture.

The client began the eighth hour with the same rather listless style of communication characterizing the earlier hours, seeming at times to have difficulty in expressing himself at all. The client slowly began to inflect his voice more, and to employ figures of speech voiced by his therapist.

By the end of the first third of the eighth hour the client, seeming to find the figures of speech (icons) voiced by the therapist pleasing, voiced figures of speech of his own. As the hour progressed, the client's language became more inflected, and more vivid, expressive, and figurative. He also began to employ expressive gestures. In contrast with the dull, lifeless client of the first seven interviews, the client, by the end of the eighth hour, seemed like a different person. His highly expressive language, dynamic and alive, gave the impression of a person who is interested and interesting; also, the client exhibited pleasure in his own figures of speech. Finally, the whole hour seemed to progress smoothly and to have a decidedly thematic structure.

From the eighth hour on, the therapy (and the client) seemed to be different. The inexpressiveness of the first seven interviews was no longer present; in the later hours of therapy the client was decidedly more self-expressive. This self-expressiveness seemed to be self-generated. Indeed, the client seemed to be stimulating experience in the therapist as much as creating it for himself. This self-creation of icons and self-stimulation continued until therapy was terminated.

The excerpts from the eighth interview, quoted below, although not explicitly showing expressive gestures and changes in voice inflection, do explicitly show the development of more icons during the hour. The actual recording leaves the impression that the therapist was initially the more expressive member of the dyad.

T5   What do you do *now* after saying that?

C6   Yes. This leaves me where I stopped the other day.

T6   *What* does *that mean really*? [with emphasis on each word italicized]

C7   What does it mean to, to do something.

T7   What does it *really mean* for me to be *participating*.

C8   Yeah. A, a phrase that Tillich used this morning. I heard him for the first time. Participate in history. In my own little history, participate in it. What does it mean to participate in it. Um, where this—where this left me the last time was when I stopped, was two phrases that popped up into my mind. Does he like me and will he help me. And I guess, no, and I guess this thought came into my mind that maybe this is some sort of insecurity that I ask these questions means that I'm not ready to take something—that I'm not ready to act on faith. To love or hate, either one. On faith. [Note that his inner experience seems to be happening to him; he does not appear to be creating the phrases]

T8   You can't *overcome fear* just by *saying it*, huh?

C9   Yeah. Just by saying; by saying—what?

T9   It's time for me to *participate*.

C10   Yes. No. No. No.

T10   What you're saying—basically I can't *participate*. I can't overcome my own fears. Are you saying I should?

C11   Right. I—I—I guess it's something you've got to experience, begin to have an experience, to begin to build upon, and . . . The next thought that came into my mind was—was, I was thinking that things might go faster here—here, if there are, if I would build, try something. A relationship with somebody outside, maybe. This would sort of, this idea came to me as I was reading this case last night. It said something in there about a woman who was married, a couple of children. More motivation perhaps. Something to test what she was doing in therapy against something out there. A relationship, uh, I'm not sure. My God it's not the same. [Again thoughts seem to come to his mind and client is speaking slowly and with seeming effort.]

T11   That's what a tryout is.

C12   It gets back to the same thing. You just can't, I can't just say I should participate.

T12   If I could *try out* and *really* do it, it probably would be . . .

C13   Yeah, yeah, I think so.

T13   I'm not so sure I *can*.

C14   Yeah, as I look back over it I've tried a lot of times. And I took a beating. Yet, I never really gave too much to it.

. . .   .

C49   He—I was talking about asking about you to myself. But he—way out there. [makes pushing gesture with hands and arms]

T49   Um hum.

C50   Does he like me?

T50   Do those objects way out there like me, huh? [leans back and then leans forward making pushing gesture with hands and body]

C51   Yeah.

T51   Uh, pushed away even your question, huh? [pushing gesture with hand]

C52   Yeah. Um—in therapy, talking just you and I here, way out there. [extends right arm]

T52   I'm way out here and you're way back there, huh? [repeats above gesture]

C53   Yeah.

T53   You know, there's a distance for you even while you're trying to lessen the distance.

C54   I know. Talking to you rather than with you, the way I talk. Uh.

T54   How come these things that I can listen to ———I can regard.

C55   Yeah. With the girls too. Most things in life.

T55   It's really *grained deep.* [with emphasis]

C56   I think so. But I know damn well it's bad though.

T56   I gather that you experience it like a fog, almost. That uh—

C57   Yeah.

T57   . . . it's hard to push.

C58   Yeah.

T58   . . . through—it closes in around you. [makes enclosing gesture with arms]

C59   Just a few minutes ago, just a few minutes ago I just stopped there for awhile. I don't think it's *it*—this is what we're talking about—I don't think it's *it*—I think it's [Voice becomes much louder in last sentence]

T59   *Me,* huh?

C60   Yeah.

T60   Um hum.

C61   [laugh] This is what we. . . talk. . .

T61   It surrounds you because you're carrying it with you, huh? [enclosing gesture with arms]

C62   Right. Exactly. Yeah, I carried it everywhere—still. You know. My own smoke screen.

T62   Um hum.

C63   Mobile smoke screen.—Refrigeration unit.

T63   Um hum. You're hidden or you're frozen wherever you go.

C64   I freeze others, yeah.

T64   Um hum. I see.

C65   I was thinking the image came to my mind of a comic strip freeze gun. Freeze you! Freeze you! [uses hand like gun]

T65   Um hum. Freeze you, freeze you . . . out of your smoke screen, but you're lost. Huh?

C66   Yeah, yeah. Trying other's attempts, attempts at relating to me but freezing them. Uh. I kill myself, my own emotions. Uh. It's like a mirror. [makes gesture of shooting himself]

T66   It works pretty well, huh?

C67   Right. But the point is that it's not an "it" fog out there. It's something *I* do, I think. [taps chest with finger on "I do"]

T67   On the other hand, you experience it as an "it." [cups hands close together, as though clasped around small, hard object]

C68   Very often, yeah. [pause]

T68   The only thing is—I'm *doing*. It's not just there.

C96   Um. Um. Spreading it. I'm . . . I'm throwing it out. [throwing gesture with hand)

T69   Um. Hum. The net effect for you is you have no experience.

C70   Yeah.

T70   Or impoverished experience.

C71   Yeah. Like the Nautilus running along under the ice for a long time and popping up here and there. Once in awhile—experiencing.

T71   Right back down under, huh? [diving gesture with hand]

C72   But again that's the wrong analogy because that makes it "it."

T72   Um hum.

C73   Cause I—throw it—

T73   That really removes—even that way of putting it really removes your experience from you, which is—you're withdrawing from experience. [shrinks backward in chair]

C74   Yeah, yeah. Which isn't quite right. I'm really pushing experience away from me. Freezing everyone from me. Making my own icebergs rather than the icebergs *being made* with holes in them. [laugh]

T74   Your figure of speech pleases you.

C75   [laugh] The, the, the figure of speech pleases me.

T75   Yeah.

C76   It pleases me because—why?—recognition of an old friend? Or enemy? Awareness?

T76   It may be friend and enemy.

. . . .

C80   I have no suicidal tendency as far as I know. Although I'm pretty self-destructive in some ways. But, uh, oh I don't know, it's suicidal in a way—I mean—limited—cold [laugh] cold warfare, [laugh]

T80   Mm hm. Suicide of absolute zero.

C81   Yeah, yeah, I guess way down below zero isn't it 200 and some degrees down?

T81   No motion.

C82   Uh. No motion. I don't, I feel like kicking off right now and it, I'd sort of like to sort of enjoy myself right now—that's where no motion—it preserves monsters [shouting] through the ages out in California and . . .

T82   *Stay* as you *are.*

C83   Yeah, stay as you are. It's fine for that.

T83   And there's something appealing about that, huh?

C84   Uh—no longer. It must be or I wouldn't know it—I mean

T84   Without its sense of attractiveness—I mean, no longer attractive.

C85   No longer attractive. Right. [pause] My dislikes, my hates—I don't like my studies right now. I—I met a very honest guy this afternoon for about an hour—my advisor, Mr. H. I can't pull any punches on him. But he's my—that's why I'm wondering what I'm going to—always taking that risk. Again I'm talking to you rather than with you. That means that words are running away from what I want to say. [Voice becomes louder with last sentence.]

. . . .

C92   It's a good hiding place also from—not only from risks and, and sinking toward zero, but, but from relating to anyone too, somehow. Maybe not so much but it is in a way.

T92   I see. And at the university you kind of exist in a . . .

C93   Yeah. You can stay . . .

T93   . . . without being in it.

C94   You can stay in your room and study. [cough] Excuse me and have trivial conversations—trivial because you make them trivial in a way, uh, that is, I don't give my—I'm not active in them. Um—I'm beginning to recognize this—but—it takes time—it keeps your mind busy, but without getting your heart into it too much.

T94   It's a good place to stay where you are . . .

C95   Yeah.

T95   When you start to sink you can come out of your room and pull yourself up a few notches and . . .

C96   Yeah. Talk to somebody and go back again, yeah. Yeah, yeah, yeah.

T96   I see. It's a good place to keep your head above water, but just your head.

C97   [laugh] Yeah, yeah, . . . yeah, yeah. [laugh] Yeah, you've got it. [laugh]. You're high up as a cloud and that makes a pretty long neck. [laugh] [attitude is playful]

T97   Um hum.

C98   But uh, uh—from, from, from water to the clouds is a pretty long neck, but uh, you have demands on your long neck since the distance is so great that uh it's, it's nothing more above water. [pause] [playful attitude in first sentence] And yet the rest of the body keeps squirming around [laugh]. In spite of itself it's going to live. In spite of the head it's going to live. [laugh] Sit at the desk and try to study and think of this girl and then that girl or you walk the floor or you beat the wall once or twice, turn on the jazz music and dance a little bit, cuss yourself out in the mirror or, uh, take off downstairs for an ice-cream cone or a bottle of milk and so on.

T98   You really want to be out of water—all of you, huh?

C99   Yeah.

T99   And part of you is *fighting* to be all the way out.

C100   Yeah. In spite of my head. And the "oughts"—the "ought to's."

T100   Um hum.

C101   [laugh]

T101   In a way you didn't really feel like that before, huh?

C102   Very—

T102   You're fighting too.

Curiously enough even though the client was consciously pleased by his figures of speech, his comment after the hour was over was: "I feel as though we really shared something today." In other words the creation of icons was not a primary goal during the hour. The client wanted, it seemed, closeness in relationship, and so experienced the hour.

Wexler (1970) did an empirical study assessing the expressive output of client and therapist excerpted immediately above. He found that the level of client expressiveness was greater in interviews subsequent to interview eight than it was in interviews before interview eight. The therapist expressiveness was higher in interview eight than in interviews earlier than and subsequent to the eighth interview. The level of difference between the two parts of a therapist–client dyad (T–C) was greater in interview eight than in interviews subsequent to and earlier than interview eight. Therapist expressiveness was greater than client expressiveness up to and through much of interview eight; client expressiveness was greater than therapist expressiveness after interview eight. There were differences in client expressiveness between the first and last halves of the eighth interview but not between the first and last halves of the seventh, ninth, and twentieth interviews. When (in interview eight) a therapist response was more expressive than the immediately preceding client response, the succeeding client response was more expressive than the preceding client response; otherwise it was not.

Wexler concluded, on the basis of his findings, that the effect of the therapist intervention in the eighth hour was to increase the expressive level of client response in the eighth hour and in subsequent hours of therapy. He also concluded that after the eighth hour the client became a self-stimulator; a source of new experience to himself (and to his therapist). He suggested that his results supported the hypothesis of Butler and Rice (1963) that low prognosis clients who are relatively inexpressive and cannot generate positively reinforcing new experience for themselves may crucially need the intervention of therapists who are able to be stimulating to them; that is, to be stylistically independent of their client's mode of self-expression and to be able to be more expressive than their clients.

SUMMARY

Feeling processes are integral aspects of neural processes that appear when a sufficiently high level of neural excitation has been reached. The province of the objective is constituted by feelings that appear to result from impact or encounter, and the province of the subjective has to do with those feelings that appear to originate from within and to go outward into expression. Feelings, whether appearing to be self-originated (in the province of the subjective) or to be arising from impact (the province of the objective) are often not amenable to understanding by way of discursive communication. Such feelings must be rendered or depicted. This is especially true of self-originated feelings. Such renderings are objectified images (icons) directly perceived by self and other, and are not "understood" in the usual sense.

Icons, as representations of feelings of self, are symbols, and encounter of self with icons of self's feelings lead, almost by definition, to a kind of self-knowledge. Such encounter with the iconified representations of one's own feelings is an actual encounter of self with self's own subjectivity, the subjectivity being, however, objectified and *out there in the world*, perceivable by self and others. Thus a person can be said to be in a self-encounter when he perceives an icon of his own feelings whether or not the icon is created (or expressed) by self or other.

With respect to psychotherapy, self-encounter with iconic representations of the client's own feelings may be an important avenue of self-comprehension for a client. Self-encounter with iconic representation of his own feelings is peculiarly characteristic of Rogerian psychotherapy although it is not necessarily limited to any one approach to psychotherapy.

When a person iconifies his feelings, especially his self-engendered feelings, he can be said to be existentially present in the world with his iconification of feelings being in the province of the objective for both self and others. Then something truly new has come into being, and both self and others can encounter self because self is existentially present. The process of therapy for a client can be conceived as deeply involving the iconification of self and the subjectification of both self and therapist. The subjectification of both client and therapist by the client occurs when the client subjectifies the reiconification of client feelings by the therapist. Thus it is that direct comprehension of self is facilitated.

Client creation of icons of his own feelings can be facilitated by a therapist who reiconifies client feelings as well or better than the client iconifies them. Such a reinconification tends to decrease the interruptions to development of the form of client feelings that occur because such a development is typically anxiety-evoking.

The creation of iconic representation of client feelings, either by the client or the therapist (or both) consitutes a self-supply of stimulation, which is in the province of both the subjective and the objective, and thus meets the biological need for new experience demonstrated by psychological research during the last 20 years. Because icons are symbols that have features of the feelings that they represent, the creation of icons of client feelings not only satisfies the need for experience, but also involves the elaboration and differentiation of cognitive processes that the writer and others regard as being central to the operation of the tendency of the organism toward self-realization and self-actualization.

Self-actualization has usually been thought of or discussed in abstract terms, but with understanding of the process of iconification of feelings, it should be clear that in speaking of iconification of feeling, we are speaking of concrete events that happen in the world. These concrete events literally constitute the realization of self in the world. When realization of the self in the world is based on the self-generation of experience, when the person becomes a self-supplier of experience in a mode leading to self-knowing; when he can dually encounter self and other in the embodiment of his own experience via self and other; he becomes part of that universal process of becoming conscious so nobly described by Whitehead (1929).

REFERENCES

Appelbaum, S. A. Speaking with the second voice: Evocativeness. *Bulletin Menninger Clinic*, 1966, **14**, 462–477.

Berlyne, D. *Conflict, arousal, and curiosity.* New York: McGraw-Hill, 1960.

Bullock, T. H. The origins of patterned nervous discharge. *Behavior*, 1961, **17**, 48–59.

Butler, J. M. The interaction of client and therapist. *Journal of Abnormal and Social Psychology*, 1952, **47**, 366–378. (a)

Butler, J. M. A psychological consideration of freedom. Unpublished lecture, University of Chicago, 1952. (b)

Butler, J. M. The goals of counseling. Paper read at the meeting of the Missouri Guidance & Personnel Association, 1953. In *Counseling Center Discussion Papers*, **2**(20). Chicago: The University of Chicago Library, 1956.

Butler, J. M. Client-centered counseling and psychotherapy. In D. Brower & L. Abt (Eds.), *Progress in clinical psychology.* Vol. 3. New York: Grune & Stratton, 1958.

Butler, J.M. Client-centered counseling. *International encyclopedia of the social sciences.* Vol. 10. New York: Macmillan, 1968.

Butler, J. M., & Rice, L. N. Adience, self-actualization and drive theory. In J. M. Wepman & R. W. Heine (Eds.), *Concepts of personality.* Chicago: Aldine, 1963.

Butler, J. M., Rice, L. N., & Wagstaff, A. K. On the naturalistic definition of variables: An analogue of clinical analysis. In H. Strupp & L. Luborsky (Eds.), *Research in psychotherapy.* Vol. 2. Washington, D.C.: American Psychological Association, 1962.

Butler, J. M., Rice, L. N., & Wagstaff, A. K. *Quantitative naturalistic research.* Englewood Cliffs, N.J.: Prentice-Hall, 1963.

Cassirer, E. *Language and myth.* New York: Harper, 1948.

Duncan, S., Rice, L. N., & Butler, J. M. Therapists' paralanguage in peak and poor psychotherapy hours. *Journal of Abnormal Psychology*, 1968, **73**, 566–570.

English, H. B., & English, A. C. *A comprehensive dictionary of psychological and psychoanalytic terms.* London: Longmans, Green, 1958.

Fine, H. J., Pollio, H. R., & Simpkinson, C. H. Figurative language, metaphor, and psychotherapy. *Psychotherapy: Theory, Research, and Practice*, 1973, **10**, 87–91.

Fiske, D. W., & Maddi, S. R. (Eds.). *Functions of varied experience.* Homewood, Ill.: Dorsey, 1961.

Gendlin, E. T. The experiential response. In E. F. Hammer (Ed.), *Use of interpretation in treatment.* New York: Grune & Stratton, 1968.

Gendlin, E. T. Focusing. *Psychotherapy: Theory, Research, and Practice*, 1969, **6**, 4–15.

Goody, W. On the nature of pain. *Brain*, 1957, **80**, 118–131.

Kiesler, D. J. *The process of psychotherapy: A review of research.* Chicago: Aldine, 1973.

Langer, S. *Mind: An essay on human feeling.* Baltimore: Johns Hopkins, 1967.

Lenrow, P. Uses of metaphor in facilitating constructive behavior change. *Psychotherapy: Theory, Research, and Practice,* 1966, **3**, 145–148.

Mandler, G., & Watson, D. L. Anxiety and the interruption of behavior. In C. Spielberger (Ed.), *Anxiety and behavior.* New York: Academic Press, 1966.

Maslow, A. H. Higher and lower needs. *Journal of Psychology,* 1948, **25,** 433–436.

Maslow, A. H. The expressive component of behavior. *Psychological Review,* 1949, **56,** 260–272.

Maslow, A. H. Self-actualizing people: A study of psychological health. In W. Wolff (Ed.), *Personality symposium.* No. 1. New York: Grune & Stratton, 1950.

Maslow, A. H. *Toward a psychology of being.* New York: Van Nostrand, 1962.

Reik, T. *Listening with the third ear.* New York: Farrar, Straus, 1948.

Rice, L. N. Therapist's style of participation and case outcome. *Journal of Consulting Psychology,* 1965, **29,** 155–160.

Rice, L. N., & Wagstaff, A. K. Client voice quality and expressive styles as indexes of productive psychotherapy. *Journal of Consulting Psychology,* 1967, **31,** 557–563.

Riesen, A. H. Stimulation as a requirement for growth and function in behavioral development. In D. W. Fiske & S. R. Maddi (Eds.), *Functions of varied experience.* Homewood, Ill.: Dorsey, 1961.

Riesen, A. H. Sensory deprivation. In E. Stellar & J. M. Sprague (Eds.), *Progress in physiological psychology.* Vol. 1. New York: Academic Press, 1966.

Rogers, C. R. *On becoming a person.* Boston: Houghton Mifflin, 1961.

Rogers, C. R. Actualizing tendency in relation to "motives" and to consciousness. In M. R. Jones (Ed.), *Nebraska symposium on motivation.* Lincoln: University of Nebraska Press, 1963.

Schafer, R. Generative empathy in the treatment situation. *Psychoanalytic Quarterly,* 1959, **28,** 342–373.

Vognsen, J. A. Need for new experience, client vocal style, and psychotherapy. Unpublished doctoral dissertation, University of Chicago, 1969.

Wagstaff, A. K. Successive set analysis of verbal styles in psychotherapy. Unpublished doctoral dissertation, University of Chicago, 1959.

Wexler, D. A. Therapist stimulation of client expressiveness. Unpublished minor research, University of Chicago, 1970.

Wexler, D. A. Style and meaning in emotional experience: An exploratory study on the nature of self-actualization. Unpublished doctoral dissertation, University of Chicago, 1971.

Wexler, D. A. Expressiveness as a variable in therapeutice process and a scale for its measurement. Unpublished manuscript, Rutgers University, 1972.

Wexler, D. A. Self-actualization and cognitive processes. *Journal of Consulting and Clinical Psychology*, 1974, **42**, 47–53.

White, R. W. Motivation reconsidered: The concept of competence. *Psychological Review*, 1959, **66**, 297–333.

Whitehead, A. N. *The function of reason.* Boston: Beacon, 1929.

Part III

PRACTICE

The practice of client-centered therapy, as each of the authors in the following chapters describes it, seems to be moving further and further away from a strictly "school" approach, and toward the use of a variety of different techniques with different clients and at different times with the same client. This, of course, is a trend that has characterized a number of therapy orientations in recent years (cf. Hart, 1970; Lazarus, 1971). The striking aspect of the ideas presented here, however, is that this move away from orientational orthodoxy does *not* seem to be leading in the direction of becoming atheoretical. The theoretical formulations are simply taking a different form. The trend is not toward dealing in whole orientations, but toward the *specification* of different kinds of therapist operations, and identifying the kinds of client styles or process units with which these therapist operations would be particularly facilitative. There is a tendency to turn to theoretical formulations based on empirical investigations in psychotherapy and other areas of psychology in an attempt to understand the mechanisms whereby certain kinds of client and therapist participation lead to reorganization. These writers are trying to answer such questions as: What are the active ingredients in therapy? What kinds of therapist interventions make sense for which clients at which times?

But this leads us to a basic paradox. On the one hand, the attempt to pin down the kinds of questions mentioned above suggests an almost mechanistic approach to therapy. There is a suggestion that, ideally, the therapist should know the appropriate strategy to use at any given moment and should direct the client accordingly. How can we reconcile such a trend with the kind of relationship that has always been at the core of client-centered therapy? We have always felt that the essence of therapy is a relationship in which the client can count on certain consistencies on the part of the therapist. It is a relationship where the client can feel increasingly sure that he will be consistently prized, cared about without the imposition of conditions. He comes to realize that the therapist is not focusing on his defenses and how to penetrate them, but is intent on trying to experience his world as he experiences it. In recent years the client-centered therapist has felt increasingly free to share his own inner world with the client in a relationship that is spontaneous and human, but the emphasis is on the therapist's sharing a part of himself, not on making a judgment about the client.

Is this combination of using a variety of different therapist operations precisely and knowledgeably within the matrix of a client-centered relationship indeed too paradoxical to be reconciled? Each of the chapters included in this section has taken a different approach to the resolution of this seeming paradox; yet there is considerable common ground to their solutions. There are at least three characteristics common to all these proposals, commonalities that promise to characterize client-centered therapy as it continues to change and develop.

The first of these common aspects is particularly well stated by Gendlin in Chapter 7. He points out that the client-centered reflective response that attempts to stay constantly in touch with what the client is experiencing is the basic fabric of client-centered therapy. It is the point from which all other kinds of responses take off, and to which they should return, if the "inward process of change" is to be facilitated and not impeded. The client is asked to check all the therapist's responses against his own "concretely sensed experience" and it is this experiencing that serves as a touchstone both for the accuracy of the content of the therapist's responses, and for evaluating the fruitfulness of a particular kind of therapist process. "[It] should be the baseline, the single precondition on which the use of all other kinds of responding should be built." (See p. 216.) It is this that makes the client feel not alone and not manipulated. Thus, the fabric of the client-centered relationship is maintained, although there may be many different attempts to maximize ingredients that promise to be particularly facilitating for any given person at a particular point in time.

The second common aspect is related to the first, but warrants separate emphasis. The client and therapist are seen as engaged in a joint process of exploration and reorganization. To some extent the two have differentiated roles (although Noel and De Chenne contend in Chapter 8 that this need not be the case), but they share the responsibility for the kind of process generated. Early writings on client-centered practice emphasized the value of some preliminary structuring on the part of the therapist concerning the form the therapy would take. Later this precept was largely abandoned, with the rationale that the best way of conveying the ground rules of the process was by having the client experience it. It was even felt that structuring might interfere with the development of the relationship. To some extent there seems to have been another reversal, though with a difference. In the older kind of structuring the therapist told the client what he himself would and would not be doing in the hour. The idea now is that the therapy situation should be understandable as a *process*. This process is made up of different modes of participation that give promise of taking the participants where they want to go. It is not something that only works if one participant knows what is going on and the other doesn't, but a process in which the choice of modes is implicitly or explicitly shared by both participants. Thus Noel and De Chenne quite explicitly explain to their clients the process they call *cycling*. Rice (Chapter 10) asks the client at certain points to participate actively in the process of "unfolding reaction points." Cochrane and Holloway advocate in Chapter 9 suggesting to the client from time to time that he participate in Gestalt "experiments," and show that this fits in with and enriches the less-active client-centered position. And as Gendlin points out in Chapter 7, the client is the therapist's best consultant on the question of whether or not the things he is doing at any given moment are facilitative at that point. It is this quality of two colleagues engaging in a variety of tasks that are acceptable and understandable to both that is crucial.

The third common aspect is that the theories of therapy are theories of process and not theories of personal contents. Client-centered therapy has always been committed to the demystification of psychotherapy. Yet it has always been true and clearly continues to be the case that it is the process and not the client that we seek to demystify. It is about the process that hypotheses are formed and generalizations are made, not about the personality dynamics of the client or the things that he ought to explore. Each client must be free to move in whatever idiosyncratic direction he needs to go. Thus, there can be a technology of process together with a fluidity and spontaneity about what is explored and what is changed. This is evident in the kinds of research undertaken, in the kind of therapy done, and perhaps most evident of all in the way training and supervision are carried on.

Those of us who have responsibility for training and supervising therapists, counselors, and other facilitators in settings that are not primarily client-centered discover that our approach to supervision (or consultation, as most of us prefer to call it) is very different from that of most of our colleagues. Although frequently puzzling to our colleagues, it is taken for granted by people who have been intensively trained in client-centered methods. And yet this approach has never been made explicit in client-centered writings, and has led to several misconceptions. Therefore it seems appropriate to digress a bit here and elaborate on consultation methods.

The things that guide the therapist in decision-making about what to do and when to do it are not formulations concerning the personality dynamics or focal conflicts of the client, the kinds of things that were referred to above as personal contents. The therapist is not guided by a hypothesis that the client needs to work on his relationship with his father, or that he has a conflict about the expression of hostility. What the therapist does use as guides are the stylistic and structural aspects of the client's participation in the therapy process. Thus we teach those we are training to listen to the voice quality, the use of language, the quality of the experiencing process at any given moment, as guides to what is important to the client, to the things that must be heard and responded to. This is what determines the focus of the therapist's response. Similarly, when the therapist's responses do not seem to be getting through to the client in a productive way, we do not ask questions about areas against which the client may be defending. We encourage the therapist to ask himself another kind of question: What is it about my responses that seems to make them unusable for this client? What is it about the client's process that is making it difficult for me to listen and to shape responses that are truly facilitative?

The therapist makes many moment-by-moment process judgments, but he also needs to learn to make longer-range strategy decisions, at least for a particular point in the client's development. When a client is taking a consistently external stance toward his own experience, evident in voice quality, manner of expression, and the like, the therapist has a number of different courses open to him. He can suggest to the client some other mode of participation, such as *focusing* (Gendlin, Chapter 7), or the use of a dialogue using two chairs (Cochrane and Holloway, Chapter 9). Or he can intervene in the client's recounting of events outside himself, and bring to life some fragment of the client's reactions, thus putting the client vividly back into his own experience (Rice, Chapter 10). Or he can share his dilemma with the client in a nonjudgmental fashion and discuss alternatives (Noel and De Chenne, Chapter 8). Or he may do all these things. And of course it is equally important for the therapist to be able to recognize when a client has changed in his process level, so that he will not himself get stuck in an earlier mode of relating when the client is clearly beginning to process his experience more richly and complexly.

This use of process guidelines rather than guidelines based on personal contents is often misunderstood in two ways. The statement is often made that client-centered therapy does not concern itself with personality theory. It does, of course, but it is a theory that concerns itself with the ways in which perceiving, construing, remembering, reconstruing, and the like take place. It is partly for this reason that so many of the writers in the current volume seem to be recognizing the potential importance of cognitive theory as an appropriate base for client-centered personality theory. Thus as Wexler (1974) suggests, the way in which an individual characteristically engages in the differentiation and integration of meaning in the ongoing processing of information has decisive and enduring consequences for his abilities, attitudes, behaviors, or whatever else one considers to be the dimensions of personality.

The second misconception that arises is that client-centered therapy, because of its stress on moment-by-moment listening, is essentially direc- tionless, that there are no guidelines for the directions in which change could and should take place. That there are such guidelines, stated in terms of processes, is evident in many of the chapters in the present volume, especially perhaps in the papers by Anderson, Wexler, Zimring, Pearson, and Beck.

Now, having pointed out some of the common ground, it seems appro- priate to give a brief preview of some of the specific ways in which each paper has handled the seeming paradox involved in maintaining a client- centered relationship while using a variety of techniques with judgment and precision. Gendlin reformulates the client-centered response in experi- ential terms, and maintains that this is a way of being that can characterize the therapy of any orientation, as well as the most potentially powerful ingredient in client-centered therapy. The seemingly paradoxical combina- tion of the emphasis on the spontaneous human relationship with an in- creased precision of therapist-responding is especially visible in this chapter. The way in which Gendlin combines the two should be particu- larly helpful for anyone engaged in training therapists.

Noel and De Chenne contend that staying in the client's internal frame of reference is one-sided, not only as a therapy process but as a way of relating to other people in the world, and they advocate engaging in two other kinds of processes. The therapist explains all three modes to the client, and then works out with him a way of *cycling* among the three. Thus dealing with the therapist's frame of reference and dealing with the relationship itself are made legitimate and explicit parts of the total process.

Cochrane and Holloway contend that a combination of client-centered and Gestalt methods would yield a more complete and productive process than either can offer alone, because the strengths of each can compensate for the weaknesses of the other. For instance, one of their suggestions is that the intensive listening characteristic of the client-centered orientation can profitably be supplemented by the "activist skills" of the Gestalt therapist. Thus the therapist suggests "experiments" at times when the client seems to be engaged in a shallow process of "talking feelings." However, they also emphasize the idea that such a merger is possible only because the two orientations share basic philosophical agreements about the nature of man, such as the conviction that each individual must live by his own subjective truths. Thus, we have a richer, more flexible array of strategies together with an emphasis on the client's following his own unique directions.

Rice suggests that there are for each client certain crucial classes of situations in which maladaptive, unsatisfying reactions take place over and over again. These classes are idiosyncratic to each client, but the presence of such reaction points can be recognized by certain process markers. At such points the use of *evocative responding* can lead to a reexperiencing and reprocessing of crucial internal and external data. Rice asserts that this is a very different operation from an interpretation, which supplies to the client a new construction within which to organize the new data. The evocative response does not attempt to supply the construction, but is a method for letting the client into his own experience, so that he can reprocess it and form his own more adequate construction.

Although each has focused on different aspects and operations, there is one attitude that pervades every chapter. Each conveys the clear conviction that the therapy process is essentially understandable and specifiable. Furthermore, this is important, not just as a springboard for research. It is important to be able to make the process understandable to therapists in training, to people in the community who want to be more facilitative, and to our clients, who can then function as our colleagues in the therapy task.

REFERENCES

Hart, J. T. The development of client-centered therapy. In J. T. Hart & T. M. Tomlinson (Eds.), *New directors in client-centered therapy.* Boston: Houghton Mifflin, 1970.

Lazarus, A. A. *Behavior therapy and beyond.* New York: McGraw-Hill, 1971.

Wexler, D. A. Self-actualization and cognitive processes. *Journal of Consulting and Clinical Psychology,* 1974, **42**, 47–53.

CHAPTER 7

Client-Centered and Experiential Psychotherapy

Eugene T. Gendlin

In this chapter I will first discuss client-centered, and then experiential psychotherapy. Both, in different ways, have special roles, and are not just methods among others.

In discussing client-centered therapy, I will first add some new developments, making it much more specific. I will then ask just what, if anything, our field still has to learn from client-centered therapy. I will argue that despite its great familiarity, despite the fact that most therapists think they have "reflection of feeling" as part of their repertory, the essence of client-centered therapy has not been learned and absorbed. Most therapists, even the latest, still miss this vital essence.

The experiential method, discussed later in this chapter, is a way of using many of the different therapeutic approaches. It is a method of methods. It enables me to show just how client-centered therapy ought to be a part of every therapist's way of working. It is a systematic way of using various vocabularies, theories, and procedures, among them client-centered therapy. When I have offered some details of its theory and practice, it will then become clear how my rendition of client-centered therapy (in the first section of this chapter) is really a reformulation of it in experiential terms. As so reformulated, it ought to be a part of every therapist's way of working.

Currently the difference between different therapeutic orientations has lessened very much. They used to be separated by great gulfs. Each group of therapists worked and thought quite isolatedly from others with different views. Each group held that only what it did was therapeutic and well-founded, and that what others did was destructive, or at best useless, and founded on no scientific or theoretical basis. Currently the differences between therapeutic orientations are far less sharp. Many therapists define their orientation hyphenatedly, for example, "psychoanalytic–experiential" or "client-centered–existential." It is widely said that the person of the therapist is a more important factor than his official orientation. More exactly, how the therapist lives personally toward the client is more important and *much more specific* than anything the methods cover. It matters more *how* something is done, than just what general procedure is used. Many therapists borrow each other's procedures freely, fortunately more concerned with what works, than with what fits preconceptions.

The experiential method, of which I will say more in the second part of this chapter, has played a special role in making the different orientations more related to each other. The experiential method is not just another body of concepts and procedures. Rather, it is *a certain way of using* any and all of the older methods. Therefore, the older orientations are now cut across by a new division between those who practice experientially whatever orientation they come from, and those who do not as yet practice their older orientation in the experiential way. At least for those who do, the distinctions between the older methods become less important, even though one continues to think and talk in the words of one's old vocabulary. Therapists who practice experientially understand each other, even though some talk psychoanalytically, and some existentially, some in Jungian, and some in Sullivanian terms.

The basic principle of the experiential method is that whatever is said and done must be checked against the concretely felt experiencing of the person. There are no words or sentences, speculations and inferences, which are in themselves correct. Rather, do they make touch with the person's directly felt concrete body sense of what is being worked on—or do they fail to make touch with it? If they do touch it, this might be because there is some directly felt power to the words; they result in the person feeling a sharpened sense of what was being worked on, or there might be a release and a new step emerging. In some way the words are more than words, they also engender some directly experienced effect. If not, then these words are not the right ones for now, however interesting and generally true they might be.

In the second section of this chapter, I will have more to say about the experiential method and theory. It should be clear here, however, that this method undercuts the differences between various vocabularies and procedures—any of them might be tried and have experiential effect, or in a given instance they might fail at achieving such an effect. The experiential psychotherapist could use them all at times, and would use none of them as absolute but always keep the directly felt experiencing of the patient as absolute.

My discussion of client-centered therapy, here, will be from the experiential perspective.

CLIENT-CENTERED THERAPY: A CURRENT VIEW

In today's much less sectarian climate, what significance is there still in client-centered therapy?

Many people think that client-centered therapy has made its contribution, and has been absorbed. Hardly anyone practices only client-centered therapy, purely. Most therapists know and use other techniques that are helpful as well. The richly varied field of Gestalt, transactional, existential, and reevaluation techniques tends to appeal to the same nonpsychoanalytic, nonorthodox therapists whom client-centered therapy first freed from the near-priestly cult of psychoanalysis. It was client-centered therapy (and Sullivan) who first broke the dominance not only of psychoanalysis, but also of the pseudomedical idea that a therapist practices techniques, and that it is these that get someone well. Rogers (1961) emphasized the therapist as a genuine person, rather than techniques. But all this is now well-known, and held widely. Is there still something to learn from client-centered therapy?

Other contributions of client-centered therapy too, have been absorbed. To mention a few: research with unashamed tape recording of ongoing therapy is no longer exclusive to client-centered therapy, as it used to be. Similarly, most therapists today accept emphasis on the present, and reject the total focus on the past that characterized psychoanalysis. The emphasis on feeling, and the rejection of pure intellectualizing, which client-centered therapy began, is widely shared today. Similarly, the client-centered idea that the therapist's feelings toward the client are not necessarily an unreal "countertransference" is now widespread. Real relating is widely attempted. The face-to-face way of doing therapy, rather than the infantilizing couch, is used today by all but orthodox psychoanalysts. I recall a textbook of the 1940s that carried a photograph of client-centered therapy! It was a picture of two people, one behind a desk, and another sitting at the side of the desk. Today such a picture would hardly be necessary, nor would it be characteristic only of client-centered therapy.

Has client-centered therapy then been fully absorbed in today's plethora of similar, newer methods? Or is there still something that requires us to go back to it?

I would argue strongly that the essence of client-centered therapy has not yet been learned by the field. Indeed, looking back over the many years of my own work in the field, devoted mostly to experiential psychotherapy,

I could now express some hindsight: I did not devote enough effort to point up, and retain, and take with us into new developments the essence and crux of client-centered psychotherapy. Although I never ceased using this crux in practice, I have not written enough about it.

This is a good time to do just that, first because it is necessary, and second, because we are experiencing a kind of renaissance of client-centered therapy. It is being rediscovered by plain people. In our community here in Chicago, we call it *listening*, and that has become a common word. People use such phrases as "I feel upset, I need to be listened to . . ." which is a request to the person spoken to. In our community we understand this request and know how to meet it.

Everyone in the field of psychotherapy knows about the client-centered response, saying back to the person what the person has said. This "reflecting" has become part of the common tools of all therapists, and is known to help clarify and articulate what someone feels. In this rather unexciting form, it is well known.

Two New Additions to Client-Centered Therapy

Currently, two very vital further aspects characterize our listening.

1. First, there has developed a great sense for *exact specificity*. A round, vague approximation is not yet really listening. Today, looking back, I think that 90% of the client-centered therapy I have seen in the last two decades was only round approximation. The client's distinctly felt experience, rather than being articulated, was obscured and deprived of its specific edges by such responding. Accuracy is most important as an aim of the therapist. Let me explain.

If therapists lack a keen sense that they are making *an attempt at* accuracy, then they fail to grasp that the client's reaction to the therapist's response is often due to the therapist's inaccuracy. The client's reaction, most of the time, is one of trying to *hold on to* what is felt, despite the inaccurate response. In trying to hold on to the felt datum, the client tries somehow to deal with the therapist's inaccurate response. "It's not so much this and so way," the client now says, "because after all, such and such, and this and that, are the case, and therefore, well, it isn't so." (It isn't the way the therapist said.) Now the therapist, not realizing that this is all a comeback to the inaccurate response, "reflects" this comeback. The therapist restates the reasons the client gave (for why the earlier therapist response doesn't apply). But again, the therapist doesn't quite get it right, so the client is now forced to tighten up these inaccurately stated reasons. Again the therapist responds to what was just said, and both people are now so far off, so far away from the original felt datum the client had, that they never return, at least not unless the client is very hardy.

"Don't you realize," I will say in supervising such an interaction, "that *you* were the one to raise all this stuff in the first place, not the client? The client was trying to get into this feeling, but had to explain why what *you* said wasn't right."

A very great deal of so-called therapy in the past had something like the quality of the above example, and all because therapists were not keenly aware of the task of accuracy.

Today we don't stand for that, we want to say it exactly as the person feels it, and we don't mind trying three times. We have not become somehow cleverer, we are still often inaccurate the first time, but because we know that we *wanted to be accurate,* we recognize that the client's reaction is a comeback to our inaccuracy.

This recognition enables us to stay with the person's felt datum and with whatever the person actually says, until we get it.

2. We are also aided in this regard by a second, rather new addition: We talk a lot about the responsibility of the person being listened to. We give the person exact instruction always to check inside. Whatever is said back, the person is asked always to check inside, to sense if the response is just exactly what is felt. Without this inner checking by the person listened to, there is no way to become exact, and no way to make really direct contact with what's there in the person.

We have found that not only listeners, but also the people being listened to, have the terrible tendency to give up on what is inside, and to settle for round words and concepts. The person is likely to agree easily, "Yea, I guess so, yea, that's what I said." This is instead of referring inwardly and sensing what's there, and noticing how what was said is *not* it.

We therefore push the rule that the person being listened to must check each response inwardly. Then it can be felt quite directly and unmistakably, what wasn't right, or what just now shifted, and what must be said further.

This rule also gets around politeness. It seems impolite to tell someone that the response is wrong, knowing that this listener is trying hard and being very nice. But if inward checking is the rule, then one cannot settle for a string of round words; one is brought directly in touch with what is there and therefore also with what needs to be added or corrected in anything that was said. The rule also makes the therapy more experiential. If the person being listened to checks inwardly at each step, not only is the accuracy of the response checked, but the client can find the further step now arising in what is concretely felt.

Thus both of these two new specifications have been added to client-centered therapy from an experiential perspective. Rather than viewing themselves chiefly on the level of talk, both the listener and the person being listened to consider themselves working on some inward level of the person being listened to. It is there that the response is checked and the next step to be found. It is there, that the listener awaits the response being checked. And it is there that the person will find the next thing to say.

With these two specifications a new client-centered therapy has arisen— one much more powerful and yet capable of being done by ordinary people. There is no need, we make quite clear, to get anything right the first time. There are no points lost, we all agree, by one's response being checked and people saying their thing over again, or saying it more exactly. As long as they hang on to it, as long as we help them get into it, it doesn't matter if it is a moment sooner or a moment later. Thus the great specificity and devotion to what the person actually has there does not require super-human beings and certainly it does not require professionals (who are not, as a group, more able than others to put up with being corrected all the time, anyway).

Client-Centered Therapy: The Essence

If it is now clear how the experiential approach has led to a tightening of client-centered therapy in these two respects, I can now explain what, it seems to me, is the essence of client-centered therapy, and why I think our field has not yet learned it.

It is true that most therapists have heard of, and sometimes use, "reflection of feeling." They consider it as one technique among many, and thereby they miss the point. I am not arguing that one should never do anything else, I agree that there are many other things it is important to do. And yet, as I say, the main essence and point of client-centered responding has been almost entirely missed by most of the psychotherapy field. My reason for saying this is that the client-centered response should not be one among many types, but should be the baseline, the single precondition upon which the use of all other kinds of responding should be built. Here is more exactly what I mean:

For the therapist, all other kinds of responding should take off from, and return to, client-centered responding. Only in this way can the therapist stay constantly in touch with what is occurring in the person, and thus know and help make good use of whatever beneficial results other therapeutic procedures may have. Only on this baseline can the therapist know exactly how to use all other therapeutic procedures.

Indeed, one can and must do very many other things besides responding reflectively, but never without quite quickly again picking up and really listening to where that leaves the person, what has happened in the person, what the person is now feeling and saying.

Without being able to listen, to hear, to respond exactly, to help the person share what is felt, the therapist is actually leaving the client basically alone. However useful the other things a therapist does may be, if the therapist can't hear, the person is left alone inside. What the person is really up against is not dealt with, is not even brought in, is not even touched. Without listening, the inward sense of the person is not expanded, it remains not only alone, but compressed, sometimes nearly silent, dumb. That way there can be no relationship. A lot of pushing and pulling may occur and look very interactional, but genuine relating is simultaneously a coming to be of each person, an opening up and being carried forward into interaction. Without making real touch with what is there in another, one cannot relate to that other.

Some people are not silent inwardly, but in fact have long and complex inward processes. Nevertheless, if the person were in interaction, what is in the person would be different. (Later I shall explain how the quality of the ongoing process determines what "contents" one will find.) If one leaves the person untouched, unrelated to, what is in the person is (what I call) autistic. Instead of steps of carrying forward into living by action and interaction, the person supplies all the responses. The results are not the same! Self-responding alone, in the absence of interaction, tends to circle and make problems and contents that are nothing but this aloneness, although they have technical names and are treated by our field as if they were some sort of inward things. It is thus a very serious charge, when I say that most therapists leave their patients inwardly alone. It means also that what most needs to change, will not change.

Another result of not listening is that one does not know what is happening for the person just now. Thus, one is blind. If inviting the person to say what is happening and then responding listeningly for a few steps is not your usual procedure, just try it sometime when you're certain you know what is happening. It won't be what you thought! You will be glad you did not go on in the direction you had intended.

Responding in a listening way is a baseline prerequisite for any other modes of responding. It is not just one of many ways, but a precondition for the other ways. It is for therapy what watching the road is in driving a car. One does many things—shift gears, look at signs, engage in conversation, think private thoughts. Driving a car is by no means nothing but watching the road. However, it is quite unwise to forgo watching the road, for any other activity. A glance now and then at something else is fine, even necessary to find one's way. Also, watching the road does not take all one's attention and time; one can also think and converse—*but watching the road has priority!* As soon as the situation out the windshield gets murky the conversation must stop, one's thinking must cease, one must slow down and attend entirely to what's in front, until that becomes clear again. Unfortunately many therapists drive without watching the road. They don't even want to see it! They think they already know what is in the person just then (but, without listening responses, they can only know in a very general, unsatisfactory way).

Therapists may say some challenging thing, some effect may happen, but where it fits, how it leaves the person, what (if any) further steps are now opened—none of this can be known without a quick return to client-centered responding. Thus, no continuous process arises. At best there is a spark here, and then, later, another one there, but no self-moving therapeutic process. Or, if there is one, it is solely in the individual person's lone autistic space, unshared. Blind therapy, I call it. Poking here, and then later poking there. It's the latest thing. Therapists have found ways that do have some effect and aren't just talk. That is excellent. But they use these ways, for the most part, discontinuously, and are not aware that there is such a thing as a therapy process, a continuous movement. And they use their methods in such a way that patients can't share them, and cannot proceed further from where it left them.

A few years ago I was on a workshop panel with a number of other therapists, and we did demonstrations (by calling someone up from the audience). Some of the therapists on the panel fitted a description I sometimes use accusingly; they were "sharpshooters." They were more interested in hitting dead center on some mark (invisibly painted on the patient, I suppose), than in helping anyone. They were good at saying something impactful, undoing the person who had bravely come up from the audience. "There . . ." and they would self-satisfiedly stop. It was as if to say "The prosecution rests." When it was my turn I worked with a volunteer from the audience, more or less as I always do, staying close to what he felt, every few seconds. I also did other things but always followed each of my other kinds of moves with an inquiry where that left him, to which I would again respond listeningly. When it was over I was acclaimed for being incredibly sensitive and gentle and a wonderful person. The panel wanted to imply that it was all due to my own personal qualities, which of course meant that no other person would need to look more closely at what I did, because, presumably, only rare people like me could do this. I had done experiential focusing (which will be elaborated upon later), which anyone can learn to do.

I had also done other things—all of them on a baseline of client-centered therapy. The marvelously sensitive quality was all due to the client-centered baseline; my return, constantly, to what he was feeling, asking him about it and responding to it. If that seemed so rare and gentle in the midst of what was currently being demonstrated, it is clear that the essence of client-centered therapy has not yet been widely understood.

It is very well that we have developed ways that are impactful. It is a good thing that we are no longer "just talking," month after month, helplessly hoping that something more than words will somehow occur. It is excellent that so many therapists are aware of the relative uselessness of talk, and are seeking more and more to make a clearly felt difference. It is quite right that something the person can actually feel has to happen, or else it is only talk, and worth little. But this emphasis on felt impact is insufficient alone. There must also be a sense for therapy as a continuous process, as a movement of a person, rather than just shots here and then later shots there. Whatever else one does will be more useful if one also stays in touch at all times with the person's own felt sense of what is happening on a moment-by-moment basis inside. Then a moving process arises, and continues.

If listening were accepted as a baseline prerequisite for all other forms of responding, as I propose, this would not need to mean that therapists would constantly be saying "You feel . . ." or "Let me see if I understand you, you're saying . . ." These verbal routines are unnecessary. There is a much more natural way of wanting to be in touch constantly with where a person "is at," at any moment. Natural ways are asking the person (What do you feel now? Where did that leave you? What are you thinking?), or of saying back what one understands (for instance, "So, you . . ." or "Damn right, I can see how that would be . . ." or "Yes, it makes sense to me, that . . ." or "Sure, that would be heavy, if they . . ."). The dots here refer to one's own statement of what one thought one understood. Many other forms come naturally, once the principle is established not to respond routinely with "You feel . . ." but to respond so as to express where the person "is at."

Years ago (Gendlin, 1964, 1970) I reformulated client-centered therapy from negative to positive, from *don't* rules, to *do* rules. The old rules were: don't ask questions, don't answer questions, don't say your own feelings, don't interrupt, and so on. I changed it to "make sure you do say what you understand, and let that be checked out, so you stay in touch with the person. Given you do this, you can do anything else also." The therapist's own self-expressing, for example, is welcome, provided that the person is really listened to before, after, and continually.

It was from my experiential philosophical basis that I could reformulate client-centered therapy from *don'ts* to *do's*, because only in experiential terms can one think about what must happen in a psychotherapy process. The essence of client-centered therapy is not well-stated as "Say back what the person said," it is much better stated as "Stay in touch at all times with the person's directly felt concrete experiential datum—and help the person also to stay in touch with that, and get into it." (If doing that is the baseline, every other procedure and idea can also be tried out, and one returns quickly again to finding out, listening, and responding to where it leaves the person.)

These days we introduce listening on an experiential base. We do not first give therapists the puzzling instruction to repeat what their clients say. Rather, we convey what it is like to get into oneself, to accord oneself a friendly hearing, to allow, without rebutting, the coming up of anything that will be there inwardly. We convey that, in one's relation *to oneself*, one must not immediately argue with what comes, or put oneself down for it, or explain it; rather one must gently allow it to be there, just exactly in whatever way it comes up to be felt. When this attitude is understood, listening is presented as how one would help other people take that kind of attitude toward themselves within themselves. To help them do it, we would say back exactly only what they said, try to get it exactly as they felt it and said it, help them "lay no trips on it," and thus certainly also ourselves "laying no trips" on what the person has there.

In the next section, I shall explain experiential focusing and more of the experiential approach. It will then be clear how the present rendition of client-centered therapy was made possible by the experiential approach. Given that that is so, however, the baseline I propose is still the client-centered response—done more exactly, done with a positive sense for the person's inward process and felt data as the ultimate referent, constantly checked there, but otherwise the same client-centered response.

Someone in a training group said to me recently, "It feels so odd to repeat what someone said, but it feels so powerful when someone does it for me." This contrast is worth mentioning. For us helping types, listening often seems too little, almost embarrassing. We are all so bright, we can think of many ways of doing things—should we really remain limited within what the person said? It makes us uncomfortable. Exactly the other side of this question is that if we do remain within what the person said, we accord the person all the space. There is enormous power in letting a person say what is inside. There is no other way to let them do it, than to allow them to do it.

When I say that a therapist can also do anything else, just so there is always a swift return to the listening baseline, I mean that a therapist can occasionally do any other thing. If something else is done every minute, then of course people are again not permitted to get into, and lay out, what is within them.

Isn't it absurd, that one finds so many patients in psychotherapy saying such things as "If only I could make my therapist understand this . . ." or "I try to tell this to my therapist but he won't hear of it . . ." and other such statements? Despite so many advances in our field, more than half of therapy is still only talking, and at that, mostly a matter of not being heard. People would not put up with this kind of thing from their friends. It is because they falsely believe that professionals have some sort of magic that they continue to go for years of hours of being essentially insulted, unheard, and left alone inside.

But, as I say, even those newer therapists who know how to make something happen that isn't just words, even these usually fail to engender a continuous process in their patients. Listening, responding exactly to what the person has here, and aiding the person "to process" this, are vital to the good use of any other impactful methods.

Recently a visitor asked me, "What does this word mean, 'to process' . . . everybody here is 'processing' all the time. What is that?" A closer description will be given in the next section, but for now I want to emphasize the fact that client-centered responding *has steps*. This is roughly what is meant by "process" and "processing." It isn't a question just of listening so that the therapist will know where the person "is at," and so the person will feel heard and unalone, unautistic. Rather, having been heard, checking further inwardly, something new and further will arise there for the person. Having that also responded to, will let still further steps arise. Thus there is a process of many steps further and further into what is there—and also thereby a changing and resolution of what is there.

Without such continuous steps, the inward process of change does not arise, and therapy remains occasional puzzling impacts, disconnected openings here and there, leaving people unable to make use of these impacts and openings, without a continuous and concrete internal change process of their own.

Listening, therefore, is never a one-shot response, but involves at least a few steps: a listening response, then again hearing, and again responding. When that first thing is really heard, wait. Let the person see what now arises. Respond to that. Several such steps, not just one turn, are listening in this sense of the word.

In my recent writings (Gendlin, 1969) I have argued strongly against "just talking," as though any therapist who did not in a few interviews reach an experiential process level with his patient must be quite foolish.

And I still think that most therapy is relatively useless talking. A therapist must strive (and I will show how) to help the person allow directly felt referents to form, to attend to a bodily felt sense, and to let that live further in words and interactions. However, I must also say something in favor of patience.

It is well even in first interviews to ask a person to remain quiet outwardly and inwardly, and to see if there isn't right there a felt sense of what is being talked about. Often just this simple request helps the person's attention move down, as it were, many floors, to a coming into touch concretely.

However, if that does not succeed, one should go on responsively, and try again later or next time. One should also respond verbally on the feeling side of anything the person says. In writing about how to help a person move down into concrete felt sensing, I do not want to say that this always works immediately, or that one should feel one is not helping when it doesn't. It is something to keep moving toward, and may require a period of time in which to be discovered by the person. Until then, one can also be very helpful. It may take some time before some people allow themselves into their own experiential insides. It won't do to blame them for this; it is for the therapist to sense how and when best to help. But therapists should be careful to retain their energy and impetus to aid the person to focus experientially when that becomes possible. Therapists have a tendency to accept a lesser level of process, and to stop trying, with the given person.

Another qualification of client-centered therapy concerns therapist self-expression. The old client-centered therapy forbade it. My writings have urged it strongly. Therapists should always be visibly the people they are—and I still think that. An invented person who does not exist in the room cannot relate to a client. The client's experience cannot be carried forward by responses that are not the responses of a real, other person present. Therapists who cannot permit themselves to be seen off balance, who cannot share even seemingly undesirable experiences inside, cannot be very fully lived with. And the client needs to live *further* with the therapist, than is possible with most other people outside. This often requires the therapist's self-expression—saying what the therapist feels.

But, to be accurate, I must mention that this more expressive mode may not at first fit every client. Some people will let the careful listener know very quickly that *any* input is confusing and obstructing to them. If the therapist expresses some feeling, this burdens them. If a therapist said anything, they remember it 5 years later and are still puzzled about it. If the therapist asks something, they feel pushed, as if what they now feel is not being taken in fully. Wise therapists will need only one or two such signs to allow the person to proceed for some time *only* as the inward process itself moves, and with nothing whatsoever added by the therapist.

Gently asking the person to stop and sense what is right there, is quite safe, if done now and then in an hour. But whatever the person then says or does next should be accepted and responded to.

Miss L. found exact client-centered listening enormously powerful. Every little while it would make her cry to have her exact feeling restated out loud. The crying went with a feeling of inward movement. Once she experienced this powerful effect, nothing else would do. She would get unhappy and frustrated with any other response from me. "Why don't you reflect my feeling?" was a constant reminder. Furthermore the words had to be exact, all the main words had to be the ones she'd used. Then only would she have the sense of powerful impact, and only through these moments would she get to a further step. There were times when she would tell me exactly what to say, and then, when I said it exactly, it would make her cry.

When I asked her a question there would be a blank look, as if she were saying, "That's a stupid question, how would I know?" When I asked her for a further step ("What's in that?" or "See what *that* is"), which works well with most people, she would say: "Don't ask for something further, I just got to *this!*" When I would at last be again willing to respond purely listeningly, she would feel a flood of relief, and the process would move again. Miss L. has engaged in other therapeutic modes quite successfully, both with me and with others. She has profited from operant situational restructuring, Jungian imagery, and reevaluation techniques. But when she says her feelings then the response must be client-centered.

Mr. O. remembers a number of his previous therapist's utterings, which he has brought up now and then, as if to say "How could anyone have said *that* to me, when I was saying so and so?" It is clear that he will always remember these things, and that they were major disruptions that foreclosed further movement along a given line. Yet the therapist most probably said these things offhandedly and perhaps would have felt and thought something quite different only moments later, had the process continued. Mr. O. was obstructed by his therapist's self-expression in another way: when the therapist told him some personal troubles, Mr. O. felt flattered at being trusted but also burdened and misused. Mr. O. is the sort of person one can talk to, and people share their problems with him. He feels the need of some place where this won't happen to him, where he won't be "used," where all the space will really be open and his own.

These people have an extreme sensitivity to others, as if they cannot be at ease and deeply into themselves if another person also uses the space. They find their whole being shifted by the pull, upon them, of another person's needs, statements, or interactional moves. They can use relational space for themselves only if the other person really puts nothing else in and allows that space to stay totally empty until they in some way fill it.

I want to make a plea for people like this. We don't want to become useless to them if we become freer, more self-expressive therapists. We want to be able to hear when the oldest form of client-centered therapy happens to be the only form they can use at the given time. Look at it this way: such people are regularly able to move in a powerful therapeutic process if we do no more than listen and respond exactly. They are the easiest and in many ways most rewarding people to work with, so why not?

It was only some 20 or so interviews later, that Mr. O. demanded more realness from me, and commented very sensitively on some of my shortcomings. Then was the time for me to express how these really are in me (which was quite similar to what he had sensed). An open and self-expressive therapist, a visible and real person who can be lived with, was also right for him, *when* he wanted it and *exactly where* he wanted it. (Perhaps still later in our relationship he may criticize me for never initiating anything, and from then on I surely will.)

With most people, however, I would not wait in this careful fashion, but would say something of my own now and then, when it seems to want to be expressed. Most people appreciate knowing what sorts of things go on in me, and there is a fresher interaction as a result. It all depends on the reactions I get when I first do whatever I do, and I can know these only because I also respond to the person's own felt sense, because that is my constant baseline. It is foolish to say only "fit your way to the individual person . . ." as is so often said. Every therapist wants to do that. The point is that constant listening and responding to feeling, as a baseline, *enables* one to fit oneself to the individual person at a given time.

Having said this, I would like to convey the ease with which I can employ other procedures, ranging from those I have learned from Gestalt or operant work with a person's situation, all the way to very spontaneous expressions of myself. Especially when things are stuck, when a person goes round in circles and we have been around a circle many times, I feel quite free to try one thing after another. It is then best not to be too invested in any one way. Again, responding to the person's own sense between every two tries lets one know that what one has tried has failed, and enables one to return to the person's own process. ("Now, let's see, the last live thing we said was . . ." is a very frequent response of mine.)

Above all, I need to be honest. I don't need to (nor could I) express everything that goes on in me, but I am willing to let it all show. I am willing to share anything that is asked about. I may insist on expressing something, if the person implies that I am or feel some way I'm not. For example, when Mr. O. told me about his previous therapist's sharing personal troubles, I felt Mr. O. implying that *I* would know better than to do a thing like that. But I often do that, and have written a good deal in favor of it. Therefore, even though I grasped that I am not to do that, at this time, with Mr. O., I had, at that very moment, to express myself after all. For me not being dishonest is ahead of anything else, because I cease to be here at all, if I am not here as I am. (And if I am not, then nobody is there with the client.) Therefore I said, very briefly "I want you to know that some people *would* want the therapist to express things like that, and I *do* sometimes do it too." Then, when he had taken that in, I said something like "But for you it was . . ." and returned him to his own track (as I usually do, when I am the one to interrupt).

I find quite often that my feelings and reactions are of help. People have usually had too much of "professionalistic" attitudes. Also, people imagine what goes on inside the other person; if I don't say what is in me, they will imagine it quite differently.

It also helps to confirm, to validate, to say "Damn right" or "I'm with you on that" or "It feels good to me that you were able to do that." I often affirm the person, when I feel that reaction. "Good for you . . ." I say, "talking up for yourself." Conversely, I find that it helps to say "I don't think they would take the time to have meetings to talk about you" or "Yes, I've been with other people who had that sense, that everybody was mad at them, and that every little thing had some weird significance—but it's not right. That's the crazy part. But I know you experienced it that way." (Of course I wouldn't push that again and again; I offer it once for whatever it is worth. We both live here now and can both say what we feel, not only the client. One side doesn't negate the other. Usually people need very much to know how I feel about the things being said, and I make it clear that I do respect how something is experienced by them, even if I do say what I think.)

In short I may say or do most anything that seems helpful, but with constant responding to the person's own feeling. I always bring the person back to that when something of mine got us off and then led nowhere.

The current renaissance of "listening" stems from the fact that it is something ordinary people can learn. The method is therefore adaptable to the current development of youth networks, communes and communities, free clinics, rap centers, and other alternate institutions. Ph.D. or M.D. or M.S.W. or D.D. professionals are generally no better at listening than ordinary people with a little training. Learning listening is unrelated to one's other knowledges, and requires a good deal of careful practice.

It is safe to let ordinary people learn and practice listening—it is much safer than *not* training them in this regard! People do all kinds of things to each other, some of them sometimes harmful. If listening becomes a baseline precondition for whatever else one does, everything else is safer. One will find out, and take in, whatever effects one is having on another person, and one is able then to change what one is doing accordingly.

Thus, ordinary interactions, no less than therapeutic procedures, need listening as a baseline, or else one blindly has all kinds of effects on others, which one doesn't get to hear about, at least not until much later. In our community (called *Changes*) in Chicago, I have been impressed with the ease with which listening can become an ethos of a group. There is a legitimacy, a right to validation, that goes along with it and seems natural to people once they experience it. "May I be listened to?" is an expression of a valid human need. It fits into living.

Professionals, like myself, often find that we respond therapeutically in our therapy hours, and fail to do so in most of our personal lives. This is not the case with the people who learn listening without becoming professionals. It is striking and lovely in a large group, that there is always someone who wants to listen and say exactly what someone is trying to get at—especially when I myself have totally forgotten to do that.

Before leaving this topic I want to summarize: I consider listening a baseline requirement making all other forms of interaction safer and more effective. Listening these days does not mean some round restatement, but a very exact set of steps wherein the listener states exactly what the person said, and the person being listened to is expected then to correct the response, or to move another step. Without doing this fairly continually, no other methods of therapy are likely to provide a continuous therapy process, or to be very effective.

Our field has yet to learn that listening is absolutely essential during any therapeutic work. This conclusion implies that listening in its experiential specificity should be universally adopted, universally taught, professionally and nonprofessionally. It should probably be freed of being one orientation among others; it should be a baseline, not a sect. Above all, unfortunately, it is still very very new to most people and most therapists.

EXPERIENTIAL PSYCHOTHERAPY

Experiential psychotherapy stems from a philosophy (Gendlin, 1962) that holds that direct experiencing is "implicitly" rich in meanings, but is never equatable to words or concepts. Experiencing is the organism's interaction with all the environment, therefore it is implicitly very rich.

One must always "directly refer" to felt experience, and if one does, then words and concepts can be of help in articulating it and carrying it further. To say what one feels is not a mere telling about it, but is itself a *further* experiencing. When one articulates it rightly, one feels an experiential movement.

People say "Now I know what that was, which I felt," but in that very act they have changed, experienced further, lived past some blockage. They don't only "know," they *are* differently, in the very saying of how it has been. In contrast, purely conceptual, so-called insight makes little difference. Experience is a process, it is experienc*ing*, and therapeutic change is a further experiencing, where there was blockage.

Philosophically, one must recognize that experience is therefore never equal to some conceptualized version. Experience is not made of conceptual units. (In that sense all theories are wrong. For all theories it can be said that my experience is mostly *not* whatever the theory says it is.)

Conversely, one can use any (and all) theories to help one articulate one's experience, if one clings to the experience itself, as directly felt. Accept nothing that is *merely* logical or merely conceptual. It must also resonate unmistakably with what one feels directly, and it must have a distinct felt effect. If saying it makes no difference to the knot in one's stomach, one has not yet found an experiential step, and must go on seeking one. Weaving concepts on alone, without felt effects, is of little use in therapy or personal growth.

The experiential philosophy has a good deal to say about a kind of science that could be about people—about a method of thinking in which concepts wouldn't be "about," but are themselves steps of experiencing. The philosophy relates feelings and thought.

A first step to notice is that a person's experiential felt sense of a difficulty is not the same as what is called *emotion*. Emotions are "felt," but an emotion is all one, it is anger or joy or shame; there is nothing else inside it but what it is. A moment's experiencing, on the other hand, though also felt, is a rich maze of implicit aspects, all of them felt together in one conceptually unclear "this." For example, if I am angry, then concentrating on the emotion of anger will make me angrier and angrier. If I have never been able to express anger, it might do me some good to shout or pound the wall with my shoe. However, if I have no trouble doing this, it will only leave me tired out, and no different. Something quite different is focused on if I ask myself "What is that whole thing, which is now making me angry?" Of course, the answer to this must not be solely words or concepts. Instead I must let the feel of the whole thing come home to me. Then "it" will tell me what is involved in it. At first, "it" will be a conceptually unclear feel of a whole complexity, involving what happened, what always happens, why it gets me, what I ought to do about it and can't, why I can't, who else is involved, how I feel about them, what I'm afraid of, what I hoped for, why it's disappointing, how I got hurt, and much else. The felt sense is this implicit complexity. Emotion is something else.

The experiential philosophy refuses to equate experiencing with any set of convenient concepts or units. Only the directly felt actual experiencing is the real thing, and it is always a complex maze of very specific aspects that are just what they are. What is central among these can be found, and can be lived further, if one first allows the directly felt sense of the trouble to form. To allow that, one has to remain quiet (not talk out loud, or inwardly), and sense, while waiting for one's feeling to clear and form. "It all" then comes home to one as a felt sense. Very quickly, also, certain quite distinct felt aspects stand out, usually not what one would have expected or figured out. But this is not merely a finding out. It is a letting oneself live further, and *feels good,* even if one doesn't like what one finds. It feels like relief, easing.

I term this process *focusing* (Gendlin, Beebe, Cassens, Klein, & Oberlander, 1968; Gendlin, 1969). If clients do not, of their own accord, engage in this every few minutes, I try to bring it about. I ask people to stop talking and to sense inwardly into themselves. Let it form and let it tell you what it is.

Without this experiential focusing, little therapeutic movement usually occurs. People talk helplessly, far above their feelings, without ever going directly and concretely into them. To be sure, they have what look like feelings, emotions of anxiety, fear, and anger, but they rarely get quiet enough to let themselves down beneath these, into *the concrete experiential complexity.* Without doing so, little changes.

Sometimes I say something like "All right, now we have said what you *surmise,* now go see how it actually is and *feels.*" Then I ask the person to attend inwardly and let the feel of it come. It is a distinct act, and many people will never do it while they are talking with another person, or, perhaps, ever, unless they are asked to do it, and shown how.

People spend most of their time *talking about,* rather than *getting into.* Even if what is said is deep, genuine, and courageously confronts every issue, one can also ask oneself whether the person has a direct felt sense at that point, and do these things being said arise out of it? Or is the person just telling about something inferred, something that must be in there somewhere, but hasn't been concretely encountered? If the latter is the case, one can try to aid the person to focus experientially. Here is one set of more detailed instructions, called the *Focusing Manual* (Gendlin, 1969, pp. 5–6). Both in therapy, and in our community, this manual and many variations of it have been widely used.

Focusing Manual

· ·

This is going to be just to yourself. What I will ask you to do will be silent, just to yourself. Take a moment just to relax. . . . . 5 seconds. All right—now, just to yourself, inside you, I would like you to pay attention to a very special part of you. . . . . Pay attention *to that part where* you usually feel sad, glad or scared. 5 seconds. Pay attention to that area in you and see how you are now.

See what comes to you when you ask yourself, "How am I now?" "How do I feel?" "What is the main thing for me right now?"

Let it come, in whatever way it comes to you, and see how it is.

· ·

30 seconds or less

· ·

If, among the things that you have just thought of, there was a major personal problem which felt important, continue with it. Otherwise, select a meaningful personal problem to think about. Make sure you have chosen some personal problem of real importance in your life. Choose the thing which seems most meaningful to you.

· ·

10 seconds

· ·

1. Of course, there are many parts to that one thing you are thinking about—too many to *think* of each one alone. But, you can *feel* all of these things together. Pay attention there where you usually feel things, and in there you can get a sense of what *all of the problem* feels like. Let yourself feel *all of that.*

· ·

30 seconds or less

· ·

2. As you pay attention to the whole feeling of it, you may find that one special feeling comes up. Let yourself pay attention to that one feeling.

· ·

1 minute

· ·

3. Keep following one feeling. Don't let it be *just* words or pictures —wait and let words or pictures come from the feeling.

. . . .
1 minute

. . . .
4. If this one feeling changes, or moves, let it do that. Whatever it does, follow the feeling and pay attention to it.

. . . .
1 minute

. . . .
5. Now, take what is fresh, or new, in the feel of it *now*. . . . . and go very easy. Just as you feel it, try to find some new words or pictures to capture what your present feeling is all about. There doesn't have to be anything that you didn't know before. New words are best but old words might fit just as well. As long as you now find words or pictures to say what is fresh to you now.

. . . .
1 minute

. . . .
6. If the words or pictures that you now have make some fresh difference, see what that is. Let the words or pictures change until they feel just right in capturing your feelings.

. . . .
1 minute

. . . .
Now I will give you a little while to use in any way you want to, and then we will stop.

This manual is also used one step at a time; one need not give the steps all at once. One can rephrase any part of it in one's own language, once one knows what specific step is intended.

In addition, we have developed a set of instructions (Gendlin & Hendricks, 1972) for our community. These include, among much else, the following section on making an experiential process happen, when a person is talking of troubles. In these instructions a felt sense is called a *place,* and these instructions, written in terms as plain as possible, will probably communicate better than anything else can, one simple and straightforward way of using the experiential method.

Making Places
Often people seem not to go down into themselves at all. Many people can tell you their thing just as far as it is clear to them, but then they stop, or they go on to something else. Yet it's just where feelings and

situations aren't clear, that a good process needs to happen. It can happen, if people will first *make a place* out of what's unclear, or unresolved, and then feel their way into that.

Making a place is like saying to oneself, "That, there, that's what's confused," and *then feeling that there.* Or, *"There* is that whole big confusion." Or, "It's just *this* part about it, that's scary." Or, "Yeah, it's that I'm so disappointed, that's what's getting me."

A place is not just the words, but something in the person that is directly felt, and can be pointed to inwardly. *"There, this, that's* what the worst of it is."

It is necessary for the person to keep quiet, not only outwardly, but also not to talk inside, so that a feeling place can *form.* It takes a couple of seconds, maybe even a minute.

Some people talk all the time, either out loud or at themselves inside, and they don't let anything directly felt form for them. Then everything stays a painful mass of confusion and tightness.

When a place forms, the person also feels better. There is some relief. It's as if all the bad or troubling feeling goes into one spot, right there, and the rest of the body feels easier and freer, and one can breathe better.

Once a place forms (and this happens by itself, if one keeps quiet and lets it), then people can relate to that place. They can wonder what's *in* that, and can feel around it and into it, and can let aspects of it come to them one by one.

When to help a person let a place form: When people talk round and round a subject and never go down into their feelings of it;

when people say things that are obviously very personal and meaningful to them, but then they go on to something else, and again to something else, and don't get *into* any one of these things;

when people have said all that they can say clearly, and from there forward it is confusing, or a tight unresolved mess, and they don't know how to go on;

when people can't get out of just describing the situation, what one could have seen from the outside, and don't go into what it adds up to, in them, or how they feel it, where it gets them;

when a person tells you nothing meaningful, but seems to want to;

when there is a certain spot that you sense could be gotten into further.

How to help a place form: There is a gradation of how much help you have to give, to enable the person to get a place: Always do the least amount first and more only if that doesn't work.

(a) Some people won't need any help except your willingness to be silent for a minute now and then. If you don't talk all the time, and if you don't stop them or get them off the track, they will feel into what they need to feel into. Don't interrupt a silence for at least a minute or two. Once you have responded and checked out what you said and gotten it exactly right, be quiet.

(b) The person may need one sentence or so from you, to make the pause in which a place could form. Such a sentence might simply repeat the last important thing you already responded to, it might just point again to that spot, it might be just one important key word. Or you can make a simple global sentence, like, "Yeah, that feels heavy," and then stay quiet.

Whatever people say after your attempt to enable them to form a place, say the crux of it back. Let them and you go on as usual, and try again a little later. If you, in this way, don't get hung up on the fact that you hoped and tried for a silent deeper period, your efforts have cost nothing. You can try again soon. Therefore don't refuse to go with whatever comes up, even if the person didn't do what you said.

(c) If, after quite many tries the person still isn't feeling into anything, then, the next time you try, say explicitly, "Sit with it a minute and feel into it further." Say something like, "For the next minute don't say anything to me, or to yourself either. I'd like you to just hang on to that one spot and keep quiet and let the feel of it come to you, see what's in it. It takes a minute of keeping quiet to let that come in more."

(d) You can also make a question for the person, and tell them to ask this question inwardly, to ask not the head but the gut or feelings. "Stay quiet and don't answer the question in words, just wait with the question, till something comes from your feeling."

Questions like that are usually best open-ended. The following examples are all the same: "What really *is* this?" "What's keeping this the way it is?" "Why is this still this way?" "Just where is it really hung up?" "Why am I still hung on that?" "If it's still not all OK yet, why not?" (These questions refer to the specific thing or place just talked about.)

Another type of question applies to the "whole thing;" use it when everything is pretty confused, or when a person doesn't know how to begin. Tell the person to feel the whole thing, let the whole mess come home to them and ask (but not answer in words) the question "Where is this really at?" or "Where am I really hung up in this whole thing?"

(e) Some people won't know what you mean by "let yourself feel it" or "let the feel of it come home to you and just see what it feels like." They know only about words. In that case, repeat the person's last most meaningful words, and ask them to say this to themselves again and to sense what they are feeling when they say these words. In this way they can notice the fact that there is something there besides words that they can let themselves get or have.

Usually, if the person has a felt place, by sensing into it and letting it be, a next step will come, some aspect of it not had before, will emerge, and the whole thing will shift a little, and then more. The deep kind of process will go forward.

(f) If nothing like that is happening, and a person *has* let a felt place form but is stuck, it may help to ask the person, "How would it be different, if it were all OK, what ought it to be like?" Then, after that, tell the person to ask inwardly "What's in the way of that?" and to not answer the question, just to get the feel of what's in the way, and let that talk.

All these different ways need the person to stop talking out loud and inside, and to let the feel of whatever it is get sensed.

This stopping of deliberate talking, inwardly as well as out loud, is a sharp change. One stops what one was doing. One does nothing further. One *lets come*, instead of doing it oneself. One keeps only the focus, the topic, or question.

Even more globally, one can use this way to ask oneself, "Where's my life still hung up?" You can ask yourself this now, and see how fast it gives you the places, if you ask and don't answer with words but wait for the places to come to you in a felt way.

You can also pick the two or three most important things the person said, if you feel they go together into one thing, and tell the person, "When I say what I'm going to say, you don't say anything to me or to yourself, just feel what comes there." Then, say the two or three things, each in one or two words.

(g) These ways could help when a person doesn't want to say some private or painful thing. They can work on it with you even without your having to know what it is; they can get into, and say how it is, without telling you what it is about.

How you can tell when it isn't working, and when it is

(a) When people look you straight in the eyes, then they aren't yet focusing inward. Say, "You can't get into it while you're looking at me, let me just sit here and get with yourself."

If the person speaks immediately after you get through asking them to be quiet, they haven't done it yet. First get, and say back the crux of what they say, then ask them again to make a place as described above. If you've done a very "heavy trip" on it, let it go fifteen minutes or so, and then if the person still isn't into anything, try again.

If, after a silence, the person comes up with explanations and speculations, ask how that point feels, and what's *in* that, to feel it out. Don't put the person down for "just head stuff." Rather, pick up what people do say, and keep pointing into feeling, so they get there eventually.

If people say they can't let feelings come because they are too restless, tense, feel empty, discouraged, trying too hard, etc., ask them to focus on *that*. They can ask themselves (and not answer in words), "What is this rattled feeling?" "What is this tense feeling?" "What is this empty feeling?" "What is this 'trying too hard' thing?"

(b) How can you tell when a person has a place, and when referring to this place is working? One has a place when one can feel more than one understands, when what is there is more than words and thoughts, when something is quite definitely felt, but it hasn't opened up or released yet.

Referring has worked, when something further has come up, something one hasn't just thought up, or figured out. This way a person feels something directly, and doesn't only figure that it must be so.

Anything whatever, which comes in this "from the gut" way, should be welcomed. It is the organism's next step. Take it and say it back just the way the person tells it.

It feels good to have something come directly from one's feeling, it shifts the feelings slightly, releases the body slightly, even if one doesn't like what has come it feels good. It is encouraging when more is happening than just talk. It gives one a sense of a process, and movement from stuck places [pp. 4–6].

In the above instructions, a person talking about troubles is made experiential. The persons is aided to focus, to make a place, to let a felt sense form (these phrases all have the same meaning). Because the person is talking about troubles, the felt sense is formed in that context, as the feel of this whole thing, or this specific thing, now being talked about.

Other procedures of psychotherapy too, not only a person's talking of troubles, can be made experiential.

For example, the same instructional manual from which the above excerpt was taken, also includes a way to make experiential that famous therapeutic procedure, interpretive guessing. It contains the following paragraphs:

If you get a hunch as to what the person is feeling, by putting together a lot of theoretical reasoning in your head, or if you get it from a long set of hints, don't take up time saying all this to the person. Just ask yourself what one would feel if your line of inference were right. For example, don't say, "Because of these and these and those and those reasons, which I put together this way and which indicate this and this because of that and that, I think you must be afraid of such and such." Just ask, "Are you maybe afraid of such and such?"

Example: If you conclude that this man's relation with his woman is "oedipal" (say you're right into that theory), ask yourself what sort of a feeling edge might he then find in himself, then skip the oedipal theory and ask him "Do you maybe feel small or something, as if she is the adult and you aren't quite?" or "Do you have something there like you could be punished, some threat or something?"

You can say any hunch or idea in an asking way, sometimes you might add another possibility, to insure that he knows it's not a conclusion but an invitation for him to look how it is in him. "Is it like you're scared of so and so . . . or maybe ashamed? How does it feel?"

Here interpretation is made experiential, both negatively, by *not* putting upon the person any of the inferential and thinking steps of the therapist, and positively, by asking oneself (when one has an inferential hunch or interpretation) "what would the person concretely feel or find within, if I'm right?" Then, asking the person whether such a feeling is there or not takes only a moment, and is itself again an invitation for the person to check inwardly. (Of course, the therapist should now continue with whatever the person *does* find, however close or distant to what was expected it may be. The worth of the interpretation may well lie in the person's finding something opposite or very different; what counts is the experientially concrete.)

The determining crux, from the experiential point of view, is whether or not the theory and the thinking are used to help get at the person's concretely sensed experience right now, as the person can find it right now. Anything that fails in this must be immediately discarded so that much time isn't lost uselessly rebutting false leads and explaining at great length why they do not serve right now. The experiential method rejects a use of theory in which concepts are substituted for the person, so that, instead of dealing with what is concretely there (what must be sensed into, directly, in order to find what is there), the two people deal *instead* with the inferential concepts. The experiential way is to keep one's inferential concepts in one's head, and ask only about the concrete felt datum that might be there to be found, if one happend to be right.

In this way any and all interpretive theories can be experientially used. One need not discount all theories, nor limit oneself to one only. It is not the theory that matters, but what it helps one find concretely—and at various times various theories and lines of thought can happen to aid in this inward finding.

The inward finding I call focusing always involves the person's letting something come. It cannot be manufactured, argued, made to come. Focusing seems like a kind of magic; something happens that the person does not control. The directly felt sense itself "comes." It also opens, and tells the person what's what. One man phrased it challengingly after I instructed and led him step by step through focusing. He asked me, "What happens there—is that a crease in my brain opening up, or what?" Because I had instructed him to do the steps, he assumed that I knew the answer to that question.

But I can give only a very general answer as to how and why focusing works. Experiencing is a bodily process, and the body is the vast number of interactional aspects that we live. The body is also one system. Our troubles are constrictions upon our living, felt as constrictions in the body. In focusing we allow the body to live further on a new level, a new plane, a new space, an inward space. Here we can live forward the step we have been unable to live in the world. In letting the next felt sense form, we live the next step we need.

The body forms any next behavior from all relevant aspects, but in troubles there is no way to live all the aspects further; one is held up, hung up; there is no way to act or speak so that all that is involved can be lived. Only on the plane of inward space and the forming of a felt sense is there a way for the body to produce a next step that takes everything relevant into account. Therefore a felt sense of the whole thing, its very formation, its coming, is a further step of body life such as could not otherwise happen. It is therefore felt as a relief, as "It feels so good to get in touch with myself."

As one *then* finds, from out of the felt sense, what exactly is salient in it, this again is experienced as a relief. It is again a living forward, now into words or images.

The body is wiser than all our concepts, for it totals them all and much more. It totals all the circumstances we sense. We get this totaling, if we *let* a felt sense form in inward space.

Other therapeutic methods also require something that happens of its own accord, beyond the person's willful ego control. The Jungians employ imagery and daydream, which must be allowed to form as they come to the person, not as willfully made by the person. Freud used free association, again so that something could come, which the person would not be able to produce deliberately. Role playing, too, involves a person in spontaneous actions that would not arise deliberately.

But it is relatively easy to get "something" to happen that is beyond the person's control; it is done every night in dreams, and in any regressed condition. This isn't enough. The patient on the regression couch may come up with associations, but, as Jung recognized, such coming up is only the half of it. The person must also actively respond, react, and for this the person must be all there, wide awake and *not* regressed.

A therapeutic process oscillates along the regression line, across it, and back again. For some moments one allows something to form, and as soon as it does one must be fully there to notice it and receive it and ask it further questions. Drift and passive sluggishness do not serve well. We must stay very much awake, so that when we let something come we can immediately again return to deal with it. But how does one deal with it? What does one do, to make a therapy process from something that has come, that was not made deliberately?

As we saw, different methods engender different kinds of such comings —images, thoughts, role actions, and so on. It is my contention that allowing a directly felt sense to come is the most powerful type of coming. However, the other types can also help, but only provided one then moves toward a felt sense. This can be done as follows: instead of getting fascinated with the inherent interest of the image or association, and interpreting it (as Jungians and Freudians were long in the habit of doing), the person should be asked "What does the image make you feel?" Or, "What does this sentence make you feel?" This allows a felt sense to form. When that felt sense is first allowed to be and then quite quickly opens so that its salient aspects emerge, a step of experiential process will have been achieved with the aid of the image or sentence.

The mere emergence of something odd and interesting is no step of therapy. Only its role in an experiential movement makes it therapeutic, if one engenders such a step of therapeutic movement. To do so, one must always involve the experiencing process, in this case by letting a sense of the image or sentence form.

When a person feels regressed, sleepy, or alone and autistic, or rejected or put upon or constricted, then the contents—what the person finds inwardly—will also tend to be negative. Contents are results of the quality of ongoing process. Our inward psychic data are not just things inside, they are aspects of experiential process. This process is our interaction with the universe, with the situation, with others. When the interaction process has a negative or constricted character, it will not resolve or change the contents in a desirable way. Let me say more about this.

To let a felt sense form is not even possible except in a quiet and accepting gentle allowance, a letting, a friendly attitude toward one's insides. What comes may at first seem negative, but will soon shift in an adaptive way, because the body will live further, and will thus live certain aspects that until then were held up and could not be lived onward.

Therefore one's allowing the inward coming of a felt sense is itself already an overcoming of every stoppage. It is as if before we even find out what was wrong, we change in the act of allowing the further living, which till then we could not allow. (But, of course, in inward space one can allow what may not be possible in situations. In inward space a feel of "all that" can form, whereas in speaking and action only specific words and acts are possible.) Therapeutic process is itself a kind of further living —and the best kind, better and fuller than ordinary, not less awake and less fully present. After all, therapists must recall that they depend upon something they do not understand: therapists assume that by bringing out and facing, becoming aware and saying what is wrong, something good will happen. How does it? On what is founded their faith that saying the bad will make something good? Why is not the ordinary person right, who assumes that the less seen and said of bad things, the better? In short, that facing it and saying it won't help, because one won't know how to change it? It isn't enough, therefore, to produce pathological content. Hospitals have people who do that all the time. The crux of therapy is to engender a process in which what sounds bad becomes resolved and changes—and most therapists lack the method for making this process happen.

The experiential theory holds that change depends upon whether the ongoing living and experiencing process moves fuller and further, in just those respects in which previously it was held back. Experience is basically process, it is liv*ing*, and not just this or that content. Contents are not basic, they are made from process, they are aspects of living, and they change if liv*ing* changes. If the process engendered now is the living that was stopped before, then the contents that form will also change and in a good way.

Thus it is well and safe to let a person come up with whatever comes, if the person is living a process in a free manner: the very letting come what comes is already a free living. Whatever comes, however bad it may at first sound, will be changed and released. But letting anything whatever come is not at all safe, when it is not the person freely letting something come, but rather is something that is done to a person, conjured up while the person is passive and helpless. To deprive someone of sleep for several nights, for example, will surely make for a lot coming, but not a positive process of their fuller living. Rather, the person will be attacked and invaded. That deprives us of the factor on which all therapists count. After all, therapists believe that to let bad things come to awareness will somehow be a good thing. But it is the quality of the ongoing living experiential process that is the only thing that guarantees that. Just by having these bad experiences, they will not turn good, or be resolved. The manner of the process must be positive or the results will not be. (Of course, there is also the therapist's interacting with the person. On that avenue, too, the manner of the process can be made a positive one, if the personal relating is close and gentle.)

It should be clear that good manner of process does not mean "nice" rather than "bad" content. It means letting come whatever felt sense comes. However, this letting is itself a wider and better process than one is usually engaged in. In the spirit of this kind of letting, even the worst things emerge with a sense that one is more than just this—and indeed, just then one is! One is the wider process, of which contents are only products. Just now the product may be the very first clear emergence of what was wrong, but already one's capacity to produce this is a result of a large change, which will show more clearly as one awaits one's next step.

Thus the basic crux of experiential psychotherapy is the richer, fuller experiential process that occurs when one lets a felt sense form, when one lives and stays with that until the next step of speech or action emerges from that—and when one then returns again to the level of felt sense to take still further steps.

In this basic crux, the interpersonal relationship is very important. Human experiencing is an interactional process, our living and our bodies *are* interactions. It is not that one is a certain way, and then enters into interaction. Rather, how one is, is from interaction, and to interact further *is* already a being different, if the manner of that further interaction is different. Most people find it very much easier to let a felt sense form, much easier even to make themselves willing to try to do so, if another person is with them. But of course that other person must be welcoming and must wish to aid this process, must also be willing to let whatever will come, come.

If allowing a felt sense to form, and taking steps from it, is our basic principle, how would other older methods be reformulated, how would they be different, if used in the service of this principle?

When these other methods let something that isn't in the person's own control come, we can now see exactly how they miss the experiential process. Not only have most other systems neglected to specify that the person must be awake, and must actively react to what comes, but they also fail to let a *felt sense* form. What comes can give the person a felt sense if the person stops and asks: "In regard to this (image, etc.), what felt sense does this give me?" Only so can one process experientially what came.

For example, in free association the patient says everything that comes to mind. The analyst then interprets. All this is instructive to the analyst, but the patient goes home with an interesting puzzle, with only intellectual leads. Freud did not do it that way. Freud used free association differently, but one has to read carefully to notice. Freud had the patient free associate until the patient came to a block. When such a block is hit, free association stops. The patient, it seems, can think of nothing further. Not so; he can think of many things, but *feels* clearly that they do not move the block. The block is *felt!*

Freud would then attempt to interpret the block—thus Freud had a criterion for his interpretations. He could try out quite a number. When he got the right interpretation, the felt block would be released and the patient would find a flood of new material, an opening up, and unfolding.

Only this movement gives a criterion for interpretation. When there is a "dynamic" shift (I call it an experiential shift, a felt shift), the interpretation is effective. Thus, the basic factor is the patient's attention to, and a felt shift in, what is directly felt.

The same point can also be made about Jungian imagery and daydream. Only very occasionally does Jung make it clear that the patient must move his attention *from* the image *to* direct feeling. Only if the patient works with directly felt concretes will there be change. Jung called this the *transcendent function*, but he said little about it. If it is ignored, people watch chains of images go by, or speculatively interpret an image, and very little happens. The real changes and concrete shifts occur when one first lets the image form and then moves to what it makes one feel. There, concretely, is then something to work with. When one focuses on that, and allows that to be lived and to move, change occurs (see Gendlin & Olsen, 1970).

Another example might be taken from Gestalt therapy, where one good method is to ask the person to speak from just one side of some conflict or problem. Then, when that is over, the person is asked to move into the opposite chair and speak from the other part, as it were, to answer to the first part. This method is powerful. But quite often people make up what to say, invent what seems reasonable for that part to say. This does not have any effect. The right way (not specified, not made clear, but sometimes found and sometimes not) is to pause and let oneself get a felt sense of the given part. Then, to one's amazement, words come from the felt sense. These words are powerful to express.

The "motor" that powers psychotherapeutic change is a direct sensing into what is concretely felt (not emotions, but implicitly complex felt sense); the allowing that to form and to move.

Every different method of therapeutic techniques can be made to work well, if this is done. None of them work if it is not done. The best exponents of these methods do this, but they have lacked the words and theoretical ideas to make it plain.

It should be clear that a very specific and rather unusual level of awareness is required by the experiential method. It is not at all enough that there are all sorts of ideas, emotions, images, and so on. Only if one moves from these to let a felt sense form, can one expect the experiential process I am discussing.

The experiential method centers on this basic motor of therapeutic change. It can employ all theories, concepts, and techniques. All types of human productions such as words, images, actions, can be used as I just described. The experiential method cuts across other orientations and allows one to keep one's older orientation, but shows one how to use it experientially. It explains why the incidence of success is roughly the same for all therapies despite grand claims, and it may go a long way to explain when psychotherapy does work, and when not.

Research findings bear this out. When people during therapy are high on the Experiencing Scale (Klein, Mathieu, Kiesler, & Gendlin, 1970), they are successful. A series of studies (Gendlin et al., 1968) has now replicated this finding. It represents the only measure of the effectiveness of *ongoing* therapy. This repeated finding does not tell us how to make therapy experiential if it is not. Newer findings show that the experiential level can be raised by focusing instructions, but these findings are still tentative. It takes many years to bring in a rigorously established finding of something that one knows well from practice (but that has the advantage that it checks one's prejudices).

A felt sense is both psychic and bodily, but not in a way in which the two are separate. For example, in working with muscles, body and psyche are separate. Reich, for example, works in that way. However, the most effective therapeutic process occurs when one does not separate psyche and body, but senses directly into one's physically felt bodily sense of one's situations and troubles—something quite directly and distinctly felt and concretely there in both a bodily and psychologically relevant way.

For example, at a recent convention there was a lady in my group who had just been in a Gestalt group. When I asked her how she felt now, she said, pointing at her chest "I feel easy here," and then pointing at her chest lower down she said "I feel tense here." I asked her what personal meaning or life feeling she sensed in these places, and she could find none. To her it was just the body, like how the clothes felt on her. There was nowhere to go with this purely bodily sense. So I asked her where her life was at, just now. Then she said that the convention was nearly over and she still hadn't met anyone and was so disappointed and began crying. I asked her to feel into that whole thing, in a bodily way so she could feel it as a big heavy weight, felt all together and implicitly rich. This time she had the opposite difficulty, namely to sense the whole thing in a bodily way—it seemed simply her situation. But we do feel our situations with our bodies, we live them bodily. If one stays with only defined concepts, there is not much movement from a statement of a situation. But as felt by a living bodily person, the felt sense of it all soon comes, and produces a step.

Psychotherapy is a psyche–body process. The unconscious is not a vague realm. The unconscious is the body. It is that vast amount more that we are, but have not formed in concepts. It is not really *un*conscious, for it can be felt, if one allows a felt sense to form.

To allow a felt sense to form, one must stay quiet, and one must let it form. The letting part is only half of it. Another half of this process is (very deliberately to make room for it) like holding a frame over the dark, so that then something can be let to form within that frame. One deliberately asks oneself: "How do I feel now?" or "Where is this really at?" or "What's in this?" and then one does *not* answer the question in words. Posing the question is like holding the frame over one's feelings. Then one must wait and let a felt sense form, and that felt sense will be the answer, not words.

Thus the unconscious isn't really unconscious, for it can be felt. However, one feels only a step at a time. If one allows that felt sense to open up and to be lived forward into words, images, or acts, then there is change and shift. When next one lets a felt sense form, it will be different.

The steps one goes through in this way are a process. No one step is the truth, for in the very getting it, it shifts—and we want and need it to shift. But it shifts as *it* will, and not as we predirect.

In the concretely felt bodily sensing there is a genuine direction, one that neither client nor therapist chooses. Whatever the next step is, that is what comes, and everything else that one may say or think leaves one unchanged.

Focusing on a felt sense that is allowed to form, and then letting this felt sense tell one what's what, is the source of basic change and is the motor of any psychotherapy.

Why wait for it to happen by accident, haplessly going along with only talk, or stabbing this way and that? There can be a systematic way of engendering this process, the experiential method.

At its simplest, it consists of no more than asking people to keep quiet both outwardly and inwardly, and to let themselves sense into what it all feels like. Asking them to do this every little while (if they aren't doing it) is often enough to make the therapy experiential.

More complexly, the experiential method means putting anything you use (words, body muscles, emotions, Gestalt roles, images) into direct relation with a concrete felt sense that must be allowed to form, and is then worked from.

It can now be clear why, if one adopts the experiential method, it becomes much less important whether one talks in psychoanalytic or Jungian words, whether one uses operant or family therapy procedures, whether one uses some Gestalt techniques or some body work, whether one calls it the "parent" or the "super-ego," for all these words and procedures are so many fishing lines, not fish. All sometimes work. Why would one want to be ignorant of any of them? Why would one not wish to be proficient in all of them? Especially when a person is stuck, why not try a procedure not yet tried? All are equally aiming at that person's directly sensed concrete experiencing, and they are all equally empty if they fail to hook into it.

The experiential method thus gets us beyond the empty arguments as to whether these or those abstractions best describe the human person. None of them do that at all well; the real person is infinitely richer than any of our systems. The experiential method provides a different base. It is not a relativism, not an eclecticism, it does not say everything is relative. Rather, the experiential method says that words and procedures are *relative to* the concretely felt experiential process, implicitly complex and capable of steps. Only the next bodily felt step is what we can go by. Therefore all the methods and concepts can help.

This is not to say that they are all the same; if they were, one would need only one of them. Experiential process is interaction, but only some of the older methods focus on interaction, both between person and therapist, and also between person and situation. Sometimes I must be an operant or a family therapist for this reason. The psychoanalytic and Jungian approaches provide the richest vocabularies for trying out different distinctions and ways of articulating. Thus, various methods do not all offer the same tools, and therefore one wants many of them. But it is as tools, that the experiential method regards them, not as renditions of human nature, nor as ultimate procedures that must work just by being instituted. Stated positively, this means that any method must constantly be attempting to reach, to let form, and to enable a step in, the directly felt experiential sense of the person. Any statements and procedures must get to that, or else one should try others. Thus the differences between the older methods becomes less important not only because no concepts and procedures are absolute (an easily agreed-upon statement), but for the positive reason that these methods can be altered so as to make each of them a way to get to the experiential process.

I have already indicated what client-centered therapy, Gestalt, psychoanalytic free association, and Jungian active imagination look like, when done experientially. I also mentioned that operant situation-restructuring can be done well in an experiential way. The operant method (Goldiamond & Dryud, 1968) includes, among other useful principles, the seeking of small steps to an external behavioral goal. Like family therapy and every interactional view (including the experiential view), operant therapy emphasizes that problems are not really in one's head or body but in one's living. I have found it very helpful with some people to suggest setting up small steps, for example on the task of finding friends or a mate. (First listing places, then going to one—just going, then going and looking people in the eyes so one could notice if someone seemed nice.) When the person then, as is usual, can say and feel what is so hard about doing any of this, we can work directly on the felt sense of that. Each aids the other because more doable steps are devised if the person focuses. Some steps become doable when at first they were not. At other times seeing just what is undoable about a proposed step lets us think of different ones.

I want to emphasize that this is no mere addition of methods, although it may sound like that. Rather, each of these methods can be done in such a way that the steps and procedures of the older method are genuinely experiential—really what the older method always intended them to be, but was unable systematically to make them be.

Thus the proponents of each method I have mentioned can be expected to say "But this is just how we intend our method to be used." Yes, I reply, but you have not been able to explain how to do it, and therefore all but the very few do not do it that way. Even to say how to use any method effectively, you must have some words that refer to the experiential process, to what is directly felt and is not this or that but a feel of an implicit richness, the bodily felt whole of "all that," relevant to a difficulty. Without that you are trapped on only words and what *they* mean, and any procedures work only haplessly.

My version of client-centered therapy in the first section of this chapter was, itself, one of these applications of the experiential method. I reformulated client-centered therapy in experiential terms; it is the only way I can specify how it works. As in the other cases, how could one explain that a therapist response must be checked by the person against a felt sense, if one cannot use words about something concretely and bodily experiential? Also, it cannot be explained that client-centered therapy (when it is done correctly) involves steps. The whole point is not to say exactly what the person says or felt, but that so doing enables new aspects to arise when next the person checks into the felt sense. Saying these again makes for more movement.

But again, such movement is possible only if both people are working on something they both know to be not as yet fully defined, not consisting of just these or those ideas or emotions or contents. One must be in touch with the implicitly complex and not conceptually clear felt sense. The listener too, must know that that is what is being worked with, although only the person being listened to can feel it directly. Even so, the vocabulary and concerns of client-centered therapy, like those of the other methods, cannot get at the experiential method. One can do therapy experientially, and use them all for aids, but in their terms one cannot say how. In this respect client-centered therapy is one method among others, and the experiential method is no more related to it than to any other. Client-centered therapy *is* special in providing listening responses that are needed as a constant baseline for staying in touch with the person, whatever else one does.

In conclusion, today I would not propagate client-centered therapy as a single orientation any more than I would propagate any other. Like the others it can be done badly. Then it results in years of rambling talk. Like the others it can be done well, if one makes the experiential method one's basic method.

On the other hand, I would wish that everyone would personally experience the effect of good client-centered listening and thus learn from inside the power of that kind of responding. I would wish that every therapist made listening a precondition for anything else.

REFERENCES

Gendlin, E. T. *Experiencing and the creation of meaning.* New York: Free Press, 1962.

Gendlin, E. T. Schizophrenia: Problems and methods of psychotherapy. *Review of Existential Psychology and Psychiatry,* 4 (2), Spring 1964.

Gendlin, E. T. Focusing. *Psychotherapy: Theory, Research and Practice,* 1969, **6,** 4–15.

Gendlin, E. T. A short summary and some long predictions. In J. T. Hart & T. M. Tomlinson (Eds.), *New directions in client-centered therapy.* Boston: Houghton Mifflin, 1970.

Gendlin, E. T., Beebe, J., Cassens, J., Klein, M., & Oberlander, M. Focusing ability in psychotherapy, personality and creativity. In J. M. Shlien

(Ed.), *Research in psychotherapy*. Vol. 3. Washington, D.C.: American Psychological Association, 1968.

Gendlin, E. T., & Hendricks, M. *Rap manual*. Unpublished mimeograph by *Changes*, Chicago 1972.

Gendlin, E. T., & Olsen, L. The use of imagery in experiential focusing. *Psychotherapy: Theory, Research, and Practice*, 1970, **7**, 221–223.

Goldiamond, I., & Dryud, J. E. Some applications and implications of behavior analysis for psychotherapy. In J. M. Shlien (Ed.), *Research in psychotherapy*. Vol. 3. Washington, D.C.: American Psychological Association, 1968.

Klein, M. H., Mathieu, P. L., Kiesler, D. J., & Gendlin, E. T. *The Experiencing Scale: A research and training manual*. Madison: University of Wisconsin, Bureau of Audio-visual Instruction, 1970.

Rogers, C. R. *On becoming a person*. Boston: Houghton Mifflin, 1961.

CHAPTER 8

Three Dimensions of Psychotherapy:
I–We–Thou

Joseph R. Noel
Timothy K. De Chenne

The purpose of this paper is to sketch a system of psychotherapy based on the explicit use of three distinct dimensions, which we refer to as I, We, and Thou. I–We–Thou therapy is in part an attempt to combine the strengths of client-centered therapy and encounter groups. It grew upon reflection and recollection of what we believe to be critical personal growth events in our own lives. These were times when we felt different internally, for example, more relaxed or resolved. I–We–Thou therapy also sprang from the weaknesses in strict Rogerian therapy, and from the deficiencies, interferences, and obstacles to growth we experienced in encounter groups. This therapy is in part an intentional and structured system focusing specifically on the growth dimensions of both individual therapy and encountering modalities.

First we will focus somewhat on the deficiencies and strengths of I–We–Thou forerunners. Then we will describe I–We–Thou dimensions or structures. We will close with some theoretical implications.

Two main criticisms of traditional client-centered therapy are that it is unnecessarily slow and incomplete. As individual client-centered therapists we frequently encountered a variety of complaints that ran in three main areas: methodological inexplicitness, the lack of mutuality, and covert interpersonal issues. The concern with methodological inexplicitness is a desire for the therapist to share his conscious intentions in the relationship, to share what he hopes to do. Clients consider the therapist to be an expert in solving problems, and become anxious when he does not do what he is "supposed to do." Inexperienced clients who are not sufficiently acquainted with their internal process do not understand why the therapist does not intervene. It is hard for clients to believe that the therapist has no hidden agendas, no expectations and preferences concerning the relationship. It is difficult to trust a therapist fully if he avoids making the groundwork of therapy explicit. It is like hiring a guide who avoids telling you which way he would like to go.

The client's complaint over the lack of mutuality concerns his sense of being controlled, manipulated, or condescended to in the relationship, and the related feeling of being isolated from the therapist as a person. It is a call for a more symmetrical relationship; more important, it is a desire to participate in the exploration of the therapist. It is a genuine concern, which can be traced to the one-sided structure of many therapy approaches. There is a temptation to dismiss the client's complaint about the lack of mutuality as romantic or ideological. But the complaint is associated with behavioral consequences. In addition to intrapersonal exploration, therapy serves as a model for living in the world, for interpersonal relationships. When the therapist only listens to the client's feelings, the client's sensitivity to his internal processes improves both in therapy and in everyday situations. He is more in touch with himself and can relate more effectively. But he simply does not know how to be sensitive to another person's feelings and process. He has not learned how to listen to someone else. In therapy, the model promulgated was entirely one way, and that model carries over to everyday interaction. Thus, the lack of mutuality complaint is legitimate, because traditional therapy really only teaches incomplete relationship skills.

More abstractly it may be thought of as a means–end problem. Therapy needs to be a means toward the achievement of an ideal relationship. As much as possible the process of therapy should be the example of a good way of interpersonal being. It must be an attempt at a perfect relationship. Minimally it should strive toward having the structural properties and variety needed in a growing relationship.

The client's concern with covert interpersonal issues centers on the feeling of being blocked by vaguely perceived disturbances working somehow between the client and therapist. For instance, the client may feel blocked when something important he was about to say eludes him, or when he finds he has been avoiding matters of importance and can only "small talk." There is more to this feeling than "something the therapist is doing is keeping me from going on;" there is also "something I am doing is contributing to why the therapist is acting this way." It is a sense of dual responsibility for a covert interpersonal disturbance, a disturbance that must be dealt with openly and collaboratively. In other words, there are feelings the client has about the therapist and feelings the therapist has about the client that become obstacles to the therapy and need to be recognized, invited, aired, and heard. As they are accurately heard by both the therapist and the client, they become resolved and become another important aspect of therapeutic growth. Furthermore, in addition to the interpersonal feelings of the therapist and client that may deter therapy, there are often process obstacles. The therapist may be misunderstanding the client and making inaccurate responses, or the client may not know how to focus on his feelings. Or the therapist, because of his own fears, may unconsciously avoid responding to some of the client's problems. These obstacles also need to be given time and attention so they may be dealt with and thus improve the therapy. Neither the working through of interpersonal feelings between client and therapist from both sides, nor the discussion of incomplete or inadequate therapeutic procedures have a purposeful focus in traditional client-centered therapy.

As therapists in traditional client-centered therapy we experienced feelings complementary to these client concerns. For instance, as a complement to the concern with mutuality, we have often felt that although we were expressing our feelings openly with the client, he was not really "picking up" on our feelings. We were trying to be as genuine as possible, trying to communicate that we were not hiding behind a facade, and yet we felt frustrated, because we received no sense that he actually considered or understood our feelings. We also need to feel that we are accurately heard. We came to realize that this frustration often lay behind our boredom, our irritation, the undifferentiated "sick" feeling we had inside. When the therapist is stuck with these feelings, it is much more difficult to provide facilitative conditions for the client. We tend to tune out, to become less empathic. We began to feel increasingly that there was certainly more the client could do, and that we would probably both be happier if he did it. We began to wonder if there wasn't an answer to the client's question "Isn't there something I can help you with?"

Another source for the development of the approach was our experience with encounter groups. Although we have experienced growth through sharing experiences, receiving honest feedback and support, encounter groups often develop counterproductive norms. When a person is vulnerable and open, his personal functioning can be manipulated toward the normative behavior of the group. Depending on the group, a participant may have to show raw emotion, submit to analysis, take imposed risks, receive advice, be interrogated, be pressured to self-disclose, and so on, in order to be accepted, included, and appreciated. In these cases growth occurs with great difficulty, if at all, and the experience may in fact be deleterious. A second group complaint concerns the chaos that exists when more than one person simultaneously acts out an agenda, with the resulting diffusion of focus and disconnectedness of discourse. In these cases, frustration increases, hostility erupts, and the group process becomes dysfunctional to personal growth.

Our reaction to these various complaints has been the construction of a system that merges into a coherent whole, combining the benefits of the three perspectives: that of a client, a therapist, and a member of an encounter group. Our approach builds in the time and space that permits the client to experience what is unique to Rogerian therapy. He experiences the sense of responsibility for himself in the relationship, the exploration of denied attitudes, the reorganizing of the self, and the like. He is also given opportunities to have the rewards of acting as a therapist. For example, in a 1964 speech at Stanford University, Carl Rogers told what he personally got out of being a therapist. He said that as a counselor he learned everything he knows about interpersonal relations and general laws of behavior, and that being a counselor has got him in touch with aspects of the awesome. More concretely, the empathy skills developed as a therapist are critical in everyday life. From encounter groups, we include the abilities to become aware of how we affect others and in turn are affected by others, and the ability to perceive interpersonal process and change it. We recognize the unique values of these three types of experience, but we propose that putting the three together enhances the value of each, while tending to overcome their limitations when taken separately. In systematically using the three dimensions, we have modified each and created mechanisms for linking them together.

DIMENSIONS IN THERAPY

I–We–Thou psychotherapy involves three dimensions or perspectives that are made explicit in a preliminary interview and consciously focused upon in the therapy sessions. The first focus, what we call the I dimension, has similarities to the basic features of client-centered counseling. In this dimension, the events of therapy are made relevant primarily in relation to the client's psychic framework. It is an attitude of the counselor that says, in effect, "The most important matter before us is how you feel, and the best thing I can do is try to get in touch with those feelings." As behavior, this dimension usually involves statements by the client followed by a therapist statement that attempts to reflect or point to the emotional content or underlying meaning of the client's remarks.

When the therapist feels he understands the experiential thrust of the client at the moment, he tries (perhaps several times) to respond empathically. We consistently stress that the client also has a responsibility in this process: namely, to aid the therapist in his search for understanding, to restate feelings if necessary in order to bring the therapist to a fuller discernment. In other words, the client acts as a consultant for the therapist, helping the latter to refine his empathic remarks until there is a shared acknowledgment of accurate empathy.

The importance of this process for the client, as Rogers (1951) has noted, lies in the nonthreatening empathic atmosphere in which the client can examine those parts of himself inconsistent with his self-concept. Rogers (1961) has observed that clients move toward recognizing and "owning" a variety of constantly changing feelings, experiencing in the present moment, holding more tentative constructs concerning the meaning of their experience and developing a self that is not viewed as an object, but that is synonymous with subjective experience. The I dimension is an important third of our approach.

The second focus of our approach, the Thou dimension, also takes about one-third of therapy time. Again, we define it in terms of attitude and behavior. The attitude places a primary importance on the therapist's perspective; the events of therapy are made relevant primarily in relation to the therapist's psychic framework. It is an attitude of the therapist that says, in effect, "At this point in therapy the most important matter before me is how I feel, and the best thing you can do is try to get in touch with those feelings." As behavior, the Thou dimension usually involves statements by the therapist followed by a client statement that attempts to reflect or point to the experiential thrust of the therapist's remarks.

This attitude of the therapist involves a genuine respect for the client. It is a kind of prizing that accepts the client as an equal, which says "I value you enough to give myself over to you, to let you help change me by coming in touch with me."

In the Thou dimension the exchange proceeds more or less as a mirror image of the I perspective. The therapist tries to communicate his feelings and the client tries to empathize with them. Because it is reasonable to assume that most clients will not be as good in the empathic process as the therapist himself, the therapist will more often be acting as a consultant or coach on the Thou process, at least in the early stages of therapy. When the client misses the mark the therapist will need to reexpress himself, and to help the client come closer to his feelings. Of course, "correcting" a client's response may, especially if the client feels uncertain about the whole process, lead to a feeling in the client that he should keep his mouth shut. It is important therefore not only to help the client over his misreading of your remarks, but to express your valuing of his attempt to enter your world.

Our confidence in the Thou dimension rests on a fundamental assumption. Rogers (1961) has assumed that at base each person is capable of exploring his own problems and of dealing with them. As a corollary, we have assumed that each person is capable of coming closer to the feelings of others, thereby helping the other to grow. In short, every client is a potential helper. Further, communication of acceptance and empathy is helpful not only to the person receiving these communications but also to the person giving them. Some of the advantages of the Thou dimension for the client, and for the therapeutic relationship as a whole, are:

1. *Increased mutuality in relationships.* The Thou perspective is a step in the direction of alleviating the sterile one-sidedness that may prevail in therapy or extratherapy relationships. It moves away from viewing the therapist or any significant other as an expert in human relations, and moves toward a view that stresses openness and sensitivity in a more democratic relationship.

2. *The internalization of listening abilities.* From the outset the legitimacy of the therapist's self-disclosures and the valuing of the client's empathic responses are stressed. In the Thou dimension the therapist strives not only to disclose his inner life, but also, in a manner that shows valuing and respect, to help the client focus on and become more sensitive to the person before him. We hypothesize that these efforts result not only in interpersonal sensitivity but in intrapsychic sensitivity as well. They foster listening abilities that can be turned inward to enhance the client's contact with his own fluctuating experiences.

Once these empathic skills are learned, the client is encouraged to incorporate them into his everyday conversations and to observe their impact on others. These skills then are refined daily. Thus, not only expression of feeling but also being a facilitative person to others is explicitly fostered within each counseling session. The client begins to realize that he has more mutually beneficial alternatives when in difficult conversations than arguing or distancing. He begins to realize interpersonal effectiveness while reflecting others' feelings.

3. *The therapist as an effective model.* Therapist self-disclosure legitimizes and stimulates similar activity or processes in the client. By focusing on and differentiating his inner life, the therapist provides concrete examples to which the client may refer in his own self-exploration. Learning how to focus on one's internal bodily references comes much easier if the therapist is an unambiguous model. He can be an exceptionally good influence, if during the Thou stage, he asks his focusing questions to himself out loud so that the client can hear him. In addition, occasionally we have even found it useful to give clients written lists of focusing instructions that have in the past facilitated the therapist's process. In any case, at some point, the client becomes aware of his own sets of internal instructions.

4. *An increase in the client's sense of personal worth.* As clients become more proficient in the Thou dimension, the therapist becomes more at home in expressing his experience to his client. Such shifts, we believe, are highly visible and of great importance to the self-esteem of the client. He gains a sense of helping, of being not only needed but effective in the way he meets the needs of another. And since so many clients must struggle with estrangement from their fellows, with a sense of disconnectedness and uselessness, we see the Thou dimension as contributing significantly to the actualization of therapeutic goals.

5. *The Thou dimension sets aside a legitimate space for therapist expressivity.* It allows the client to perceive therapist genuiness and allows the therapist to externalize his concerns, freeing him to focus more clearly on the client's self-exploration. After freeing himself of unexpressed affect, the therapist experiences a sense of renewal. His therapeutic facilities are enhanced and enriched and thereby made more readily available to the client.

In the early sessions, about one-third of our time is devoted to the third focus of our approach, which we call the We dimension. As the name implies, this perspective does not place primary relevance on either one of the members' psychic framework. Rather, it involves discussion of processes occurring *between* the client and therapist, processes which are co-owned and must be dealt with collaboratively. Thus, a broad definition of this perspective is the discussion of interpersonal processes. This kind of discussion is strongly associated with T-groups, encounter groups, or sensitivity training, particularly with human relations groups whose major learning focus is on how the here-and-now behavior of the participants affects one another. It is difficult to define precisely the content of the We dimension, as its focus may range from long-term patterns in interaction to the immediate, affective impact of one individual on the other. The We dimension includes, for example, giving and receiving feedback, problem-solving on the therapy process with both participants acting as if they were outside observers, and the immediate expression of emotions catalyzed by the interaction.

One major purpose of the We dimension is to alleviate interpersonal issues, that is, problems between the client and therapist that are seen as hindering the acceptance and empathy characteristic of the I and Thou dimensions. It appears that barriers to mutual empathy arise less because of the content of the issues than because the issues are operating *covertly* in the encounter. By explicitly making the We dimension a significant third of the therapy process we believe interpersonal issues come to the fore and are resolved more quickly. By presenting their issues, coming to a mutual understanding of them, discussing the relations among them and keeping alert to the way the issues change as they are discussed, interpersonal distance tends to be bridged.

The range of content of interpersonal issues is highly varied. It is clear that "approach" tendencies such as erotic attraction or the striving for dependence can interfere with the empathic process as much as avoidance issues such as distrust. Further, the possible range of issues must be extended to include individuals outside the interaction; that is, either client or therapist may have encountered similar difficulties with other individuals. When this is true for the client, the therapist may well point it out, but this is not the interpretation of transference in the classic sense. It is a statement of similarities, phrased in terms of the client's consciousness and closely tied to the previous statements of the client.

The advantages of the We dimension go beyond the reduction of empathic barriers. First, this dimension is an anchor to the here-and-now situation, an anchor that the participants agree to drop regularly and frequently in every session. Further, through this perspective, both client and therapist become increasingly aware of the effects their actions have on one another. Finally and perhaps most important, through the We perspective, the client becomes aware that his objections to the way therapy is proceeding are legitimate and valued. In a fundamental sense, he has more control over the course of his therapy because he has a say on the manner in which the therapist approaches him.

THE COURSE OF THERAPY

In our approach, the course of therapy begins with a preliminary interview, a sharing with the client of procedures and goals. In the initial contact the therapist briefly describes the three dimensions, augmenting his explanation with examples illustrating the kind of activity to which each dimension refers. He then turns to a discussion of *cycling*, the various modes by which client and therapist may shift among the three perspectives.

From the beginning, it is stressed that the client holds the decision-making powers over the cycling process. The dimension to which client and therapist proceed and the amount of time they spend there rest upon the decision of the client. However, this fundamental ground rule does not preclude the negotiation of the cycling process in any given session. The therapist indicates that he shall inevitably have preferences about where to go at any point in therapy, and that he will feel free both to suggest a focus and to negotiate this suggestion with the client.

The therapist goes on to explain that there are different ways of shifting among the three dimensions. The different kinds of cycling can be placed on a continuum according to the amount of explicit structuring involved in each. For instance, a highly structured mode would be the pattern I–We–Thou, and so on, with the explicit agreement to shift the focus as frequently as possible without losing some sense of "closure" or experiential shift in each dimension. A highly unstructured mode would simply be the decision to change dimensions whenever comfortable, with no prearrangements as to the sequence of the perspectives. Our preference is to begin therapy in the highly structure mode, primarily so that the client may learn through experience that all three modalities are available to him and are of equal legitimacy and value. Through frequent dimension exposures and shifts the client begins to gain facility with the system. When a minimum level of such facility has been acquired, we then feel more comfortable in adopting an unstructured mode of cycling. Generally, we believe that a minimum level is evidenced when the client himself begins to suggest dimension shifts.

The therapist concludes the preliminary interview by summarizing what he hopes will occur as a result of therapy: that the client will be aware of all his fluctuating feelings, capable of empathizing with another, and able to recognize the process of interaction between himself and others. During the explanation, the therapist checks to see if the client has understood, and remains willing to explain his concepts more fully if necessary. Inasmuch as we are advocating an essentially symmetrical relationship, it is important that the client has all the information he needs to fully understand and operate within the model, rather than just a brief or abstract introductory note.

This kind of initial interview has two important advantages. First, it tends to alleviate the many difficulties arising from methodological inexplicitness. As mentioned earlier, procedural ambiguity often serves as a subtle divisive influence in the relationship. Second, the initial interview is the first step toward concentrating on the therapeutic relationship. By discussion of some of the structures in the interaction, the dyad begins to develop the awareness characteristic of the We dimension. One important result of this awareness is the built-in, ongoing mechanisms for making the therapeutic method explicit, teachable, and negotiable.

For the most part, our therapy sessions are characterized by the kind of process described in the foregoing pages. However, it is possible to conceive of the dimensions less as specific procedures than as general frames of reference. Thus, we have remained open to the use of other specific techniques that may foster the kinds of awareness characteristic to these dimensions. For example, as an aid to the I dimension we have employed Gendlin's (1969) *focusing* procedure, through which the client attends to the bodily sense of his problems and lets the words come from these felt meanings. As an aid to the We dimension, we introduce a third party or consultant at an early point in therapy and recommend using a consultant in every third meeting. If a consultant is used early, before client and therapist become resistant to any intrusion from the outside, the effect of even one or two consultation sessions can be remarkable. Our consultation model is similar to other models in that we advocate that the consultant attend to the participants' feelings, behaviors, voice quality, and to the relationship between these elements. Our consultation differs in that the consultant also attends to and relates back to the participants such matters as sequence and quality of the dimensions and the amount of time spent in each. The consultant shares his observations when he has been asked to do so and when he feels comfortable doing so. His objective is not to convince the dyad that his observations are correct, but rather to elicit responses to those observations, to focus the members' attention on one another, and to help clarify the feelings that arise from that focus. In many ways he functions as the facilitator of an encounter group; another way of saying it is that he energizes the We dimension of psychotherapy.

We have also used therapist–client role reversal, a technique in psychodrama and Gestalt work, because it has the peculiar quality of bringing all three dimensions together simultaneously. But we must emphasize that all these special procedures occupy only a small percentage of our time in therapy. We believe the system as presented is a better solution to the problems inherent in client-centered therapy than any of these specific techniques; through it, client and therapist focus on what are likely to be the three essential dimensions of healthy personal relationships. Further, it is possible that a good deal of "psychopathology" can be traced to the persistent failure in, or avoidance in everyday life of, one or more of the I–We–Thou dimensions of being.

A brief description of the I–We–Thou system as it is applied to group psychotherapy is as follows: It begins with a mutually shared We dimension, where the first decision concerns which participant is to be the helper, and if the individual agrees, the session proceeds with the rest of greatest urgency, that is, the person with the most pressing problem or anxiety. Next, the helpee chooses another group member to be the primary helped, and if the individual agrees, the session proceeds with the rest of the group assuming the role of consultant. After an agreed upon period of time, usually 10 to 20 minutes, the personages of helpee and helper are renegotiated. Sometimes more than one person simultaneously feels that his urgency should take precedence (i.e., two or more people want to be helpee at the same time). At this point, the group may split into smaller groups. Another useful arrangement involves one person as helper, another as helpee, and a third as consultant, while the rest of the group function as observers to the triad. The observers remain silent for an agreed amount of time and then give feedback to the triad. Other combinations are also useful, but will have to await a fuller description at a later point.

In closing, we will summarize why we think I–We–Thou counseling is an advance on the traditional client-centered approach, and point to a revised view of personal growth. We hypothesize that I–We–Thou counseling is faster, provides a greater range of interpersonal skills, and yet retains the essential value system of client-centered thinking. Theoretically, Rogers' necessary and sufficient conditions need to be revised to include the mutuality principle. In brief, personal growth is better facilitated if both participants agree to focus on, prize, and empathize on each other's accept) each other's inner life. Personal growth is further enhanced if both participants agree to focus on, prize, and empathize on each others view of how they are with each other at every meeting.

REFERENCES

Gendlin, E. T. Focusing. *Psychotherapy: Theory, Research, and Practice.* 1969, 6, 4–15.

Rogers, C. R. *Client-centered therapy.* Boston: Houghton Mifflin, 1951.

Rogers, C. R. *On becoming a person.* Boston: Houghton Mifflin, 1961.

CHAPTER 9

Client-Centered Therapy and Gestalt Therapy: In Search of a Merger

Carolyn T. Cochrane

A. Joanne Holloway

The responsibility of the therapist is to influence maximally the probability that a certain kind of process will occur in the individual who comes to him for help. Accordingly, the individual who elects to become a therapist takes on a lifelong concern with how to grow in the actualization of his potential as a therapist, that is, in his capability for influencing the growth process in his clients.

All actualization requires an attitude of re-viewing every second afresh. The re-viewing in which we invite our concerned therapist-readers to join us is of two therapy systems, client-centered and Gestalt, that we consider incompletely developed as systems. We take the position that each of these therapy systems could play a significant role in increasing the actualization of the other. We also take the position that a therapist's own development within any therapy system is constrained by the degree of actualization of the total system he has accepted as the basis for his operations. Hence, before we can look meaningfully at how individual therapists might become more therapeutic, we must first work on recasting the overall therapy system in directions that are system-actualizing. Keep in mind, however, that the attention we devote at this point to the therapy system is only preparation for our primary focus on the tangible *practice* of therapy.

For us, the starting point for examining a therapy system is to ask three questions: (a) What is man's basic nature? (b) What is nonfulfillment of his nature? (c) What restores man to fulfilling his nature? Each therapy system provides its own answers to these questions and its answers form a conceptual definition of that system.

The first question, What is man's basic nature? is phrased in a way that would be recognized in all therapy systems. However, the phrasing of questions two and three is already an outcome of the answer supplied to question one. To illustrate, if the description of man's nature includes the concept of pathological mechanisms, then question two must be phrased, What is the pathology (sickness) that affects his nature? And question three becomes, How is the sickness (pathology) cured or removed?

Thus, the manner in which we have phrased questions two and three for client-centered and Gestalt therapies, referring to nonfulfillment and restoration of fulfillment, indicates that these therapies have in common a view of man's nature that is different from the psychoanalytic view reflected in the illustrative phrasing above.

MAN'S BASIC NATURE: HOW IT IS VIEWED

The particular view of man's nature embraced by client-centered and Gestalt therapies is traditionally called the humanistic view. Although the term "humanistic" in itself may convey little—as who doubts that man is human—a body of understanding has grown up around the term that makes it a useful label. Thus, as humanistic therapies, the client-centered and Gestalt approaches emphasize first and foremost that every human being is a unique individual. Man's uniqueness is an inevitable outcome of his operation in a subjective mode. Carl Rogers' (1959) belief in the fundamental predominance of the subjective, in comparison with the objective, is unmistakable. He says:

Man lives essentially in his own personal and subjective world, and even his most objective functioning, in science, mathematics, and the like, is the result of subjective purpose and subjective choice [p. 191].[1]

Frederick Perls (1969) is equally definite about the predominance of the subjective. He says:

I personally believe that objectivity does not exist. The objectivity of science is also just a matter of mutual agreement [p. 12].[2]

Perls takes the position that our only knowing of the universe is through the particular sense organs we happen to come equipped with. The particular nature of these organs automatically affects the scope and quality of

[1] Quotations from Rogers (1959) in this chapter reprinted by permission of McGraw-Hill.

[2] Quotations from Perls (1969) in this chapter © 1969 Real People Press. Reprinted by permission of the publisher.

the impressions we receive. What is "really" out there is only speculation. What is perceived within the person is the only reality anyone can be in contact with. This conception of the nature of reality is expressed by Gestaltists in a strong valuing of subjective living through a here-and-now focus. If reality can be known only through the senses, it follows that the best possible means of staying in contact with reality is for a person to maintain a continuous contact with the impressions flowing in through his sensory receptors. It also follows that for a therapist truly to know his patient, he must be prepared to receive the unique subjective self the patient represents rather than seek to impose so-called objective perceptions on him.

We see that our two theories are alike in believing that no absolute reality, no statement as to "what is" can be universally established. Both theories view each person as having his own truth regarding himself, his environment, his preferred ways of interacting with his environment, and so on. This aspect, the uniqueness that arises from locating reality within the person's internal perceptions, allows both theories of therapy to qualify as phenomenological.

Though our two therapy theories view each person as unique in his own constellation of being, they also see each person as sharing common life processes. Man is a part of nature and all men share in those processes that characterize their level of being. For man, the significant common processes at the psychological level are motivation, organismic responsiveness, and consciousness.

Before we describe the nature of these basic life processes, we would like to emphasize the critical significance of the *process* concept to the understanding of these theories. Both the client-centered and the Gestalt therapy theories are first and foremost process theories of man. As such, they are concerned with the *how* rather than the *why* of behavior—that is, with functional laws rather than with historical causality. The process nature of our theories is evident in their lack of interest in viewing the organism in terms of structures, traits, and other static, content-oriented characteristics. Process theories exhibit a preference for describing the organism in movement-oriented terms such as exchanging, emerging, unfolding, flowing. The latter terms do not suggest content-oriented goals or criteria for the organism to achieve, but instead suggest a concern with the effectiveness of the organism's functioning in its own right.

Process theories are not concerned with either input or output, but rather with what is going on in between these two points—that is, with what affects being able to get from here to anywhere. In spatial terms, process is concerned with how to get moving, not with where to go. In temporal terms, process is strictly a matter of now, not of then or when.

Process has its own internal lawfulness in terms of which it is continuously operating. Rules need not (and cannot) be imposed upon process from outside; through its working, process reveals its own order. There is no point in asking why a process operates in the way it does. It merely is what it is. To get with it is to discover its own lawfulness and to attune one's actions and expectations to what is. Process is trustworthy in that it is consistent and predictable because it is being lawful unto itself. As such, what it produces is also beyond question. A lawful process produces what it can (or must), nothing else. Hence the only thing left to be concerned with about a process is whether anything is in any way hindering the natural working out of the process—that is, interfering with its functioning.

The process model described above is integral to the reasoning of our two theories. Both client-centered and Gestalt theory take the position that people can be understood psychologically in terms of the lawfulness of three general life processes: motivation, organismic responsiveness, and consciousness or awareness.

The first of these, man's motivation process, consists of a tendency to fulfill himself, to strive to realize his potentiality as the human being that he is. The directing of life is toward actualization. Life is growth—continual, unending, open process. Man is appropriately termed constructive; he is becoming as well as being. Man is never finished in the sense of having a final identity. Each achievement in realizing his potentialities becomes a new base from which to grow and further realize himself.

In client-centered theory this single motive force or directing tendency is termed the *actualization tendency*. Rogers (1959) defines the actualizing tendency thus:

> This is the inherent tendency of the organism to develop all its capacities in ways which serve to maintain or enhance the organism [p. 196].

The actualizing tendency is the only motive postulated by Rogers. The actualizing tendency has a central function as a criterion in the organismic valuing process. That is, experiences are valued in accordance with how well they serve the actualization motive of the person—that is, as to how much they help it meet its needs to exist and grow.

Perls (1969) posits an identical self-regulating tendency directing the organism's activities. As he says:

> . . . with full awareness you become aware of this organismic self-regulation, you can let the organism take over without interfering, without interrupting; we can rely on the wisdom of the organism [p. 16].

Perls views the organism as a system that is in balance. Any imbalance is felt as a need to correct the imbalance. Any number of imbalances may be occurring simultaneously. The most urgent of these emerges as the "emergency" that takes precedence over all others. This emergency becomes the director at that point in time. It occupies the center of attention until it secures relief or restoration of balance, or what Perls (1969) terms the "end-gain." He describes this process very simply:

> ...from within, some figure emerges, comes to the surface, and then goes into the outside world, reaches out for what we want, and comes back, assimilates and receives. Something else comes out, and again the same process repeats itself [pp. 21–22].

The figures that emerge into the foreground and render the remainder of the field background are the *gestalts*. A good gestalt is one that progressively dominates the field by gathering unto itself the resources of the field until it is unified, bright, sharp, and clear. Gestalts may be either perceptual or motor. That is, behavior on both the perceptual level and the motor level is organized by the felt imbalance to permit the individual to engage in activities that will satisfy his needs. These perceptual and motor behaviors are said to be *gestalt-motivated*. When a need is satisfied, its domination of the perceptual field is ended and the need next highest in the hierarchy of needs moves in to organize perceptual experience and behavior. As Perls (1969) says:

> ...our life is basically nothing but an infinite number of unfinished situations—incomplete gestalts. No sooner have we finished one situation than another comes up [p. 15].

Up to this point we have a better picture of how the motivational process operates to maintain the organism than we do of how this process enhances the organism. Perls (1969) sees the overall direction of all life as toward actualization rather than mere maintenance.

> Every individual, every plant, every animal has only one inborn goal—to actualize itself as it is [p. 31].

This complete actualization Perls (1969) terms *maturity*. And, as he says:

> ...maturation is never completed. It's an ongoing process for ever and ever.... There's always a possibility of richer maturation [p. 64].

By Perls' own estimate, most persons are using only about 5–15% of their potential at the most. By that calculation, the possibilities for increased actualization are substantial indeed, if persons would but allow themselves to grow.

Thus, we see that both Perls and Rogers are essentially optimistic about the motivational direction of man's life. They see actualization as a process of increasingly assimilating experience into one's being. The only limit to actualization for any person is his own death, or—within life—the level of functioning of his process. While alive, each person has the possibility of actualizing his being limitlessly.

A second major process that all persons have in common is an experiencing process. Experiencing is the immediate registering by the organism of all that is happening in it and around it from instant to instant. Rogers (1959) provides this definition of *experience*:

> This term is used to include all that is going on within the envelope of the organism at any given moment which is potentially available to awareness [p. 197].

Rogers goes on to note that experience refers to the given moment, not to some accumulation of past experiences. He puts this concisely:

> ... to experience means simply to receive in the organism the impact of the sensory or physiological events which are happening at the moment [p. 197].

Gestalt theory also has a well-developed belief in the existence of an experiencing process within man. Perls identifies two systems with which man relates to the world: the sensoric system and the motoric system. The *sensoric system* includes orientation and the sense of touching and serves to get us in touch with the world. The *motoric system* is our way of coping, our system of action through which we do something with the world. Together they provide orientation and ability to act. Perceptual and motor events register in the organism in the form of gestalts—that is, emergent figures. The gestalt is the ultimate experiential unit. It is what is experienced phenomenologically. Gestalts cannot be analyzed or broken down further.

Thus, both Perls and Rogers see experiencing as the process by which the organism receives reports of ongoing events both from within itself and from the surrounding environment. Rogers' definition appears to limit experiencing to perceptual events, whereas Perls' definition includes motoric events as well. Perls' inclusion of the motoric system in experiencing has significant counterparts in his emphasis on body (muscular) sensations and activity as data for therapy exploration.

A third major process that all people have in common is that of *awareness* of their experience. Awareness according to Rogers is the symbolization of experience at the conscious level. The conscious representation of experience need not be verbal. Experience is available to awareness whenever it can be allowed in—that is, symbolized without defensive denial or distortion. The self-concept serves as the criterion by which the organism decides which experiences it will permit to be accurately symbolized in awareness. When the self-concept or self-structure of an individual can permit *all* experiences to be accurately symbolized in awareness, self and self-experience are considered to be in a state of congruence. A congruent indivdual is completely open to his experience in the sense that the self does not perform any alterations or censoring on what is received. Pure awareness of experience occurs.

Gestalt theory is highly involved with the concept of awareness. For Perls, awareness is so fundamental and powerful a phenomenon that he proposes it be considered a third dimension of matter, alongside of extension and duration. Awareness is the key to the organism's healthy functioning. Awareness is the process of attending to experience. Awareness encompasses both attention to self in the form of needs and attention to the world in regard to means of meeting needs. Awareness as consciousness works to assist the organism to meet its needs by coordinating its exchanges with the environment. Enright (1970) provides this concise definition of awareness:

Awareness is a state of consciousness that develops spontaneously when organismic attention becomes focused on some particular region of the organism–environment contact boundary at which an especially important and complex transaction is occurring [p. 107].[3]

He adds:

. . . in healthy life awareness is . . . simply there, flowing along with behavior [p. 118].

Perls (1969) refers to a continuum of awareness. He defines it as simply being aware from second to second as to what is going on. As he sees it:

This continuum of awareness is required so that the organism can work on the healthy gestalt principle: that the most important unfinished situation will always emerge and can be dealt with [p. 51].

We cannot complete our discussion of awareness without looking further at the use of the term "self" in each of our theories. For Perls, self is merely a referent or indicator of who is doing something, a way of delimiting this being from that being or from what is other. Self is not a repository of known characteristics that ensure consistency; on the contrary, the creative self is essentially unpredictable. For Perls, the concept of a center of awareness comes closest to filling the function that the congruent self fills in Rogers' theory. Perl (1969) describes the center as providing a place

[3] Quotations from Enright (1970) in this chapter reprinted by permission of Science and Behavior Books.

from which to work and to cope with the world. To be centered is to have anything that happens register immediately. Perls says:

This achieving the center, being grounded in one's self, is about the highest state a human being can achieve [p. 37].

If Perls' centeredness is comparable to the aware being of one's ongoing experience, and Rogers' congruence calls for including all experience in the self, then our two theories agree as to the existence and value of an awareness process paralleling experience.

As we conclude our section on man's basic nature, we see that according to the humanistic viewpoint shared by client-centered and Gestalt therapy theories, the basic nature of man is to be unique, actualizing, experiencing, and aware. These four characteristics appear in only slightly different guises in the theoretical structure of each of these therapy theories.

When these characteristics are present in the ideal form, they generate the model of the fulfilling person. In client-centered theory, this model individual is termed the *fully functioning person*, and is one who is maximally creative and self-actualizing. In Gestalt theory, the model individual is described as the *whole person*, and is one in whom attention and awareness are fully integrated.

WHAT IS NONFULFILLMENT?

Our second major theoretical question is, What is nonfulfillment? To be consistent with our groundwork, any description of this less-than-ideal condition must have its genesis in the basic structure of man's nature that we have just finished sketching. We find just such a continuity. For example, Rogers (1959) defines nonfulfillment, which he calls maladjustment, as follows:

Psychological maladjustment exists when the organism denies to awareness, or distorts in awareness, significant experiences, which consequently are not accurately symbolized and organized into the gestalt of the self-structure, thus creating an incongruence between self and experience [p. 204].

Once the self-structure has become incongruent with experience, the way is open for a self-actualization tendency to work at cross-purposes to the actualization tendency. That is, the individual acts to actualize a self that is no longer congruent with experience. His goal becomes maintenance of the current structure of the self at the expense of allowing experience into awareness.

Perls arrives at a comparable picture of maladjustment, though through a quite different terminology. Perls (1969) conceptualizes maladjustment as a growth disorder, namely the failure of the organism to mature:

> . . . *maturing is the transcendance from environmental support to self-support.* . . . The *impasse* is . . . the crucial point in growth. . . . The impasse is the position where environmental support or obsolete inner support is not forthcoming any more, and authentic self-support has not yet been achieved [p. 28].

Maladjustment reflects an incomplete transition from environmental support to self-support. The maladjusted individual is unable to mobilize his own resources. He is incomplete, or as Perls puts it, has holes in his personality. The holes are the missing parts of himself that he has alienated and given up to the world. This blindness to one's own potential reflects a blockage in the development of awareness.

Perls indicates four main ways in which a person blocks awareness. One is retroflection, in which the person opposes, puts off, and holds back wishes, impulses, and behaviors, resulting in unfinished business. Another is desensitization of sensory and physical messages. A third way is introjection of others' shoulds. A fourth, and perhaps the most important, way is projection of expectations, criticisms, and so on onto other persons. When awareness is blocked by one of these devices, the person is in effect acting on needs that are not based in the organism. Perls terms this behavior self-image actualizing. Self-image actualizing individuals are trying to actualize a concept of what they should be like rather than actualizing themselves. They are living for their image. Self-image actualization is to be contrasted with what Perls terms self-actualization,[4] the latter being actualization of the particular being that one is with full awareness of experience.

Structurally, Perls and Rogers have much the same definition of maladjustment. Experience is not being allowed into awareness. Something from outside the organism has been allowed to take a guiding role in behavior and organismic valuing has been tuned out. The organism is operating from an external locus of control rather than from an internal one. The awareness process is clogged and blocked. A maladjusted person acts out of only part of the data that are potentially available to him. Because he is limited perceptually, his behavioral choices are narrowed.

[4] Note the possible confusion of terms between Perls and Rogers. Rogers' actualizing tendency is equivalent to Perls' self-actualizing tendency. And Rogers' self-actualizing tendency is equivalent to Perls' self-image actualizing tendency.

WHAT RESTORES FULFILLMENT?

What restores the nonfulfilling individual to his basic nature of fulfilling himself? We will deal with this question of restoration on both the theoretical and the operational levels. In our theoretical review, we will establish first what the state of restored fulfillment is like, which is equivalent to specifying the goal of the therapeutic effort. Secondly, we will establish what it is that needs to be available theoretically to bring about the desired effect. The latter task is equivalent to specifying the necessary and sufficient conditions for therapy, a kind of analysis originated by Rogers and one that we feel every therapy theorist would do well to emulate. Gestalt therapy has yet to undertake this task.

The goal of the client-centered therapist is to create complete congruence of self and experience, a state equivalent to complete openness to experience. The therapist wishes to assist the client to revise his concept of self in such a way that all experiences can be accurately symbolized and assimilated.

Rogers' formulation of the conditions that need to be established for the therapy process to proceed are so well known as not to need full quotation here. Briefly put, the therapist must be congruent in the relationship, show unconditional positive regard for the client, and demonstrate an empathic understanding of the client's internal frame of reference. Furthermore, the client must experience the regard and empathy.

Rogers' (1959) position is that the presence of the stated conditions is both necessary and sufficient for the therapy process to get underway, regardless of the particular characteristics of the client. He says:

> . . . it is not necessary nor helpful to manipulate the relationship in specific ways for different kinds of clients [p. 214].

However, in a footnote to a compendium of his theoretical position, Rogers (1959) recognizes that findings from a study by Kirtner may have implications for his position. He notes Kirtner's findings as follows:

> . . . the client who sees his problem as involving his relationships, and who feels that he contributes to this problem and wants to change it, is likely to be successful. The client who externalizes his problem and feels little self-responsibility is much more likely to be a failure [p. 214].

As we will see shortly, the client's feeling of self-responsibility to which Rogers refers is a central concept in Gestalt therapy theory.

Perls (1969) has this to say about the goal of Gestalt therapy:

> What we are after is the maturation of the person, removing the blocks

that prevent a person from standing on his own feet. We try to help him make the transition orfm environmental support to self-support [p. 36].

Perl continues:

So what we are trying to do in therapy is step-by-step to *re-own* the di-owned parts of the personality until the person becomes strong enough to facilitate his own growth . . . [p. 38].

Expressed another way, the goal of the Gestalt therapist is to reintegrate organismic attention and awareness so that the need-fulfillment process can operate freely. Furthermore, the Gestalt therapist wishes to do this in a manner that develops the patient's own problem-solving capacity. An essential job for the Gestalt therapist is to establish the conditions under which the patient can best use his own problem-solving abilities and "be in his own support." The therapist does not directly solve the problem. Instead he works to free the process by which the patient may solve his own problems and be in his own support. The therapist seeks to help the patient overcome the barriers that block awareness, and as Enright (1970) says:

. . . to let nature take its course (that is, let awareness develop) so he can function with all his abilities [p. 108].

Although the idea of furnishing certain conditions is implied in the statements above, to our knowledge no expressed list has ever been formally assembled for Gestalt therapy. In reading the Gestalt literature, we nonetheless find strong hints as to what these conditions might be. We will present our inferences, with the caution that they are just that.

1. The patient must be willing to work. Perls (1969) identifies one necessary condition for therapy as being within the patient's domain. He labels this condition "goodwill." By this term he seems to mean a willingness to work toward being cured rather than a desire to strengthen one's neurotic skills. Perls puts it thus:

Basically, I would say that we encounter two types of clients or patients, and roughly speaking there are the ones who came with goodwill and the others, those who are clever [p. 75].

In Perls' (1969) view working with patients who are not themselves willing to work tends to be unproductive. Regarding the clever people, he in fact says:

And whatever one tries to do will run off, like the water off the famous duck's back, and nothing will penetrate. These people need quite a bit of work. Very many people do not want to work [p. 75].

It was not uncommon for Perls to dismiss a volunteer patient who in his opinion was not willing to work.

2. The therapist must be aware, responsible, and direct in his communication with the patient. Paralleling Perls' (1969) demand that the patient provide goodwill is his demand that the therapist take responsibility for his contribution to the relationship. He describes his stance as follows:

. . . I want to clarify my position. I am responsible only for myself and for nobody else. I am not taking responsibility for any of you—you are responsible for yourselves [p. 74].

Perls was essentially stating the requirement that the therapist be an aware person himself in order to be therapeutic with the patient. Otherwise, according to Perls, the therapist was liable to play out his own neuroses with the patient or to become an accomplice in the patient's manipulative games.

3. The therapist must be able to experience the patient's total communication. Perls (1969) is outspoken regarding the therapist's need to look and to listen in ways that go beyond merely receiving the particular verbal message the patient is aware of sending:

Verbal communication is usually a lie. The real communication is beyond words. So don't listen to the words, just listen to what the voice tells you, what the movements tell you, what the posture tells you, what the image tells you . . . [p. 53].

The ability to take in the panorama of the patient's communication provides the therapist with much of what he needs to work effectively with the patient. Perls (1969) goes on to say:

. . . there is so much invaluable material here that we don't have to do anything else except get to the obvious, to the outermost surface, and feed this back, so as to bring this into the patient's awareness [p. 54].

4. The therapist's interventions must build on actual present behavior, that is, a present concern of the organism. Perls (1969) makes this declaration:

My function as a therapist is to help you to the awareness of the here-and-now, and to frustrate you in any attempt to break out of this [p. 74].

5. The therapist's interventions must operate to expand the patient's

claiming of responsibility for his own living. Perls (1969) describes the implementation of this condition as follows:

> Then the therapist must provide the opportunity, the situation in which the person can grow. And the means is that we frustrate the patient in such a way that he is forced to develop his own potential. . . . the patient is forced to . . . discover that *what he expects from the therapist, he can do just as well himself* [p. 37].

6. The therapist must recognize that the ultimate meaning of any organismic experience is founded in the patient's permitting it to come into his awareness, and thus that interventions should be noninterpretive. Perls (1970) is quite definite on this point:

> The more you refrain from interfering and telling the patient what he is like or what he feels like, the more chance you give him to discover himself and not to be misled by your concepts and projections [p. 29].

Perls' (1969) confidence in the patient's capability for generating meaning for himself is expressed thus:

> But the person has to discover this by seeing for himself, by listening for himself, by uncovering what is there. . . . And the main thing is the listening. To listen, to understand, to be open, is one and the same [p. 38].

The idea of frustrating the patient expressed by Perls in some of the preceding quotations is so strikingly different from anything expressed in Rogers' writings that we would like to elaborate on this idea. At first glance it might seem that Perls' central objective is that of frustrating the patient. However, for Perls frustration is instead an inescapable accompaniment to his basic therapeutic stratagem, which is not to help the patient. By not helping the patient, Perls means not supplying the patient's needs, not doing his work for him, and not filling in the patient's missing pieces. Perls' intention is to get the patient in touch with his own resources. Perls feels this can happen only when the therapist refuses to allow himself to be used for things the patient can do for himself. Perls' unwillingness to allow the patient to play out uninterruptedly his hidden agenda is inevitably experienced as frustrating by the patient.

We will postpone our comparison of the necessary and sufficient conditions for therapy posited by our two therapy systems until we reach the point in this chapter at which we consider how client-centered therapy and Gestalt therapy might be merged into a single, more productive system.

IN THE HOUR: IMPLEMENTATION

It is one thing to know what one's goals are and quite another thing to know what to be doing to achieve these goals. Once again we make our statement regarding the therapist's mission: it is his responsibility to influence maximally the probability that a certain kind of process will occur in the individual who comes to him for help. At this point we are concerned with the implementation of the theoretical positions that have been set forth. What does the therapist do in the hour to restore the fulfillment process in his client or patient? What kinds of responses and interventions does each therapy orientation supply to its practitioners, and what is each intervention or response intended to accomplish? We will deal with both intentions and pitfalls. Intentions are what is planned to happen. Pitfalls are what disrupt the working of the plan.

Intentions

It is difficult to find much written about implementation or technique in client-centered literature, particularly in the earliest writings. This paucity of tactics may well be a function of the belief that what makes therapy happen is indeed supplying the necessary and sufficient conditions. If this is the case, then we must return to our statement of these conditions to see what the therapist does or is in the hour that is crucial. Another way of putting the question about implementation is to ask what makes a particular encounter between two persons therapeutic for at least one of them, as compared with an encounter in which no therapy occurs.

Rogers (1959) comes to the following conclusion:

> . . . for therapy to occur the wholeness (congruence or genuineness) of the therapist in the relationship is primary, but a part of the congruence of the therapist must be in the experience of unconditional positive regard and the experience of empathic understanding [p. 215].

Thus, the therapy process unfolds as a result of the therapist's ability to be completely and fully himself, with his experience of the moment being accurately symbolized and integrated into the picture of himself during his contact with an incongruent client. As part of his congruence in the relationship he experiences unconditional positive regard for and empathic understanding of his client.

The primary means by which the client-centered therapist manifests empathic understanding of the client's internal frame of reference is reflection of feeling. The reflection of feeling response has at times been equated by outsiders with an almost mimicking paraphrase. Reflection should not, and need not, be so limited as such an equation suggests. The origin of the reflection of feeling response lay in the desire to stay within the client's internal frame of reference and to be noninterpretive. It also arose from a belief that the client's inner feeling life was the most important item in bringing about change. Hence reflection of feeling was intended to bring out feeling, to let it flow, and to carry the person along into fuller experiencing of himself.

Over time, the reflection of feeling technique has been enriched considerably, as for example by Rice's (1970) evocative reflection, Gendlin's (1970) focusing tasks, and Butler and Rice's (1963) poetic imagery. The serious student of client-centered therapy technique needs to acquaint himself directly with these recent elaborations.

The primary means by which the client-centered therapist manifests unconditional positive regard is by the constancy of his interest in and receptivity toward the entire range of the client's experience. No one part of this experience is valued more or less than any other. The therapist's *prizing* (Butler, 1965) of the whole person of·the client is seen as an extremely potent element in the therapeutic relationship. Rogers is not particularly explicit as to how this prizing attitude is conveyed into the client's awareness. Nonverbal communication, as in voice quality, posture, and the like, may be particularly important. Rogers (1959) does have much to say, however, about what this attitude is like inside the person of the therapist:

> If the perception by me of some self-experience in another makes a positive difference in my experiential field, then I am experiencing a positive regard for that individual. In general, positive regard is defined as including such attitudes as warmth, liking, respect, sympathy, acceptance [p. 207].

Thus, therapist congruence, positive regard, and active empathy appear to be the main operants in the client-centered approach to therapy.

The specific tactics employed by the Gestalt therapist flow out of the elemental goal of reintegrating organismic attention and awareness and out of the further goal of having the patient develop his own problem-solving capability. In the Gestalt (Enright, 1970) view, the patient is continually demonstrating the following:

> . . . just how he avoids being in full contact with his current actuality—how he avoids awareness of ongoing matters of organismic importance to him [p. 108].

Perls' (1969) description of his basic therapeutic strategy is this:

So what I do as a therapist is to work as a catalyst both ways: provide situations in which a person can experience this being stuck—the unpleasantness—and I frustrate his avoidances still further until he is willing to mobilize his own resources [p. 52].

In contrast to client-centered therapy, Gestalt therapy abounds in specific methods of implementation, frequently referred to as exercises, experiments, or games. Possibly the main problem with such an abundance of techniques is that of organizing them in a way that is meaningful rather than arbitrary or ineffective. The writers are not alone in this problem in that Gestalt therapy faces it as well.

One possibility we are experimenting with for categorizing the multiplicity of Gestalt techniques is classifying them according to the extent to which they are intended primarily to (a) increase the accessibility of the flow of organismic experience or (b) increase the sense of owning one's experience. The former we term *awareness-generating* techniques; the latter, we term *responsibility-generating* techniques. Many exercises contain both elements; others, containing mainly one facet, must be combined in practice to reach both goals of Gestalt therapy. Table 9.1 illustrates how such a categorization might look.

Pitfalls

A pitfall, by definition, is a concealed danger or source of error. We believe the practice of any of our imperfect therapies is subject to various

Table 9.1.   A Categorization of Some Gestalt Techniques

Primarily Awareness-Generating	
Focus on the now	Amplification
Communication in the present tense	Use of the awareness continuum
Dream-telling in the present tense	Exaggeration and repetition
Event-telling in the present tense	Can you stay with this feeling?
Primarily Responsibility-Generating	
Semantic games	Games of dialogue
I language rather than it language	Top-dog and underdog
I won't rather than I can't	Centering—the reconciliation of
Making statements in place of	opposites
asking questions	
Interpersonal directness	Direct claiming
Talking to instead of talking at	. . . and I take responsibility for . . .
Talking to instead of talking about	Asking, How do you . . .?
(no gossiping)	Asking, May I feed you a sentence?

pitfalls, the staking out of which may help save the unsuspecting from some rather rude shocks and unproductive captivity.

Pitfalls may spring from either of two sources: therapy theory or therapist role execution. Most pitfalls probably have their source partially in each. By saying that a therapy theory is a source of pitfalls, we mean that the theory may not have accurately conceptualized certain events or may even have omitted consideration of them. For example, one classic therapy event is the so-called transference situation. When the client or patient produces feelings toward the therapist that the therapist feels are not earned by his own behavior, what does he do, and what is his rationale for so doing? If a therapy theory does not have something to say that is productive about this and other therapy events, the theory can be held responsible for allowing the therapist who attempts to operate on the basis of its elaborated concepts to fall into a hole.

On the other hand, if the therapy theory has dealt adequately with the event at issue and the practitioner for one reason or another has not grasped the essential implication of the therapy theory for his situation, then his failure to deal satisfactorily with the situation is a personal failure —that is, one of role execution. It can readily be presumed that role-execution errors are most often a function of the relative inexperience, lack of traning, or incongruence of beginning therapists. However, role-execution errors can be proliferated and perpetuated by therapy theory errors that make learning of effective modes of response difficult to come by. We will focus exclusively on what we feel are therapy theory pitfalls, recognizing at the same time the difficulties these pose for novices.

THE GIVING PITFALL

The classic client-centered concern with providing the conditions for therapy largely through the relationship or climate engendered by the therapist can lead the therapist into what we are labeling the *giving* pitfall. When the therapist has fallen into the giving pitfall, he is proceeding as if he had defined his role as, "It's my job as therapist to see that you get all you want." The client may assist the therapist in getting into the giving pitfall by communicating in one way or another: "No one has ever really loved me, but perhaps you will," to which a sympathetic therapist can readily respond, "Yes, I will." The therapist in this pitfall becomes involved in literally giving the caring in a naive attempt to fill the client's need.

The probability of a nontherapeutic outcome from the collusion of the therapist and client in such an arrangement is self-evident. By becoming overly concerned with providing the conditions of therapy, rather than with the nature of the client's perceptual problems, the therapist ends up confirming whatever lifelong distortion the client has used to imagine that no one ever cared. The client is maintained right where he is. Further, and worse, in accepting the assignment of bringing in love to serve up to the client, the therapist reinforces the client's dysfunctional notion that the solution to his problems lies outside of himself. This therapist stance helps focus the client's efforts on rearranging the outer world rather than on the more productive restructuring of his inner world as a basis for coping with the world as it is. The client who is already inclined in this direction will readily accept the therapist's help. The two can work together on building a warm, padded nest of a therapy relationship. The client will encourage the therapist's efforts to nest-build for him by communicating something like this: "If you loved me, you would provide a safe (meaning riskless) warm nest for me to nourish myself in (that is, to hide in)." The hook for the therapist is the "If you loved me . . . ," because he does not think of himself as an uncaring person nor wish to be perceived as such by the client. To get out of this bind he may assume a confluent stance, doing whatever is required by the client's perception. The net result of this interaction is that the client can assume, "You the therapist will take care of me, so I won't have to take care of myself."

THE TALKING–FEELINGS PITFALL

The labeling of this pitfall as the *talking–feelings* pitfall is meant to indicate the danger that exists in verbalization about feeling as contrasted with direct experiencing of feeling. As one theorist (Wallen, 1970) put it:

> There is a great tendency, it seems to me, for words to get in the way of experience [p. 12].

In his antagonism to the interpretive stance of the psychoanalytic therapist and in his insight that something had to come from within the client, Rogers made a lasting contribution. However, the basic technique that he instituted to tap the inner resource, namely that of reflection, has been found to have limitations. There is something about classic reflection that is a step removed from the here-and-now. The "you feel" readily fades into the equivalent of "I think" or "I observe my feeling (noun)" on the part of the client. The client who is not already in touch with his experiential–behavioral level tends to persist at a perceptual–cognitive level even though the content of his communication may ostensibly be in regard to feelings. His reported experience is veritably "packaged" and unchanging, as it is not really his live ongoing experience that he is reporting from.

The pitfall of maintaining the client at the level of nonexperienced feeling is particularly well-recognized by the neo-Rogerians such as Rice and Gendlin. Their extensions of client-centered theory emphasize therapist techniques for expansion of awareness through evocative reflection and focusing on experience. The common goal of these techniques is to bring more immediacy into the client's expression. It is as if the client-centered therapist were now saying, "I will work hard to make a big fresh stimulus for the client that might have the effect of turning him inward to his experience."

We would like to note, however, that this solution has the potential for leading into a new pitfall. The *leakage* pitfall, as we will call it, occurs when the therapist attempts to supply all the energy to get a process going. When the therapist attempts to pour energy in to fill the client's emptiness, it may merely leak out again. A more conserving approach involves finding out whether the client is willing to make his own energy source available to resonate to the therapist's input. Perls' recognition of the existence of the leakage pitfall is indicated in his requirement that the client come with a willingness to work, which we have stated as an initial condition for Gestalt therapy.

THE TAKE-CHARGE PITFALL

Because the Gestalt therapist is highly skilled at detecting splits between organismic attention and awareness, upon hearing such a split he may preemptorily rush in and insist the person start doing something immediately to heal the breach he has detected. The person with the split may not have identified himself as a patient, or at least not in regard to the newly discovered fracture, and may drop out at this point out of a sense of being overwhelmed or bulldozed by the suddenness and intensity of the therapist's desire to heal him. The experience is akin to being struck by lightning or caught up in a floodwater. The therapeutic efficiency of such a tactic is comparable to that of the driver who forgets to pick up his passenger and doesn't even miss his presence until he arrives alone at what was to have been their joint destination.

The existence of a take-charge pitfall in Gestalt therapy practice is quite understandable and perhaps could have been predicted. The Gestalt therapist sees himself as an active agent in the change process. By this very token he is vulnerable to forgetting the partnership dimension in that process. One of the basic conditions of Gestalt therapy as we have listed them is that the meaning of an experience must be accepted by the patient if it is to be useful. Thus, a therapist cannot simply "do" therapy on a patient in the manner that a doctor might perform an operation on an anesthetized body. For Gestalt therapy to work, the patient must be conscious and participating. Participating means consentfully joining in. The Gestalt therapist's task is not to lead the patient around by the nose, but rather to stimulate the patient's exploration.

In attempting to avoid being overly aggressive in relation to the client, the Gestalt therapist may leave himself vulnerable to another danger, that of being overly considerate of the client's wishes. We are calling this the *backing-off* pitfall; the timid Gestalt therapist who proposes an experiment to the patient and has it rejected may then back off and fail to explore with the patient his unwillingness to undertake the experiment. Reluctance is also a communicative behavior, one with which the therapist should help the patient get fully in contact.

THE SCATTER PITFALL

Another pitfall into which the Gestalt therapist is prone to fall is what we are terming the *scatter* pitfall. The scatter pitfall is akin to mistaking the trees for the forest in that the therapist responds to a miscellany of cues without ever recognizing the flow of the patient's experience. Gestalt therapists pride themselves in not arbitrarily keeping the patient on any given point and instead going with shifting organismic attention. However, if the therapist does not form a Gestalt of his impressions of the client's stream of experience but rather views the patient's continuing expressions as disconnected events, he runs the risk of sending the patient in all directions at once. At the very least he will perpetuate the patient's unfinished business at the feeling level.

The scatter pitfall may be gotten into as a result of the therapist's prematurely attempting to bring about reintegration of awareness and experience without first fully developing the patient's sustained awareness of his immediate experiencing. Only when the patient can really touch in at this level will there be any place to go in an experiential reintegration sense. The patient must be helped to find the current. Then the direction for induced movement will be evident.

The pitfall we are describing could also be seen as resulting from a lack of empathy on the part of the therapist. An empathic therapist has a full and accurate perception of the client's inner experience of himself. He can more or less go into the client's world and sense what is salient for him.

In Table 9.2, we have classified the major pitfalls that we described into two categories: (a) those related to the facilitation of client/patient awareness and (b) those related to the facilitation of client/patient responsibility. Organizing the pitfalls in this framework points up some interesting parallels. The giving pitfall in client-centered therapy and the

Table 9.2.   A Categorization of Therapy Pitfalls

Client-Centered Therapy	Gestalt Therapy
Facilitation of Awareness	
Talking–feelings pitfall: therapist does not get with flow of experience	Scatter pitfall: therapist does not get with flow of experience
Facilitation of Responsibility	
Giving pitfall: therapist loses sight of own role	Take-charge pitfall: therapist loses sight of patient's role
Leakage pitfall: therapist loses sight of client's role	Backing-off pitfall: therapist loses sight of own role

take-charge pitfall in Gestalt therapy can be seen as different distortions relating to maintenance of the client's or patient's sense of responsibility for doing something himself to solve problems of which he has become aware. The giving pitfall opens for the client-centered therapist when he has an investment in personally solving the client's problems by being the answer. The take-charge pitfall opens for the Gestalt therapist when he has an investment in personally solving the client's problems by creating the answer. Both pitfalls involve ego trips for the therapist wherein he can feel what a wonderful, helpful person he is. Both pitfalls also involve a mistaken goal of attempting to develop solutions rather than developing the client's or patient's problem-solving process so that he can work out his own solutions.

The talking–feelings pitfall and the scatter pitfall have in common an acceptance by the therapist of invalid data from the client. The invalid data is nonfelt data. Unless the therapist can distinguish experiential data from nonexperiential data, he will fall for the counterfeit currency. Training and growth experiences that bring the therapist in contact with genuine experience in himself and in others are probably the best corrective.

The less important leakage and backing-off pitfalls have their genesis in attempts to correct the original pitfalls. Both represent the therapist's losing sight of the joint contribution to be made to the therapy process by patient and therapist. The pitfalls we have described are not the only pitfalls into which the therapist may fall. Rather, they are the ones we believe to be central to these therapies.

INFLUENCING THE PROBABILITIES

Can we establish that these two therapies need each other in order to exert maximal influence on the probability that a therapeutic process will occur in the help seeker? Or is each therapy a fully adequate vehicle in its own right? We will point out what we feel are the limitations or areas of minimal influence of each of these therapies by itself as preparation for recommending their combination.

Minimal Influence

As we see it, the greatest danger in the practice of client-centered therapy is *sterility*. If the therapist's only tool is bare reflection, how often is it that nothing new is added to bring life to the process? How often is it that nothing new opens up for the client? The client's likelihood of moving beyond where he is is limited by lack of new input. The client's experience is likely to be that he is right where he started, and that although he has not lost his bearings, he has in fact gotten nowhere. The client's complaint to the therapist would then appropriately be, "Can't you *do* anything?"

By way of contrast, the greatest danger we see in the practice of Gestalt therapy is *gimmickiness*. If the therapist is caught up in running innumerable experiments without reference to the flow of the patient's experience, how often is the result for the patient a sense of massive inner confusion and disconnectedness from his own experience? The patient's likelihood of moving productively is limited by the random quality of the therapist's input. The patient's experience is most likely that of having been led around, of having moved but of being lost and nowhere. The patient's complaint to the therapist would then appropriately be, "Can't you *hear* me?"

Neither approach as described is fully successful in bringing about the sought-after reprocessing of blocked experience. Both are ways, though different, that can result in nonexperiencing. They can fail to bring the client/patient into full ongoing awareness of his organismic experiencing as a basis for living and choice-making. The client-centered way of constant listening appears overly quiet. The Gestalt way of constant doing appears overly noisy.

At this point we would like to focus again on our main thesis, that it is the responsibility of the therapist to influence maximally the probability that a certain kind of process will occur in his client/patient. In our examination of client-centered and Gestalt therapy theory and their operational implementation, we have observed that each of these therapies does a less-adequate job than the other at particular points in facilitating the therapy process. Let us share with you, therefore, what we think the combination of these two promising approaches could accomplish.

Maximal Influence

We will suggest only the bare outlines of what the merger of these two therapies might be like; to attempt to do the entire job would be presumptuous at the very least. We will look first at some major areas of overlap and agreement that already exist and require little or no movement on the part of therapists of either orientation to assimilate. Then we will suggest the manner in which the areas of difference might be brought together to enhance the influence of the therapist in bringing about the maximum in therapy process.

We believe an effective therapy consists of both a set of basic beliefs and a set of operations that flow from and are consistent with these beliefs. Hence, in our integration of client-centered and Gestalt therapy theories, we will establish relationships both at the level of beliefs and at the level of operations.

We see the two therapy theories as wholly consistent in their basic beliefs about the nature of man. A merged theory would view the person as (a) unique by virtue of his valid subjective reality; (b) motivated by a single actualizing tendency that operates to maintain and enhance the organism; (c) an experiencing organism constantly registering all its contacts with events within and without; and (d) having access to experiencing through the process of awareness. A merged theory would select the same ideal person—one who is completely open to his experiencing in the moment.

In a merged view, the nonfulfilling person would be one who is not allowing some portion of his organismic experiencing to enter awareness in an accurately symbolized manner. He would be one who has cut off some part of himself from his knowing it. The goal of therapy in a merged view would be to free the natural processes in the person for authentic living, wherein organismic experience becomes the guide within awareness for knowing and valuing.

The first content area requiring significant work on our part to achieve a rapprochement of the two theories is that of the necessary and sufficient conditions for therapy to occur. We believe that *all* of the conditions proposed by each of our therapy approaches are essential in a merged approach, and that none can be done without. However, despite differences in language, several of the conditions appear to be getting at the same thing and can be equated without doing violence to the intent within either approach. After this equating, we have a total of nine nonoverlapping requirements, meaning that each therapy approach must take in three previously unidentified postures. In this expanded perspective we find one of the growing edges created by the merger. Listed in Table 9.3 in tandem

Table 9.3.   Merger of Necessary and Sufficient Conditions

Client-Centered Statement of Condition	Gestalt Statement of Condition
The two persons are in contact	
Therapist must show unconditional positive regard	
Therapist must show empathic understanding of the client's internal frame of reference	Therapist must recognize that the ultimate meaning of any experience is founded in the patient's permitting it to come into his awareness, and thus his interventions should be noninterpretive
Client must experience the therapist's regard and empathy	
Client is in a state of incongruence, being vulnerable or anxious	Patient must be willing to work
Therapist is congruent in the relationship	Therapist must be aware, responsible, and direct in his communication with the patient
	Therapist must be able to experience the patient's total communication
	Therapist interventions must build on the here-and-now
	Therapist interventions should operate to expand the patient's claiming of responsibility for his own living

are the nine necessary and sufficient conditions for a merged client-centered and Gestalt approach. Conditions coming from client-centered therapy to expand the Gestalt perspective are mainly those dealing with the relationship and trust, for example, client and therapist being in contact, therapist showing positive regard, and client perceiving the therapist's regard and empathy for him. Conditions coming from the Gestalt approach to expand the client-centered perspective are mainly involved with particular kinds of interventions, such as, experiencing the patient's total communication, building on the here-and-now, and expanding the patient's claiming of responsibility for his own living.

Having completed our outline of the repertoire of beliefs that a client-centered and Gestalt therapist would espouse, we are ready to consider the nature of the full set of operations that would flow from and be consistent with these beliefs. Here we will skip almost all detail in order to focus on the singular contribution that we feel each therapy could make to the other. If we consider this merger as a marriage about to take place, these singular contributions could be considered the respective dowry of each. This specific contribution is not all each will bring to the other, but it is the most obvious initial benefit. When these two therapies truly get together, we feel much more will result.

We see the singular client-centered contribution as being in the area of knowing how to *listen* (and hear). We see the singular Gestalt contribution as being in the area of knowing how (and what) to *do*. These respective contributions have the potential for remedying certain weaknesses described earlier in the separate practice of each of the therapies. For example, client-centered operations tend to place the therapist in a stance of listening with insufficient doing. Gestalt operations can carry the therapist along into doing with insufficient listening. We would envision our client-centered Gestalt therapist as both a listener and a doer.

The listening skill developed in client-centered training allows the therapist to tune in deeply to the client's experience, to feel out where the client really is, to get inside the person. The therapist's ability to hear what the client's experience is like to him and to communicate empathically about it with him is most likely one of the events that contributes to the growth of the client's trust and willingness to risk more. Empathic listening skill in fact contributes to the making real of quite a few of the combined necessary and sufficient conditions for therapy that we have cited.

Good listening, with its inherent recognition of what is salient for the client and which way the flow of experience is going, avoids the scatter pitfall to which the Gestalt therapist is liable. Good listening, with its recognition of the extent to which experience is owned and available to the client, helps prevent falling into the take-charge pitfall of leading the client on the surface rather than going with him into depth. Good listening, with its attentiveness to where the client is at the moment, can save the therapist from the backing-off pitfall by providing him with a fresh focus. Good listening and alive reflection of what is heard can contribute to amplifying and expanding the volume with which the client's experience is trying to speak to him. Good listening, with its tracking of the experience beam, can help the client go deeper along his awareness continuum. Good listening and reflection of what is heard can help the client learn to differentiate the experience of congruent versus incongruent communication as it issues from himself.

When the listening therapist hears deadness, incongruence, fragmentation, stuckness, or whatever, it becomes important that he do something to influence the patient's process rather than merely witness the self-perpetuating condition. The activist skill developed in Gestalt training impels the therapist to engage the patient in some kind of doing that has the potential for removing the block between his organismic experience and his awareness of it. The activity may be as little as merely steadfastly encouraging the patient to give additional attention to what he is doing, seeing, or feeling in order that he may be as much in the here-and-now as possible. Or the initial activity might be one chosen to encourage the patient to own his here-and-now experiencing by having him employ different grammatical constructions, such as substituting "I" for "it" to describe his own doing, seeing, or feeling.

The active therapist's ability to conduct the patent through experiments that are successful in allowing experience to flow into awareness and become integrated, with the concomitant release of energy, can only contribute to the patient's willingness to allow himself to be processed further. The therapist in this sense has what Fagan (1970) has termed *potency*— namely, the ability

> . . . to assist the patient to move in the direction that he wishes, that is, to accelerate and provoke change in a positive direction [p. 96].

A potent therapist fulfills a number of the necessary and sufficient conditions for therapy that we have listed for our combined therapy approach.

Activism is a great help in staying out of the talking-feelings pitfall, as it dispenses with much talk and seeks a mode of getting with and being in feeling. Activism also makes a contribution to avoiding the giving pitfall. The active therapist refuses to take on the role of becoming a permanent environmental support for the patient who thinks of himself as helpless, stupid, and generally lacking resources. Activism seeks ways to mobilize the patient's awareness of how he gives his power away to others, thereby placing himself in a weak position. Activism seeks ways to get the patient in touch with the feel of his own self-support and how he can take charge of his life. By this same token, activism helps keep the therapist from being sucked into the leakage pitfall. Activism forces the patient to make visible choices regarding participation or nonparticipation in the therapy work.

Activism can be particularly helpful in developing the patient's own problem-solving capabilities, as it increases the patient's recognition of his own agency or I-ness in the events of his life. Activism, with its capacity for freeing the experiencing process to flow unblocked and to allow cycles to complete themselves without interruption, can increase the patient's overall confidence in the contribution that his natural process of experiencing can make to the living of his life. Activism can help the patient come to value being fulfilled rather than unfulfilled, and to seek to grow continually toward a fuller realization of his being.

THE MERGER IN PRACTICE

The manner in which a therapist who seeks to bring together these two approaches might operate is suggested by the following excerpt from a therapy session conducted by a therapist equally well trained in both client-centered therapy and Gestalt therapy. The illustration will be offered without commentary. We prefer that the therapist-reader make his own connections with the example. Review of the preceding section outlining the major contribution each therapy can make to a merged approach may be helpful in this regard.

Suzy, as we will rename her, is an eight-year-old patient who lives with foster parents. She is being seen for individual therapy after expressing suicidal preoccupations and making a suicidal gesture in the form of attempting to suffocate herself with a plastic bag. This is her second interview with the therapist.

Suzy comes into the office, goes to the toy box and pulls out several toys. She picks up drumsticks and plays the drums. The therapist makes some reflections about the drumming. Suzy then begins to set up the bowling pins and the following dialog takes place.

Patient (P)   Why don't you bring up something for me to talk about?

Therapist (T)   You want me to suggest something for you to talk about.

P   Yes. You say something to talk about.

T   You want me to name something to talk about, and my feeling is that I want you to say what you want to talk about. I don't. . . .

P   I just don't know what to talk about. I don't have anything.

T   You don't know anything in the world you want to talk about.

P   Well, I could talk about why my Mommy and Daddy don't want me any more.

T   One thing you could talk about is why your Mommy and Daddy don't want you any more. I'm not sure, are you saying you feel puzzled about their not wanting you?

P   I don't know why they don't want me anymore. They just don't want me.

T   Your sense is they don't want you, you don't know why and I'm not really sure how you feel as you say they don't want you . . .

P   I feel sad. (eyes begin to moisten)

T   I am aware as you say you feel sad that a tear comes into your eye. You feel sad and like crying.

P   Mhmm. (More tears come. She tries to stop tears. Sniffles.)

T   Seems like you're trying to stop yourself from crying and inside you feel sad, though.

P   (cries more fully, emotionally)

T   (sits with patient until crying ceases)

P   I don't want to cry any more.

T   You're through crying.

P   Yes. I just don't know why they don't want me.

T   I have an idea of something we might do that might help find out. Would you be willing to try something?

P   Mhmm.

T   (pulls up two empty chairs) Put your Mommy and Daddy in the chairs. Can you see them? Imagine them both sitting there.

P   Mhmm.

T   Now, tell them how you feel and ask them what you want to know.

P   I don't know why you don't want me any more. I feel sad and I want to stay with you. I love you.

T   Now, sit in one of the chairs and be your Mommy or Daddy. Tell Suzy how you feel as Daddy.

P   (as Daddy) I didn't know you loved us. You've never said you loved us before. I didn't know you wanted to be with us.

T   Sit over here now, and be your Mommy. Tell Suzy how you feel as Mommy.

P   (as Mommy) I didn't think you cared about me at all. I asked for you to leave because you fight with Jenny [another child] all the time.

T   Come sit back down here and say how Suzy feels.

P   (in own chair) But I love you and I want to be with you. I don't want to leave you or Jenny, Mary, Tommy, and Jimmy. (silence)

T   How do you feel?

P   Good.

T   You feel good. Anything else you want to say?

P   I could tell Mommy I love her.

T   One thing you could do is tell Mommy how you feel about her and what you want.

P   Mhmm.

T   I guess you're saying you've never done that?

P   Mhmm. (silence) (picks up bowling ball) Let's play now. I want to bowl.

T   You want to play bowling now?

P   Mhmm. (set up pins) [5]

REFERENCES

Butler, J. M. Client-centered counseling and psychotherapy. *Counseling Center Discussion Papers,* 11 (7). Chicago: University of Chicago Library, 1965.

Butler, J. M., & Rice, L. N. Adience, self-actualization and drive theory. In J. Wepman & R. Heine (Eds.), *Concepts of personality.* Chicago: Aldine, 1963.

Enright, J. B. An introduction to gestalt techniques. In J. Fagan & I. Shepherd (Eds.), *Gestalt therapy now.* Palo Alto: Science and Behavior Books, 1970.

Fagan, J. The tasks of the therapist. In J. Fagan & I. Shepherd (Eds.), *Gestalt therapy now.* Palo Alto: Science and Behavior Books, 1970.

Gendlin, E. A theory of personality change. In J. Hart & T. Tomlinson (Eds.), *New directions in client-centered therapy.* Boston: Houghton Mifflin, 1970.

Perls, F. S. *Gestalt therapy verbatim.* Lafayette, Calif.: Real People Press, 1969.

Perls, F. S. Four lectures. In J. Fagan & I. Shepherd (Eds.), *Gestalt therapy now.* Palo Alto: Science and Behavior Books, 1970.

Rice, L. N. The evocative function of the therapist. Unpublished manuscript. York University, 1970.

Rogers, C. R. A theory of therapy, personality, and interpersonal relationships, as developed in the client-centered framework. In S. Koch (Ed.), *Psychology: A study of a science.* Vol. 3. *Formulations of the person and the social context.* New York: McGraw-Hill, 1959.

Wallen, R. Gestalt therapy and gestalt psychology. In J. Fagan & I. Shepherd (Eds.), *Gestalt therapy now.* Palo Alto: Science and Behavior Books, 1970.

[5] The following week, the patient came in and reported that she told her foster parents she wanted to stay and she was staying. During the week, the placement agency had contacted the therapist and indicated the foster parents had made a dramatic turnaround, that they were wanting to keep the child and come for therapy themselves.

CHAPTER 10

The Evocative Function of the Therapist

Laura North Rice

Client-centered therapists sound very much alike to outsiders but very different to themselves. On the one hand, we share a view of the nature of man, and some assumptions about the kinds of interpersonal encounters that facilitate growth. On the other hand, as we build up experience in implementing the principles, we begin to maximize behaviors that seem to facilitate the client's work. The result is a working theory concerning the active ingredients in therapy. This can then be viewed as a specification and extension of client-centered therapy, or as a new approach to therapy. This chapter presents one such formulation, the method of *evocative reflection.*

The presentation rests on three assertions:

1. The technique usually called *reflection of feeling* is potentially one of the most active and powerful tools available to a therapist. This potential can be realized through the use of evocative reflection, which leads to a reprocessing of experience. Probably the clearest statement of the general client-centered position is Rogers' (1957) statement of the necessary and sufficient conditions for therapeutic personality change. The three guidelines for therapist participation are (a) that he be congruent in the relationship, (b) that he experience unconditional positive regard for the client, and (c) that he communicate to the client quite explicitly an empathic understanding of his internal frame of reference. Although the specification of these three therapist conditions has had a sweeping influence on the whole psychotherapy field, the tendency has been to accept them as perhaps necessary but certainly not sufficient. They are seen by those not trained in client-centered therapy as useful in establishing a climate of trust and nondefensiveness, but as a background for other interventions, rather

than as active agents of change. Even by therapists within the client-centered orientation, the technique of reflection is often seen as one effective means of implementing the expression of unconditionality of regard and accurate empathy, but as essentially a passive mirroring process whose chief value lies in establishing a background within which the actualizing tendency can be presumed to operate. A more negative view put forward by Carkhuff and Berenson (1967) is that reflection of feeling is often a technique by which the therapist avoids a true human encounter with the client. Even those who make liberal use of reflection find it difficult to explain how a method that makes use of noncontingent reinforcement (unconditional positive regard) and feeds no new information into the system (reflection of client's message), can lead to change.

The first assertion of the chapter, then, is that although much reflection is indeed at the maintenance level, which encourages the feeling of safety, of being understood and accepted in one's own terms, the method of *evocative* reflection is a more active and powerful tool. Furthermore it is possible to spell out a theoretical rationale for the way in which the use of this technique can lead to therapeutic personality change.

2. Evocative reflection is *not* the same as an interpretation. Although a "good" interpretation and a "good" evocative response may sound very similar, the aim of the reflection is different; attempts to demonstrate their similarity only serve to blur a worthwhile distinction. This distinction will be clarified later, and only stated in general terms here. The aim of an interpretation is to go beyond the client's statement, to point out patterns and connections, and to offer to the client new ways of viewing his experience. The aim of an evocative reflection is to open up the experience and provide the client with a process whereby he can form successively more accurate constructions of his own experience.

3. One's theory of psychotherapy and personality change does and should make a difference in one's moment-by-moment behavior in the interview. Spinning theories is not simply a luxury to be indulged in during the intervals of doing therapy by the seat of one's pants. A good theory, together with its underlying view of the nature of man, need not be something that comes between two very human participants, but a set of ways of engaging in the complex and demanding dialog designed to take the client from where he is now to where he wants to be. The gap between therapy theory and therapy practice in most orientations is too well known to be belabored. One of the most appealing features of some of the learning-theory derived methods has been the conceptual clarity with which theory and practice are connected.

If the choice of therapeutic method for a given client at a given time is to be based on something more substantial than current fashion or past role models, we should be able to spell out quite explicitly the answer to the following questions:

1. What needs to be changed? This could involve a single behavior or a whole stance toward life. Although the question is specific to each client, the way in which the answer is stated stems directly from the theory, and has immediate implications for therapeutic method.

2. What are the mechanisms of change? How can we conceptualize the process whereby those elements (target structures) deemed to be in need of change are altered in the chosen directions?

3. What kinds of therapist operations will maximize change? The answers here need to be almost as concrete as the proverbial cookbook. The criteria for good therapist responses should not be vague and global, especially if the propositions of the theory are ever to be tested.

The remainder of this chapter will spell out the method of evocative reflection within the framework of these three questions. There will be no attempt to expound the whole fabric of client-centered therapy, but the present formulation does not seem to be inconsistent with that body of theory.

WHAT NEEDS TO BE CHANGED?

Client A says: "I'm not studying even though I know I'll fail if I don't. I have a big paper to write, but every time I sit down to do it, I find an excuse to get up and do something else. I just can't study and it panics me." Client B says: "I keep getting into jobs where the boss is a very domineering guy, who tells me how to blow my nose. Why do I keep getting into that kind of situation?" Client C says: "I'm not interested in anything. I just walk around going through the motions. I'm miserable even when there's nothing wrong. What's the matter with me?" These three examples, chosen more or less at random, are fairly typical of the kinds of statements clients make about their problems. The nature of the problem is specific to each client, but the kind of answer given to the question, "What needs to be changed?" stems directly from one's explicit or implicit theory of therapy. The way in which each theory identifies the "targets" of the therapy will have a substantial influence on the nature of the process in which the client and the therapist engage.

Behavior therapists, would, of course focus on the inappropriate behaviors, attempting to establish contingencies of reinforcement whereby more appropriate responses would be substituted for those felt to be unsatisfactory. From the client's standpoint, this view of the therapy as a frontal attack on the undesirable behaviors is likely to seem logical and understandable. This statement of the target is a satisfying one for the therapist also, inasmuch as the therapist operations seem to follow directly from the theoretical statement.

The dynamically oriented therapist would tend to focus on motivational questions, primarily unconscious motivations. This intention to help the client to achieve insight into unconscious motivations guides the therapist's overall strategy, but is less directly related to the actual therapist operations than is the case with the behavior therapist. The route to "true insight" is seen as a long and tortuous one. Many clients, particularly those from the middle class, tend to focus on this kind of question spontaneously. They ask, "Why don't I write those papers? Is it because I want to fail?" "Why do I keep getting jobs with domineering bosses?" Whether this is the general influence of our pervadingly deterministic culture or the more direct influence of the motivational preoccupations of the psychoanalytic thinkers, many clients are all too ready to play the "maybe it's because" game.

The client-centered therapist would tend to focus on the way in which situations are perceived and conceptualized by the client. Rogers makes the assumption that the client's perceptions are filtered through his concept of self. The aspects of the client's experience that seems to pose a threat to the congruence between the self-concept and experience are distorted or denied symbolization in awareness. The assumption is made that if the self-concept is brought more into line with experience, then new situations that are encountered will be more accurately perceived. If such situations are more accurately perceived, then behavior will automatically be more appropriate. The client is encouraged to explore himself under conditions of acceptance and greatly reduced threat. Under these circumstances new and previously unacceptable aspects of the self can emerge and can be integrated into the self-concept. The implications of this for the conduct of therapy are rather general. For the client the implicit prescription to explore himself as deeply as possible often seems to have little clear relevance to the process of change and may be a puzzling one to implement. Even for the therapist, the prescription for congruence, empathic understanding, and unconditional positive regard gives only general guidance toward the kinds of operations he should seek to maximize in his own behavior.

It seems increasingly clear that the appropriate theoretical base for understanding the operations of client-centered therapy and the mechanism of change involved is some kind of information-processing model. This conclusion has been somewhat obscured by Rogers' use of "threat" and "perceptual defense," terms, which suggest a conflict model similar to that of Freud. Nevertheless, it seems quite possible to formulate the client-centered position in a way that does not depend on the concepts of unconscious motivation or defense mechanisms but rather conceptualizes the mechanisms of change in the framework of information processing. This will be more than a semantic exercise. It is designed to lead to rather specific prescriptions for the kinds of operations on the part of both client and therapist that are likely to lead to maximal positive change. The remainder of this section will attempt to sketch the general outlines of this viewpoint. The argument will be stated more precisely and illustrated more fully in the next section.

The basic assumption is that for any person there are some classes of experience that have never been adequately processed, and for some people, there are many such classes. Because of the conditions, both internal and external, under which certain situations have been encountered, the various aspects of the experience have been construed in ways that are inadequate, in the sense that they are not veridical representations of the actual structure of the situation. As one continues to encounter such situations under such distorting conditions, a more or less enduring construction or set of constructions is formed, which filters one's experience and guides one's behavior whenever situations of that general class are encountered. An obvious example of this would be a response to authority figures as invincible and implacable people with whom one can never win, but only lose everything by trying. The assumption is that whenever one encounters situations perceived as involving authority, one reacts in ways that are inappropriate and unsatisfying. It is not the repressed memory of the early experience with the father as an authority figure that is troublesome in the present, but the enduring constructions or "schemes" that are brought to bear on each new experience. Certainly strong motivational forces are assumed to have been involved in the formation of the inadequate construction. However, currently active motivations are assumed to be less decisive in the inappropriate reaction than the fact that all new experiences are processed by means of schemes that may be inadequate in crucial ways.

The obvious implication of all this is that the targets of therapy are the sets of schemes that are relevant to the recurrent situations in which the client reacts in unsatisfactory ways. The problem for therapy, then, is to find a method by which the client can reprocess an important experience from such a problem class in a way that is relatively undistorted. It is this new, full, undistorted experience that is precisely what is needed to force reorganization of the old schemes. Such reorganized schemes would be relevant to a wide variety of situations (situations falling in the same general class) and as the client's responses are organized by his schemes, the result should be that he would react differently in a wide variety of situations.

One crucially important assumption should be mentioned here. The class membership of various situations will be quite different for different clients. In other words, the dimensions along which situations are reacted to as similar will often be idiosyncratic. Therefore, it would usually not be productive to form external judgments concerning the experiences that are likely to be members of crucial classes. Rather, one should deal with whatever is live for the client. Anything that is felt by the client as problematic or "loaded" is inevitably a member of some problem class, although often neither client nor therapist has any idea where it will lead. And of course it is just such situations that will be brought up by the client because he will be currently experiencing trouble with them. If the client can fully explore his reactions to *one* such situation and become aware of the elements in a more accurate and balanced form, that is, can *reprocess* the situation, the effect will be to force reorganization of all the relevant schemes. This in turn should lead to different responses in many different situations, generalizing in ways quite unpredictable from outside.

Each of the three clients quoted at the beginning of the section is reporting that his reactions within a class of situations are inappropriate and unsatisfying. These reactions may show themselves as feelings or overt behaviors. The situations may be limited and specific or as broad and pervasive as finding no pleasure in a world that others find exciting. But in each case the client feels himself to be responding in ways that do not make sense. The task of the therapist is to listen for reactions that are problematic in some way, and to help the client to turn around on his own experience and to reprocess it in ways that are more veridical representations of the actual structure of the situations encountered.

This formulation is not intended as an attempt to account for all maladaptive reactions, nor is it meant to imply that all therapeutic change takes place in this one way. It is asserted, however, that this formulation accounts for much of the change that takes place in client-centered therapy. Furthermore, the amount of positive change could be maximized by more systematic and extensive use of the evocative function of the therapist.

WHAT ARE THE MECHANISMS OF CHANGE?

The present section is an attempt to spell out some of the mechanisms by which favorable psychotherapeutic change takes place. This discussion could well be cast in the more rigorous and theoretically neutral terms of information-processing theory. In a forthcoming publication this will be done, using Pascual-Leone's (in press) theory of constructive operators. In the present chapter the terms used will be defined in a way that is consistent with this approach, but the ideas will be presented in a more discursive fashion, with a variety of clinical examples.

In the previous section it was suggested that the client's problem is that he reacts in inappropriate and unsatisfying ways to certain classes of stimulus situations because of the relatively enduring schemes that are brought to bear on the construing of each new situation. That is, the client continues to behave maladaptively because he has built up over time schemes that are faulty, in the sense that they fail to take account of the reality structure of the situations to which they are relevant. It was further suggested that the way to change such faulty constructions is to explore fully the client's reaction in any one such situation, and thus to reprocess the experience in such a way as to force reorganization of the relevant schemes. The term "scheme" is used here to refer to the relatively enduring clusters of cognitive and affective structures that serve to assimilate input and organize output.[1] This translation of Piaget's term *schème* as "scheme" rather than "schema" follows the usage advocated by Pascual-Leone and Smith (1969) and Furth (1969) and recently accepted by Piaget (1970) as representing his thinking.[2] When the terms "stimulus" or "stimulus situation" are used, we are referring to a combination of two kinds of input, that coming from within the organism as well as that coming from the environment. In the discussion that follows, the language of stimulus and reaction is not intended to imply a rigidly reactive organism. Rather, it is a recognition that behavior takes place in a context of continuous external and internal stimulation. The nature of the client's response in each new situation will depend on his repertoire of schemes, together with his characteristic approach to information processing. This characteristic approach is determined by a number of higher-order func-

[1] A scheme is defined by Piaget and Morf (1958, p. 86) as "an organized set of reactions susceptible to being transferred from one situation to another by assimilation of the second to the first." These reactions can be sensorimotor or perceptual–conceptual. They can be either cognitive or affective.

[2] The following statement by Pascual-Leone and Smith (1969) clarifies the use of this term in the present paper. "Piaget's French label *schème* is usually translated into English as 'schema' and less frequently as 'scheme.' However, it is our opinion that the latter constitutes the only acceptable translation. The word 'scheme' suggests a plan of action (internalized or external) which is precisely the core meaning of Piaget's predicative psychofunctions or assimilatory schemes. The word 'schema' in its modern usage suggests too strongly the idea of a template, a schematic form or an image [pp. 329–330]."

tions, but the only one of concern in the present paper is the mental capacity, the central processing space.[3] This is of direct concern in psychotherapy, because the functional size of this central processing space at any given time depends not only upon the developmental level but on such momentary conditions as anxiety level and level of activation.

The client's schemes have been built up over time, sometimes gradually and sometimes from one or two crucial experiences under high drive conditions. In each situation a person perceives a mass of data, data that are extremely complex, idiosyncratic, often having contradictory aspects. In order to act efficiently he must organize this complex flow into units and must group together into a single class data that are similar but not identical. He pays a high price for this efficiency and stability in terms of loss of richness and complexity and new experience. When his schemes are relatively adequate in relation to the actual structure of the situations encountered, the result is adaptive, but when the schemes involve distortion as well as simplification, they tend to perpetuate maladaptive reactions.

It seems probable that there are a number of ways in which a situation may come to be inadequately construed. It may have been primarily a matter of the complexity or ambiguity of the stimulus situation in relation to the size of a relatively undeveloped central processing space, or mental capacity. Or put in the language of field forces, a few salient features may dominate the whole construction, particularly with individuals with certain response biases. And, presumably, all these processes would have been altered by the presence of strongly aroused needs.

According to this formulation the problem of change in psychotherapy is the problem of changing inadequate and distorting schemes. Although the person has assuredly been exposed to a wealth of relevant new situations in the course of his ordinary life, such data have not forced change, probably for several reasons. In the first place, schemes, by definition, serve as filters and organizers of input, thus serving a selective function that is cumulative in its effect. Secondly, the arousal of anxiety and other aversive states tends to distort the client's construction of the situation, so as to make it less veridical by drastically changing the focus—that is, the salience (or weight) of the different features of the situation. Indeed, clients who tend to avoid anxiety-arousing stimuli also tend to take themselves out of the situation either bodily or as a distraction of attention away from the focus on what the situation is like. Clients who tend to focus excessively on the anxiety-arousing features (the so-called "sensi-

---

[3] Other higher-order functions would be a learning construct variable, a field factor, and various individual response biases.

tizers") tend to disregard too many other relevant aspects of the situation, which are needed for a veridical construction. In the third place, if new data do force their way in, it is usually under conditions of stress and lowered mediational capacity, which make adequate construction unlikely.

How can change that has not been possible in ordinary life be affected in therapy? How can new data become accessible in a form that will force reorganization of key schemes? Between the initial encountering of the stimulus, and the response that is seen as concluding the given sequence, there is a complex series of events in which the stimulus is scanned, input is assimilated, and output organized; the output thus organized may, in the form of affects or images, serve as input into further construction systems, followed by further scanning assimilating and organizing. This complex series of events is defined here as the client's "reaction." This reaction may be very much condensed, seeming to consist only of the stimulus and the terminating response. Nevertheless, much of the reaction is potentially available to awareness. Furthermore, it contains a wealth of information about the total situation, information that is often more complete and complex than the final response that is organized by (consistent with) the relevant schemes. The parts that are left out may be aspects of the external stimulus situation, or they may be internal stimuli such as affects or kinesthetic cues. All of these things may be part of the memory traces of the experience, and yet not encompassed by the way in which the situation is construed.

A simple example of this is the client who reports that he has had a fight with his boss, got scared, and just gave into him "in my usual cowardly way." The client's total reaction was far more complex than this. If he can reprocess some of these events, the tension in his arms, the clenching of his jaw and so forth, he will be in a position to take seriously his own rage in the situation. He doesn't need any interpretation about the fear of his own impulses. Compelling new data have become available, information that forces reorganization of his schemes pertaining to disagreement with authority figures.

In a second example, the new data concern features of the external situation. A client complains that he feels desperately uncomfortable when he walks into a room full of people and sees the faces turn toward him. He just stands there blankly or turns and rushes out. The therapist chooses to reflect this in such a way as to put the client back into the situation at a high level of intensity. "You open the door, walk into the room and all heads swivel. The eyes focus on you, they get big and terrifying." In this case it is as if the client stands in the room, feels the staring eyes and his own sweat, but he also sees the looks of indifference rather than sneers, perhaps even receptive interest. In other words, in the therapy situation he "stays in the room" and processes the situation in a very different way.

Let us now focus on what the therapist is trying to do here. How does his role differ from that of an interpretive therapist? We come now to what is meant by the evocative function of a therapist. This function is precisely that of reevoking in the client the client's own reaction to a key situation in such a way that the client can successfully reprocess the total experience. What is unique about this function? How does it differ from the role of the interpretive therapist or the more orthodox client-centered therapist? The latter distinction will be brought out more clearly in the next section, and the former will concern us here.

At this point we can contrast two methods of helping the client to reprocess his experience in such a way as to develop more adequate schemes. In the first approach the therapist would listen to the client's recounting of his experience of the situation. As he listened, he would analyze the situation, bringing to bear on it his accumulated knowledge of the client, together with his own theoretical knowledge, and would attempt to pinpoint wherein the client's construction of the situation was faulty. The therapist would then attempt to formulate a more adequate construction —what the client was really feeling, what must have been happening in the situation, and so on—and then proffer this to the client. Hopefully, the client is able to accept this, substitute it for his own construction, and explore its implications. This of course is the method of interpretation.

A second approach would be for the therapist to listen as freshly and openly as possible to the client's whole description, and not simply his conceptualization of it. He then attempts to synthesize all these bits into a whole that attempts to capture the flavor of the original experience. Whereas an analysis implies a breaking up into parts in order to abstract and find relationships or order, the term "synthesis" means putting parts together to form a whole. It is the client's *whole reaction* that the therapist's synthesis attempts to capture. The therapist does not try to analyze what it means in terms of historical or causal connections. He simply tries to sense as accurately as possible "this is what it was like to *be* the client at that moment." It is this flavor of the total experience that he tries to give back to the client as concretely and vividly as possible. Hopefully, the client can then use this reflection to deepen and enrich his own awareness of the total experience and thus to broaden his construction of it. The method of evocative reflection is designed to provide a means whereby the client can form successfully more accurate constructions of his own experience.

Some examples may help to clarify this distinction. The client has a small brother who spends the week in an institution and comes home weekends. She mentions that on Sunday nights when the family drives him back to the hospital she herself gets very depressed: "He's such a pest, I can't stand having him around, you'd think I'd be just delighted to be rid of him, but I cry and feel so depressed all evening, I just can't pull out of it." The client senses the discrepancy between her judgment of the situation and her emotional response to it. She feels overwhelmed by a reaction that is so isolated from the rest of her thinking that it cannot be assimilated. At this point the object of the therapist's reflection is to evoke as vividly as possible what it is like to be the client as the little brother is returned to the hospital. As the client has been talking about the little brother getting out of the car, turning, and marching toward the hospital door, the therapist picks up a rather poignant image and this is included in the reflection: "You're sitting there, just seething with irritation, and yet there is something about the rigid little figure walking up to that blank, impersonal, fortress that just *gets* you." The client recognizes the quality of the experience and says, "Yes, it's awful." The next time she comes in she remarks in passing, "Sunday night was okay this week, I felt all right about it." She had evidently assimilated the total experience in a way that no longer disturbed her.

What seems to have happened here is that the helplessness and loneliness of the little brother was a part of her memory of the experience, and therefore came across to the therapist in a fragmentary fashion, but was not included in the client's construction of the situation. When the therapist listened freshly and receptively, he was able to hear all of this, and was thus able to synthesize more of the total experience out of the fragments.

When evocative reflection is successful, it is as if the client goes back into the situation with a more or less deliberate suspension of his usual automatic construction. He is able to respond freshly to the full complexity of both the internal and external aspects of the situation. Parts of the reaction that have been isolated can become integrated with the rest. Aspects that have been felt with less than their full intensity can be fully experienced. In the example above there seem to be two aspects of the situation that have become more available to the client. The first is the realization that the little brother is not only pesty, but pitiful too, and even a bit courageous. This helps to close the gap between the apparent stimulus and the reaction that was previously felt to be inappropriate. The second aspect that emerged was the client's feeling that taking the brother back was a kind of desertion on the part of the adults. This idea was very frightening to the client and she was later able to explore the full force of the fear.

A second example concerns a client who tells a story to illustrate the fact that he had a rugged childhood. He tells about going off to school for the first time, all innocent and unsuspecting, and meeting persistent cruelty. He tries to find adult protection, which fails him, and finally concludes that the only safety lies in having weapons of his own and never leaving himself open. It is this conclusion that the client stresses, and the therapist might well focus on his need to be hard and tough. This would be accurate, but would close off the experience, dealing only with its conclusion. On the other hand an evocative reflection would focus on the beginning of the experience, the vivid picture of the vulnerable, hopeful little kid walking in and—wham! This leaves the client in the middle of the experience, just at the transition, when he is experiencing the pain and fear and deep disillusionment. Now, when he goes back into this intense experience, he automatically brings to it an organism with more complex schemes and more mature processing capacity. Reorganization of the scheme that was reasonable at the age of five, is forced by the current impact of the experience, and the older scheme is progressively replacd by a more mature one.

The argument thus far contains an apparent paradox. We have said that the therapist's goal in forming his responses is not to offer to the client his own, presumably more adequate, construction of the situation, but to *bring to life vividly what it is like to be the client in that situation.* And yet, we have said that the client's construction is inadequate—salient parts are overemphasized, others are left out. How then can the therapist reflect more accurately and vividly what the client's experiences were like, than the client himself was able to do? Isn't the therapist of necessity drawing on his own reactions? The answer is that the client's memory of the experience is fuller than his construction of it. As a client talks about an experience, his account will be a mixture of levels, including both his construction of the experience and also some material much closer to the original experience that is not encompassed by the construction. This extra material may not be inconsistent with the construction, but simply was left outside the original scheme, displaced by other materials that were more salient at the time when the original experience took place. If the therapist listens with a fresh and receptive surface to the client's description, and not simply to his conceptualization of it, he can receive a variety of sensory impressions and synthesize them into a whole that more closely approximates the client's original experience than does the client's own construction. Thus, we have something more complex, more difficult to conceptualize, but more closely resembling both the external and internal features of the original situation.

Several aspects of evocative responding should be clarified here. In the first place, this is not a one-stage process, but a series of approximations, a very active way of stimulating the client to focus on and reprocess his own experience. Whenever the therapist offers his synthesis to the client, the implicit or explicit message is always "Is this what your experience is like?" Usually the client recognizes it immediately as clearly having the characteristics of his own experience, new in its impact and differentiation perhaps, but clearly his own. Often it evokes in the client a fuller awareness of the experience, from which he can expand or correct the picture, or become aware of a new facet of it, and the therapist in turn responds to this. The purpose of the therapist's response is to stimulate the client to become aware of the idiosyncratic edges of his own experience and to include these data in his constructions. Often a vivid fragment is more likely to evoke the whole reaction in an intense and accurate form, than is a whole map of the territory. The response should be accurate in the sense of being a real and recognizable part of the client's experience, but it need not and cannot attempt to encompass the whole experience. Although the therapist tries to grasp each new attempt of the client toward more adequate construction, he avoids any attempt of his own toward closure. The client, rather than the therapist, attempts the new constructions. The client uses the successive syntheses in relation to his own memory traces, and attempts to process the experience more adequately, and the more adequate the schemes the client brings to bear on the memory, the more accurately can the remembered experience be recaptured and reconstrued.[4]

I am assuming here that it is important for the therapist to avoid closure of his own, leaving the client free to explore his total reaction in the situation and to reconstrue it for himself. This is important for several reasons. In the first place, although the therapist picks up and synthesizes impressions that are fuller than the client's construction, the client is the *only* one who can fully know what it was like in the total situation. Therefore, by helping a client to get further and further into his own experience, encouraging him to check each new synthesis against this experience, the therapist is less likely to build in his own distortions and oversimplifications. In fact, when evocative reflection is functioning well, and the client's experience is unfolding, many aspects of it will come as a surprise to the therapist. He could often have predicted the general direction it would take, but not the particular flavor, and it is this particular flavor that provides the crucial new data needed for reorganization.

A further reason why it is important for the client rather than the therapist to arrive at the new constructions concerns the nature of insight or

---

[4] Evidence for this statement is found in experiments of Inhelder, in which the ability to reproduce from memory various configurations of objects actually improved rather than deteriorated after a 6–8 month interval, presumably because of the more mature schemes the children were able to bring to bear on the memory image (Inhelder, 1969).

proof. To be told that waves are big, powerful, crests of water, carrying sand and pebbles, is very different from being caught and overwhelmed by one. To be offered a new scheme, however logical, by the therapist is less compelling than reexperiencing the sights and sounds and feels, that by their very nature compel belief. An old experience becomes a new experience that has fresh impact in the moment.

A second point that should be clarified is that it is not the aim of the therapist to focus on parts of the experience that are contradictory to the main construction, unless they are clearly part of the client's "message" (i.e., of his implicit interpretation of his own experience). The purpose of the therapist's response is to evoke more of the experience for the client. The emphasis on what is contradictory to the client's focus would tend not only to produce defensiveness, but to focus both participants on a more abstract level of analyzing similarities and differences, and not on the experience itself.

Much has been said here about the way in which new data become available to the client, but little mention has been made about the way in which the client uses these new data to reorganize his schemes. Often this seems to happen spontaneously, without an explicit focus on the reorganization process. The client simply finds himself reacting differently in a variety of situations. Other clients seem to want to discuss the meaning of the new experience and try out verbally new ways of viewing situations and exploring their implications. It is not clear whether the latter process is really a necessary step to responding differently, or whether it is simply the client's need to understand what has happened spontaneously. In either case, the crucial point is that once the old organization has been disrupted by the new data, the reorganization almost always leads to schemes superior to the old ones. They will be more adequate just because they are based on more complete information, and because reorganization takes place under optimal conditions for processing, when threat is low and concentration is high.

The client-centered procedures seem to be ideally suited to producing just this combination of lowered threat and high concentration. In the first place, the unconditional positive regard of the therapist and the fact that he tends to stay within the client's internal frame of reference serve to reduce the interpersonal anxiety and establish conditions of relative safety. Thus, anxiety remains at a tolerable level, even though the experience is evoked in an intense and real form, with a high level of arousal. This is crucial, because the functional size of the central processing space, the mental capacity, is usually markedly reduced by intense anxiety. In the second place, the client is not simply responding to his intense experience by shouting, crying, hurting, running, and the like. He is not just acting on the experience, but his energy is focused on exploring the nature of his own reactions. The therapist's reflections within the internal frame of reference, particularly the kinds of evocative reflections to be desired, tend to induce in the client a kind of *inner tracking*, an intense concentration on what it's like. It seems probable that this intense concentration, made more intense by the effort to convey it to therapist, together with the lowered threat, maintain the client's mediational capacity at the highest functional level of which the client is capable. Thus, optimal conditions for information-processing are established.

WHAT KINDS OF THERAPIST OPERATIONS WILL MAXIMIZE CHANGE?

It has been asserted that it is possible for the client to turn around on his own experience in such a way as to transcend the limitations imposed by his own repertoire of schemes. He can be helped by the therapist to engage in a sequence of steps whereby he becomes aware of more of his own reaction, and is thus able to form more adequate schemes. This in turn permits further accurate and differentiated awareness. Although evocative reflections always deal with particular reactions in particular situations, it is assumed that these situations are members of classes of situations that are recurrent and troublesome. In a real sense, any member of a class is as worthwhile exploring as any other. Neither the past nor the present has priority, but rather the vividness with which an experience can be recounted by the client. After all, the more vividly an experience is recounted, the more likely it is to be an experience that is emotionally important to the client. More adequate processing of any one experience should lead to more adaptive responses in a whole range of specific situations.

How, then, should the therapist participate in order to maximize this reexperiencing and reprocessing? One central point that underlies much of what follows concerns the selection of units to which to respond. The therapist is, of course, guided to some extent by the client's implicit "turning the floor over" to the therapist, and yet the therapist will also rely on his own judgment that there is a chunk of material, a message to which he wishes to respond. *The first principle for evocative responding is that the therapist should listen for and respond to reactions, either explicit or implicit.* A reaction was defined in the last section as everything that intervenes between the encountering of the stimulus situation and the response that terminates the sequence. Sometimes a reaction is clearly the focus of the client's message, as he dwells on it quite explicitly. For instance, a client says, "After I talked with her, I felt sort of itchy and uncomfortable."

At other times, the reaction will be only implicitly present. A client says, "I went there and found a note saying she would be back in a week, and then I jumped into the car and drove around, and then a cop gave me a ticket for speeding." In this case, the reaction that starts with going and finding the note and leads to fast driving is merely implied, but might, nonetheless, be an important focus for the therapist's response. In each case there is something about his own reaction that is sensed by the client as being problematic. And it is these problematic reaction points that alert the therapist to the importance of using evocative reflection to help the client to unfold (reconstruct) his own reaction.

There is a further question of selection, however. When a client is talking about himself, there are many reactions to which one could choose to respond. How is the selection to be made? We have assumed that there are key classes of situations that are not handled adequately, and that an intensive exploration of any one member will generalize broadly in its effects. The decision that a certain situation or class of situations is crucial is not a matter to be decided on the basis of a personality theory or even on the basis of an analysis of the person. These classes seem to be formed on idiosyncratic rather than obvious logical lines. The criterion of poignancy, or liveness seems to be the therapist's best guide. How then is poignancy recognized? How can we recognize that the client is moving into an "unfinished" experience? In some cases, the signs are very clear to both client and therapist; in others the therapist must attend to minimal cues. The most obvious sign is that the client feels something inconsistent or discomforting in the situation. In other cases, a kind of intensity comes through in the voice. On the other hand, the feeling may not be especially intense, but the client may feel that he somehow can't quite assimilate the experience. For instance, a client has seen, on his way to the Center, a dog that has just begun to realize that it is lost, and is beginning to panic. The client does not attach much importance to it, but still he finds it hard to forget it. Another signal to which the therapist might well attend is his own sense that a reaction does not make sense. Of course many reactions do not make sense to the therapist as a way in which he himself would react, but he does get a feel for the internal consistency of the situation from the client's viewpoint. It is at times when he cannot achieve this understanding that exploration may prove fruitful. In fact, an evocative question at that point is often met with a statement, "I don't quite get that either," and is followed by an attempt to explore.

Clients differ markedly in the quality of their participation in the search we are talking about. Some pursue the search in a purposive and self-directed way, feeling for poignancy, and sensing when to explore a reaction out to its very edges. As one client put it, "I start out each hour, skating along, deliberately feeling for the ice to crack, and then I plunge in and start exploring." Other clients are less able to focus on the quality of their own reactions but are still expressive enough to enable the therapist to hear and attempt to synthesize live experiences. Other clients seem to have their reactions almost wholly condensed, in the sense of being almost totally without awareness of the experiential aspect that precedes or accompanies the observable behavior. Here the therapist must actively listen for and attempt to unfold the implicit reactions. The client may be recounting a series of fairly routine happenings, and her account of something that happened at the checkout counter at the market comes to life momentarily for the therapist. It is this one live bit that he attempts to unfold.

In this discussion of the evocative function of the therapist, we are assuming that the three basic therapist conditions of client-centered therapy are present. It is these basic conditions that provide the climate of safety and concentration that makes other therapist operations effective. In fact it seems probable that there is some kind of optimal balance for each client between evocative and maintenance responses from the therapist. It seems worthwhile, therefore, to distinguish between evocative reflections and maintenance reflections, even though they are not always sharply distinguisable in practice. A *maintenance reflection* is a response that is accurate, empathic within the client's internal frame of reference, and *conveys an interest in and acceptance of the client*. It makes the client feel received and understood, and therefore maintains a safe climate for exploration. An *evocative reflection* should also be accurately empathic within the internal frame of reference and should convey interest and acceptance. It is primarily designed, however, to let the client into his own experience, to unfold rather than to package the experience. It is focused on the reaction in a form that (a) has particularity rather than being generalized or abstracted; (b) has reflective subjectivity rather than objectivity; and (c) is sensory and connotative rather than denotative. Each of these qualities will be discussed in detail below. The general distinction may be clarified by an example. Client A, quoted earlier, says, "I'm not studying, even though I know I'll fail if I don't. I have a big paper to write but every time I sit down to do it, I find an excuse to get up and do something else. I just can't study. It panics me." From the point of view of what to reflect, this is an embarrassment of riches. The most salient reaction is that of being panicked in response to the situation of not being able to study. This is certainly a real feeling and could legitimately be reflected. The client would feel understood and accepted. This would be a maintenance reflection, however, in that one would not be responding to the reaction that is felt by the client to be inappropriate, the reaction of not studying when she knows she will fail if she doesn't. It is, rather, a reflection of a reaction (probably felt by the client to be reasonable) to another reaction, felt by the client to be *inappropriate*. Another kind of maintenance reflection would be to pick up the key reaction, but in a generalized form, "Even though the consequences may be disastrous, you just cannot make yourself study." Here again the client would feel understood, but the problem is that it is a generalized statement. It is a condensation of the innumerable times the client has sat down at her desk, had her mind go blank, daydreamed, sharpened pencils, and finally remembered errands that needed to be done. The thing to focus on would be a *particular* experience of trying to study. Neither client nor therapist has much feel yet for what it is like, but there is something that comes before getting up to sharpen the pencil or do the errand. In this case the therapist's response would have to be an open, exploring one, designed to help the client catch an inner glimpse of herself in this situation.

One crucially important caution concerns the directive nature of this process. An evocative reflection often has a demanding quality, pushing toward awareness and active differentiation. It is not directive in terms of a *specific content* to be chosen; but in terms of the quality of the *process* to be engaged in, it is directive. Inasmuch as it is a powerful tool, it could be used in ways that are quite inconsistent with the client-centered philosophy, which leaves to the client the responsibility for regulating for himself the pace at which he broaches his own defenses. In the method suggested here, an evocative reflection would be offered to the client as a stimulus to his exploration, as part of the ongoing, active effort to understand. If the client does not feel ready to use it, he can, as always with a reflection, ignore it and respond with a meaningless "yes" or "not exactly," or change the subject. The therapist should not in any sense pin him against the wall, but should continue with maintenance reflections, following the client's lead with respect to content. At intervals the therapist would continue to offer evocative reflections, opportunities which might or might not be used by the client.

The remainder of this section is an attempt to provide a cookbook for evocative reflection. This is obviously not a push-button task, to be performed by rule. It is an art, demanding a full cognitive–affective involvement, whereby the therapist applies his own mediational capacities to the task of synthesizing the parts in a way that recaptures the substance of the experience rather than abstracting from it. Nevertheless, there are some principles for identifying and evaluating evocative reflections. A knowledge of these can guide the therapist in the art of listening actively and responding evocatively.

Particularity

An evocative response is an attempt to focus on a single incident and apprehend what it is like as concretely as possible. Although generalization to a wide range of situations is a long-range goal, our assumption is that reprocessing can be done most effectively by intensive exploration of a single experience. To abstract from it or to generalize about what is common to several similar experiences seems to lead away from the new meanings needed for reorganization. This is directly contrary to the procedures of many therapists who attempt to spot similarities in patterns and choose to respond in such a way as to interpret these similarities to the client.

The rationale for particularity in responding rests on our assumption about the nature of reprocessing. An experience can be reentered at a high level of arousal, but with a good deal of the client's energy concentrated on observing and reprocessing the experience. It seems to be precisely this high level of arousal that enables the client to get in touch with the idiosyncratic quality of his own experience. A generalized statement about a class of experiences seems to move the client to a level of abstraction at which this level of awareness is more difficult to achieve. For instance, the client is talking about a recent incident that involved a burst of anger at a colleague. He feels that this is happening in different situations, and speculates that maybe it happens when someone acts superior. If the therapist responds, "Whenever anyone acts superior, you get terribly angry," he is responding to the client's attempt to find patterns in his behavior. Such a response will usually be followed either by the giving of several more examples or by an abstracted attempt at insight. On the other hand, if the therapist responds to the incident rather than the generalization—"When he looked down his long nose at you, you just exploded"—the client may well explore further the impact of this situation, what it felt like to be viewed as a speck of dirt.

After a client has grasped an experience freshly in this way, he may begin to explore similarities and patterns, and get very excited about the new avenues that are opened up. However, the generalization follows rather than leads to a new experience.

Subjectivity

In an earlier section it was stated that one of the things that prevents the the reprocessing of reactions is that the reactions themselves are condensed. Another way of stating it is that many people tend to objectify their transactions with the world and with themselves. There has been strong cultural pressure toward that which is objective and abstract (i.e., intellectualized or analytically considered in the client's consciousness), and away from the subjective and particular (i.e., direct experiencing or synthetic affective reacting to the concrete situation). One route to the goal of unfolding and reprocessing, then, is to make subjective that which has become objectified. The term "subjective" is used here as defined by Webster (1952), "arising out of or identified by means of one's awareness of his own state and processes." "Objective" is defined by Webster as "not subjective, hence detached, unprejudiced."

There seem to be two different aspects of objectification, closely related but worth looking at separately. The first characteristic of objectification is that the meaning of an object or event is felt as inhering in the object, or automatically defined by its class membership. One speaks automatically of "that ugly building" rather than of one's reaction to particular aspects of it. Or if expressing disagreement with someone is defined as a hostile act, then by definition it is a lousy thing to do. The therapist's push toward subjectivity would involve helping the client to become freshly aware of the stimulus qualities to which he is responding, and consequently of his power to scrutinize and regroup these qualities. For instance, he may become aware that the "ugly building" is heavy gray stone, of Gothic architecture, decorated at each corner with a gargoyle, from whose snout water drips on innumerable rainy days. At this point he is in a position to assess the impact that these aspects are having on him.

The second characteristic of objectification is that one is aware only of the resultant behavioral response, and is only slightly if at all aware of the experiential element, the immediate impact on the self. It is this awareness of one's own state and processes that is often short-circuited. This aspect is, of course, what we mean by feelings, and yet "responding to subjectivity" is intended to imply something beyond "reflection of feelings." In the first place, it implies the major part that the person himself plays in generating meaning. Secondly, it implies that we are less interested in identifying a feeling that can be labeled than in focusing on the more personal, idiosyncratic aspects of what it is like to be in that situation. Rather than the usual condensed feeling words like "anxious" or "guilty" one might pick up a sense of the client feeling "stretched tight" or of feeling "dubious and slimy." Or, rather than putting a facile label on the situation being described, the therapist might make an exploratory response—"When he said that and you resigned—I'd like to get the flavor of that. Can you tell me more about what it is like?"

An evocative response is particularly effective if it involves both these aspects of subjectivity; the qualities of the stimulus situation and the differentiated inner awareness of impact. In most therapist responses one aspect is subordinated to the other, but often client and therapist move back and forth, exploring both aspects. For instance, the client is reporting that she can never stay in hotels because of those "awful impersonal corridors." She just has to leave the place. One might try to focus on the stimulus quality of the corridors, with only a brief reference to personal impact—"There is something that hits you about that corridor—all the doors firmly closesd, no furniture but an echo, maybe an odd smell—I don't know—" Here the therapist is more or less free associating to the word "impersonal" to see if anything hits. On the other hand, the therapist might focus on the impact of these impersonal corridors—"Those impersonal corridors sort of close in on you I guess—a feeling of 'let me out.'

There is some research evidence of a relationship between the amount of this kind of exploring of subjectivity on the part of the client and favorableness of outcome of therapy (Rice & Wagstaff, 1967). Moreover, it seems intuitively to be true that one of the valuable things to be learned in therapy would be an appreciation of the special qualities of one's own reactions, and to see these reactions as intervening decisively between what impinges and what one does. In other words, one becomes aware of oneself as a processor, and aware that meaning can be generated by one's interaction with the situation. One would then become more independent of the impinging world, in the sense of not being controlled by it, and yet, paradoxically, one would become more freshly and vividly aware of one's world.

Use of Sensory, Connotative Language

The purpose of the evocative response is to stimulate the client to get deeper and more accurately into his own experience. The therapist tries to register the fragments and synthesize them, not to label the experience, but to open it up. The language that he uses is an important determinant of his stimulus value for the client. Some language serves a denotative function, that of pointing, of marking out. On the other hand, connotative language suggests various associated impressions and possibilities beyond the explicit meaning. It is not a matter of vagueness, but of richness of associations. Language based on sensory imagery (auditory, kinesthetic, etc., as well as visual) is especially connotative in its impact. Metaphorical language seems particularly suited to the task of accurately evoking an experience while leaving open all sorts of possibilities that are not yet clear. *Metaphors can be both concrete and open.* For instance, a client has been talking about feeling utterly alone, trying to understand how everything can be going so wrong, and the therapist responds, "You feel as if you are all alone in a cavern shouting, 'What's wrong! What's wrong!' " This is extremely effective in conveying to the client the imagery his message has evoked in the therapist, which in turn evokes more vivid experience in the client.

Another client has been saying that she needs to be independent from her husband, but whenever he comes home, she drops everything and follows him around. The therapist responds, "And there goes the little puppy dog pattering after him." This picks up her sense of dependence, but also suggests other possibilities of faithful devotion, hunger for affection, even fear of desertion. Another client has been talking about a nagging fear, and the therapist responds, "It's always there nibbling at the edges." This turned out to express very clearly the client's sense of being eaten away by worry. This sort of response is particularly effective when a client find its difficult to focus inward, and describes people and things outside himself. For instance, a client is describing how difficult his mother makes it for anyone to explain things to her, because she won't respond. The therapist focuses on an example the client has given. "You tried over and over to explain, but your mother just sat there like a great Buddha." Even though the description is of something external to the client, it picks up a vivid fragment of the client's experience. The use of metaphorical language must rest on a base of active empathic listening for the flavor of an experience. Otherwise it may well slip into the use of analogies, which draw attention to the structural similarity between two referents, rather than intensifying the client's own immediate experience.

The three characteristics of evocative reflection discussed above bear a striking resemblance to the qualities that distinguish poetry that is moving and impactful. Such poetry has the quality of particularity that captures the uniqueness of an experience, and yet somehow leaves one knowing oneself and the world more broadly than before. It has the inherent subjectivity that strips away the confinement of labels and pigeonholes and enables one to feel the impact of familiar things with newborn senses. And of course connotative language, rich with possibilities, is the very stuff of poetry. It would be unreasonable to expect every therapist to become a poet. On the other hand, anyone can learn to avoid labeling and packaging, and dare to use words freshly.

REFERENCES

Carkhuff, R. R., & Berenson, B. G. *Beyond counseling and psychotherapy.* New York: Holt, Rinehart & Winston, 1967.

Furth, H. G. *Piaget and knowledge.* Englewood Cliffs, N.J.: Prentice-Hall, 1969.

Inhelder, B. Memory and intelligence in the child. In D. Elkind & J. H. Flavell (Eds.), *Studies in cognitive development*. New York: Oxford University Press, 1969.

Pascual-Leone, J. *Cognitive development and cognitive style: A general psychological explanation*. New York: Heath, in press.

Pascual-Leone, J., & Smith, J. The encoding and decoding of symbols by children: A new experimental paradigm and a neo-Piagetian model. *Journal of Experimental Child Psychology*, 1969, **8**, 328–355.

Piaget, J. Piaget's theory. In P. H. Mussen (Ed.), *Carmichael's manual of child psychology*. (3rd ed.) New York: Wiley, 1970.

Piaget, J., & Morf, A. Les isomorphismes partiels entre les structures logiques et les structures perceptives. In J. S. Bruner, F. Bresson, A. Morf, & J. Piaget (Eds.), *Logiques et perception*. Paris: Presses Universitaires de France, 1958.

Rice, L. N., & Wagstaff, A. K. Client voice quality and expressive style as indexes of productive psychotherapy. *Journal of Consulting Psychology*, 1967, **31**, 557–563.

Rogers, C. R. The necessary and sufficient conditions of therapeutic personality change. *Journal of Consulting Psychology*, 1957, **22**, 95–103.

Webster's new world dictionary of the American language. (College ed.) New York: World, 1952.

Part IV

BEYOND INDIVIDUAL
PSYCHOTHERAPY

The focal concern of client-centered therapy has traditionally been the individual. As a therapeutic orientation, its roots lie in traditional one-to-one psychotherapy, and it is in this context that it has grown and flourished. Beyond its principal form of practice, there is another sense in which its main emphasis lies with the individual person. As a system of ideas, client-centered therapy is also a psychology of the individual. It is a psychology that has focused on the uniqueness of each person, the way he processes his subjective experience, and his basic push for freedom and autonomy from forces that control him from without. The traditional concern with the individual, both in theory and in practice, is well represented in the chapters contained in Parts II and III of this book.

There is, however, another side to client-centered therapy—a side that is the focal point for the chapters in this section. Since its beginnings, client-centered therapy has also sought wider spheres of influence, beyond the individual, both in attempting to explore the relevance of its ideas in contexts broader than traditional dyadic therapy and in seeking to apply its approach to wider social milieus. Thus, spearheaded by the efforts of

Rogers and his colleagues, client-centered ideas have been extended and applied to areas as diverse as parent training (Gordon, 1970), groups (Hobbs, 1951; Rogers, 1970), education (Rogers, 1969), families (Raskin & van der Veen, 1970), leadership (Gordon, 1951), to name but a few. In its efforts to go beyond the confines of individual counseling, client-centered therapy has met with much success. In these broader social contexts it has found receptive audiences, and client-centered principles relevant to the facilitation of personal growth have achieved considerable popularity in diverse areas of interpersonal relations.

There are several aspects of Rogers' psychology that in all likelihood have contributed to the efforts to extend client-centered therapy to wider spheres of application. The first lies in the Rogerian view of psychological health and the implications it has for therapeutic practice. In Rogers' psychology, health is fundamentally conceptualized in positive terms; it consists of the fuller use of the individual's potentials and capacities and the heightening of both his autonomy and the subjective richness of his experience. In this view, health becomes synonymous with continuous change and growth, and is almost limitless by definition. Such a position represents a marked departure from the model of psychological health offered by traditional psychoanalytic theory. Born from a medical model, psychoanalysis saw health in terms of the relative *absence* of pathology. With this view comes a medical approach to treatment and all that it implies. Thus, the goal of treatment is the removal of pathology, with treatment being called for only upon the detection of pathology and restricted only to the individual who is sick, either by his own report or that of others. Moreover, the treatment setting also tends to be restricted to situations where pathology can be readily isolated, identified, and corrected. In contrast, viewing psychological health in positive terms leads one to consider treatment in a very different light and also in a variety of contexts. The term "treatment" becomes something of a misnomer, for therapeutic intervention is not concerned with the correction and removal of pathology, but with the facilitation and enhancement of growth. Inasmuch as growth can be a continuous process, and one that can be enhanced in all individuals, the principles that foster it have continuing relevance, and diverse areas of human relations become fertile ground for its facilitation. Thus the encounter group, the classroom, the community are all equally viable areas for the application of growth-promoting principles.

A second factor that probably contributes to the effort to extend client-centered practice to wider social contexts is Rogers' (1962) conviction that the dyadic therapeutic relationship is only one isolated instance of a growth-promoting relationship, and the qualities that make this relationship facilitating are indeed relevant to all other areas of social interaction where the enhancement of growth is of concern. Moreover, the therapist attitudes that are conducive to growth are not seen to lie in the exclusive province of the professional, but are seen as basic human qualities that can be effectively developed and used by any individual. Thus, those attitudes that make the therapist a potent facilitator in the traditional therapy context are the very same attitudes that can also help individuals facilitate growth in a group, a classroom, or any other larger social unit.

A final aspect of Rogers' work that has provided an impetus for the extensions of the client-centered orientation into diverse areas of human relations is his contention that the knowledge that has been gained through the study of psychotherapy concerning the components of individual growth and the factors that impede its expression also has relevance to the understanding of larger social collectivities. Using his model of therapy as a basis, Rogers (1959) not only developed a theory of personality, but also a theory of interpersonal relationships. In so doing, he established a trend that has as its focus the search for principles governing behavior in larger social groups, principles that parallel those found in the traditional therapy context. The continuance of this trend is particularly evident in Chapter 13 by Bebout, Chapter 14, by Beck, and Chapter 15, by W. Rogers. These chapters extend client-centered principles to groups and to the community. It should be noted, however, that the extensions of client-centered thought to larger social units do not simply involve taking principles pertaining to the individual and blindly imposing them on broader social areas. Rather, they involve modifying and transforming these principles in order to deal adequately with the complexities and unique characteristics of these larger social areas.

Having considered aspects of Rogerian psychology that have provided an impetus for these extensions, we shall now turn to the substance of the individual chapters in this section. Chapter 11, by Homans, which begins this section, is not an attempt to extend client-centered thinking to a wider social milieu. It does however, help provide a sociological context for further understanding why such extensions have been attempted and also why they have been well received. Falling within the domain of what has been called the *sociology of knowledge*, Homans' chapter addresses two questions with respect to Rogerian psychology, questions that are all too frequently neglected in examining psychological theory: What are the social forces that influence and mold the direction and substance of psychological theory? and, What are the sociological factors that might in part be responsible for the popularity and growth of one theoretical perspective rather than another? Homans formulates the answers to these questions with respect to Rogers' psychology, by examining his theoretical system in the context of mass society. In his sociological analysis, Homans paints a vivid picture of the plight of the individual in mass society—his loneliness and alienation, his lack of a sense of individuality, his inability to make sense out of a complex and perplexing world, and his experience of being controlled by forces from without. Homans cogently argues that Rogers, in his theorizing, basically assumes as a starting point the psychological impact of mass society upon the individual. More important, however, as a system of ideas, Rogerian psychology also offers a potential solution to the plight of modern man, for it holds out to the individual the possibility of discovering and developing his own individuality in a manner whereby he is not estranged and alienated from his fellow man, but deeply and intimately related to him. Thus, Homans contends that part of the appeal of Rogerian psychology lies in its timeliness; it not only helps the individual make sense out of his dilemma in the modern world, but also provides a world view that holds out the promise of a potential solution to this dilemma.

The remaining chapters in this section also assume as a starting point the plight of modern man as described by Homans. Explicitly or implicitly, each assumes man alienated both from himself and from other persons. In attempting to apply and extend client-centered principles to wider social milieus, each author, in different ways and in different contexts, is also attempting to counteract the deadening impact that mass society has had upon the individual. The focal point for Chapter 12, Gaylin's chapter, lies in the fostering of creativeness. First dispelling the common association between creativity and madness through illuminating historical analysis, Gaylin argues that creativeness and psychological well-being are synonymous. In depicting the unique synthesis and organization of information as the wellspring of creative activity, the view of healthy functioning described here is quite consistent with that advanced in several of the chapters in Part II (see Chapters 2, 3, 5, and 6), where the emphasis was on the active seeking and assimilation of new information in the ongoing processing of experience. Gaylin does not view creativeness as something reserved only for the gifted, but rather as something within the grasp of all individuals. Indeed, it is the cultivation of the individual's basic creativeness, that, according to Gaylin, can be of crucial importance in helping to counter the existential meaningless and anomie that prevail in contemporary society.

The chapters by Bebout and Beck (Chapters 13 and 14) concern the extensions of client-centered principles to groups. The last decade or so has witnessed a remarkable growth of various forms of groups having as their aim the facilitation of personal growth. In enormous numbers individuals have come to groups seeking the interpersonal contact, intimacy, and the deep sense of emotional involvement that are so sorely lacking in contemporary society. Bebout discusses the idea that encounter groups are a natural outcome of developments and changes in client-centered therapy over the years, and his chapter attempts to reinterpret central concepts in client-centered therapy in light of experiences with these groups. He outlines how encounter groups are a natural consequence of the client-centered emphasis on the experiential, and more particularly the recent trend in client-centered therapy toward stressing the mutual sharing of the experiential processes occurring within the therapist as well as those occurring within the client (see also Chapters 7 and 8). Bebout contends that experiential communality, the mutual coexperiencing of functionally equivalent affective responses between two or more persons, represents the active ingredient in encounter groups that helps to dissolve interpersonal distance and alienation, and enhance growth in its participants. He illustrates in detail the workings of experiential communality as it occurs in groups, and discusses its relation to the concept of empathy. Bebout also discusses how client-centered concepts pertaining to the individual find parallel expression in groups, thus illustrating the usefulness of these concepts in illuminating the group situation.

Beck's chapter also shows the general trend toward seeing groups as organized social units, with processes and organization paralleling those occurring in the individual. Just as the individual is a system interacting with his environment, with orderly development and organization evolving from that interaction, so too, Beck contends, a group is an organized system that develops and takes on structure as it interacts in its environment. Pushed by individual needs to establish workable patterns of social interaction and a need for social belongingness, groups search for identity as a whole. Beck presents in her analysis a detailed model of basic phases in group structure, goals, and roles that seem to be invariant across successful groups as they develop and search for this identity.

The chapter by W. Rogers, Chapter 15, represents an extension and application of client-centered principles to community psychology, an area that also has grown enormously in the past few years. Rogers poses an important challenge to psychotherapists with his contention that they should be concerned not only with the psychological health of individuals, but also with influencing those factors in the social structure that affect the psychological health of individuals existing within that social structure. In setting forth a model by which this might be done at the level of the community, Rogers also clearly demonstrates the trend toward conceiving of larger social groups almost as organisms to which some principles of individual functioning may be profitably applied. Rogers posits that just as the individual possesses a basic force to develop his unique identity and potentials, so too does a community seek to develop a sense of common belonging and identity that is unique to it. Presenting a detailed list of propositions, with respect to the development of community identity, decay, and reorganization, that closely parallel the Rogerian formulation of these processes as they occur in the individual, this chapter demonstrates the potential usefulness of client-centered concepts in understanding complex social processes in the community. More important, perhaps, Rogers also presents a detailed model for how, from a client-centered perspective, community reorganization and change can be facilitated.

Relative to the magnitude of what is involved, the attempt to extend psychological principles to larger social groups and to the solution of complex social problems is something that has barely begun. It is an enormous task, but yet it is an important and challenging one. It is the persistent attempt of workers in the client-centered tradition to meet this challenge that is in part responsible for the continuing vitality of client-centered therapy.

REFERENCES

Gordon, T. Group-centered leadership and administration. In C. R. Rogers, *Client-centered therapy*. Boston: Houghton Mifflin, 1951.

Gordon, T. *Parent effectiveness training: The no-lose program for raising responsible children*. New York: Wyden, 1970.

Hobbs, N. Group-centered psychotherapy. In C. R. Rogers, *Client-centered therapy*. Boston: Houghton Mifflin, 1951.

Raskin, N. J., & van der Veen, F. Client-centered family therapy: Some clinical and research perspectives. In J. T. Hart & T. M. Tomlinson (Eds.), *New directions in client-centered therapy*. Boston: Houghton Mifflin, 1970.

Rogers, C. R. A theory of therapy, personality, and interpersonal relations as developed in the client-centered framework. In S. Koch (Ed.), *Psychology: A study of a science*. Vol. 3. New York: McGraw-Hill, 1959.

Rogers, C. R. The interpersonal relationship: The core of guidance. *Harvard Educational Review*, 1962, **32**, 416–429.

Rogers, C. R. *Freedom to learn: A view of what education might become*. Columbus, Ohio: Merrill, 1969.

Rogers, C. R. *Carl Rogers on encounter groups*. New York: Harper & Row, 1970.

CHAPTER 11

Carl Rogers' Psychology and the Theory of Mass Society

Peter Homans

Today, Rogerian psychology is a major theory of psychotherapy and personality in America. Within a few short years following the close of World War II, Rogers published the basic concepts of his thought and the client-centered theory and practice of psychotherapy took shape. His major statement, *Client-Centered Therapy*, appeared in 1951, and the most sustained, cooperative work was done at the Counseling Center of the Department of Psychology of the University of Chicago during the period 1945–1957. Before the end of the 1950s, many survey texts in theories of personality, theories of psychotherapy, and schools of psychology contained "a Rogerian chapter." By the end of the decade Koch's (1959) authoritative survey of the science of psychology appeared, and included a chapter by Rogers. Koch placed the chapter in the volume entitled, *Formulations of the Person and the Social Context*—a significant editorial choice, in the light of the purpose of the present chapter. The appearance of Rogerian psychology was of course implemented in a more general way by the postwar rise in popularity of two new genres of psychological work, personology and psychotherapy.

Rogers' thought has generated philosophical speculation (Gendlin, 1962), and his colleagues have attempted to link its central concepts to biological processes (Butler & Rice, 1963). He has addressed himself to educational problems, problems of social and international relations, and his writings have become a resource for the emerging sensitivity groups movements. Even ministers (e.g., Oden, 1966) have attempted to use his thought, although often in a thoroughly misguided way.

But Rogers' psychology is more than one theory alongside others. It is also an approach, or orientation, or point of view. Survey texts usually classify it with the humanistic psychologies, which are of American origin, or with the existential psychologies, which are of European origin. In either case, Rogers' psychology belongs to a cluster of theories that share ideas and principles—both sociological and epistemological—of considerably wider general significance than those at issue within the theory itself. It is fair to speak, I think, of Rogerian psychology as a movement, or as part of a movement, much in the sense in which Freud originally spoke of his own work as the psychoanalytic movement.

Despite the prominence of Rogers' psychology, its range of applicability outside psychology, and especially its character as a movement, the social forces that may have contributed to the formation and propagation of Rogerian concepts, assumptions, and practices remain undiscussed. This highly significant issue must not be confused with the integration into a sociological framework of psychological theory, in order to create a general theory of personality and society. Nor does it refer to the attempt on the part of social psychology to discern the social determination of personal attitudes and opinions. Rather, the issue is what kind of social forces produce one particular theory of personality rather than another one?

Psychologists are often aware of the psychological forces that produce psychological theories, and they often speak of the social forces that produce psychological distress. But they have little regard for the relation between social forces and the formation of personality theory. Such a lack of confidence in the sociological bases for psychological theory-making is all the more surprising in the light of two facts. First, we now have considerable sociological discussion of Freudian theory, albeit conducted mostly in the light of mass society theory. A major interpretation of modernity, the theory of mass society has not, on the whole, impressed those working in psychology. Second, most of Rogers' psychological concepts bear such striking likeness to Freud's as to force the somewhat cynical observation that for each Rogerian word there is a Freudian one. Rogerians have not as a rule spoken of such similarities, a costly choice that has rendered them inaccessible to valuable sociological analyses of their work.

The best way to approach the sociological implications of Rogerian thought lies, therefore, in extending sociological discussions of psychoanalytic theory and therapy to include the Rogerian viewpoint. We will see that Rogers' psychology has to a large extent been shaped by those social forces that are best described by the theory of mass society. On the one hand, Rogerian theory implicitly assumes those social forces described by the theory of mass society. On the other hand, Rogerian theory also takes its particular shape from its attempt to resolve or reverse the effect of such forces.

This argument can be cast in terms of the process of psychological growth. Rogers' diagnosis of the conditions that limit all human becoming is fundamentally identical with the diagnosis of society that the theory of mass society offers. However, Rogers also offers a solution for overcoming these conditions, and this solution constitutes his own creative response to the sociological realities of which the theory of mass society speaks. The theory of mass society is, then, the foundation upon which Rogerian theory is built, but the superstructure of Rogerian theory is innovative and significant in its attempt to meet the challenge of the problem of a mass society.

MAJOR TENETS OF ROGERIAN PSYCHOLOGY

What are the basic tenets of Rogers' psychology, and to what extent do they owe their beginnings to Freud? Rogers' theory is at bottom an experiential theory of human becoming. Therefore its central tents derive from two questions: What defines the limits of human becoming? What makes possible human becoming? Rogers' answer to the first determines his answer to the second.

Conditions of worth and *organismic valuing process* describe what is limiting and engendering in the Rogerian view of becoming. Conditions of worth are patterns of preference regarding types of behavior and experiences, patterns that originate in others but are adopted nonetheless by the individual. These introjected values throw into motion a series of ominous consequences for the future organization and coherence of the self. They split the actualizing tendency from the self-actualizing tendency, and the self from the self-structure. They are, consequently, at the root of all anxiety, incongruence, vulnerability, denial of experiencing to awareness, and inaccurate symbolization—in short, of all psychological maladjustment. Conditions of worth develop early in life and are the cause of the need for therapy. However, inasmuch as they are also unavoidable according to Rogers (1959), they constitute a tragic dimension in all of life, "the basic estrangement in man [p. 226]."

The concept of the organismic valuing process is the logical, psychological, and developmental opposite of conditions of worth. Through this notion Rogers conceives a mode of experiencing in which valuing of specific behaviors and experiences arises from within the organism and cannot be derived from external conditions. Valuing is grounded in visceral and sensory sources of stimulation, includes their full and accurate symbolization within awareness, and results in the integration of self or self-structure and experience, and of actualizing tendency with self-actualizing tendency.

Three other concepts of considerable importance lie midway, so to speak, between these two primary ones. "Denied and distorted symbolization" and "accurate symbolization within awareness" both refer quite directly and specifically to the further experiential consequences created by either the imposition upon the organism of conditions of worth, or the reverse. A third notion, *unconditional positive regard*, refers to a type of attitude taken by a social other that is prerequisite for the development of accurate symbolization and organismic valuing, and without which conditions of worth are likely to occur.

The notion of conditions of worth is deeply biographical in character, a fact rarely mentioned by Rogerians, although clearly stated in Rogers' own biographical remarks. This is an important point, because the theory of mass society gives considerable emphasis to the experiential effects upon individual persons of specific aspects of the social order. In Rogers' case the experiential process denoted by the concept of conditions of worth is clearly apparent in three major phases of his life—childhood, vocational decision, and development of professional work-techniques.

Although we cannot develop this point at length, we should note its major features. First is Rogers' struggle against his parents' religiously based ethical life style, a struggle that began in childhood but extended well beyond it. Rogers grew up in a rural community that imposed harsh, religious ideals of behavior upon him, and he accepted these as a matter of course, without questioning them. This nonreflective acceptance formed, in childhood, the first biographical context for the concept of conditions of worth. We should note the close relation between religion and parental authority.

Rogers' struggle with religion culminated in a vocational decision, to attend Union Theological Seminary in New York City, a training school for ministers. However, there he became as doubtful about the truth claims of religious doctrines as he had been earlier about the behavioral claims of religious ideals. Rogers created his own discussion group in order to work through a vocational conflict, which he described (Rogers, 1961) quite succinctly: "It seemed a horrible thing to *have* to profess a set of beliefs, in order to remain in one's profession . . . [p. 8]." We can regard this phase of Rogers' life, in which beliefs were imposed from without, as a second experiential context for what later became conceptualized as conditions of worth.

Rogers turned to psychology in the hope of finding a profession in which he would have more freedom of thought. During his training and early years at Rochester he was exposed to Freudian theory and technique. This was a period of intense inner activity, relatively uninfluenced by the thoughts of others. As Rogers became more experienced as a therapist, he felt more conflict between the orderliness he found to be discoverable *in* experience and the Freudian theories that were imposed *upon* his clinical experience. His well-known rejection of Freudian theory is based exactly upon this perception of it as a kind of condition of worth, at the level of thinking.

In each phase of Rogers' life he felt something static and preformed imposed from without, upon something arising from within that had its own intrinsic character and direction. Certain parts of his life were being preferred over other, more unique portions. Parental religious attitudes restricted a search for a unique life style, the seminary constricted ideological innovation, and the Freudian concepts restricted reliance on his own clinical experience. Each phase was, in its own way, a condition of worth. It is the last of these, representing as it does the relation between personal experience and psychological theory formation, that most concerns us.

Rogers and Freud—Similarities and Differences

Rogerians as a rule do not feel indebted to Freud. When they turn their attention to psychoanalysis, it is more for purposes of correction than appreciation. Rogerians are not an ungrateful lot, nor does Freud deserve unqualified admiration; rather an assent on differences has obscured important likenesses. Rogers' psychology does articulate directly with Freud's at major points. As we shall soon see, both likeness and difference in the case of the two theories require sociological as well as accurate comparative discussion.

Freud's understanding of personal becoming has of course been interpreted in many different ways. Recent efforts (e.g., Bakan, 1966; Brown, 1959; Marcuse, 1965; Ricoeur, 1965; Rieff, 1966) have stressed the analysis of social and cultural symbols as a major concern underlying the entire range of Freud's writings. These views differ considerably from the more established views of psychoanalysis as scientific psychology or personality theory. But all interpretations, conventional or otherwise, acknowledge the pivotal character of the superego, and its progressive modification, in Freud's estimate of the possibilities and limitations of personal becoming. The concept of conditions of worth strongly resembles that of the superego. Both refer to a process whereby socially derived evaluations or preferences with regard to psychological and especially bodily processes have been appropriated by the individual as if they were his own. Both therefore stipulate a form of alienation in which one dimension of self-relation becomes strange or contrary to self-relation as a whole.

It is also true that, in many respects, the concept of an organismic valuing process resembles Freud's description of successful therapy. "Organismic" means visceral and sensory processes, and captures much of Freud's emphasis upon affect and perception in his discussions of instinct. "Valuing" signifies self-initiated preferencing with regard to feeling-states, behaviors, ideas, and objects, capturing much of Freud's phenomenological emphasis upon libido as interest and intention. And the concept of "process," juxtaposed as it is by Rogers to rigidity and stasis, shares much of Freud's emphasis upon the free, though fundamentally ordered, interplay of feeling, perception, and thought so necessary for insight and integration. The Rogerian notions of experiencing denied to awareness, and accurate symbolization within awareness, are so similar to Freud's concepts of repression and insight that elaboration is unnecessary.

But there is an equally important difference, regarding the extent to which socially derived alienation can be reduced or eliminated. Freud of course believed that the superego was a constitutive element or structure in society, history, and culture, as well as in the individual personality. The psychoanalytic process, and growth and life experiences that produce equivalent effects, could reduce its opacity to insight and consequent moral harshness. Still, Freud's moral psychology frees the individual from society only in order to return him to it—more wary, more prepared to decide against it in specific instances, but fundamentally committed to the making and maintaining of civilization with like-minded men. This is the first premise for all discussions of Freud's ethics.

Rogers stipulates no such "return." Like Freud he considers internalization of social valuing the problem of all personal becoming. However, Rogers' theory of psychotherapy makes no proposal to strengthen the individual's capacity to tolerate, in any intrinsic sense, introjected value systems. Rogers' moral psychology is a radical approach to the problem of the superego. For instead of simply mitigating conditions of worth, the organismic valuing process calls for their very dissolution, a dissolution that presupposes a collective or universal form of sociality, grounded in the character of experiencing itself. The organismic valuing process provides all persons with equal access to a similar kind of experiencing process.[1] Consequently, all special types of experiences are in principle equally acceptable to all persons. On the one hand Rogerian therapy releases the individual from social restraint, in the form of conditions of worth; on the other hand it returns the individual to a deeper, more

---

[1] Rogers (1951) concluded his discussion of the organismic valuing process with the following words: "One of the ultimate ends, then, of an hypothesis of confidence in the individual, and in his capacity to resolve his own conflicts, is the emergence of value systems which are unique and personal for each individual, and which are changed by the changing evidence of organic experience, yet which are at the same time deeply socialized, possessing a high degree of similarity in their essentials [p. 524]."

organic, more universal form of sociality.

Rogers has not explicated as fully as he could the fact that the very structure of the organismic valuing process is social, perhaps because of the unavoidable emphasis placed upon individual autonomy as a major goal of any form of psychotherapy. Therefore some have viewed his theory as a rejection of social norms in the interests of individual autonomy. Psychological well-being is not achieved, according to Rogers, at the cost of either an heroic or nihilistic rejection of sociality, in favor of the individual *over* society. It is achieved through the discovery by the individual that socially derived conflicts do not constitute the deepest level of experiencing. To cast this conclusion in the fashionable language of some linguistics and anthropology: conditions of worth are diachronic, but the organismic valuing process is synchronic.

Rogers fails, however, to account for the source or origin of conditions of worth, beyond the transactional immediacies of family life. A sociological framework, and more particularly that of the theory of mass society, is particularly useful and convincing. Rogers assumes this theory, although he does not mention it. If we apply this theory to Rogers' thought, we can entertain the following speculation: The source of such preferential valuing as is found in conditions of worth lies in the breakdown of a generalized, culture-wide valuing framework sufficiently broad and diverse to permit the positive valuing of many types of experiences within the same culture. Only a social organization characterized by an established center, a recognizable periphery, and by continuity rather than conflict between the two can support such a valuing framework. That the fragmentation of a culture-wide valuing framework creates social and psychological alienation is the major tenet of the theory of mass society. Rogers assumes as much in his theory of conditions of worth, and further, his concept of an organismic valuing process must be viewed as an attempt to overcome the effects of such alienation. Rogerian psychology implicitly views society as mass society.

To support this argument we now apply specific sociological discussions of mass society theory to Rogers' psychology. These discussions focus on the Freudian notion of the superego and, as we have already seen, what can be said of the superego can be said of conditions of worth. We begin with a brief characterization of the theory of mass society itself.

ROGERS' PSYCHOLOGY AND THE THEORY OF
MASS SOCIETY

The theory of mass society is as much a conceptual leitmotif running through the many different types of modern thought as it is a series of easily recognizable propositions.[2] All versions, however, possess in one form or other, and in varying degrees, the following features. First, the Middle Ages, more than any other period in Western history, provided a strong, firm, mutually supportive relation between social solidarity and epistemological and ontological consensus. A single, generally accepted view prevailed as to what constituted objective reality, the nature of the world, in both an ultimate and a practical sense. This consensus permitted considerable stratification of groups within the society, without weakening loyalty to society as a whole. The medieval church supervised social variation through its ecclesiastical practices, and ensured ontological and epistemological consensus through its theology.

Second, this continuity between social stability and a common view of objective reality was broken at the time of the Reformation. The breakdown of social stability established by the medieval church went hand in hand with a corresponding fragmentation of a shared sense of what was objectively true. The Reformation was, therefore, the period of preparation for the later formation of a mass society. Third, these sociological and ontological changes affected corresponding shifts in the pattern of integration between self and society, forcing the burden of psychological integration away from institutionalized mechanisms and placing it more and more onto the psychological systems of the individual. Certain psychological processes that were formerly structured and maintained by institutional practice were handed over, so to speak, to the individual. Fourth, this shift created great strain on the psychological functioning of the individual. This shift, the theory of mass society argues, accounts for the subject-oriented character of modern epistemology, which in turn is directly related to the rise of the science of psychology. An epistemology of the subject and the science of psychology are inseparable from increased psychological strain.

The last of these four propositions is of course the most germane to our discussion. It is usually rendered by the notion of *alienation*. This famous notion received its modern philosophical statement from Hegel, its sociological rendition from Marx, and its psychological formulation from Freud. It has recently been carried forward most explicitly with regard to the relation between the theory of mass society and psychology by Erich Fromm (1955) and Herbert Marcuse (1965).

[2] The theory of mass society has been ably summarized, both historically and systematically by Giner (1969). In addition to Giner's summaries, two specific texts of special value for the following discussion are Mannheim (1936) and Kornhauser (1959). One of the most representative modern philosophical statements of the theory of mass society is Marcel (1962). See especially his chapter on the "fanaticized consciousness."

This concept has, however, been overgeneralized to an extraordinary degree. A term that retains much of what is meant by alienation, while making more explicit its psychological implications, is the term "massification." Mannheim (1956) used the term massification to mean the loss of individuality and identification with society as a whole, resulting in the appearance of traditionlessness, aimlessness and lack of individuality. Lack of individuality refers to the fact that because men tend more and more to do things collectively, they interpret their own actions as simple repetitions of what others are also doing. Kornhauser (1959) has spoken of the breakdown of intermediate relations in creating such personal isolation.

Freud's psychology is inseparable from this type of analysis. His is a psychology of alienation as massification. Freud's metapsychology provides an account whereby the individual's wishes and desires, so constitutive of his being and so familiar to his consciousness, are rendered strange and alien to him, at the hands of the cultural superego. The cultural superego imposes its alien forms upon the instincts, creating the mechanism of repression, the individual superego, and the inevitability of guilt.

Rogers' conditions of worth is really an American version of the oppressive superego. However, his solution to the oppression differs markedly from Freud's. Freud provided his patients with the capacity to distance themselves sufficiently from both social form (cultural superego) and inner desire (id) to bring about some sort of working compromise between the two. Massification was not avoided, but its effects were considerably mitigated. Rogers provides a process whereby the individual need *never* compromise himself at the hands of an alien society. Conditions of worth do impose upon the self-actualizing tendency forms alien to the experiencing process itself. Such alienation is an inevitable and tragic consequence of the process of becoming. However, the accurate symbolization of experiencing in awareness, as it is facilitated by the unconditional positive regard of the client-centered therapist, frees the experiencing process from alien social effects, permitting a congruence between actualizing tendency and self-actualizing tendency. This congruence owes its possibility, both energetically and structurally, to the organismic valuing process. That process is therefore a Rogerian answer to the threat of massification.

If the individual's consciousness is organized by the organismic valuing process, he is beyond the possibility of massification, for he is in touch with a type of experiencing that is common to all men, that is social, but has no special social derivation. Rogers' conception of the fully functioning person presupposes social forces such as those described by the theory of mass society.

Three well-known sociological discussions of psychoanalysis and modernity further illustrate and support this conclusion. Each contains the basic assumptions of the theory of mass society; each finds psychoanalysis central to that theory, especially to the split between present and past; and each provides a sociological context for the argument that Rogerian psychology both assumes the diagnosis of mass society theory and attempts to "cure" the presumed effects of that diagnosis.

Rogers' Psychology and David Riesman's Other-Directed Social Character

David Riesman's (1954, 1955, 1964) theory is well-known and well criticized. (See Lipset & Lowenthal, 1961.) It is concerned with the relation between changing historical conditions and types of social character. Many elements go to make up social character, but the source of authority to which the individual conforms is crucial. Riesman speaks of the "voices" to which the individual listens, in referring to the most compelling source of conformity. At the time of the Reformation, Western history underwent a shift from a tradition-directed type of social character to an inner-directed type. Parental figures replaced oral traditions as the locus of authority and conformity. The appearance of inner-direction set the stage for the development of a mass society.

The actual appearance of a mass society required a second major shift in Western society, from inner-direction to other-direction. The locus of authority, the voices one listens to, shifted for Western society from parental figures to social peers, that is, to extrafamilial persons contemporary to oneself. This shift resulted from a breakdown of the mechanisms of inner-direction, a breakdown facilitated by industrialization and urbanization as well as by the rise of electronic communications media.

Other-direction requires exceptional sensitivity to the actions and wishes of others, and threatens to produce behavioral conformity. Clearly, the other-directed social character is Riesman's term for a mass society. The nature of other-direction is directly juxtaposed to the problem of autonomy, a problem that Riesman posed at the end of his classic study, but never really resolved. Although autonomy is always possible and desirable in all periods of history and for all types of social character, it is most problematic for the other-directed type. Without it the individual has little sense of himself apart from society. This condition is clearly an instance of the phenomenon of massification. At this point psychology, especially the psychologies of Freud and Rogers, take on special moral significance.

Riesman rightly named Freud the psychologist par excellence of inner-direction. Freud's work gives psychological clarity to the social character of inner-direction, because the mechanism of inner-direction depends upon the psychological process of identification. By means of identification, parental voices, which are the locus of authority, become internalized as a structure of personality, the superego. But Freud is the psychologist of inner-direction in another sense. He also gave psychological transparency to the motivation of the inner-directed, thereby making possible a decision against this mode of functioning. By availing himself of Freud's interpretative techniques, the inner-directed individual can free himself to a considerable extent from the coercive power of a "blind" superego, and thereby modify the strength and pattern of identification. Parental voices lose their power over the individual, and the voice of contemporaries becomes a source of authority. So Freud also created the possibility—and to a considerable extent the necessity as well—of other-direction.

Freud's conviction that the force of the superego should be reduced though never eliminated prevents him from ever being held responsible in any simple sense for the creation of other-direction. But no such exception can be made for Rogers. They do agree: conditions of worth, the superego, both derive from parental introjects. From Riesman's sociological viewpoint, however, what Freud considered intrinsic to all culture and what Rogers calls the unavoidably tragic character of human growth are simply psychological descriptions deriving from the far less dramatic fact that one is born into a period of history that is so organized as to support the inner-directed type of social character.

The innovative significance of Rogers' psychology lies in its reparative strategies, not its diagnosis, and the character of that strategy is best disclosed by reflecting on its social reference. Consider those situations in which persons can no longer maintain their inner-directed orientation, but are as horrified as Riesman of simple, other-directed adjustment as the only alternative. The well-organized, inner-directed social character lacks the experiential capacity to know that his self-understanding is guided by conditions of worth, but he also lacks the capacity to endure the ambiguity that such recognition would force upon him. Freed from parental voices, what is to protect him from the voices of his peers? In the face of such a dilemma the Rogerian concept of an organismic valuing process is a fortunate one, indeed. Rogers' psychotherapy breaks down inner-directed psychological organization while at the same time obviating other-direction by way of the organismic valuing process. It describes and seeks to produce the kind of autonomous other-direction that Riesman commended.

But Rogers' psychology goes beyond simply completing an aspect of Riesman's dilemma. Autonomous other-direction assumes social conformity of some sort. But the organismic valuing process filters all social adaptation, so the fully functioning person need not conform to social conditions, regardless of their character. This is a radical position because it removes immediate experiencing beyond any simple distinction between self and society, and, by implication, beyond the distinction between good and evil. The organismic valuing process is beyond social control, it is incapable of evil, it is *transmoral*. There is something Nietzschean about this gentle and apparently modest insistence that personal self-awareness entirely transcend the world of institutional demands. But who would choose otherwise, when that world is the world described by the theory of mass society?

Rogers' Psychology and Philip Rieff's Therapeutic Character-Type

Philip Rieff's (1966) sociology of culture is based on a lengthy analysis of the way Freud's psychology has undermined traditional Christian culture, transforming it into a modern, secularized society.[3] What we call mass society is the direct result of Freud's deleterious impact upon the structure of moral awareness in the West. After writing a thorough interpretation of Freud's work, Rieff applied the same argument eight years later to three modern figures—Carl G. Jung, Wilhelm Reich, and D. H. Lawrence—arguing that the meaning of their work lies in their struggle to repair the moral damage done by Freud to Western thought. He could have added another chapter, one on Carl Rogers.

According to Rieff every culture has two main functions: to control men's feelings, binding them together, and to provide occasions for the release from control and conformity. Religious symbols, consisting of dogmas, ceremonies, systems of casuistry and principles for the cure of souls, moderate these two functions. Stability in the West has depended upon the collective validity of certain psychological processes described all too well by Freud—repression, sublimation, group psychology—but especially upon the psychology of authority and of the cultural superego. Rieff believes that the forces that created community in the West were always largely unconscious in the Freudian sense, and therefore were based upon illusion.

The significance of Freud's psychology lies in his method of exposing these unconscious forces and their illusory claims. By making use of his interpretive method, men in the West could, for the first time, actually choose for or against the authority of the past. Freud's system of interpret-

---

[3] For further discussion of Rieff's work in relation to Christian culture and the theory of mass society, see Homans (1970).

ing the relation between person and culture gave full precedent to remission or release over control. The result has been a reversal at the very foundation of Western ethics, which Rieff calls "deconversion." Religious conversion created a community of faith, but Freud's therapy created a *negative community*, the reverse of a community of commitment, without positive loyalties between people. Freudian therapy convinces the individual that he must protect himself from the demands for commitment on the part of his leaders and his fellows, and it provides him with the only means for doing so, because the interpretive method is the only way to reduce the demands of the cultural superego. As a consequence, a new structure of social consciousness and a new type of social character were born.

The new, Freudian consciousness is one of scientific detachment and moral neutrality toward desires and wishes, in imitation of the attitude the psychoanalyst takes toward all the desires and compulsions of his patients. This attitude therefore produces a new type of social character, free from primary group moral passion, as this has been typically engendered first in the family and then carried over into various forms of social organization, especially churches. He allows himself no commitments beyond an intensely private sense of well-being. Well-being is not, as in the case of the Christian ethic, the by-product of a wider, more primary communal loyalty. So self-interpretation and its benefits become ends in themselves, the basis of a new ethic. Hence the "triumph" of the "therapeutic."

There is much in Rieff's analysis agreeable to Rogers. His autobiographical remarks show how he experienced religion as the primary source of an alien moral demand system unmistakably deleterious not only to the optimal workings of personality, but also to ways of thinking about it. Just as Freud's interpretive method was calculated to neutralize religiously supported moral imperatives to obedience, as these took the form of a confrontation between the developing ego and the ever-present cultural superego, so Rogers also rejected religion. His techniques of self-expression serve to mitigate the force of conditions of worth, those alien, controlling demands through which social authorities permanently anchor their wishes in the lives of their children.

But Rogers offers a remedy far more radical than Freud's for those circumstances described by Rieff. Rogers and Freud agree without question that religion unnecessarily limits human becoming. However, Rogers believed that Freud himself had simply replaced one form of alienation (the moral demand system of religious ethics) with another (the theory that the superego remains both necessary and alien in normal, everyday life). Both religious attitudes and Freud's techniques create conditions of worth. Rogers' clinical techniques do not serve merely to mitigate the negative effects of religious attitudes and the harsh superego, they are calculated to transform those effects, in a very fundamental sense.

The key to such transformation lies in the concept of the organismic valuing process. Freud's therapeutic strategies erode the restraining forces in Western culture, creating a kind of sociological deconversion. Rogers' methods also strongly accent the release of feeling, but they also contain a way of restructuring feeling without recourse to the notion of the superego. As such they create a kind of reconversion. The fully functioning person, valuing as he does his own visceral and sensory processes unconditionally, is hardly alienated from his own feelings, nor is he socially isolated. On the contrary, he is morally committed and has a positive relation to collective life.

The organismic valuing process underwrites a new view of consciousness, of social character and of social organization. Rogerian man has the best of both worlds, at least as Rieff defines the alternatives. He can allow the remissive process to occur, he need not fear its socially negative consequences. Who could imagine a better form of "therapy" for the effects of mass society? Rogers' psychology has a triumph all its own—a triumph "over" the triumph "of" the therapeutic.

Rogers' Psychology and Peter Berger's Sociology of Everyday Life

Quite possibly the most inventive and disturbing sociological criticism of psychoanalysis, and of psychology generally, has come from the writings of Peter Berger and his colleague, Thomas Luckmann (Berger, 1963, 1965; Berger & Luckmann, 1964, 1967). Much of the force of his approach is due to his view of sociology. Unlike Riesman and Rieff, Berger's approach is best characterized by an existential or subjective orientation. It assumes that the rise of the discipline of sociology itself was due to personal need on the part of those who began it for organized reflection upon their own social self-understanding. Therefore the first business of sociology is with the nature of self-consciousness and its relation to everyday life, with how people come together on the basis of commonly agreed-upon modes of understanding and interpreting everyday life. The sociologist begins with the here-and-now of the workaday world. He is interested in collectively agreed upon versions of everyday reality, the official self-interpretations of groups. In pursuing such inquiry, the sociologist bears a double relation to the everyday world. As a member of society he shares an interpretation of it. But as a sociologist he must also distance himself from his own social world. He is both subjective and objective.

Such an approach requires that all sociology be in effect a sociology of knowledge, wherein "knowledge" refers to ways of defining everyday reality, and "sociology" refers to the social forces that create and determine these particular definitions of everyday reality. It also follows that all such definitions of reality are historically relative. Each period in the history of a people will have its own particular view of what is especially real in everyday life. This is in fact the sociological definition of epoch or period. Berger is concerned, however, with the differences between traditional and contemporary forms of social life, as they can be studied in Western society.

Berger understands the development of mass society as the result of the loss of a single symbol system for knowing the world and rendering life meaningful. He views psychoanalysis, Catholicism, and communism as alternate symbol systems that explain to the believer what is real, why other views are less real, how the real view can be discoverd, and why it must be maintained. Further, each offers techniques of thought for evaluating both other persons' behavior and the vicissitudes of one's own inner life. Psychoanalysis performs this task by insisting upon acceptance of the following tenets about everyday reality (Berger, 1965): (a) part of the human mind is unconscious; (b) the unconscious is the locus of what is truly real and deserving of attention in mental life; (c) the contents of the unconscious are largely sexual in character; (d) sexual motives derive their unconscious character during childhood; (e) unconscious motives are apt to be concealed in adult life, especially by means of the mechanisms of projection and repression.

As a theory of everyday life and reality, psychoanalysis resolves the problem of pluralization of world-views at its most crucial point, that of industrialization and its consequences. Industrialization is the major structuring force in modern social organization, and its major effect has been the creation of a permanent splitting of everyday reality into public and private realms. Therefore men need a theory of everyday life that makes sense of this split, a theory that will convince them first that each realm has its own peculiar value and meaning, and second, that no fundamental contradiction exists between the two sets of meanings. Freud's theory provides just this. In placing great emphasis upon sexuality and family life, psychoanalysis enriches the private sphere, and by commending attention to the mechanisms of projection and repression it also supports the public sphere. Psychoanalysis defines the first realm generally under the rubric of the pleasure princple, and the second realm under that of the reality principle. The goal of psychoanalytic therapy is the reconcilation of these two principles, and through them of the private and public spheres of modern, everyday life.

Berger offers the further, provocative observation that the concept of the unconscious, so crucial to all Freudian theory, arose as a result of the increasingly complex social arrangements of industrial society. Formerly persons evaluated each other in terms of general knowledge of social location. Today, such knowledge is often unavailable—"one runs into so many different kinds of people these days." Some concept must render plausible this otherwise distressing and counterproductive feature of everyday life. If "everybody has an unconscious," one has in advance psychological knowledge that replaces the needed social information about them. Thus, the opacity of social organization has created a psychological concept.

Rogers' psychology is, even more than Freud's, a theory of everyday reality.[4] It asserts that (a) every individual has the potential capacity to experience himself and his world—in short, his life as a whole—fully and completely, without distortion; (b) this capacity for experiencing oneself and one's life nevertheless does become distorted during the early years of growth; (c) distortion is due to a tendency on the part of all people to manipulate one another; (d) such manipulation consists of the imposition by society of role expectations—individuals representing institutions demand specific patterns of experiencing and behavior, giving little attention to their relation to the inner tendencies of the individual; (e) freedom from such distortions, and from the institutions they are grounded in, can be achieved through constantly symbolizing one's experiencing—one's feelings and perceptions of oneself and others—directly to oneself, but often directly in the midst of perplexing social relations; and (f) such symbolizing leads to a definite and enduring sense of one's own personal reality, which is more dependable and authentic than social definitions of personal reality.

What sociological force might lie behind the appeal of the notion of conditions of worth? This concept, so central to Rogers' psychology, renders more plausible what so many people experience to be the central dilemma of modern life—the perplexing, manipulating character of the society in which they live. On the one hand, different world-views or views of everyday reality press upon him, demanding his loyalty, and he can interpret this as manipulation, as conditions of worth. On the other hand, nothing within his social experience serves as a guide for the selection of one view against another. The issue must be resolved at the psychological level, and the concept of the organismic valuing process does just this. It explains that no such selection is necessary, that the real guide to the nature of social reality lies deeper within the individual himself, rather than at any particular point in the social world about him. The task is only to find this

---

[4] In the Preface of *On Becoming a Person*, Rogers informed the reader of his purpose in writing the book: to communicate something of what he had learned "in the jungles of modern life, in the largely unmapped territory of personal relationships."

guide. This source transcends and obviates all the perplexing, relative views that surround him, providing clarity and integration in a world of ambiguity and diffusion.

If Freud's psychology is, in Berger's terms, the result of industrialization, then Rogers' psychology is "postindustrial." The splitting of private, inner life and public, social expectations is no longer problematic for Rogerian man, for Rogers' theory explains that, although this tension is a real one, it is also imposed upon him, and is of less significance than the more fundamental forces within him. The fully functioning person, convinced that the full range of his experiencing process is unconditionally valuable, is sufficiently grounded in his own inwardness that he need not "return," psychologically, to the public sphere in order to complete his search for a reliable view of the social world and a theory of his relation to it. For this reason Rogers' psychology has no need of a concept such as the unconscious. The organismic valuing process has a social or collective dimension all its own, experientially deeper than conditions of worth. Rogerian theory is not hostile to socialization, nor do Rogerian therapists and their clients live merely private lives. But they do conceive themselves to a considerable extent free, thanks to their theory, from conflicts created by the alienating social structures and shifting social expectations of a highly industrial society.

Rogerian psychology offers the pearl of great price sought by all modern men: a set of techniques for thinking about everyday reality that convincingly protects them from the pervasive pluralization of worlds—protects, that is, from the vicissitudes of a mass society.

CONCLUSION

Three sociological discussions of psychoanalysis, each in their own way, serve to exemplify the theory of mass society. All three largely agree that psychoanalysis has an important function in the transition from earlier periods in Western history, in which religious institutions served to coordinate a unified social structure and personal experience, to the modern period, characterized by its declining religious institutions, its fragmented social structure, and its consequent psychological alienation.

The diagnostic portion of Rogers' psychology fits lock-and-key with the diagnostic portion of these theories of mass society. Rogers' description of psychological maladjustment (concept of conditions of worth) assumes and depends upon the view of social reality highlighted by the theory of mass society. However, the positive side of his psychology (concept of the organismic valuing process) attempts to overcome the effects of mass society, be they the dilemmas of other-direction, of a remissive psychological process, or of a perplexing series of competing world views. It is as though Rogerian man had been designed exactly for the purpose of living successfully in a mass society.

What can we conclude from such compatibility between the theory of mass society and the Rogerian system of psychology? First, the continued presence of Rogerian theory will depend upon the persistence of the split between public and private—between work life and family life, between vocation and avocation—and in particular upon the persisting strain that such a split places upon the private sector of life. As we have seen, this fundamental sociological factor has created this type of psychological thinking. As long as the public sphere continues to be perceived as the locus of alienation, hostile to personal fulfillment, then Rogers' psychology will meet an important need, and, one would expect, will maintain or even increase in prominence.

But our discussion also forces a second conclusion, one that follows in large part from the first but also seemingly contradicts it. Quite possibly the mode or structure of experiencing commended by Rogers could become more and more, rather than less and less, institutionalized. Each of our sociological discussions agreed that Rogers' psychology moved against institutional norms, that it accented the primacy of the inner life over social, public forms in relation to that life. But suppose, to use Berger's terms, for example, the Rogerian view of everyday reality became more institutionalized? Such circumstances exemplify the very essence of irony.

This latter eventuality is, however, hardly restricted to Rogers' psychology. It pertains to many other intellectual systems current in contemporary society, each of which in its own way defines personal fulfillment in opposition to social conformity. In a broader and more accurate sense, the future of Rogerian psychology lies with the future of these movements.

REFERENCES

Bakan, D. *The duality of human existence.* Chicago: Rand-McNally, 1966.

Berger, P. *Invitation to sociology.* New York: Doubleday Anchor, 1963.

Berger, P. Toward a sociological understanding of psychoanalysis. *Social Research,* 1965, **32**, 26–41.

Berger, P., & Luckmann, T. Social mobility and personal identity. *Archives Europeennes de Sociology,* 1964, **5** (2), 331–334.

Berger, P., & Luckmann, T. *The social construction of reality.* New York: Doubleday Anchor, 1967.

Brown, N. O. *Life against death: The psychoanalytical meaning of history.* New York: Random House, 1959.

Butler, J. M., & Rice, L. N. Adience, self-actualization and drive-theory. In J. M. Wepmen & R. W. Heine (Eds.), *Concepts of personality.* Chicago: Aldine, 1963.

Fromm, E. *The sane society.* New York: Holt, Rinehart & Winston, 1955.

Gendlin, E. *Experiencing and the creation of meaning: A philosophical and psychological approach to the subjective.* New York: Free Press, 1962.

Giner, S. *The theory of mass society: Its history and nature in social thought and sociological theory—A critical appraisal.* Unpublished doctoral dissertation. University of Chicago, 1969.

Homans, P. *Theology after Freud: An interpretive inquiry.* New York: Bobbs-Merrill, 1970.

Koch, S. (Ed.) *Psychology: A study of a science.* New York: McGraw-Hill, 1959. 6 vols.

Kornhauser, W. *The politics of mass society.* New York: Free Press, 1959.

Lipset, S., & Lowenthal, L. *Culture and social character: The work of David Riesman reviewed.* New York: Free Press, 1961.

Mannheim, K. *Ideology and utopia: An introduction to the sociology of knowledge.* New York: Harcourt, Brace, & World, 1936.

Mannheim K. *Essays on the sociology of culture.* New York: Oxford, 1956.

Marcel, G. *Man against mass society.* Chicago: Henry Regnery, 1962.

Marcuse, H. *Eros and civilization.* Boston: Beacon Press, 1965.

Oden, T. *Kerygma and counseling.* Philadelphia: Westminster, 1966.

Ricoeur, P. *De l'interpretation: Essai sur Freud.* Paris: Seuil, 1965.

Rieff, P. *The triumph of the therapeutic.* New York: Harper, 1966.

Riesman, D. *The lonely crowd.* New York: Doubleday, 1954.

Riesman, D. *Individualism reconsidered.* New York: Doubleday, 1955.

Riesman, D. *Abundance for what?* New York: Doubleday, 1964.

Rogers, C. R. *Client-centered therapy.* Boston: Houghton Mifflin, 1951.

Rogers, C. R. A theory of therapy, personality and interpersonal relationships, as developed in the client-centered framework. In S. Koch (Ed.), *Psychology: A study of a science,* Vol. 3. New York: McGraw-Hill, 1959.

Rogers, C. R. *On becoming a person.* Boston: Houghton Mifflin, 1961.

CHAPTER 12

On Creativeness and a Psychology of Well-Being

Ned L. Gaylin

> *An ulcer, gentlemen, is an unkissed imagination taking its revenge for having been jilted. It is an unwritten poem, a neglected music, an unpainted water color, an undanced dance. It is a declaration from the mankind of the man that a clear spring of joy has not been tapped, and that it must break through, muddily, on its own.*
>
> **JOHN CIARDI**

Basic to the foundations of client-centered therapy and theory is the conviction that within each individual is an inherent thrust toward maximizing his potential. The implications, though rarely clearly enunciated, are that psychological health and basic creativity border on being synonymous and that both are embodied in the fully functioning person. Few would argue against the merits of psychological health. Yet ironically, although creativity in the abstract is considered one of the most highly prized human attributes, many of the most creative people are regarded with a specialness that is far from positive. That is, despite recent research and theoretical arguments to the contrary, the clichéd association between genius and madness persists. This paradoxical association has both historical and phenomenological bases that derive from increased societal constraints upon the individual and from the implications of the present-day practice of psychotherapy. An understanding of the impact these forces have, both upon the development of psychological theory and upon individual behavior is necessary to the acceptance of a positive psychology of human potential: one that promotes the enhancement of human development in its highest sense, rather than one that seeks to cure maladaptive behavior when it occurs. This chapter is intended not simply as another argument for preventive mental health as it has come to be understood, but rather suggests an approach based on the following premises: (a) when successful, psychotherapy is in essence a facilitator of an inherent creativeness in the individual; (b) this creativeness by its nature is therapeutic and enhancing; and (c) this creativeness is the same process that Rogers (and others) has referred to as the actualizing tendency.

The chapter is divided into three parts. The first section briefly traces the parallel development of the concepts of mental illness and creative genius in an attempt to elucidate the forces that shaped their association through time; it introduces an alternative approach to the examination of human potential via the client-centered framework. The second section stresses the conceptualization of a general theory of creativeness and explores its relationship to a positive approach to psychological development and functioning. The last section introduces empirical justification for the intimate association between creativeness and psychological well-being, and gives some of the possible ramifications and utilizations of this association.

OF GENIUS, MADNESS, AND HISTORY

Traditionally, the practice of psychotherapy has been thought of as a means of making whole the psychologically infirm. It was conceived in the framework of physical medicine, and despite attempts to conceptualize it in more positive terms, the illness-treatment model remains in the minds of most people, including those who are actively engaged in its practice. This is perhaps natural, as those who tend to seek out psychotherapists are generally looking for relief from emotional anguish that impairs their functioning. But to equate health solely wtih the absence of infirmity is similar to asserting that love is merely the absence of hate. Although the absence of obvious disease may be a starting point for a definition of health, health carries with it the implications of a kind of robustness from which the organism may enhance its future growth and potential.

Historically the concept of mental illness is a relatively recent one. The Greeks as far back as Plato showed a certain tolerance—even a reverence—for aberrant mental states. However, as Western society grew more complex, it correspondingly became less able to tolerate the aberrant individual.

During the Middle Ages the insane were viewed as receptacles of evil and their behavior was considered a sign of consort with the devil. In the Renaissance, psychopathology was viewed primarily as a moral failure; the most extreme cases were treated much as criminals; punishment was considered an appropriate form of "therapy." According to psychological historians[1] it was with Pinel in the latter half of the 18th century that the insane were first considered "mentally sick;" with that their separate institutionalization, via the creation of mental hospitals, began.

The early pioneers of psychology and their more recent counterparts saw in the concept of mental illness a means of dealing more humanely with the problems of individuals who were socially maladaptive. This was an attempt to perceive the aberrant psychological condition as one not to be despised but, like physical illness, one that might evoke a response of sympathy and concern while at the same time imply the hope of treatment and cure. From all I can gather, this noble effort has been by and large a failure. As recently as 1961 *The Final Report of the Joint Commission on Mental Illness and Health* makes note of just this: "mental illness is different from physical illness in [at least] the one fundamental aspect that it tends to disturb and repel others rather than evoke their sympathy and desire to help [1961, p. xviii]."

The medical sciences have traditionally focused upon malfunction as a means of determining normal functioning behavior; it was thus natural for the study of mental illness to follow this methodology. However, that which originally helped to clarify has become a source of confusion, as was aptly pointed out by Zubin in a 1968 compendium on definition and measurement of mental health:

> Disease is usually defined in terms of etiology, structure, and symptomatology. In most mental disorders etiology is unknown, the structure of the organs of the patient as far as we know is unaffected, and symptomatology is the only available basis for the definition. Mental diseases whose etiology and structural defects become known are usually lost to psychopathology. Thus disorders like general paresis, pellegra with psychosis, epilepsy, even PKU are now largely in the hands of other disciplines. Only the diseases of unknown origin remain in the field of psychopathology. Furthermore, there is also the question of whether mental disorders are in fact diseases or merely reaction patterns [Zubin, 1968, p. 71].

It was with Freud in the early 1900s that the mental illness paradigm became fully conceptualized. Freud's dissection of the psyche led to a structural and nomenclatural system analogous to the biological systems of medicine. Despite initial difficulties in its acceptance, its definitiveness made

---

[1] The reader is referred to Zilboorg and Henry (1941), and White (1956) for a fuller explication of the subject.

Freud's system attractive and for many practitioners today the metaphors he developed to account for the conflicting forces that shape the personality (e.g., id, ego, superego) have come to be virtually existing organs.

Freud's theory is inherently a drive-reductionistic, conflict-based one. All behavior is grounded on the satisfaction of the instinctual drives, which in turn are seen in conflict with the constraints of the social system. The best that can be hoped for under such a theory is a dynamic (and precarious) balance or equilibrium. The emphasis on pathology is preeminent and its potential is always an impending threat. Furthermore, despite Freud's emphasis on the importance of the first five years of life and his enhancing the thoughtful study of children's psychological development, he himself never worked with the young. It was natural that his views of child and human development should be slanted toward psychopathology, considering that he reconstructed them from the recounted experiences of patients whose early childhood, by definition, had been problematic.

While remaining associated with the Freudian conflict-based model, others, primarily those working directly with children (e.g., A. Freud, 1946; Hartmann & Kris, 1945; Spitz, 1945) began to perceive a more positive, or at least, a more neutral formulation of psychic development through their explication of such constructs as the *conflict-free ego sphere*, *regression in service of the ego*, and so on. These "ego" theorists (as they came to be known) developed their ideas during the 1930s and 1940s. Simultaneously, the locus of psychological activity (both theoretical and practical) was shifting from Europe to the United States, where the ongoing emphasis was on experimental and behavioral psychology.

Psychological thinking was becoming subject to more and more empirical observation; it was being tested in light of recent animal studies, and couched in terms of educational psychology. Sociology and anthropology began incorporating and applying many of the heretofore unchallenged "universal" concepts regarding personality development. It became increasingly apparent that even with continued reworking, there was much in analytic theory that could not account for certain behaviors exhibited by apparently healthy individuals in various societies. The impact of these divergent schools of thought coming together in a climate totally different from that of Victorian Europe generated a new ideational approach—that which Maslow has referred to as the *Third Force* of psychology.

Although the Third Force school has no one prophet, it is probably best embodied in the theorizing of Maslow (1954, 1962) and the empirical and clinical work of Rogers (1951, 1954), and Rogers and Dymond (1954). It is heavily grounded in the philosophy of William James (1890) and the observations of Kurt Goldstein (1963) in that it presents a more positive and holistic view of the development of the personality. It postulates a drive considered but later rejected by Freud—that of a push toward growth or actualization by the organism. This drive is present in all human beings, both healthy and ill. The tendency is ever present. Basically it is a humanistic view and an optimistic one of the human condition. Its stance is that psychological health is more than the mere absence of disease but, rather, a condition in which the individual approaches the acme of productivity—that is, creativity. Where Freud's metaphor for the human condition is a blank slate upon which society writes its mark, for Rogers the self is more like the metamorphosis within the chrysalis.

The self theorists, as members of this school have been dubbed, stress the process of becoming. This functional approach may, in part, account for the lack of an elaborate theory of personality as rich in embellishment as that posited by the analytics who stress the structural components of the psyche. Thus, for the analytics, there exists a highly technical delineation of psychic components, the appropriate development of which is considered critical to adjustment and normative social behavior; for the self theorists no such dissection is attempted. The tenets of the analytic school tend to lead to theorizing regarding structural deficiency, those of the self theorists do not.

In part this may well explain why the mental disease modelists can best launch their ideas when discussing the kind of population observed in mental institutions where the behavior of the individuals tends to be extremely differentiated from that of those who appear able to function at least adequately within society. As suggested by Zubin (1968), there may indeed be in these institutionalized individuals some biological structural deficiencies or anomalies, that continued research may disclose. The mental health modelists, however, whose work has been with far better functioning populations, although somewhat at a loss to explain extreme psychopathology, seem better able to cope with more common adaptational problems.

As broad spectrum psychology becomes more and more a tool of society at large (particularly through its use in schools and other social institutions dealing with children and families) the process of healthy growth becomes more germane. Thus in the last decade or so there have been numerous attempts to establish mental health rather than the mental disease model as a focal criterion for psychological study. There are indications of a growing awareness of some positive preventive uses for many of the techniques employed heretofore primarily by psychotherapists. The use of these methods in training parents, educators, and executives in communication skills and the use of groups for brainstorming are but a few indices of this cognizance. In our society we have a great need to facilitate, increase, and enhance human effectiveness—not only to make the sick well, but to make the competent even more so.

This increased emphasis on human potential and its enhancement has led to a fresh look at the creative individual, not so much as an accident of genetic and societal forces, but rather as the possible idealized combination of these forces, which might be systematically facilitated and encouraged throughout growth and development. To understand the development of thinking regarding creativity and to unravel the reasons for the stubborn persistence of the specious correlation between creativity and emotional disturbance, it is necessary to trace the history of man's attitudes regarding the creative process and its manifestations.

On the surface the connection between genius and madness is patently absurd. To make this association is to suggest that through the course of history everything that man has treasured in the arts, all that the technology of the sciences has made possible, and indeed, all of man's augmented understanding of the world around him are the products of his derangement. Yet despite the obvious illogic, the clichés of the mad scientist and the tempermental artist linger on. Virtually no research has been done on the subject. Although Freud undoubtedly aided and abetted the notion by (a) his continued use of the artist's work as clinical case material (e.g., Da Vinci (Freud, 1932), Dostoevsky (Freud, 1956a), Michelangelo (Freud, 1956b)); (b) his final justification of the common relationship between the products of artists and their neuroses via the concept of *sublimation* (Freud, 1958), he merely loaned a semblance of scientific credence to a preexisting societal prejudice.

More likely, the myth arose somewhere during the late 18th or early 19th century. For the early Greeks the word "ars" (from which our word "art" developed) bore little resemblance to its modern counterpart. Rather, it meant a specialized skill or craft. Carpentry, cooking, and surgery as well as poetry and sculpting (all kinds of handiwork) were embodied in this notion and little or no distinction was made among them. In medieval times the Latin "ars" took on the idea of any special form of knowledge gained from books (e.g., astrology and magic as well as logic and mathematics). With the Renaissance the word again took on its older meaning. Most art historians mark the Renaissance as the time when the artist took on his special identity (as a craftsman). The refinement of this definition into the fine arts, as opposed to the useful arts, did not fully become crystallized until about the 19th century in the West (see Collingwood, 1958).

Socially the Renaissance was also the demarcation of the shift from a medieval agrarian economy with its lack of specialization, to an emerging industrial–commercial era. Simultaneously Calvinism, with its belief in a divine calling, gave rise to the Protestant work ethic. The respectability of the earning of money and the corresponding emphasis upon thrift, responsibility, and sobriety radically changed man's view of his role on earth. For the first time worldly success could be associated with a divine morality, and the lack thereof associated with moral frailty or failing.

With the 19th century and the industrial revolution (really the final consolidation of the evolution noted above), the transition from a stable agrarian/trade life style to an urban factory-centered one was complete, and with these events the advent of economic and human labor specialization produced our technological society with its highly refined division of labor. It was also at this time that the role of the artist as separate from the productive craftsman was finally synthesized. He was no longer the interior decorator of the church, the photographer of the nobility. Technology had freed the artist from any such defined job in the production–consumption spheres. Although elements of his former image lingered, the idea of art for art's sake, for better or worse, had arrived. With this transition, the artist was separated from the mainstream of life and a kind of dilettantism developed surrounding his work.

It is more than chance that the shift in our thinking about creativity and the arts coincided with the tremendous social and economic changes occurring. In similar ways the artist and the madman became alienated from society at large. Neither could play a productive part nor had a defined role in the production-oriented society, which thrived and relied upon burgeoning specialization and role definition. Add to this the similarity of their behavior at times—the eccentricity of the artist and his singular driveness when in the throes of his endeavors (which often had none but remote and abstract relevance to the world around him). All of this loaned him the aura of onanistic behavior associated with the deranged. Furthermore, his insistence at times, even in the face of poverty and rejection by his immediate society, on the merits of his efforts tended to corroborate the association. It was also easy to point to examples of the coexistence of severe emotional disturbance and genius (e.g., Van Gogh, Kafka, Beethoven) to lend credence to the argument, while in the process forgetting those who lived a less flamboyantly notorious and relatively stable existence (e.g., Dickens, Renoir, Haydn). Few thought to question the possibility that for those who experienced emotional anguish, the disturbance may have been the result of familial and social lack of acceptance of their impelling life direction rather than a result of their ill-understood talents.

It was but a short time after the industrial revolution, in a Victorian Europe noted for its emotionally repressive atmosphere, that Freud developed his theory of personality. As a product of his milieu it was perhaps natural for him to perceive work and love as the primary parameters of successful adaptation. Yet it would seem a paramount irony that this creative pioneer of personality theory, who was quite taken with the productions of creative men, has had so much to do with the continuing association of genius and mental illness through his conceptualization of artistic works as the process of a basically neurotic defense diversion of libidinal energy.

It was nearly 30 years later that Kris (through his work with children) developed a consistent theory regarding creativity. This involved the evolution of a less-conflict-based model of the impulses via an elaboration of the preconscious rather than unconscious, and a new concept, that of regression in service of the ego (1952). Further exposition by Hartmann (1958) and Kubie (1958) led to such refinements as the conflict-free ego sphere. This was the foreshadowing of a fresh approach to the study of creative behavior—one of potential rather than conflict. It is this stance that will be elaborated upon in the following sections.

ON CREATIVE SYNTHESIS AND PSYCHOLOGICAL INTEGRITY

In lieu of that which has commonly been termed mental health, the phrase "psychological well-being" is introduced and employed here because (a) unlike the concept of mental health it is not associated with a converse concept (i.e., disease or illness), and (b) it has a certain easy to understand, straightforwardness. It tends to avoid negative concepts such as the *problems in living* suggested by Szasz (1960) or the implications of ability such as those of *effectiveness* (Smith, 1968) and *competence* (White, 1959)—although I think all are attempting to define similar states.

For many of the same reasons I prefer to use the term "creativeness" rather than creativity, because the latter has been colored with the specialness of genius, a connotation that, more often than not, confuses discussions of a more universal capacity I believe to be inherent in all individuals.

The conceptualization of psychological well-being draws heavily on the formulations of Allport (1955), Hartmann (1958), Jahoda (1958), Szasz (1960), and Sells (1968). No attempt will be made to describe here some of the elaborate but well-developed detail in the above-cited works. Instead, the reader is referred to Rogers (1959) for summation and for a more complete explication of the basic premises and terminology.

The major assumptions are relatively few. The *"actualizing tendency* [italics added] is the only motive which is postulated in this theoretical system . . . [Rogers, 1959]." Although it includes such concepts as ". . . need-reduction, tension-reduction, drive-reduction [e.g., Maslow's, 1954, deficiency needs] . . . It also includes however the growth motivations which appear to go beyond these terms: the seeking of pleasurable tensions, the tendency to be creative, the tendency to learn painfully to walk when crawling would meet the same needs more comfortably [Rogers, 1959, p. 196]." It is a holistic approach reflecting the entire state of the organism at any given moment in time. This idea of a positive drive as opposed to a drive reductionist model recently referred to as *adience* or *stimulus hunger* has been empirically and experimentally demonstrated by investigators who go so far as to suggest its superseding the more basic homeostatic drives (White, 1959; Butler & Rice, 1960; Fiske & Maddi, 1961).

Rogers (1959) continues to define a special form of the actualizing tendency—*self-actualization.* "Following the development of the self-structure, the general tendency toward actualizing expresses itself also in the actualization of that portion of the experience of the organism which is symbolized in the self [p. 196]." The hypothetical goal of the actualizing tendency is the fully functioning person. The process of becoming more fully functioning is emphasized and is characterized by another focal concept, increased openness to experience. As the exact opposite of defensiveness, this openness means that every stimulus, be it internal or external to the organism has entry to the individual's awareness without filtering or distortion. Although this concept strongly implies perceptual elements of reality testing and relating to the environment in an adaptive manner, there is the noticeable lack of any of the usual criteria often found in discussions of the "normal" or "adjusted" individual.

Based upon these premises the operational definition of psychological well-being used herein will be taken to mean a sense of personal worth or self-esteem. This is not to imply a state of smug self-satisfaction, but rather an ever-fluctuating awareness of who one is in relationship to one's environment (both physical and interpersonal). It is a relative concept, that is, one that contains upper and lower limits (the toleration of which varies for individuals) rather than a static endpoint. Self-worth also implies a constellation of values (some conceptualized, some amorphous), an ideal toward which the individual strives and against which the perceived self is evaluated. There is always some discrepancy between these perceptions; when the discrepancy is tolerable the individual experiences psychological well-being (also relative), when intolerable, psychological anguish or distress is experienced.

Such a definition generally articulates with society's standards as they are often incorporated into the individual's value system. However, it allows for possible exceptions as in the case of men of vision or genius who may be psychologically more sound than their environment. Psychological well-being stresses adaptation, rather than adjustment. It includes, as well as the adaptive and perceptual elements of self-actualization and openness to experience, a third focal concept: that of the internal locus of evaluation.

Within such a framework, the notion of psychological well-being depends primarily upon the individual for definition. It has valuation at any given moment in time by some internal rather than external valuing center. True, that locus implies that no distortion of the world around the individual is taking place, if he is truly open to his experience, and allows room for societal influence in terms of his assessment, acceptance, or rejection of the values of his milieu. As a consequence psychological well-being allows for change and growth in a positive manner not readily accounted for by other theoretical stances. The kind of person described by such a state is summarized by Rogers (1961): "He would not necessarily be 'adjusted' to his culture, and he would almost certainly not be a conformist. But at any time and in any culture he would live constructively, in as much harmony with his culture as a balanced satisfaction of needs demanded. In some cultural situations he might in some ways be very unhappy, but he would continue to move toward becoming himself, and to behave in such a way as to provide the maximum satisfactions of his deepest needs [pp. 193–194]."

It should come as no surprise that for Rogers (and others like him) the similarity between psychological well-being and creativeness borders on equivalence. "The mainspring of creativity appears to be the same tendency which we discover so deeply as the curative force in psychotherapy—man's tendency to actualize himself, to become his potentialities [Rogers, 1954, p. 253]." Barron (1963) puts the relationship as follows: "The moment of health is the moment of unconscious creative synthesis, when without thinking about it all we know is that we make sense to ourselves and to others [p. 5]." For Schachtel (1959) it is the essence of growth: "The problem of creative experience is essentially the same for all the human capacities . . . it is the problem of the open encounter of the total person with the world [p. 240]."

There is an elegant simplicity to this relating of psychological well-being and creativeness. The relationship implies a growing integrity of the organism with its environment, that of maximizing potential with all the powers available to the being. It goes beyond the simple correlation of the two, implying (though few have directly explored the possibility) that indeed the very curative force of psychotherapy is a kind of self-integrating creativeness, which is the embodiment of the actualizing or growth motive within us all. Although it may become temporarily thwarted, this creativeness continually seeks expression in its drive toward wholeness. Such a formulation also implies a conscious and deliberate growth or enhancement rather than a passive one. It requires self-awareness, which to our knowledge is uniquely human. It is perhaps just that awareness that is the referent for the biblical poets' inference that God created man in his own image.

Because of the difficulties in defining or operationalizing the kind of creativeness discussed above, investigators have often turned to the study of "successful" artists, writers, scientists, and so on—those individuals who appear best to embody creativity. As a consequence the focus of much inquiry in the area has become field-specific and dependent upon products defined by society as creative. Herein, it would seem, is the root of much of our confusion with regard to the kind of creativeness discussed above and creativity as it is commonly thought to be. It is this distinction that the rest of this chapter will attempt to elucidate.

Individuals engaged professionally in the activity of creating generally combine with their inherent creativeness special talent and skills—qualities that are often related to, but not synonymous with, creativeness. It is this kind of expression Maslow (1962) refers to as *special talent creativeness*, and that will be heretofore referred to as creativity. It tends by its nature to be rather easily identified and is often defined as the epitome of creativity or genius. Thus the process and state of creativeness become confused with the attributes of skill and talent and the end products thereof.

However, Maslow suggests another kind of creativeness not unique to individuals in special fields and consequently not so easily identified. He calls this *self-actualizing creativeness*. It is a pervasive process found in all individuals and is thought to be closely related to the process of becoming less defensive, more open to experience, and more fully functioning—the process of becoming more psychologically healthy. Maslow distinctly divorces these two types of creativeness, claiming in his dichotomy a lack of concern with creativity. The suggestion offered here is that creativity as found in the talented is but a special form of creativeness, and that the latter underlies all creative activity regardless of field of endeavor be it cooking or sculpting.

Creativeness is the driving force, inherent in the human organism from birth, that leads to creative acts and experiences. These creative acts and/or experiences need not be those that, in the past two centuries, have been defined as the work of the artist or scientist, but may be observed in the developing child as he grapples with all the motor tasks involved in actualizing his human condition.

Thus, the act of walking, although a universal human behavior. is also inherently a paradigm of an individual creative act and experience requiring the synthesizing of a multitude of more basic skills. It is the precursor to the dance. If one doubts this one has only to regard the toddler executing his first connected steps. The accompanying delighted expressions may range from distinct wide-eyed surprise to gales of laughter from the moment that the awareness of synthesis and mastery has registered. And careful observations show that no two infants pursue this process in exactly the same way, despite the similarity of the end result. Correspondingly one might call all true learning (as distinguished from training) a representation of creativeness, but not creativity. Creativity requires the added dimensions of originality or uniqueness, as well as the implementation of creativeness through expression (as will be explained below).

What is being suggested here is that a creative act or experience is an extension and representation of the inherent creativeness of the individual that is directly related to his actualizing tendency. It may be an action or some form of experience that as a consequence does not imply a product and correspondingly has little or nothing to do with societal or cultural values inherent in defining it as esthetic, worthwhile, or innovative. The recognition and identification of the creative act or experience is totally dependent upon the individual. The locus of evaluation is totally within. And indeed, it is the very essence of our humanness, for only the human organism appears capable of awareness of his consciousness.

Such a formulation is similar to Goldstein's (1963) *biological knowledge,* Maslow's (1957) *peak experience,* and also to the often-discussed *eureka!* or *aha!* phenomenon. It is learning in the true sense of the word, meaning discovery and synthesis, not training or memorization (which includes little, if any, of the above-mentioned attributes). It is this kind of experiential learning that Dewey (1939) so vehemently advocated. And most important, it is the kind of learning that is the prelude to the creativity that has advanced our culture (see Werner, 1948). It is the impetus for the actualizing process. Thus, as creativity is the actualizer of society, creativeness is that for the individual.

As each creative act or experience becomes synthesized and incorporated, it becomes a part of the organism's repertoire to be further built upon by additional and often more complex acts or experiences. If the individual combines these acts and experiences with talents and skills, they may lead to some kind of product creativity. An example is in order. When the child spontaneously makes his first scribbles on a piece of paper his acts are an expression of his individual creativeness. No matter that these first scribbles, like the first halting imbalanced steps of the child learning to walk, are a universal human phenomenon—to that child they are unique at that moment in time. The experience of pleasure that this typical act of creative synthesis engenders impels the child to continue exploration and experimentation discovering the nuances of control, until at some point or another basic mastery is attained. At this point the experience/expression loses the novelty of the creative. At this plateau the child is practicing. However, generally before this juncture, new discoveries overlap the old, pushing the drawing experience forward. Somewhere hidden within those very early scribbles are the rudiments of first the eggshape, then the circle, square, etc: each discovery of which will be a basic creative act or experience and an expression of creativeness—each discovery accompanied by a sense of excitement and satisfaction. These are the very same rudiments first at two, then at three and later at six which pull the child toward the elements of design, composition and pictorial representation. Once the basic shapes have been mastered and incorporated, they will never be forgotten. This is the same process which produces the five year old's "potato and stick" self-portrait and which produced that of Rembrandt's. The major difference is of a highly sophisticated combination and recombination of the same basic elements found in the latter.

As Kellogg (1967) has so astutely and handsomely pointed out, there is a universalism to all children's art. No matter what the country of origin, all children develop the same graphic configurations, the same basic representations and at about the same age levels, much in the same way that all children walk (whether cradleboarded, bound, or free) at the same age and go about the process in roughly the same manner. It is this same universal elegance embellished with simple touches of individuality that makes children's art so appealing and communicative. These are the same features evident in cave paintings and in the folk art around the world, and we are only just beginning to understand their fundamental creativity.

Frequently folk art is referred to as primitive art—in my opinion a deceptive misnomer. In these works, there is a simultaneity of earnestness and playfulness that conveys a uniquely personal message. Often, perspective and natural size relationships are ignored. Colors may have little to do with those found in nature. Representationalism is secondary to self-expression. It is apparent that the artist, be he caveman, peasant, or child, is endeavoring to please himself first and foremost. That the results may or may not be pleasing or communicative to others is secondary. The locus of evaluation is the self, not society.

As the child grows more sophisticated (i.e., becomes socialized), he becomes aware, often through unempathic criticism, that in the graphic arts there are naturalistic rules that are to be obeyed. His locus of evaluation at this juncture often begins shifting from internal to external. Too frequently this occurs in the early school years, coincident with the time when children's art begins losing some of its characteristic uniqueness.

The child learns to adjust his artistic production to that which becomes expected of him. He may begin to deem himself a good or bad artist, which when paired with developmental differences in visual motor coordination abilities may preclude further joy in the activity and thereby deflect pleasure and further exploration in this area. He may shift to another area (e.g., music, sports, language) of endeavor if supported. The analogy between artistic reproduction and psychological development appears plain. Too often we stress conformity or adjusting as opposed to creative adaptation in our approach to children.

If the child is dealt with empathically and warmly in the early years his actualizing tendency continues to maintain itself from one synthesizing creative act to the next. He is impelled forward with regular progression. As his physical competence as well as his psychological sense of well-being increase, his creativeness is enhanced and vice versa. One reinforces the other much as a chain reaction creating a perpetuation of the actualizing process. Such an individual is more likely to produce creatively. He is not afraid to do something that is different. He is not afraid to combine elements that appear to be contradictory. He is not afraid to stand alone at times, yet takes satisfaction from contact with others—not being afraid of either. The threat of failure has little meaning or impact upon such a person's self-esteem, because failure is more of an experiment leading to creative synthesis, and from which something is to be learned. For such an individual the simple may become infinitely complex and the complex may merge into benign simplicity, each with its own inherent fascination. He may grow where he is transplanted or transplant himself elsewhere if enhancement in his present spot does not materialize.

This is not to imply that creative endeavors take no training. Mastery over techniques, knowledge of tonal scales, chemical balances, and blending of pigments require certain degrees of training. But, like the simpler creative acts, these become (to borrow from Hartmann, 1958) *automatized* —second nature. As in walking, there was creative synthesis first, but through repetition and consequent incorporation into the organism's repertoire, the originally creative acts become rather the enlarged foundation from which the self may actualize.

TOWARD VALIDATION AND APPLICATION

Despite the interest in both creativity and psychological health, particularly in the last two decades, research, primarily on the latter, has not been abundant. Mental illness is far easier to examine than mental health, let alone the notion of psychological well-being. For investigative purposes there is usually a captive population in mental hospitals and/or in clinic offices. Usually a relatively well-defined group of people, their behavior is either crazy enough to get them put away or sufficiently self-distressing to cause them to seek help and relief. Therefore they are either unable to protest their being studied or so much in need of help that they will put up with a lot—even the psychological poking and prodding of a psycho-diagnostician. Furthermore, they generally present a relatively easy-to-describe set of behaviors (symptoms), which are labeled *maladjusted*, the elimination or reduction of which serves as evidence of therapeutic effectiveness.

In contrast, research on creativity in the past few years, at least, has been somewhat more plentiful. There are generally two tacks taken here: the first being investigations of character traits of successful artists, writers, scientists. These are exemplified by such studies as those of Roe (1946, 1960), Drevdahl and Cattell (1958), Eiduson (1958), Hammer (1961), and Myden (1960). There are problems with this approach, as noted by Barron (1963) and Kubie (1958). Often those actively engaged in the creative arts and sciences are concerned that the dissection and under-standing of their "gift" might dissipate it in some way or another, and are therefore reluctant to participate. It is an extension of the continued asso-ciation in the minds of many between neurosis and talent, the former being assumed the wellspring of the latter. Further, this kind of research again focuses on creativity (i.e., special talent creativeness), confounding creative process with evidence of tangible production in combination with notions of special talents and skills rather than elucidating the kind of creativeness discussed in the preceding section.

The other tack has been to study normal groups such as high school and college students (also, in part, because of their availability and captive quality). In these studies creativity is first operationally defined by some parameter such as originality in problem solving, and an appropriate test is then administered. These studies are best exemplified by the work of Getzels and Jackson (1962), Barron (1957), and Maddi, Charlens, Maddi, and Smith (1962). Problems here center around the validity of the defining parameters: that is, the choice of tests of creativity, which range from the choosing of the more esthetic of a pair in a series of drawings, to listing as many conceivable uses for a simple object, such as a brick.

None of these approaches can be faulted, considering our present state of knowledge concerning both the creative process and states of psycho-logical well-being. And although consistencies are few and contradictions abound, from the results of one study to the next there are certain con-sistencies, which recur with relative frequency. For example, observations persist among investigators using a variety of techniques, that common to most individuals deemed as creative there exists a group of factors or qualities. Briefly stated these are: memory, imagery, originality, organization (including organizational complexity) and energy (Barron, 1957, 1958; Brittain & Beittel, 1960; Drevdahl & Cattell, 1958; Ehrenzweig, 1957; Guilford, 1957; Hart, 1950; Horney, 1947; Porterfield, 1941; Spearman, 1931; Stein & Meer, 1954). These five qualities (often more, sometimes less) recur in the literature regardless of the diverse vocations of the individuals being observed (e.g., artists, business executives, scientists).

Let us assume that the five qualities noted by behavioral scientists under numerous conditions are indeed identifiers of creativity (which in turn is a special form of creativeness), and that we could measure these qualities in some way in all people. Furthermore let us assume, as has been contended in the previous section, that psychological well-being and creativeness are intrinsically related and positively correlated. Could we not then anticipate these same qualities to become more evident for individuals who can in some way increase their level of psychological well-being?

On the basis of the continued popularity of psychotherapy as a means of easing psychological distress, it would appear to be a safe assumption too that psychotherapy is a means of increasing psychological well-being. Studies that validate this claim are far too numerous to cite here, but the interested reader is referred to Rogers and Dymond (1954); Strupp (1963); and Shlien (1964) as a starting point. Given these assumptions we might then examine a number of people undergoing psychotherapy, assess the degree of their improvement in level of psychological well-being, and also the creativeness of those individuals before and after therapy to determine if the proposed relationship does, in fact, exist.

Such a study was performed at the University of Chicago Counseling and Psychotherapy Research Center. It was part of a larger research design determining the effects of short-term (20 sessions, generally twice a week) psychotherapy (see Butler, Rice, & Dicken, 1960). A group of clients who had applied for outpatient psychotherapy were administered a battery of tests individually prior to entering and following 20 sessions of client-centered psychotherapy. Among the tests administered to these clients were the standard Rorschach test, the Butler–Haigh Q-sort, and the Therapists' Rating Scale. The last of these was administered only at the end of 20 sessions.[2]

Any attempt to go into elaborate detail is inappropriate here, but some explanation of the use of the Rorschach scores is in order to convey the

---

[2] Only a small portion of the design, its rationale, and the results are presented here. The reader is referred to Gaylin (1966) for a complete description of the study.

full implications of the study. Since its inception over 50 years ago, the Rorschach test has been the object of much controversy, and psychotherapy outcome studies employing it have been contradictory and confusing. The various scores that are derived to obtain a total picture of the subject's personality functioning are based on previous research comparing normal and clinic populations. Some of these scores are therefore heavily loaded with what are considered normative-adjustment criteria. These scores stress the absence of psychopathology and the presence of conformity to societal norms (e.g., good reality testing, control over affect, peer group identification, consistency in problem solving).

On the other hand, there is another group of scores that place little emphasis upon normative adjustment criteria. Previous to the study under discussion here little attempt to distinguish selectively or separate these two kinds of scores had been made. In addition, and most important for this study, many of the same scores that were least related to adjustment criteria had been shown to tap and measure those same five qualities associated with creativity as listed above (i.e., memory, imagery, originality, organization, and energy).

For this study, the creativity-associated scores were grouped into a subscore called the *Function score*, so labeled because it emphasized ongoing dynamic processes within the individual. This Function score was distinguished from the *Structure score*, so labeled because it stressed the organizational components of the personality structure and included those scores commonly associated with adjustment criteria. This was the first time any such distinction had been made. It should be noted that this is *not* a totally new scoring system but rather a selective division of classical (primarily Beck, 1950) Rorschach scores with few changes made solely for ease of quantification.

To assess change in level of psychological well-being two other measures were employed. The first of these was the Butler–Haigh 100-item Q-sort. The subjects completed a Self and an Ideal sort, which were correlated. The S–I correlation has proven to be a most effective means of assessing psychological well-being or lack thereof (Butler & Haigh, 1954). As for the Rorschach, S–I correlations were obtained before the subject entered therapy and again upon the completion of 20 sessions. Although with the S–I sort, like the Rorschach, much work has been done in the establishment of optimal normal levels, no attempt was made to do this in the present study as the concern was with improvement for each individual rather than any specific level that might be considered psychologically healthy, or, conversely, psychologically ill. The S–I correlations obtained before the onset of therapy were subtracted from the correlations obtained after 20 sessions to obtain a measure of change in level of psychological well-being. The same procedure was followed for the Rorschach Function (creativeness) scores and the Rorschach Structure (adjustment) scores. The final measure used, the Therapists' Rating Scale, is a simple nine-point scale on which each subject's therapist was asked to rate the amount of gain made by his or her client at the end of 20 sessions of psychotherapy.

On the basis of S–I change scores and therapists' ratings two groups of clients were arrived at: one group who significantly increased their level of psychological well-being (according to themselves and their therapists) and one group who (on the same basis) had not. For each of these there were two sets of Rorschach scores: a creativeness (Function) score and an adjustment (Structure) score. The success group contained 20 people, the failure group 13. Each group was first compared with regard to sex, age, education, occupation, and experience of their respective therapists. Essentially no significant differences were found among any of the groups on these variables. By and large the groups were quite similar and there seemed little to distinguish them from the usual outpatient clinic population. Furthermore there were no significant differences found among the groups in their pretherapy Structure or Function scores. Thus any changes found in the creativeness scores and the adjustment scores could be attributed solely to the clients' changed levels of psychological well-being. The pretherapy/post-20th session Rorschach change scores were then compared for the groups.

What was discovered was simply this: although the failure group showed no change in their creativeness (Function) scores, the success group showed tremendous positive gains in creativeness as reflected by the Function scores, and in only 2½ months of therapy. These results were evinced at statistical levels well beyond those deemed acceptable for such research. Furthermore, and this was not anticipated, the Structure scores—those used routinely by previous investigators and clinicians to assess level of psychological health or relative amounts of psychopathology—not only showed little change, but indicated a slight (though not statistically significant) downward shift for the entire sample. Lastly, when the two sets of scores (Function and Structure) were combined for the entire sample into a total Rorschach change score, the dramatic positive results were minimized to an almost negligible change; that is, the actions of these two scores tended to cancel each other out.

Thus, not only could it be said that the results of this study demonstrated a positive relationship between psychological well-being (as perceived by both participating therapists and clients) and creativeness (as measured by previous investigators), but, furthermore, that these factors had little to do with adjustment criteria heretofore commonly used to determine psychological health and improvement in psychotherapy. In fact, it could be inferred from these results that the healing force—that which enhances the individual's growth toward some higher level of functioning—lies somewhere in his innate creativeness and its push toward expression, rather than in his adjustment and fitting into the world around him. The process of psychotherapy in some way (and for some clients) facilitates the mobilization of this force. In summary then, what is being suggested is that self-actualization and creativeness are virtually synonymous and that the maximization of both leads to increased psychological well-being.

These results are obviously only a beginning and are presented primarily as a stimulus to explore the ramifications of applying client-centered theory and technique beyond the psychotherapeutic hour. To begin, let me suggest a few implications that seem most immediately relevant. With regard to psychotherapy: we generally think of psychotherapy in negative terms, that is as a means of alleviating psychological distress—of making the impaired more "normal." But if the psychotherapy process can augment creativeness in clients who by definition are experiencing psychological distress, what might be the potential for these techniques, when used with people who are already moderately well-functioning, productive individuals? Such applications have been suggested and advocated in the work of Shlien (1956), Rogers (1969, 1973), Gordon (1970), and Lerner (1972), among others. Each in turn has suggested the use of psychotherapeutic techniques as a means of increasing creative productivity in industry, higher education, parenting skills, and community development. Some of these suggestions have catalyzed methods such as brainstorming (Osborn, 1960) and synetics (Gordon, 1961), which have been employed in industrial settings to enhance creative productivity; others relate to a more student-centered approach to learning through open classroom techniques, which are gaining favor with educators; still others evidence broader application via local community help services such as "FISH,"[3] and hotlines, which have sprung up throughout the United States.

The relationship between creativeness and psychological well-being, if established through these and other practical applications, could indeed remove the long-standing unilateral association between the psychopractitioner and mental illness. We could begin conceptualizing an applied psychology of human potential rather than one solely of deficit. Szasz' (1960) suggestion of the establishment of clinics for problems in living—thought by many to be a crackpot notion—might begin to seem a bit less so. After all, what is really wrong in seeking a little boost for one's productivity,

---

[3] A recently activated church-affiliated network of volunteers community-help services (see Howell, 1968).

particularly if one feels caught in a rut? During times of stress we seek help from relatives and friends (sometimes even strangers sitting next to us on a bus or plane). Various cultures build in such helping devices during identifiable periods of normative crisis. One example is the *wake*, and other rituals that surround grief and mourning and serve as an aid to the bereaved following the loss of a loved one. This should not be misconstrued as yet another crisis-intervention approach. Crisis intervention has come to mean the attempt to quell difficulties once they have become full-blown and unmanageable problems (which generally speaks to why these programs have proven relatively unsuccessful). On the contrary, actualizing techniques would be habilitative rather than rehabilitative: inventive rather than interventive. They would prepare the individual for crises before they arise and act as an aid in mobilizing his own restitutive forces. They would help alleviate the anxiety of such times by making the individual aware of the indigenous human support structures available to him and perhaps, most important, they would offer legitimacy while minimizing shame in the need for such support.

There is, of course, much to be done. We must first discover those qualities of the successful therapeutic encounter that are growth-enhancing, as well as determine how and where their analogs occur in more mundane interpersonal encounters. Harlow and Harlow's (1962) monkey studies have certainly suggested conditions under which exploration and psychological well-being are engendered or inhibited through controlled differences in mothering. These appear to have great relevance to parallels in human infant care and development. There are other experimental studies (e.g., Platt, 1961; Thompson & Melzack, 1956; Levine, 1960) that bear on the relationship between the actualizing tendency and positive psychological growth. Direct studies of the therapeutic milieu have disclosed variables such as empathy, unconditional positive regard, and their communication as conditions promoting changes in level of psychological well-being as creativeness (Lorr, 1965; Cartwright & Lerner, 1963; Truax, 1963).

Indeed, we have been slow to recognize and evaluate those regularly occurring aspects of human contact that are enhancing and growth-producing. Preventive mental health is a misnomer that misguides us in our pursuits. True prevention in the area of avoiding loss of human potential means continual facilitation of psychological well-being in all human dealings, from parenting to burying. With social institutions (e.g., the family and the community) in the tremendous state of flux in today's rapidly paced world, the need for a reexamination of our support structures is perhaps more crucial today than at any other point in human history. When we lived in closely knit communities and among larger extended families we were trained in sensitivity to others through everyday dealings with those around us. With the proliferation and expansion of our urban complexes made up of highly mobile nuclear families, much of the informal interpersonal learning has been systematically eliminated. Psychological development now takes place in an extremely coarctated emotional life space, thus increasing the need for greater understanding of communication skills within and between generations. The growing popularity of family life education, parent preparedness and effectiveness training, and the like, speaks to this felt need. Simultaneously, the ease of world travel and international communication systems make the need for interracial empathic understanding a focal and very practical issue.

Increases in the amount of leisure time, and the extension of life-span are forcing us to be more aware of the need for enrichment of our lives beyond that of the simple work ethic. There is developing what some social critics have termed *the crisis of leisure*. Little has been done to prepare us for the assumption of these new and less-well-defined roles. This hiatus creates a form of personal and social malaise in young and old alike, which stems from lack of practice in mobilizing our internal creativeness and a corresponding inability to draw upon those resources within ourselves. The application of creativeness-enhancement techniques could be used to foster the aforementioned conceptualization of habilitative flexibility (as opposed to passive rehabilitation) as a basic human skill to be cultivated along with specific skill training.

Above all else, the need for continual awareness of the inextricable interrelationship between creativeness and psychological well-being is most germane to our educational institutions and their policies. Here we seem to have all but lost sight of the goal of developing responsible, self-reliant, creative individuals. Rather, there has been emphasis on training as opposed to educating, on competitive achievement rather than satisfaction derived from the joy of discovery and personal productivity. The resulting apathy and lack of excitement in learning, as well as (and far worse) the distress and pain created with our young and future citizens by such an atmosphere are reason for great concern, as has been aptly noted by Bettelheim (1965), Leonard (1968), and Holt (1964, 1967) among others. It is in our schools (which have taken over much of the educational responsibilities that were once under the purview of the family and community) that personal enhancement must be prized and fostered. The desire to learn and to actualize onself, if protected and nurtured, will cause the student to educate himself. Within such an educational and developmental framework the distinction between creative problem-solving (which we think of as technologically oriented) and solving one's problems creatively (which we think of as psychologically oriented) might well begin to disappear, while establishing a base for a true psychology of well-being and human potential.

Finally, from here we might begin to explore the relationship between creativeness and creativity, and the eventual manner and modes in which creativeness can and does express itself through creativity. If creativeness is the experience and process (i.e., the "Function") that is the wellspring of creative production, what factors shape the end result? How does a Mozart, a Planck, or a Michelangelo come to be? It is in these individuals that the interplay of constitutional and social factors are inextricably woven with the psychological to produce a tapestry that we call personality. Herewith are a few speculations on this interplay, among some other concluding considerations.

There is strong evidence (e.g., Getzels & Jackson, 1962; Chess, Thomas, & Birch, 1965) that supports the position that there are constitutional and genetic givens with which the individual begins, and that they not only help determine certain directions throughout his life, but cause him to be an active part of his environmental interrelationships from birth. Thus, that which has been referred to as talent may well be an inherent biological disposition toward a sensory modality (see Meier, 1939). For example, in the musician it may be the auditory–vocal modality over the visual–motor. Such dispositions are encouraged through exploration at first by the organism, and then by the environment (both interpersonal and physical). If, for instance, a child learns to distinguish tones, begins humming and deriving pleasure from it, he may take pleasure in music, if encouraged. If not, such germinative talent may indeed become submerged in favor of other modalities that _are_ responded to. Undoubtedly in the worst of circumstances such inclinations may be lost altogether if actively suppressed or if creativeness is not enhanced along with them. Talent without creativeness may lead to craftsmanship but not creativity. Possibly if the thrust of these dispositions is great enough and they are continually thwarted by the environment the result may be that of an unhappy marriage between creativity and psychological distress.

At the other extreme, little has been said in this chapter about the severe pathological limits of human behavior—those so bizarre that they fall beyond the range of acceptable—the psychotic. In part, that is because I believe this to be a different realm of study than that of psychological well-being. It well may be that in the future continual discovery regarding brain activity and chemistry will disclose a biological basis for mental illness (in the narrowest sense of the word) just as was the case for general paresis in the 19th century. Studies of early childhood autism are beginning to disclose perceptual imbalances (e.g., "structural" deficiencies) that have previously gone unnoticed but can help account for schizophrenic-like behavior in children (Tousieng, 1957). Our whole conceptualization of mental retardation is beginning to shift its emphasis from a once-hopeless, wastebasket category, to a differentiated schematization regarding remediation and enhancement of human potential (see Stevens & Heber, 1964).

Concern with these issues is rapidly becoming more than the esoteric focus of but a few behavioral scientists. Our society is growing larger and continually more complex. It has gained immense technical capacities in but a short period of time. Yet knowledge regarding ourselves and how we function when at our best and in relation to our fellows has lagged far behind. The effects of this lag have been delineated incisively by recent analysts (Slater, 1970; Toffler, 1970) whose predictions for the human condition are rather disquietingly apocalyptic with regard to the future. Increasing desperation is reflected by the loneliness, disconnectedness, and consequential violence that continue to grow and spread within and from our large urban centers. In our frenetic need to cope with and maintain the pace of modern existence, we have tended to ignore the fact that man is more than an appendage to the machinery he has created—indeed he is man in search of himself, who is in turn, man the creator.

REFERENCES

Allport, G. A. *Becoming*. New Haven: Yale University Press, 1955.

Barron, F. Originality in relation to personality and intellect. *Journal of Personality*, 1957, **25**, 730–742.

Barron, F. The psychology of imagination. *Scientific American*, 1958, **199**(3), 150–170.

Barron, F. *Creativity and psychological health*. Princeton, N.J.: Van Nostrand, 1963.

Beck, S. J. *Rorschach's test. Basic processes*. (2nd ed.) New York: Grune & Stratton, 1950.

Bettelheim, B. Teaching the culturally underprivileged child. Unpublished manuscript, University of Chicago, 1965.

Brittain, W. L., & Beittel, K. R. Analysis of levels of creative performance in the visual arts. *Journal of Aesthetic Art Criticism*, 1960, **19**, 83–90.

Butler, J. M., & Haigh, G. V. Changes in the relation between self-concepts and ideal concepts consequent upon client-centered counseling. In C. R. Rogers & R. F. Dymond (Eds.), *Psychotherapy and personality change*. Chicago: University of Chicago Press, 1954.

Butler, J. M., & Rice, L. N. Self-actualization, new experience, and psychotherapy. *Counseling Center Discussion Papers,* **6**(12). Chicago: University of Chicago Library, 1960.

Butler, J. M., Rice, L. N., & Dicken, C. F. Process and outcome in psychotherapy: A controlled study. *Counseling Center Discussion Papers,* **6**(6). Chicago: University of Chicago Library, 1960.

Cartwright, R. D., & Lerner, B. Empathy, need to change and improvement with psychotherapy. *Journal of Consulting Psychology,* 1963, **27**(2), 138–144.

Chess, S., Thomas, A., & Birch, H. G. *Your child is a person.* New York: Viking, 1965.

Collingwood, R. G. *The principles of art.* New York: Oxford University Press, 1958.

Dewey, J. *Intelligence in the modern world.* New York: Random House, 1939.

Drevdahl, J. E., & Cattell, R. B. Personality and creativity in artists and writers. *Journal of Clinical Psychology,* 1958, **14**, 107–111.

Ehrenzweig, A. The creative surrender. *American Imago,* 1957, **14**, 193–210.

Eiduson, B. Artist and nonartist: A comparative study. *Journal of Personality,* 1958, **26**, 13–28.

Fiske, D. W., & Maddi, S. R. (Eds.) *Functions of varied experience.* Homewood, Ill.: Dorsey, 1961.

Freud, A. *The ego and the mechanism of defense.* New York: International Universities Press, 1946.

Freud, S. *Leondardo da Vinci—A psychosexual study of an infantile reminiscence.* New York: Dodd, Mead, 1932.

Freud, S. Dostoevsky and parracide. In *Collected papers.* Vol. V. London: Hogarth, 1956. (a)

Freud, S. The Moses of Michelangelo. In *Collected papers.* Vol. IV. London: Hogarth, 1956. (b)

Freud, S. *Creativity and the unconscious.* New York: Harper, 1958.

Gaylin, N. L. Psychotherapy and psychological health: A Rorschach function and structure analysis. *Journal of Consulting Psychology,* 1966, **30**(6), 494–500.

Getzels, J. W., & Jackson, P. W. *Creativity and intelligence.* New York: Wiley, 1962.

Goldstein, K. *The organism.* Boston: Beacon, 1963.

Gordon, T. *Parent effectiveness training.* New York: Wyden, 1970.

Gordon, W. J. *Synetics.* New York: Harper, 1961.

Guilford, J. P. Creative abilities in the arts. *Psychological Review,* 1957, **64**, 110–118.

Hammer, E. F. *Creativity: An exploratory investigation of the personalities of gifted adolescent artists.* New York: Random House, 1961.

Harlow, H. F., & Harlow, M. K. Social deprivation in monkeys. *Scientific American*, 1962, **207** (11) , 136–146.

Hart, H. H. The integrative function in creativity. *Psychiatric Quarterly*, 1950, **13**, 1–16.

Hartmann, H. *Ego psychology and the problem of adaptation.* New York: International Universities Press, 1958.

Hartmann, H., & Kris, E. The genetic approach in psychoanalysis. In A. Freud, H. Hartmann, E. Kris (Eds.), *The psychoanalytic study of the child.* Vol. I. New York: International Universities Press, 1945.

Holt, J. *How children fail.* New York: Pitman, 1964.

Holt, J. *How children learn.* New York: Pitman, 1967.

Horney, K. Inhibitions in work. *American Journal of Psychoanalysis*, 1947, **6**, 18–25.

Howell, R. *Fish for my people.* New York: Morehouse-Barlow, 1968.

Jahoda, M. *Current concepts of positive mental health.* New York: Basic Books, 1958.

James, W. *The principles of psychology.* New York: Holt, 1890. 2 vols.

Joint Commission on Mental Illness and Health: *Action for mental health*, Final report of the Joint Commission on Mental Illness and Health. New York: Basic Books, 1961.

Kellogg, R. *The psychology of children's art.* Del Mar, Calif.: CRM, 1967.

Kris, E. *Psychoanalytic explorations in art.* New York: International Universities Press, 1952.

Kubie, L. S. *Neurotic distortion of the creative process.* Lawrence: University Press of Kansas, 1958.

Leonard, G. B. *Education and ecstasy.* New York: Delacorte, 1968.

Lerner, B. *Therapy in the ghetto: Political impotence and personal disintegration.* Baltimore: Johns Hopkins, 1972.

Levine, S. Stimulation in infancy. *Scientific American*, 1960, **202** (5) , 80–86.

Lorr, M. Client perceptions of therapists: A study of therapeutic relation. *Journal of Consulting Psychology*, 1965, **29** (2) , 146–149.

Maddi, S. R., Charlens, A. M., Maddi, D., & Smith, A. Effects of monotony and novelty on imaginative productions. *Journal of Personality*, 1962, **30**, 513–527.

Maslow, A. H. *Motivation and personality.* New York: Harper, 1954.

Maslow, A. H. Cognition of being in the peak experience. *Counseling Center Discussion Papers*, **8** (14) . Chicago: University of Chicago Library, 1957.

Maslow, A. H. *Toward a psychology of being.* Princeton, N.J.: Van Nostrand, 1962.

Meier, N. C. Factors in artistic aptitude: Final summary of a ten-year study of special ability. *Psychological Monographs*, 1939, **31** (5) , 140–158.

Myden, W. An interpretation and evaluation of certain personality characteristics involved in creative production. In M. H. Sherman (Ed.), *A Rorschach reader*. New York: International Universities Press, 1960.

Osborn, A. F. *Applied imagination*. New York: Scribner, 1960.

Platt, J. R. Beauty: Pattern and change. In D. W. Fiske & S. R. Maddi (Eds.), *Functions of varied experience*. Homewood, Ill.: Dorsey, 1961.

Porterfield, A. L. *Creative factors in scientific research: A social psychology of scientific knowledge studying the interplay of psychology and cultural factors in science with emphasis upon imagination*. Durham, N.C.: Duke University Press, 1941.

Roe, A. Artists and their work. *Journal of Personality*, 1946, **15**, 1–40.

Roe, A. Painting and personality. In M. H. Sherman (Ed.), *A Rorschach reader*. New York: International Universities Press, 1960.

Rogers, C. R. *Client-centered therapy*. Boston: Houghton Mifflin, 1951.

Rogers, C. R. Toward a theory of creativity. *Etc.*, 1954, **11**, 249–260.

Rogers, C. R. A theory of therapy, personality, and interpersonal relationships, as developed in the client-centered framework. In S. Koch (Ed.), *Psychology: A study of a science*. Vol. III. *Formulations of the person and the social context*. New York: McGraw-Hill, 1959.

Rogers, C. R. *On becoming a person*. Boston: Houghton Mifflin, 1961.

Rogers, C. R. *Freedom to learn*. Columbus, Ohio: Merrill, 1969.

Rogers, C. R. The person of tomorrow. Paper presented at Lisner Auditorium, Washington, D.C., February 22, 1973.

Rogers, C. R., & Dymond, R. F. (Eds.) *Psychotherapy and personality change*. Chicago: University of Chicago Press, 1954.

Schachtel, E. G. *Metamorphosis*. New York: Basic Books, 1959.

Sells, S. B. (Ed.) *The definition and measurement of mental health*. Washington, D. C.: U.S. Department of Health, Education and Welfare, 1968.

Shlien, J. M. Creativity and psychological health. *Counseling Center Discussion Papers*, **2**(27). Chicago: University of Chicago Library, 1956.

Shlien, J. M. Comparison of results with different forms of psychotherapy. *American Journal of Psychotherapy*, 1964, **28**, 15–22.

Slater, P. *The pursuit of loneliness*. Boston: Beacon, 1970.

Smith, M. B. Competence and "mental health;" problems in conceptualizing human effectiveness. In S. B. Sells (Ed.), *The definition and measurement of mental health*. Washington, D.C.: U.S. Department of Health, Education and Welfare, 1968.

Spearman, C. *The creative mind*. New York: Appleton, 1931.

Spitz, R. A. Hospitalism. An inquiry into the genesis of psychiatric conditions in early childhood. In A. Freud, H. Hartmann, & E. Kris (Eds.), *The psychoanalytic study of the child*. Vol. I. New York: International Universities Press, 1945.

Stein, M. I., & Meer, B. Perceptual organization in a study of creativity. *Journal of Psychology*, 1954, **37**, 39–43.

Stevens, H. A., & Heber, R. *Mental retardation*. Chicago: University of Chicago Press, 1964.

Strupp, H. H. Psychotherapy revisited: The problem of outcome. *Psychotherapy*, 1963, **1**, 1–13.

Szasz, T. The myth of mental illness. *American Psychologist*, 1960, **15**, 113–118.

Thompson, W. R., & Melzack, R. Early environment. *Scientific American*, 1956, **194**(1), 38–42.

Toffler, A. *Future shock*. New York: Random House, 1970.

Tousieng, P. W. Childhood schizophrenia and cerebral damage—reflections on diagnosis. Paper presented at the annual meeting of the American Association of Psychiatric Clinics for Children, Chicago, March 1957.

Truax, C. B. Effective ingredients in psychotherapy. *Journal of Counseling Psychology*, 1963, **10**, 256–263.

Werner, H. *The comparative psychology of mental development*. New York: International Universities Press, 1948.

White, R. W. *The abnormal personality*. New York: Ronald Press, 1956.

White, R. W. Motivation reconsidered: The concept of competence. *Psychological Review*, 1959, **66**, 297–333.

Zilboorg, G., & Henry, G. W. *A history of medical psychology*. New York: Norton, 1941.

Zubin, J. Clinical, phenomenological and biometric assessment of psychopathology with special reference to diagnosis. In S. B. Sells (Ed.), *The definition and measurement of mental health*. Washington, D.C.: U.S. Department of Health, Education, and Welfare, 1968.

CHAPTER 13

It Takes One to Know One:
Existential–Rogerian Concepts in Encounter Groups[1]

Jim Bebout

> *We do not need a new theory so much as a new experience of the data [but a new experience of the data leads to a new theory].*
>
> **R. D. LAING**

For a decade and more, Carl Rogers concentrated his professional practice and thinking in the small-group field, specifically on basic encounter groups (Rogers, 1970). By now, thousands of small groups have undergone an encounter process following certain Rogerian principles.[2] Of this development, Rogers' (1968) well-known statement is:

> One of the most rapidly growing social phenomena in the United States is the spread of the intensive group experience . . . a "grass roots" movement. . . . It has permeated industry . . . education . . . families . . .

[1] I am most grateful to Carole Marks for persistently listening to my ideas and contributing her own. My generalizations depend in part on the data collected in the Talent in Interpersonal Exploration Groups Project, so my thanks to NIMH Grant MH-17330 and all those who made it possible.

[2] Through the programs of such organizations as the Western Behavioral Science Institute and the Center for the Study of the Person at La Jolla, the Personal Encounter Group Program in Berkeley, Esalen in Big Sur, the National Training Labs at Bethel, Me., and hundreds of growth centers and training workshops given throughout the country and internationally.

professions. . . . Why? I believe it is because people—ordinary people— have discovered that this group experience alleviates their loneliness and permits them to grow, to risk, to change. It brings persons into real relationships with persons [p. 265].

If encounter groups improve relationships, produce growth, and alleviate loneliness in so many individuals, it follows that this movement is therapeutic. Does this "social invention," then, represent a long-awaited breakthrough in mental health service—a royal road to personal growth? Does the encounter group movement mean to supplant traditional forms of treatment—individual psychotherapy, counseling, community mental health work?

The answer is both yes and no: this chapter will try to show that the theory underlying encounter groups, at least in the Rogerian school, is part and parcel of the client-centered conception of psychotherapy in general. In this sense, encounter groups are a logical extension of what Rogerians already believe about therapeutic relationships and are nothing new. To support this argument several redefinitions of client-centered concepts will be offered here—in my view, an updating of basic principles. Certain new concepts are introduced, for example *encounter* and *experiential communality*, which may tend to make the original tenets of Rogerian theory less recognizable. I will try to elaborate on the connectedness between these newer concepts and the more familiar theory.

On the other hand, encounter groups *are* a new phenomenon. Taken as a whole, basic encounter groups do not resemble traditional psychotherapies. The style of encounter groups, their technical innovation and their image bear little relation to standard forms of therapy (even earlier Rogerian therapy). They appear the antithesis of institutionalized medical practice and established clinical programs.

Encounter groups tend to be anti-institutional; they depart radically from medical models of treatment and accompanying role behaviors of doctor and patient (with their implications of the constituted authority of "professional-healthy-expert" and the dependency of the "mentally-sick-consumer"). They do not assume *official* responsibility for others' lives; they do not ordinarily attempt following-up their clientele. Most encounter groups do not screen or select their membership, and seldom reject applicants. Their assumption is usually that of realizing the potential for growth of any number or kinds of individual members through unplanned (spontaneous) interpersonal interaction in the here-and-now, rather than programmed case management. Diagnosis does not matter in encounter groups. The setting for these groups is almost always informal, sometimes recreational. Socially defined identities and statuses are shunned. Group encounters can be nude, physical, violent, en masse, silly, mystical, and as brief as one day or one weekend. At present, the target population for the encounter group movement is the mainstream of society—the great, washed, white, middle-class segment of society interested in self-improvement (although many applications are now being made within ethnic, community, criminal, sexual, and intellectual subgroups). Traditional therapies and the encounter group movement may be in competition for services to this broad element of American society.[3]

The media is new. The promise is appealing. Conservatively, some 5 million people have sought out this unconventional avenue of learning and change since its popularity began 10 or so years ago. As against established methods of helping people, there may be distinct advantages to the encounter media—in time, depth, focus, and impact.

Recent research indicates that an encounter process can and does effect significant positive changes in the emotional and relational lives of people, using briefly trained nonprofessional leaders (Bebout, 1973; Bebout & Gordon, 1972), or even tape-recorded programs in place of any leader (Berzon, Solomon, & Reisel, 1972; Lieberman, Yalom, & Miles, 1973). It is not surprising to claim, therefore, that the technology of. encounter groups constitutes a remarkable innovation in the mental health field.

In this chapter I will try (a) to review briefly the development of the client-centered theory of psychotherapy in order to show a natural progression toward the "invention" of encounter groups; (b) to provide a preliminary definition of the encounter from the point of view of this tradition; (c) to reanalyze the core notion of empathy in Rogerian theory in terms of the operation of a more fundamental human transaction—experiential communality; and, finally, (d) to portray the role of group self-deceit as related to the concept of incongruence, and to describe self-actualization in encounter groups.

RECYCLING: SOME BACKGROUND

Rogers' advocacy of the encounter group as a vehicle for personal growth did not appear overnight. The encounter group movement was born of many parents, Carl Rogers being one of the primary godfathers. There

[3] One group of investigators reports there is little significant difference between the adult neurotic psychotherapy client population and those seeking groups at growth centers (Lieberman, Yalom, & Miles, 1973); evidence from the Talent in Interpersonal Exploration Groups Project indicates numerous distinctions (Bebout & Gordon, 1972).

have been many others. As early as 1920, J. L. Moreno described the value of intensive small-group interaction through psychodramatic methods. The group therapy field parented the Tavistock Institute in England and applied psychologists and management and educational consultants combined the learnings of Lewinian and general social–psychological research into group dynamics theory to produce sensitivity training and process groups at the National Training Laboratories at Bethel, Maine after World War II. Borrowing heavily from these schools and from Gestalt (Perls, Goodman), and body–mind theorists and practitioners (from Reich, Selver, and Lowen to Assagiolli, Alexander, and Rolfe), the Esalen Institute at Big Sur generated a potpourri of intensive small groups dedicated to deep personal and interpersonal exploration, some of the earliest of which were highly Rogerian (see Back, 1973; Lakin, 1972; Schutz, 1973; Yalom, 1970).

Hart (1970) (see also Shlien & Zimring, 1970) describes the changes that have occurred in client-centered therapy in terms of three stages. The first stage contained an unbroken focus on clients' concerns, problems, and even specific sentence-statements to the nearly total exclusion of therapists' personal participation in what was called *nondirective* therapy. In a second stage (circa 1955–1960), the therapist was seen as more personally active and interactive; still, there was a singular restriction of therapists' response modality in practice—through the nearly exclusive use of *reflective* statements, those intending to communicate empathic understanding through strict adherence to the terms and tone of the phenomenal field of the client (Bebout, 1961). When therapist congruence was at stake, deviation from this mode of response was theoretically justifiable; and, in this case, focus on the therapist's experiencing allowed his or her emergence as a more initiating and participatory individual. The third period of development, according to Hart, focused more on therapy process (Shlien & Zimring, 1970), especially the affective–motivational experiencing of *both* the client and the therapist (Gendlin, 1970). The therapist became more free at this point to introduce his own here-and-now feelings, concerns and perceptions, independent of the sanction of remaining congruent.[4]

Rogers began intensive study of small groups at the Western Behavioral Sciences Institute in the 1960s, and in this context he stated:

I find that I have changed in the willingness to express myself and my feelings openly, as data for the other person to use, but not as a

---

[4] The reflection response underwent some changes although it is still a mainstay of practice. In this third stage of theory, one staff member's reflective response to his client's outburst "fuck you," was "fuck you, too;" a rather confrontive reflection.

guide or an imposition. If I am angry, I will express that anger as something within myself . . . I am much more free-wheeling in stating personal feeling reactions to what the other person has said or done. I have been amazed . . . [in groups] by the confrontation of others with my feeling reactions, [and] by the *extent to which I become a participant, expressing problems and concerns of my own.* [Italics added.] Only when I sense that someone in the group is . . . groping to find himself, do I find myself expressing primarily the empathic feelings I experience . . . [Rogers & Hart, 1970, p. 519].[5]

In its inception, the client-centered school established an identity by subtraction—by rejecting therapeutic models based on transference and externally superimposed insight. The movement discovered in practice the importance of empathic understanding, and quickly adopted an interaction process that led to the unfolding and expression of personal meanings and feelings attaching to a client's here-and-now moment. This empathic, acceptant climate encouraged clients, by themselves as it were, to develop their emotional concerns to a natural conclusion and a new level of growth.

In work with schizophrenics and in small groups, it was found that therapists needed more initiative and personal visibility. With groups it became increasingly clear that it was not possible to preserve the somewhat delicate and one-sided concentration on a single individual's psychological "trip" (Gordon, 1951). With "well-motivated neurotics," in a dyadic clinical relationship, the therapist and client have abundant space and time within which to sensitively track the client's experiencing and intuitive awareness. In group settings this borders on a luxury.

Probably for these reasons, fundamental changes occurred in the interactional nature of the therapeutic relationship, hinging on release of the therapist's spontaneity and natural responsivity. But, when one person initiates feelingful statements or actions with reference to a face-to-face other, and the other responds *in kind,* then the *medium of exchange is basic encounter.* In Gendlin's (1970) terms:

Therapy must be "experiential". . . . Experiencing is . . . a moving directly felt process. . . . *Interpersonal relationships carry the experiencing process forward,* as the therapist *expresses his own* actual *reactions . . . and at the same time* gives room, attention, and reference to the client's felt reactions . . . [p. 93; italics added].

Inasmuch as the focus here is on the *conjoint experiential process between client and therapist,* I suggest either "*co*experiential" or "en-

[5] Reprinted by permission of Houghton Mifflin.

counter" therapy as a suitable name for this most current form of client-centered practice. The major dynamic of client-centered psychotherapy, then, has shifted to a kind of doubling of empathic and expressive components in interpersonal interaction, rendering a fuller and a more authentic, two-way relationship. In coexperiential or encounter therapy, a new basis for the dynamics of change is possible—beyond insight, catharsis, reeducation, acceptance, transference, or individual introspection. This new concept is that *the overlapping and reciprocal sharing of momentary emotional experience is an event that in itself generates growth and change.* The phenomena and dynamics implied by this concept will be discussed under the heading Experiential Communality below. Before that discussion, some definition is needed.

SOME PREDEFINITION: ENCOUNTER AS CONTACT

An encounter between humans is first of all psychological touching. It is a meeting of emotions and minds. The first prerequisite for encounter between persons is *contact*. To follow the physical image, to be touched is to be felt (and feelings are the ingredients of emotion). But, in being physically touched by the other, one "feeling" another is also felt by the other. In touching (feeling) me, I also feel you and your touch if I allow it. Our feelings occur together. So it is psychologically—or it can be so. I can feel you feeling me in an encounter, and you can also feel me feeling you. Contact is made.

Encounter happens psychologically without physical touching—it is mental contact, lasting or momentary. It requires two or more people being equally emotionally open, direct, expressive, and personal in communicating with each other. This conscious (more or less aware) contact can be described as a state in itself. A state of contact can be considered independent of content. The emotions involved can be of almost any nature or quality. There is one clear exception: the psychological state of alienation and feelings of loneliness. Alienation is a phenomenal representation of Sartre's "existential nausea" (and Sartre's "hell" was made of people who could neither contact nor escape each other).

Martin Buber (1958) tells us that, in the language of Tierra del Fuego, the term "far away" translates:

> They stare at one another each waiting for the other to volunteer to do what both wish, but are not able to do [p. 18].

Contact dissolves interpersonal distance or alienation—alienation is just that state of being in which there is the conviction that no one is close to you, in touch with you, or meaningfully shares your feeling-life. (When people are "there" but not in touch, Buber characterizes the interpersonal situation as an I–It relationship.)

Contact with another at an emotional and personally meaningful level —one of the original preconditions of therapy cited in a lesser sense by Rogers—is a necessary ingredient for human psychosocial survival. People become desperate in its total absence. Disorientation occurs given complete sensory deprivation, and derangement occurs with human contact deprivation (Harlow, 1958). People feel out of touch first with others, secondly with themselves, and finally with the world. By itself the condition of contact in interpersonal encounter specifies no particular kind or combination of emotional material—we may be in contact when I am saddened by your rage, which makes you angrier; or I am anxious about your depression, which makes you sadder; or I am overjoyed at your failure, which makes you disgusted. Even physically, in touching each other, my reaction may be delight and yours fear but nevertheless contact and closeness between us has been momentarily effected.

The embeddedness of feeling in the concept of encounter may be understood by reference to Plessner's and Strasser's descriptions of the nature of feeling itself. Plessner (1950) defines the essence of interpersonal feeling as:

> Direct intimacy with the other or self-*awareness* of a *contact that excludes all distance (distanzlose sachverhaftung)* [p. 17; italics added].

How should we understand this direct intimacy or contact? It clearly is the obverse of Buber's example of the two "far-away" Tierra del Fuegians. Strasser, adopting Plessner's definition, believes that feeling itself constitutes the primary mode of interpersonal understanding or knowledge of another, just as Rogers holds the empathic mode of understanding as primary in psychotherapy and Polanyi gives epistemological priority to "personal knowledge" (Polanyi, 1958). Strasser (1970) states:

> Our original feeling and emotional mode of awareness . . . rises to the surface whenever the situation appears to the ego in such a manner that he cannot *maintain a distance* [italics added] (emotion) or whenever, *in the nature of things no distance exists (feeling). When I am present to the other, no distance exists* [italics added]. The most elementary of all human experience—we together in surrounding world

—is not at first perceived, thought or sought after; it is primarily lived, through feeling [p. 306].

In contact there is feeling; moreover, feeling is at the essence of and arises out of contact.

The most popular conception of encounter relies on the quality of confrontation present in the psychological contact between people (with accompanying deep levels of emotional involvement and expression).[6] It is certainly true that in confrontation there is usually contact, as described above; however confrontive interactions imply an intentionality and a driven aspect of behavior—a quality of clash or struggle between people—which is not an essential component. Further, the idea of confrontation posits a necessary conflict and tension in interaction; these characteristics are more epiphenomena then definitional elements. Some writers and practitioners seem to view meaningful contact as existing only within states of interpersonal conflict, but it should be apparent that intense contact is possible also in the contexts of joy, reverie, with peace of mind and in loving relationship.

Intimacy is a related concept and another form of closeness similar to what is meant here by encounter. However, intimacy implies a positivistic, private, and somewhat delicate relationship between people. This relationship frequently occurs as a product and part of the process of encounter but is not substantive to it. Rapport and empathy have similar connotations but do not require the mutuality inherent in this definition of encounter. One may have strong rapport with a pet animal and empathy with an infant without ever achieving a condition of encounter.

Contact is a necessity for human social survival and a precondition for interpersonal growth; it is the least common denominator of whatever virtues there are in encounter groups—the value of the encounter movement would be assured if it only continued to be a vehicle whereby people could be brought in touch with people. The primary social drive for human closeness can be fulfilled through encounter even though the emotional transactions that occur are not further satisfying; even though the existential emotional life of a group member is not further matched, appreciated, or reciprocated by any other member of the group. The condition of contact is necessary but hardly sufficient to fulfill what we believe to be the human potentiality, and there is yet another, and a critical, definitional element in the concept of encounter in the Rogerian framework.

[6] "Basic encounter, marathons, and sensitivity . . . training are confrontation techniques that are capable of mobilizing powerful inter- and intra-personal forces in a most constructive manner [Blank, Gottsegen, & Gottsegen, 1971, p. 499]." (See also Burton, 1969; Perls, 1969; Schutz, 1973.)

ENCOUNTER AS EXPERIENTIAL COMMUNALITY

Most people have the capacity to become more closely "together" than merely being in touch or in contact. It often happens in encounter groups and in encounter therapy that the participants will live through moments in which their feelings are mutual and coexperienced. This event lies at the base of a definition of encounter unique to the Rogerian school—in Rogers' (1970) own example:

> The basic encounter . . . a man tells, through his tears, of the tragic loss of his child, a grief which he is experiencing fully for the first time, not holding back his feelings in any way. . . . Another man says to him, also with tears in his eyes, *"I've never before felt a real physical hurt in me from the pain of another. I feel completely with you." This is a basic encounter* [p. 33; italics added].

A much earlier example comes from Hobbs' (1951) illustration of a group therapy session in which the therapist and the group are reviewing the previous meeting and talking about a member who is now absent:

Mr. H.   I thought that there was so much difference in our two ages that there might be a gap there. Somehow he closed the gap the other day. *I feel that underneath we all have the same feeling* . . .

Therapist   I am not sure, Mr. H., that I understand just how you see that relationship.

Mr. H.   Well, I had the feeling that somehow I couldn't quite understand the scope of his problem and how much this problem really meant to him. Yet, *as he spoke* on Monday, *I had the feeling of great empathy with him.* Not so much that I have the same problem, but because I could see how another person feels carrying a burden like that around with you all the time. *Because even though we may have different problems, the feelings these problems create are pretty much the same,* and, uh, the feeling that he is going around carrying the same burden all the time—well, thinking about it *made me feel much closer to him.*

That is better said . . . that is what I was trying to say.

You feel closer to him not because of a similarity of problems but because of a similarity of feeling.

Mr. H.   *By and large, I think that has been typical of the whole group* . . . [p. 288; italics added].[7]

---

[7] Reprinted by permission of Houghton Mifflin.

In these examples, what seems most important and new to the participants is the sharing of emotional experience or experiential communality. Let's trace some of the characteristics of this event:

In both examples it appears that the simultaneous sharing of feeling is unpremeditated, unplanned. Although the members involved may have wished to become closer together, their statements suggest that this happened spontaneously, without a phenomenal sense of cognitive mediation. In the words of Mr. H., "Somehow he closed the gap. . . ." If these men had been striving to make their emotional experiences similar, with a deliberate and self-aware intent to empathize, the freshness and completeness of the experience would have been diminished. Intentionality interferes with feeling spontaneity (see definition of "feeling" above by Strasser).

Also apparent is the fact that the feelings the members shared occurred at the same time, that is, *simultaneously* (though in Hobbs' group it was described later). It would have been possible for the two men quoted to state that over the past week they found that they felt the same as their fellow members. Such reports would not be the phenomena discussed here as experiential communality, because the emotional coexperience did not happen in the same moment. Further, the coexperience would not have been *conscious* in the same moment. The examples above describe an emotional coexperiential event that the members *live through at the same time*. The existence of experiential communality is not usually verbally articulated ("in so many words") but more often inferred from context and behavior. Although verbal statement may be highly desirable, most often expressive, nonverbal signs are taken to indicate the presence of emotional coexperience (the tears in the eyes of the respondent in Rogers' example) (Butler & Rice, 1963; Soskin & Kauffman, 1961).

The feelings that the participants share are *functionally equivalent.* In Rogers' example, one man feels the loss and grief of another as physical pain or hurt. He is not angry at the other's emotion, reacting to him as a cry-baby or a weakling. He is not merely depressed by the other's grief, but shares the state of the other to the point of feeling pain in his body. Mr. H. shares another's feelings of burden in having a problem, but not the problem itself. In his words, ". . . the feelings these problems create are pretty much the same. . . ." Though less complete, we again have a case where similar feelings are paired together and the result is the same: a state of greater, sometimes intense, closeness and contact, as defined earlier.

The feelings that these group members share are not simple sensations; rather, they are *affective-meaning* gestalts (see Gibson, 1959). Each person discovers an identification between himself-as-experiencer and another self-as-experiencer.[8] The feelings involved are personal and have nearly the same personal meanings for each member (Walker, Rablen, & Rogers, 1960). Bodily felt sensation without personal significance, with no "self" participating as part of the experience, cannot be coexperienced of itself. Both a physical state of arousal (felt sensation) and a self-meaning context must be isomorphic to arrive at experiential communality.

This set of observations contributes to a formal definition of experiential communality (Bebout, 1971/1972) as follows:

> The spontaneous, simultaneous, and more or less conscious coexperiencing of functionally equivalent (isomorphic) affective-meaning processes (gestalts) in two or more people in face-to-face interaction and contact, which contact implies the perceived lack of psychological distance [p. 104].

In experiential communality a *direct intimacy* between people is established—a direct "feeling-together-with" another person—because the feelings are recognized as mutual in one existential moment. At these times, as in Strasser's definition above, the knower knows another "as well as himself" by virtue of the other being "the same" as himself. When *both* experiential communality and contact, as previously defined, exist, people are in the process of encounter as it has come to be conceived in the Rogerian or client-centered school. In fact, the concept of contact mentioned previously includes the possibility of degrees of psychological distance, and it is theoretically possible for people to realize experiential communality but achieve only a muted form of contact (and the converse is also true).

Consider this example. For three years Colin Turnbull lived with and studied a society of starving people called the *Ik*, a hunting tribe in the mountain ranges on the northeast border of Uganda. He records the final erosion of all their social mores and institutions—the family, marriage, cooperation, morality, the young caring for the old, and the old caring for the young. Yet, Turnbull (1972) suggests, there was one form of social contact left:

> With the Ik the family does not even hold itself together, much less serve as a model for a wider social brotherhood of Ik. Economic interest is centered on as many individual stomachs as there are people, and cooperation is merely a device for furthering an interest that is

---

[8] Such an identification is different from traditional concepts of identification, imitation, or role-modeling, which require hierarchical, nonsimultaneous, asymmetrical, or unconscious transactions between people.

consciously selfish . . . I used to come across little groups of them sitting silently on their *di* [a rocky ledge near their village overlooking the mountain valley] . . . One is tempted almost to suppose that they join together and sit in each other's presence on a common *di* without talking to each other, merely for the pleasure of ignoring each other. That might well be an appealing idea to the Ik, but hardly enough to justify in their eyes the considerable expenditure of energy involved. Sometimes men walk for over two hours simply to sit at a *di*, they are there inescapably as a social unit. *It is possible that they receive some comfort in the communal sharing of the pangs of hunger, in their lethargic but anxious quest for the telltale vulture, in their despair as they search the skies for rain, in their fear and mistrust of each other* [italics added]. This taking of comfort in a shared misery would at least help preserve the fragile sense of need for each other that is one of the bases of society [p. 158].⁹

When the entire tribe verged on starvation, Turnbull notes:

Villages were villages of the dead and dying, and there was little difference between the two. People crawled rather than walked—the very young and the very old all crawled . . . *It was their destination that intrigued me, for really they were going nowhere, these semi-animate bags of skin and bone, they just wanted to be with others, and they stopped whenever they met.* Perhaps it was the most important demonstration of sociality I ever saw among the Ik. *They just gathered during the morning and stayed until late afternoon. Once together they neither spoke nor did anything together, they were together and that seemed enough* [p. 223; italics added].

The Ik who manage to crawl together do so in search of experiential communality, because it is better to starve with someone than to starve alone; even though their noninteraction implies a state of minimal psychological contact, the contact is sufficient, and the result should be called an encounter.

Traditionally, client-centered theory has used concepts of empathy to describe the therapeutic process of sensitively listening and responding to another's feelings. Experiential communality and empathic processes are intricately associated. How they are different may already be apparent from the above definitions and examples but further distinctions will be drawn in the next section. Before discussing empathic processes it may be helpful to cite examples of and references to experiential com-

---

⁹ Quotations from Turnbull (1972) in this chapter copyright © 1972 by Colin M. Turnbull. Reprinted by permission of Simon and Schuster.

munality from other literature and theories so as to show a broader picture of the phenomena in question.

Related Concepts and Other Examples

The presence of and need for some form of contact and experiential communality so strongly portrayed above in Turnbull's description of the Ik can also be seen in the "collective mind" of crowds in situations of panic or emotional contagion interpreted by other anthropologists and social theorists. Brown (1965) summarizes concepts of this "mental unity:"

> How does it happen that emotionality and irresponsibility, once they arise in a crowd, prove so powerfully contagious as to produce a kind of "mental unity." Le Bon referred vaguely to suggestion and hypnotic effects. McDougall suggested that a kind of "primitive sympathy" operates. "The principle is that, *in men . . . each instinct . . . is capable of being excited in one individual by the expressions of the same emotion in another* [italics added] by virtue of a special congential adaptation of the instinct on its cognitive or perceptual side" (1920, p. 25). F. H. Allport (1924) wrote of "social facilitation," Park and Burgess (1921) of "rapport" . . . and Blumer (1951) of "circular reactions." These concepts are largely equivalent to one another and to Le Bon's "contagion" [p. 735].[10]

The sweeping release of rage during a riot, the stampede of a group toward a single exit during a theatre fire, perhaps the frenzy and resultant despair accompanying a stock market crash—these are all behaviors suggesting the presence of experiential communality.

Through ritualization, preindustrial societies provide for experiential communality in the most basic themes of human life and emotional concern (birth, puberty, marriage, death, war, and security, for example). These rituals usually obtain a moving and positive level of group feeling, experienced by the participants as in itself uplifting, self-transcending, and reaffirming of social bonds. Collective ritualized ceremony and belief are often considered potent enough to cure individual illness (physical or psychic).

In other words, experiential communality can by itself evoke an expanded sense of self. For the duration of this interactional process, and often for some time to follow, people can feel one component of a larger

[10] Quotations from Brown (1965) in this chapter copyright © The Free Press. Reprinted by permission of the publisher.

whole, of a group. If we ignore the content, theology, and structures of such rituals, we still have the fact that people undergo a significant emotional experience in the same place at the same time and attribute similar personal meanings to this event—for example, awe, reverence, power, or purity of spirit. G. H. Mead (1934) goes somewhat further in believing that mind itself is primarily a social phenomenon and that the "processes of experience which the human brain makes possible" are only possible given the group life of interacting individuals. The Ik who struggle to be together in their starvation, when they are sitting on their communal cliff, become significant symbols to each other. In Mead's terms, this implies a gesture that is "reflexive, presupposes another person, anticipates . . . response, and involves some sense . . . of how another person will feel."

Angyal refers to this human need and associated behavior in his concept of *homonomy*[11] and Polanyi describes it more simply in terms of *diffuse emotional conviviality.*[12]

There are more common and lighter examples of experiential communality in everyday life. There is often a peculiar increase in subjective feelings of closeness and sharing (encounter) when strangers are thrown together into similar transient environments, such as an elevator, airplane, or ocean-liner trip, or even when they are bunching together in a doorway to avoid a sudden rainstorm. The least common denominator of these situations is that groups of people, previously strange to each other, are undergoing similar affective-meaning events. It is notable that these most often happen in a group context. Brown (1965) gives another familiar example:

A common fate is also a similarity that can give rise to friendly sentiments and cooperative or altruistic behavior . . . *solidarity can also arise from the sharing of a very trivial hardship.* One day in the winter of 1960 a blizzard struck Boston and very few people went to work in the

[11] "Human behavior cannot be understood solely [in terms of] . . . the trend toward increased autonomy . . . [Man] seems rather to strive to surrender himself and to become an organic part of something that he conceives as greater than himself . . . The super-ordinate whole may be represented for him by a social unit—family, clan, nation—by an ideology, or by a meaningfully ordered universe . . . the important fact is that the trend toward *homonomy, the wish to be in harmony with a unit one regards as extending beyond his individual self, is a powerful motivating source of behavior* [Angyal, 1965, p. 15; italics added]."

[12] Diffuse emotional conviviality merges . . . into the transmission of specific experiences in the . . . physical sympathy . . . [one feels] at the sight of another's sharp suffering . . . good fellowship within small groups of people . . . is a direct contribution to the fulfillment of man's purpose and duty as a social being . . . [Through] ritual, the members of a group affirm the community of their existence . . . as transcending the individual [Polanyi, 1958, pp. 210–211]."

building at M.I.T. where I then had my office. Among these few *there was a curious euphoria, a sense of fellowship, of the self extended. People congratulated one another on their hardihood, shared lunches, helped dig out one another's cars, and only barely refrained from group singing. Next day the weather cleared and the mood vanished* [p. 75; italics added].

On a one-to-one level the reader may remember this childhood game:

Much of the charm [of children's sayings] seems to stem from the sense of participation in group ways ... The sense of fraternity-like membership is well demonstrated when two children catch themselves *saying the same thing at the same time* [italics added] and instantly fall into the ritual of hooking their little fingers together, making a silent wish, and then exchanging the prescribed phrases before they break the hold with a ceremonial flourish and remain mute until a third person speaks to one of them and so breaks the spell. If they forget and speak without this release, the wish is lost [Stone & Church, 1968, p. 375].[13]

Previous generations may also recall that when two friends or lovers walked side by side together and were physically separated by an obstacle in their path, they would jointly say "bread-and-butter" as if in recognition of their essential unity but temporary separation.

Buber (1947) imagines an instance of experiential communality between two people in its most extreme form in this way:

A man belabours another, who remains quite still. Then let us assume that the striker suddenly receives in his soul, the blow which he strikes; the same blow; that he receives it as the other who remains still. For the space of a moment he experiences the situation from the other side. Reality imposes itself on him. What will he do? ...

A man caresses a woman, who lets herself be caressed. Then let us assume that he feels the contact from two sides—with the palm of his hand still, and also with the woman's skin. The twofold nature of the gesture, as one that takes place between two persons, thrills through the depth of enjoyment in his heart and stirs it ...

I do not in the least mean that the man who has had such an experience would from then on have this two-sided sensation in every such meeting ... But the one extreme experience *makes the other person present to him for all time. A transfusion has taken place after which a mere elaboration of subjectivity is never again possible or tolerable to him* [p. 90; italics added].[14]

---

[13] A West-Coast version is to say: "Poke, you owe me a coke."

[14] Reprinted by permission of Routledge & Kegan Paul Ltd.

Buber characterizes such a relationship as "I–Thou" or encounter. I do not think that Buber intends to be fanciful in this example; rather he is pointing, through metaphor, to the real possibility of experiential communality.

Throughout Western philosophical and cultural traditions runs the premise that internal subjective experience is impermeable; that every man is an island. This premise substantiates the cultural themes of rugged individualism; the lonesome cowboy; the profit motive; the Protestant ethic of solitary work, personal responsibility, and private worship. Nonutilitarian collectivities (e.g., communes, cooperatives, sects) are disfavored at best, outlawed at worst, suffered for the sake of our constitutional imperative ensuring equal rights to maintain individual sovereignty and balances of power (e.g., state's rights). Our ideological enemies are said to be communism and socialism. This societal *weltanschauung* is well illustrated by our first flag of independence—a coiled rattlesnake with the motto "Don't tread on me."

In this light, the recognition of experiential communality as a natural psychological phenomenon seems opposed as well to the philosophical traditions underpinning modern behavioral science. Bakan describes the problem in suggesting that behaviorism inherited a doctrine of epistemological loneliness from Locke, Berkeley, and Hume, in effect:

> . . . a philosophy of individualism in which community had little or no part . . . in which the single individual was supreme.

and he focuses directly on the question raised here:

> Is it possible and in what sense is it possible for one person to "know" another person's experience, if experience is, as a certain traditional outlook would have it, utterly and unalterably private? [Bakan, 1967, p. 111].

In characteristic style, Bakan recommends an alternative assumption, that "after all, we are all pretty much alike." In a major work Bakan (1966) argues for there being a duality of existence in human nature, the first modality of which is "*agency* for the existence of an organism as an individual . . ." and the second, "*communion* for the participation of the individual in some larger organism of which the individual is a part [p. 15; italics added]." He draws the distinction between these elements in this way:

> Agency manifests itself in self-protection, self-assertion, and self-expansion . . ., in isolation, alienation, and aloneness; . . . in the urge to master. . . . Communion manifests itself in the sense of being at one with other

organisms . . . in contact, openness, and union . . . in noncontractual co-operation [p. 15] .

Bakan specifically relates the process of psychotherapy with that function in the therapist that entails communion. He cites Rogers' concept of a helping relationship:

. . . to carry on psychotherapy . . . is to take a very real risk. . . . If you really understand another person . . . if you are willing to enter his private world . . . without any attempt to make evaluative judgments, you run the risk of being changed yourself. . . . If I enter, as fully as I am able, into the private world of a neurotic or psychotic individual, isn't there a risk that I might become lost in that world? [Rogers, 1961, p. 333] .

Such an "entering into" another's world, and the understanding achieved, is accomplished by a union with another and by overcoming the separateness of each to the other.

The healer-role is one which entails understanding. The first meaning [of understanding] . . . entails the separation of the knower from the known, tending to make an object of that which is known. . . . The second meaning . . . is that of *coming into intimate contact with* [the other]. . . . The first sense of the word . . . is related to splitting. . . . In the healing relationship there is a suspension of judgment, the characteristic of the ego which decides what it will entertain and what it will not. . . . [*In*] *the healing relationship the separation between the two people is overcome as the paradigm of the overcoming of all other separations* [Bakan, 1966, pp. 99–101; italics added] .

Such an understanding comes close to what is known, stereotypically, as "woman's intuition" as Helene Deutsch (1944) has characterized it ("men's intuition" can't be far behind) :

Woman's . . . intuition is the result of an unconscious process through which the subjective experience of another person is made one's own by association . . . [in which] the other person's mental state is emotionally and unconsciously "reexperienced," that is, felt as one's own [p. 136] .

Experiential communality would seem to be a specific enactment of Bakan's fundamental mode of human existence, and a general instrumentality whereby contact and union and understanding take place. Through the communion aspect of therapeutic relationships the separateness of the individual and his prepossessive "agentic" feature become mitigated.

Bronowski (1966), a philosopher–mathematician, comes close to this position in his summary statement of the mind's "logic:"

> Each man has a self, and enlarges his self by his experiences. That is, he learns from experience; from the experience of others as well as his own; from their inner experiences as well as their outer. But he can learn from their inner experience only by entering it. *We must have the gift to identify ourselves with other men, to relive their experience and to feel its conflicts as our own . . . in order that we shall feel in their lives what we know in our own; the human dilemma* [p. 12; italics added].

One can choose to believe that another's subjective experience can never be *exactly* the same as one's own; it can equally well be argued that one's experience is never entirely different from someone else's. The first position leads easily to a preoccupation with individual differences, and the second to a concern with collective similarities. Debate between these positions seems more a matter of epistemological bias than evidence.

The postulation of experiential communality entails the proposition that one can know (and be known by) another through direct contact and co-experience; that this coexperiencing is only conceivable given that there can be some isomorphic identity between the subjective, emotional states of interacting individuals; and, also, that contact and experiential communality are the phenomena underlying much of the basis of group life and group activity, particularly what is called encounter.

Some group members themselves give evidence for these assumptions. After an experience in a successful encounter group—sometimes months after—in answer to questions on the value of their experience, group members have made these statements: [15]

> It has had great value. I've never been close (intimate) to people—not even in family situations. I've always held [people] at arm's length. The group was and in part still is a family—the family of man is what I needed to feel and see . . . [Now] I think I *will* much more.
>
> Interacting with the other members, listening to them, made me aware that my feelings are not that different from everyone else's. That I was not alone in my feelings.
>
> The encounter group has been valuable for me in a number of ways. I feel . . . able to be closer to people and to share our common feelings. I feel very moved by the need I've seen for closeness and support. . . .
>
> Listening to other people's problems and how I felt toward them made me realize the uniformity of human experience . . . I feel that I can now talk about my experiences freely without the fear of shocking the hell out of anyone—without being "forever" rejected.

[15] Data from the T.I.E. Project (Bebout & Gordon, 1972, pp. 109–112).

I'm able now to be more direct with other people, more honest, I'm more in touch with my feelings, I'm better able to "see" myself in relation to others. I understand how very similar all human beings really are in terms of basic needs.

An Example from a Group

The interaction to follow is taken from the sixth meeting (of 10) in an encounter group.[16] In this interaction there are many examples of experiential communality. Mostly, people do not directly comment on its presence; it is evidenced better by tone of voice, gesture, mood, meaningful silence, and similar cues, but throughout this transcription I will try to point to the significant events members are sharing as the group meeting unfolds. In this meeting Jack becomes the center of a group-wide confrontation. The leader began the meeting with the suggestion that members reveal what they had been withholding from each other, if anything. It is Jack's turn:

Jack I've just been going through my mind a couple of thoughts about Nancy and Brian and I thought about some other things . . . About . . . Barry's trip—the time he was attacking both of you . . . And I've been worried that if I come out now and said that, you're obviously going to immediately react . . . put me off, and it shouldn't be that way . . . I don't know which of you to talk to first—I guess Brian. (to Brian) I feel bad about you because you seem—I see you giving almost as a game. I can see you, like you give to people and that's the way of getting something back. Giving to get. And I'm sure that envy enters into it somewhat . . . I don't know if you felt this . . .

Gerry Jack, tell him what you're withholding from him.

Jack I feel—I just, wow, you just work too smooth. You look too relaxed and calm and you've got it all together and you're making sure that everybody likes you. I can relate to that . . . [but] that's something that I resent. I'm really waiting for a reaction.

Brian I think that—I have a problem taking things for myself but I resent your saying that I'm too smooth—that pisses me off. I don't know what I have together . . . I feel I have a lot of

---

[16] The names cited in this and other examples are invented.

	stuff to give. And I feel good about it. It helps me get through a lot of shit.
Jack	Do you feel you could ride on it?
Brian	Not necessarily. I just feel comfortable about some things. About the way I relate to some people. It's like I'm beginning to understand what the hell I'm all about . . .
Jack	Yeah. I mean I—I don't know. I felt your sensitivity at times. I've seen you being really, really sensitive. Wow. It really only happened once that I can remember off hand. That was at the end of the encounter group during the marathon . . .
Leader	What are you saying, Jack?
Jack	What I just said.
Leader	I don't get your meaning.
Nancy	You don't have to take back . . . I thought you were saying now that you were sort of backing off from what you were saying originally.
Jack	I didn't take it back—no, no, I'm saying that that's something that I did see good in him but very often I feel—I feel contemptuous or envious.
Charlotte	Do you mean contemptuous or do you mean envious? Or are you saying that contempt is what is outside and envy is what is inside?
Jack	No, I think they're really both the same. I can feel really mad at him, you know, and then when I think, I think, wow, that must mean that I'm being envious of him (*Charlotte*: O.K.). And that's just not true.
	And then I feel, wow, I feel really mad at Nancy, because I don't know, wow—you come on, you come on really intimidating people. You try to intimidate me and I see you doing that with other people. It really bugs me sometimes because other people do that. For instance when Gerry threw a pillow at Charlotte, you know, you said, "Ah, that must mean he likes her" and that really kind of bugs me— (*Nancy*: What?). I felt that you were manipulating.
Gerry	You know I've said this to you before—when you say things to people you put this incredible trip on other people. It's what you are perceiving, not what other people are doing. There's no way for you to have information what another person is feeling—it's impossible!
Jack	Oh, come on get outa here!

Gerry	And you're putting the most incredible trips . . . (to Nancy) Did you feel that way at all?
Nancy	I haven't the slightest . . .
Gerry	I didn't feel manipulated.
Nancy	I can't even know where to be . . . you know, where to react to that.
Leader	*You* (to Charlotte) feel manipulated by *Nancy*—but not by that.
Gerry	(to Jack) Don't tell me that I felt that way.
Jack	She wasn't putting it on to me at all. I didn't feel manipulated but I reacted to her as manipulating.
Charlotte	But why? What was going on inside of you? I don't understand. We didn't feel manipulated and we were the ones it was done to. Therefore—
Jack	She just kind of put it out to the group, you know, and—
Nancy	I didn't put anything onto the group. I was kidding around with Charlotte is what I was doing. She just got a pillow thrown at her and I thought it was very funny that Gerry had done it and I just wanted to say something kidding and teasing that's all.
Jack	Yeah. Well, I just really took it differently. Not all the time, you know, I've seen good things in you. But, well, I don't know, I just see you as intimidating and manipulating—it just bugs the hell out of me.
Charlotte	I can't follow you anymore.
Jack	God, you do that all the time, why do you do that?
Charlotte	Because I'm getting really frustrated with you.
Jack	Uh-h-h. (mimicking Charlotte) I'm doing something!
Nancy	Yeah, that's right.
Jack	You do that all the time, you know.
Charlotte	I don't do it all the time.
Jack	Well, pretty often.
Charlotte	Jack, you're really pissing me off!
Jack	You're pissing me off too! (pause) We're not getting anywhere. That's what I feel when you do that. Because you've done it before.
Brian	(angrily, to Jack) I don't feel I'm getting anywhere listening to you (*Jack*: O.K.).

                    MOMENTARY SILENCE

Charlotte   (to Jack) I felt what you said to Brian was straight—part of it anyway—and then you were saying what you were feeling and it was coming out straight, you said you resented him because sometimes you felt that he was being too nice or too smooth and that you thought maybe that was envy and that was when . . . but I don't know what you're saying.

Jack   O.K. I feel much more in contact with what I'm saying about Nancy.

Charlotte   But we don't—I don't understand—?

Leader   I heard you when you were talking to Brian and you sounded straight and in contact when you were talking to Brian but something happened when you started talking to Nancy. All I can say is I couldn't get a *hold* of anything—I couldn't get a hold of your voice and the words you were saying, you know, and I got more and more frustrated because it kept going on, and on, and on until I still wasn't hearing anything straight, you know. And I resent when you do that. (*Jack*: O.K., wow.) Because I know you can be straight, Jack, that's the thing.

Jack   No, no, no, I see it as you just in a different enough place that you can't relate to me. I don't think it's either of our—

Leader   I *am* relating to you. I'm telling you you piss me off.

Jack   Yes, *now*, but you're talking about . . .

Leader   And before I was telling you I was frustrated.

Jack   Right.

Leader   That's not *not* relating—that's relating.

Jack   No, no, no—you are not relating to me.

Leader   Oh, fuck off!! (shouting)

Jack   You're not listening.

Leader   That's right I'm not listening! I don't feel like listening to you now! (shouting)

                    SILENCE

If one is accustomed to an orderly logical process in individual therapy, the above interaction may seem like bedlam or the blind leading the blind. Everyone is frustrated and angry with Jack. Nancy is angry at being called manipulative, Brian at being called too slick. The leader and Charlotte are frustrated with Jack's apparently confusing messages, and they respond with irritation. Gerry is riled by Jack's "incredible" projections. Jack gets angry in return. They are all squabbling and "pissed off." The group seems to be getting nowhere.

But where they have gotten to is a state of experiential communality. They are fighting together and angry together and frustrated together. They are in the process of sharing, openly, these emotional experiences and this is the critically important point. Having shared this much, and agreed that they are stuck, the interaction takes on a different note:

Brian   (to Jack) I think you're really sensitive. You feel an incredible amount here. But at the same time when you try to relate to those feelings you speed up. You're really not in contact . . . And I'd like to see you slow down a lot.

Nancy   You know what I'm getting from you, Jack? That I tick you off somehow because this is the third time you've singled me out in this group for some—as reacting to you in some way. I don't think you're in touch exactly with what it is that bugs you about me but you keep laying this trip on me. Now I'm out of touch entirely with what you're talking about and I'm just really angry at you, furious at you. And I wish you'd just stop doing this to me. And I'm *not* intimidating. Right now I'm really furious. If that's intimidating then I'm intimidating, well, too bad!

Jack   Right. Well, I can dig what you're saying right now. You are mad now and I can dig that.

Nancy   You want me to react to you and you keep singling me out so I'll have to react to you.

Jack   (overtalking) Yeah, yeah, maybe I do.

Nancy   You force me to react to you.

Jack   I really—You're being mad now, I can dig that. It's just something—at other times it's not—it's not real—I can't—I just can't relate to you.

Nancy   What the hell are you talking about? I don't know what you're talking about!

Jack   I'm talking about when you're manipulating or when you're trying—

Nancy   I'm not manipulating. I refuse to accept that.

Jack   (overtalking) Not now.

Leader   What's happening now?

Jack   Now, I just said she's being mad and I'm enjoying that.

Gerry   You're enjoying it? (pause)

Nancy   That's lovely! (disgusted)
           GROUP BREAKS INTO HELPLESS LAUGHTER

Nancy   I know why I'm laughing: I feel like telling you you're an idiot.
           MORE LAUGHTER

Brian   Remember what Charlotte said at the beginning of the group: that things can get so bad that we can laugh about it—

Jack   Yeah, yeah. (laughs genuinely)

Gloria   (to Jack) A couple of sessions ago or maybe last time, I don't remember, Jack, you said that you wanted to get to know Nancy better. That you'd like to get behind her. That she was a deep person. Do you single her out because she isn't letting you get to know her better? *I* think you single her out because she doesn't let you get closer.

Jack   I don't know. It doesn't strike me off hand as being—although, yeah, I did, a couple of different times, you know. Um, I don't know, I just get really angry, you know, really angry when people put pressure on me, and that's what I feel.

. . . .

Nancy   What I want to say is that I think that for a lot of the time, particularly when I've had positive things to say to you, I usually do ignore you. And it feels good to me to get pissed off at you like I did just now. *Because I feel I'm being much more straight with you and I can move on,* you know.

Jack   Yeah. Because you really—you really seem to have a lot in you that really resents when I come out, or when I get attention, you know. And I just, wow, you know, so it's really—it's really great.

Mark   (to Jack) I just felt like, last week I thought you were beautiful. I was in a high mood myself. I look at you as a surrealistic manifestation.
           GROUP BREAKS UP IN LAUGHTER
           Yeah, I'm really cookin'—you know, I think we have an underlying rapport between us. I say those things to you, and you'll smile.
           EVERYONE LAUGHS MORE, INCLUDING JACK

Leader   I think you do amazing things for this group (to Jack). I really like having you here. I feel that what's happened is that the air is cleared somehow. There's a new atmosphere in here. I don't know how everyone else feels . . .

The focus centers on Jack and Nancy's relationship or lack of it. At first

Jack's pleasure at Nancy's anger seems a ridiculous incongruity and the tension in the group is broken by hilarious laughter. But why should this break the tension? I think it is precisely because it is when Jack and Nancy are seemingly most incongruous, showing the least experiential communality, that they are most in contact with each other—in Nancy's words, "being much more straight." Another member believes that Nancy withholds herself from Jack; from Jack's point of view it is her resentment of him "getting attention" that has been hidden, and Nancy seems to acknowledge this. In effect, they have agreed they are "enemies" and can now move on. Even hostile feelings can be shared in experiential communality; in fact it is crucial to a group's progress that negative *interpersonal* feelings be expressed and coexperienced when they are present. As so often happens, when hostility is shared it is reduced.

Jack, the cause of so much frustration, now comes in for some sideways support from Gerry, Mark, and the leader (who recognizes that "the air is cleared somehow"). The group takes a still more positive turn:

Ned	Jack, I'd like to know what you want from *me*. (to the group) Jack called me last night. We talked for about 20 minutes on the phone and he asked if he could come by some time and I said, "Well, what are you doing right now, why don't you come up?" And he came up immediately . . . and we talked for, what, a couple of hours?
Jack	Yeah, it was about 11 or so.
Ned	I could really talk to you when you were dealing with things that seemed very close to you. He talked a lot about rock climbing . . . and he gave me a lot of his feelings about that. And, you know, I really felt close to you then . . .
Jack	Well, about what you say, when I was talking about school and philosophy and everything; I was searching, looking around, struggling and everything. When I was doing the rock climbing thing it was—wow—really loose, you know . . . It felt good to relate to you.
Ned	That's when I got your real feelings. When you were talking about rock climbing and when you were talking about skiing. And not anything else. (*Jack*: Yeah.)
	But I'd like to know why you called me. You know, what you want from me.
Jack	Well, I guess I see a friend in you, so, uh . . .
Ned	I feel awkward and I feel a little bit pressured by that. But I feel I want to be patient with you.

Jack	I've been looking around for a friend. And I thought about calling various other people and then, and then, I just flashed on you—like that.
Ned	*But you just said something that I wanted everybody to hear: that you're looking around for a friend.* I really feel that . . . (pause)
	THE GROUP SEEMS TO "HEAR" THIS. THERE IS A SHORT SILENCE.
Jack	I was thinking of calling Charlotte.
	THE GROUP BREAKS UP LAUGHING BECAUSE THEY HAD JUST GOTTEN THROUGH FIGHTING AND BECAUSE OF THE CONTRAST BETWEEN THEM.
Ned	Women!
Charlotte	I'm surprised. (more laughter) I didn't mean that as an insult. I mean I'm really surprised. I'm feeling better so I'm getting cocky! (Earlier Charlotte was very depressed.) Tell me why you were going to call *me*.
Jack	I wanted to talk to you about your relationship with your husband.
	GROUP COLLAPSES IN LAUGHTER.
Charlotte	Were you planning on getting married?
Jack	No! No way!
	GROUP HAS ANOTHER FIT.
Charlotte	I've never seen you get a genuine little-boy look on your face, like when you said that. I really enjoyed that. I really got a glimpse of Jack. Well, I'd *like* to talk to you about that sometime. (more laughter)
Jack	That's good.
Brian	It feels really good to laugh. I feel like farting around and I don't feel like giving anything to anybody. Not a fucking thing to anybody and I really want to not be myself!
	GROUPS BREAKS UP AGAIN.
Leader	Good!
	LAUGHTER
Jack	You're doing a good job of it.
	MORE HELPLESS LAUGHTER.
Brian	Fuck off!
	MORE LAUGHTER

Jack's own frustration with the members of the group is put in the context of "looking for a friend." His reaction to Nancy's rejection becomes more meaningful in this light. His need is answered here by Charlotte's invitation and later by Ned and others in the group. Everyone heard Jack, and experienced contact with him. This was an immense relief to them and their reaction—in the bunglingly beautiful way of encounter groups—was hysterical laughter, shared in even by Jack. The affective-meaning events that are shared in these group episodes are frustration and anger, confusion and hostility, tension and relief, loneliness and the need for a friend, distance and closeness, understanding, silliness, abandon, and compassion; and the very process of working from the "bottom" of negative relationships to the "top" of joyful ones. These emotional states obviously contain personal meanings for the participants; they spontaneously unfold from the concerns the members have at present and they are equivalent states for most members of the group. Such interactions cannot be characterized through the usual conceptions of empathic response; this problem will be discussed next.

SOME REDEFINITION: EMPATHIC PROCESSES AND EXPERIENTIAL COMMUNALITY

It is to Rogers' permanent credit that he stressed empathic understanding as a fundamental therapeutic principle in the relationship between therapist and client. As Rogers defined empathy it has the same meaning as the dictionary definition of "vicariousness:"

taking the place of another person; endured, suffered or performed in the place of another; or enjoyed or experienced . . . through . . . imagined participation in another's experience. [*Webster's*, 1959, p. 1164].

A more textured and lifelike description is provided by Rogers in quoting Raskin:

. . . counselor participation becomes an active experiencing with the client of the feelings to which he gives expression, the counselor makes a maximum effort to get under the skin of the person with whom he is communicating, he tries to get within and to live the attitudes expressed instead of observing them . . . in a word, to absorb himself completely in the attitudes of the other . . . *Because he is another, and not the client, the understanding is not spontaneous but must be acquired, and this through the most intense, continuous and active attention to the feelings of the other* . . . [Rogers, 1951, p. 29; italics added].

One of the best and most frequently cited illustrations of this vicarious empathic interaction between therapist and client is Rogers' own:

Client   And then, of course, I've come . . . to see and to feel that over this, see, I've covered it up with so much bitterness, which in turn I had to cover up. (weeps) That's what I want to get rid of! I almost don't care if I hurt.

Therapist   (gently) You feel that here at the base of it, as you experience it, is a feeling of real tears for yourself. But that you can't show, mustn't show, so that's been covered by bitterness that you don't like, that you'd like to be rid of. You almost feel you'd rather absorb the hurt . . . than to feel the bitterness. (pause) And what you seem to be saying quite strongly is "I do hurt and I've tried to cover it up."

Client   I didn't know it.

Therapist   M-hm. Like a new discovery really.

Client   (speaking at the same time) I never really did know, it's almost a physical thing. It's . . . it's sort of as though I—I—I were looking within myself at all kinds of nerve endings and —and bits of, of . . . things that have been sort of mashed. (weepy)

Therapist   As though some of the most delicate aspects of you—physically almost—have been crushed or hurt.

Client   Yes, and you know, I do get the feeling, "oh, the poor thing." (pause).

Therapist   Just can't but feel very deeply sorry for the person that is you. [Rogers & Dymond, 1954, pp. 326–327].[17]

Empathy is important in the operation of encounter groups, not, as it has been pictured, as an end in itself. But it is important because this basic psychological process is a precursor to, and a facilitator of, experiential communality. Empathic processes lead one to a position where coexperience is more likely to happen, if it's going to happen at all. It is a predispositional factor. In this light I want to review the client-centered concept of empathy and show its distinctiveness from experiential communality and also its application in groups.

Vicarious Empathy

This form of empathic response is the one just cited above in reference to Raskin's statement and Rogers' interaction. Vicarious empathy has been and is still a "primary process" in client-centered therapy. This form of empathy comes closest to experiential communality. It is also most similar to standard definitions of empathy.[18]

There are several features in this traditional use of a concept of empathy that highly resemble experiential communality. Any concept of empathy contains the assumption that some constituents of people's experience are similar. Empathic interaction is usually thought to generate closeness between people, that is, greater contact. The phenomenon is conscious, even at times deliberate. Yet, there are important differences between experiential communality and empathy.

Most definitions of empathy are careful to note an indirect quality in the empathizer's emotional experience. This indirectness stems from several sources:

1. An empathic response is usually conceived as *unidirectional*; that is, *by* one person *for* another. Coempathic states where feelings are shared mutually are not considered. Presumably, the person empathized with is appreciative, but there is no necessity, or even probability, of two-way coexperience.

2. Empathy is viewed as *reactive* rather than proactive; this specifies a sequential, rather than simultaneous, process of affective interaction. As Stotland, Sherman, and Shaver (1971) point out, the empathizer's emotional state is an outcome of his perception of another. In the example from the Ik culture there is an emotional coexperience because both or all of those collected together are starving—their hunger is in no way reactive.

3. In empathy there is proximity of internal feeling–meaning states. This proximity is not supposed to be identicality or functional equivalence (Coleman, 1969; Rogers, 1951). Rather, most authors indicate that the empathizer responds with what I would call *harmonic* states of feeling. By harmonic feeling I mean a lesser affective state, which is sympathetic to,

---

[18] One's "Perception of [another's] 'inner' aspect is called *empathy*. In a broad sense empathy involves sufficient understanding of his feelings, attitudes, motives, and general frame of reference to see a situation from his point of view and *enter into* his feelings about it . . . In an intimate relationship . . . empathy means that we are aware of and *to some extent* share in the desires, hopes, expectations, and worries of the other person. . . . [Coleman, 1969, pp. 422–423; italics added]."

"Empathy: Understanding another person by putting oneself in that person's shoes and sharing his thoughts and feelings [Kagan & Havemann, 1972, p. 589]."

"In empathy an individual projects his feelings and emotions into the object of his experience [Bonner, 1953, p. 87]."

". . . empathy is defined as an observer's reacting emotionally because he perceives that another is experiencing or is about to experience an emotion. . . . In empathy . . . the individual perceives the other's emotional state first; his own reaction, both subjectively and physiologically, is an outcome of his perception of the other person [Stotland, Sherman, & Shaver, 1971, pp. 2–8]."

and allied with, a more primary affective state, such as pleasure with joy, surprise with shock, irritation with rage, distaste with disgust, and so forth.

4. Similarly, there is *differential initiation* in the typically empathic therapy interaction. Initiation of the to-be-experienced emotion comes from another (the client), not oneself. In experiential communality, the affective coexperience is mutually sought after and joined in.

5. Most definitions of empathy suggest an *imaginal* transposing or projection of one's feelings over onto the other person or object (Bonner, 1953), or a putting of oneself into another's shoes (Kagan & Havemann, 1972). In experiential communality and direct contact, the participants are already in each other's shoes and no imagination or irreality is required. Notions of projection, of course, always evoke the possibility that the material projected is alien to the object projected upon. Would it be possible for me to project my feelings onto you when in fact they are identical?

6. As Raskin so clearly points out, the practice of empathically responding in a deliberately therapeutic situation is *effortful*, requiring the "most intense, continuous and active attention." Some forms of empathy just happen but for the most part *intentionality* plays a crucial role in achieving an empathic understanding. This intentionality of itself attenuates contact. In experiential communality a coexperiencing of internal feeling–meaning states occurs unpredictably, without intention, without premeditation, and usually without the aid of structured relationships (Goodman, 1973). Experiential communality is more immediate, unorganized, uncontrolled, and spontaneous.

In the general model of empathy, a therapist is supposed to have a set of his own, "real" feelings, and distinct from these, a set of "as if" feelings that take their cue and character from another (the client). In the early history of client-centered therapy, strict adherence to this model led many therapists to be viewed by their clients as "surrealistic manifestations," to use Brian's earlier phrase, because they felt so well understood by someone whom they understood not at all (Bebout, 1961). In tracing some of the developmental history of Rogerian therapy earlier, it was pointed out that the use of empathic response has expanded broadly to include more two-way interaction between therapist and client in the form of encounter. In group interactions, some of this more spontaneous quality of interaction actually derives from another form of empathy altogether.

Physiognomic Empathy

Familiar to many people are psychology textbook photographs showing spectators at a pole-vaulting event lift and strain along with the movement of an athlete who is striving to clear the crossbar. There is a frequent impulse, when perceiving some danger as a passenger in a car, to press one's foot against the floorboard as if applying the brakes; this, even though there is clear intellectual knowledge that pushing on a floorboard will not stop a car. The rider is acting "as if" he were the driver applying the brakes. Many simple physical responses are "catching;" for instance yawns, scratching (itching), laughing, postural mimicry, stomach noises, coughing. Some obvious features of these physical responses are their automatic, compelling, spontaneous, and usually semiunconscious nature. This "body language" communication, when interpersonal, is representative of physiognomic empathy.

Heinz Werner (1957) and Kurt Goldstein (1939) further suggest a process of physiognomic perception—the infusion of emotional and expressive qualities in the act of perception—as an integral and developmentally primary property of psychological organization (see also Arnheim, 1949). Thus, lights "dance," stars "twinkle," and the color red is "angry." If this is apparent in perception of the object-world, it should be an even more dynamic influence in perception of the Mitwelt—the people-world. George Klein (1970) states:

> . . . perhaps a gift for physiognomic organization is implied in behavior usually described as "empathic" . . . the coloring of percepts by subtle affects may be a precondition of "empathic experience" . . . to be able to perceive physiognomically is probably essential to rich and responsive communication between people . . . its complete *loss* may be accompanied by narrowing or dulling of emotional responsiveness of the sort . . . frequently observed in the brain-injured [pp. 152–154].

One of the more striking examples of physiognomic empathy leading to experiential communality is found in the desire in sex partners to achieve simultaneous orgasm. For many people this requires a sensitive synchronization of physical movement, realized mostly through physiognomic empathy rather than verbal instruction. An orgasm is an orgasm and intensely pleasurable for nearly everyone—why this craving for unison in the experience? I think it is precisely because a coexperienced pleasure is more fulfilling, more pleasurable. This sexual interaction provides a model for the relationship between empathy and coexperience in that it is necessary for some degree of physiognomic empathy to be present in order to realize experiential communality.

Dancers get to know each others' bodies in a kinesthetic, physiognomic sense and reveal this knowledge in the harmony of their performance; aerial acrobats and ballet duos rely upon an intuitive matching of body movements impossible to achieve via purely cognitive perception and analysis. Musicians refer to "swinging" together. A physiognomic sense of rhythm and meter is required. When musicians' sense of the beat seems in perfect synchrony and their creative–affective moods are matched, they "swing" ("groove," "rock"). In these examples, the rarefied "as if" criteria in traditional definitions of empathy is inappropriate.

Getting "in touch with" someone (Gunther, 1968) by physical–sensual communication can be a deep and meaningful contact with people.[19] Rogers (1970) cites the reaction of a woman in one of his groups:

> . . . the real turning point for me was a simple gesture on your part of putting your arm around my shoulder one afternoon when I had made some crack about you not being a member of the group—that no one could cry on your shoulder . . . I *received* the gesture as one of the first feelings of acceptance—of me, just the dumb way I am . . . I have (never) felt just plain *loved*. I actually felt *loved*. I doubt that I shall soon forget it [p. 34].

Only to the extent that the language of another's body (body English) is similar to one's own is this kind of communication possible. Again, like Mead's *significant symbol*, the meaning of another's gesture is accurately recognized only to the extent that that gesture has a similar or identical meaning in terms of one's own body. R. D. Laing, Phillipson, and Lee (1966) point to the jungle of misinterpretation possible when one person mistakenly infers another's intention-reading nonverbal signals:

Peter	*Paul*
1. I am upset.	1. Peter is upset.
2. Paul is acting very calm and dispassionate.	2. I'll try to help him by remaining calm and just listening.
3. If Paul cared aboue me and wanted to help, he would get involved and show some emotion also.	3. He is getting even more upset. I must be even more calm.
4. Paul knows that this upsets me.	4. He is accusing me of hurting him.
5. If Paul knows that his behavior upsets me, he must be intending to hurt me.	5. I'm really trying to help.
6. He must be cruel, sadistic. Maybe he gets pleasure out of it, etc.	6. He must be projecting [Laing, et al., 1966, pp. 21–22].[20]

[19] I am lumping together processes of input and output under the term physiognomic empathy—motoric identification may be distinct from perceptual "coloration" of stimuli, but it is peculiar to this concept that percept and impulse become fused into one gestalt.

[20] Copyright © 1966 by R. D. Laing, H. Phillipson, & A. R. Lee. Reprinted by permission of Springer Publishing Co.

Eugene Gendlin (1970) points to the necessity for conscious reference to a therapist's or client's *bodily* felt sensation in his theory of experiential focusing:

> . . . even when people are speaking quite articulately, we want to respond not to the words we hear and know, but to the felt experiencing, the felt referent, the mass of inner momentary felt meaning [p. 285].

This mass of inner momentary felt meaning cannot be directly perceived, but its perception can be built up from a number of empathic responses. Central among these responses is physiognomic empathy.

One does not observe the "tight ass" of a person who is felt to be holding back his emotional life and himself. But one can see a tight mouth, narrowed eyes, and stiffness in the walk, or hear constriction in the voice and parsimony in the words (and most people feel "uptight" in response) (Lowen, 1967). The data of body tension (flaccidity, tiredness, restraint) may often be subceived as elements of what Rogers terms organismic experience, not often readily available to awareness.

In a Rogerian approach to encounter groups, communication with and about body English can be a valuable aid to understanding and sharing another's total felt experience. Other approaches to intensive small groups (for example, psychosynthesis, bioenergetics, some applications of Gestalt therapy) use such material as grist for the interpretive mill—explaining the other person to himself. This is a critical difference in practice. It is a radically different human transaction to use physiognomic empathy to become closer to or encounter someone than it is to use it for directing, molding, or diagnosing another's psychic life from a professional distance.[21]

Below is an example of a group interaction which begins with much conflict of interpretation between Wendy and Yoli. To help get around their impasse the leader introduces a nonverbal exercise that requires the two of them silently approaching each other from opposite corners of the room while looking directly at each other and paying special attention to how their own and the other's body feels. When they are as near as they wish to be, they act out physically what they want to do with each other's body.

Leader   The reason I think it was unresolved at that time is because there is a third party you are leaving out of the discussion.

Wendy   You mean because we are competitive about Rob.

---

[21] It should be apparent that physiognomic empathy or communality need not correlate with Graduate Record Exam scores, I.Q., or grades. It is likely that the selective bias in graduate schools for intellectuality works toward recruiting professionals who are much out of tune with their bodies. Future therapists and group leaders might practice sensitivity to their own and other people's physical presence to learn physiognomic response as a mode of empathy.

Leader   Right, and Rob was not there at that time.

Wendy   Yeah, but that is a different fantasy that you and Hal wanted—you wanted us to fight it out over him.

Yoli   (overtalking) That is true!

Bill   OOOOH!! That is *your* fantasy (lots of overtalking) . . .

Wendy   I feel that it is delightful to be turned on to Bruce; it is delightful to have him turn on to me, but it is clear in my mind that it is a flirtation and that is all it is and that doesn't change the fact that I am jealous of other women when men I am attracted to are turned on to them . . . I was jealous of Hal paying attention to you. I am that kind of woman; I react that way . . . I am a very sexual, very volatile person, and I just react on that gut level most of the time. One of the reasons I feel uptight with you is that you don't react that way and you make me feel I am with my mother. You are too nice, you know. My groin is there and I know it . . . You see we are in two different places entirely—but there are things about you that I dig very much, but you know I am not comfortable being with you.

Yoli   I don't feel jealous with you—I don't and I feel—

Wendy   I am saying—you don't like my feeling jealous about you, right?

Yoli   Because that makes me uncomfortable, I don't know what for, personally I feel like, does that mean that I am having something that you don't have. That is not true. I just don't get that clearly because I feel my relationship with Hal, my relationship with Rob—it is sort of a package in itself . . .

Leader   (To Wendy and Yoli) Are you ready to deal with it now? Are we going to talk about what happened last week at the restaurant?

Bill   (to anyone) I think it is a way of avoiding the issue.

Wendy   (to Yoli) You feel something toward me that—it's not clear to me what you feel—and I would like to know what you feel and what you would like from me in order to feel more comfortable.

Yoli   As clear as I can say—often I felt some jealousy feeling and I couldn't say whether it was jealousy or not and, with that was resentment feeling and—I just wondered if it was my trip or not, and I was really trying to check.

Wendy   I thought I had expressed openly that I felt jealous of you and felt competitive toward you and envied you at certain times—I didn't feel that I hid that at all.

Yoli	(overtalking) It didn't get at all dealt with—O.K., you might have let it out, you know.
Wendy	Well, I couldn't do any more than say it, I mean I don't want you to change, I love the way you are. I wish I was more like that—that is all I can say . . .
Yoli	(overtalking) Yeah, but you said then, yes it was an unresolved thing.
Wendy	What?
Yoli	At the restaurant—it was an unresolved thing.
Wendy	No, no, no, I meant our discussion that night was unresolved, not this feeling. No, that is not what I am saying.
Wendy	I think part of the problem is, Yoli, that I have never felt close to you—I have never felt that you shared with me the way you shared with other people in the group, and I feel that it was not because I was competitive with you for other men . . . I felt very early in the group that you were holding back and that somehow you would never sit next to me, you would never initiate conversations with me. Often, I would be talking with you and I would feel you were drifting off to other people. I felt you holding back from me, too, and that hurt . . .
Yoli	I felt that it seemed the other way, because I wanted to talk to you but it was like I always had to initiate it which really made me feel, wow, I always had to go to you—
Wendy	No, I felt really rebuffed when I did go to you . . .
Leader	I think it is time for something nonverbal—I really do . . . (group overtalking—tense laughter) I guess what I would like to see is you two starting at opposite ends of the room and walking together, and see what we get . . .
Wendy	Do you want to do that (to Yoli)?
Yoli	O.K. (They carry out exercise, slowly coming together. When face to face, they impulsively hug each other. Yoli begins crying quietly.)
Yoli	(crying) I am sorry if I did that—I am.
Wendy	(also tearful) I love you—you are beautiful. (short silence between them and in the whole group while they hold each other) And, I would like you to sit by me—O.K.? (They sit down together—Yoli still sobbing softly.)
	(The whole group is silent "together.")

Yoli and Wendy sense the more positive feelings behind their words by a nonverbal appreciation of each other's physical attitudes—thus the willingness to embrace and become closer is perceived through a physiognomic empathy and successfully acted upon; their verbal interaction was leading only to further knots.

There is still another form of empathy useful in groups but separable from vicarious and physiognomic empathy. I call this *cognitive empathy*.

Cognitive Empathy

The prototype of physiognomic empathy is the gut reaction one has when watching, say, a surgical amputation. The response is usually strong, physical, immediate, and preemptory. Cognitive empathy, on the other hand, encompasses the empathizer's feelings only at the peripheral level of fascination, challenge, curiosity, or puzzlement. It is the most consciously intentional. It involves data-processing and is, therefore, mediate (and therefore tenuous contact by previous definition). Cognitive empathy refers to the ability to arrive at integrative understandings of another's perceptual field by a predominantly cognitive assimilation of the other's values, meanings, symbols, stated or implied intentions, and ideation. When successful, the empathizer knows the organization of another's world or self-view. In this case a therapist or group leader needs to give his or her mind over to the data presented in the manner of a high-speed computing machine.

Perhaps cognition seems clear in this sense, but how should one empathize cognitively? What connection is there between the rather emotional activity called empathy and the intellectual assimilation of ideas, organization, and so on? Normally, we make a consistent division between these two activities:

> If [a] group is assembled for an intellectual task, feelings are denied, though they are often painfully evident. If the group is assembled for personal encounter, ideas are often strongly rejected as having no place in such a group . . . We still tend to dichotomize these two aspects. I have observed this so strongly in groups . . . It seems that we live on an either/or basis. We are aware of and express, our emotional reactions. Almost never are the two sides of our life brought together [Rogers, 1973, p. 384].

In fact, the connection between idea and affect, cognition and emotion is intimate. Harris (1962) points out:

> The immediate objects of consciousness are not material things but feelings. Different philosophers [Spinoza, Hegel, Collingwood, the

empiricists] recognize this in different ways, but there is a large measure of agreement between them . . . It may further prove to be the case . . . that the activity involved in cognition is a sharpened and heightened degree of an isomorphic activity occurring at a lower level which is also involved in feeling. Becoming aware of the feeling may be no more than feeling it more acutely (not necessarily more intensely, but with greater precision and in more significant relation to other experiences) [pp. 484–485].

Piaget concludes, with Escalona, that, with regard to cognitive and affective aspects of behavior:

. . . while these two aspects cannot be reduced to a single aspect, they are nevertheless inseparable and complementary. For this reason we must not be surprised to find a marked parallelism in their respective evolutions . . . [Piaget & Inhelder, 1969, p. 21].

And,

My data suggest the possibility that what Piaget proposes for cognition is true for all adaptive aspects of mental functioning; namely, that the emergence of such functions as communication, modulation of affect, control over excitation, delay, and aspects of object relation, and identification, are all a result of a developmental sequence in sensori-motor terms, before they can emerge as ego-functions in the narrower sense [Escalona, quoted in Piaget & Inhelder, 1969, p. 25].

In encounter groups and in psychotherapy, the data presented are not usually simple. Most frequently the stuff of communication in groups and therapy involves feelings about feelings, values about feelings, feelings about thoughts about values about feelings, and so on. Thus, one individual may refer to his or her frustration with anger that leads to a sense of inadequacy in dealing with goals A or B in situations X, Y, or Z. These networks of motives, values, percepts, affects— in sum, *personal meanings*—may be difficult to grasp and still more difficult to communicate.

It is in this concept of personally experienced meanings that cognition and emotion have their most direct synthesis. This has been referred to as connotative meaning by Osgood (1957) and experiential meaning by Gendlin. Gendlin (1970) says:

I call this reliance on experiential as well as conceptual steps the "experiential use" of concepts . . . Steps of experiential differentiation intervene between one concept or set of words and the next . . . An experiential use of concepts still requires that concepts retain their logical precision and meaning . . . It is an error to drop . . . language, definition, and logical precision . . . Concepts and intellectual differentiations play a vital role both in psychotherapy and in civilized man generally . . . Thus the process of felt experiential steps is involved not only in our own experiential use of concepts, but also in the client's change process in therapy. This process of felt steps helps to explain the value of the personal relationship in psychotherapy [pp. 78–79].[22]

Within the encounter movement, group approaches can be divided according to the emphasis given the exploration and integration of personal meanings and the "referral systems" offered within which one is to understand his experience. In a large, naturalistic investigation, Bebout (1973) found that *meaning exploration* accounts for an estimated 40% of all group activity. Lieberman, Yalom, and Miles' (1973) study of various encounter group technologies indicates that meaning attribution, or the inclusion of cognitive understanding in group interactions, was one of the factors most highly associated with benefit.

Skill is required in understanding the complex organization of someone else's life; skill is also needed to communicate this kind of understanding of personal meaning. In small groups, the leaders' awareness must also be heightened by a factor equal to the number of people there are in the group, and the time available for any one person is limited by that factor. If it takes forever for a client or a group member to be understood or to explain what he is saying, much time is wasted and unnecessary frustration gained.

Cultural anthropologists come to specialize in cognitive empathy. In field work they are specifically required to immerse themselves in another culture's language and belief system, norms and values, to the point of being able to think in that culture's terms. It is acknowledged that a broad system-level comprehension and flexible thinking-orientation, as well as emotional availability, is prerequisite. The process is no less empathic because it is also highly rational. Castaneda (1972) reports his initial failure to comprehend the Yaqui Indian "way of knowledge." At the height of his exposure to the "teachings of Don Juan," he felt as though he was losing his "mind."

But it is precisely this losing or at least, loosening, of one's mind that is necessary in cognitive empathy, in the sense that an anthropologist (or therapist) temporarily relinquishes his conceptual organizations of his personal-meaning-world and assumes the meaning world of another or others. The experientially based conceptual organization of personal meaning is one's reality; through cognitive empathy one adopts a different reality. No easy trick.

What usually impede this process are the imposition of one's own values onto another's experience, prior investment in a theoretical (rather than empathic) understanding of another, the threat value of being wrong or having to change one's mind, the lack of appreciation (through inexperience) of the experience underpinning another's concepts, and similar factors. In effect, a group leader (and many in his group) must be open to experience at both a cognitive and emotional level in order to achieve cognitive empathy, implying a capacity to open one's mind to entirely different values, percepts, constructs. It is possible in animals, as Polanyi (1958) points out in his concept of *conviviality*:

> A true transmission of knowledge . . . takes place when [a chimpanzee] shares in the intelligent effort which another animal is making in its presence . . . chimpanzees watching a fellow animal's attempt to perform a difficult feat [reveal] by their gestures that they participate in another's efforts. Such interpersonal transmission seems at work whenever animals learn something by example, which they obviously do when a trick invented by a more intelligent chimpanzee is immediately taken up by another. Kohler . . . convincingly asserts that it is no blind parrotlike imitation, but . . . a real communication of knowledge on the inarticulate level [p. 206].

In the computer analogy, if there need be a program in the group leader's or therapist's head, it should accommodate as many options and branches, as free and as wide a range of possibility as can be imagined, in order to arrive at a correct estimation of another's phenomenal world. Of this kind of machine, Bronowski (1966) suggests:

> The brain as a machine is certainly not the kind of machine that we understand now. It is not a logical machine, because no logical machine can reach out of the difficulties and paradoxes created by self-reference. [Its logic] differs from formal logic in its ability to overcome and, indeed, to exploit the ambivalences of self-reference, so that they become the instrument of imagination . . . I am asserting, so that there is a mode of knowledge which cannot be spelled out formally to direct a machine . . . a machine is not a natural object; it is a human artifact which mimics and exploits our own understanding of nature . . . we cannot now conceive of any kind of law or machine which could formalize the total modes of human knowledge [p. 9].[23]

[23] Reprinted by permission of *American Scientist*.

One reflexive and imaginative mode of interpersonal "knowledge" is attainable through cognitive empathy; and although this cannot be formulated mechanistically, neither can it be completely divorced from present theories of cognition (see Jessor & Feshbach, 1967).

GROUP INCONGRUENCE OR DECEIT

The process of therapy has been described as the effort to "become the self that one truly is." Rogers' concept of congruence applies equally well to the *process of movement* in encounter groups, although here it is the whole group that must "be itself." Therapist or leader incongruence acts as a suppressor variable. As originally conceived, congruence implied that awareness, behavior, and experience were matched or balanced for one person in the context of a relationship. This principle can be expanded to apply to small groups: When the behavior, awareness, and experiencing of people in a group are coordinate or matched with each other, the group is in a state of interpersonal or relational congruence. This factor obviously influences the degree of experiential communality that is possible.

The most important form of relational congruence can be described simply as honesty; the most popular brand of group or relational incongruence derives from group self-deceit (Shlien, 1961). Honesty entails openness, candor, and risk-taking; relational incongruence involves keeping secrets, deviousness, role playing, game playing, or simply lying. Other kinds of relationship incongruence exist—differing expectations or preferred modes of interaction, incompatable styles, and the like—but these are not considered here.

There is power in numbers and there are numbers in groups. The power of collective sanctions can work toward intensifying and massively affirming a particular "truth" about a given individual or the group itself, or this force can be used to intensify and institutionalize a "lie."[24] Group congruence becomes a precondition for the occurrence of experiential communality and most empathies; group self-deceit becomes a limiting factor. In a group one is open to attack from many sides; there is no initial guarantee that other members are there to be empathic, supportive, and insightful confidants. In a group context it becomes more difficult to realize that vulnerable, groping process of self-search and truth-seeking that is characteristic of and nurtured in good one-to-one therapy relationships.

---

[24] A not so shiny contemporary example is the administrative "team" involved in the Watergate scandal.

Therefore, some form of deceit is much more likely to be present throughout the early stages of developing encounter groups. In fact, the history of a successful encounter group can be seen in terms of an unfolding cyclical process of gradually relinquished interpersonal facades and deceptions (what Rogers has called *becoming unmasked*) (Rogers, 1970). Each step in this unveiling process, if successful, is accompanied by a deeper trust in and attachment to the group. With little exception, groups that fail do so because of an inability to expose and undo a significant group self-deceit; the most difficult group disclosure is avoided and this leads to other diversionary tactics that build to a point of complete impasse.

Below is an example of the emergence of a group lie in the first hour of the first meeting. The group self-deceit is initiated by the leader and stems from her extreme insecurity in her role. In the simplest language, the group deceit that the leader would enforce is: My motives are pure and therapeutic; I will use my considerable authority and expertise to good purpose in helping you find the way. What is hidden is the feeling: I want power and control over you.

I have used the language of *double-bind* theory (Bateson, Jackson, Haley, & Weakland, 1956) to interpret the messages in this group interaction. In much simplified form, a double-bind exists when double-message statements by significant others are repeatedly given an individual in a condition of need. A double-bind is, then, a form of incongruent deceit. The conflicting messages are usually communicated through different channels, for example, positive-approach statements in one's words simultaneous with negative-withdrawal messages implied by one's gestures. Such messages are labeled *injunctions* because they are implicit commands potentially reinforced by emotional approval or disapproval even though they are contradictory. Accompanying these "push–pull" communications is an implied suppression injunction that forbids disclosure or reference to the primary injunctions. Here is what happens:

First injunction: I am the business manager.   The group slowly collects together in the meeting room; people are either silent or having short quiet conversations waiting for everyone to arrive. The leader is propped against one wall, sitting in a Buddha style on several pillows (there are no chairs); she is one of the first in the room. When most members are present, she begins giving administrative details for the conduct of the group, pointing out the presence (in another room) of observers, microphones, tape recorders. *This takes some 25 minutes* during which she talks rapidly in a rather businesslike fashion. She answers questions about research requirements; reading from a printed handout she outlines the rules and policies of the program. At no point during this "instruction" is any member asked if they concur with the rules or conditions. One member wonders how to get to know everyone so the leader suggests an exercise called *dyads* in which people pair off and introduce themselves, reassembling afterward to introduce their partners to the whole group. The leader calls this one thing they could do that is *not very far out.* There is some hesitant questioning by the members and they first exchange names; then at someone's suggestion they begin the exercise. After exactly four minutes, the leader interrupts the partner conversations saying:

Second injunction: Do what I say.

"Would everyone just stop for just a second and close your eyes, stay the way you are sitting, get into the way you are feeling. Think of something that you could say . . . that you are close to, that would be sort of hard for you to say. Get into the way you are holding your body, and think of something that is within your mind . . . that you can say to the person you are talking with that would sorta be risky for you or hard to talk about. Then go on talking and say whatever you find."

Her tone of voice is neutral, hurried, flat, somewhat strained.

After a slight pause the group continues talking but in a more subdued tone. There are some giggles. They talk for two more minutes and then stop. The leader prods: "Is there any couple that would like to start?" Slowly, quietly, one-by-one, members begin a very brief resumé of what each partner said about themselves. These introductions are superficial and externalized, with many references to "credentials" in terms of past groups.

Sharon tries to confront the leader's injunction.

One member, Sharon, who has had some prior group experience, expresses some resistance to the leader and her own ambition to lead groups, but these comments go unexplored. There is a long pause after the last person is introduced; Larry comments to the leader:

Larry tries to confront the leader's injunction.

"You got any other great ideas?" Spoken flatly to the leader.

"Do you?" she responds.

"No," he says.

There is more silence.

The leader turns to another female and in a friendly tone comments about her and asks questions; soon the members begin a more lively but generally shallow discussion of prejudices attached to names—one member thinks his name is unusual. After this light talk, the leader states:

Third injunction: Remember, I'm the leader.

"In this situation my corresponding fear is that I am going to get tight because *I am leading this group.*"

A male comments generally and then, to the group as whole, the leader says:

Fourth injunction: I take liberties.

"There is one rule, if I can take the liberty of writing down one rule ... it's that the group stays on what is called the here-and-now, which means that it is easier to associate with things in the past, things in the future, especially when we are uncomfortable with impasses in here. While we are together, it has got to be here-and-now and what you are feeling now and what you are thinking now. As much as possible stay away from discussions about abstractions ..."

Members then begin a discussion about how they feel about coming to an encounter group and some of their background fears. One member, when questioned by the leader, says she had heard criticisms about encounter groups

in terms of realizing change only for the duration of the group; another is afraid that nothing will happen, a third is anxious to see what
will happen. One woman is uneasy about the
possibility of being put on a "hot seat" as had
happened in another group. While these people
are talking, the leader is writing things on
cards and when asked about this explains that
it has to do with an exercise. The episode ends
in silence.

*Fifth injunction: I know
what's going to happen.*

At this point, the leader states:
"Yeah, there is going to be a lot of silence in
here, I expect."

*Larry again tries
confronting injunctions.*

The leader's neoantagonist, Larry, responds to
this by saying that he was originally relaxed but
became more uncomfortable as the group went
on. He adds that a previous group had been
really great, but this one probably would not
measure up to that experience. Someone states
that his humor is sarcastic; he acknowledges
this and attributes it to his own nervousness.

*First suppression
injunction.*

Leader: "It didn't feel like humor, it felt sorta
like hostile."

Larry: "I really don't think that was in it."

Sharon and another female thought his remarks to the leader were funny and not hostile
and they say so. Others partly recognize the
possible hostility in Larry's comments.

*Second suppression
injunction.*

The *leader continues in slightly hurt under-
tones* to the effect that Larry's jokes *left her no
response*; that *they were passive, maybe an
anxious rejection of her ideas*; that, perhaps
*the exercise didn't work because Steve and
others didn't close their eyes* in the exercise
(he did, some didn't); and that, *consequently,
she felt*, in effect, *mistrusted*. She comments:

*Locks positive and
negative injunctions:
Leader completes the
double-bind with Larry.*

"Your name is Dick?"
"No, Larry."
"Ok, Larry, *would it be good if people spoke
up when you seemed to be making a hostile
or sarcastic remark?*"

Larry: "If somebody feels, you know, threatened or that I am being aggressive, yeah, I would appreciate it because I don't like to put people off that way." (acquiescently)

Attempts same with Sharon: If you, Sharon, are so smart, you would help me—Sharon resists injunctions; Larry has been emasculated by the double-bind.

The leader then turns to Sharon, saying: "I feel like I have something to say to you. I definitely would like help, like, you know, *if you feel, you know, where the situation should go.*"
Sharon: "I think that should be an open problem."
Larry: "But she is trying to talk to you."
Leader: "Yeah, I am trying to talk to you."

Sharon rejects primary injunctions, tries to unlock the double-bind. Implies leader is "out of touch."

The leader goes on in a conciliatory tone stating that she feels Sharon is aggressive, needing a lot of attention, which she will get and feel good about, and that constitutes a challenge to her (the leader) in that Sharon will want to do a lot of things. The leader will try to help (but) has had a lot of experience. . . . Sharon declaims the expertise, commenting that she is involved in antagonisms with the leader of another group that she is in concurrently; that that other group is more in touch with what is going on in the group than the leader, who is a professional, and thinks he knows it all. She doesn't like him at all; but now she realizes, in this group, that the leader doesn't have that position.

The leader, then, seeming to agree, procedes to define her position as an authority in the group in terms of being responsible for keeping an eye on the group as an organism, and in following through, but beyond that it is up to everyone. Following another solicitation for Sharon's opinion by another member, there is some silence and an interlude in which several people change positions.

Other members try to reject the lie.

A male states his wish that the leader would change her position and is joined by two others, commenting that she "looks like a queen," "looks too authoritative" propped up

Fifth injunction.   on her pillows alone against the wall. But the leader says she will stay and retorts that what people are saying is "super indirect" and she wishes that they would come to the point.

This particular group never overcame the level of self-deceit established from the first meeting and, although some member benefit was realized (through interaction with each other), it failed to reach significant experiential communality or depth.

Shlien (1961) and Bakan (1954) (and Sartre before them) have well described the self-denying and defensive consequences of maintaining self-deceit. In order to lie, one must know the truth, but if the truth is impossible to live with, or cope with, it must be denied and the knowledge of lying itself forgotten or suppressed. It is the same in encounter groups. A group originally struggling for the self that it truly is, collectively, can never achieve it when, through fear of the power inherent in the group itself (and/or of the leader), complicity in a lie is maintained. Given half a chance, however, groups will fight hard for authenticity and combat emerging forms of deception. Rogers calls one extreme version of this process the *cracking of facades* (Rogers, 1970).

At each presentation of a form of deceit, the validity of the group is thrown into question in the minds of the members. Each unfolding lie is a test of the integrity of the group, and its failure to meet the challenge thereby defines its limitation—this is as true in groups as it is in an individual's struggle for growth. The themes that most often stall or defeat the progress of a group are problems fundamental to all human relations: sex, power, leadership, responsibility, negative or hostile feelings (particularly seen in race hatreds), and love.

The important point suggested here, though, is that the succession of group self-deceit followed by its exposé, followed by another deceit and its exposé, and so on, is a basic mechanism underlying the dynamic process of encounter groups, and this spiraling process leads to ever deeper levels of trust, honesty, and risk-taking.

GROUP SELF-ACTUALIZATION

It is just the motive force behind this spiraling process leading to greater authenticity that makes me believe that the concept of individual self-actualization applies as well to groups. Self-actualization has been a fundamental tenet in Rogerian theory, and refers to the innate tendencies of organisms to respond to their total environment in such a way so as to

enhance their holistic functioning.[25] Underneath it all, client-centered therapists trust that clients have an abiding motivation to solve their own problems, to grow, and to do the best they can for themselves. The concept
applies particularly to a "self" (ego, adaptive response), and can be witnessed even in such molecular behavior as the persistent urge in an individual to search in words for a resolution to his experience in a given
conflict area. The notion of a group mind implied in experiential communality and group self-deceit suggest the possibility of a group self or
identity—another level of abstraction. Is there such a thing, then, as
group self-actualization? Do groups exhibit a natural impulse toward
collective growth?

Members enter an encounter group with an original anxiety about
whether or not "this group is for me" (Will this be *my* kind of group?
Can I be myself in this group?). Then, it is as if a group must borrow its
identity by taxing individual members' identities. It is in this sense that
every group is different, a unique event. As part of the series of studies
carried out in the T.I.E. Project, Gordon (1972) found member composition to be a highly influential factor in encounter group outcome. Members
are concerned about how much of their selves they must give up to belong
to this new group identity. With representation comes taxation, in that
order. Most theorists single out the importance of this identificatory process—"Inclusion" after Schutz, the "work culture" of Bion, what Rogers
calls "the development of a healing capacity," Freud's view of "group life,"
for example.

In the early meetings of most intensive growth groups, members will
likely be in different places with respect to identification with a group as
a whole. Some will over-identify, others will under-identify. As the group
gropes toward establishing what they have in common and what they are
to be, certain individuals emerge as over-eager or not interested enough.
Invariably, role positions are assigned, if only implicitly—he is the rebel,
she is the mother, he is the clown, she is the facilitator. A cast of characters is invented as an initial means of coping with individual and collective
identities (Berne, 1961; Gibb, 1969; Schutz, 1973). Left to themselves
these role definitions could persist insufferably long (because they are
safer), but in a successful process of unraveling group self-deceits and
persistent attempts at emotional openness and coexperiencing, members
reach a stage described by Rogers as a *self-healing capacity*. Here the
personal risk is intense yet it is taken to achieve a deeper growth. This
signals an important movement toward actualization.

---

[25] The level of abstraction is not unlike Darwin's theory of natural selection, Freud's
life instinct, or Maslow's theory of growth.

In the beginning there is no group (except in fantasy); there is no group identity, just as there is no "family" for relatives who are only role-playing and there is no "community" for collectivities that are simply bartering. There is only a disordered collection of single, dyadic, or triadic feeling gestalts. In the beginning it is everyone for themselves. As trust or safety or frustration builds, individuals increasingly risk being the self that they truly are, and from this effort a true group self emerges.

A Rogerian approach to encounter groups relies on this group self-acutalizing process. Other approaches do not—they may rely on the leader's charisma or expertise, on methods or exercises, or they may discredit or distrust entirely the value of group self-direction. There are three dynamics that most often defeat (at least impede) the emergence of growth as a group.

The most frequent of these dynamics is the achievement of a quasi group-identity through dependence on the leader. Unfortunately, many leaders consciously or unconsciously promote this dependence out of ego needs (this is the case in the previous example of group interaction). Group identity is founded, ingenuinely, on the premise: "We are all followers; our leader will show the way." Some groups actually subsist on a fawning adulation of a minor dictator. Should the leader leave the room, interaction stops, encounter ends. At their best such groups will wait passively for someone to take charge of them and take responsibility for the group. The leader may even appear as a nonparticipant, unresponsive, authoritarian observer, and members can neither lead themselves nor ignore the omnipresence of their silent "benefactor." Lasting individual and interpersonal growth is practically ruled out when members thus relinquish their identities and responsibilities. My studies increasingly suggest that, although some mutual admiration is possible, self-reliance and self-actualization are seldom, if ever, achieved, in this group setting.

Another ineffective solution to the problem of the formation of a group self is scapegoating. It is fairly well established in theory that some groups define themselves by subtraction; that is, by a process of eliminating or attacking "undesirable" characters. In the prescription of what is undesirable there is an implicit statement of consensuality as to what "our" group norms and identity should be. Often, the person chosen to scapegoat is one who has revealed some deviation in terms of underidentification or overeagerness, or in terms of local subcultural expectations. Conformity ensues. Threat is heightened. The forced group identity that results pleases no one and cannot allow for group or individual self-actualization.

The third most frequent negative dynamic in terms of emergent group self-actualization that I have found is the flight into coupling (whether sexual partnerships ensue or not). Although sexual and friendship needs are among the most prominent for encounter group volunteers, when a movement toward sexual pairing occurs it is invariably at the expense of the development of a completed group identity and of the fullest potential for experiential communality, that is, encounter. The possibility of a self-transcendance and of interpersonal growth through the encounter process is temporarily lost to those individuals who separate themselves. The most common cause for the flight into coupling, and its most frequent point of occurrence, is a group's failure to undo a significant group self-deceit, typically a sexual dishonesty. If prolonged, this impasse leads members to abandon their search for growth through the group media and to look elsewhere for satisfaction.

Groups who avoid these traps, who are genuinely motivated toward growth and allowed the freedom to develop their own sense of identity and direction; who also find the strength to unlock and resolve their own complicity in self-deceit, will discover many moments of intensive emotional coexperience—group "highs," in the encounter idiom—and so realize positive, enduring personal change.

Turnbull's observations on the social and physical crisis faced by the starving Ik are again appropriate. He concludes his study this way:

> The Ik have successfully abandoned useless appendages . . . such as family, cooperative sociality, belief, love, hope and so forth, for the very good reason that in their context these militated against survival . . . they have replaced human society with a mere survival system that does not take human emotion into account . . . And the symptoms of change in our own society indicate that we are heading in precisely the same direction. . . .
>
> The sorry state of society in the civilized world today, which contrasts so strongly with the still social society of the "primitive," is in large measure due to the simple fact that social change has not kept up with technological change. . . . The Ik have relinquished all luxury in the name of individual survival, and the result is that they live on as a people without life, without passion, beyond humanity. We pursue . . . trivial, idiotic technological encumbrances and imagine *them* to be the luxuries that make life worth living, and all the time we are losing our potential for social rather than individual survival, for hating as well as loving, losing perhaps our last chance to enjoy life with all the passion that is our nature and being [Turnbull, 1972, pp. 289–295].

Encounter within a group can be an immensely revitalizing, resocializing process. At its best it can reestablish the meaning of people for each other. It recreates a discovery of man's humanity, going far beyond the epistemological loneliness inherent in individual searches for individual meaning in individual therapy. Encounter may even promise to produce social change. But this remains to be seen.

REFERENCES

Angyal, A. *Neurosis and treatment: A holistic theory.* New York: Wiley, 1965.

Arnheim, R. The gestalt theory of expression. *Psychology Review*, 1949, **56**, 156–171.

Back, K. W. *Beyond words.* New York: Russell Sage, 1972.

Back, K. W. The experiential group and society. *Journal of Applied Behavioral Science*, 1973, **9**, 7–20.

Bakan, D. A reconsideration of the problem of introspection. *Psychological Bulletin*, 1954, **51**, 105–118.

Bakan, D. *The duality of human existence.* Chicago: Rand McNally, 1966.

Bakan, D. *On method.* San Francisco: Jossey-Bass, 1967.

Bakan, D. Psychology can now kick the science habit. *Psychology Today*, 1972, **5**, 26ff.

Bateson, G., Jackson, D., Haley, J., & Weakland, H. Toward a theory of schizophrenia. *Behavioral Science*, 1956, **1**, 251–264.

Bebout, J. On reflection in client-centered psychotherapy. *Counseling Center Discussion Papers, 7*(16). Chicago: University of Chicago Library, 1961.

Bebout, J. The use of encounter groups for interpersonal growth. *Interpersonal Development*, 1971/1972, **2**, 91–104.

Bebout, J. A study of group encounter in higher education. In J. Vriend & W. W. Dyer (Eds.), *Counseling effectively in groups.* Englewood Cliffs, N.J.: Educational Technology Publications, 1973.

Bebout, J., & Gordon, B. The value of encounter. In L. Solomon & B. Berzon (Eds.), *New perspectives on encounter groups.* San Francisco: Jossey-Bass, 1972.

Berne, E. *Transactional analysis in psychotherapy.* New York: Grove Press, 1961.

Berzon, B., Solomon, L. N., & Reisel, J. Audio tape programs for self-directed groups. In L. Solomon & B. Berzon (Eds.), *New perspectives on encounter groups.* San Francisco: Jossey-Bass, 1972.

Blank, L., Gottsegen, G., & Gottsegen, M. *Confrontations in self and interpersonal awareness.* New York: Macmillan, 1971.

Bonner, H. *Social psychology.* New York: American Book, 1953.

Bronowski, J. The logic of the mind. *American Scientist*, 1966, **54**, 1–14.

Brown, R. *Social psychology.* New York: Free Press, 1965.

Buber, M. *Between man and man.* London: Kegan Paul, 1947.

Buber, M. *I and thou.* New York: Scribner, 1958.

Burton, A. (Ed.) *Encounter.* San Francisco: Jossey-Bass, 1969.

Butler, J. M., & Rice, L. N. Adience, self-actualization and drive theory. In J. M. Wepman & R. W. Heine (Eds.), *Concepts of personality.* Chicago: Aldine, 1963.

Campbell, J. P., & Dunnette, M. D. Effectiveness of t-group experiences in managerial training and development. *Psychological Bulletin,* 1968, **70,** 73–104.

Castaneda, C. *Journey to Ixtlan: The lessons of Don Juan.* New York: Simon and Schuster, 1972.

Coleman, J. C. *Psychology and effective behavior.* Glenview, Ill.: Scott, Foresman, 1969.

Deutsch, H. *The psychology of women: A psychoanalytic interpretation.* New York: Grune & Stratton, 1944.

DiMascio, A., Boyd, R. W., & Greenblatt, M. Physiological correlates of tension and antagonism during psychotherapy. *Psychosomatic Medicine,* 1957, **19,** 99–104.

Dittes, J. E. Galvanic skin response as a measure of patient's reaction to therapist's permissiveness. *Journal of Abnormal and Social Psychology,* 1957, **55,** 295–303.

Egan, G. *Encounter: Group processes for interpersonal growth.* Belmont, Calif.: Brooks/Cole, 1970.

Gendlin, E. T. Existentialism and experiential psychotherapy. In J. T. Hart & T. M. Tomlinson (Eds.), *New directions in client-centered therapy.* Boston: Houghton Mifflin, 1970.

Gibb, J. R., & Gibb, L. M. Role freedom in a TORI group. In A. Burton (Ed.), *Encounter.* San Francisco: Jossey-Bass, 1969.

Gibson, J. J. Perception as a function of stimulation. In S. Koch (Ed.), *Psychology: A study of a science.* Vol. I. New York: McGraw-Hill, 1959.

Goldstein, K. *The organism.* New York: American Book, 1939.

Golembiewski, R. T., & Blumberg, A. *Sensitivity training and the laboratory approach.* Itasca, Ill.: F. E. Peacock, 1970.

Goodman, G. *Companionship therapy.* San Francisco: Jossey-Bass, 1973.

Gordon, B. Typological analysis of encounter groups. Paper presented at the annual convention of the American Psychological Association, Honolulu, September 1972.

Gordon, T. Group-centered leadership and administration. In C. R. Rogers (Ed.), *Client-centered therapy.* Boston: Houghton Mifflin, 1951.

Greenblatt, M. Discussion. In E. Rubinstein & M. Parloff (Eds.), *Research in psychotherapy.* Vol. I. Washington, D.C.: American Psychological Association, 1962.

Greif, E. B., & Hogan, R. The theory and measurement of empathy. *Journal of Counseling Psychology*, 1973, **20**, 280–284.

Gunther, B. *Sense relaxation below your mind.* New York: Collier, 1968.

Harlow, H. F. The nature of love. *American Psychologist*, 1958, **13**, 673-685.

Harris, E. Mind and mechanical models. In J. Scher (Ed.), *Theories of the mind.* Glencoe, Ill.: The Free Press, 1962.

Hart, J. T. The development of client-centered therapy. In J. T. Hart & T. M. Tomlinson (Eds.), *New directions in client-centered therapy.* Boston: Houghton Mifflin, 1970.

Hobbs, N. Group-centered psychotherapy. In C. R. Rogers (Ed.), *Client-centered therapy.* Boston: Houghton Mifflin, 1951.

Jessor, R., & Feshbach, S. *Cognition, personality and clinical psychology.* San Francisco: Jossey-Bass, 1967.

Kagan, J., & Havemann, E. *Psychology: An introduction.* (2nd ed.) New York: Harcourt Brace Jovanovich, 1972.

Klein, G. *Perception, motives and personality.* New York: Knopf, 1970.

Laing, R. D. *The politics of experience.* New York: Ballantine Books, 1967.

Laing, R. D., Phillipson, H., & Lee, A. R. *Interpersonal perception.* New York: Harper & Row, 1966.

Lakin, M. *Interpersonal encounter: Theory and practice in sensitivity training.* New York: McGraw-Hill, 1972.

Le Bon, G. *The crowd.* New York: Viking, 1960.

Lieberman, M., Yalom, I. D., & Miles, M. B. *Encounter groups: First facts.* New York: Basic Books, 1973.

Lowen, A. *Betrayal of the body.* New York: Macmillan, 1967.

Marks, C. Encounter group observation methods. Paper presented at the annual convention of the American Psychological Association, Honolulu, September 1972.

Mead, G. H. *Mind, self, and society.* Chicago: University of Chicago Press, 1934.

Montague, A. *Touching.* New York: Harper & Row, 1971.

Moreno, J. L. *Who shall survive?* New York: Nervous and Mental Disease Publishing Company, 1934.

Osgood, C. E., Suci, G. J., & Tannenbaum, P. H. *The measurement of meaning.* Urbana: University of Illinois Press, 1957.

Perls, F. *Gestalt therapy verbatim.* Lafayette, Calif.: Real People Press, 1969.

Piaget, J., & Inhelder, B. *The psychology of the child.* New York: Basic Books, 1969.

Plessner, H. *Lachen und weinen.* Bern: A. Francke, 1950.

Polanyi, M. *Personal knowledge.* Chicago: University of Chicago Press, 1958.

Reich, W. *Character analysis.* New York: Orgone Press, 1949.

Rogers, C. R. *Client-centered therapy.* Boston: Houghton Mifflin, 1951.

Rogers, C. R. *On becoming a person: A therapist's view of psychotherapy.* Boston: Houghton Mifflin, 1961.

Rogers, C. R. Interpersonal relationships, 2000. *Journal of Applied Behavioral Science,* 1968, **4,** 265–280.

Rogers, C. R. *Carl Rogers on encounter groups.* New York: Harper & Row, 1970.

Rogers, C. R. Some new challenges. *American Psychologist,* 1973, **28,** 379–387.

Rogers, C. R., & Dymond, R. *Psychotherapy and personality change.* Chicago: University of Chicago Press, 1954.

Rogers, C. R., & Hart, J. T. Looking back and ahead: A conversation with Carl Rogers. In J. T. Hart & T. M. Tomlinson (Eds.), *New directions in client-centered therapy.* Boston: Houghton Mifflin, 1970.

Schutz, W. C. *Here comes everybody.* New York: Harper & Row, 1971.

Schutz, W. C. *Elements of encounter.* Big Sur, Calif.: Joy Press, 1973.

Shlien, J. M. A client-centered approach to schizophrenia: First approximation. In A. Burton (Ed.), *Psychotherapy of the psychoses.* New York: Basic Books, 1961.

Shlien, J. M., & Zimring, F. M. Researh directives and methods in client-centered therapy. In J. T. Hart & T. M. Tomlinson (Eds.), *New directions in client-centered therapy.* Boston: Houghton Mifflin, 1970.

Smith, H. C. *Sensitivity training.* New York: McGraw-Hill, 1973.

Solomon, L. N., & Berzon, B. (Eds.) *New perspectives on encounter groups.* San Francisco: Jossey-Bass, 1972.

Soskin, W. F., & Kauffman, P. E. Judgment of emotion in word-free voice samples. *Journal of Communication,* 1961, **11**(2), 73–80.

Stone, L. J., & Church, J. *Childhood and adolescence.* New York: Random House, 1968.

Stotland, E., Sherman, S. E., & Shaver, K. G. *Empathy and birth order.* Lincoln: University of Nebraska Press, 1971.

Strasser, S. Feeling as basis of knowing and recognizing the other as an ego. In M. Arnold (Ed.), *Feelings and emotions: The Loyola symposium.* New York: Academic Press, 1970.

Truax, C. B., & Mitchell, K. M. Research on certain therapist interpersonal skills in relation to process and outcome. In A. E. Bergin & S. L. Garfield (Eds.), *Handbook of psychotherapy and behavior change: An empirical analysis.* New York: Wiley, 1971.

Turnbull, C. *The mountain people.* New York: Simon and Schuster, 1972.

Walker, A., Rablen, R., & Rogers, C. R. Development of a scale to measure process changes in psychotherapy. *Journal of Clinical Psychology,* 1960, **16**(1), 79–85.

Webster's new world dictionary of the American language. (College ed.) New York: World, 1959.

Werner, H. *Comparative psychology of mental development.* New York: International Universities Press, 1957.

Yalom, I. D. *The theory and practice of group psychotherapy.* New York: Basic Books, 1970.

CHAPTER 14

Phases in the Development of Structure in Therapy and Encounter Groups

Ariadne Plumis Beck

HISTORICAL PERSPECTIVE

This chapter is, of necessity, only a place to pause on the road to creating a more complete theory about the developmental process in small groups. It presents some highly distilled observations on the characteristics of the formative phases of development in time-limited therapy and encounter groups. It does not present a completed or systematized theory of group development because that is somewhere ahead on the road. The problems to which this work is addressed can be described as follows: A collection of individuals comes together for a purpose, perhaps only vaguely defined at first, and many meetings later emerges as an organized whole, with functionally related parts. We call it a group. How does this come about? Is there any similarity in the process experienced in different groups? Are there certain problems that all groups must cope with or to which they must find solutions? How do members retain their individuality while finding ways to combine meaningfully with others? How does personal change come about in a group context?

This chapter represents an attempt to deal with these questions within a framework for understanding group process. The framework is a developmental one, analyzing change in the context of phases in the evolution of the group's structure: its efforts to organize itself to fulfill its goals. Ultimately, via careful analysis of recordings of groups, the formal phases of development will be defined in terms that attempt to capture the way the group members themselves defined them. For the purpose of this chapter however, we are confined to a prior stage of theory development, which is based primarily on the experiences and observations of the author as leader, member, observer, and supervisor of therapy groups, and on discussions with colleagues at the University of Chicago (Beck & Keil, 1967).

Client-centered therapy and its theory moved us from a position as external observers and analysts of the mind, the personality, and the motives, of the patient to a position as both empathic and active participants in the becoming process. In the best of client-centered therapy the client and the therapist emerge more fully into becoming who they can be and more fully into relationship. In client-centered theory Rogers (1957, 1959, 1961a, 1961b) gave us a description of the therapeutic relationship in terms that moved us closer to the process as it is perceived by the participants. This attempt to have theory in some way characterize the essential qualities of the process of human interaction fits into a larger movement in the development of the human sciences in this century. The important changes that have taken place and are relevant to this chapter can be summarized as follows:

1. The shift from seeing man in static terms including mechanistic analyses of his motivation toward seeing man in process terms, both as an organism and in interaction (see Simmel, 1908; Parsons, 1961; Stark, 1962).

2. The shift from seeing man as tabula rasa toward seeing man as an *open system* in continuous dynamic interaction, and further as organizing his perceptions and experiences and giving meaning to his world, *as structuring his own process* (cf. Gray & Rizzo, 1969; von Bertalanffy, 1956; Schroedinger, 1956; Merleau-Ponty, 1964).

3. The shift from seeing man's behavior in groups as either mechanistic or chaotic toward seeing man's structuring of his process as *orderly and systematic, developmental or regressive* (cf. Bales, 1953; Parsons, Bales, & Shils, 1953; Tuckman, 1965).

4. The shift from seeing theory as based on objective, external views toward seeing theory as potentially reflecting the process it describes, or better, *combining the objective and experiential perspectives* (cf. Langer, 1964; Merleau-Ponty, 1964).

The major overriding theoretical development in this century is the elaboration of General Systems Theory, first introduced by von Bertalanffy in biology. This approach made it possible to understand living systems in terms that are consistent with theories of physics and chemistry, and to describe living systems in terms of their interaction processes both internally and with their environs. Although the present paper is not, strictly speaking, a systems analysis, it does attempt to delineate those areas that must ultimately be analyzed in order to produce a comprehensive theory of group development, and its language and approach are consistent with a systems analytic viewpoint.

In particular, the present chapter begins the undertaking of a multi-faceted view of the systematic development of small groups. This view combines objectively analyzed or observable phenomena with subjectively perceived or *experiential phenomena* in group process. It sees man as a *self-organizing system* that values, feeds on, and creates order. It sees man and group as open systems in interaction with their environs, actively involved in organizing their experience and their realities with respect to their goals. This organization is seen as evolving in an orderly developmental process at both individual and group levels. The view being developed here is based on informal observation of a wide range of groups and careful observation of 13 therapy groups conducted at the University of Chicago.

The system we call a group will ultimately be analyzed by the theoretical description of five important, systematic sources of influence:

1. The purpose for which the group comes together as this is elaborated into a system of goals over time.

2. The personalities of the members and their particular skills and developmental needs at the time they participate in the group.

3. The structure of the group (roles, norms, etc.) and the developmental process by which it evolves.

4. The qualitative aspects of group life (style of leadership, style of members in group participation, accuracy and inclusiveness of communication, depth of emotional significance of communication, etc.) and the methods for facilitating or hindering them in the developmental context.

5. The environment or context within which the group and its members exist.

The present chapter has as its primary purpose the presentation of the phases of development of group structure (see pp. 435–455). It will briefly develop the personality (see under Individual Development) and qualitative issues (see pp. 462–430; 455–458 in order to clarify the development of structure, but it will not develop the goal and environmental issues at this time, although they are alluded to in passing.

INDIVIDUAL DEVELOPMENT

A group has an existence in its own right in the sense that there are processes and properties that can describe it; in the sense that it has a history, and in the sense that its members not only have commitment to participation in it but have a conception of it as a unit that is somehow separate from their perceptions of each member. However, it is composed of individuals who are themselves complex systems. It is appropriate therefore to present first some thoughts about individual development, functioning, and malfunctioning.

The personality of the individual refers here to the patterns of his internal processes such as perception, imagination, cognition, and experience; his external processes such as his characteristic responses, habits, behavior mechanisms, and styles; and his intermediating processes such as attitudes, goals, curiosity, and the like. The personality is formed in a complex interaction between the individual's genetically determined biological qualities, skills, needs, and impulses to act; his physical environment and interpersonal environment, as these impinge on him, are perceived, given meaning, and dealt with by him. These experiences are sorted out and ordered into hierarchies in terms of their significance to the person himself, as they occur. There is a tendency over short periods of time for this organization to be maintained in the same pattern, but periodically, as new experience makes it relevant to do so, the individual reexamines these patterns and reorganizes his understandings and meanings so that particular past material may be found newly sorted into different hierarchies. At certain critical periods in the life-span, due to the impetus of dramatic biological changes or heightened social pressure, these reorganizations and reevaluations occur at a very intensive rate and cover many major areas crucial to the individual. To develop this point further: In the life span of the individual there are a number of basic changes or reorganizations in the collective patterns of his personality that are initiated and timed by genetically determined biological changes (completion of neuron development, maturation of muscles critical to macromovements of the body, puberty, disease, etc.). In the intervening periods, there are a number of critical periods for development, which have been largely socially determined and often initiate reorganizations of at least some patterns in the individual (such as entrance into a peer-work world when school starts; the necessity to make a commitment to a work role in young adulthood or even earlier; marriage; parenthood, etc.). We think of all these as potential experiences for growth in individuals. The direction of these changes in the first third of life is generally one of increased physical strength and dexterity; increased ability to manipulate and understand symbolic forms, such as language, number, abstract levels of organization of ideas and people, emotional meaning, gestural communication; increased capacity to cope with any particular experience, and capacity to cope adequately with increased diversity in experience. This direction can potentially continue throughout life (with the exception of physical strength). However, increasingly, as life continues, there are changes that threaten to deteriorate or even destroy previously gained capacities. The concept of growth in these contexts then tends to focus on the emotional and intellectual dimensions of the person, with the assumption that it is at least possible in principle to deal with changes that are potentially or actually detrimental in a way that in fact allows the individual to emerge with a net gain in the dimensions outlined above.

The major consequences of the biologically triggered set of changes are explored, developed, and assimilated by the individual in the interactions he has with other persons. The achievement of the socially triggered set of changes is almost entirely dependent upon the interactions the individual has with others, because their very nature is basically interpersonal. Relationships become the critical medium through which development proceeds and is integrated into the personality.

Therefore, at any particular time, the individual's ability to make use of the persons available in his environment to create functional relationships in which the process of development can proceed is a critical factor. The difference between persons who are functioning adequately (in terms of the values and expectations of the subsociety of which they are a part) and those who are not depends very largely on their ability to make use of relationships that cross their path either to maintain currently developed patterns or to consolidate new levels of organization in the patterns of their personality. Persons not functioning well are unable to relate and communicate with others in a way that accomplishes this development. The ability to respond to others in a functional and productive way, or at least in a nondestructive way, is a product of previous experience and learning. In the field of psychology, and more particularly in psychotherapy, there have been many attempts to conceptualize about the nature of the problems in personality development that lead to malfunction. A great deal of this thinking has focused attention on the presence of a basic conflict at one level or another: between parts of the personality (Freud, 1949); between awareness and experience (Rogers, 1959); between self and others (Sullivan, 1953); between different needs or forces (Lewin, 1935; Murray, 1938); between self and subgroup (Asch, 1952; Bion, 1961); between self and larger culture (Durkheim, 1938; Kluckhohn & Strodtbeck, 1961). In addition to the issue of conflict at these various levels there may be difficulty due to inadequately developed communication skills. Each of these levels involves some form of communication process, which usually includes verbal abstraction (but may not), certainly includes the production of physical and/or physiological cues, includes the interpretation of perceived patterns and the ability to form into a pattern the inputs from several different sources, which may or may not be discrepant. In more general terms, then, there are skills involved in understanding oneself, one's internal processes, needs, and experiences in such a way as to represent these in awareness with a fair degree of accuracy; there are other skills involved in the understanding of other individuals, for themselves; still other skills in the recognition of relevant dimensions in the relationship between self and other; and still other skills involved in the recognition of relevant group processes and patterns and one's own part in these. As I see it, then, the adequacy of the communication skills and the presence or absence of conflict in the individual in relationship to these levels are the primary determining factors in whether or not the person is able to develop the kinds of relationships that lead to growth for him. In certain instances individual work is necessary to help cope with the conflicts or the development of basic communication skills. Many clients, as well as persons not seeking therapy, can, however, profit from the use of growthful or therapeutic groups to work on these issues. Because the outcome for any individual is determined by the relationship he has to his social environment, group therapy allows the client and the therapist the unique opportunity to work directly with the problems the client has in relating to others in mutually facilitative ways. Increasingly, practitioners are exploring the usefulness of group therapy for the entire range of psychological problems, and for a wide range of groupings including families, organization staffs, communities, as well as total strangers. Encounter and training groups offer comparable experiences to therapy groups, but usually do not offer the continuity of a therapy group or (more important for change issues) the opportunity to go back and forth between their life outside the group and the group itself. This process allows for assimilation and integration of new experiences, which is probably important in successfully reorganizing behavior and life style, and keeping the intensity of emotional experiences within a range that can be readily processed. With the amount of group activity increasing in this field it has become a more significant challenge to attempt to characterize its crucial dimensions and to develop a better understanding of how or why or when it works.

THE CONTEXTUAL AND QUALITATIVE ASPECTS OF THE GROUPS THAT WERE OBSERVED

The task of the remainder of this chapter will be to present an initial distillation of observations that have been made by this author over a period of years of small, time-limited therapy, training, and encounter groups. In that setting, a time-limited group agreed to meet for 15 or 20 sessions before starting. There were from six to nine members, and usually a leader and coleader.

The major body of data has been collected on therapy groups that were conducted at the University of Chicago Counseling and Psychotherapy Research Center during the period 1960–1970. Clients were interviewed beforehand, but were essentially unselected for groups. They were assigned to groups in the order in which they came in, with no attempt being made to arrange them in any particular grouping. In addition to observation, some sociometric data, postmeeting rating scales, and pre- and post-group personality tests were collected on a subset of the groups. This material will be summarized elsewhere. Thirteen of the groups were audio-tape-recorded, and serve as the data base for observation. In addition, the tapes of one group, which is considered prototypical, are completely transcribed and being used for detailed analysis.

As indicated earlier in this chapter, the qualitative dimension of influence in the group's process includes the skill and point of view of the leader, the style of his leadership, and the type and quality of the communication in the group. It is pertinent, therefore, that these characteristics in the sample of groups that were observed, should be at least briefly described here.

The groups on which data have been collected were led by members of the staff or interns in training in a client-centered counseling center. The therapist–leader related to the group as a facilitator, neither defining topics or specific tasks nor directing the group except to initiate the process at the beginning. The group essentially selected its own issues. The leader did act in a variety of ways to improve the communication, and to develop trust, thus influencing the qualitative aspect of the group's life. This is an essential characteristic of client-centered or existential leadership style. As in any group, the values and expectations of the leaders influence the development of the norms and values in the group.

The following summary of the values, goals, and expectations that characterized their leadership is based upon discussions among the therapists who worked on the groups at the University of Chicago. These derive from the values and views of individual therapy in the client-centered framework, but include issues that are raised by the fact that the unit is a group, rather than a dyad.

1. An important goal of the therapist–leader is the facilitation of individuals (and in this case, the members of the group) to take responsibility for themselves in whatever ways this is realistically possible at any particular time. First, this is true with regard to the content issues they wish to

deal with; that is, the client is encouraged to raise whatever issues are currently pressing to him. Secondly, it is true with regard to the feelings and attitudes expressed about issues of concern. Operationally, the method of response that tends to accomplish this is one that focuses sharply on the client's statements as expressions of what he is experiencing, with the result that pressure is put on the client to seek a closer identity between what he says and what he experiences. The third sense in which the therapist attempts to facilitate each member's taking responsibility for himself is in terms of increased initiative within the group; that is, the therapist intends (as an explicit goal) that the group members should develop the capacity for taking over the leadership functions of the group process as they become ready to do so.

2. The therapist–leader believes that problems and conflicts can be clarified and solved via a process of self-understanding, and the development of an empathic understanding of others. The primary mode of response of the therapist is therefore one that elicits a good deal of self-reflection from the client, and of checking perceptions with each other between clients. The therapist's behavior is characterized in early sessions by regular responding to both individual and group expression. An effort is made to respond to the communication that is relevant to the issue at the center of the group's attention at any particular time. The primary goal here is to keep communication fluid. Regular responding is a means of maintaining a higher level of accurately perceived communication, minimizing the accumulation of fantasy, misperception, and misunderstanding that eventually block communication.

3. The therapist holds the view that one of the conditions for producing growth is the recognition of the client as he is, a recognition of his reality as he sees it. A willingness on the part of the therapist to seek to understand the client in terms of his real potentials and real limits, in the moment, is also very important to this style of leadership and therapy.

Parallel to the attitude toward the individual is the therapist's attitude toward the group as a group. Consistent with a viewpoint developed by Gordon (1955), these therapist–leaders are focused on the development of the group's own issues. It is possible that this aspect of their leadership greatly facilitated the clear emergence of the dynamics involved in the formative stages of group development. Responded to in this way groups seem to have a clear sense of what they want to work on.

4. Closely associated with condition 3 is the evaluative attitude of the therapist. He attempts to offer an attitude which is nonjudgmental, in order to facilitate exploratory and self-reflective behavior in the client.

However, it is recognized that no person can act, ultimately, without making evaluations. The important thing is the basis on which these evaluations are made. The clients evaluate themselves and each other in the group. The therapist tries to influence them in such a way that they will take greater account of the functions that their behavior is serving, in terms of their own needs, perceptions, intentions, and feelings. For example, when an individual reacts to someone else, his response may or may not be based on an accurate understanding of the other person; it may or may not be simply a reflection of his own feelings about that person or the topic raised by him; it may or may not be intended to foster understanding and so on. The intention here, then, is to bring about a shift from responses that condemn or glorify to responses that give the other person a more accurate understanding of the effect he has on others, or that let him know more clearly how his own perceptions and experiences compare with those of others. The process and progress of the group tend to push the limits of conditionality back, so that each individual becomes willing and able to accept more in others than he did at first. This will be seen to be one of the basic aspects of the group's developmental process.

5. The therapist recognizes the significance of maintaining as high a degree as possible of clarity about his own views, feelings, and reactions while he is in the therapeutic relationship. This is considerably easier to accomplish in a situation in which one is responding to and focusing on a single individual. In a group situation, and particularly in one in which the therapist is actively participating in the interpersonal communication process, it is more difficult to maintain internal clarity. There is too much going on at one time, in terms of the simultaneous behaviors of the various members, their interactions with each other and the therapist's own reactions, for him to be able to sort out all that is important on the spot. You might say that the nervous system becomes overloaded. This is not a matter of inadequacy of the therapist (although for an inexperienced therapist this is an added problem) but a practical reality of complex situations. Under these conditions it becomes extremely important for the therapist to be aware of, and accepting of, his own limits. The degree of his willingness to know this and to communicate about it to the group, even though it may elicit disappointment or anxiety from them, is a significant dimension in his effectiveness as a leader. On the other hand, he must be prepared to spend a fair amount of time between sessions of a therapy group doing the thinking and sorting out that cannot be done during each session. This is especially important in the formative stages of the group's development. Issues that were misunderstood or left hang-

ing have a way of returning or even of becoming exacerbated when the therapist and members leave them unnoticed.

The developmental phases to be presented here have already been observed in groups led by leaders with different styles, values, and expectations. Ultimately, of course, the validity of this phase analysis will have to be tested empirically in a variety of contexts, with a variety of leadership styles and a variety of group compositions.

INVARIANCE IN THE DEVELOPMENT OF GROUP STRUCTURE

As with the individual, groups are seen to evolve through a sequence of changes in the course of their existence, and these changes are characterized by discernible patterns. And as with the individual, a group is determined by the interaction of a number of sources of influence: the group's purpose and goals; the personalities of the individuals; the structure of the group; the qualitative dimension; and the context in which it exists. A complete theory would need to develop each of these sources of influence and their dynamic interactions as well. In an important contribution to summarizing the state of knowledge on small groups (as of 1962), Golembiewski (1962) organized the existing theories and studies into "three panels of variables:" structural, style, and population. The present paper was influenced by that summary in the clarification of the structural and personality sources. The concept of qualitative dimensions does not parallel Golembiewski's style panel, however.

In this study, structural issues include the development of leadership, the articulation of roles and functions in a group, the critical issues focused on in each stage of development, the critical work tasks and goals a group chooses, the creation of norms, and the process by which that is done. The structure of a group is its skeleton, which strongly influences its overall form. Qualitative issues include the style with which leadership and other roles are exercised, the amount of conflict experienced in differentiation of roles, the way in which work is done (in a therapy group for example, the depth of emotional issues that are dealt with, and the adequacy of the resolution that is achieved), the comfort and meaningfulness of the group's norms for the members, the skill with which the group progresses through its formative stages. Qualitative issues determine how one feels about the group, how one's experience takes shape. If the structure is the skeleton, the qualitative input is the texture of the flesh, the color, the tone of voice, and the "feel." The personality has already been outlined above, but for the purposes of group behavior, would include here the developmental stage of the individual and therefore the salient issues for him at the particular time of his participation, the competence of the person with respect to the goals and activities of the group (particularly as these are perceived by other participants), and the readiness or neediness of the individual to use the group to achieve or facilitate his own growth.

The entire system (group) is, in addition, immersed in an environment that impinges on the group process in two primary ways: the physical–interpersonal setting in which it meets defines certain limitations, codes of behavior, or criteria for participation, and the entire complex of each member's life outside the group determines his complex state upon entering (and reentering) the group and may influence the group in a variety of ways, but primarily through the perceptual sieve of the member himself.

Each of these aspects is seen as "in process," and in interaction with each other; none is static. The output of any group in terms of productivity and effectiveness and the outcome of a group experience for any member is determined by an interaction of all these levels of input. Moreover, these levels of input interact in lawful ways, characteristic of all living systems. The many processes, inputs, and outputs of a group that have been described by a large number of researchers are seen here as having a variety of meanings, a variety of consequences and impacts on the group as a system, depending on when it is that they occur in its history. The initial thesis of the theory being developed here is that there is a discernible pattern consistent across groups in the developmental process by which a collection of individuals structures itself into a relatively stable organization that we call a group; and that the various levels of analysis will take on greater meaning when they are seen in the context of this developmental sequence. The interaction of the inputs from the five sources of influences determines the rate at which a group progresses through the phases of development, the effectiveness of what is accomplished at each phase and the usefulness of the experience to each member. This interaction also determines whether or not a group is successful in organizing itself, for there is the possibility of failure or detour in this enterprise as in all others in which living systems participate.

In order to develop a complex theory dealing with the various sources of influence outlined above, we must first identify the *invariant* developmental process that holds all the variable sources together. It is in the development of a structure that has the capacity to function adequately for the members as individuals and for the members as a group with a goal that an invariant pattern can be identified. Although the particulars of structure in each group are unique, there are phases in the development of the group's structure that occur in an invariant sequence, when a group is successful in coping with each phase. This unifying framework allows us then, to integrate meaningfully, the variable influences in a particular group from the purpose and goals, the personality, the specific structural characteristics, the qualitative dimension, and the environment. It also allows us to understand and describe the processes of groups that do not succeed, or develop incompletely or in an aberrant fashion. The developmental process of the successful group becomes the norm against which we can compare and understand a wide range of variations in group process.

The question of whether or not there is an invariant sequence of developmental phases has been debated for some time in research on groups. Unfortunately there have not been enough studies using either careful clinical observation or systematic schedules of categories to settle the question. Those that are available seem to corroborate the idea that phases do indeed exist. In one of the earliest studies, Heinicke and Bales (1953) found distinct phases in short-term laboratory work groups. More recently Tuckman (1965) summarized the theories (of which there are several: Bach (1954); Bennis (1956); Hill and Elmore (1957); Schutz (1958); Mann (1967)), the clinical descriptions, and the empirical studies on phases of development in task and therapy groups. He identified four overall phases of group development for which the literature provides considerable agreement. A subsequent study (Runkel, Lawrence, Oldfield, Rider, & Clark, 1971) found some support for Tuckman's sequence in observing classroom, task-oriented groups.

In another, very ambitious study by Mann (1967) the relationship between the members and the leader was observed using systematic techniques inspired by Bales. They found certain phases in group development whose major characteristics were apparently accounted for by the behavior of the dominant subgroups, within the larger group. They too were observing task-oriented classroom groups. In spite of these kinds of evidence many group leaders continue to question the validity of the idea of developmental phases in groups.

Although a number of studies have now been completed on this topic, Howard and Orlinsky, in their review of Psychotherapy Research for the *Annual Review of Psychology* in 1972, said:

> Phases or temporal stages also concern the group psychology of the therapeutic process, as the participants contribute to and are affected by the phenomenon of therapeutic "movement." . . . The development of a phase x aspect matrix for the description of conjoint processes would provide a useful framework within which to consider the subtle factors involved in dynamics [p. 618].

And then, later in the same chapter,

> Perhaps the most challenging problem for research in this area is the empirical definition of phases of therapeutic process, but in this review period there was no advance over work previously done [p. 645].

Before adequate empirical work can be done, however, the relevant dimensions must be defined. The summary to be presented here is an attempt at defining the relevant issues. It is by no means complete as yet, but is offered here for its suggestive value.

DIFFERENTIATION AND COHESION WITHIN DEVELOPMENTAL PHASES

In addition to the invariance of phases in successful development of group structure, there is an invariant pattern that characterizes each phase of development. At the phase level the group participates in processes that seem to have as their goal the integration of the diverse positions expressed in the group and cohesion of its members on an emotional level. In other words the group's structure emerges out of a process by which the members are structuring their own experiences with each other. The group's behavior in each phase is characterized by a pattern of alternating differentiation and cohesion. Each phase poses a problem or a set of issues that draw varied responses from the individual members; the members *differentiate* themselves with respect to the issue(s) being dealt with. This tends to create a higher level of activity and anxiety. The members must then cope with the variety in views and needs among them, and, in developing a resolution, find a way to have everyone remain meaningfully related to the group and capable of living with the solution. When they achieve this, tension reduces, and the group is drawn together in a *cohesive* experience.

Bales has described this process as he observed it in laboratory task-oriented groups. According to Bales (1953), coping with instrumental issues tends to strain the group's integration, bringing about tensions sufficiently high that the group then turns its efforts to emotional issues and thus becomes reintegrated. Bales developed the idea that the group moves back and forth between these issues attempting to maintain equilibrium in the process. He introduced the idea that role differentiation occurs in the group as a natural outcome of this movement and that the role differentiation increased the efficiency of the group. Bales (1970) went on in his later work to elaborate extensively on the variety of group roles and personality characteristics of those who tend to take each role.

The model being developed here is based in several of its concepts on Bales' work. He observed very-short-term laboratory-created task groups. In the longer-term, natural group, the process he described takes on implications that he did not have the opportunity to observe or document. The model presented here attempts to develop this aspect of the process further.

The process of differentiation and cohesion occurs over a variety of critical issues pertinent to the developing group culture and structure. Each phase of development has a different issue as its focus. Each of these issues has both covert and overt aspects. Some of the division of labor regarding leadership functions that this model describes is caused by the need to attend to both covert and overt levels of issues, process, and communication in the group. The issues focused upon in each stage occur in a sequence. When each is coped with successfully the sequence is invariant across groups (under certain conditions to be specified below). Specific individuals in specific leadership roles emerge as the critical participants at each of the phases of the group's development. The particular issues being dealt with relate meaningfully to the nature of the emergent roles. A group that evolves smoothly through the formative developmental phases to the termination point and achieves certain characteristics (to be outlined later) is considered successful for the purposes of this study. Groups can fail to evolve by becoming held up at various phases in the sequence, and therefore not develop through all the phases described here. In addition, the entrance of new members after the group's development has begun usually requires beginning again and retracing those phases already completed. In a well-established group this process may be accomplished much more rapidly than it was accomplished originally or may even be done in almost symbolic terms. However, in groups where the membership is in regular flux one would predict that the group would continually be dealing with issues characteristic of the early phases of development, a point of some significance when dealing with the open-ended milieu therapy group that many in-patient facilities are using. The question of success will be developed further after the presentation of the phases of development.

The action in a group develops in a complex manner; it is not always clearly in one phase rather than another. One or two individuals may be experimenting with phase IV behavior while the majority of the members are clearly in phase III behavior. And when most of the group is ready to go on to phase IV one person may be holding back trying to resolve or complete some unfinished aspect of phase III. In presenting this summary of observations, however, phases will be outlined as though they were clearly separated and discretely defined, because there are crucial events that do identify the important characteristics of each phase in which all the members participate in some way, and all phases do end with a discernible experience of cohesion.

THE PHASES IN THE DEVELOPMENT OF GROUP STRUCTURE

The model presented here is a description of the developmental phases in creating a functional structure in a time-limited therapy or encounter group. It is written from a perspective that combines the viewpoints of an external observer, and a participant in the process. This model is focused on the formative period of group development. It assumes a beginning with a number of individuals (most often strangers) who come together with a general goal and a variety of expectations among them; i.e., a potential group. It describes the evolution of these individuals to a point where they have a set of relationships that allows them to relate functionally to each other and to the tasks and goals to which they address themselves as a group; i.e., they become a functional group. The data on which this model is based were obtained from time-limited therapy groups. An ongoing group such as a work organization or even a long-term therapy group can, in principle at least, develop through the formative period and go on to a different set of developmental issues. The current model does not cover all the levels of functioning or stages of development that are possible, nor are the phases described here in any way related to specific amounts of time. Groups vary in the amount of time they spend in any particular phase, and they may fail to develop through all the phases to be described. A later section will speak to the issue of incomplete or aberrant development. The current section will describe the stages of development of a potential group that successfully evolves into a functional group. The time-limited groups we observed did not go beyond this process but many of them did achieve this level of development in 15–20 sessions. Termination of the group at this point was experienced by its members as a natural and appropriate closure of the group process. When groups did not achieve all these phases there was a good deal of frustration expressed and various methods were sought to prolong contact in one way or another.

The description of the sequence of phases of development will be formulated at a level that aims to help the reader make immediate connections to actual group experiences. It focuses only on the critical and invariant aspects within each phase of development of group structure. Any actual group will be experienced as being much more complex and unclear than this description indicates. There will be some mention of both qualitative and personality influences but these will not be fully developed in this chapter.

This section will outline the phases of development of group structure that are characteristic of groups that meet the following conditions:

1. Between six and 10 members. (Groups that are larger have been observed informally and seem to have some variations on the same pattern. For example, they typically have two emotional leaders.)

2. Are meeting together for the purpose of personal growth. (The developmental sequence has been observed informally in work groups, classrooms, committees but no data has as yet been collected on these.)

3. With a time limit agreed upon in advance. (The same stages have been observed in ongoing groups but the time limit seems to press the group so that phase development is faster in time-limited groups.)

4. With no addition of new members once the group has actually started. (See discussion above on this issue.)

5. With no external influence on the organizational structure of the group. (Except with respect to the preconditions of meeting place, cost of participation, selection of leader(s) and members, and the time limit.)

6. With a therapist-leader who is nonauthoritarian and capable of facilitating shared or distributed leadership.

For each phase there will be: (a) a description of the critical issue(s) in the group's focus; (b) a description of the characteristic process in that phase; (c) a definition of the significant leadership role(s) that emerges in that phase (leadership roles sometimes have significant changes at other phases than the ones where they emerge—when this happens the role will again be described at that point in the group's development when it again becomes significant); and (d) a summary of the phase and its connection to the next phase of development. A leader here is defined as a person whose influence on the group is ongoing over some period of time in its life (not just in one phase) and has a pattern and particular direction.

Phase I: Making a Contract: The Agreement to Work on Becoming a Functional Group

GROUP LEVEL ISSUES

The initial tasks facing a newly collected group of people are related to the question of survival. We mean that in terms such as, "Can I tolerate being in this situation—can I function in it in a way that will, at least minimally, get me what I need, and can I tolerate the other members in the group?"

The first session gives everyone a chance to size up the situation, himself, and the others, including the therapists, and to decide whether or not he is prepared to participate in a process with this particular set of people.

Phase I has as its focus the creation of an initial contract to become a group, given that it begins with a collection of individuals who are usually strangers to each other or who do not already define themselves as a collectivity. It also has as its task the initial clarification of both individual and group level goals, and the identification of certain limits or expectations, thus beginning the norm creation process. On the experiential level the group participates in a process that at least minimally identifies each member to the others and in which a basis is sought for integration of the members.

PROCESS

In the first meeting of the group the therapist sets a style for the group's participation (this is true whether he is active or passive). In the groups studied here this session usually included some form of a round of introductions in which members tended to identify themselves in sociocultural, economic, or educational terms and indicated something about their purpose in coming to group therapy. In addition most first sessions included some demonstration on the therapist's part of how he would deal with personal exploration by an individual in the group and the group interaction in response to this. This was not necessarily a deliberate demonstration, as the occasion usually arises quite naturally. However it occurs, it tends to be perceived by the members as a model of the leader's idea of appropriate style for interaction in the group.

If the communication up to this point is reasonably congruent, and if the therapist has participated in a reasonably supportive way and each person has to some extent identified himself and his goals, a strong feeling of involvement develops.

As the phase nears its close, there seems to emerge a strong impulse or pressure to exchange or share some emotionally meaningful content, as though there is a mutually felt need to establish a bond in terms of experiences that are common to everyone there. In one group this was initiated by one member suddenly asking the group if they had ever had the experience of waking in the middle of the night in a state of panic and anxiety only to realize that there wasn't anyone in the world whom they felt they could call, or turn to. Other members in the group responded to this by relating some feeling or experience that expressed their sense of aloneness or isolation in the world. This exchange took place very rapidly with each member putting his version in without hesitation. It was a deeply felt encounter that generated a strong feeling of cohesion. Although the specific issue over which this experience is generated is different from group to group, the common aspect is that the group members seem to be saying, "Although we are separate and different we have a common bond in experiences that are very similar." With the establishment of that similarity, a contract is in essence made to work together in this group.

LEADERSHIP ROLES

Designated Leader. The Designated Leader is the official or appointed leader of the group, who usually convenes the group, and may also be the one who has selected the members. In the therapy group, he is expected by the members to be the most skilled in interpersonal processes and communications. In addition, he is the basic supportive person to all members. He gives overall guidance to the emerging structure and strongly influences the level and degree of emotional self-disclosure in the group by his style and the degree of his emotional maturity. He corresponds to Bales' (1958) taskleader in a laboratory task-oriented group, although in the groups observed here he intends that his function will be shared by others in time. As Bales indicated, this is an essential functional role and it appears that every group has such a person. In the group that starts as a leaderless group this role would emerge very early in the group's experience.

Emotional Leader. This person is very important to the group throughout the group's life. This term is borrowed from Bales (1958). In his analysis of this role in task-oriented groups he identified the emotional leader as a kind of manager of the group's emotional life, helping to give expression to their concerns and acting as an integrator of the task leader and the rest of the group. In an ongoing natural group, the Emotional Leader does perform these functions but in addition plays an even more significant role. He tends to be the person in the group who is most ready to make use of what it offers. In a therapy group that means he is ready for a significant experience of personal growth. He is usually turned-on by the group process almost immediately. He tends to have a high level of interaction in phase I. Very early in the group's contact he begins the development of an especially deep, warm, and intense relationship with the Designated Leader. This relationship and the generalized support and liking that other group members give him facilitate a dramatic growth spurt for the Emotional Leader. He becomes a model of the change process in the early phases of the group's development. Later, his function changes. The selection of the Emotional Leader occurs during phase I. The development of the role takes place over a number of phases. Therefore, the description of the role of Emotional Leader will be continued at those points where it again appears as a critical event in the development of the group.

SUMMARY OF PHASE I

During phase I, the members must first, indicate something about who they are, and second find a basis of similarity between them that will allow some discernible degree of cohesion to be experienced by all. In addition, the style of the Designated Leader is identified and responded to, and the beginnings of group structure are seen in the creation of norms, the selection of the Emotional Leader and the achievement of a contract. The communication style of the group, the issues dealt with, and the achievement of cohesion set the tone for the qualitative dimensions of the particular group. If some basis for coming together that is not too threatening is found in this initial encounter, then the members are in a position to face the problem of organizing themselves into a functional group. This immediately raises the most crucial issues of goals, the development of norms, and the establishment of a group identity.

Phase II: Establishment of a Group Identity and Direction

GROUP LEVEL ISSUES

The question of an identity raises many crucial issues, whether a group or an individual is seeking clarification. In the group's formative process this throws into sharp relief the issues of (a) purpose for the group; (b) style of communication (competitive–cooperative, authoritarian–democratic, and so on); (c) conditions for participation or limits; and (d) leadership.

Any newly collected group of people who are planning to accomplish some task together, whether work oriented or personal-growth oriented, are faced with the problem of organization. This involves the development of role relationships, the clarification of limits of operation, or goals and subgoals, and the establishment of mutually acceptable norms. This process was tentatively begun in phase I but is entered into in full force during phase II. In all the groups observed, scapegoating was a characteristic behavior at this phase of development. Scapegoating is a group experience that brings together all these issues and solidifies the group at the same time. Differentiation in phase II, therefore, is stereotyped and positions tend toward polarization. The dominant mode of interaction is competitive. The two most critical issues become (a) the question of the criteria for membership, and (b) whether the group can establish a cooperative mode of interaction in solving their problems of development.

PROCESS

In the early phases of a therapy group, the members have had a minimum amount of time to get to know each other, or to clarify their own desires; during this period there exists the maximum amount of ambiguity regarding the issues just outlined. This is a source of anxiety to each member, which is further increased by the ambiguity at this time about the potential for intimate relationships in the group. Under this pressure the members seem to feel pressed to find quick solutions to as many of the problems of organization as possible. Not knowing each other makes it difficult for them to make wise decisions. An immediate problem is that each one tends to push for that kind of order that will make him most comfortable. Therefore, the predominant style of interaction is competitive at this time.

In the initial phases of organization it is probably fair to say that the therapist or Designated Leader is the only person in the group who has the perspective and the ultimate interest in seeing that very person in the group finds the possibility of functioning in it in a beneficial way. He exemplifies then the norms and conditions that have the potential of encompassing the entire collection of characteristics and needs of the group members. The members, in turn, also feel concerned that the group should not fly apart, and that it should find a commonly acceptable direction. In their struggle with each other, they are all concerned with the question of how the Designated Leader will assert himself in this situation, yet they usually do not dare to confront him directly.

The characteristic response to these problems and pressures is the creation of a strong in-group feeling by selecting one member as the scapegoat. Often (thought not always), he is openly attacked. This is usually so intense and effective a mechanism that the person attacked wants to leave the group, and the other members generally wish he would. The group exerts great pressure during this process, trying to hold everyone together and these pressures can be very compelling to therapist and member alike. The therapist can be caught up in the apprehension that the scapegoat is somehow damaging to the group or in some way holding it back. We have found that only deliberate preparation and experience allow the therapist to maintain separateness from the group pressure. In some cases the therapist is drawn into the process so intently that he actively supports or leads the group's efforts to get rid of the scapegoat. In those instances where the group survives this conflict intact and the scapegoated person is accepted as a member of the group, he goes on to serve an important function for all, which will be described below. The resolution of this conflict almost requires the presence of at least one person (usually, but not necessarily, the leader) who does not get caught up in it. The therapist who is able to act as a reality check regarding the communication of the scapegoat and who can help the members to get in touch with the larger group issues that are causing anxiety can help a group to resolve this issue constructively.

In the process of these discussions norms are established regarding the appropriate basis for membership in the group, goals are clarified, and the method for handling conflict in the group is established.

LEADERSHIP ROLES

Scapegoat.   The characteristics of the person selected: the major interpersonal characteristic of the scapegoat is his awkwardness in dealing with the subtle and often nonverbal cues that people use as a way of identifying each other (in terms of social characteristics) and of keeping communication smooth and fluid. He seems unable to tune in on this level of communication, or not to recognize or agree with its content. Despite this fact, however, he asserts himself and seems to flaunt both his own style of participation and his lack of sensitivity to this subtle dimension of communication. In addition to this he has less control over the spontaneous expression of his observations and reactions than have other members. The net result is a tendency to focus on material that is significant, but not commonly exposed so openly by others. He seems especially prone to veer toward aspects of a situation that are obvious but not generally admitted or discussed by others. He is openly vying for leadership, but is unacceptable to that group, at that time.

Ongoing role of Scapegoat.   In the scapegoating process the group punishes him for all these things. If they survive that phase intact, and do accept him as a member, these same qualities serve a constructive function in the group. His insensitivity to nonverbal organizational cues presses the other members to communicate more explicitly and more verbally about this, and therefore makes all of them more aware of the process they are involved in and the assumptions they tend to make about others. His tendency to express his feelings more spontaneously seems to serve the function of initiating new phases and new directions within phases, once the group is prepared to use them in that way. He is, in other words, an excellent example of how a peripheral person can help a group to know itself better, if they accept his presence as legitimate and make constructive use of the differences in his perception of shared events. It should be clear at this point that the scapegoat is not necessarily a disruptive or inappropriate person in any general sense. His clear characteristic is that he is operating on different assumptions from the majority of the group regarding values, norms, and cues. This same person may be an accepted Designated Leader or Emotional Leader in a different group or at a different time.

SUMMARY OF PHASE II

Phase II achieves its goal of establishing a direction for the group, in the process of successfully handling the basic question of the conditions that will determine participation. In resolving this question norms have been established such that persons in the group are welcome because they are human, are interested in being there, have something to contribute, have agreed to join others in a process of group development and in the hope of achieving an experience of personal growth rather than on norms based upon class, economic, racial, or educational determinants, which tend to characterize the initial stereotyped images members form of each other. Probably the most crucial resolution in phase II is the issue of competition or cooperation as modes of operation in the group. In solving this problem the skills and values of the Designated Leader are usually solidly tested. Progress into phase III is dependent upon a shift to a cooperative mode of interaction. Many groups have been observed to fail at this phase of development, unable for a variety of reasons to shift out of a competitive mode. The successful completion of this phase brings cohesion based on dissolution of the polarities posed and on constructively devising norms for this group with its specific goals and needs now made clearer.

Phase III: The Exploration of Individuals in the Group

GROUP LEVEL FOCUS

The focus of this phase is on the development of effective work skills in the group and on the recognition of individuals, their differences, their unique problems, and their potential contribution to the group. This phase is in dramatic contrast to phase II, being characterized by cooperation, interest in others, and considerably greater reflectiveness.

PROCESS

The achievement of some group norms regarding participation and the successful handling of competitive process in phase II seem to lead naturally to the question of how individual differences will be handled in the group.

If the tasks of phase III are successfully accomplished the group achieves a cohesion based on a mutual recognition of individual differences among the members and different personal goals for growth. Because personal growth is the "work" of a therapy group, this stage must also deal with the problem of developing a communication style that leads to the accomplishment of the work to be done. The basic conditions must therefore be created which are conducive to personal growth. Phase III, then, is characterized by (a) the exchange of information of a personal kind with everyone having an opportunity to express and to expose himself, and (b) an experimentation with various modes of communication and their interpersonal implications, ranging from facilitative listening to confrontation. This work-oriented stage has the special feature of allowing everyone to emerge more openly and fully in his uniqueness, in an atmosphere that tends more toward cooperation and caring than the previous two phases. In this process the information and experience is generated that then allows the group to develop a more functional set of relationships later on. It is dependent, however, on the successful resolution of the scapegoating problem because it is this resolution that allows anxiety to subside sufficiently for a cooperative atmosphere to develop.

During this period of work on personal growth, the Emotional Leader is recognized clearly by everyone as experiencing a growth spurt. The Emotional Leader usually makes significant changes in his life outside the group either in work commitments or in intimate relationships and to some degree shares these accomplishments with the group, acknowledging the significance of their support to him.

It seems to be important to the group that everyone participate in the work on personal growth and in the self-disclosure process in particular. Therefore, everyone is expected to participate in some meaningful way (the group of course deciding what is appropriate). There is a sense of establishing a basic equality as "known" individuals at this time. The Designated Leader is the only person on whom this demand is not made explicitly. His own ability to convey openness within appropriate limits is pertinent to his being perceived as facilitative in this process, however. Most often his self-disclosures occur in his interactions with the Emotional Leader.

As phase III comes to an end, the group reviews characteristics, views, experiences, and problems they share. The members reestablish a group emotional bond on a basis that now recognizes individual differences and on the basis of a feeling of equality.

LEADERSHIP ROLES

Emotional Leader (Continued). One of the important dimensions of the Emotional Leader's leadership stems from the fact that he becomes a strong model for the main task at hand for clients in a counseling group:

namely, that of personal change and growth. The individual in this role is someone who comes to the group in a period when he is ready to take some significant developmental step in his growth, but for some reason is fearful, and needs the support and safety of a group.

He is often ready to make immediate use of the general support he gets from the group as well as the very concrete and positive response he gets from the therapist. The kind of change that takes place in this individual cannot be accounted for by the minimal contact he has had with the group. It is as though the support of the therapist and the group are the final conditions needed to trigger a dramatic movement. It is the culmination of much prior preparation. It can be described as a discontinuous change, requiring the integration and reorganization of many different trends in the personality, so that, at this point, all these elements can be translated into real-life decisions that deeply affect his work or personal life. There is great likelihood that this person would have moved in this direction even without the help of the group, but with its support, the quality of this experience is changed. The therapist has the feeling of having given flight to someone in a way that is rare and exciting. Because this development takes place during the early part of the group's experience together, the Emotional Leader becomes an active, dramatic model of the pressures, conflicts, work, and joys of significant growth.

SUMMARY OF PHASE III

The important accomplishments of phase III are the establishment of a cooperative mode of interaction, the creation of an atmosphere in which each person is able to express his own views and himself, and the experimentation with various communication styles and their effects on others. This phase is often quite long as compared with the previous two and is the place and time where a basic trust is built in the group. A cohesion based on the creation of space for and caring about each individual as he is, has profound effects on a group, most important reducing barriers and anxieties regarding closeness.

Phase IV: The Establishment of Intimacy

GROUP LEVEL FOCUS

The demonstration that there is space for and interest in each individual during phase III leads to an atmosphere in the group that allows for the possibility of intimacy to develop. The term is used here in a relative meaning, i.e., intimacy as compared with earlier phases. There are two aspects to the issues dealt with: (a) coping with sexuality as a problem area in life, and as a dimension in the group's relationships; and (b) the expression of tenderness and closeness in the group. The cohesion achieved at the end of phase IV creates the potentiality for a new commitment in the group based on mutual choice to work together.

PROCESS

The more realistic base for cohesion in phase III seems to free people to move toward each other in a more positive way than before. This phase of the group's communication focuses on questions of love and intimacy. The pattern usually followed in therapy groups initially involves a discussion of important, close relationships that individuals have outside of the group—to parents, friends, and spouses. This often gets into some of the problems that they experience in these relationships and from this it is a quick step to a discussion of sexual relationships and problems they may have in that area. In the groups observed here this is usually the most touchy of topics for the members to deal with openly. Perhaps for this reason the fact that it can come up and be dealt with reasonably has several important consequences. Those members who feel that their biggest problems are in this area are now freed to participate more fully in the group. Because the subject is also an important one for everyone else, it is very meaningful to all members that there is a possibility of communicating openly about it. The net result is a noticeable reduction of tension and an impulse to move toward each other more positively. This impulse raises a general problem for the group. How will they relate to each other in terms of intimacy? What about the sexual dimension of relationships within the group? Can tenderness be a part of the experience within the group? The wave of good feeling usually carries the group rather quickly through an exchange of positive feelings via words and gestures that clearly acknowledge warmth and attraction between the members, and including the therapists.

As would be true in any relationship, this initial expression of deep caring and attraction creates feelings of relaxation and expansiveness. Interaction is characterized by freer playfulness and more subtle humor than before. The open acknowledgment of warmth, affection, and physical attraction between members takes place within sensitively observed limits (which would of course vary from group to group). This experience creates a new feeling of cohesion based on an integration of the group on a physical–emotional dimension.

LEADERSHIP ROLES

Designated Leader (*Continued*). During phase IV the role of the Designated Leader begins to change in visible ways. Although his support to the group is crucial during this phase because of the sensitivity of the issues, he nevertheless begins to participate or to be perceived by the members as a more complex person, not just as an authority figure or professional in the group. This change seems both necessary and appropriate, as this phase pulls everyone in the group into closer emotional contact.

Emotional Leader (Continued). Often the changes in the Designated Leader's role are expressed most openly in the relationship to the Emotional Leader. It is during phase IV that the Emotional Leader's position becomes more publicly acknowledged. Because he has experienced a fairly dramatic positive development already, the Emotional Leader has a good deal to give others at this point. His warmth and support of the other members is as crucial as the Designated Leader's in this phase.

SUMMARY OF PHASE IV

Phase IV introduces several significant changes in the group's life. The changes in the Designated Leader's and Emotional Leader's roles parallel the capability of the group members to relate to each other more openly and about issues that normally are difficult to share in group discussion. The ensuing expressions of warmth and attraction imply the potential of a new base for relationships in the group. However, before this becomes a reality, the intimacy must be tested.

Phase V: The Exploration of Mutuality

GROUP LEVEL FOCUS

Phase V is characterized by feelings of vulnerability. The open expression of liking in phase IV implies a mutual commitment to create a deeper relationship. A certain amount of testing and clarification of limits must include the question of how dependency needs will be handled in the context of that relationship and how frustration and hostility will be handled when needs are either not met or not understood. The natural direction to resolving these issues is the development of mutual relationships based on equality and the acceptance of responsibility toward one another. Of necessity this implies a reduction of the dependency on the Designated Leader and the movement toward greater autonomy both individually and as a group.

PROCESS

As phase V begins, it seems as though the individual asks himself and the group "Will this person, or group of persons, use me; will they take advantage of the caring I have offered; will they make unreasonable demands for my support and loyalty; will they find my own demands unreasonable; and most important of all, will there be a mutuality in this relationship: will my needs be met in return for what I give?"

As a result of this shared anxiety regarding their vulnerability, there is strong pressure on everyone in the group to demonstrate his good will.

The nature of the vulnerability that is experienced at this time creates a great problem (and in a sense almost a trap) for anyone who may be experiencing deep fear, hostility, or ambivalence about participating in such mutuality in the group. These feelings are of course being experienced to some extent by everyone, but it is characteristic for one member in particular to experience a crisis at this time.

LEADERSHIP ROLES

Defiant Member.   The person who fulfills this role is usually in a period of intense psychological and social alienation. Often, he has no particular community group or set of friends (outside the therapy group) to whom he feels deeply related and/or from whom he feels he is currently getting meaningful support. The individual in this role is usually experiencing some form of identity crisis of the sort that makes intimacy threatening. He seems to sense that he is at a point in his life where he must change if he is to develop closer and more meaningful relationships with others.

At the same time he tends to feel, and at times to express, intense feelings of rejection of the group and a good deal of self-protectiveness. In a number of the groups observed the person in this role was someone who was not born or raised in the United States and who was experiencing an intense version of culture-conflict when his own values were confronted by the group. The Defiant Member presents the group with a contradictory set of responses at this point in its development. He conveys an inability (or unwillingness) to participate in a mutual relationship with peers, and an inability to let go of his dependency on an authority figure, the Designated Leader. He often places exceptional demands on the Designated Leader during this crisis, in effect punishing him for going along with the change in the group's structure. At the same time he takes the opportunity, created by the expression of caring and good will by others, to expose the full intensity of his fear, hostility, and alienations; that is, to make a demand that is experienced by group members as unreasonable. His needs to be cared for seem to go beyond the limits established by the group regarding dependency. On the other hand, he is frustrated by the demand that he participate in a mutual relationship with peers in order to have his needs attended to.

The personal conflict of this individual helps the group to remain sensitively aware of the dangers of conformity based on seeking fulfillment of dependency needs. He asks to be dealt with as he is, which means that he can only partially participate in the group-level process in a facilitative way at this point.

PROCESS (CONTINUED)

The group must find a way to cope with the issues regarding dependency and frustration in a way that establishes some reasonable expectations for all. In addition they must find a way of coping with the personal crisis of the Defiant Member. Groups are very often unsuccessful in handling the personal crisis and this member leaves the group. When he does stay it is characteristic that a separate "contract" is made with him. That is, some accommodation is arrived at that allows him to express his ambivalence about participation overtly, often including the privilege of not attending meetings of the group regularly, but not being challenged or punished for this. On the other hand, this member relates to the group less punitively, freeing them of the guilt they might otherwise feel about their inability to take care of him adequately.

SUMMARY OF PHASE V

In the process of coping with the crisis of phase V the group's limits for dealing with dependency are explored and clarified. The possibility of expressing hostility and having that dealt with without rejection is also demonstrated in those groups that successfully cope with this phase. The resolution of these problems establishes a dominant norm of equality among peers and a new sense of cohesion develops. The special contract with one person will be seen in the next phase to be the model for all relationships in the group, in the sense that each person is unique and the group's needs change from meeting to meeting, therefore expectations must be flexible.

The achievement of mutuality, at least to a minimal degree, becomes the basis for a reorganization of the group's structure. If the group does not settle the issue of mutuality in one way or another, it can prevent this reorganization from taking place at all.

Phase VI: The Achievement of Autonomy Through Reorganization of the Group's Structure

GROUP LEVEL FOCUS

Phase VI involves the reorganization of leadership structure in the group including major changes in the Emotional Leader's and Designated Leader's roles. It also involves a significant change in the style of participation of all members from this phase on, in the direction of a more function-oriented set of relationships, and a greater fluidity regarding roles.

PROCESS

The personal commitment that has been made in the preceding phases has several noticeable and immediate consequences. There is a friendlier atmosphere characterized by trust, intimacy, and comfort. Sessions from phase VI onward begin in a more jovial mood, with an increase in the playful interaction that allows everyone to get a feeling for the general state of everyone else that day. One has a feeling that there are fewer personal controls operating and as a result more complex and subtle interaction is possible. Probably most dramatic of all is the fact that the new basis for commitment to the group makes possible a change in the leadership pattern of the group. It is at this point that we have a shift of some responsibilities from the therapist to the members. That is, the members take over some of the responsibility for initiation and for control, and as a result the therapist's role changes in the direction of becoming more like an equal partner or member in the group. None of this is meant in absolute terms, however. The therapist is still seen as the one who can be counted on to provide a constructive or therapeutic response to individuals and to problem situations, but the clients are now more inclined to try to handle both things themselves with the therapist becoming a backup or resource person. The quality and the content of the therapeutic process in the group changes. There is evidence of more openness to others and more honesty about self.

This is a major reorganization of the group in the sense that the potential for leadership that has existed among the membership is now overtly asserted. Although several people now share in directing the group's progress, and this is visible on a sociometric ranking, there seems to be a need for an acknowledged leader from among the membership to serve as a coordinator and to offer the generalized emotional support to others that the therapist has been responsible for previously. During this phase, the Emotional Leader emerges into a central, active role.

The basis for reorganization of responsibilities and roles is a more functional one for everyone involved. It reflects an awareness of each member's real needs and real skills. From this point on the group's pattern regarding roles is much more flexible and fluid from session to session, and issue to issue, with each member contributing on the basis of his interest and competence with respect to issues rather than on the basis of a stereotyped role pattern in the group. The Emotional Leader, however, continues to provide an ongoing emotionally supportive function.

The role changes are completed when the Designated Leader gracefully acknowledges the group's emergent responsibilities and continues to support the new functions of the Emotional Leader. In addition, however, his own participating must change in ways that are discernible to the membership, and particularly important is his own self-disclosure on an emotional level that is perceived as comparable to the other members. This, then is finally a complete group of equals as far as their participation in the group is concerned.

LEADERSHIP ROLES

Emotional Leader (Continued).   The selection of the emotional leader is not a discrete event. The process evolves slowly from the first day the group meets, and the Designated Leader influences the choice as much as the members do, and perhaps more in the beginning. The jelling of this decision within the group probably takes place in phase V, when the expressions of affection and caring are open.

The Emotional Leader is well liked by the members and Designated Leader. The liking between him and the Designated Leader is mutual (as expressed on sociometrics and interpersonally). This person is quite responsive to the feeling aspect of any issue that is raised and usually can be quite articulate about such content. In addition he tends to express an interest and concern for all the other members of the group and enjoys a high degree of rapport with the therapists (even when there is more than one). An individual with an active sense of humor makes the most effective Emotional Leader. His sensitivity and caring monitor his use of humor so that it is a positive group experience and not something used at the expense of the group. Although this person often stands out in some ways from the very beginning of the group's interaction, it is in phase VI that his leadership is clearly acknowledged. This leadership is not to be confused with dominance. The responsibility for determining the direction of group action and the attitudes of the members in decisions is shared by all the members to some degree with the dominant action shared by a group of three or four persons. The main functions of the Emotional Leader from phase VI on are to act as a low-key coordinator and to be the main support person to the other members, including the Designated Leader.

SUMMARY OF PHASE VI

The significance of phase VI is that the changes that occur bring the group to a point where they now feel that the process is theirs. They can "own" what goes on in the group and see themselves as determining the process as well as reaping its results. The group achieves separateness from the Designated Leader as authority and/or guardian and it achieves a sense of directing itself. The cohesion that ends this phase brings a deep sense of contentment and satisfaction to the members.

Phase VII: Self-Confrontation and the Achievement of Interdependence

GROUP LEVEL FOCUS

As in phase III, the group again participates in an intensive differentiation experience. The entire atmosphere and goal seem to be different in phase VII, however. In this phase the group is acting more explicitly as a support structure for each individual to take a hard look at himself and the issues that brought him to therapy. The cohesion that ends this phase seems to be based upon (rather than in spite of) an awareness of each member's profound complexity and a sense of sharing the experience of struggle with oneself that is involved in personal change. In arriving at this cohesion the group develops further a fluid pattern of behavior that tends to disperse the earlier role structures. Through sensitive communication the group achieves a pattern of comfortable interdependence.

PROCESS

The sessions that follow the reorganization of the group are marked by a serious attention to the critical issues that each client has brought to the group. The attitudes expressed are more clearly oriented to coping with reality. Each client again receives some significant amount of time and attention from the group. During this phase each member deals with a more tender or painful level of the issues that concern him, and a marked increase in mutual trust can be seen during these sessions. This new differentiation of members often leads to a group level sense of involvement in each person's personal battle with his limits and fears. Characteristically the problems dealt with here are deeper and more difficult psychological issues than have been raised before. This is a time when each member has an opportunity to become more aware of his growing edges, and with the help of the group to work on his personal development in concrete ways.

It is characteristic in this phase for certain members to suddenly become far more self-disclosing than they have been previously, indicating that they perceive the group to be at a different, more trustworthy level of communication. In fact, the group has achieved a state in which many functions and responsibilities are shared, and role behavior is no longer rigid but in fact is taken up freely by one person or another as the situation changes from moment to moment and session to session. By this point in the group's development the members have learned to attend to each other's verbal and nonverbal cues in a sensitive manner. They deal more realistically with each other's moods and issues and are in fact more helpful as mutual problem solvers. They are capable of combining and recombining as the issues and needs change in a fluid, nondefensive manner. The achievement of interdependence in the group's functioning pulls the members together in a comfortable feeling of accomplishment shared by all of them. The emotional level issues dealt with in this phase add a deep sense of sharing in processes of personal growth. This is the group's highest point of functional integration as a work group (the work of a therapy group being personal change).

LEADERSHIP ROLES

Scapegoat (Continued). Although the interaction between this person and the others changes dramatically after the end of phase II, and he is certainly a participant in the intimacy developing phase, it is not until this phase in the group that the member reorganize their perceptions of the scapegoat in a fundamental way and come to see his problems in realistic terms and as only one aspect of him as a person. When a group successfully reaches this point, many members report the changes in their understanding of the scapegoat as one of the significant experiences of participation in the group. The person in this role often experiences a great deal of change in himself as well. It does not appear to be a developmental change as in the Emotional Leader's case but rather a change in his ability to cope with and relate to others, in particular a reduction in defensiveness.

Emotional Leader (Continued). The Emotional Leader experiences an integrative experience during this phase. He has not only asserted himself within the group but now finds himself facilitating rapid movement in his peers. It is a significant experience of appreciated leadership and often has an impact on the Emotional Leader in terms of reorganizing his image of what he is potentially capable of doing elsewhere as well as in the group. In this respect he is again anticipating the general movement of the group as a whole.

SUMMARY OF PHASE VII

During phase VII the group achieves the organizational basis for creative and intensive work. Not only are role dynamics freed and more fluid but each individual comes to a more realistic encounter with himself and his strengths, limits and potentials. If this were to be an ongoing group it would have achieved the kind of functional interdependence that facilitates a high level of productivity over sustained periods of time. In a time-limited group it brings the members to a crucial issue: the relevance of what they have learned in this experience to their life outside this group in the future.

Phase VIII: Independence, the Transfer of Learning

GROUP LEVEL FOCUS

During phase VIII the group members consider the potentiality for close relationships outside of the group. The review the various issues that they dealt with in the group, the way they handled them and their outcome, and attempt to extrapolate about the meaning of their experience in the group for their relationships elsewhere. They are rehearsing their independence from this group and seeking problem-solving help and support for the transfer of new learning into their ordinary life process.

PROCESS

In the last sessions of the group, attention turns to close or potentially close relationships to persons outside the group. In one group, the members explicitly discussed the problems of forming friendships; how they develop or deteriorate; what would be considered reasonable in a friendship, etc. They seemed to be attempting to formulate what they had learned in the group that could be taken to other old and new relationships outside the group. The tone of the group is collaborative in this process in spite of the fact that the issues raise anxiety levels again. As in many other phases each member explores his version of this issue to some extent during phase VIII. One of the interesting dynamics that was observed in the time-limited groups was that the scapegoat was one of the people who most readily and articulately coped with the issue of transfer of learning. He seemed ready for the change. On the other hand, the Emotional Leader, who has had a profound and exciting experience in the group seems to find some difficulty in making the transition. The chances are good that this person will seek contact with the Designated Leader on an individual basis after the group is terminated to address issues in his personal life that have been directly influenced by the profound changes initiated in him by the experience with the group. In effect he has more to transfer than anyone else in the group. The interdependence that the group developed in the previous phase becomes the foundation for now working on the resolution of dependency in this phase. This resolution is an important step in the group's development. As the members deal with their issues in this area the group becomes prepared to deal with termination.

SUMMARY OF PHASE VIII

Phase VIII is a critical experience for group members, in that it allows them the opportunity to relate their experience and learning in the group to their important relationships in their ordinary life. Many encounter-group experiences end before reaching this developmental stage and as a result leave their members with intense feelings of incompleteness. With the achievement of a sense of independence from the group the members are ready to cope with separation, and in the process of that, to cope with unfinished business between pairs of individuals.

Phase IX: Termination of Group and Separation from Significant Persons

GROUP LEVEL FOCUS

The group participates in a process of saying goodby which involves the completion of unfinished (or leftover) business between pairs of individuals and the acceptance of the termination of the group. When the group has been relatively successful, members are ready for termination. They have usually had a fairly significant emotional and developmental experience and shared some deep feelings with each other. In this context the critical issue is coping with ending the process and with separation from important persons. This is achieved by maintaining openness to one's own feelings and to others, by resolving frustrations not attended to earlier, by expressing the warmth and meaning that was shared. The danger in termination is that people may resort to denial of the significance that others have had to them as a way of coping with their pain or tension regarding separation experiences. When the group can maintain an atmosphere of openness and honesty regarding their experience in this phase, they achieve what in some ways is the ultimate or prototypical of cohesive experiences: a deep sense of togetherness even as they part.

PROCESS

The group often rearranges itself a number of times so that various pairings can touch base and deal with their unfinished business and their parting process. The group as a whole participates in some interaction dealing with the same issue and sharing some observations on the meaning and outcome of the experience for each member and for them as a group.

As we mentioned at the beginning, all of these groups were time-limited. The limit was determined before the sessions began, and all the members chose to participate, knowing when the group would end. For those groups that actually evolved through all the phases described, there was complete comfort with the termination. There was not even a hint that the members felt they should continue to meet; on the contrary, there was a unique sense of resolution, a sense of having experienced a satisfying completion.

For those groups that did not arrive at this point in their development, there were varying degrees of dissatisfaction and a noticeable lack of resolution. Members in many of them pressed the therapist to extend the meetings. In at least two cases the members reconstituted the groups informally and met without therapists for a while.

As the final meeting comes to a close one can observe a fair amount of eagerness in many people in the group to go on about their normal business. One of the positive outcomes of a successful group experience is a feeling of integration within oneself and a greater clarity in one's relationship to his work and interpersonal contexts. There is also more awareness of one's "incompleteness" and need for new experiences to continue the work on development, accomplishment, contemplation, or whatever process the particular individual is involved with at the time.

This description of phases represents only a part of the interaction process that goes on throughout the group's experience together. These are highlights or bench marks that help to clarify the context within which a great many other issues are dealt with by the members. When one is participating in an ongoing group, he attends to a great many details that are not on the same level of abstraction as this analysis. It is not always easy to recognize these patterns as they are expressed in the group, until one has had the experience of looking for them in several groups so that he can begin to differentiate those characteristics that are common to all groups from the myriad details that are unique to a particular group. The leader who is aware of the structural development issues in a group is better able to understand the significance of communication that might otherwise seem confusing, and is in a position to ask questions (of himself as well as the group) that bring clarification to the entire process.

INCOMPLETE AND UNSUCCESSFUL
GROUP DEVELOPMENT

The sequence of phases that are followed by a successful group depict the simplest version of group development. Many groups of course do not follow this pattern through all the phases. Some develop problems at an early phase, such as scapegoating, and recycle through that phase several times. If they finally succeed in resolving their issues they may then move on to a smooth developmental process. Among the groups in the data base for this study there are some that did not achieve the degree of development called a functional group. In all cases, however, it was possible to understand and describe what did happen to each group in terms of this analysis of the phases of development.

On the basis of observing this same data, the conclusion was reached that there was a particular point that a group had to reach in its development before the members felt comfortable about termination, and that a group paces itself so that it will reach this point in time. This is true, provided that the group is able to solve each problem of organization at least to a minimal degree, and provided that the leader does not interfere with the process. It would be possible (and in many long-term groups, this does occur) to spend more time in each phase than time-limited groups do. If the time limit is too severe, however, a group may not in fact reach the separation phase described here. This tends to be the case with weekend growth groups and intensive marathon groups. If the group has evolved smoothly through a number of phases, the lack of completeness is not necessarily a bad experience at all, and in fact is perhaps fitting to that kind of group. It is, however, a different experience from participation in a group that does evolve to the point where separation is the developmental issue as well as the necessity imposed by time limitations.

In addition to problems raised by severe time limitations, there are a great many ways in which groups may not develop through the complete sequence of phases that have been described in this chapter. It is not possible to catalog here all the deviations or problems that might develop. However, an attempt will be made to illustrate this point by referring to variations observed in the data.

The most general problem that can occur is that a leader may not recognize the particular level of group process we have described, even when it occurs in a dramatic form. Many times of course, it is not dramatic but rather subtly buried in a variety of things going on at the same time. Problems can be caused by the Designated Leader's previous commitments to a different level of behavioral analysis; for example, one based on intensive training in individual therapy. This perspective can present a serious problem to the leader and his group, if he feels overwhelmed by his concern for attending to several clients simultaneously.

As an example of problems related to leader functioning, the scapegoating process is a very intense experience in the group and a great deal of pressure is brought to bear on everyone to maintain a united front in opposition to the Scapegoat. Many Designated Leaders find it difficult to develop a sufficiently long-range view and a sufficiently deep understanding of the significance of this process to feel comfortable standing separate from the group on this issue, so that they can help the group and the scapegoated person to regain perspective.

When a group succeeds in getting rid of the scapegoated member all the issues remain unresolved and the competitive mode continues to dominate. Groups go on to choose another Scapegoat in that case. In fact the Designated Leader has even been observed to lead the group in the attack. The analysis that was made earlier of the multiple meanings of this group process indicate the long-range significance of the Designated Leader's unsuccessful handling of this problem, whether he leads the group or simply joins it in the attack. A group can become so ensnarled by these consequences that it never develops its structure beyond this point.

Even if the Designated Leader recognizes the issues in a particular group process, he may or may not be in a position to facilitate a constructive solution due to his own feelings about the issues involved. For example, in one of the groups in this sample the therapist recognized the scapegoating process immediately and was quite prepared to support the scapegoated person, but had very punitive feelings toward the group. In consultation later we found that the therapist felt the group was trying to "tame" the Scapegoat. As we have already mentioned the Scapegoat is often someone who differs from the majority of the group either in national or class origins, in educational or vocational achievement, in some crucial aspect of identity or values, and therefore is someone who often feels and acts awkwardly in the group situation. In this case the therapist happened to be in a similar position (i.e., just becoming a part of the American culture) and was strongly identified with the Scapegoat and strongly resistant to "being tamed." In this particular instance the therapist recognized the problem well enough to seek consultation and was open enough to deal with the personal issue involved and therefore to help the group. In another situation, the therapist might not recognize the issue, or might not have help available and would therefore be limited in his ability to deal with the group.

Because the relationship between the Designated Leader and the Emotional Leader is basically one of positive attraction, when they are not of the same sex their perception of each other on a sexual level becomes an important dimension in the development of the group and can be another source of difficulty. In particular if either one is threatened by the other because he perceives him as sexually aggresive, rather than attractive, warm, and basically supportive, a disruption in the development of leadership in the group is likely to occur. Instances of both kinds have been observed; i.e., where the Designated Leader was threatened and where the potential Emotional Leader was threatened. In neither case did the reorganization of the group's leadership take place when the appropriate time for it came.

In addition to the problems that can arise from the therapist, there are many problems that can result from certain group compositions. Particularly when a group is small or extremely unbalanced in its ratio of men and women, there is the possibility that the same person seems to be most available or best suited to both the Scapegoat and the Emotional Leader roles. As we mentioned earlier, the Scapegoat is someone who does indeed seek leadership and asserts it throughout the group's life. However, we have not yet seen a group that was able to change their attitudes sufficiently to accept the person they scapegoat as their Emotional Leader. This problem can have disastrous results on group process, and on the accomplishment of the therapeutic goal.

These are examples of the wide range and great number of problems that can develop that may prevent the group from finding an adequate way of handling some crucial aspect of its development. There are of course many others, and, indeed, there may be a number of characteristic patterns in unsuccessful groups that will eventually be identified.

CRITERIA FOR SUCCESS IN DEVELOPMENT OF GROUP STRUCTURE

At this point, it is important to remind the reader that the description of phases of development is characteristic of a group that has progressed rather smoothly through all of the problems and processes involved in developing a functional structure. It is also important to repeat that this entire sequence is seen as the formative period in development. It represents the process of establishment of a functional group from the components of a potential group. If the same group were to continue for some time beyond phase VIII, it is certainly conceivable that this sequence would be followed by a different set of phases, posing different issues and creating the necessity for new forms of organization in the group. It must be remembered, however, that the introduction of new members tends to recycle the group into the formative process again. Therefore, many group situations in which we participate are characterized by new beginnings at regular intervals, in the context of ongoing organizations.

The successful group is characterized by modal changes during its developmental process with respect to certain crucial issues. These issues are not processed equally during the various phases of the group. Each issue has its own history in the sequence, usually reaching a peak when it becomes the central focus in the group's attention during a particular phase. At that point it becomes a critical condition for further development that the group cope adequately with the issue.

In general, a successful group is seen as shifting modally, during this sequence of phases, with respect to the following issues:

1. Movement from a focus on the therapist (or Designated Leader) as central leader in the group, to a distributed leadership structure.

2. Movement from relationships based on stereotyped role definitions of members to relationships characterized by fluidly changing, functionally oriented role behavior.

3. Movement from concern with a past or future orientation to a concern with the here-and-now.

4. Movement from a predominantly competitive to a predominantly cooperative style of participation in the group's communication and problem-solving.

5. Movement from a superficial level of naming problems, ideas, and feelings to the capability of doing productive work on individual and group-level emotional and instrumental tasks.

6. Movement from a sense of separateness and highly diversified goals to integration, coordination of differences, and a partial overlap of goals among the members.

The achievement of each of these group-level characteristics enhances the group's effectiveness for work in the areas of personal growth and group problem solving. Before discussing the seventh criterion it would be valuable to summarize what evidence there is in the literature for the relevance of the first six criteria.

Although this view of characteristics of an effective and functionally related group of individuals has been developed largely by observing successful groups, the view also receives support from the literature on group relations. For example, Bales and Strodtbeck (1951), Bales (1958), and Guetzkow (1960) observing task groups, and Mann (1967) observing self-analytic classes in social relations, found systematic evidence regarding the diversification of roles over time as a group develops. Many writers have pointed to the fact that groups develop role interdependence in the process of becoming effective and productive organizations. Thomas' (1960) experiment found support for his idea that mutual facilitation was a critical aspect in the development of cohesion, a stronger sense of responsibility, and faster movement toward goals in the groups he studied. Related to the development of mutual facilitation is the shift in successful groups from a competitive style of behavior to a cooperative one. Among the many studies now in the literature on the effects of cooperation and competition, Deutsch's work still stands out for its erudition regarding this significant issue. From his earliest work (1949a, 1949b) his hypotheses regarding the negative effects of competitiveness on productivity in a group endeavor were supported. Cohesion, harmony, and open communication are also generally hindered. Therefore the need to get work done pressures a group to resolve those differences and conflicts that foster competition. Many writers (Bach, 1954; Bennis, 1956; Mann, 1967) have noted that aggressiveness, hostility, and the use of highly stereotyped styles of relating are characteristic of earlier sessions of groups, and that the development of the capacity to get more work done, efficiently, is related to changes in behavior in the direction of greater openness in communication and more flexibility in relating in terms of here-and-now issues rather than in terms of stereotyped images of each other.

7. The sequence of phases that has been described here is characterized by a seventh kind of movement in addition. Each phase was seen to pose an issue or set of issues, with respect to which group members differentiated themselves. In exploring and clarifying their differences and the various meanings of the issues to them individually, they also sought a basis for integration of the range of their diversity and when they succeeded in finding that, they experienced a strong sense of cohesion. It is this process, in which each individual becomes more clearly who he is to himself and others (differentiation) in a context in which he is then drawn closely into a unifying and supportive experience with others (cohesion), that makes group therapy (or any successful group experience) so powerful and growth-producing for the individual. The group is seen as moving from a relatively superficial basis for cohesion based on stereotyped differentiation to a realistic, highly complex basis for cohesion based on a sensitive understanding of each person in the moment as well as in general. The cohesions achieved at the ends of the phases can be seen as being at different levels. The successful group handles each process of differentiation in such a way as to achieve a creative integration at a higher level than the previous phase achieved until finally a functional group has been created in which work can be done effectively and efficiently and individuals can grow without inhibiting the growth of others.

REFERENCES

Asch, S. E. *Social psychology.* Englewood Cliffs, N.J.: Prentice-Hall, 1952.
Ashby, W. R. What is mind? Objective and subjective aspects in cybernetics.

In J. Scher (Ed.), *Theories of the mind.* New York: Free Press of Glencoe, 1962.

Bach, G. R. *Intensive group psychotherapy.* New York: Ronald Press, 1954.

Bales, R. F. The equilibrium problem in small groups. In T. Parsons, R. F. Bales, & E. A. Shils (Eds.), *Working papers in the theory of action.* New York: Free Press, 1953.

Bales, R. F. Task roles and social roles in problem-solving groups. In E. E. Maccoby, T. M. Newcomb, & L. Hartley (Eds.), *Readings in social psychology.* New York: Holt, Rinehart & Winston, 1958.

Bales, R. F. *Personality and interpersonal behavior.* New York: Holt, Rinehart & Winston, 1970.

Bales, R. F., & Strodtbeck, F. L. Phases in group problem-solving. *Journal of Abnormal and Social Psychology,* 1951, **46**, 485–495.

Beck, A. P., & Keil, A. V. Observations on the development of client centered, time-limited therapy groups. *Counseling Center Discussion Papers,* **13** (5). Chicago: University of Chicago Library, 1967.

Bennis, W. G., & Shepard, H. A. A theory of group development. *Human Relations,* 1956, **9**, 415–438.

Bion, W. R. *Experiences in groups and other papers.* New York: Basic Books, 1961.

Deutsch, M. Experimental study on effects of cooperation and competition upon group process. *Human Relations,* 1949, **2**, 199–231. (a)

Deutsch, M. A theory of cooperation and competition. *Human Relations,* 1949, **2**, 129–152. (b)

Durkheim, E. *The rules of sociological method* (Ed. by G. E. Catlin; trans. by S. A. Solovay & P. H. Mueller). Chicago: University of Chicago Press, 1938.

Freud, S. *An outline of psychoanalysis.* New York: Norton, 1949. (1st German ed., 1940.)

Golembiewski, R. T. *The small group, an analysis of research concepts and operations.* Chicago & London: University of Chicago Press, 1962.

Gordon, T. *Group-centered leadership.* Boston: Houghton Mifflin, 1955.

Gray, W., & Rizzo, N. D. History and development of general systems theory. In W. Gray, F. J. Duhl, & N. D. Rizzo (Eds.), *General systems theory and psychiatry.* Boston: Little, Brown, 1969.

Guetzkow, H. Differentiation of roles in task-oriented groups. In D. Cartwright & A. Zander (Eds.), *Group dynamics.* New York: Harper, 1960.

Heinicke, C., & Bales, R. F. Developmental trends in the structure of small groups. *Sociometry,* 1953, **XVI** (23), 7–38.

Hill, W. F., & Elmore, M. A. Toward a theory of group development: Six phases of therapy group development. *Journal of Group Psychotherapy,* 1957, **7**, 20–30.

Howard, K. I., & Orlinsky, D. E. Psychotherapeutic processes. In P. Mussen & M. Rosenzweig (Eds.), *Annual Review of Psychology*, 1972, **23**, 615–668.

Kluckhohn, F., & Strodbeck, F. L. *Variations in value orientation.* Evanston, Ill.: Row, Peterson & Co., 1961.

Langer, S. *Mind: An essay on human feeling.* Vol. I. Baltimore & London: Johns Hopkins, 1964.

Lewin, K. *A dynamic theory of personality. Selected papers* (Trans. by D. K. Adams & K. E. Zener). New York & London: McGraw-Hill, 1935.

Mann, R. D. *Interpersonal styles and group development.* New York: Wiley, 1967.

Merleau-Ponty, M. The primacy of perception and its philosophical consequences. In J. M. Edie (Ed.), *The primacy of perception and other essays.* Evanston, Ill.: Northwestern University Press, 1964.

Murray, H. A. (and collaborators). *Explorations in personality.* New York: Oxford University Press, 1938.

Parsons, T. An outline of the social system. In T. Parsons, E. A. Shils, K. D. Neagele, & J. R. Pitts (Eds.), *Theories of society: Foundations of modern sociological theory.* New York: Free Press, 1961.

Parsons, T., Bales, R. F., & Shils, E. A. Phase movement in relation to motivation, symbol formation, and role structure. In T. Parsons, R. F. Bales, & E. A. Shils (Eds.), *Working papers in the theory of action.* New York: Free Press, 1953.

Rogers, C. R. The necessary and sufficient conditions of therapeutic personality change. *Journal of Consulting Psychology*, 1957, **21**, 95–103.

Rogers, C. R. A theory of therapy, personality, and interpersonal relationships, as developed in the client-centered framework. In S. Koch (Ed.), *Psychology: A study of a science.* Vol. III. *Formulations of the person and the social context.* New York: McGraw-Hill, 1959.

Rogers, C. R. The characteristics of a helping relationship. In C. R. Rogers, *On becoming a person.* Boston: Houghton Mifflin, 1961. (a)

Rogers, C. R. To be that self which one truly is: A therapist's view of personal goals. In C. R. Rogers, *On becoming a person.* Boston: Houghton Mifflin, 1961. (b)

Runkel, P. J., Lawrence, M., Oldfield, S., Rider, M., & Clark, C. Stages of group development: An empirical test to Tuckman's hypothesis. *The Journal of Applied Behavioral Science*, 1971, **7**(2), 180–193.

Schroedinger, E. *What is life? and other scientific essays.* Garden City, N.Y.: Doubleday, 1956.

Schutz, W. C. *Firo: A three-dimensional theory of interpersonal behavior.* New York: Holt, Rinehart & Winston, 1958.

Simmel, G. *Soziologie.* Leipzig: Duncker & Humbolt, 1908.

Stark, W. *The fundamental focus of social thought.* London: Kegan, 1962.

Sullivan, H. S. *The interpersonal theory of psychiatry.* New York: Norton, 1953.

Thomas, E. J. Effects of facilitative role interdependence on group functioning. In D. Cartwright & A. Zander (Eds.), *Group dynamics.* New York: Harper, 1960.

Tuckman, B. W. Developmental sequence in small groups. *Psychological Bulletin*, 1965, **63**, 384–399.

von Bertalanffy, L. General systems, theory. *General Systems,* 1956, **1**(1), 1–17.

CHAPTER 15

Client-Centered and Symbolic Perspectives on Social Change:
A Schematic Model

William R. Rogers

It is not remarkable that the dominant emphasis in the theoretical formulation of client-centered therapy has been on the individual. The therapeutic interests and research attention have properly been focused on the development of personality; the qualities of feeling or experiencing; the nature of incongruity, distortion, denial, threat, and breakdown in psychopathology; and the process of psychotherapy.

If there were a central dictum in client-centered therapy, it would probably be something like this: Above all else, remain attentive to the experiential feeling realm of each individual's unique internal frame of reference! From this has stemmed much of the therapeutic skill and personality theory innovation in the 30 years that have passed since Carl Rogers' first publications.

What is remarkable is that, until very recently, little attention has been given to the therapist's responsibility for understanding and influencing the determinants in the social structure that have a direct bearing on the psychological functioning or dysfunctioning of individuals. Social psychology has not been without influence, but in spite of occasional references to an objective reality environing the subjective reality of individual experience, the main responsibility of the client-centered therapist has continued to be perceived directly in relation to the individual client seeking help in personal or group therapy.

One possible exception might be the work of Batten and Batten (1967) relating client-centered approaches to group work and communities; however, this still has more of a focus on individual personal growth than on fundamental change in community structures. Even as late as 1970, with the publication of the excellent Hart–Tomlinson volume, *New Directions in Client-Centered Therapy*, we find only scanty attention to social dimensions of therapeutic practice. There is one note recognizing this dimension (Hart & Tomlinson, 1970, p. 31). But the preponderance of the book is given to principles in psychotherapy, process scales, client–therapist interaction variables, developmental theory, group experience, and phenomenological and experimental methodologies. Little is again mentioned about the environmental responsibilities of the therapist.

My impression is that this relative neglect of social dimensions is not so much a theoretical or moral oversight as it is a relatively conscious decision to delimit methods and theories to the processes of individual dysfunction and growth with which the therapist has the greatest daily contact and expertise. Besides, there was something at stake in preserving awareness of the immediacy of unique personal experience amidst the clamor to develop and regularize social bureaucracies, increase social planning, and generalize about the nomethetic features of personality. Rogers, like Gordon Allport (1955) and Robert White (1966), championed the call to understand the individual integrity and idiosyncratic development of each human life.

Yet Rogers was also aware that the freedom of individual growth could easily be stifled by routine, conformity, and conditional positive regard common in the education, socialization, and vocations of thousands of people. In the essays collected in *On Becoming a Person* (Rogers, 1961), he emphasizes the qualities that educators and community developers should have in common with the psychotherapist (or good parent): the patience to listen carefully and accurately to others' feelings and ideas, the willingness to be known, the courage to let others grow in ways that respond to their own deepest potentialities, honesty in interpersonal communication, and enduring trust in deeply human striving for self-actualization.

Rogers has also repeatedly emphasized the importance of a person's immediate situation over extensive analysis of past determinants as critical in therapeutic understanding. "Field theory has won out over theories rooted in the sequential past [Hart & Tomlinson, 1970, p. viii]." And field theory certainly lays stress on the multiple social and interpersonal relationships that interact with reciprocal force and must be addressed with more comprehension of these systems than has yet been obtained. Furthermore, I would argue that it is in the interests of psychotherapeutic responsibility to do so, because these systems have a direct bearing on the psychological well-being of literally millions of persons who have neither the access nor the financial resources to reap any benefits from standard modes of individual and group therapy.

We should not leave this invitation begging. It is our moral and therapeutic challenge, as well as of theoretical interest in itself, to seek some fresh understanding of the processes of social dysfunction and recovery that complement and interact with our psychological analyses. It may be that such understandings, and the accompanying strategies of engagement in social change, could have a far broader effect on optimal development of human lives and relationships than the more remedial effects of therapy as traditionally conceived.[1]

I would like to suggest in this chapter that client-centered therapy has not only the rudimentary suggestions of the importance of this task, but also a variety of suggestive values and approaches that could substantially deepen our understanding of social phenomena and of optimal modes of involvement for those interested in facilitating social change.[2]

A second theoretical framework that informs this chapter could be identified as a symbolic and moral consciousness, which for me has roots in an understanding of the religious and value-orienting functions of communal experience. These frames of reference, as modified by my own community and psychotherapeutic involvement, form a meaningful base for extrapolation when reflecting on empirical instances of both community breakdown and constructive change. Such reflections, and subsequent new insights into social change, were stimulated for me in a course presenting case studies in public psychology, taught by my colleagues Ira Goldenberg, David McClelland, John Shlien, and myself in 1971–72. Hence, I see this present endeavor as combining both empirical analysis and theoretical extrapolation in the interests of generating a model suggestive of new principles in the emerging field of public psychology.

The model-building proceeds in two basic stages:

1. A client-centered and symbolic analysis of community identity and community decay (pathology).

2. A client-centered perspective on the facilitation of social change (therapy)—with special reference to a case study of social change in Boston. This stage will be illustrated by a detailed schematic diagram.

[1] It is largely in response to such concerns that the new interdisciplinary program in Clinical Psychology and Public Practice at Harvard, and similar programs at Wright Institute and elsewhere, have emerged.

[2] I refrain from using the term "social change agent," for, as in psychotherapy, the real agency, that is, empowering initiative, must derive from relationships to client populations.

A CLIENT–CENTERED AND SYMBOLIC ANALYSIS OF COMMUNITY IDENTITY AND COMMUNITY DECAY (PATHOLOGY)

Following in part the approach of Carl Rogers (1951) in *Client-Centered Therapy*, I find it appropriate to construct a series of propositions that may be useful in specifying features of community identity and decay. These propositions incorporate the therapeutic and symbolic considerations alluded to in the preceding statement of method. My hope is that they will deepen our analysis of community identity and decay, augmenting other available sociological analyses of these phenomena.

1. *Individuals seek a community of belonging, understanding, and mutual support that will enhance the actualization of life.* It is so clear as to be almost banal to observe that individuals find relationships necessary to meet not only physical needs but also needs for a common identity. This sense of belonging seems to be directly related to what Rogers has called the self-actualizing principle. For without the realization of a community of belonging, it would be impossible to conceive of the emergence of a self-concept, of personal identity, of genuine warmth and acceptance, or a productive work. It is particularly apparent in a religious understanding of personal development that people seek common identification in what is variously called A People of God, a Gathered Community, a Community of Faith, or some other form of self-identification as congruent with a context of "sacred space." In one sense, every community has its sacred space —that is, its geographical and psychological territory with protected boundaries and a core sense of mutual coherence. It is also clear that communities, once formed, tend actively to attract persons through various forms of proselytizing, or chamber of commerce image building (whether positive or negative), or simply personal attraction of other like-minded persons, families, or racial and ethnic groups.

2. *Every community develops its own distinctive symbolization or myth of itself.* The imaginative self-consciousness that contributes to this myth-building may have a variety of forms. For instance, some communities view themselves as relaxed, sunny, private, spacious, secure; others may have an image of decay, dirt, distrustful relations, and apprehension; others may see themselves as large, extended, ethnic tribes—volatile, loving, self-protective, loyal. A number of the classical sociological studies of communities like Park Forest, Illinois; Muncie, Indiana; Wellesley, Massachusetts; Phoenix, Arizona; and Glens Falls, New York, have articulated the shape of this symbolic consciousness, at the same time demonstrating the incongruity of components in the life style that either directly or

obliquely violate the dominant self-image. The symbolic consciousness has mythic dimensions in that it frequently interprets the history of how that particular community came to be, with tales of founding heroes, the tribulations in its social and ideological history, anticipations of its burgeoning directions, as well as the sense of the common ingredients making it coherent. At times these elements are symbolized by critical incidents, significant persons, or geographical and fabricated monuments that either set boundaries or point to the center of the community's self-consciousness. The mythic consciousness for a community can be understood as parallel to the self-concept in personality formation.

3. *Persons within a community are potentially better able to understand and articulate the identity and hopes of that community than are persons from outside.* Parallel to client-centered therapy's notion of the internal frame of reference of the individual and of each individual's unique potential access to that frame of reference, it is possible to speak of the priority and accuracy of internal self-awareness on the part of residents of a neighborhood that frequently supersedes the analyses and observations of researchers or "interveners." The subtleness of the folk wisdom, patterns of communication, historical awareness (or historylessness), and scope of the community's self-consciousness should be given extended and sensitive attention by anyone seeking to understand the community. The necessity for deep and careful listening is no less present in a community than with individuals, especially when those communities seem increasingly distraught, chaotic, or disruptive.

4. *New residents in a community gradually adopt and identify with the dominant symbolic awareness of that community.* A process of acclimatization occurs when people at first identify with a small portion of the mythic consciousness of the community and gradually adopt more and more of its features into their own awareness and style of living. Frequently those features of the community—whether a spacious lawn, chic housing, ethnic solidarity, access to services, or whatever—that meet individual or living-group needs are subsumed into a broader consciousness or "feel" of the atmosphere of hopes and disappointments that are the affective components of the community's self-consciousness.

5. *Some elements of the community are "owned" as important to the identity of that community, while other elements are denied or distorted in the common awareness.* Depending on the dominant myth of the community, some may see the high quality of schools, the care of yards and houses, preservation of historic homes and parks, preservation of quiet and privacy as the elements to be owned. Others may view nearness to family and relatives, proximity to employment, ease of public transporta-

tion, and immediate access to shopping and human services as the elements most to be owned. In each case these elements stand as congruent with the predominant group-consciousness of the community. The elements of community life that are denied or distorted tend to be those elements that stand in conflict with the dominant image and potentially threaten loyalty to the community. In one case these elements may include felt isolation and loneliness across the boundaries of the spacious lawns, perpetual guilt in the quiet participation in economic systems that deny other people's rights and opportunities, the deceit and apprehensive competitiveness that mark what David Bakan (1967) calls the *mystery–mastery complex* in which people have to keep their lives hidden (mysterious) from each other in order to maintain the mystification that supports a pretense of authority and mastery over one's own life as well as over other people. In another case the distorted awareness may conceal the extent of the destruction of persons and property, of alcoholism and drug use, of air and noise pollution, or fear of radical change. It may also be that in communities with "low" group-images, the distorted elements would include positive dimensions of community strength, stable employment, neighborly self-sacrifice, and multiple incidents of human compassion.

6. *These distorted or denied elements can be brought into awareness within the community.* Occasionally journalistic investigations carried on by the press or other media can expose elements that have been concealed because of a negative valence in relation to the dominant self-consciousness. Also, block organizations and neighborhood councils, such as those instigated by the Industrial Areas Foundation, and other activities of people like Saul Alinsky, can increase consciousness of subterranean and potentially damaging elements of a community's incongruity. New simulation games such as "Starpower," "Blacks & Whites," and "Suburbia," also have dramatic power in raising a community's awareness.[3] Church, school, lodge, or gang members may draw the attention of the community to similar distortions or injustices that violate the common myth of the community's well-being.

It can be further observed that the modalities in which attention is brought to denied elements can vary between what might be called *legalistic* and *epigenetic* modes. In the legalistic mode, the chief concern is with the question, Who is to blame? And the apparent intent of bringing the element to awareness is that of exposing criminal neglect, personal hypocrisy, professional fraud, or communal irresponsibility in such a way as to generate guilt, and possible indictment, retribution, or amelioration. In

[3] See especially some of the community-awareness games developed by Community Change, Inc., Wakefield, Mass.

the *epigenetic* mode, there is a ground swell of awareness emerging within the community itself as private conversations and informal groups come to identify more accurately incongruous performance in the community, taking responsibility for their common blindness in the past and instigating projects of social change based on this expanded consciousness.[4]

7. *The extent of subliminally perceived threat from the distorted or denied elements of the environment is directly proportional to a decreased scope of participation in, or relationship to, that environment.* The perception of threatening elements within the community may be accentuated through the legalistic or epigenetic modes mentioned above, but it may also be accentuated through repeated experiences of individually felt insecurity in the community. Frequently this insecurity may be generated by threats to one's safety, exaggerated by increased crime rates, poor lighting, personal property damage, and the like. But beneath this, there may be a more insidious threat, only dimly perceived, to the relatively unconscious myths that have in the past identified and solidified the community. When, for instance, an ethnic group has established traditions of personal interaction, shopping, laundry, worship, and so on in a community, and then finds itself gradually cornered and overwhelmed by persons with divergent backgrounds, the sense of solidarity and self-identification diminishes and there is increasingly less participation in the political, religious, and social life of the community. Typically, such individuals and families respond to the threat by increasing their isolation, preferring to stay at home, often fixated on television, or in private clubs. Thus a vicious cycle develops in which feelings of loss of safety lead to protective isolation that (a) diminishes prior identification with the persons and myths that have given solidarity, (b) increases feelings of fragmentation in the community; (c) generates increased feelings of apprehension; and (d) leads to further isolation.

8. *There is an optimal level of diversity in the homogeneity–heterogeneity spectrum of a community.* When homogeneity is too high, there may be increased lassitude, boredom, self-indulgence, and quiescence. This phenomenon not only isolates the community from growth and change, but may also permit decay or reification of the symbolic images that have given vitality and meaning to the community. Forms of worship, recreation, or intercommunication within the community may become so sterile as to lose any potency in organizing the experience of the residents.

[4] This epigenetic mode is close to a new model emerging from "Greenhouse" organized by Phil Slater and others in Cambridge, who are concerned with expanding and deepening the group awareness of communities in ways that increase self-generated consciousness of new goals and new identity as opposed to capitulation to externally manipulated social planning.

When heterogeneity becomes too great, there is an increase of suspicion, fear, distrust, guardedness, political maneuvering, and subgroup alienation. This condition sometimes leads to the embattling of competing myths regarding life style, meaningful behavior, and community goals. The potential clashes resulting from this heterogeneity may increase the sense of threat and the possibility of violence when one group tends to maneuver its values into political or economic forms that subjugate and depress other elements in the community. Any sensitive model of community development must take as one of its early tasks the responsibility of increasing the accuracy of communication among such threatened subgroups within a community and of finding modes of ameliorating differences while not destroying the integrity of minority myths and hopes. Without such attention, optimal levels of diversity may be lost and pluralism may turn into either chaos or conformity.

9. *The overuse of space tends to exaggerate the effects of both homogeneity and heterogeneity.* In crowded inner city areas where there is a gradual erosion of recreational space, school yards, and green belts, with a simultaneous subdividing of existing housing into multiple units or into compacted public housing and high-rises, there is an increase in the threat of both boredom and violence at opposite ends of the spectrum. Some overcrowding of space, particularly in homogeneous communities, tends to accentuate positive as well as negative elements of the homogeneity. There may be more front-stoop visiting, more sense of solidarity and power in the face of external threats, more feeling of rapport and common self-identification. But there may also be an increased sense of common impotence, fear for common survival as a group or as individuals, shallowness of political engagement, and increased quiescence in the face of feelings of ensnarement and helplessness in the social, economic forces of the larger city–state–federal complex. Alternatively, there may be in crowded heterogeneous populations an increased awareness of irresolvable differences and the possibility of overt and violent struggles for dominance in either the political sphere, the control of schools, the looting of businesses, police–community relations, or the territorial warfare of gangs.

10. *Particularly under conditions of abrasive and conflicting heterogeneous groups in a community, along with political irresponsibility, a sequence of deterioration develops.* Increasingly the self-image of the community breaks down. There is the loss of a unifying cultural symbolic that had given meaning and centeredness to that community. Divergent, competing images develop and fade. Frequently a sense of mythic sterilization develops in which individuals feel no sense of common belonging around any patterns of meaning, life style, or sense of history.

There is increasing isolation of diverse subgroups from one another. Persons tend to seek alliances only with others like themselves. Employment, community services, eating, transportation, worship, and recreational patterns tend to follow stricter subgroup boundaries.

The common sense of responsibility for order and protection of the community decreases as subgroups become suspicious of one another and lose a sense of responsibility for the whole. There is a loss of what have been called "block watchers," persons aware of when other families are in or out of town, of personal details of residents' lives, of whose car is parked where, and of who can be called on in times of need. Responsibility for the protection and welfare of the community is increasingly given over to formal guardians; police, welfare agencies, community service organizations. This phenomenon tends to generate increased resentment and misunderstanding about the values that such formal agents should be protecting and increasing doubts about the extent of accountability to the community. Personal rights and personal freedoms are perceived as threatened. And the sense of fear and apprehension in relation to persons with differing meanings and values from one's own increases.

To understand what is behind this sequence of deterioration, it is important to see that the defensive parameters of the constricted range of life space have become simultaneously (a) *more rigid* in order to protect against subsumed and increasingly obvious threats, and (b) *more vulnerable*; that is, more susceptible to explosive collapse. The collapse may come also in one of two ways: (a) as *depression* or inward collapse, in which persons feel individually defeated, hopeless, trapped in a situation that is uncomfortable and isolating but which seems to have no resolution. Or, (b) *violence*, or outward explosion in which there is direct individual and group attack on other groups or their symbolic representatives, such as the housing complex, the police station, the ethnic club. In cases where the threat is perceived in terms of a total economic or political system, the form of violence again may take symbolic form; but in this case toward diffuse and subsidiary representatives of industrial, business, or political power accessible within the communities of those protesting. Increasingly the energies of persons responding to threats of a repressive nature on their life space tend to be organized and focused more coherently on particular industries, institutions, or government practices seen as especially responsible in the perpetuating of social injustices.

11. *Chronic decay in the community accelerates when individual helplessness and depression, as well as episodes of violence, fail to restore a sense of common identity, growth, and cohesiveness.* This process is generally marked by the abandoning of buildings, poor trash removal, poor lighting, decreased police protection, increased housing code violations, the

retreat of personal services to more stable locations (drug stores, groceries, restaurants, physicians, dentists, mental health agencies, and the like), the retreat of industry to more spacious or economically viable areas, and a decrease in the construction of new schools, churches, or recreation facilities. Amid these phenomena there is a conscious breaking of the gestalt of any coherent myth about the community. The breaking of the gestalt of the community self-definition is analogous to the breaking of the gestalt of the self-concept in individual psychopathology. Once the self-concept is broken, frightening feelings of loss of control and a simultaneous onrush of previously denied or distorted experiences leave the individual in a desperate and helpless condition usually referred to as pathological breakdown (or psychosis). This sometimes eventuates in a self-constructed dissociated inner world of protection utterly devoid of interpersonal communication. Similarly in the community experience, no hope seems left to restore the integrity, the history, or the optimism about a meaningful future of the community, but rather there is desperate and noncommunicative retreat. With this a series of alternatives may follow:

(a) An increased sense of *depression* with concomitant feelings of isolation, hollowness, and abandonment of any originally compelling myth about a sense of belonging or cohesiveness in the community.

(b) An increased sense of *bitterness*, trappedness, and resentment in the face of forces that seem impending and uncontrollable. Such feeling may be more active and more painful than the experiences of depression.

(c) Increased *fear* of being attacked or overwhelmed by persons, ideas, or forces alien to oneself. Sometimes this fear is identified as a kind of paranoia, but more accurately it may be a clear symbolization in awareness of the dangers to survival present in the situation.

(d) Increased fantasies of *escape*, often followed by abandoning the community literally to seek one apparently more stable, or one that has nostalgic reminiscences of childhood or a home country. Or abandoning the community psychologically through sensual–sexual or psychoactive drug excesses, or through the wonderlands of the media or even a medium.

(e) *Psychotic* developments generated by an overwhelming sense of meaninglessness and loss of the community of belonging. The components of anxiety in this experience can lead to unrealistic images, both of oneself and the community, that idealize desired elements in the community but collapse the real distance from those elements and permit the self-deceit that the elements really are present. These unrealistic images may attempt to preserve some remnant of a previous symbol of belonging and understanding in the community, but do so at the risk of unrealistic alienation from massive forces that in fact threaten both individual life and community identification. This is an example of desperate attempts to rebuild a gestalt of community coherence on a much smaller ground in order to replace that which is shattered but too painful to deal with in its shattered state.

A CLIENT–CENTERED PERSPECTIVE ON THE FACILITATION OF SOCIAL CHANGE, WITH SPECIFIC REFERENCE TO A CASE STUDY OF SOCIAL CHANGE IN BOSTON

Interest in constructive social change is clearly motivated by a concern to reverse processes of community decay as discussed in the preceding section. Like therapy, however, which is more than remediation, social change is also a proactive responsibility among those concerned with facilitating optimal conditions in which persons can thrive together. It is my belief that whether social change is instigated as a corrective (for instance at a point such as item 6 in the above-listed propositions) or as a fresh developmental process, it is best carried on by persons who see themselves as actively listening to, facilitating, and augmenting the energies and hopes of the persons themselves who live within that community. I relate this to the epigenetic model in that both the awareness of needs to change and the germs of ideals toward which growth may be directed emerge from potential resources and cooperation within the community itself. A number of interesting attempts have been made to deal structurally and theoretically with the dynamics of social change in communities. Among the more successful attempts have been Alinsky (1971), Caplan (1964), Cox (1970), Klein (1968), Ruoss (1968), Tornatzky, Fairweather, and O'Kelly (1970), and Wileden (1969). Although some of these positions are attentive to the dynamics of community involvement in the planning process, many of them have abstracted the process to a level of theoretical analysis, which then becomes too diffuse or generalized to be of real help to persons involved in a change process. In the discussion that follows in this chapter, I want to be attentive both to the involvements in what I have called the epigenetic process, and to the need for clarity and specificity in articulating concrete steps that can be taken by persons wishing to facilitate community change processes.

To make these steps, and the critical decisions they involve, more vivid, I have developed a schematic diagram (see Figure 15.1). The discussion will also be illustrated by allusions to the South End Urban Renewal

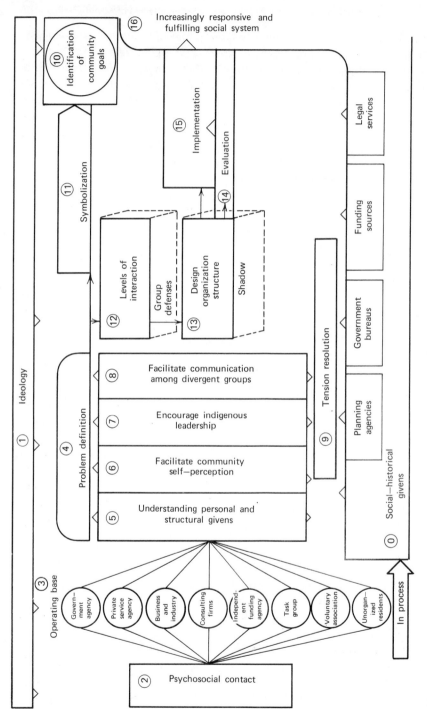

Figure 15.1. A schematic diagram of interactive systems in planning for social change.

Project of Boston, with special attention to the involvement of an organization called Cooperative Metropolitan Ministries (CMM).[5]

First of all, underlying and imbedded in any community change is a multitude of social–historical *givens* (Schematic No. 0, Figure 15.1). Although it is true that all communities are in the process of change continually, one can, for purposes of structural understanding, point to existing agencies, geographical boundaries, transportation patterns, social interaction patterns and the like, which characterize the structure of life in a community. Of particular importance in the beginning of any planned social change process is an assessment of the *readiness to change*. Somewhat parallel to the psychotherapeutic importance of individuals coming to some awareness of their own anxiety, discomfort, or incongruity prior to meaningful initiation of therapy, so communities must in some way come to an awareness of their own difficulty or decay, or to some consensual awareness of their desire for a new possibility, prior to active engagement in constructive social change. It is perhaps unfortunate but true that crises within a community often precipitate the greatest sense of urgency and highest dedication to constructive work in rebuilding common strength from blight and brokenness.

Also, the givens of social–economic background, ethnic and racial life styles, divergent hopes and despairs of existing community institutions, employment practices, and so on are directly related to the process of community development. In particular, as the base of Figure 15.1 suggests, given institutions such as metropolitan planning agencies and governmental mechanisms (welfare and health delivery, mental health, veterans' services, child services, job training services), funding agencies (private foundations, banks, endowed institutions), professional consultants (lawyers, economists, architects, psychiatrists, psychologists), and legislation governing regulatory mechanisms and individual rights and responsibilities, must all be taken into account knowledgeably and seriously in any planning for constructive social interaction.

In the case of the South End Urban Renewal Project, there was a clear sense of readiness for change, both among the residents and in the Boston

[5] Documents dealing with this project have included the official urban renewal plan published by the Boston Redevelopment Authority (B.R.A.) (1964) under the general chairmanship of the Right Reverend Monsignor Francis Lally; specifications for the plan and a message to the residents prepared by Richard Green for the B.R.A. (Green, 1964); and reports prepared by the Director of the Cooperative Metropolitan Ministries (CMM), the Reverend Charles Harper (Harper, 1971). The South End Urban Renewal Plan was first presented by the B.R.A. in 1964, with specifications for an area of 566 acres, housing approximately 31,500 residents. CMM, an interfaith organization involving eventually 39 metropolitan churches and temples, became active in community development relative to the plan in 1965–1966.

Redevelopment Authority. This area had dropped in population during a period of 50 years from 76,000 to roughly 31,500. All seven of the public schools had been built prior to 1884. There were only approximately 9 acres of playgrounds for 7500 children. Housing for the elderly was grossly inadequate. Housing was increasingly being taken over by nonresident landlords. There were increasingly heavy concentrations of liquor stores (over 116 liquor licenses). There were at the same time sources of strength in the churches, medical units, settlement houses, and industries in the area. And though nonresident ownership and lodging houses were increasing, still roughly 50% of residential structures were owner-occupied.

Most important, various groups in the community were interested in seeing blighted areas rebuilt and were interested as well in greater communication and a sense of common identity within their geographically as well as politically defined area. The emergence of CMM, Community Action Project representatives, and settlement-house groups discussing large-scale redevelopment in the community were as important as the declaration by the Boston Redevelopment Authority and the Boston Housing Authority that the South End was a redevelopment area.

Community groups not having the money to do serious architectural or construction planning prior to approval of plans by the Redevelopment Authority and the Department of Housing and Urban Development (HUD) in Washington—a circumstance that stymies many grass-roots planning efforts—turned in this case to local churches and synagogues. Special endowment monies from denominational sources were released, and these became instrumental in early funding of local neighborhood groups. It enabled professional assistance from lawyers, architects, contractors, and "packagers" in order to develop ideas into a plan that could be funded by state and federal allocations. Knowledge of legislation governing public land acquisition, financing, federal housing subsidies for rent and construction, formation of holding corporations and realty trusts was important in the successful development by CMM in the area.

For any individual or group contemplating active involvement in constructive social change, there are significant questions of ideology (Schematic No. 1)—political, social, and ethical—which have a significant bearing on one's perspective on social change, one's choice of an operating base, the definition of community problems, the choice of levels of intervention, and the perception of goals (as indicated by the arrows from Schematic No. 1, in Figure 15.1). By ideology I mean a thought-out set of assumptions and ideas concerning the nature of human life and community existence, the nature of social change processes, and the optimal modes of relationship between social change agents and community constituents.

One such assumption may have to do with what might be called a *community growth principle*. Analogous to the assumption of a self-actualing principle in individual organisms, it might be argued that given optimal possibilities for inner communication among groups and awareness of the needs for survival, welfare, and fulfillment for individuals with all their diversity, communities can and will make wise choices in the direction of their mutual well-being and growth. An alternative asumption might be that communities are chaotic and competitive social systems in which individuals seek only self-interests, and where competition and chaos must be carefully managed and controlled by administrative authority. My own position champions the first assumption, recognizing that this has considerable bearing on the whole scheme that follows, just as assumptions of a growth principle directly (and positively!) affect constructive movement in the process of therapy.

Another important assumption has to do with the *ethical prerogative* of a majority to govern while balancing the rights of minorities to representation and optimal fulfillment. Assumptions about change and justice must eventually be based even more profoundly on considered views of the nature and destiny of human experience itself and of the ontological context in which life takes its shape and participates in historical meaning.

As is illustrated in Figure 15.1, there are a number of points at which one's ideology becomes important in decisions relating to social change. One is the point of original contact with the community. It makes considerable difference, for instance, whether a person interested in facilitating change goes into a community or institution at the request of that community or institution and works in terms of the tensions, goals, hopes and self-images of those constituents; or whether he/she has a carefully prepared set of strategies and goals worked out in advance, and then seeks communities in which intervention strategies may be employed to actualize the preconceived goals. Of course there is a strategy in between these two in which a person may enter an institution or community as a consultant to work on a particular problem, but may in midstream change roles from that of an operating technician in meeting externally defined ends, to that of a moralist attempting change within the institution or community according to goals that seem more humanizing in the view of the change facilitator (or, in this instance, change agent).

It is my belief that a responsible facilitator of social change must have both (a) some profound sense of the optimal conditions in which human life moves toward fulfillment and maturity, and (b) some sense of the importance of *listening deeply* to the needs and concerns of individuals and groups within constituent communities where he/she is engaged. The tension in this double sensitivity most frequently comes when the interests of a primary contracting agency or government office seem to be operating to the detriment of unrepresented or disenfranchised groups—usually minorities, children, the poor, or transient persons. In the interest of actualizing the conditions for well-being among all persons, it may be necessary at points to challenge or even deny the self-serving interests of agencies that have the political and/or financial power to terminate one's activity in a particular project. At the least one must always strive to understand the felt meanings on both sides and improve communication between policy administrators and constituent persons.

Such ideological questions also control to some degree the selection of an operating base or professional affiliation (Schematic No. 3). For instance, quite variant responsibilities would accrue from identifying oneself with a profit-making, consulting organization, a government department, a social service agency, or a task-oriented voluntary association. Implications with regard to funding, accountability, professional relationships, and overall goals would differ considerably from one to the other.

Matters of ideology also affect the way in which problems are defined in the community setting—certainly the degree to which matters of understanding and facilitation of communication within diverse subgroups in the community are undertaken. It also affects levels of intervention (Schematic No. 12) in ways that will be discussed later. Ideology also affects the specific modalities that are utilized in the processes of symbolization of community life and social goals. Within some ideologies, attention to symbol-making and communal development of a *meaningful* myth of local history and purpose seems unimportant. Within the view I present here it is a matter of considerable importance. The degree to which symbols reflect accurately both the honest needs of persons within a community and the experience of cohesiveness of persons with diverse backgrounds determines the power of a shared vision of desired ends, and concomitantly, the possibility of sustained work toward those ends.

In the case of the Cooperative Metropolitan Ministries a religious ideology comprising Christian and Jewish religious traditions led both neighborhood and suburban persons to become engaged within an ethic of love, willingness to suffer on behalf of another, a redemptive concern to actualize new potential for creativity and reconciliation in the midst of brokenness, and a wisdom about the "belongingness" of all persons. They specified as one of their goals the intent to engage as broad a spectrum of community residents as possible in the process of decision-making regarding the future of their community. Their energies were directed through an operating base (CMM) that was unencumbered by specific political obligations. As voluntary associations they had special freedom in this regard. They also had the freedom to organize unrepresented citizens in the neighborhood, particularly a group of Puerto Rican tenants, so that they too could be active in the decision about the future of the community.

Both in the initiation and throughout the duration of any social change process it is crucial that there be genuine psychosocial *contact* (Schematic No. 2) among persons interacting in the change and development process. Without real *identification and involvement* between social change facilitators and their communities there can develop a horrendous form of social rape. It is all too easy for consultants in institutional or community projects to enter at the behest of some parochial interest group, especially one with administrative power; then proceed to assess the situation, write reports, make recommendations, and leave, without bearing any responsibility for the social consequences of their behavior! The appropriate responsibility to the community may not be as clear as in the case of therapeutic responsibility to an individual client, but it is nevertheless close to the heart of both community trust and professional ethics to attempt as full a sense of understanding and identification as is possible within the processes one is engaged in altering. Furthermore, there is a limit to the diversity of client communities that can be responsibly understood and aided by any given individual or group.

In the case of the Cooperative Metropolitan Ministries, a sense of identification and responsibility for long-range consequences of community change were obvious in the local churches and their membership. Residents were involved throughout the community planning process and housing debates. Though persons from surrounding metropolitan communities became engaged as volunteers in housing renovation, funding operations, and community planning discussions, they did so under the policies and guidance of the local residents and at some sacrifice of their own financial interest and personal convenience.

The *operating base* or *professional identification*, (Schematic No. 3) represents a significant decision for anyone involved in community change. The lines between items 2 and 3 on the schematic suggest that the nature of one's psychological involvement with the community, as well as one's ideology and professional training, have a bearing on how one develops an appropriate and ethical operating base. A number of options are indicated in the schematic model: government agencies, private service agencies, business or industry, profit-making consulting firms, independent task-oriented voluntary associations, ongoing voluntary community institutions, or previously unorganized residents. The selection among these carries weighty implications regarding primary loyalties and systems of accountability for persons working in community development. The situation is somewhat analogous to the importance of the professional context in which counseling and psychotherapy takes place. If, for instance, a counselor is perceived as working for the local welfare agency, or for an independent child guidance clinic, or for a local church, the kinds of problems that are discussed in the counseling sessions will be somewhat different (cf. Colston & Hiltner, 1961). Similarly if one is working on problems of housing, community planning, or residential youth centers, it makes some difference whether the operating base from which professional support comes is a government or a private agency, a previously organized or unorganized group, an indigenous community institution or an externally controlled institution.

One obvious problem in operating from agencies in the public sector is that they are very dependent on what often turn out to be capricious funding allocations from governmental legislators. Another problem that demands political and moral skills in nearly all agency settings centers around types of bureaucratization which demand certain hierarchies of status, salary, and accountability within the system. At times loyalty to that bureaucratic line of authority, hence employee security, stands in direct conflict with one's responsibility to the real needs and expectations of persons the institution is designed to serve. Service agencies experience tension in meeting self-expressed needs of community persons, especially the psychological and political needs to experience potency in decision-making within organizations affecting their lives; at the same time these agencies must maintain responsibility to professional standards of training, certification, and service delivery priorities. Greater attention is now being given to the composition of governing boards including consumers of the services rather than simply persons with the available freedom and financial independence to become engaged in such "public-spirited" governance positions. Business and industrial programs may have great strength in encouraging better employment possibilities and in some cases sponsoring educational and community growth activities, but in the final analysis the profit margins of the corporations will dictate the extent of involvement in such programs and their duration. The same may be true for consulting firms, which have the additional disadvantage of involving persons for only temporary periods of time in a community, and then most likely without the requisite sense of identification and ongoing responsibility discussed under Schematic No. 2. To engage in independent funding agency decision-making may help facilitate community projects and by agency policies dictate the areas in which community growth can proceed. But such agencies and their personnel rarely get involved in the actual work of ameliorating tensions and reversing decay in particular communities. In most cases of successful community change the funding for specific action projects has been drawn from combined resources of foundations, governmental programs, interested businesses, and the contributions of local citizens.

With the Cooperative Metropolitan Ministries, initial funding for community planning and hiring of professional consultants in law and architecture came from private religious and foundation resources; the money for rent subsidies, for the repayment of planning costs, and for demolition and some construction purposes came from federal agencies; most construction money came from local banks, with HUD mortgage insurance backing; and money for the purchase of some houses for renovation and resale to low- and middle-income families came from private individuals and local churches pooling their resources in a realty trust.

Another option in the selection of an operating base is an ongoing community institution such as a lodge, church, or fraternal organization. Although none of these may have as its original and primary intent community development and reintegration of factioned subgroups, nevertheless elements of this responsibility may be present. Often the energies of such voluntary institutions are drawn into small, specific, and manageable projects within the community. But such groups could, with additional funding and imagination, play a much larger role in community development.

In the case of CMM the 39 churches and temples extended their responsibility from multiple programs in housing and community development to social services, voluntary referral programs, community leadership training, scholarship assistance, and social welfare legislation. The work of this cooperative group of voluntary religious institutions maintained its credibility, planning capabilities, and actual implementation of community changes long after the time when the more elaborate redevelopment authority activities had met with frustration and partial failure owing to limitations in legislative allocations and controversies among competing planning groups.

The option of working as an organizer with previously unorganized residents in the community is at the heart of the model developed by the Industrial Areas Foundation, and is typical of the work of Saul Alinsky (1971). Its advantage is solid community representation and participation in policies and programs affecting that community. The disadvantage may be the lack of professional resources in planning, funding, administration, medical, psychological, educational, and legal areas.

In the case of CMM, it was discovered that although many residents in the South End were already participating in institutions and agencies involved in the planning and development process, there were substantial groups of relatively disenfranchised persons not engaged at any level in planning the future of the community. Part of the work of CMM was to engage a community organizer to help primarily Puerto Rican tenants to form an Emergency Tenants Council. This gave them a voice and eventually funds to develop an area—so-called Parcel 19—in ways that would be in accordance with their particular interests and desires.

The overall point of this section of our discussion is to indicate something of the consequences that accrue from identifying oneself with a particular professional or institutional base. The consequences of identification may have a direct bearing on the later tensions, sense of credibility and trust, availability of funds, access to additional services, and provision for continuing responsibility in the community development process.

Problem definition (Schematic No. 4) is ideally a task that involves a coincidence of (a) the energy and imagination of individuals concerned about community development with some conceptualizations stemming from their fundamental ideology (Schematic No. 1); (b) the institutions or agencies identified in the preceding section (Schematic No. 3); and (c) the involvement of citizens in the specific community articulating their concerns, planning, and image-producing processes. Because of the importance of this kind of involvement, the task of problem definition as indicated on the schematic model overarches items 5, 6, 7, and 8. Obviously the importance of community participation in the definition of problem areas for that community presupposes one solution to the question considered earlier regarding points of origin of community change projects. Projects that start from an ideology of change, with predefined problems the community *should* be responsive to, lead to forms of coercion, manipulation, and external decision-making, which may not only violate the integrity of the specific community, but which also may forecast ultimate disaster in the following through of plans so generated from outside the population for whom they are intended. At the same time it is the experience of many people engaged in community development that passive waiting for indigenous groups to arise with the energy and imagination to identify significant problems and act constructively on them may not be realistic. Frequently, as we have seen from the model of community decay, the patterns of depression, lethargy, or subgroup rivalry may foreclose possibilities for self-renewal. The combination of serious community participation in self-discovery and local planning, along with forms of leadership and funding that draw on the imagination and resources of broader-gauged agencies may be the wisest combination.

Initial stages of planning always call for the *gathering of information* (Schematic No. 5). Demographic information on the nature and proportion of dominant and minority populations, population trends over several decades, social–economic class levels, along with information on governmental structures, service agencies, employment possibilities, traffic patterns, population density and mobility, and so on are all important background information in assessing the possibility for constructive change in a community. However, this information is far from sufficient if one is really concerned with the self-image of the community and with genuine understanding of life styles, hopes, depressions, conflicts, and potentialities for constructive growth.

This is somewhat analogous to the psychotherapeutic contrasts between a diagnostician's medical or social history-taking, and a therapist's receptivity to idiosyncratic individual presentations of felt experience in significant problem areas. One can have a great deal of external data about an individual or a community and still miss the spirit of persons struggling with everyday issues and hoping for specific goals. In the final analysis, residents in a particular community have the greatest potential access to significant knowledge about life in their community. And it is extremely important for anyone concerned about social change to try to understand as fully as possible those internal self-perceptions of individuals, living units, and dominant as well as subdominant groups.

In attending to the internal self-perceptions of community residents, it is also possible to help increase the clarity of those self-perceptions for the persons involved (Schematic No. 6, *facilitating community self-perception*). In the process of listening and understanding the needs and desires of a community of persons, one may help bring into awareness dimly perceived, or in some cases denied, needs and distorted communications that have damaged cooperative possibilities for growth in the community previously. Such self-perceptions change in the process of time. There are also transient characteristics of increasingly mobile populations that cannot be captured in a simple time-limited sample of community attitudes. It may be that especially under the conditions of threat to a community there will emerge previously concealed attitudes and desires of special subgroups, and perhaps simultaneously an increased consolidation of the total community's sense of self-awareness and mutual need for survival if not constructive growth. If these needs can be identified and clarified in the consciousness of the entire community, a change toward cooperative work in a newly conceived environment, congenial to the greatest number of interests of all residents, may become possible.

In the South End Renewal Project, the community's self-perceptions of the needs were enhanced not only by block meetings and neighborhood meetings in churches and community centers, but also by several creative strategies involving the development of simulation games outlining alternative futures of communities. These put in a game format some of the economic, real estate, political, and personal pressures that people had to contend with in making new planning decisions.

As individuals and groups increasingly clarify their self-perceptions and hopes for the community, there is an increasing *recognition and encouragement of indigenous leadership* (Schematic No. 7). A critical juncture in most community development experiences comes when there may in fact be competition for leadership among different resident persons, as well as competition between resident leaders and institutional or professionally affiliated community change agents. How one responds to this potential competition goes back to matters of basic ideology (Schematic No. 1). In almost all current urban change projects, the importance of indigenous leaders is well recognized, but there are frequent attempts to co-opt these leaders into programs that have been developed a priori by city or state agencies. This in the long run creates either resentment and consequent sabotage of previously developed plans, or a gradual erosion of the real leadership quality of those persons through their submissive participation in externally controlled programs.

On the other hand, community facilitators who see their work primarily as supportive of the growth and planning of residents, and encouraging to indigenous leaders, may sometimes put unrealistic confidence in the administrative, interpersonal, and organizational skill of community persons prior to the time when they are genuinely ready to accept such responsibilities. Persons in a number of Community Action Projects, Model Cities programs, Residential Youth Corps programs, and the like, have been disappointed and frustrated when it was found the citizen-control groups lacked some aspects of legal, financial, or planning skills that were essential to successful completion of the projects. What is needed is trusting and open cooperation between professional planners, lawyers, architects, community organizers, and the like and local leaders who know, love, and understand the needs and hopes of the community. It is still my belief that the ultimate balance of such cooperation must be strongly weighted in the direction of the needs and desires of community residents.

The community desires must also be balanced, of course, with the multiple interrelationships with wider metropolitan, state, and national interests. And those larger interests, which often have to do with psychologically and ethically important matters like equalization of educational opportunity, economic justice, environmental control, and satisfying employment possibilities, must be taken seriously even if in some instances defensive interests of community elitism or self-protection might resist them.

In the process of facilitating self-perception and the growth of the community leadership, it is likely that there will be clashes among groups with differing self-interests. Hence, another task that is extremely critical in constructive community change is the *facilitation of the communication among divergent groups* (Schematic No. 8). This may mean discovering some mechanism of community forum or some new media of communication that will enhance sensitivity to differing points of view in community debate. In some cases it may mean legal arbitration of divergent claims on community resources or on state and federal program money. The nexus of differing needs may be in racial, social, or ethnic self-definitions; but the clashes may sometimes be closer to unanticipated financial or psychological needs. The fact that such differences may emerge in forms that are very difficult to resolve by compromise leads me to posit the importance of developing community or institutional plans that will legitimize alternative *options* for such things as housing, educational opportunities, and recreational or vocational choices.

Not only is there potential tension among divergent community groups, but there is sometimes even more severe tension between the self-definitions of a community and the desires of governmental, professional, funding, or planning agencies with headquarters outside of the immediate community. Care must be given to providing modes of *tension resolution* (Schematic No. 9) between such intrinsic and extrinsic interests. Sometimes this can be done through mediation or conciliation boards. Most often it is handled crudely on an ad hoc basis as crises emerge. Unfortunately, in such crises it is usually the extrinsic interests that have the greater power and financial leverage. Insofar as this is the case, community development programs must find good ways of ensuring that the interests of the local community be forcibly represented. In some states this representation is being attempted by citizen advocacy groups, though increasingly even these may be funded by state agencies.[6]

A significant factor related to problem definition is the *identification of community goals* (Schematic No. 10). Such goals may well emerge as a remedial or corrective understanding of abuses and problems identified in the community consultations discussed above. But it is also important to think of goals not as remedial but as *imaginative lures* that draw a community toward new conceptions of its potentiality. Just as it is inadequate to think of psychotherapy simply as remediation from pathology, so it is inadequate to think of the goals in community change as simply redressing deficits and resolving tensions. There is a function of goal setting that excites creativity and fresh growth in communities that may or may not have had severe problems in the past. It is my conviction that not only new communities such as Columbia. Maryland, or Gananda, New York, profit from this creative planning, but also do many existing

---

[6] The Citizen Advocacy Program established recently under the State Secretary of Human Services in Massachusetts, implemented through the work of Robert Terry.

communities that have a rich heritage and memory, as well as inevitable disappointments.

The goals, and responsibility to those goals, should probably be seen as a convergence of expectation growing from at least three sources: (a) the ideology and hopes of those active in the change process (Schematic No. 1); (b) the ideals of existing agencies and planning groups responsible for the community (Schematic No. 0); and (c) the self-identified goals of the community worked out in processes of self-definition (Schematic No. 6, No. 7). Clearly this all becomes a part of problem definition (Schematic No. 4) and particularly as the goals are gradually articulated they stand in direct line as the object of the problem definition and design intent.

Insofar as there is commitment to indigenous hopes in the establishment of community-change goals, there is conveyed an *ethic* of responsibility to those hopes. This ethic may stand in conflict with extrinsic expectation at some points, and should serve as a guide to decision-making in situations involving conflicts of interest—just as the therapist's responsibility to individual clients serves as an ethic when private practitioners experience conflicts of interest.[7] One's accountability should be first to the population for whose benefit the community development processes have been initiated.

It is noticeable that new groups, communities, institutions, even nations in the past have found succinct ways of *symbolizing their hopes* for new direction and integration (Schematic No. 11). Sometimes that symbolization has taken the form of dominant heroes, architectural styles, or mythic stories of the struggle toward a new life envisioned by the community. It is apparent at a more mundane level that practically all industries strive for identifying trademarks or corporate symbols that will be valuable not only for the sake of sales visibility, but also for coherence and identification within the organization. The symbols for new community identity, at least in our country, have been varied; the "melting pot," the "village green," the "outpost," the "watering hole," or the "new metropolis." Carl Jung (1959), Paul Tillich (1952), Philip Rieff (1966) and others have pointed to the increasing symbolic impoverishment in Western cultures. Many symbols become sterile or separated from any depth of meaning to

---

[7] It is at this point that the appropriateness of extrapolating from psychotherapeutic models to social contexts may be most suspect. It would appear that principles of the "greatest good for the greatest number," or the necessity of open communication, would contradict the therapeutic championing or discrete individual goal setting, and confidentiality of private interests. The toughest problems in community change come precisely where a greater good for a metropolitan area, or for a dominant racial/ethnic population, place the integrity and interests of minority groups in jeopardy.

which they are intended to point, and in which they once participated. Unfortunately, for instance, in many communities it would appear that the only unifying image remaining might be the name of the high school athletic mascot. The facile choosing of such images, and their almost universally aggressive nature demonstrates further the poverty of symbols available now for consolidating community hopes. Will it be possible to revive images like that of William Penn in Philadelphia: The City of Brotherly Love?

Following from community problem-definition processes and the symbolization of goal-setting, there comes an important set of decisions relating to possible *levels of interaction* (Schematic No. 12). Decisions must be made regarding the extent of interaction in the social system consonant with the goals and with the energy and resources of persons or groups concerned about constructive change. There are several possible levels of interaction, moving from the more limited toward the more extensive.[8]

1. *Providing information:* one can give information on sources of referral for health services, methods of home decorating, nutrition and family-planning assistance, vocational rehabilitation, referrals, information on rights of persons displaced by urban renewal demolition projects, and so on.

2. *Action for individuals:* direct help can be given to individuals in the area of health counseling and medication, welfare assistance, negotiations with landlords, legal assistance in personal problems, child care, food programs, assistance in relocating or renovation of housing, scholarship assistance, and so on.

3. *Block organization action:* group assistance can be given in insisting that landlords meet housing-code standards, in political organization, or referenda, among others.

4. *Development of independent groups or co-ops:* clearly defined subgroups may seek funds for building projects, food supply, generation of new health services, development of equity in housing, or the pooling of

---

[8] What I am referring to here as levels of interaction is referred to in some literature as levels of intervention. I resist the term "intervention" on the grounds that it implies external manipulation of the persons and systems of a particular community in the interests of ideals and strategies worked out in what I have here called *extrinsic* fashion. When such extrinsic goals and strategies are introduced, "intervention" is an appropriate term, for it means interrupting normal developing procedures of the community and requires techniques of salesmanship, persuasion, or outright coercion generating new systems, or new institutions, or new attitudes consonant with the extrinsically defined ideology. Interaction, on the other hand, connotes mutual engagement of the ideology of change agents with the indigenous hopes, ambitions, frustrations, and diverging goals of members of a specific community.

common labor in the construction or maintenance of desired community institutions.

5. *City planning:* joint efforts may be established among local communities, city, and state governments related to total design or redesign of community structures. Efforts to seek funds for construction and other modalities of change may be implemented.

6. *Altered economic or social system:* basic changes may be initiated in the distribution of wealth and services, movement toward equalization of income, alteration of tax bases and inheritance rights, alteration of job incentives and training programs, equalization of educational opportunity, and so on.

Interaction with a social system at any of these levels depends on clarity of perception, available energy, sustained vision, and at least minimal group cohesiveness. As we have seen in the processes of community decay, however, limited vision, discouragement, and the desperate attempts to preserve marginal self-interests may be exaggerated under conditions of *threat*. And these conditions may lead to a manifestation of *group defenses*, somewhat analogous to individual defenses that are operationally resistant to change in the constricted self-structure. Such defenses militate against serious interaction in altering social structures, especially at the broader levels (e.g., levels 4, 5, or 6, above).

In a tentative way I think at least four such defenses could be identified:

1. *Anonymity.* A typical mode of group behavior that ensures evasion of either self-criticism or corporate action is the retention of disparate anonymity among its members. Indeed, this may be the social manifestation of massive individual withdrawal—a response we have previously identified as one of the major reactions to an experience of communal disintegration. Anonymity, when justified under the banners of personal privacy, or individual rights, may become a self-destructive form of perpetuating mutual irresponsibility in the denial of impotent isolation.

2. *Linguistic Privacy.* Ethnic maintenance of primary language patterns from prior national identifications, or subgroup dialect structures within the dominant linguistic arena, may constitute a barrier against participation in constructive community change. From one perspective this may be essential to the preservation of historical identity and dignity within a group otherwise repressed by the dominant cultural forms. But from another perspective it may gradually ensnare the subgroup in illusory pretenses of self-sufficiency, however minimal, cutting off either appropriation

of benefits from the broader culture, or (more important) the internal awareness of potency in affecting changes that would improve the communal structures to the advantage of all.

3. *Capitulation to Strong Leaders.* Fear of, and consequent acquiescence to, powerful spokesmen of *some* of the concerns of a group may also mask deeper tendencies toward withdrawal, and toward denial of one's own unique needs and contributions. Of course vigorous commitment to causes championed by genuine leaders, Martin Luther King, for example, may give indelible strength to a people. But often in community contexts there emerge vocal and demanding figures who articulate some common needs, but primarily seek personal ego gratification. Others may be less self-aggrandizing, more representative, and more facilitating of broad-scale participation. Such participation is quite distinguishable from *capitulation* —a point that is important here as well as in our earlier discussion of Schematic No. 7 in Figure 15.1. In cases of capitulation, the defense may be a form of fantasized identification with power and corollary distortion of one's own organismic valuing processes.

4. *Polarization Strategies.* Under conditions of simultaneously perceived threat and invitations to participate in significant levels of social-change interaction, there appear at least two forms of polarization. This may occur between ethnic, racial, or ideological subgroups, or between a consolidated community group and an extrinsic political planning or funding agency (as in Schematic No. 9, Figure 15.1). One form of polarization is directed *outward* and emphasizes the "we–they" dichotomy in which massive, unbridgeable gulfs are sensed with a concomitant loss of recognition of the variations within the "they" or of their potential value for "us." Discriminations of discrete positions and feelings among different individuals within the "they" is blurred or neglected in the anxiety of the felt threat, so that it becomes impossible to draw on the potential conciliatory individuals or attitudes within the opposing group in attempts at convergent mediation. The other form of polarization is directed *inward* and emphasizes the owned and disowned components of the internal reality of a relatively homogeneous community group. There may be real but denied differences, for instance, about the best form of child care facility, or the preferred mode of housing, or the optimal form of political strategy. But at times these differences must be obscured in the interests of maintaining at least minimal strength for the group, leaving only a gnawing sense of unresolved ambivalence. In either case the polarization may generate a paralysis in regard to action; in the first case because of resistance to being overcome by "them," and in the second because of subliminally perceived inner contradictions. In either case, action, if it were taken, would most

likely be inappropriate because of the fundamental self-deceptions involved in the rigid maintenance of the polarizations.

Assuming effective ways are found to deal constructively with these defenses if they occur (see Schematic Nos. 5–8 again), the next step in social change involves *design and programmatic structure* (Schematic No. 13). Although many changes are piecemeal and often ill-considered, what I am arguing for here is a thoughtful construction of plans based on the preceding decisions regarding problem definition, goals, and levels of appropriate interaction. Programmatic structure involves the assigning of responsibility for specific tasks, the exploration of alternative modes for achieving desired ends, the design of innovative subsystems, strategies for continued planning incorporating evaluation and informal feedback from ensuing stages over time, some approximation of a time line for anticipated developmental steps, and attention to appropriate modes of organizational structure and process. Obviously such planning must be done in relation to existing legal, professional, governmental, and financial contingencies in the social context (Schematic No. 0). And it is here that wise selection of operating bases (Schematic No. 3) and modes of adjudicating conflicts of interest (Schematic No. 9) pay off.

It may also be important as an aspect of the design to incorporate features of an experimental control. It may be possible to compare the effects of community development projects with the results of alternate policies (or no policies) in other communities of similar composition and similar indices of health/ill health. Because the problems of matching are so difficult on this scale, however, it may be more useful to incorporate a *self-control* in which measures of psychosocial well-being/dysfunction are taken during a period prior to intentional alterations of the social structures in education, housing, government, health services elsewhere. It may also be possible to compare the differential effectiveness of varying approaches to the same problem in the same community at the same time. This was possible with CMM, for instance, as some six to eight neighborhood groups were functioning simultaneously in the preparation of housing critiques and proposals, all incorporating slightly different modes of participation and coming to different psychosocial as well as architectural conclusions.

Each design also has what might be called its *shadow*. I borrow this term from the psychology of C. G. Jung (1959) who incorporates it to designate that unwanted, dark, hidden element of personality that is not congruent with the moral image of the self. The closest analogy in client-centered theory is the notion of experiences that are not owned within the self-concept. Similarly, I would argue, every community or institution has a set of dimly subceived, hidden, or disowned designs, and compensatory unacknowledged urges lying in its shadow. Some designs may be thought through partially and rejected relatively explicitly. Other potential designs or dimly conceived strategies may never come fully into awareness. But they cause considerable strain in relation to the explicit conceptualized design, generating unproductive resistance in ways that are not understood. It may be true in some cases that the shadow side of a community consciousness contains elements that are exactly antithetical to the articulated goals of that community. In such cases there may even be subtle dynamics working for the failure of a conscious design. To put it differently, there may be a dimly symbolized or distorted awareness of significant, felt ambiguities, reticence, desires for privacy, nostalgia for old ways, and so on, which stand in the way of active engagement and commitment in the direction of community perceived plans. The obvious implication of these observations about the shadow is that such hidden motifs should be brought to light and considered in the corporate awareness of the community. As in therapy, genuine growth occurs only when elements of experience previously distorted, denied, and hidden are brought into an expanded awareness. Such processes lead to health in both individual and communal terms, as well as to the greater possibility for genuinely moral decisions.

Another aspect of successful design, which continues beyond stages of implementation but must be considered early in planning is *evaluation* (Schematic No. 14). The evaluation of social change involves the ability to translate goals and projects as corporately conceived into operational terms, which in turn allows for some measure of assessment. In some ways actual completion of a project or an organizational change may in itself be evidence of success, though often that stops short of answering the real question of whether the initiated program is really meeting the intended goals. Provision for extended feedback from constituent populations involved in communities or institutions is an important evaluative procedure. Assessment of changes in relation to experimental controls discussed under Schematic No. 13 is also possible. And obviously regular meetings of responsible planners and participants is important, with attention given to group process as well as to task completion.

Beyond this it is important for persons involved in community-change projects to have a broad perspective on community indices of health—that is, indices of the degree to which the environment of the community or institution supports and encourages the optimal development of individuals in its domain. Some of the traditional indices have been related to the educational level of citizens, crime rate, suicide rate, accessibility of human services, level of transiency in residential units, extent of participation in

school committee meetings and other citizen groups, incidence of alcoholism, drug addiction, or other sociopsychological–medical difficulties. It
is my conviction that we need to drive even deeper than this to get at
items indicative of the health of a community or institution. For instance,
one could assess the level of felt and real participation in community decisions, community government, and community planning. We could assess
the level of mutual trust among divergent subgroups, the sense of freedom
and seriousness in decision-making in individual living units and in neighborhood areas. We could assess the ability to understand divergent viewpoints on issues related to the common development of the institution or
community. We could assess variables related to general satisfaction with
the life styles permitted within the constraints of the social systems that are
emerging. And we could assess the degree of loyalty, the sense of belonging, the level of identification with persons in their social setting, analyzing
these indications over time. In early research on the process and outcomes
of psychotherapy, new measures needed to be developed to ascertain individual success in movement toward the self-realization of significant goals.
Now attention has to be given to outcome measures of successful social
change in community development if we are to have confidence that the
designs undertaken do in fact improve the quality of human life and meet
the needs of persons and groups in varying settings.

Implementation of these designs (Schematic No. 15) depends on continuing support from the constituents whose lives are involved in the
changes anticipated, as well as on continuing support from political and
funding agencies where their help and authorization is necessary. It is my
conviction that implementation also depends on continued growth of a
vision of new wholeness and possibility that sustains hope even in the
midst of defeat and failure. If a community or institution is to work through
the difficult periods of delay and controversy, it must be sustained by some
preliminary experiences of success, as well as by the attractiveness of a
forward-looking anticipation. It is here that the importance of symbolization is again apparent. Those graphic, artistic, architectural, or personal
symbols of the community help to renew energies at times when progress
seems miserably slow.

In the South End Urban Renewal project only a portion of the originally
developed items of the redevelopment plan came into being. Others have
been left dormant for either lack of agreement, lack of funds, or both.
In the Cooperative Metropolitan Ministries' participation in and beyond
the Renewal Project, there has been significant achievement in the direction of the goals articulated earlier. CMM has been involved in the creation
of 1080 units of new and rehabilitated housing, 455 completed, 220 under
construction, and 405 in planning. It has fostered two significant com-

munity development projects in the South End and the Roxbury–Dorchester area. It has stimulated new economic development in black business operations. New scholarship assistance has been given to minority young people. Consultation services with suburban community action programs and broad metropolitan planning has begun. There has been work on legislative action relating to urban support systems and metropolitan planning. There has been an active educational program raising the awareness of people throughout the area to conditions in the South End and to the needs for total metropolitan involvement. And finally there has been an extensive volunteer program in multiple projects in the community.

The result of such designs and implementation should be an *increasingly responsive and fulfilling social system* (Schematic No. 16), though in the process of events, a result is also a new beginning. Historically, that which is the outcome of today's growth and planning becomes the object of tomorrow's reassessment and realteration in the light of newly perceived needs and realities. In this sense all social systems, as all personal lives, are intricate flowing processes. And though it would be a naive positivism and historical blindness to assume that social change always moves in the direction of greater fulfillment and meaningful individual growth, I think we can assume that without profound hope for such growth, and dedicated work toward it, we would have very little assurance of viable futures in communities worth living in.

The scheme of sequential steps and critical decision points presented in this chapter is intended to clarify this process of intentional and constructive community change. At times there is deep frustration, fatigue, and dismay, as persons working for promising new developments find some of their work failing, or even exacerbating the conditions of injustice and brokenness they had hoped to heal. At other times there seems to be an inchoate process pulsing toward creativity and new community wholeness in spite of transiency and a plurality of desires. Hopefully the scheme of analysis given here will increase our recognition of the elements of this process so that greater care can be given to ensuring more constructive outcomes. And it is clearly my intent to argue that for any outcome to be truly constructive, it must be profoundly responsive to the internal frame of reference, the indigenous symbolizations of experience, and the self-defined goals of the given community.

REFERENCES

Alinsky, S. *Rules for radicals.* New York: Random House, 1971.
Allport, G. *Becoming.* New Haven: Yale University Press, 1955.

Bakan, D. *On Method.* San Francisco: Jossey-Bass, 1967.

Batten, T., & Batten, M. *Non-directive approach in group and community work.* New York: Oxford University Press, 1967.

Boston Redevelopment Authority. *South End urban renewal plan.* Boston: Author, October, 1964.

Caplan, G. *Principles of preventive psychiatry.* New York: Basic Books, 1964.

Colston, L., & Hiltner, S. *The context of pastoral counseling.* Nashville: Abingdon Press, 1961.

Cox, F. M., Erlich, J. L., Rothman, J., & Tropman, J. E. *Strategies of community organization.* Itasca, Ill.: F. E. Peacock, 1970.

Green, R. Specifications for the South End urban renewal plan, and Message to the residents of the South End. Boston: Boston Redevelopment Authority, October, 1964.

Harper, C. Director's fifth annual report to the Cooperative Metropolitan Ministries. Boston: CMM (Mimeo), March 1971.

Hart, J. T., & Tomlinson, T. M. *New directions in client-centered therapy.* Boston: Houghton Mifflin, 1970.

Jung, C. G. *The archetypes and the collective unconscious.* New York: Pantheon, 1959.

Klein, D. C. *Community dynamics and mental health.* New York: Wiley, 1968.

Rieff, P. *The triumph of the therapeutic.* New York: Harper & Row, 1966.

Rogers, C. R. *Client-centered therapy.* Boston: Houghton Mifflin, 1951.

Rogers, C. R. *On becoming a person.* Boston: Houghton Mifflin, 1961.

Ruoss, M. *Citizen power and social change: The challenge to churches.* New York: Seabury Press, 1968.

Tillich, P. *The courage to be.* New Haven: Yale University Press, 1952.

Tornatzky, L. G., Fairweather, G. W., & O'Kelly, L. I. A Ph.D. program aimed at survival. *American Psychologist,* 1970, **25**, 884–888.

White, R. W. *Study of lives.* Chicago: Aldine, 1966.

Wileden, A. F. *Community development: The dynamics of planned change.* Totowa, N.J.: Bedminster, 1969.

Contributors

WAYNE ANDERSON is a faculty member of the Psychology Department in the Neuropsychiatric Institute, University of Illinois Medical School, and is also engaged in private practice in Chicago. He was formerly Assistant Director of the Community Mental Health Program at the Illinois Institutes of Mental Health, and an Assistant Professor in the Psychology Department at the University of Chicago, where he received his Ph.D. His current interests center on the application of the concepts and research of cognitive and perceptual psychology to psychotherapeutic, educational, and organizational development practices.

JIM BEBOUT is Director of the Talent in Interpersonal Exploration Groups Project at Berkeley, a five-year study of encounter groups sponsored by NIMH, and is also Associate Professor of Psychology at California State University at San Francisco. He received his doctorate from the University of Chicago. After some years of practicing therapy and conducting encounter and sensitivity groups in the Bay Area and for the Peace Corps, he became Research Editor of the *Journal of Humanistic Psychology* and Chairman of the Research Committee for the Association for Humanistic Psychology.

ARIADNE PLUMIS BECK is currently Director of the Counseling Center and Instructor in the Department of Psychology and Education at the Illinois Institute of Technology. She did her undergraduate work at Cornell and her graduate work at the University of Chicago where she served on the staff of the University of Chicago Counseling Center. Her interests include theory and research on group development, family therapy, and the supervision and training of counselors.

JOHN M. BUTLER is a Professor at the University of Waterloo, with appointments in the Departments of Human Relations and Counseling Studies, and Psychology. He is interested in the practice and theory of psychotherapy, exploratory and naturalistic research, motivation and personality, psychometrics, and factor analysis, and has published in all these areas. He is author (along with Laura Rice and Alice Wagstaff) of *Quantitative Naturalistic Research*. His most recent interest is in memory of conversations by participants. After obtaining his Ph.D. from the University of Minnesota, he served on the faculty at the University of Chicago from 1947 until 1969.

CAROLYN T. COCHRANE did her undergraduate work at Emory University and received her Ph.D. from the University of Chicago. She is presently Director of Psychological Services at the Family Service and Mental Health Center of South Cook County where her interests center around individual and group child psychotherapy, couples therapy, and family therapy.

TIMOTHY K. DE CHENNE did his undergraduate work at Occidental College and is currently a Ph.D. candidate in Clinical Psychology at the University of Chicago. He has also served as a psychology intern at the Southern California Permanente Medical Group in Los Angeles. His interests center principally in psychotherapy research and cognitive models of personality.

NED L. GAYLIN received his B.A. and Ph.D. degrees from the University of Chicago, after which he joined the staff of the Institute for Juvenile Research in Chicago. He then went to the Center for Study of Child and Family Mental Health of the National Institute of Mental Health where he served as Research Coordinator and Chief of the Section on Youth and Student Affairs. Presently he is Professor and Chairman of the Department of Family and Community Development, College of Human Ecology, University of Maryland, where he maintains an active interest in the area of the individual within the family and the application of creativeness enhancement through education for living.

EUGENE T. GENDLIN received his Ph.D. from the University of Chicago. After being associated with the University of Wisconsin, Gendlin returned to Chicago where he is currently an Associate Professor of Psychology and Director of the program in Philosophical Psychology. He is the author of *Experiencing and the Creation of Meaning* and is editor of *Psychotherapy: Theory, Research and Practice*. His current interests are focusing, experiential psychotherapy, and community psychology.

A. JOANNE HOLLOWAY received her doctorate from the University of Chicago and is currently Senior Project Director at Science Research Associates. Her current interests include career education curriculum development and career awareness assessment.

PETER HOMANS is an Associate Professor of Religion and Psychological Studies at the Divinity School of the University of Chicago. His undergraduate work was at Princeton and his Ph.D. is from the University of Chicago. He is interested in the historical origins of psychology, theories of modernity and mass society, the relation of psychology to religion, different approaches to the theory of myth, and recent discussions of hermeneutics. He has edited *The Dialogue Between Theology and Psychology* and has authored *Theology After Freud: An Interpretive Inquiry*.

JOSEPH R. NOEL received his Ph.D. from the Committee on Human Development at the University of Chicago. He has served as an Assistant Professor at the University of Chicago and as Associate Study Director at the National Opinion Research Center. Currently he divides his time between faculty responsibilities at the California School of Professional Psychology in Los Angeles and consultation to the Topanga Center for Human Development. His present research interests include client-centered and body movement therapies.

PAMELA HOWELL PEARSON received her Ph.D. from the University of Chicago, and after teaching some years at the University of Illinois, Circle Campus she is now at Colorado State University where she is an Associate Professor of Psychology. Her major interests are theory in humanistic psychology and transpersonal psychology.

LAURA NORTH RICE received her Ph.D. degree from the University of Chicago. She is presently a Professor of Psychology at York University in Toronto and has taught previously at the University of Chicago, Roosevelt University, and Springfield College. She is author (with John Butler and Alice Wagstaff) of *Quantitative Naturalistic Research*. Her interests include task analysis of psychotherapy operations in different therapeutic orientations, analysis of vocal aspects of therapeutic communication, and intensive single case studies of psychotherapy and personality change.

CARL R. ROGERS is well known as the founder of client-centered therapy. He has formerly been associated with Ohio State University, the University of Chicago, the University of Wisconsin, and the Western Behavioral Sciences Institute. He is presently Resident Fellow at the Center for the Studies of the Person in La Jolla, California, where he continues his work in interpersonal relations. In addition to authoring numerous books and articles, he has served as President of the American Psychological Association and has received both the Distinguished Scientific Contribution Award and the Distinguished Professional Contribution Award from that organization.

WILLIAM R. ROGERS received his Ph.D. from the University of Chicago. After teaching at Earlham College, he went to Harvard University where he is currently both Professor of Religion and Psychology in the Divinity School and the Graduate School of Education, and Faculty Chairperson of the Clinical Psychology and Public Practice Program. His interests include the symbolic contents of psychotherapy and personality change; working on the development of neighborhood-based planning mechanisms for organizing state and federally funded human services operations; and developing a multimedia curriculum in depth listening for church groups and secondary education.

DAVID A. WEXLER is an Assistant Professor of Medical Psychology in the Department of Psychiatry, School of Medicine, University of California, San Francisco. He received both his B.A. and Ph.D. degrees from the University of Chicago and has also served as an Assistant Professor at Rutgers University. His current interests focus both on the development of an information-processing framework for viewing personality and on human communication.

FRED M. ZIMRING holds both a J.D. and a Ph.D. from the University of Chicago where he also served both as an Assistant Professor and as a staff member of the Counseling Center. He is currently an Associate Professor and Director of Clinical Training in the Department of Psychology at Case Western Reserve University. His interests started with the question of what changed in successful psychotherapy, focusing on the possibility that it is a change in the way people think. This led him to his current interests, which include the study of cognition and the organizational processes common to both cognition and emotion.

AUTHOR INDEX

Alinsky, S., 470, 475, 483
Allport, F.H., 379
Allport, G.A., 346, 466
Anderson, W., 16, 17, 18, 21, 209
Angyal, A., 380
Arnheim, R., 22, 397
Arnold, M.B., 84
Asch, S.E., 425
Auerbach, A.H., 89
Austin, G., 128

Bach, G.R., 432, 460
Bachrach, H.M., 89
Back, K.W., 370
Bakan, D., 323, 382, 383, 412, 470
Balcombe, J., 93
Bales, R.F., 422, 432, 433, 434, 438, 459
Barrett-Lennard, G.T., 110
Barron, F., 348, 353, 354
Bartlett, F.C., 24, 56
Bateson, G., 407
Batten, M., 465
Batten, T., 465
Bebout, J., 315, 316, 317, 367, 369, 370, 377, 384, 396, 404
Beck, A.P., 421, 422
Beck, S.J., 209, 315, 316, 317, 355
Becker, E., 21
Beebe, J., 57, 228
Beittel, K.R., 354
Bennis, W.G., 432, 460
Berenson, B.G., 290
Berger, P., 332, 333, 335, 336
Berkeley, G., 382
Berne, E., 413
Berzon, B., 369
Bettelheim, B., 359
Bion, W.R., 425
Birch, H.G., 360

Blank, L., 374
Blumer, H., 379
Bolgar, H., 12
Bonner, H., 395, 396
Boston Redevelopment Authority, 477, 478
Brittain, W.L., 354
Broadbent, D.E., 25, 26, 126
Bronowski, J., 384, 405
Brown, N.O., 323, 379, 380
Bruner, J.S., 22, 128
Buber, M., 11, 372, 373, 381, 382
Bullock, T.H., 173
Burgess, E.W., 379
Burton, A., 374
Butler, J.M., 18, 19, 44, 79, 87, 90, 91, 101, 111, 171, 173, 179, 180, 192, 199, 273, 319, 347, 354, 355, 376

Cannon, W.B., 84
Caplan, G., 475
Carkhuff, R.R., 95, 97, 290
Cartwright, R.D., 358
Cassens, J., 57, 228
Castaneda, C., 404
Cattell, R.B., 353, 354
Chandler, M., 89
Charlens, A.M., 353
Chess, S., 360
Church, J., 381
Clarke, C., 432
Cochrane, C.T., 207, 208, 210, 259
Cohen, J., 89
Coleman, J.C., 395
Collingwood, R.G., 344, 402
Colston, L., 482
Coombs, A., 11
Cox, F.M., 475

De Chenne, T.K., 207-209, 249

Deutsch, D., 126
Deutsch, H., 383
Deutsch, J.A., 126
Deutsch, M., 460
Dewey, J., 350
Dicken, C.F., 354
Dreudahl, J.E., 353, 354
Dryud, J.E., 244
Duffy, E., 66
Durkheim, E., 425
Dyk, R.B., 69
Dymond, R.F., 44, 129, 342, 354, 394

Ehrenzweig, A., 354
Eiduson, B., 353
Elmore, M.A., 432
English, A.C., 177
English, H.B., 177
Enright, J.B., 265, 269, 273

Fagan, J., 284
Fairweather, G.W., 475
Faterson, H.F., 69
Feshbach, S., 406
Festinger, L., 66
Fiske, D.W., 66, 146, 149, 150, 161, 162, 163, 347
Freud, A., 342
Freud, S., 41, 42, 62, 63, 236, 240, 293, 320, 321, 323, 324, 326, 327, 328, 329, 330, 331, 332, 333, 334, 335, 341, 342, 343, 344, 345, 413, 425
Fromm, E., 326
Fromm-Reichman, F., 41
Further, H.G., 295

Galanter, E., 59, 62, 128
Garner, W., 22
Gaylin, N.L., 79, 87, 88, 316, 339, 354
Gendlin, E.T., 16, 52, 56, 57, 58, 77, 79, 81, 83, 84, 86, 121, 122, 123, 128, 149, 156, 190, 206, 207, 208, 209, 211, 219, 221, 227, 228, 229, 240, 241, 255, 273, 277, 319, 370,
371, 399, 403
Getzels, J.W., 353, 360
Gibb, J.R., 413
Gibson, E.J., 22, 28, 33, 34, 35, 39
Gibson, J.J., 22, 24, 25, 27, 28, 31, 33, 34, 39, 46, 376
Giner, S., 326
Goldenberg, I., 467
Goldiamond, I., 244
Goldstein, K., 342, 350, 397
Golembiewski, R.T., 430
Goodenough, D.R., 69
Goodman, C., 370, 396
Goodnow, J., 128
Gordon, B., 369, 384, 413
Gordon, T., 314, 357, 371, 428
Gordon, W.J., 357
Gottsegen, M., 374
Gottsegen, G., 374
Gray, W., 422
Green, R., 477
Guetzkow, H., 459
Guilford, J.P., 354
Gunther, B., 398

Haigh, G.V., 355
Haley, J., 407
Hammer, E.F., 353
Harlow, H.F., 358, 373
Harlow, M.K., 358
Harper, C., 477
Harris, E., 402
Hart, H.H., 354
Hart, J.T., 205, 370, 371, 466
Hartmann, H., 342, 346, 352
Havemann, E., 395, 396
Hayek, F.A., 43
Hebb, D.O., 66
Heber, R., 354
Hegel, G.W.F., 326, 402
Heinicke, C., 432
Hendricks, M., 230
Henry, G.W., 341
Hill, W.F., 432
Hiltner, S., 482
Hobbs, N., 314, 375, 376
Holloway, A.J., 207-210, 259

Holt, J., 359
Homans, P., 315, 316, 330
Horney, K., 354
Howard, K.I., 432
Howell, R., 357
Hume, D., 382
Hunt, E., 60, 62

Inhelder, B., 30, 301, 403

Jackson, D., 407
Jackson, P.W., 353, 360
Jahoda, M., 346
James, W., 84, 342
Jessor, R., 406
Joint Commission on Mental
  Illness and Health, 341
Jung, C.G., 488, 492

Kagan, J., 29, 395, 396
Karp, S.A., 69
Kauffman, P.E., 376
Keil, A.V., 422
Kellogg, R., 351
Kelly, G.A., 62, 63, 66
Kiesler, D.J., 79, 241
Kirtner, W., 268
Klein, D.C., 475
Klein, G., 397
Klein, M.H., 57, 79, 228, 241
Kluckhohn, F., 425
Koch, S., 319
Koffka, K., 66
Kohler, W., 405
Kornhauser, W., 326, 327
Kris, E., 342, 346
Kubie, L.S., 346, 353

Laing, R.D., 28, 367, 398
Lakin, M., 370
Langer, S., 172, 422
Lawrence, M., 432
Lazarus, A.A., 205
Le Bon, G., 379
Lee, A.R., 398
Leonard, G.B., 359
Lerner, B., 357, 358
Leuba, C., 66

Levine, S., 358
Lewin, K., 65, 425
Lieberman, M., 369, 404
Lindsay, P.H., 60
Lipset, S., 328
Lorr, M., 358
Lowen, A., 370, 399
Lowenthal, L., 328
Luborsky, L., 89
Luckmann, T., 332

McClelland, D., 467
Maddi, D., 353
Maddi, S.R., 66, 90, 149, 150,
  161, 162, 163, 347, 353
Mandler, G., 76, 189
Mann, R.D., 432, 459, 460
Mannheim, K., 326, 327
Marcel, G., 326
Marcuse, H., 323, 326
Marks, C., 367
Marx, K., 326
Maslow, A.H., 342, 347, 349,
  350, 413
Mathieu, P.L., 79, 241
May, R., 12
Mead, G.H., 380, 398
Meer, B., 354
Meier, N.C., 360
Melzack, R., 358
Merleau--Ponty, M., 422
Miles, M.B., 369, 404
Miller, G.A., 22, 24, 59, 60,
  61, 62, 127, 128
Moray, N., 28
Moreno, J.L., 370
Morf, A., 295
Murray, H.A., 425

Nauman, C., 93
Neisser, V., 22, 25, 27, 30,
  39, 41, 44, 56, 59, 60
Noel, J., 207, 208, 209, 247
Norman, D.A., 25, 27, 56, 59,
  60

Oberlander, M., 57, 228
Oden, T., 319

O'Kelly, L.I., 475
Oldfield, S., 432
Olsen, L., 240
Orlinsky, D.E., 432
Osborn, A.F., 357
Osgood, C.E., 403

Park, R., 379
Parsons, T., 422
Pascual-Leone, J., 295
Pearson, P.H., 17, 18, 139,
 140, 144, 145, 167, 209
Perls, F.S., 141, 143, 161,
 260, 262, 263, 264, 265, 266,
 267, 268, 269, 270, 271, 273,
 277, 370, 374
Phillipson, H., 398
Piaget, J., 22, 24, 29, 30, 39,
 62, 64, 295, 403
Platt, J.R., 358
Plessner, H., 373
Polanyi, M., 373, 380, 405
Porterfield, A.L., 354
Posner, M.I., 26
Pribram, K.H., 59, 62, 128

Rablen, R., 377
Raskin, N.J., 314, 393, 394,
 396
Reich, W., 241, 330, 370
Reisel, J., 369
Reitman, W.R., 62
Rice, L.N., 44, 79, 87, 88, 90,
 91, 101, 154, 165, 166, 171,
 173, 179, 180, 192, 199, 207,
 208, 210, 273, 277, 309, 319,
 347, 354, 376
Ricoeur, P., 323
Rieff, P., 323, 330, 331, 332,
 488
Riesen, A.H., 179
Riesman, D., 328, 329, 332
Rizzo, N.D., 422
Roe, A., 353
Rogers, C.R., 1, 3, 4, 5, 7,
 12, 15, 16, 18, 22, 23, 33,
 34, 35, 36, 37, 38, 39, 44,
 49, 50, 51, 52, 53, 54, 55,

 56, 57, 62, 63, 80, 89, 95,
 96, 109, 110, 111, 120, 121,
 128, 129, 139, 140, 141, 142,
 143, 144, 145, 146, 150, 153,
 157, 158, 159, 160, 168, 176,
 213, 250, 251, 257, 260, 262,
 263, 264, 265, 266, 267, 268,
 271, 272, 273, 276, 289, 292,
 293, 314, 315, 316, 319, 320,
 321, 322, 324, 325, 327, 328,
 329, 330, 331, 332, 334, 335,
 336, 340, 342, 343, 346, 347,
 348, 354, 357, 367, 369, 370,
 371, 375, 376, 377, 383, 393,
 394, 395, 398, 399, 402, 406,
 407, 412, 413, 422, 425, 465,
 466, 468
Rogers, W.R., 315, 317, 318,
 465
Runbel, P.J., 432
Ruoss, M., 475
Russell, C., 41
Russell, W.M.S., 41

Sartre, J.P., 412
Schachtel, E.G., 28, 348
Schacter, S., 84, 85
Schroedinger, E., 422
Schultz, D., 66
Schutz, W.C., 370, 374, 413,
 432
Sells, S.B., 346
Shaver, K.G., 395
Sherman, S.E., 395
Shils, E.A., 422
Shlien, J.M., 96, 354, 357,
 370, 406, 412, 467
Simmel, G., 422
Simon, H.A., 94
Singer, J., 84
Slater, P., 361, 471
Smith, A., 353
Smith, J., 295
Smith, M.B., 346
Solomon, L.N., 369
Soskin, W.F., 376
Spearman, C., 354
Spinoza, B., 402

Spitz, R.A., 342
Stark, W., 422
Stein, M.I., 354
Sternberg, S., 93
Stevens, H.A., 361
Stone, L.J., 381
Stotland, E., 395
Strasser, S., 373
Strodtbeck, F.L., 425, 459
Strupp, H.H., 354
Sullivan, H.J., 425
Szasz, T., 346, 357

Talland, G.A., 29
Thomas, A., 360
Thomas, E.J., 459
Thompson, W.R., 358
Tillich, P., 488
Toffler, A., 361
Tomlinson, T.M., 466
Tornatzky, L.G., 475
Tousieng, P.W., 361
Truax, C.B., 95, 97, 111, 120, 358
Tuckman, B.W., 422, 432
Turnbull, C., 377, 378, 379, 415

van der Veer, F., 314

Von Bertalanffy, L., 422

Wagstaff, A.K., 44, 79, 87, 154, 165, 166, 192, 309
Walker, A., 377
Wallen, R., 276
Watson, D., 189
Weakland, H., 407
Webster, N., 308, 393
Werner, H., 350, 397
Wexler, D.A., 16, 17, 18, 19, 49, 79, 87, 88, 93, 181, 198, 199, 209
Wheeler, L., 84
Wheelis, A., 21
White, R.W., 341, 346, 347, 466
Whitehead, A.N., 200
Wileden, A.F., 475
Witkin, H.A., 69
Wittgenstein, L., 19, 118, 124, 125
Wohlwill, J., 22

Yalom, I.D., 369, 370, 404

Zilboorg, G., 341
Zimring, F., 17, 18, 19, 52, 93, 117, 209, 370
Zubin, J., 341, 343

SUBJECT INDEX

Acceptance, 372, 468
Activation theory, and assimilation,
  process, 149-151, 161, 162,
  296
Actualization,
  of organism, 144
  Perls' view, 263, 264, 266
  Rogers' view, 264, 266
  self, 144
  self-image, 268
Actualizing tendency, 16, 260,
  261, 290, 321, 327, 340, 343,
  346, 347, 352, 358
Adience, 90, 179-181, 183, 347
Affect,
  bodily processes in, 83, 85
  disorganization, 81, 83, 85
  generation of, 53, 54
  nature of, 19, 53, 54
  processing mode, 85, 88, 91,
  99
  production of, 80-83
  productive process, 55, 80-82
  restructuring, 81, 83, 85
Affective-meaning gestalts,
  376
Alienation, 324-327, 331, 335,
  372, 373
American psychology, 5, 9, 10,
  11
Anxiety,
  as boredom, 188, 189
  defense, 142, 143
  definitions of, 144, 145
  iconification, 183, 188, 189
  interpersonal, 3
  intrapersonal, 3
  level in therapy, 302
  processing style, 75, 76, 88,
  89, 296, 302
  roots of, 120, 321

Assimilation process,
  activation theory, 149, 150,
  161, 162
  active, 147, 148
  conditions of worth, 140, 162
  defense, 140, 151-158, 162-169
  frequency, 161-169
  in growth, 149, 150
  identity function, 140, 146,
  147, 150, 151, 156, 157
  information function, 140,
  146, 147, 150, 151
  in maintenance, 149, 150
  meaningfulness, 161-169
  measurement of, 161-169
  multidimensional, 148, 149
  pseudoassimilation, 156-161
  self-relevant experience, 147,
  161, 162
  therapist conditions, 167, 168
Attention,
  focal, 28, 40, 42
  selective, 27, 28, 32, 33, 40,
  41, 45, 46, 127
  therapist selectivity, 40, 41,
  97, 98
Attention-recognition phase of
  assimilation, 151-153, 164,
  165
Attentive capacity, 23, 25-29
  allocation of, 18, 33-43, 45,
  46, 69-80, 93, 98
  personal growth and, 39
  retraining of, 39-41
  structured exercises and,
  46
  therapist, 98, 110, 111
Autonomy,
  in groups, 448-451
  problem of, 328
  therapeutic goal, 325
Awareness, 126, 364-366

Becoming, 321, 323, 324, 327, 343, 422
Behavior therapy, 291, 292
Belonging, 468
Bioenergetics, 399
Boston Redevelopment Authority, 478
Butler-Haigh Q-sort, 554

Centeredness, 265-266
Central processing space, 295, 296, 302
Central processing unit, 61, 62, 68
Change,
  dynamics of, 372
  mechanisms of, 205, 227, 238, 239, 291-303
  therapeutic, 93, 225, 226, 290, 291, 296
Channel capacity, 24, 25
Character,
  inner-directed, 328, 329
  other-directed, 328, 329
  tradition-directed, 328
Client,
  constructions, 297-301
  frame of reference, 125, 209, 465
  operations, 293
  processing style, 18, 67, 68, 71-79, 87-113
  style of participation, 205, 208, 209
Coexperiential therapy, 371, 372, 413
Cognition and client-centered therapy, 49-113, 209
Cognitive,
  consistency, 66
  processing, 118, 126-137
  psychology, 16
  theory, 117, 126, 128
  see also Information processing
Communication,
  skills, 426
  styles, 442, 443

theory, 23
Communion, in psychotherapy, 382, 383
Community,
  decay, 318, 467, 468, 473, 475
  depression, 472, 474
  deterioration, 473
  diversity level, 471, 472
  fear, 474
  goals, 476, 487
  group-image, 470
  identity, 318, 467, 468, 473
  myth, 468, 469, 474, 480
  mythic consciousness, 469
  psychosis, 474
  rigidity, 473
  self-awareness, 469
  self-concept, 474
  self-perception, 476, 485, 486
  violence, 473
  vulnerability, 473
Community-awareness games, 470
Competence, 346
Concretely sensed experience, 206
Conditions of worth, 51, 140-143, 163, 164, 321-325, 327, 329, 331, 334, 335
Confrontation, 374
Congruence, 19, 95, 96, 109, 111, 112, 269, 273, 282, 292, 327, 470
Connotative language, 305, 309, 310
Consensus,
  epistemological, 326
  ontological, 326
Construction,
  of experience, 290
  inadequate, 293, 296, 300
Constructive,
  nature of information processing, 18, 56, 57, 59, 80
  operators, 295
Contact,
  community, 476, 481
  in encounter, 372-374, 377
  point of, 476, 479

Cooperative Metropolitan Ministries, 477, 478, 480, 483, 484, 492, 494
Creativeness,
client-centered therapy and, 10, 340, 354-358
creativity and, 346, 349, 350, 360
development of, 316
education for, 359, 360
enhancement of, 359
need for, 10
psychological well-being, 339-361
self-actualizing in, 349, 350, 357
special-talent, 349
Creativity, 339, 343, 344
and the arts, 344, 345
character traits in, 353, 354
creativeness and, 346, 349, 356, 360
information processing, 32
research in, 353
Crisis intervention, 358
Cybernetics, 23
Cycling, 207, 209, 254, 255

Defense, 51, 206
assimilation and, 150-157, 162-169
consequences of, 146
experiential space, 149, 150
group, 490
mechanisms of, 293
perceptual, 292
versus openness to experience, 140-143
Demystification of psychotherapy, 15, 207
Denial to awareness, 63, 64, 141, 143, 144, 469-471
Desensitization, 267
Developmental needs, 423
Diagnosis, 368
Differentiation,
exactness of, 34
of feelings, 33-37, 40

group, 433-434
of meaning, 69-79, 87, 209
recognition, 33-35
therapist response, 102-109
therapy, 68-79, 87
Disorganization of client's field, 81-85
Double bind, 407-412
Dreams as information, 34, 35, 41, 45
Dualities, 54-56, 118-120, 124-126, 128

Ego, 131, 342
conflict-free, 346
psychology, 2, 342
regression in service of, 346
Emotions,
nature of, 25, 227, 228
processing of, 129, 136
Emotional leader, 438, 439-460
Empathic,
listening, 310
participation, 422
responding, 19, 96-113, 396
understanding, 112, 289, 292, 370, 371, 393
Empathy,
accurate, 290
. cognitive, 402-406
experiential communality compared with, 369, 378, 385-392
function of, 160
nature of, 18, 95, 101, 175, 176, 374, 393-406
physionomic, 396-402
therapeutic change, 358
vicarious, 394-396
Encounter, 368
basic, 371, 375
contact, 372-374
definition of, 375
experiential communality, 374-379
psychological touching, 372
social change, 416
therapy, 371, 372
Encounter groups, 11, 46, 255,

317, 367-416
client-centered base of, 369
medical model, 368
mental health services, 368
phases in, 421-460
research in, 369
Rogerian principles in, 367,
 368
target population of, 369
therapy groups compared, 426
weaknesses of, 249, 250
Epigenetic mode, 470, 471, 475
Events of therapy, 17
Evocative reflection, 210, 216,
 273, 277, 289-310
Existentiality, 50-53
Existential,
 approach, 11
 dilemma, 188, 189
 nausea, 372
 orientationa, 332
 presence, 189
 therapy, 312
Existentialism, European, 12
Experience,
 definition of, 141, 264
 responsibility for, 147, 148,
 151
 self-relevant, 144, 145
 structured, 144, 145
Experiencing,
 changes in, 52, 53
 in client-centered therapy,
 211, 212, 244, 245, 264, 266
 cognitive processes, 56, 59-
 66, 79, 83, 89
 definition of, 227, 236
 dynamics of, 59, 60, 66-84, 87
 of feelings, 19, 96
 Gestalt therapy, 213, 240-244,
 264, 266
 implicit feelings, 56, 57
 information processing view
 of, 16, 50, 56-61, 66-80, 94,
 129-136
 Jungian imagery, 240, 243,
 244
 operant methods, 223, 244

optimal modes of, 18, 66, 67,
 74, 77-79, 81, 90, 91, 94,
 96, 99-102, 109
 process of, 49, 52, 57-60,
 121-123, 125, 128, 208, 327,
 333, 336, 371
 psychoanalysis and, 213, 243,
 244
 quality of, 49, 51, 54, 66
 remoteness in, 36, 37, 53
 Scale, 241, 245
 therapist, 370
 therapist style, 96-109
 traditional view of, 50-59, 80
Experiential communality, 317,
 368, 372
 agency in, 382-383
 behavioral science, 382, 383
 communion in, 382, 383
 empathy compared with, 369,
 378, 393-406
 encounter, 374-379
 example of, 385-392
 homonomy, 380
 nature of, 375-385
 perspectives, 422
 space, 151
Experiential,
 method, 211, 212, 216, 236,
 239-243, 255
 philosophy, 212, 227
 psychotherapy, 227-245
Experimental psychology, 118,
 342
 client-centered therapy and, 4
 new trend in, 22
Experience,
 cognitive processes, 59
 creation of, 75-78, 80, 90, 91
 transformation of information,
 59, 60
Exploration-closure phase of
 assimilation, 151, 152, 156,
 157, 164, 166, 167
Expressiveness,
 client, 45, 192, 193, 198, 199
 therapist, 45, 171, 192, 193,
 198, 199

Fantasies as information, 34, 35

Feelings,
as constructs, 53, 54, 123, 124, 133, 134
as information, 35, 41, 57, 80, 81
awareness, 54, 55
cognitive organization, 54
communication of, 174-178
differentiation of, 40
emotional, 174, 175
emotions, 53, 54, 84, 372
experiencing of, 53, 54, 80, 81
functional equivalence of, 376
iconification of, 178, 179, 186, 189-191, 200
implicit, 56, 57, 86, 87
nature of, 19, 373, 374, 171-174, 199
objectification of, 173-178, 190, 199, 200
reflection of, 40, 96, 97, 99, 134, 289, 308
self-engendered, 173, 174, 180, 181, 189, 200
subjectification of, 175-178, 190, 199, 200

Felt datum, 212, 214, 215, 220, 221, 235

Felt sense, 222, 228, 236, 237, 240-242, 244, 245

Field Dependent, 69

Field theory, 466

Focusing, 122, 208, 218-220, 222, 228-230, 235, 236, 241, 252, 253, 416

Free association, 2, 240

Freudian,
conflict model, 293, 342
interpretation, 240
theory, 3, 320, 322, 323, 327, 341, 342, 345
training, 7

Fully functioning person, 36, 122, 140, 147, 149, 266, 327, 330, 332, 339, 347, 349

General systems theory, 422

Genius and madness, 339, 344-346

Genuineness, 11

Gestalt,
activist skills, 210
experiments, 207, 210

Gestalts, 263, 264, 395
as experiential units, 397
incomplete, 395

Gestalt techniques, 273, 274
awareness-generating, 274, 279
contributions, 281-284
pitfalls, 276-279, 283
responsibility-generating, 274, 279

Gestalt therapy,
and client-centered theory, 210, 213, 240-244
experiencing in, 240-242, 244
information processing view, 40, 44-46, 399

Goals of therapy, 39, 118, 119, 121-123, 268, 269

Group,
communication, 427
deceit, 406-415
identity, 414, 439
lie, 407
self-actualization, 412-416

Group defenses,
anonymity, 490
capitulation, 491
linguistic privacy, 490, 491
polarization strategies, 491

Group dynamics, 11, 370

Group level focus, 435-437, 439, 442, 444-446, 448-451, 453, 454

Groups,
contextual aspects of, 426-430
developmental process in, 421, 437, 438
goals of, 423
qualitative issues, 426
quantitative issues, 430

structure of, 421, 423
structural issues, 430
successful, 45(-460
time-limited, ⸘26-427
unsuccessful, 4⸮5-4⸮8
Growth,
drive toward, 8
facilitation of, 314, 315,
428
information processing view
of, 16
personal, 443
potential for, 369

Health,
creativeness and, 316, 340,
343
medical model of, 314, 340
Rogerian view of, 314, 340
Humanistic psychology, 10, 49,
319, 343
Human potential,
information processing view,
10, 31, 32, 39
mental retardation, 360
psychology of, 339, 344, 357,
359, 360
Human relationships, need for,
10, 11

Icon, 177, 178, 199
Iconic mode,
and anxiety, 183, 188, 189
experiencing in, 189, 190
nature of, 177, 178, 191
thematic development in, 182,
183, 186, 187
Id, 327, 342
I-dimension, 250, 251, 255,
256
Identification, 329, 377
Identity, need for, 468
Idiology, in social change,
476, 480, 481, 486
I-it relationship, 11, 382
Ik, 377-380, 395, 415
Incongruance,
experience versus awareness,

53, 135
experience versus behavior,
142, 143
experience versus self-concept, 292, 321
group, 406-412
group deceit, 369, 406-412
therapist, 119, 120, 406
Independence in groups, 453,
454
Indigenous leadership in a
community, 476, 486
Information,
and affect, 54, 80
bits, 25
centrality of, 81, 86
coding, 26, 27
definition of, 59, 60
emotional, 129, 133
internal, 69
organization of, 54, 92
neglected, 41-43
Information processing, 4, 16,
22, 23, 26, 29, 30
capacity, 29, 30, 32, 60, 61,
67, 79, 92, 97, 98
capacity of therapist, 43
client style of, 67, 97-113
development of, 35, 36
differentiation in, 34, 69-79,
87, 92, 97
fully functioning person, 36
integration in, 69-79, 87, 92,
97, 98
internal events, 34-38
limits in, 34, 35, 60-62, 64,
67, 95-110, 149
mechanisms of change, 292, 293
model, 292, 295
optimal conditions for, 303
parallel, 27, 41
peak functioning, 33, 34, 108
in psychotherapy, 36, 37, 39,
59, 65-79, 93, 94, 97, 98-
113, 126-137
research in, 27
Rogers' Process Scale, 22,
32-39

sequential, 27, 41
stages in, 26, 27
Inner tracking, 303
Insight, 119, 129, 302, 307, 324, 371
Instinct, 324
Institute for Child Guidance, 7
Integration,
of meaning, 69, 71-79, 87, 209
in therapy, 68, 71-79, 87
therapist response, 102-109
Intensionality, 142, 146, 374, 376, 396, 402
Interaction,
of client and therapist, 16, 18, 125, 128, 216, 217, 239, 243, 244, 396
information processing view of, 129-133
processes, 422
Internal,
events, 16, 17
frame of reference, 2
processes, 5
structures, 5
Interpersonal networks in information processing, 39, 41, 43
Interpretation, 210, 235-237, 239, 240, 290, 298, 297, 330, 331
Intimacy, 374
direct, 377
in groups, 444-446
Introjected values, 321, 324
Introjection, 267
Invariance, in group development, 430-433
I-thou relationship, 11, 382
I-we-thou therapy, 247-257
dimensions of, 250-256
in groups, 256
strengths of, 249, 250

Jungian therapy, 240, 243, 244

Leadership,
expectations, 427-430
goals, 427-430
roles, 438, 439, 441, 443-448, 450, 452
values, 427-430
Legalistic mode, 470, 471
Levels of interaction, 476, 489
Life space, 65, 67
Listening, 214, 216-221, 224-226, 245
Listening to a community, 469, 479
Locus of evaluation, 51, 348, 350
Logical positivism, 10

Making places, 230-235
Maladjustment,
Perls' view, 266, 267
Rogers' view, 266, 267
Massification, 327, 328
Mass society, theory of, 315-336
Meaning,
creation of, 68, 69, 82, 83, 87, 88, 97, 309
differentiation of, 68-79
exploration, 404
in psychotherapy, 65-69
integration of, 68-79
Memory,
buffer stores, 26
coding, 126, 127, 129
image, 126, 127, 133
immediate, 25
information processing, 23, 30, 31, 39, 46, 47
long-term, 61, 62, 64, 68, 85, 98, 126, 127, 129-134
short-term, 26, 60-65, 68-72, 98, 126, 127, 129-134
Mental illness and health, 340, 341, 343, 352
Metaphors, 309, 310
Metapsychology of Freud, 327
Moral psychology,
of Freud, 324

of Rogers, 324
Motivation,
  adient, 179-181, 183
  analysis of, 422
  homeostatic, 3
Mutuality, 248, 249, 446-448
Mystery-mastery complex, 470

Naturalistic observation, 17
Necessary and sufficient conditions, 111, 257, 268-271,
  281, 282, 289, 305, 482
New experience,
  creation of, 71, 77, 78, 90,
  91
  information processing, 66
  need for, 18, 66, 68, 78, 90,
  180
Nondirective therapy, 1, 370
Nonprofessionals as therapists,
  216, 226

Objectification, 175-177, 181,
  182, 308
Objective,
  definition of, 173, 174, 199
  perspectives, 422
Ohio State University, 7, 8,
  12
Openness to experience, 9, 50-
  55, 80, 122, 347-349
  conditions of worth, 140-143
  defense and, 140-143
  fully functioning person, 140,
  141
  measurement of, 143-169
  models of, 145-147
  rational analysis of, 139-164
  redefinition of, 146, 147
  self-structure, 140-143
  stimulus selection, 143-145
  threat, 140-143
Open systems, 422, 423
Organismic,
  self-regulation, 262, 263
  trusting, 50, 51, 53
  valuing process, 51, 52, 142-
  145, 163, 164, 321-325, 327,

329, 330, 332, 334, 335
Organization, need for, 66, 68

Particularity, 305-307, 310
Perception,
  and information processing,
  23, 25-31, 44, 46, 47, 93
  change in 40, 44, 292
Personal constructs, 37, 62,
  63
Personal growth,
  attentive capacity in, 40, 41
  creative capacity, 32, 46
  differentiation and, 40
  information processing and,
  22, 23, 31-33, 35-39, 41, 43
  over-selection, 31, 32
  potential for, 31, 32
  process of, 320, 443, 444
  seven stages of, 33-37
Personality,
  change, 290
  dimensions of, 209
  individual in group, 424
  information-processing view,
  19, 20
  malfunction, 425
  structure, 18-20
  theory, 465
Phases in group development,
  421-460
Phenomenological language, 17
Philosophy of science, 9
Pitfalls in therapy, 274-279
Poignancy, 304
Potential, inherent, 50, 52
Preattentive processes, 37, 41-
  43
Primary process, 41
Proactive view of man, 5, 18,
  55
Problematic reactions, 207,
  294, 303-305, 307
Problem definition, community,
  476, 484
Process,
  guidelines, 209
  Scale, 22, 32-39, 45, 52-55

view of man, 42, 261, 262
view of therapy, 16, 44, 207
Process of discovery, 9
Processing space, 127, 128
Professional identification,
  476, 481
Programmatic structure, 476,
  492
Projection, 276, 333
Pseudoassimilation, 141-143,
  151, 156-161
Psychoanalytic,
  movement, 320
  process, 324
  theory, 66, 292, 333, 342
  theory of defense, 3
Psychoanalysis, 213, 214, 243,
  244
  and client centered therapy,
    1-3, 67, 117, 118, 323, 343
  meaning structures in, 67, 76
  sociology of, 328, 332, 335
Psychodrama, 370
Psychological field, 65
Psychological theory, sociological base for, 320
Psychological well-being, 339,
  343, 347, 348
  in education, 359-360
  equated with creativeness,
    339-361
  mental health, 346
  as psychotherapy outcome, 354-
    358
Psychopathology, 341, 342, 360
Psychosynthesis, 399
Public psychology, 467

Rapport, 374, 379
Reaction phase in assimilation,
  151, 155, 165-167, 169
Readiness for change, 474
Reappearance hypothesis, 30, 31
Reflection,
  accuracy of, 214, 215
  as technique, 2, 43, 175, 176,
    211, 214, 216, 290, 370, 272,
    273, 276, 277

evocative, 289-310, 273, 277
of feelings, 19, 96, 97, 99,
  175, 176, 211, 214, 216, 289,
  290
  maintenance, 290, 305, 306
  round responses, 214, 215
Reflective response, 206
Regression, 237, 238
Rehearsal, in processing, 61
Reinforcement in client centered therapy, 122
Relationship,
  skills, 11
  therapeutic, 217, 422
Reorganization,
  in psychotherapy, 68-79
  of schemes, 293-295, 297
Repression, 151, 164, 165, 324,
  327, 330, 333
Reprocessing of experience,
  210, 289, 293, 295, 303, 307,
  308
Restructuring of client's
  field, 81-85
Retroflection, 267
Ritualization, 379, 380
Rogerian psychology, 16, 319-
  336
  compared with Freud, 323, 328,
    331, 334, 335, 343
  related to theory of mass so-
    ciety, 319-336
  sociological base of, 320
Rogers' Minnesota talk, 7, 8
Rogers' Process Scale, and information processing, 22,
  32-39, 52-55
Role playing, and information
  processing, 45
Rorschach test, 554,
  function score, 355, 356
  related to therapy outcome,
  356
  structure score, 355, 356
Rules, 22-24, 28-33, 35, 37
  as constraints, 22, 23, 63,
    65, 70, 73, 88, 100
  in defense, 63, 64

in empathic understanding, 40, 43
enrichment of, 36, 37, 45, 46, 64, 65
impoverishment of, 32, 33, 100
use of, 22, 42, 43, 45, 61, 62, 69-79, 90-92
Safety of therapy, 226, 238, 239
Scapegoat, 414, 440, 441
Schemas, 22-24, 28-33, 35, 37, 38, 62, 295
as constraints, 22, 23
differentiation of, 64
in empathic understanding, 40, 43
enrichment of, 26, 37, 45, 46
generalization of, 29, 30
impoverishment of, 32, 33
self, 37
Schemes, 293-303
Science, and experiential philosophy, 227, 228
Scientific method, 10
Scientific psychology, 126
Self, 384
Perls' view, 265, 266
Rogers' view, 265, 266
Self-actualization,
as motivational construct, 49-51, 89, 347
as processing style, 49, 90-94, 150, 181
as structural construct, 89
biological nature of, 50
definition of, 50
differentiated complexity, 171
in encounter groups, 369, 412-416
related to iconification, 200
related to need for new experience, 90, 91
tendency toward, 321, 327, 348, 468
traditional view of, 49-59
Self-concept, 62, 63, 120, 292, 468

inconsistency with, 141-143, 264, 265
in information processing, 19, 20, 134, 135
Self-confrontation, 451-453
Self-organizing systems, 423
Self-relevant experience, 145-147
Self-schema, 37, 38
Self-structure, 140-144, 158, 321, 347
Self theory, and analytic psychology, 175, 343, 344
Sensitivity training groups, 11, 46, 255
Social-historical givens, 476, 477
Social change,
as proactive, 475
dynamics of, 475
evaluation of, 476, 493
facilitation of, 467-495
implementation, 476, 494
Sociality, 424, 425
South End Urban Renewal Project, 475-477, 494
Specification of therapist operations, 205, 210
Specificity of theory, 16
Stimulation,
as information, 23, 24, 32
imposed vs. obtained, 24, 32, 33
Stimulus hunger, 347
Structure and information processing, 24
Structuring own process, 422
Sublimation, 344
Subjective,
human being, 10
mode, 260, 261
Subjectification, 175-177, 182, 199
Subjective, 173, 174
Subjectivity, reflective, 305, 370-410
Super-ego, 62, 322, 324, 329, 342

cultural, 327, 330, 331
Supervision of therapy, 208, 209
Surrogate information-processing function, 18, 95-113
Symbolic,
  analysis, 467, 468
  consciousness, 468, 469
Symbolization,
  accurate, 322, 324
  denied, 144, 145, 321, 322, 324
  distorted, 321
  of experience, 51, 55, 82-84, 144, 145, 334
  of stimuli, 51
Symbolizing hopes, 476, 488
Synthesis, 298-301, 305, 306, 309, 350, 351

Tabula rasa, 422
Targets of therapy, 291, 293
T-groups, 11, 46, 255
Therapist,
  as surrogate information processor, 95-113
  attentional function, 97, 98, 102, 104-107
  attitudes of, 315
  evocative function of, 97, 101-107, 289-310
  information processing, 18, 19
  operations, 205, 208, 209, 291, 293, 303
  organizing function, 97, 100, 102, 104-107
  pitfalls, 274-279
  role of, 49
  selectivity, 39, 40, 42-45, 123, 303, 304
  self-expression, 112, 222-226, 371

skill, 465
style of participation, 17, 50, 94-109, 210, 423, 428
Third force, 342
Thou-dimension, 251-255
Thought,
  as information processing, 23, 30, 31, 39, 46, 47
Transactional therapy, 213
Transference, 2, 213, 371, 372
Threat, 140-143, 293, 302, 303
  in communities, 471, 490

Unconditional positive regard, 19, 95, 96, 109, 120, 122, 141-143, 273, 289, 290, 292, 302, 322, 327, 358
Unconscious,
  attentive capacity, 42
  in client-centered theory, 119, 121, 136
  definition of, 242
  Freudian, 54, 333
  motives, 2, 293, 330, 333, 334
  portion of ego, 63
Union Theological Seminary, 322
University of Chicago, 497-500
University of Chicago Counselling Center, 8, 422, 423, 427

Voice quality, of client, 79, 87, 154, 165, 166, 208, 274

We-dimension, 253-256
Western Behavioral Sciences Institute, 10, 370

Zeitgeist, changes in, 117, 118, 123, 128, 137